THE VISIONS OF THE UNIVERSITY depicted in the endpapers of this book are nearly fifty years apart.

The front endpaper shows a preliminary sketch by Brian Lewis, the University's first architect, dating from 1947, one year after The Australian National University officially came into being. Lewis provides buildings for a small university devoted wholly to research and postgraduate training. There is accommodation for four research schools, a multi-storey administrative block and adjoining library, a residential college, and houses for married academic staff and scholars. The design is based on the water axis described by the original architect of Canberra's landscape, Walter Burley Griffin, and follows the axis along Acton ridge towards Black Mountain, the most prominent feature of the nearby landscape. A tall tower, the focal point of the site plan, looks over Griffin's proposed lake.

On the back endpaper is a model of the site plan in 1995, a year short of the University's fiftieth anniversary. Lake Burley Griffin is now an established feature of the landscape. The campus is much more extensive, and most of it is occupied by buildings or playing areas. There are now eight research schools, six teaching faculties, a graduate school, over a dozen other academic schools or centres, 4800 academic and general staff and 10 350 students, including more than 8000 undergraduates. Only a few buildings survive from Lewis's original plan; the most distinctive of which, the collegiate residence known as University House, looks out towards an empty space where Lewis had planned his tower to be.

The transformation of the campus mirrors changes over half a century in the University's purposes, size and structure. This book tells how and why those changes occurred.

THE MAKING OF

THE AUSTRALIAN

NATIONAL UNIVERSITY

1946–1996

1946
96

THE MAKING OF THE AUSTRALIAN NATIONAL UNIVERSITY

S.G. Foster &

Margaret M. Varghese

E PRESS

Published by ANU E Press
The Australian National University
Canberra ACT 0200, Australia
Email: anuepress@anu.edu.au
This title is also available online at: http://epress.anu.edu.au/making_anu_citation.html

Copyright © The Australian National University, 1996
Copyright © ANU E Press, 2009

All rights reserved. No part of this book may be reproduced or transmitted in any form or by any means, electronic or mechanical, including photocopying, recording or by any information storage and retrieval system, without prior permission in writing from the publisher.

First published in 1996 by
Allen & Unwin Pty Ltd

National Library of Australia
Cataloguing-in-Publication entry

Author:	Foster, S. G. (Stephen Glynn), 1948-
Title:	The making of the Australian National University : 1946-1996 / S. G. Foster, Margaret M. Varghese.
ISBN:	9781921536625 (pbk.) 9781921536632 (pdf.)
Notes:	Includes index.
Subjects:	Australian National University--History. Universities and colleges--Australian Capital Territory--Canberra --History.
Other Authors/Contributors:	
	Varghese, Margaret M.
Dewey Number: 378.9471	

Designer: Adrian Young, Griffiths & Young Design

Contents

From the beginnings to 1960

PREAMBLE IX
INTRODUCTION XIII

1 **The planners**
A wartime meeting *3*
The idea of a national research university *4*
Education manoeuvres *10*
The idea takes shape *14*

2 **The maestros**
'Pick the men and the rest will look after itself' *20*
Oxford and Canberra *27*
Easter 1948 *33*
Designing the schools *35*
Two gentlemen on a park bench *43*

3 **Pioneers**
Recruiting *51*
The lure of Canberra *59*
Overseas scholars *61*
A shed in a paddock *64*
Academics and architecture *67*
A genuine university *75*

4 **Research begins**
Opportunities *83*
The John Curtin School of Medical Research *85*
The Research School of Physical Sciences *93*
The Research School of Social Sciences *100*
The Research School of Pacific Studies *106*
The creative imagination *110*

5 **Academic freedom and leadership**
The University and the government *113*
'No Melville, no money' *116*
Sober administration *119*
Freedom with discretion *120*
Return of the native *126*
Hancock at the crease *130*
Florey's decision *135*
Two cultures? *140*

6   **The College**
    'A University college for pass men'   *144*
    College types   *148*
    Amalgamation   *153*

    THE UNIVERSITY IN 1960   *160*

From 1960 to the mid–1970s

7   **Setting directions**
    'There can be no end to the building of a university'   *165*
    Maintaining the difference   *173*
    'Poor relations'   *176*
    Governing the University   *180*
    A new orientation   *191*

8   **Students**
    Who were the students?   *197*
    'Welcome to the ANU!'   *201*
    Life on campus   *203*
    Teaching and learning   *208*
    'Make love not war'   *212*
    The Troubles   *217*
    Graduation   *225*

9   **New initiatives**
    'Project C'   *229*
    Biological Sciences   *234*
    Earth Sciences   *237*
    New teaching departments   *240*
    Women's Studies   *246*
    Building bridges   *248*

10 **The ends of research**
    The Prize   *251*
    The homopolar generator   *254*
    Exploring the universe   *260*
    The publishing imperative   *266*
    Papua and New Guinea   *269*
    The public professor   *273*

    THE UNIVERSITY IN 1975   *280*

From the mid–1970s to the mid–1990s

11 **A new era**
    Low at the helm   *285*
    'A tighter ship'   *290*
    The University community   *292*
    Mixed reviews   *298*

12 **Change without growth**
    Managing   *307*
    Integration   *313*
    Change and resistance in the Uohn Curtin School   *317*
    Equal opportunity?   *323*
    Innovation   *332*

13 **A new generation of planners**
    The Dawkins revolution   *339*
    Amalgamation revisted   *343*
    Music and art   *347*
    John Curtin under siege   *351*
    The University in the marketplace   *356*

14 **A new generation of students**
    Who were the students?   *363*
    Student politics   *365*
    International students   *369*

15 **From dark matter to the Roman family**
    A commitment to research   *373*
    Work in progress   *376*
    Measuring achievement   *390*
    The ANU diaspora   *393*

    THE UNIVERSITY IN 1995   *396*

16 **The past and the future**
    Retirement   *399*
    The parts of the whole   *402*
    The past in the present   *407*
    Futures   *410*

    List of Chancellors and Vice-Chancellors   *415*
    Abbreviations   *416*
    Sources   *417*
    Sources of illustrations   *420*
    Notes   *421*
    Index   *447*

vii

Preamble

'*Look at the Basic Papers*' SAID ROSS HOHNEN when we first talked to him after starting work on this history. That sounded like good advice. After all, Hohnen had been appointed to the staff of the University soon after its inception, and had served it as Registrar, later as Secretary, for over 25 years. If anyone knew where best to start, surely he would be the one.

We omitted to ask where the Basic Papers were to be found. With a name like that, they would surely turn up before long. Weeks passed, then months, and still no Basic Papers. Submerged beneath other papers, we forgot his advice. Then, two or three years into the project, a senior administrator in the Chancelry invited us to rummage through a cupboard full of documents to see if there was anything worth keeping. There, along with several volumes of ancient minutes, was a binder with 'Basic Papers (with Index)' neatly written on the spine. The contents all dated from the years 1946 to 1948: a Cabinet agendum which authorised the relevant Minister to proceed with a bill to establish a national university in Canberra; the Minister's second reading speech introducing the Australian National University Bill; various memorandums and reports about the structure of the new institution and its component parts; and minutes of various meetings held in Australia and England. These were some of the key documents which got the University started and gave it its shape. By the 1990s they had evidently ceased to matter.

The 'loss' of the Basic Papers symbolises how the ANU has forgotten its past; or more precisely, how its corporate memory has been receding, as in any institution when one generation of makers gives way to the next. We hope, immodestly, this book will serve as a substitute for lost corporate memory and therefore be of use to the University's current and future makers as they reflect on the purposes of the institution and plan its future directions.

The ANU began as a university unique in Australia and the world, and — after 50 years — so it remains. Part of our story is about the reasons for that uniqueness, and how and to what extent the University has maintained its singularity in specific political and educational environments where pressures towards orthodoxy tended to prevail. Another part relates more generally to the nature of institutions: how they are founded, how they adapt to change and how they function. It is about what H.C. Coombs called 'the fragile pattern': the relationship between people and the institutions they create.

Coombs is one of many people who figure prominently in our story. Where possible, we have addressed them as they were and are known around the campus, sometimes changing the style to fit the context. Hence there are inconsistencies, as there are in everyday usage. Academic titles have been omitted throughout. The index, which gives the full personal names of people mentioned often in the text, should remove any ambiguities.

The book acknowledges the University's extensive contributions in research, teaching and, in recent years, performance in the creative arts. Yet it is not, and was never intended to be, a 50-year report, comparable with the University's annual reports to the governor-general. While we have tried to portray the breadth and depth of campus activities, we have not attempted to cover every department or research project, or to mention in a systematic way outstanding students, dedicated administrators and distinguished scholars.

Although this book has been commissioned and entirely funded by the University to mark its fiftieth anniversary, it is not an 'official' history, in the sense that it offers an authorised view of the University's past. A History Committee, whose members are listed on an earlier page, has watched our progress and offered helpful advice, but without once telling us what the book should or should not say.

The members of that committee are first on our list of people to thank, especially the sub-committee of readers, Paul Bourke, Anthea Hyslop and Ken Inglis. Ian Ross read the whole draft and commented meticulously and humorously, correcting more slips than we care to enumerate, alerting us to the occasional solecism, and unintentionally reminding us that while chemists might make good historians, the opposite rarely applies. Ross Hohnen took a fatherly interest in the project, provided much detail on the years to the mid-1970s, and tolerated our wayward interpretations.

We thank archivists and librarians in many institutions, especially the ANU's Central Records staff, who have met our requests cheerfully and efficiently over some four years, and who were even gracious on the one occasion we created havoc by misplacing a file. For assistance with photographs we thank the University's Public Affairs Division, Stuart Butterworth in the John Curtin School, and the *Canberra Times*. We also thank the several people who have looked after our administrative and technical needs, especially Diana Nelson, Jane Sutton and Donna Webster; and Phil Telford, from the Planning Unit, who provided statistical information.

In addition to those already mentioned, the following people have commented on large sections of the draft: Don Aitkin (who also let us read and quote from his unpublished autobiography), Sir Walter Crocker (who also allowed us generous access to his personal papers), H.M. Foster, Anne Gollan, Robin Gollan, W.S. Hamilton, Peter Karmel, Michael McKernan, A.W. Martin, Beryl Rawson, F.B. Smith, Peter Spearritt, Mary Varghese and Stephen Yorke.

Others have provided information or have commented on specific sections of the text: the late A.J. Birch, Sir Allen Brown, D.J. Brown, Linda Butler, Ken Campbell, L.T. Carron, J.H. Carver, Janet Copland, R.R.C. de Crespigny, Suzanne Edgar, O.J. Eggen, F.J. Fenner, Eileen Haley, Phyllis Hohnen, Thelma Hunter, Christine James, D.A. Low, Iain McCalman, Roy MacLeod, S.F. Mason, Jeremy Mould, Ann Moyal, D.J. Mulvaney, David New, Sir Mark Oliphant, T.R. Ophel, T.M. Owen (who provided extensive information relating to the Canberra University College), Stephen

Padgham, Sir Nicholas Parkinson, Patrick Pentony, Robert Porter, Ian D. Rae, R.W. Rickards, A.W. Rodgers, John Sandeman, Geoffrey Sawer, Anne-Marie Schwirtlich, S.W. Serjeantson, D.W. Smith, Robert Street, E.M. Todd, P.M. White, John F. Williams and M. Wilmot Wright. We also thank those who agreed to be interviewed for the University's Oral History Project, whose names appear on page 419.

Most of all we thank Valsa and Peter for their encouragement and forbearance.

Introduction

The Making of The Australian National University was first published in 1996 on the fiftieth anniversary of the University's formal beginnings. Within a few years it was out of print. This new edition marks no particular occasion, but ensures that the book is freely available, if not for convenient reading from beginning to end, at least for easy reference.

Except for the addition of this introduction and the brief list of errata, the electronic edition is a facsimile of the original. I have not taken the opportunity to bring the story up to date. There is room for debate about when is the best time to update an institutional history. If written too early, a history risks losing perspective by becoming absorbed in the preoccupations of the present; if too late, it can lose access to oral sources. My own view in relation to the ANU is that ten years is too short and fifty too long: perhaps twenty-five years is about right. In the meantime it is essential that potential sources, written and oral, are well preserved and kept up to date.

This much is certain. When a new history of the ANU is written, or when the current history is updated, there will be much for the historian to say. Over the past decade the University has undergone a transformation more fundamental than any time since 1960, when the original, research-only institution was amalgamated with Canberra University College to create an institution dedicated to teaching as well as research. As this history shows, amalgamation created a University in two parts; and while successive vice-chancellors tried to bridge the two, especially through University centres and the Graduate School, tensions associated with the bifurcated structure remained. Under the current Vice-Chancellor, Ian Chubb, the University is being restructured around seven Colleges, which are intended to draw together and subsume many of the functions of the faculties and research schools. One of the tasks for a future historian will be to consider how well the new system has worked.

Appointed at the beginning of 2001, Chubb is already the University's longest serving vice-chancellor. During a period of change and uncertainty in Australian higher education, his contribution will surely be a significant theme in any future history. It is also a reminder that ever since 'Nugget' Coombs and a small group of colleagues articulated a vision for the University in the mid-1940s, individuals have had the capacity to influence its shape and purpose.

Other themes explored in this history remain significant, including the University's relationship with the federal government, the function of strategic planning, and changes in the academic workplace. Issues relating to academic freedom seem less compelling than they once had been, while few people now speak of 'the two cultures' of the arts and sciences. The two cultures in universities today are the managerial and collegial, with few academics having any doubts about which is likely to triumph. Another new theme for a future historian will be internationalisation, touched on briefly in this history. Now international students make up a high percentage of undergraduate as well as postgraduate student numbers, while numerous Australian students spend part of their undergraduate years studying abroad.

Perhaps the most obvious theme to emerge since this history was written is vigorous competition within the Australian tertiary sector, ironically coinciding with more intrusive government regulation and demands for accountability. The University has taken the lead in forging a 'Group of Eight' alliance with other Australian research universities, as well as close links with a select number of outstanding universities in other parts of the world. The ANU has always been unique among Australian universities. One of the challenges now is to assert its continuing difference in an environment where every other university claims to be unique as well.

Notwithstanding the challenges of recent years, the University has maintained its ascendancy in research and teaching. Undergraduate satisfaction remains high, while international assessments consistently recognise the ANU as Australia's top research university. Soon after this history was first published, two former members of the John Curtin School of Medical Research were awarded the Nobel Prize for work they had conducted in the School during the early 1970s. Later researchers throughout the University have maintained a steady flow of grants and awards.

In the Preamble to the 1996 edition of this history, my co-author and I wrote: 'We hope, immodestly, this book will serve as a substitute for lost corporate memory and therefore be of use to the University's current and future makers as they reflect on the purposes of the institution and plan its future directions'. In 2009 it is good to know that the history has indeed been helpful, at different times and in diverse ways, as reviewers and planners have guided the University through challenging times. We trust it will continue to be so: for it is certain that there is little chance of effectively planning an institution's future directions without a clear understanding of its past.

S.G. Foster
July 2009

ERRATA

p.107 delete 'from Britain'. Before independence in 1962, Western Samoa was administered by New Zealand as a United Nations Trusteeship.

pp.214, 454 for 'Bryan Furness' read 'Bryan Furnass'.

p.295 for 'Arthur Burns, Professor of International Relations' read 'Arthur Burns, Professor of Political Science'.

From the beginnings to 1960

Herbert Cole Coombs, planner and visionary. A studio portrait taken in the 1940s by the Melbourne photographer Spencer Shier.
Coombs Papers, Australian Archives.

The planners

I

A wartime meeting

'We are all happy, are we', said Nugget Coombs as the meeting broke up late one evening, 'that it will be a full research university?'

The meeting, or rather talking session, was one of many that took place in Melbourne and Sydney during the war years, attended by some or all of the usual crowd: Pansy Wright, Alf Conlon, Coombs when he was in the country, and other intellectuals who were, in one way or another, deeply engaged in the war effort, but at the same time thinking ahead to what Australia would look like after the war had been won. Discussion at these sessions was relaxed, often lubricated by red wine, and it ranged over large issues of the present and the future: military strategies in New Guinea, new weapons of war (Wright, a physiologist, invented a new type of gun mounting), the potential of the social sciences to influence change, the need for an Australian medical research institute, and then, as the ideas flowed on, the prospect of setting up a national research university.

Alfred Conlon was at the centre of this small but influential circle. Aged in his mid-thirties, he was tall and bulky, with a penetrating gaze, a soft, persuasive voice, and a mostly unlit pipe perpetually in his hand. The philosopher Julius Stone called him 'a theoretician of the social process'. His formal status is harder to define. From 1943 until the end of the war he was head of the Army's Directorate of Research, an organisation which we might now call a 'think-tank'. This entitled him to wear an officer's uniform, which he did to such poor effect that he looked, as Wright put it, like a military tramp. Charming and charismatic, he evoked both profound affection and, especially among conventional officers of the armed services, intense dislike. Operating, as he preferred to do, outside the formal confines of power, and without formal qualifications for the positions he held, he enjoyed direct access to the Commander-in-Chief of the Australian Military Forces, Sir Thomas Blamey, and through him to the Prime Minister, John Curtin. In addition to Wright and Stone, his close friends and colleagues included the poet James McAuley, the anthropologist W.E.H. Stanner and the lawyer John Kerr. Although Conlon and Coombs spent long evenings together, Coombs was not under his spell.

Roy Douglas Wright was Professor of Physiology at the University of Melbourne and an honorary colonel attached to Conlon's Directorate. He had picked up the nickname 'Pansy' after playing on stage the part of a malodorous university attendant during his student days, and it stayed with him through to the 1980s when, as Sir

Alfred Conlon, probably about 1950.
By courtesy of Peter Ryan.

Roy Douglas ('Pansy') Wright, 1948.
Australian Official Photograph, ANU Collection.

Douglas Wright, he was the University of Melbourne's Chancellor. The sobriquet did not suit him at all well, as he was anything but soft and delicate. A journalist later remarked that he had as much use for charm as a bear has for perfume. With a drawling gravelly voice that seemed to fit his stocky, unkempt appearance, he had forthright opinions which he expressed in earthy language that was sometimes deliberately uncouth. In the 1940s, one of the opinions he held most strongly was that Australia should improve facilities for scientific—especially medical—research in order to stop its top researchers from making their careers abroad. At one time he had himself considered going overseas, but had decided instead to stay in order to lobby those in government for change.

But Coombs is the one whose words, as Wright remembered them, deserve to begin this book, as he more than anyone else was responsible for bringing the Australian National University into being. Born in Perth in 1906 Herbert Cole Coombs had, like so many other distinguished Western Australians, attended Perth Modern School. Owing to his short and stocky build (and his aversion to the name his parents had given him), he had been called 'Nugget', a name which remained with him through a long and extraordinary life of public service. After completing Bachelor and Master degrees at the University of Western Australia, he won a scholarship to the London School of Economics, where he took out a doctorate in 1934 for a thesis relating to central banking. Returning to Australia, he joined the central economic staff of the Commonwealth Bank, and shortly after the outbreak of war the Menzies government recruited him to the Treasury. When Labor took office he became a valued adviser of the new Treasurer, J.B. Chifley.

Coombs was a pragmatic idealist whose vision had been shaped by the events of the 1930s. The Depression had convinced him of the need for government intervention to prevent social disruption and individual human suffering; and in 1936 the publication of J.M. Keynes' *General Theory of Employment, Interest and Money* had convinced him, along with many others of his generation, that planning could bring about social change for the better. Coombs was the pre-eminent planner in an age of planning; and when Chifley appointed him to head the Department of Post-War Reconstruction early in 1943, he found himself in the best possible position to influence the shape Australia was to take after the war.

So when he and his colleagues concluded, after discussion on that evening in late 1944 or early 1945, that Australia should have a national research university, there was a strong chance he would be able to make it happen. This was the moment of conception, when the idea of a national research university was set to become a reality.

The idea of a national research university

Ideas about a national university for Australia (leaving out the word 'research') can be traced back to the 1870s. At that time there were three small universities in the Australian colonies—Sydney, founded in 1850, Melbourne in 1853 and Adelaide in 1874—each based on the traditional English, Scottish and Irish concept of a university whose primary purpose was to teach.

A leading educationist of the day, Edward Morris, who is now chiefly remembered for his book *Austral English*, warned of the dangers of having small colonial institutions competing with one another, and pressed for a common standard. The three universities, he argued, should really amalgamate into one; but as that seemed out of the question at a time of intercolonial rivalries, he proposed that they federate just for the purpose of examining and assessing their students.

Morris was joined in 1900 by the journalist Alexander Sutherland, who went a step further by advocating a 'University of Australia', somewhat akin to the Royal University of Ireland and the University of New Zealand, to be responsible for setting national degree standards, regulations and examinations. Writing in the spirit of the movement that was shortly to result in federation of the colonies, Sutherland suggested that 'strong and hearty co-operation' between the existing institutions promised benefits that would not occur so long as they remained apart.

Sutherland imagined his University of Australia finding a home in the federal capital, which at that time was yet to be given a location and a name. As ideas for the capital took shape in the early years of Federation, a national university became an accepted feature of the proposed city. In 1910, after the site of what was to become Canberra had been chosen, the Minister for Home Affairs, King O'Malley, agreed to set aside land for a university; and when the government launched an international competition for a design for the city, the competing architects were required to allocate appropriate areas for various public buildings and institutions, including a university. The winning design by Walter Burley Griffin placed the university in 'a situation of gentle undulation' at the foot of Black Mountain, surrounded, as he saw it, by the most attractive region of the city.

Ideas about the purposes of the proposed university and the form it should take were so far vague. For some it was sufficient to say that the national capital should be 'the centre of our intellectual life', which implied that a university should be a part of it. O'Malley, as member of a Labor government, hoped that Australia would have at least one university which served the masses in the same way that he saw the existing universities serving 'the classes'. His fellow American, Griffin, drew a diagram whose ornate logic linked 'the scientific, professional, technical and practical branches for both teaching and research'.

Except for the choice of site, Griffin contributed little to the University as we now know it. But his use of the term 'teaching and research' does give an early hint that notions about the purposes of universities were set to change, chiefly in response to developments across the Pacific. Since the Civil War, research had gradually become a part of the American university system. Johns Hopkins University in Baltimore, founded in 1876, signalled the beginnings of a new kind of institution which emphasised research and postgraduate training. By the turn of the century, these research institutions formed a distinctive group within the American system, and an inspiration to university planners in other parts of the English-speaking world.

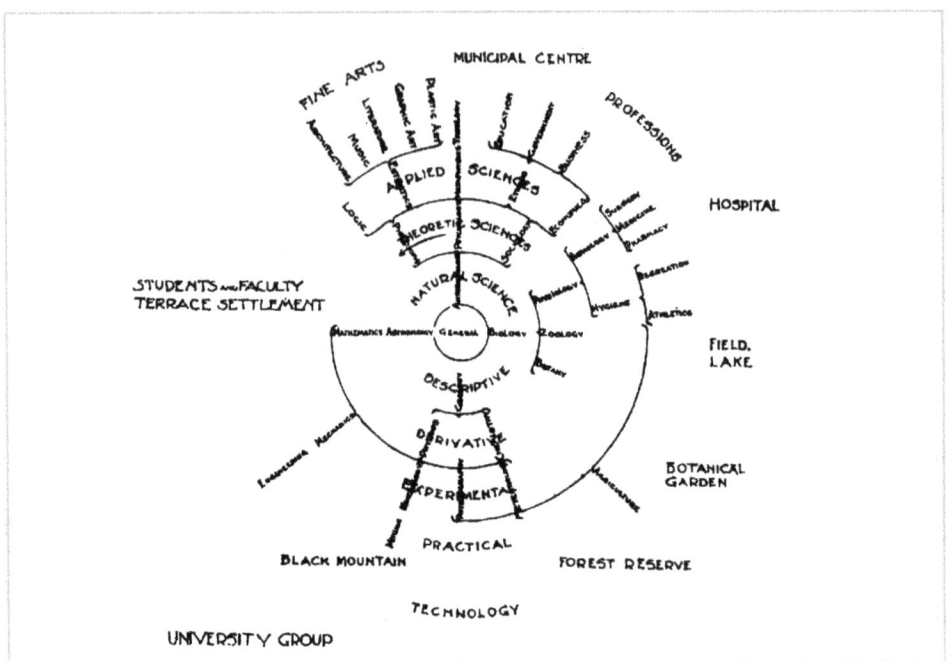

Walter Burley Griffin's plan for the 'University Group'. 'Fundamental sciences,' he explained, 'descriptive by nature, lead directly to the theoretical sciences dependent upon them along lines of derivation and through these, in appropriate combination, into the lines along which they are applied to the work of civilization'.
Griffin, The Federal Capital: Report Explanatory of the Preliminary General Plan, 1913.

In the late 1920s Canberra began to take on the role of a national capital. The federal parliament was due to move there from its temporary home in Melbourne in 1927, and with it a host of public servants, many of whom would need educational opportunities for themselves and their children. The prospect of sudden growth gave impetus to more serious debate about a university for the capital, as well as focusing attention on the purposes the university might serve. Sir John Butters, the chairman of the committee responsible for developing the capital, imagined the university serving the needs of the sons and daughters of local residents, enhancing the life of the community, and promoting the city's prestige. He was joined by Sir Mungo MacCallum, Vice-Chancellor of the University of Sydney and chairman of a committee which looked into the university question. MacCallum favoured two universities, one ('the Canberra University') for teaching and the other ('the Commonwealth University') for conducting national examinations.

Others gave priority to research, envisaging a university quite different from the state institutions. An article entitled 'Australia's Oxford' which appeared in a Melbourne newspaper suggested that Canberra did not need a 'bread-and-butter' type of institution, but rather a super-university. Its author was probably Professor T.H.

Profile of Griffin's proposed University. Tracing by Ed Rollgejser from the original wash drawings by Marion Mahony Griffin held in Australian Archives.
Tracing reproduced by courtesy of Ed Rollgejser and Paul Reid.

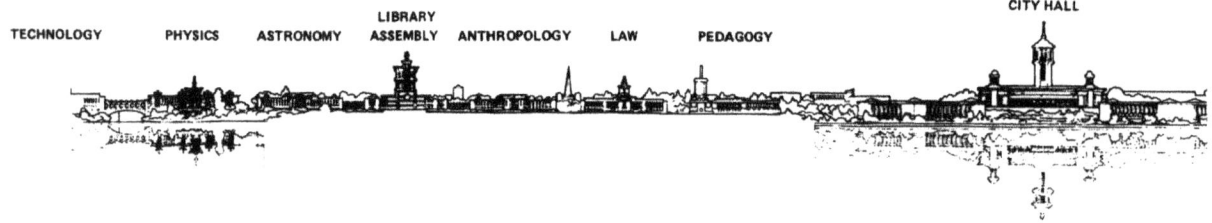

Laby, Dean of Science at the University of Melbourne and a distinguished physicist, who held the far from universal view that a university would be judged on the basis of its research. Laby told a government commission in 1927 that Canberra should have a great national research and residential university, which should be for Australia what Oxford and Cambridge were for Britain, and Harvard, Yale and Princeton were for the United States. Two years later he presented the first detailed case for a national university devoted to teaching and research, arguing that if Canberra was to have a university, it had to be justified in terms of its contribution to the nation. Certainly, it would be necessary to admit students resident in Canberra to a pass degree; but the students who would be attracted to Canberra from elsewhere should all be studying for Honours degrees or pursuing postgraduate research.

In the meantime Cabinet, recently installed in Canberra's new Parliament House, approved in principle MacCallum's proposal for a university to serve the needs of the capital, and set up another committee to take the idea a step further. This brought together two men who were to prove forceful advocates of the university concept, Sir Robert Garran and David Rivett. Garran, as a young lawyer, had played a prominent part in the constitutional debates preceding Federation; then, on the inauguration of the Commonwealth, he became the federal government's first public servant as Secretary of the Attorney-General's Department and later as Solicitor-General. In 1927, aged 60, he was one of the first public servants to move his household from Melbourne to Canberra. Lean and erect, and standing six feet four inches tall, Garran worked hard to enrich cultural and intellectual life in the bush capital.

Sir Robert Garran, 1951.
Australian Official Photograph, ANU Collection.

David Rivett was a chemist, a year or so older than Garran and nearly a foot shorter, who had acquired a taste for experimental research at Oxford and at the Nobel Institute in Stockholm before returning to the University of Melbourne, where he rose through the academic ranks to become Professor of Chemistry. In 1927 he was appointed to head the Council for Scientific and Industrial Research (CSIR), which had been set up recently by the federal government to conduct scientific research for the benefit of science and industry. Rivett accepted the need for a teaching university, but pressed for something more ambitious. Although he had never visited the United States, he knew enough about Johns Hopkins to promote it as the model for a postgraduate university which would be 'a shrine for investigators'. He also drew a link between the proposed university and his own CSIR, suggesting that the scientists in charge of the CSIR divisions might become honorary professors in the university.

Sir David Rivett, 1951.
Australian Official Photograph, ANU Collection.

Garran and Rivett, along with the third member of the committee, J.G. McLaren, who was in charge of the government department responsible for the development of Canberra, came out in favour of a university which would initially offer undergraduate courses in arts and economics to the locals, as well as conducting postgraduate research and original investigation. The government was sceptical about the prospect of a teaching university but keen about a postgraduate institution, especially if it had close links with the CSIR. On Rivett's prompting, the proposal was referred to a CSIR committee, with the distinguished chemist (and teacher of Rivett) Sir David Masson in the chair and Rivett and Garran among its members. Against Rivett's better judgement, Masson swung this committee back in favour of a teaching university: but the Wall Street crash intervened, suggesting to the CSIR that there would not be much point in spending the necessary £50 to bring the committee together for a final decision.

So the idea suffered Canberra's fate during the 1930s: stagnation. Nevertheless, that flurry of activity before the Depression ensured that it was sufficiently well planted to survive a long dry season. There was also a broad understanding that the university, when it eventually came, would be something out of the ordinary, something in keeping with the grandeur the national capital would one day certainly achieve.

In the meantime, something had to be done to satisfy the educational requirements of public servants arriving in Canberra and to reassure potential recruits that they would not be coming to an educational desert. Although Canberra's population in the late 1920s was well short of five figures, the majority were public servants and their families, better educated than most of the Australian community and more aware of the advantages education could offer them. There was also the specific problem of providing for public servants who were already part way through courses at the University of Melbourne. At the beginning of 1929 a small group of residents formed themselves into the University Association of Canberra to press for a university and, more immediately, to arrange some sort of classes for Canberra students. The Association was determined and influential: Garran took the chair, and other members included his deputy in the Solicitor-General's Department, George Knowles, and an energetic young librarian, Harold White. Without forsaking its grander ambitions, the Association decided to press for the immediate establishment of a university college. As this was a much cheaper option than a full-scale university, implying no further commitment, the government readily agreed; and an ordinance was proclaimed to create the Canberra University College.

The College, which we will visit in a later chapter, entered into a loose association with the University of Melbourne and took its first students at the beginning of 1930. It survived precariously through the next decade, with small student numbers and no permanent accommodation: however, it did provide another forum for promoting the university idea. In fact, the instrument which created it ordained that this was part of its job. There was overlap between the membership of the University Association and the College Council, with Garran occupying the chair of both organisations, and the Association having the right to nominate another two members of the Council. But overlap was not surprising in the early years of Canberra, when there were many more hats than heads to wear them.

The university's local proponents tended to base their ideas on the familiar state universities, varying the form to serve the immediate needs of Canberra and its public servants. Laurence Fitzhardinge, who joined the University Association in 1934 when he took up a job in the National Library, offered an alternative vision of a university which was national in its aims and scope, and whose form was not at all influenced by local considerations. Fresh from Oxford, where he had completed a BLitt in Classics, he described a centre for research and postgraduate study where students and teachers would work together in the search for truth. These views were sufficiently diverse to encourage a lively debate: but however much they differed among themselves, the members of the University Association and the College Council were in broad agreement that Canberra deserved, in Garran's words, 'a University with a difference; something distinctly different, in character and function, from any institution that at present exists in Australia'.

Outside the capital, detractors were ready to argue that Canberra deserved nothing, that the country needed better universities, not more of them. Long before the Australian National University materialised, the prospective university was charged with guilt through association: for example, by Queensland's Director of Education, who described Canberra as an 'excrescence on the map of Australia'. All in all, the university's advocates found the going hard. In 1934 the College Council, supported by over a dozen local organisations including Rotary, the Trades and Labour Council and the Canberra Musical Society, took the case to the Prime Minister, Joseph Lyons. But Lyons, with an eye to the wider electorate, discounted the argument that a university would encourage national unity and ruled that Canberra had no more claim to such facilities than Goulburn, Bendigo or any other town with a larger population than the capital. With the front door closed, the University Association tried other means of access. Immediately after the death of George V early in 1936, the association approached Lyons with a proposal for an Institution of International Affairs, to be named in the King's honour, which might one day form part of the national university. But Lyons concluded that the proposal would duplicate existing state organisations, and the King was left with only a stodgy statue outside Parliament House to perpetuate his memory.

After this setback, members of the University Association began to lose heart. They decided to concentrate their energies on developing the Canberra University College, though with some misgivings, as there were doubts whether the College, which appeared to be getting nowhere, would help their larger ambitions. At the same time, they continued to plan for the proposed university, keeping the question before influential people and arranging relevant talks in the Hotel Civic: for example, Harold White presenting his impressions of American universities, and the economist Douglas Copland on the university and public administration.

Following the outbreak of war, the Association put forward an extraordinary scheme for attracting 'refugee professors' from the Continent, who might then be secured 'on modest terms'. Half a dozen scholars with international reputations could form the nucleus of a first-rate research university. Not surprisingly the government's response to the idea was cool, and Australia missed the chance to start a university 'while brains were cheap'.

After more than a decade of arguing and lobbying, a national university still seemed a long way off. Garran, now in his seventies, tended to doze during meetings of the University Association or the College Council, and to wake up unsure of which group he was chairing. But by this time, the deliberations of both groups had ceased to matter, except for one decisive initiative.

Education manoeuvres

Education was an activity which the Commonwealth Constitution left to the states. Nevertheless, between the wars successive federal governments became involved in educational matters in various ways, including vocational training for veterans, an experimental system of preschool centres, and a program to encourage physical fitness for the benefit of the nation's health. Commonwealth entry into the theatre of higher education was initially through a side door labelled 'scientific and industrial research', and included the formation of the CSIR and a system of grants available to the universities through the CSIR for pursuing research and training research workers.

Despite this trend towards increasing involvement in education (which defenders of states' rights viewed with suspicion), by 1939 the Commonwealth's role relative to the states was still small. War, and then the threat of invasion, weakened the states' resistance and opened the way to more decisive Commonwealth intervention.

The conservative government led by Robert Menzies, in power during the first two years of the war, introduced a coordinated approach to training for the war effort, especially in the munitions industry. Menzies' perspective was limited by the immediate needs of wartime. It was left to John Curtin's Labor government to plan for the post-war educational needs of Australians. Curtin became Prime Minister in October 1941, two months before the Japanese attack on Pearl Harbor. He brought with him a Cabinet dedicated to the war effort, but also determined to plan for a 'new social order' in which every Australian would have the right to peace, security and employment. He had the support of an outstanding group of public servants, many of them trained as economists, who shared the government's optimism, as well as an absolute confidence in the benefits of social and economic planning. Their shared objective (as one of Curtin's ministers, quoting Keynes, declared) was to 'snatch from the exigency of war positive social improvements'.

Research was essential to realising this vision. Shortly after Labor took office, Cabinet approved a scheme of Reconstruction Research Grants which were aimed at promoting work in the social sciences just as the CSIR grants encouraged research in the physical and biological sciences. These were intended to expedite research on matters relevant to reconstruction, to supplement related work being conducted within government departments and to produce conclusions which would help the government formulate national policies. The results were disappointing. Although some of the work supported by the grants was valuable, much of it was mediocre; and the universities seemed more inclined to use the Commonwealth money for their own purposes than to participate in a cooperative research effort.

Some of the government's advisers concluded that what was needed was systematic and wide-ranging Commonwealth involvement in education and research. Towards the end of 1942, the states agreed to hand over to the Commonwealth certain powers which would allow a coordinated approach to post-war reconstruction. With its hands now untied, Curtin's government grasped the initiative and set up a Department of Post-War

Reconstruction, with the Treasurer Chifley as Minister and Coombs as Director-General. Coombs promptly put to his Minister a proposal for a Reconstruction Education Commission, which would be given the task of surveying post-war education needs. The education question, he noted, was vital to reconstruction. But Chifley was unenthusiastic: education was a state matter and, in any case, it had traditionally caused problems for the Labor Party because of its links with religion.

Coombs, never one to abandon a cause he had embraced, returned to the issue a few months later, suggesting that the Commonwealth was under great pressure to take the lead. Perhaps he had in mind the Prime Minister's Committee on National Morale, chaired by Alf Conlon. In September 1943 Conlon presented the committee's report on education, which argued that the people had to be educated for peacetime and that economic and social reconstruction would be impossible without an emphasis on education. Just a few days later, Coombs approached Chifley for the second time.

In the feverish busyness of wartime planning, there seems to have been a whiff of rivalry over who could come up with and implement the best ideas first. There was initial suspicion among other departments about the bright boys in Post-War Reconstruction, and the potential there for building empires. As it happened, the initiative for setting up an inquiry into education came not from Coombs and his departmental colleagues, but from his contemporary and fellow economist Ronald Walker, who was deputy head of the Department of War Organisation of Industry. Walker managed, with a little help from David (now Sir David) Rivett, to persuade *his* Minister, John Dedman, to raise the matter on a committee of Cabinet. Dedman then appointed Walker to chair an interdepartmental committee, comprising representatives of the main departments interested in educational matters. Conlon complained to Wright that the 'enthusiastic amateurs' in War Organisation of Industry, were 'trying to bugger our education manoeuvre'. But Coombs was made a member of the committee, and therefore remained at the centre of educational planning.

Walker's committee brought together some of the leading advocates of increased Commonwealth activity in the field of education. As well as Walker, Coombs and Rivett, there was R.C. Mills, who was Professor of Economics at the University of Sydney and chairman of the Universities Commission, which the Labor government had set up to provide financial support for students and coordinate student admissions. Coombs had known and respected Mills since his time at the Commonwealth Bank in Sydney. He was a close friend of Chifley and, according to Coombs, the only person to whom the Treasurer's door was always open.

The interdepartmental committee met several times in late 1943 and through 1944, and reviewed a wide range of Commonwealth educational activities. Initially, the idea of a national university was not on the agenda, and it appears not to have been mentioned until the sixth meeting, when Charles Daley, who had been invited to attend meetings as a representative of the Department of the Interior, suggested that it might be included in the committee's recommendations. Daley, as well as being widely regarded as the unofficial mayor of Canberra, was a long-term member of the University Association. With Garran's help, he prepared for the committee a memorandum which argued the case for a postgraduate university along the lines that the University Association had been presenting over the last decade, and emphasising teaching and postgraduate research in matters of special concern to the Commonwealth. The exact content of the proposal mattered less than the fact that the long-term advocates of a university for Canberra had now managed to project their vision before the committee directly concerned with post-war educational planning.

The committee's final report, handed down in October 1944, amounted to a decisive statement that the Commonwealth was and should be deeply involved in education. It accepted Coombs's proposal for a Commonwealth Office of Education, with overall coordinating responsibilities: this was set up under R.C. Mills early the next year. It also stated unequivocally that there was an urgent need for a national centre of higher learning, along the lines of the memorandum which Daley had slipped into the committee's deliberations; and on Daley's suggestion, the report spelt out the areas which the institution might cover, namely, government, Pacific affairs, international relations, and Australian history and literature. Daley, though not officially a member of the committee, had made a considerable contribution, which Walker acknowledged by inviting him to sign the final report.

C.S. Daley.
Canberra Times.

Dedman, pleased with these recommendations, brought them to Cabinet early in 1945 and suggested that they be referred immediately to a subcommittee of ministers. Shortly afterwards, he took over from Chifley responsibility for the Department of Post-War Reconstruction, which then absorbed the Department of War Organisation of Industry. This left Post-War Reconstruction, with Coombs still in the office of Director-General, more clearly in control of educational matters. The Cabinet subcommittee in turn referred Walker's recommendations to another interdepartmental committee, with Mills as chairman, along with Coombs representing Post-War Reconstruction, Daley from Interior, Knowles from Attorney-General's, H.J. Goodes from Treasury, and Garran present by invitation.

While the idea of a national university was being passed from one committee to the next, Wright and Conlon were pursuing their own idea for a national institute devoted entirely to medical research. Their catalyst was the Australian scientist Sir Howard Florey, who was head of the Sir William Dunn School of Pathology in Oxford. In 1940 Florey had published the results of his work on penicillin as a therapeutic agent, which made him a household name in Britain, Australia and many other parts of the world. Unlike most other great advances in medical science, the benefits of his discoveries could be understood and appreciated by anyone who had seen the effects of tuberculosis, meningitis, diphtheria or septicaemia. Eager to draw on Florey's expert knowledge, Prime Minister Curtin, prompted by the Commander-in-Chief, Blamey, invited him to visit Australia; and he spent several months in 1944 visiting all the mainland capitals and several country regions, and inspecting the major centres of medical research. It did not take him long to conclude that Australian research was in a parlous state, and he said so at various public lectures which were widely reported.

Wright was in the audience when Florey presented one of those lectures to the

Constitutional Club in Melbourne. In the late 1930s Wright had spent a year at the Dunn School, so he knew Florey well. Having had no success in arranging an appointment through official channels, he presented himself the next morning at the Melbourne Club, in his honorary colonel's uniform—looking like a rosella, as Florey put it—and asked to have breakfast with the great man. Wright thought it would be worthwhile for Florey to meet Blamey, and succeeded through Conlon in arranging a meeting for that evening. The two men got on well and talked, in company with Conlon and Wright, much longer than Wright had expected, about the role of science in modern civilisation, and the prospects for medical research in Australia. After dinner, Conlon and Wright adjourned to the Department of Physiology at the University of Melbourne and talked on into the night with the help of a case of claret, which Wright well remembered when he told the story in later years. Wright concluded that Florey was nostalgic for home and might be interested in returning to Australia. Together, Wright and Conlon drafted a letter for the Commander-in-Chief to send to the Prime Minister, arguing the need for a national medical research institute and cautiously suggesting that Florey might be willing to head it. Curtin reacted enthusiastically when Blamey raised the idea informally, assuring him that there would be no problem coming up with the £200 000 to £250 000 thought to be necessary and suggesting that the proposed institute might be located in Canberra. At the end of November 1944 Blamey delivered his letter to the Prime Minister, urging him to put a concrete proposal to Florey before he left Australia. The next day Curtin was admitted to hospital with the illness that was eventually to kill him, and the moment was lost.

But not for long: some time over the next few months Wright and Coombs, probably with Conlon and possibly with others in the Conlon network, were talking among themselves about the prospects for a medical research institute when it occurred to Coombs that the institute might form part of the national university which was then in the wind. This was the meeting that Wright remembered as crucial and with which this chapter began.

Henceforth Coombs made the running. He took his new vision to the first meeting of the interdepartmental committee chaired by Mills, in April 1945, which decided that a University of Canberra should be set up immediately, with institutes of government and social medicine. 'Government' was probably intended to include most of the subject areas that had been listed in earlier proposals; 'social medicine' was not defined. The study of social medicine, meaning the links between social, environmental and genetic factors and disease and good health, was new in the 1930s, and the term itself did not achieve wide currency until a chair of social medicine was created in Oxford in 1942. While this approach bore little relationship to the sort of medical research Florey had in mind for his proposed institute, it would have had strong appeal to Coombs and his fellow planners, including the ministers who would have to find the money.

Several meetings later, the Mills committee came back to the Cabinet subcommittee with a formal proposal that the government establish a national

R.C. Mills, 1948.
Australian Official Photograph, ANU Collection.

university, to be styled the University of Canberra, to be mainly concerned with postgraduate studies and research, and to comprise institutes of social medicine and social sciences, which were presumably seen as offering a wider umbrella than government. The subcommittee made a few amendments, adding the word 'possibly' before the names of the institutes suggested by the Mills committee, and deleting the term 'University of Canberra'. Cabinet accepted these revised recommendations without change: except to add 'an Australian' before 'National University', thereby giving the proposed university, probably for the first time, its eventual title.

The idea takes shape

The choice of the name 'The Australian National University' was immediately controversial. According to Coombs, the name's strongest proponent was Arthur Calwell, the Minister for Information, who was a staunch nationalist and one of the keenest advocates of any measure that would make the Labor government appear to be truly 'national'. Outside Cabinet, almost everyone preferred 'The University of Canberra', which was in keeping with the British tradition for naming universities and which had long been associated with the proposed university for the capital. A third alternative was to commemorate John Curtin, who died in July 1945; but Dedman proposed, and Chifley, the new Prime Minister, agreed that Curtin's name might best be remembered in the institute of medical research, in which he had so large an interest.

W.K. Hancock, whom we will meet soon as the University's Adviser on the Social Sciences school, did not much like 'The Australian National University', though he saw its merits. The name, he later wrote, was challenging, like a defiant flag: 'we are marching forward, we measure ourselves against the world!'. But the flag also challenged interests closer to home. R.S. Parker, as Honorary Secretary of the University Association, presented a case that most academics throughout Australia would have supported: the proposed title was pretentious and cumbersome, suggesting an invidious comparison with other Australian universities and implying a comprehensive character and superior status which the university might not necessarily have; and he added: 'It may not even remain unique'. Moreover, in Parker's view the name smacked of nationalised knowledge, a nexus between state and university that was alien to educational history. Rivett was more forthright, complaining to Hancock that the name was awful and that, whenever he heard it, he wanted to add 'Pty Ltd'.

But Cabinet was firm and, despite representations from the committee of vice-chancellors and all the committees set up to advise on the university's development, the name stuck. In retrospect we may ask how it could have been otherwise. A University of Canberra, so named, funded (more generously) by the Commonwealth and with grander objectives than its counterparts in the state capitals, would have been even more vulnerable to criticism than the Australian National University became. Cabinet must have realised that if the university was to survive it had to proclaim its national purpose and affirm by word and deed that it was not duplicating the work of the existing state institutions.

Coombs's main object was to define the essentials of the new institution and to get it on to the statute books lest the government lose interest. It was not that Cabinet was showing signs of uninterest, or that there was any likelihood of the government changing; rather, he recognised that other pressing post-war objectives could seize Cabinet's attention, leaving the proposed university to languish. He therefore added the university to his hefty portfolio of jobs to be done in a hurry.

Thanks to the continuing interest of the Council of Canberra University College, appropriate legislation already existed in draft form. Prepared some months earlier in the Solicitor-General's office, it owed more to the Acts which governed several of the state universities than to the intended functions of the new institution. Nevertheless, it provided Coombs and his colleagues in Post-War Reconstruction with something to work on, and it helped them to sharpen their ideas about the institution's functions and structure. By the end of 1945 a detailed proposal was ready for Cabinet.

The primary object of the university, as Coombs defined it, was to provide the opportunity for research work at the postgraduate level. This would be achieved through a number of research institutes, each with substantial autonomy. It should also be empowered to organise specialist training schools for the Public Service Board, government departments and other public authorities; and to provide undergraduate tuition through a university college, as at present, chiefly for residents of Canberra and the surrounding region.

Coombs envisaged a close relationship between the university and government, with the university able to initiate joint research projects with government departments and to appoint staff who would serve both the university and government. The relationship, however, should not be so close as to compromise the university's autonomy. Hence the value of a charter, which would give the university 'a point of view' and provide some protection against undue academic isolation on the one hand or undue government interference on the other. An early draft of the bill began with a brief but uplifting preamble—

> WHEREAS a free democracy has its basis in the decisions of the people,
> and if those decisions are to represent wisdom and maintain truth, it is
> essential that facilities be granted for the attainment of knowledge and for
> the fearless and informed discussion of vital issues;
> AND WHEREAS it is expedient for these purposes to establish a University
> at Canberra, in the Australian Capital Territory

—before proceeding to matters of substance. But the Solicitor-General was known to disapprove of preambles, so Coombs's 'bill of rights' did not get as far as Cabinet, leaving the relationship with government vaguer than he might have preferred it.

The core of the proposal lay in the description of the research schools, or 'institutes' as they were initially called. Coombs listed five institutes, including the two that had already been proposed to Cabinet, but under different titles. The medical school, which had recently been discussed by a separate interdepartmental committee, had been transformed into an institute of medical research rather than social medicine. This was a result of a long memorandum from Florey, written at Rivett's request, which set out his concept of a medical research school. The school which had started as 'government' and become 'social sciences' was briefly 'economics and politics', before 'social sciences' was restored by an unidentified editorial pen. The three new institutes were Pacific affairs, town and regional planning, and '(atomic) physics', the last two attended by question marks.

Sir Frederic Eggleston, who would soon become closely involved in the University's planning, took credit for originating the idea of Pacific affairs in a despatch he wrote from Chungking in 1943, when he was Minister to China. And Coombs thought the Minister for External Affairs, H.V. Evatt, and the acting head of Evatt's department, John Burton, were influential. But Pacific affairs in one form or another (linked sometimes with international relations or Oriental studies) had been discussed as an appropriate research area for at least a decade; and it was one of Garran's favourite themes. Garran probably saved it at the last moment when, after it had fallen off the proposal for Cabinet, he stressed how important it was as a way of proclaiming the national character of the university. Town and regional planning did not get as far as Cabinet, perhaps because it found a home once the title 'social sciences' was restored.

According to Coombs, the physics institute owed its origins to one of his flatmates in Canberra, the Commonwealth Astronomer Richard van der Reit Woolley, who ran the Mount Stromlo Observatory sixteen kilometres out of town. In conversations with Coombs about the shape of the new institution, Woolley argued that a research university must have some involvement in the natural sciences. There ought to be, he said, an institute of physics, comprising astronomers observing the southern skies, together with theoretical physicists, 'people sitting around with paper and pencils thinking highly abstract and scientific thoughts'. Perhaps Woolley imagined theoretical work in atomic physics; but more probably the word 'atomic' was introduced by Coombs and his colleagues shortly after the bombs were dropped on Hiroshima and Nagasaki, when suddenly it seemed that nuclear power might change the post-war world. Probably they had little concept at this stage of what atomic (changed by the editorial pen to 'nuclear') physics might involve; and certainly they had no notion of the experimental research that was soon to develop.

So the proposal that Cabinet approved towards the end of 1945 was firm about the institutes of medical research, social sciences and Pacific affairs, but tentative about nuclear physics. The rest of Coombs's ideas, along with a development budget totalling £325 000 (plus £150 000 for medical research in other parts of Australia), were approved in general terms and referred back to Mills and his committee for elaboration. Winning Cabinet approval soon proved to be one of the easier stages of the enterprise. The Mills committee, deciding that it needed more advice to assist with detailed planning, set up panels of five or six experts in each of the four research areas and asked them to comment on a range of matters, including the fields to be covered by each institute, relations between the institutes, ways of organising research, staff numbers and appropriate salaries, financial and accommodation needs, and relations with other universities. This opened the debate to members of the academic and research community who did not necessarily share the post-war reconstruction vision and who were as likely to see the Commonwealth institution as a rival for research funds.

The social sciences and Pacific affairs subcommittees came up with proposals which descended in detail to the size of individual salaries and the area of rooms for the various categories of staff and students. Both subcommittees devoted some time to nomenclature; both favoured 'school' over 'institute', a preference that was shortly accepted by the parent committee; and each had problems with their own school's title. S.J. Butlin, Professor of Economics at the University of Sydney and a forthright member of the social sciences committee, thought 'social sciences' was 'a rotten title', and would have preferred 'economics and government'; but that was not much liked by other committee members, so 'social sciences' remained for want of something better. 'Pacific affairs' was even more difficult, as nobody on the relevant subcommittee was sure of what it was intended to mean. The war had given 'Pacific', as in Pacific theatre, extended connotations, contrasting with the theatre of war in Europe. But it could also be construed as having a narrower application to the islands of the Pacific, including or excluding Melanesia. Opting for a broader meaning, the subcommittee suggested the title 'School of Pacific and Asiatic Studies'; but one member, R.M. Crawford from the University of Melbourne, thought this limited rather than widened the scope of the school, which should embrace areas *east* of the Pacific. Better, he argued, to keep the simple title 'School of Pacific Studies' and define its scope as 'somewhere ranging from the Americas to India'.

The subcommittee on the medical research school got off to a bad start. No sooner had it been nominated than a letter arrived, written on behalf of the potential chairman, the Commonwealth Director-General of Health, Frank McCallum, complaining testily that the intended school was headed in the wrong direction. McCallum understood the proposal to mean that henceforth *all* funds for medical research would be channelled through the university, and that the existing granting body, the National Health and Medical Research Council, was to be abolished, leaving decisions about the allocation of money in the hands of a governmental agency. Coombs stepped in to pacify him; and the subcommittee agreed in principle to Florey's plan for the school on the understanding that he might be prepared to head it. So long as that was the case, the committee would be content: but should Florey decline the appointment, it seemed that there might be further trouble.

Bad luck attended the first meeting of the subcommittee on physical sciences. Leslie Martin, Professor of Physics at the University of Melbourne, who was understood to be sympathetic to the proposal, was supposed to have flown up for a meeting at Mount Stromlo. But someone forgot to buy his ticket, leaving a committee chaired by the Commonwealth Astronomer, Woolley, but dominated by members of the CSIR who were unimpressed by grand ideas about an independent institute of nuclear research. They favoured something much more modest, and grumbled about being asked to advise on major questions in such a hurry.

But Coombs, Mills and their colleagues were not paying much attention to these squabbles. They might not have gone so far as Conlon, who dismissed the subcommittees as 'bloody silly', but they were surely wondering whether the meetings were worthwhile. Although the social sciences and Pacific affairs committees added something to the debate, the real value of all the discussions was political. Mills's committee was now able to prepare a more detailed submission for Cabinet; and once Cabinet had approved the proposal, the government was able to tell parliament, with just a hint of disingenuousness, about the process of consultation.

The draft bill passed through Cabinet with a few small changes (including a change of name for Pacific Affairs to Pacific Studies), and then passed through parliament with almost equal ease. The Leader of the Opposition, Menzies, who was—and liked to be seen as—a warm supporter of higher education, questioned the government's decision to locate schools of medical and physical science in Canberra, warned of the danger of depriving the state universities of funds, and expressed horror at the name 'The Australian National University'. Nevertheless, overall he welcomed the initiative and generously acknowledged Dedman's contribution. On 1 August 1946 the bill passed into law and the Australian National University came formally into being.

As Dedman told parliament, the bill was very straightforward. The functions of the University were defined in the Act as follows:

(a) To encourage, and provide facilities for, post-graduate research and study, both generally and in relation to subjects of national importance to Australia;
(b) To provide facilities for university education for persons who elect to avail themselves of those facilities and are eligible to do so;
(c) Subject to the Statutes, to award and confer degrees and diplomas.

It was permitted (but not required) to provide specialised training for members of the public service, and to incorporate Canberra University College, a provision which showed the influence of Garran, Daley and their colleagues during the drafting stages. The Act authorised the University to set up research schools, including the initial four, which were specified by name. There were to be a chancellor and a vice-chancellor, and a governing body to be known as the Council. This would comprise up to thirty members, including representatives of the federal parliament, persons appointed by the governor-general, the vice-chancellor, persons elected by convocation, the students and the staff, and up to three coopted members. Until the Council could be constituted, the University was to be governed by an interim council, made up entirely of members appointed by the governor-general.

The pedestrian wording of the Act gave no hint of the grand vision behind it: for that we need look to the Minister's speech when he introduced the bill. Speaking with the conviction of a Scottish Presbyterian whose own efforts to gain a degree had been twice cut short by world wars, Dedman told parliament that there were innumerable problems awaiting solution in Australia and the world if the future was to be made safe and if people were to benefit from recent developments in science and human relationships. Progress in physical science could either lead to unparalleled peace and prosperity or make them impossible. In medicine, the achievements of the war years had to be reapplied for civilian use. Human relationships had to be studied through the social sciences. And the whole field of Pacific studies demanded attention if Australians were to safeguard their own future and contribute to the councils of the nations.

In each of these areas, Dedman asserted, Australia could make a significant and perhaps unique contribution; and the means of making that contribution would be through the Australian National University, which would take its place among the great universities and would help Australia align itself with the enlightened nations of the world.

Reflecting many years later on the University's origins, Coombs remembered how he and his colleagues had looked forward to grappling with the post-war problems of poverty, waste, unemployment, social injustice, and international and racial misunderstanding:

> We believed profoundly that the will to solve these problems was within us but were conscious that much of the knowledge necessary to their solution was lacking. It was this consciousness that underlay the decision to establish the University, which we saw as a kind of intellectual power house for the rebuilding of society.

The University was an expression of the optimism of the age.

J.J. Dedman, about 1946.
By courtesy of Ruth Rodgers.

2 The maestros

 'Pick the men and the rest will look after itself'

Coombs and the Prime Minister Ben Chifley in London, April – May 1946. During this visit, Coombs approached potential leaders of the proposed university and introduced one of them, the physicist Mark Oliphant, to the Prime Minister.

Coombs Papers, Australian Archives.

In April 1946 Coombs set out on a long trip to London, Washington and Tokyo with the Prime Minister, Ben Chifley. In London Chifley was to attend the Commonwealth Prime Ministers' Conference, and Coombs was to assist him in matters relating chiefly to economic planning and international financial agreements. Coombs was also to talk to distinguished expatriate Australian scholars about the prospect of their taking up positions at the proposed national university, and if possible to arrange meetings between them and the Prime Minister.

Conlon and Wright were on tenterhooks. Ever since their meeting with Florey in 1944, they had been lobbying and manoeuvring for a medical institute. Now the moment of realisation—as part of Coombs's larger scheme—seemed imminent. But nothing should be left to chance. Conlon had a session with Coombs before he left, to remind him of Florey's requirements and issue stern instructions to bring the maestro, as he called him, back home. He wrote to Florey, introducing Coombs as the man destined to be 'Australia's No. 1 Public Servant', the only one he knew who combined intelligence, learning and imagination, and who, above all, was 'one of us'. The letter reached Florey ahead of Coombs, and Florey responded in brief, non-committal terms: sufficient, though, to encourage Conlon to cable Coombs, 'Letter from maestro—auspices good', and urge him to invite Florey to write his own ticket.

Coombs, though more circumspect than Conlon, needed no encouragement. Besides consulting Florey, who came down from Oxford to meet him, he talked with the historian W.K. Hancock, the political scientist K.C. Wheare, the physicists H.S.W. Massey and M.L.E. Oliphant, and the economist R.L. Hall. He arrived back in Australia buoyant. All these scholars, he told the Mills committee, were intensely interested in the proposed university, and if conditions were satisfactory, some of them would accept appointments in Canberra.

The high point of the discussions was a meeting between Chifley and Oliphant. Before that meeting, the prospects for a school of physical sciences looked gloomy. The physicist whom Coombs had approached first, Harrie Massey at the University of London, had reacted sceptically to his vague depiction of a school focused on theoretical studies. Massey had told Coombs that since the war and the development of the atomic bomb the main interest and excitement was in experimental physics; and if Australia was to attract distinguished people to work in that area, it would have to provide facilities comparable with those offered by institutions in Britain and the United States.

Coombs was starting to wonder whether it might be necessary to abandon the original, modest conception of the physics school, especially since the other expatriate physicist on his list, Mark Oliphant, was at the forefront of experimental research in nuclear physics. Clearly, there was no point in trying to woo Oliphant with a pittance; and if large funds were needed, the government had to be on side. Coombs concluded that Chifley should meet Oliphant, and arranged for the physicist to come down from Birmingham. Arriving in London on a warm spring day, Oliphant was greeted by Chifley who, with characteristic informality, asked him to come for a walk in the park. The two men strolled and talked for an hour or more about the problems of the time, Oliphant's view of science and the world, and so on. Each was charmed by the other. Later they met again over dinner at the Savoy Hotel, accompanied by Coombs and other members of the delegation. Chifley, already immersed in discussions at the Prime Ministers' Conference about defence strategies and the impact of the atomic bomb, was responsive; and Oliphant, as Coombs later recalled, was at his spellbinding best, conveying the excitement of his research on the Manhattan Project, speculating on a world dominated by atomic energy, and imagining Australia at the forefront of nuclear research. 'The impact on Chifley', Coombs later wrote, 'was tremendous'.

Those meetings were critical for the University's future. Besides helping to secure the talents of one of the world's leading physicists, they introduced the prospect of an institution more ambitious in scope and more generously funded than Coombs or his colleagues at home would previously have dared to imagine. Oliphant mentioned to Chifley a figure of half a million pounds or more to set up the sort of physics school he had in mind. That was over four times the amount originally suggested to Cabinet. The Prime Minister, Oliphant later recalled, was taken aback, but not overwhelmed. And when Coombs warned him that if they were to attract Oliphant to Canberra it would cost 'a hell of a lot of money', Chifley replied, 'If you can persuade Oliphant to head the school we will do whatever is necessary'.

There now seemed a genuine prospect of building the University around a group of Australian scholars of international standing. That had previously been the hope. But so far the plans of the four schools had been sketched without specific reference to the individuals who might run them, excepting the link between Florey and the medical research school; and Cabinet had approved a concept rather than a group of names. Now Oliphant's enthusiasm, along with what Coombs interpreted to be positive signals from others he consulted, transformed hope to near certainty. Bringing the great men back to Australia came to be seen as the key to success. Dedman told parliament

Mark Oliphant alongside his synchrotron in Birmingham, 1950.
Oliphant Papers, Barr Smith Library, University of Adelaide.

about the very eminent Australians who would be happy to return to Australia to work in a research university: 'We must leave no stone unturned to secure their services'. For the next few years, an absolute determination to attract established scholars with overseas reputations to head the research schools became the dominant theme in University planning. Written plans receded in importance, in keeping with the principle Conlon enunciated to Wright: 'Never mind about blue-prints, pick the men and the rest will look after itself'.

W.K. Hancock, 1948.
Australian Official Photograph, ANU Collection.

But if getting the right men was the key to success, did the converse also apply? What if some or all of them decided not to come? Would that leave the University floundering? Wright feared so, telling Oliphant, whom he had met in 1942, that because of the way the politicians had played the game, his participation was essential to getting the show under way. There were plenty of cynics, including the author of an editorial in the Sydney *Sun* entitled 'How not to win professors' who argued that the likes of Florey and Oliphant would scarcely be dazzled by what Australia had to offer.

Again Wright and Conlon determined that nothing should be left to chance, and still less to Mills and the Commonwealth Office of Education. Wright urged Florey and Oliphant not to be put off by the 'office boys', who did not have sole control of the project; and Conlon warned Coombs that the two maestros were not only famous and important, but also had minds and were human. The implication was that they should be given everything they wanted. Wright warned a friend, the Cabinet Minister Eddie Ward, that they were 'a bit like prima donnas', even though they were 'such good chaps'; and if they were mishandled on even one occasion they might sheer right off the idea of coming back to Australia.

Meanwhile, the bill passed into law and the Interim Council established under that Act came together. The first meeting took place in the Senate Committee Room in Parliament House, Canberra, in September 1946. Through Coombs's influence, Wright found himself on the Council, but not Conlon. The Mills committee made up a majority of the members: Mills, Coombs, Goodes, Garran, Daley and Rivett, along with the new Solicitor-General, K.H. Bailey. The remaining four had no connection with any government department: Wright, Sir Frederic Eggleston (who had recently returned from diplomatic postings in the United States), Eric Ashby (Professor of Botany at the University of Sydney) and Sir John Medley (Vice-Chancellor of the University of Melbourne). Mills was unanimously elected chairman, and Medley deputy chairman.

At that first meeting the Interim Council had to decide where to go next. Wright put forward the principle that the only way of getting the research schools started was to recruit men of sufficient calibre and allow them to decide what the schools should do. Accordingly, the meeting resolved to invite three expatriate professors to Australia to advise on how to proceed: Florey, Oliphant and Hancock. Although Hancock's claim to fame was not as remarkable as that of the natural scientists, he was as well known among the Australian public as any scholar in the humanities could hope to be. Many Australians had read and talked about his book *Australia*, first published in London in 1930 and reissued during the war in an edition of 30 000 copies; and others had heard his wartime radio commentaries. He was an obvious choice to advise on the proposed school of social sciences. Coombs also had someone in mind for the Pacific Studies school; but as he had not yet been able to sound him out in London, Council fixed its attention on the three other schools first.

The men who received the invitation had much in common. All had been born and had grown up in Australia: Florey and Oliphant in Adelaide, and Hancock in Melbourne. All were of similar age: Florey and Hancock were 48, and Oliphant was nearly 46. All had completed first degrees at their local universities before winning scholarships which took them to England. By the mid-1940s each had spent the greater part of his working life outside Australia and had achieved international recognition in his own field.

Florey was the best known, especially after winning the Nobel Prize in 1945. He had left Australia for England late in 1921, taken out an outstanding degree from Oxford, then served in various research and teaching positions, chiefly in Cambridge and Sheffield universities, before being appointed in 1935 to his position in the Dunn School at Oxford. Since leaving Australia he had returned only twice: first in 1936, to see his dying mother; and then in 1944, when he had talked late into the night with Wright and Conlon about the prospects for a medical research institute.

Oliphant's career had taken him out of Australia in 1927, first to the Cavendish Laboratory at Cambridge, where he worked under the Nobel Prize winner Lord Rutherford on the structure of the atomic nucleus, and then to a chair in Physics at the University of Birmingham. In 1937 he was elected a Fellow of the Royal Society. During the war years he directed research on microwave radar for the Admiralty and then contributed to the Manhattan Project. Like Florey, Oliphant had made two trips home: for a few weeks' vacation in 1931, and for several months in 1942, when he advised Australian scientists regarding the use and development of radar.

Sir Howard Florey, 1948. A keen amateur photographer, Florey carries his camera over his shoulder.
Australian Official Photograph, ANU Collection.

Hancock had divided his career more evenly between Britain and Australia. After graduating from Melbourne he spent two years at the University of Western Australia before taking up a Rhodes Scholarship at Balliol College, Oxford. In 1923 he became the first Australian to be elected a Fellow of All Souls. Repaying the duty that he understood Rhodes Scholars had to their own country, he accepted the chair of Modern History at the University of Adelaide in 1926, at the age of 28. Then it was back to England in 1934 as Professor of Modern History at Birmingham, where he overlapped for several years with Oliphant. In 1944 he was appointed Chichele Professor of Economic History at Oxford, though in fact he spent most of the war in the War Cabinet Offices in London, where he coordinated work on a series of British war histories. When the cable conveying the invitation arrived in September 1946 he had been out of Australia for more than a decade.

Each of the prospective advisers read this cable as a tentative invitation to direct one of the four schools. But their reactions were different. Oliphant telegraphed back that he would be delighted to advise the University and that he was in any case scheduled to visit Australia soon to talk about atomic energy. His enthusiasm for the project had, if anything, increased since his walk in the park with Chifley several months earlier. As he told Conlon, he wanted to see in Australia a strong and determined group devoted to the advancement of learning. He knew what Canberra had to offer, having been there several times during his visit to Australia in 1942. At the same time, he was impatient with the progress of his research in Birmingham. If the Australian government was serious about its willingness to provide ample funds, he was ready to begin his research anew.

Hancock was equally keen. His affection for Australia was as strong as Oliphant's, but more complicated. The memories of his childhood in Gippsland had a deep hold on him; but so too did the richness of culture and heritage that he had experienced at All Souls. It was not impossible, he reflected in *Australia,* for Australians to be in love with two soils. But it was difficult if both soils demanded his presence. When he had left Adelaide for Birmingham in 1934 he had felt like a deserter. Twelve years later he acknowledged a compelling impulse to return.

Other, personal reasons influenced his response. One was the sheer exhaustion he had experienced, and was still experiencing, coordinating the war histories and trying to meet the deadlines imposed by publishers and his own demanding regime. The other was the health of his wife, Theaden, who was prone to bouts of depression and who had lately collapsed under the strain of wartime work and life. Hancock hoped a return to the country of her birth and the imposition of a more relaxed way of living would aid her recovery.

No sooner had he received the Council's invitation to advise the University than he started sounding out potential colleagues. 'There are to be slap-up arrangements for equipment, salaries, leave, travel, visiting savants, research fellowships and God knows what else', he told one of them; and with the right people there was no reason why this university should not surpass the best research institutions in England or America. He also saw potential problems, relating especially to the location of the University in Canberra. Would the 'paper-planned university' repeat some of the mistakes of the 'paper-planned capital'? Was there a danger that scholars would segregate themselves from the main forces of Australian life? Could there be adequate safeguards against political interference? Above all, what would be the effects of isolation on wives (such as Theaden) who had no children, or whose children had grown up? 'What would there be for these women except gardening, golf, bridge and diplomatic cocktail parties round and round in the same narrow circle?'

Florey's concerns are more difficult to identify. His enthusiasm for a medical research institute had now almost evaporated. Perhaps this was due to changing circumstances in Britain, where the constraints of wartime were giving way to relatively generous conditions for scientific research, making it easier for him to do the work he wanted to do, but harder to attract a team to go with him to Australia. He told Wright: 'it all boils down to this: What reasons can be adduced for suggesting to anyone in this country (or the U.S.A. etc.) at the present moment that they should go and work in a non-existent Institute in Canberra?' Perhaps his attitude owed something to the award of the Nobel Prize, which had lifted his status even higher in the world of science and made Australia seem much more of a sacrifice. Also the gossip from Australia suggested that not everyone was enthusiastic about his idea for a medical research institute or the prospect of his coming home. Early in 1946 someone told him, in effect, that he would be better employed teaching people in England than 'meddling in the little affairs of Australia'. 'I took that as a hint', he told Wright, 'or more than a hint'.

But then Coombs came to see him, and Wright, Conlon and Rivett continued to write eager letters. So he maintained an interest that was half-hearted enough to worry his Australian supporters, but not sufficiently so to discourage all hope of his coming. As the concept took shape, so did his criticisms. He objected to the draft bill which Coombs sent him for comment, urging Coombs and his colleagues to frame the bill in a general way and leave the details until later. But Coombs, anxious to get the University on the statute books, took little notice. With the formation of the Interim Council, Florey became increasingly querulous—grumbling, as Wright paraphrased him, that nobody loved him and nobody told him anything. All in all, he told Wright, 'it would be a mistake to build up this Medical research Institute with too specific reference to my personal wishes'. But he would be glad to come and give advice from time to time.

Coombs, having set his course, was not to be distracted by ambiguous signals. After visiting Florey, Oliphant and Hancock late in 1946, he reported to Wright that all should be well, provided their wives could be persuaded that they were not coming to outer darkness. He recognised that Oliphant's enthusiasm offered the key to success; and when the physicist arrived in Australia on his scheduled visit early the next year, he determined that the government and the University should give him everything he wanted. Coombs advised the Prime Minister that Oliphant would come to Canberra only if he could do work of the same quality and standing as he was then doing in Birmingham. That meant a capital cost of half a million pounds over five years. Coombs explained to Chifley that 'It was difficult to assess in financial terms the benefits which may derive from the work which could be done by Professor

Oliphant in an adequately equipped research institute'; but if Oliphant's needs could be met, there was an excellent chance of attracting Florey and Hancock as well. Chifley was persuaded, and Cabinet approved the necessary funds, subject to Oliphant agreeing to come.

During Oliphant's visit, Wright worked hard to see that he did not fall into the wrong hands. He steered him towards Conlon who, during a three-hour dinner in Sydney, convinced him that the Council had a core of good people who would get things done, and managed to convey the impression that he was a prime mover in the whole enterprise. Together they concocted a cable, to be despatched by Oliphant and Florey once Oliphant reached home, asking that Wright be sent to England to talk directly, on Council's behalf, with the advisers. This was Conlon's last major contribution to the University. The sort of influence he exercised through personal contacts and backroom manoeuvres, which flourished during the exigencies of war, did not long survive the peace and the break-up of his wartime network. As he himself predicted soon after the war, his usefulness was nearly at an end. After a short and unsuccessful period as Principal of the Australian School of Pacific Administration in Sydney, he completed a medical course and practised medicine for a decade until his death in 1961, aged just 52.

Wright, by contrast, at the beginning of 1947 was playing a larger and more formal role, having got himself appointed Honorary Secretary to the Interim Council. It was therefore quite appropriate that the Council should agree to send him to England to negotiate with the advisers. The Council also decided to recruit an adviser for the Pacific Studies school. The task of picking the right man was less straightforward than for the other schools, as no Australian expatriate immediately came to mind. Conlon had put forward to Coombs two names: John Kerr, a young lawyer who had served with him in the Directorate of Army Research and who was now head of the Australian School of Pacific Administration; and Raymond Firth, who was Professor of Anthropology at the University of London. Kerr was impressive, but suffered from the drawback of being a local. Nevertheless, according to Conlon, Coombs agreed that the school could have him, provided Florey and Oliphant were certainties; and if they were not, they would have to go for Firth. As Florey and Oliphant remained doubtful, Kerr's chances slipped, leaving him free to follow a legal and judicial path that would eventually lead to the office of governor-general.

Firth was not ideal, in that he was not an Australian. He was, however, a New Zealander, the next best thing; and from 1930 to 1932 he had been a lecturer, then briefly acting professor, at the University of Sydney. Some members of Council also had reservations about whether an anthropologist was the best person to head the school. However, nobody could question his academic credentials; and he had published diversely on Pacific and South-east Asian anthropology, as well as anthropological theory. He also had an interest, which might have appealed to Coombs and Conlon in particular, in training cadets for the British Colonial Service. He was six months younger than Oliphant, and his background was similar to that of the other three advisers. After graduating from Auckland University College, he had studied at the London School of Economics and had continued his career in England.

When Coombs approached Firth with the Council's invitation, it came as a complete surprise. He responded eagerly, welcoming the opportunity to play a part in what appeared to be an exciting project, and incidentally pleased that a visit to Australia would give him the opportunity to call in to New Zealand.

So eight months after the passage of the Australian National University Act, the Interim Council had picked its men. But winning them over was proving to be a hard job. And clear differences were emerging on the Council about how the courtship should proceed. Rivett suggested, as Wright and Conlon had done, that Florey be offered a blank cheque and trusted completely to fill it in. But it appeared, he told Florey with wide-eyed innocence, that some of his colleagues—'administrators and professional organisers'—did not seem to view things 'from the same simple and straightforward point of view that is usual amongst simple and straightforward seekers for scientific knowledge'.

Already the natural and social scientists were lining up against one another, as they would many times in the history of the University. In Interim Council discussions, Eggleston wanted to know exactly what the potential directors had in mind for their schools. Oliphant and Florey were not acting like prima donnas, he told fellow councillor John Medley: it was just that the scientific members of Council were placing them in that position. Eggleston still wanted Florey and Oliphant, who would give the University a great fillip. And if they did not come he was ready to be annoyed, as he believed the Council had done everything it could to meet their wishes.

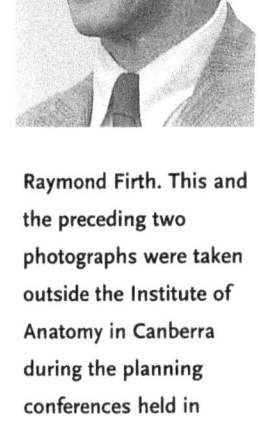

Raymond Firth. This and the preceding two photographs were taken outside the Institute of Anatomy in Canberra during the planning conferences held in Easter 1948. The Institute building later housed the National Film and Sound Archive.
Australian Official Photograph, ANU Collection.

 ## Oxford and Canberra

Wright set out for England early in 1947, fearful that he might come home as 'the boy who spilt the gravy'. He soon discovered that the maestros were not reticent in voicing their concerns. Would they be able to attract suitably qualified academic staff? Would the buildings be ready in time? Would there be an executive officer to relieve their burden of meetings and routine administrative tasks? What form of government, if any, would be appropriate for a research university? This last weighed most heavily with them, and they suggested that Wright should cross the Atlantic to find out how the American research universities went about their business.

In the course of a week, Wright trundled up and down the east coast of the USA and across the border to the University of Toronto, visiting ten universities and research institutions, including the Princeton Institute for Advanced Study, the Rockefeller Institute, Harvard University and the Massachussets Institute of Technology. According to Wright, the Rochester Medical School, founded in the 1920s, came closest to the sort of arrangement contemplated for Canberra: appoint a chief to map out general fields of activity, then chiefs of divisions as they came into view, with the buildings being erected in the meantime. The overall image he presented was one of diversity; and his message to the maestros and the Council was that 'any reasonable legal machinery is adequate for a university in which the governing body and the staff have a high moral purpose'. In other words, forget the formal structure and rely on agreed commitment and goodwill.

According to Wright, who tended to interpret responses to suit his own wishes, the maestros accepted this approach. In fact they were far less trusting, as they demonstrated at a two-day meeting at Australia House in London at the end of March, attended by Coombs, Wright, all four prospective directors, and two new arrivals in England: Eric Ashby, a former member of the Interim Council, who had been appointed to the chair of Botany at the University of Manchester; and John Foster, formerly Registrar of the University of Melbourne and now Secretary to the Universities Bureau of the British Empire, which was based in London. Ashby's influence on the development of the ANU was peripheral, but Foster came to play a central role in the planning. At Wright's request he drafted a series of statutes which enabled Florey, Oliphant, Hancock and Firth to debate and influence the details of the University's proposed organisation and administrative arrangements, including the relationship between the council and the academic board, the powers of the vice-chancellor and the directors, and the prospect of undergraduate teaching. Those discussions gave the Advisers a clear sense of involvement in the evolving venture.

The level of commitment still varied from one Adviser to the next. Only Oliphant was unequivocal: he was 'sick of the shilly-shallying' and ready to sign on the dotted line, irrespective of Florey's decision. Hancock also seemed likely, in that he stressed that he wanted to reach a decision promptly: once he received a firm offer and the issues were clearly defined, he would be quick to let the University know—though he was careful at this stage to avoid implying what that decision might be. Florey remained unenthusiastic. Firth seemed encouraging about the project, but non-committal about whether or not he would accept appointment as director. At least all agreed to visit Australia soon to advise on arrangements for the four schools.

Deciding that it would be risky to press them too hard, Wright came up with a strategy designed to turn necessity to advantage. He now argued that there were benefits in *not* pressing the prospective directors to reach a decision until more progress had been made on the University's buildings and academic structure. Until that time, the Interim Council would continue in its current form, but would function with the help of the prospective directors, who would be formally constituted in England as an Academic Advisory Committee. This committee, which would be serviced in England by an administrative officer, would advise the Council regarding the statutes, budgetary matters, design of buildings, acquisition of books and equipment, and so on. On the committee's recommendation, Council would appoint a nucleus of junior staff (meaning anyone under the rank of professor), who would work in appropriate laboratories in various parts of the world until Canberra was ready to receive them, say in 1952.

Wright's plan was not well thought through, and he seemed to have in mind only the natural science schools. But the crucial element—the creation of an Academic Advisory Committee—seemed to solve an immediate problem. As well as buying time for Florey and Firth, it would allow Council, as Wright put it, to go to 'Chif' and say 'We are acting on the advice of the committee'. So Council issued invitations to Florey, Oliphant, Hancock and Firth, each of whom readily accepted a proposal which did not appear to demand too firm a commitment. Hancock was careful, though, to decline the offered honorarium on the grounds that he didn't need it and he didn't think he would earn it.

A little carelessly, perhaps, the custodians in Australia entered into an arrangement which would shift to England a fair degree of responsibility for the University's development. Only one of them appears to have foreseen problems. L.F. (Fin) Crisp, a member of the Department of Post-War Reconstruction who was now acting as secretary to the Interim Council, warned Mills of dangers inherent in dual control, which he thought would certainly develop if the Academic Advisory Committee were given anything more than minimal secretarial assistance. For one thing, if academics were being recruited overseas there was a risk that Australians might not have an equal opportunity to compete or be considered for appointment. This was to be, after all, the *Australian* National University: and if the Academic Advisory Committee filled some of the posts with people whose connections with Australia were tenuous, the Australian taxpayers and their representatives in parliament might, rightly or wrongly, object. Crisp also warned Wright that harm could be done by seeming to abdicate control from the Australian end. But Wright was unconcerned.

By this time, the Interim Council had swung into a routine of monthly meetings, generally chaired by Mills and held in the Department of Post-War Reconstruction in Canberra. Although Wright, himself a member, was contemptuous of the Council's labours, it made significant progress with administrative and financial arrangements, appointing a Registrar, R.G. Osborne, who relieved Wright of his title of Honorary Secretary, and a Librarian, A.L.G. McDonald, from the University of Melbourne. It invited several academic visitors from overseas to lecture to Australian audiences, administered a scheme of research fellowships for established social scientists, set up an overseas scholarships scheme, and commissioned Laurie Fitzhardinge to survey the National Library's resources on Australian subjects. Before the Interim Council was due to dissolve at the end of 1947, parliament extended its life until a permanent council should come into existence, making provision for some new members as it did so.

Although the Council had a year's head start on the Academic Advisory Committee, the Committee quickly rivalled it in range of business and diligence. Mills thought it would not meet often. He was wrong: after the first meeting at Oxford in August 1947 it came together monthly for the next five months, and every two or three months after that, attended each time by John Foster and a secretary. Hancock's rooms at All Souls and Florey's office in the Dunn School became regular venues for detailed discussion of how things should develop in Canberra.

From the first meeting, the Advisers were inclined to lay down the law, insisting in particular that there should be no undergraduate or vocational teaching (except in special circumstances), and that each research school should be free to pursue its own program without interference by 'the University'. They tended to see themselves as a kind of professorial board, whose main duty was to defend academic standards and academic freedom in the fledgling institution against outside interference, which in

The Great Quadrangle at All Souls College, Oxford. Although this photograph dates from the early 1970s, the Great Quad was little different 25 years earlier.
All Souls College.

this case included interference by a Council dominated by public servants. In their view, evinced more by example than by specific declaration, the Advisory Committee should have principal if not sole control over academic matters.

The Council thought otherwise, though eagerness to retain the Advisers made it avoid a contest on specific issues. The Committee members suspected that Council was not telling them everything—which was true—and they were irritated that Council seemed to think it could interfere, as Oliphant put it, in anything it liked. Council members, in turn, became annoyed by what they saw as the Committee's contradictory statements and testy tone. Meetings in Oxford and Canberra were not coordinated with one another, and problems arose when reports crossed in the post. To add to the confusion, some Council members corresponded privately with Committee members, producing what the Registrar Osborne called some unfortunate results.

Who should be the first vice-chancellor? Everyone agreed that the matter was urgent and the choice all-important. As Florey put it, the concept was like a pack of cards: 'take out the Vice Chancellor, [and] the whole thing goes futt'. (He often mixed his metaphors.) The selection process began at the meeting in London in March 1947 and turned into a saga, partly because there was no hot candidate, but also because the choice had to be acceptable to as many of the planners as possible on both sides of the world. There was no agreed model of the ideal vice chancellor. Coombs wanted a man of high intellectual attainment, who would be a welcome colleague among the heads of the research schools. Wright hoped for a forceful leader in educational matters throughout the Australian community. The Advisers tended to emphasise administrative capacity. Florey was after a good administrator, perhaps somebody approaching retiring age, and thought there must be lots of them poked away in offices in Whitehall. Oliphant looked for someone in his mid-forties, a genuine academic who understood the nature of research, not a big man in the intellectual sense, but a bit of a social figure. All four Advisers wanted someone who would not interfere with the work of the directors of the research schools, and who would, in Florey's words, act as a buffer between them and the government, as well as people with crack-brained ideas. As Wright shrewdly remarked, they wanted a man who would relieve them of their chores, but not their authority.

Oliphant had already come up with a possibility: Charles Morris, a former don who had been in charge of the supply of war materials for much of the war, and who was now a public school headmaster. The group in London interviewed him and were reasonably impressed. But there was something about him that did not seem quite right ... and then someone said of him that he would be happier in a no. 1 position than as part of a team. Also, he was very much a Balliol man, with little knowledge of Australian conditions. How would he fit in? Many other names of people in England were bandied about, but all those who might have been suitable were unavailable. Even Oliphant was becoming disheartened as he heard a familiar set of reasons: 'Papa and Mamma are here and the children are in good schools, etc.'.

As the Advisers did not appear to be getting anywhere, the task was thrown back to the Interim Council. Mills and Coombs decided that the person appointed had to be an Australian, though the Council still toyed with some English names. Everyone concerned in Australia wanted Coombs to take on the job, and Mills and Wright pressed him hard. Although he was 'enormously attracted' by the prospect, and went so far as to discuss the matter with the Prime Minister, he decided that he could not abandon his commitment to the cause of post-war planning.

Rivett now put forward the name of Sir Douglas Copland, a 53-year-old economist who was currently Australia's Minister to China. Copland had spent most of his working life as a professor of economics or commerce, first in Hobart from 1920 to 1924, then in Melbourne until 1945. During the war he had served as Commonwealth Prices Commissioner and Economic Consultant to the Prime Minister. Copland was well known to everyone—and that was his major problem. In an academic world where the quality of one's mind was most esteemed when it was self-evident, he was seen as something of a self-promoter, and this impression was sufficient to cast doubt on his academic credentials. Even Wright, who was no friend to academic pretensions, was annoyed by an address he gave at the University of Melbourne which seemed to belittle 'stuffy academics' and endorse the virtues of 'real work' in the outside world. But Rivett, supported on Council by Eggleston, argued strongly in his favour: 'He has certain necessary qualities which will be most useful and, when they are no longer required, he will be old enough to be replaced'. Those qualities included proven administrative capacity, a flair for publicity, vast energy, and a determination to take no nonsense from anyone who might offer it. At the same time, he had characteristics which could be interpreted either as amiable weaknesses or as irritants. Some thought him overly fond of the company of important people and the status which accompanied high office. Although he was born and grew up in New Zealand, there was an Australian brashness about him. Coombs, who had shared a flat with him (and the astronomer Woolley) in Canberra during the war, liked him but thought him pompous, as well as being a pedestrian economist. Wright conceded that he might be good for the institution, but risky for relations with the maestros: 'he would bash them or they would bash him and there would be a first class dust up'.

The maestros were of two minds. Oliphant, disappointed that Coombs could not be persuaded and wanting instant action, decided that Copland was the man. 'Give us a person to bully, preferably a vigorous and rather ruthless go-getter, and we will all be happier. I have heard some reassuring things about Copland who might do well for the initial period. What about appointing him and have done with it?' But Hancock (who knew Copland) and Florey (who did not) each dismissed him privately as 'a showman' and 'not a gentleman', which probably meant that they did not think he would cut an appropriate figure in the senior common rooms at Oxford; and Hancock hinted that he would be much less interested in coming to Australia if Copland were appointed vice-chancellor. But he and Florey were hard to please, dismissing even Coombs as a possible candidate because they considered him a 'little' man who lacked both academic background and academic outlook.

Between the Council in Canberra and the Committee in Oxford, it was a wonder they managed to get anyone. Among the dozen or so names floated, Morris was too English, Copland too Australian; Ronald Walker was not an administrator; Wright was too good a researcher (which meant that nobody wanted him); Coombs was too short; and among those whom we have not met, Jackson of United Nations Relief and Rehabilitation Administration had no academic background, Wadham of Melbourne was too old and difficult, and Dodds of Oxford had 'a really terrifying wife'.

After several months of searching, and having satisfied itself that Coombs was definitely not available, Council narrowed the list of names to Copland and Leslie Melville, who had been since 1931 Economic Adviser to the Commonwealth Bank, where he had been Coombs's first employer. Coombs had introduced Melville into the discussion, and now he pressed his claims with enthusiasm, pointing out his intellectual distinction, administrative capacity and feeling for research, as well as his reputation as a cooperator. The Advisers, faced with what they regarded as a rather limited choice, expressed a firm preference for Melville. But Council, consciously or otherwise, decided that this was a matter that they were in the best position to judge and wherein they should have the final say. They chose Copland, and their choice ensured that much of the creative force in the University's development would remain in Canberra.

Easter 1948

Although the Advisers—Hancock and Florey in particular—may not have been impressed with Council's failure to accept their advice, at least the vice-chancellor was now chosen and a significant source of tension was removed. The next stage involved each of the Advisers coming to Canberra for consultations; and by a combination of good management and good luck, all of them (and all their wives) were available in the Australian autumn. The lead-up to the visit provided more opportunities for strains and misunderstandings. Florey was peeved when the Council questioned his well-considered plan for him and his wife to come to Australia at different times. The Advisers wanted Foster to accompany them or, failing him, their secretary, Joan Clemenger. When Council said no, all four were irritated and Florey was furious, complaining to Oliphant that this was the sort of thing that drives professors mad and that it would have been avoided if the Committee had some real control. Foster, caught in the middle, confided to the Registrar, Osborne, that members of the Academic Advisory Committee suspected Council's attitude towards them was not as indulgent as it once had been (which was true enough) and warned him that they were all 'rather delicate plants' who would need careful handling when they came to Australia. And he explained to Wright that 'the boys' were really seriously interested, and this made them extraordinarily touchy.

The meetings were scheduled to be held over several days before and after Easter, at the Institute of Anatomy, adjacent to the University site. Everyone hoped that Copland, whose appointment was formally announced at the beginning of March 1948, would be back in time, but difficulties in getting out of China delayed his arrival until after the first session. He made sure, however, that he was well prepared, drawing wry inspiration from his experience in China where 'you seem to gain great face if you can give continued proof that you have some capacity for scholarship and that your natural home is amongst scholars'.

The discussions were in two parts: four days of meetings between the Interim Council and the Academic Advisory Committee, which twice went into informal session for what Mills, who was in the chair most of the time, referred to as 'frank talk'; and separate meetings devoted to three of the four research schools. Each meeting lasted two days and was chaired by the appropriate Adviser and attended by senior academics and researchers from throughout Australia. Oliphant, who was already clear about where he was headed, decided that a meeting to discuss physical sciences would not be necessary. The conferences on the other schools proved to be significant occasions, giving the University its first detailed exposure to the wider academic community.

The general meetings proceeded as amiably as Mills and his Council could have wished, given that the Advisers were known to be tetchy. Discussion ranged broadly across the University's structure and objectives, narrowing occasionally to matters of detail, such as the value of scholarships, study leave entitlements and the colour of bricks to be used in building. The Council tried hard to put the Advisers' minds at ease on issues that had been worrying them, and on a few major questions discussion achieved

'Frank talk': the four members of the Academic Advisory Committee, at right, discuss basic issues with members of the Interim Council in the Institute of Anatomy, April 1948. Clockwise from the front, with backs to camera: C.S. Daley, Sir Robert Garran, Sir Frederic Eggleston, E.H. Clark (assisting the Registrar), Sir Douglas Copland, R.G. Osborne (Registrar), R.C. Mills, H.C. Coombs, A.S. Brown, H.J. Goodes, R.D. Wright, A.L.G. McDonald (Librarian), and the Advisers, Florey, Oliphant, Firth and Hancock.
Australian Official Photograph, ANU Collection.

greater precision: as, for example, in their agreement that the University's training function could be crystallised in the granting of the doctor's degree (meaning the PhD).

A few issues were left vague and unresolved, reminding participants that the structure of the University was necessarily experimental. Discussion skirted around the question of who should be responsible for appointing senior staff. Florey argued that for the first ten years appointments should be left entirely to the directors of each school. Rivett, at the opposite extreme, argued that every position should be advertised. Then there was uncertainty about the respective roles of directors and professors. It was generally agreed that directors should be responsible for the work of their schools and should be allowed as much freedom as possible to develop the schools as they wished. At the same time professors should be given the right to pursue their own research and develop their departments as *they* wished. Nobody wanted or expected a director to direct. The Advisers, who had drawn up draft conditions of appointment for professors, concluded that 'the director would not be a dictator to any professor who was capable of co-operating with others with a reasonable degree of good will'. But what of the professor who did not have that capacity? Nobody had the perfect solution as to who should have the final say.

There was nevertheless sufficient agreement for Copland to prepare a memorandum entitled 'Basic Policy for Academic Development in the University'. This stated that the function of the ANU was primarily to prosecute research and, secondly, to train research workers. With equal force, the document outlined what the University would *not* be required to do: undergraduate teaching other than genuine honours work at a high standard; postgraduate vocational training; and work outside

THE MAESTROS

The maestros listen to the Vice-Chancellor. Do Florey and Hancock look slightly sceptical? Firth is pensive, but Oliphant at least seems confident. All need to support their chins.
Australian Official Photograph, ANU Collection.

the University (in other words, for government), except when undertaken as an emergency measure and with the appropriate director's approval.

After reading the 'Basic Policy', Rivett offered Copland some wry advice, based on his twenty years as head of CSIR. The memorandum, he remarked, had been 'well and worthily drawn up'—but now was the time to forget it.

> Like all prophets or semi-prophets, its many authors suffer from the rather serious disadvantage of being unable either to see accurately into, or guess truly about, the future. Plans should always be most seriously considered, carefully written out and solemnly cremated. Their spirit will then persist but no one will be bothered with anything else about them!

Designing the schools

In Oxford as well as Canberra most of the collective work had so far been focused on the grand plan, the broad view of how the University as a whole would function. Apart from those early meetings when the Mills committee was at work, there had not been much discussion about the structure and functions of the individual schools. The Advisers, however, had been thinking independently about their schools, and by the time of the Easter conferences, each had a plan which showed, with varying degrees of precision, how his school would be composed, how much it would cost, and how it would work.

Florey had a head start, having presented his ideas in some detail in April 1945. Revisiting them over two years later, he elaborated and amended them in various ways, especially to recognise that the proposed John Curtin School of Medical Research was to be part of the Australian National University.

His starting point, when he first conceived the idea of a research institute, was the current state of medical research in Australia. In his 1945 memorandum to Rivett he quoted the microbiologist Macfarlane Burnet, who remarked on returning from the United States that if all medical research in Australia stopped tomorrow, nobody would notice the difference. According to Florey, Burnet's own institution, the Walter and Eliza Hall Institute, was the exception. The universities contributed little, apart from physiological work in Brisbane and in Wright's department in Melbourne, and bacteriological research in Sydney. To Florey the reasons for this dismal situation were obvious: potential researchers had to spend too much time on undergraduate teaching and distractions such as routine hospital visits; financial support for medical research was totally inadequate; and research institutes tended to be dominated by medical practitioners who had no concept of what was involved in medical research. Australia could and did produce first-rate scientists, but understandably most of them drifted overseas.

To combat the problem, Florey advocated 'radical procedures'. First, reconstitute the National Health and Medical Research Council with a membership who knew something about medical research. Then create a medical research institute on the basis of funding and conditions that would enable it to stand alongside the best such institutes overseas. This could be achieved, he argued, if the Australian government committed itself to providing a minimum of £200 000 to £250 000 per annum over ten years. If it were to have the necessary impact, everything—buildings, staff salaries, technical and administrative support—would have to be first-rate. From the outset, he envisaged close relations and a free exchange of staff between the proposed institute, and existing institutes and university departments, so that within a few years there would be an atmosphere of mental stimulation and competition which would benefit medical research throughout Australia.

What form should the institute take? Although Florey toyed with the idea of having an organisation devoted to a single discipline, perhaps along the lines of his own Dunn School at Oxford, he concluded that what was needed—especially once the decision was made to locate it in the barren wastes of Canberra—was a large institute with half a dozen or so departments, complementing one another but working on separate projects. While the departments, or divisions as he called them, were intended to range widely across the subject matter of medical research, the exact arrangements did not appear to be crucial, as the list put forward in 1945 differed significantly from the one he outlined nearly three years later. This second blueprint drew inspiration from the British National Institute of Medical Research, which was about to move to new premises at Mill Hill on the outskirts of London. The National Institute had seven divisions, together with a biological standards laboratory. Florey dropped the biological standards laboratory and shuffled the composition of the divisions to reflect his own experience and interests, giving emphasis to biochemistry and organic chemistry, which had proven so valuable in the development of penicillin, and including a division devoted to his own area of experimental pathology.

Florey considered his own scheme an improvement on the British model, which had been designed largely around certain individuals. He nevertheless attached prime importance to the task of recruiting the best possible men and building the school around them. The professors would each have charge of a division and would be responsible for its early development, including organising laboratories and helping select staff. Below the professors, each department would have from one to five first-rate researchers, together with a number of research assistants, people who lacked the originality or experience to work independently but who would nevertheless make valuable members of research teams.

Where would the staff come from? By the time he was preparing his second report, he had convinced himself that it would be impossible to find British researchers who would be willing to move to Australia. This left three possible sources: Australians who were then working in Britain (and he listed half a dozen possibilities); people employed at other Australian universities and institutes; and young Australians who might be groomed for professorial positions. All of these presented problems: Australians in Britain might not want to move; a raid on other institutions could lead to deep antagonism towards the ANU; and training young researchers would take a long time. Best therefore to proceed gradually, setting up the divisions only when good people became available.

Florey quite liked the idea of his institute becoming part of a larger intellectual community. But one aspect of the changed status perplexed him: the role of the director. Viewing the medical school as an independent institute, he could write comfortably that the director should be responsible for the general direction of research. But once the director became a member of a university hierarchy, with professors under him, the situation became more complicated. Presumably the director would have charge of a division. But apart from that, was there a place for him? Florey depicted him as a chairman of professors, who would have to do his best to achieve 'some uniformity of aim and some common standards of performance', though he would not formulate any general research program or be responsible for the direction of research in the various departments. He would provide the oil to lubricate the machine; he would guard against any department building itself 'a little independent kingdom'; he would ensure as far as possible that the departments worked together. In short, in Florey's proposed school the director's position would be 'one of some delicacy'—a phrase whose aptness would impress directors in the 1980s and 1990s.

At the Easter conferences, Florey presented his ideas over two days at a meeting attended by sixteen other senior medical scientists. Confronting his colleagues' anxieties head on, he announced at the outset that the main purpose of the conference was to dispel the 'fairly widespread and somewhat justified' distrust of the ANU proposal, part of which was based on ignorance. The fear was that the John Curtin School would receive generous funding at the expense of the rest of Australia—or, as Macfarlane Burnet put it, that there would be two universes of research in Australia, one of them starved for funds. Talking through these anxieties probably helped reduce them, and there was agreement that the problem could be circumvented if the University and the National Health and Medical Research Council coordinated their activities. But not everyone left the meeting convinced that the John Curtin School would benefit medical research throughout the nation.

On other matters, there was much agreement: the desirability of cooperation between the John Curtin School and the state institutions in recruiting scholars; the absolute necessity of protecting the University's research program from government interference; and the benefits to be gained from a flexible approach to departmental structure. Florey's divisional plan was generally well received; but there was also broad agreement that there should be room for an outstanding scientist—a geneticist perhaps—who might become available but who did not fit into the plan. Equally, it should be possible to accommodate new areas of research. The determining factor, said Wright, would be the interest of the individual researcher: as this was a university, good people would be appointed and they should be free to follow the course of research that they mapped out for themselves.

Although Oliphant shared many of Florey's views about the nature of the institution and how it should run, his design for the Research School of Physical Sciences implied significant differences in their thinking. Where the powers and responsibilities of directors weighed heavily with Florey, for Oliphant they were scarcely an issue. Florey, uncertain of his own position, tended to view his school's development in the abstract. Oliphant, on the other hand, saw himself from the outset as director of a school which would focus on research that he initiated. Their approaches differed too: Florey intended to cover a wide range of medical research; Oliphant wanted to concentrate on one area (if an extensive one) of the physical sciences. As the University grew, it might become possible to add other branches of physics (and chemistry) to the program of research. But for the first five years the school would need to limit its objectives.

Oliphant defined the proposed work of the school as 'research in fundamental nuclear physics and in the related branch of chemistry—the chemistry of radioactive substances'. Nuclear physics was the area that had caught Chifley's imagination as he and Oliphant strolled in the London park, and it was the basis for the government finding a vast sum of money for the Physical Sciences school, if Oliphant agreed to head it. Oliphant explained to the Interim Council that there were other developing areas of physics which might be pursued as an alternative to nuclear physics, namely, X-ray, low temperature or high temperature physics. But all of these were expensive, and none was as vital to Australia as work in the nuclear field.

Oliphant prepared his blueprint during his visit to Australia early in 1947, after he had spoken to the Interim Council and to colleagues from other parts of Australia, and he refined it after the Easter conferences. His modified scheme provided for the director, a professor of Experimental Physics ('to share direction of the experimental programme with the Director'), and professors of Theoretical Physics and Radiochemistry. Then there were to be fifteen other academic staff and fifteen research students, plus technical and administrative staff, including the essential appointment of laboratory manager. Coming to Canberra, he told the Council, would involve great sacrifice for physicists (like himself) working in Britain; but once he had thrown in his lot with the University there would be no trouble recruiting, since his decision would convince first-class men that he had 'a passionate belief in the future of the National University'. He calculated that the school would cost at least £500 000 for capital expenditure over the first five years, and £65 050 annually for salaries and other running costs.

The plan for the Social Sciences school took the form of an eleven-page letter which Hancock wrote to Mills in mid-1947. With a characteristic blend of self-deprecation and self-confidence, he explained to Mills that he had chosen to express his ideas in the form of 'epistolary chatter' because he did not want to make the screed read like 'a systematic exposition of scientific principles'. Elegantly written, the letter seemed almost deliberately imprecise. In contrast to the blueprints of Florey and Oliphant, it had little to say about money, which did not interest Hancock and which he thought ought to be left to the administrators—although a year later, during the Easter conferences, he did prepare a supplementary memorandum which estimated the annual cost of the school, three or four years after establishment, at £60 000. What the letter did provide, as the blueprints of Florey and Oliphant did not, was a detailed exposition of the work of the school and how it would be done.

'Planning to me', he later wrote, 'means not so much the imposition of a design upon life as guidance bringing gradually to view a design already implicit in healthy growth'. Avoiding the term 'departments', which he took to suggest rigidity and segregation, he presented a list of headings which he referred to as 'growing points': Economics, Statistics, Population and Health Studies, Law, Political Science, Social Anthropology, Psychology, History and Philosophy, Sociology, Geography. Not all of these areas would require early appointments. Some researchers might embrace two or more; some headings, such as Social Anthropology, might fit more comfortably in Pacific Studies; others, notably Psychology, might wait until the school could define its needs more precisely. History and Philosophy were essential, to ensure that the school did not degenerate into 'an aggregate of people myopically focussed upon their own tiny segment of place and time and research material'. But for the purposes of the school these should be seen less as subject areas than as fundamental training essential to many branches of social research.

So Hancock narrowed his list to half a dozen chief researchers, in Economics, Statistics, Demography, Law, Political Science and Anthropology. Hoping at first to escape the term professor, he soon decided it could not be avoided (though he did not say why). In addition, there were to be thirteen other staff of varying status, including a geographer, a cartographer, and a philosopher who would do 'gadfly work' around the school, stimulating his colleagues about methodological questions and encouraging them to set their research in a wide context. A year later, however, after comparing ideas with Firth and other colleagues, he moved towards 'a more coherent grouping of subjects', comprising Economics, Politics and Sociology, each of which would have a professorial head. And to provide a basis for historical research, he now advocated a readership in the Sources of Australian History. He concluded that the school at maturity should number at least twenty to twenty-five staff.

There was always some ambiguity about what Hancock meant by 'growing points'. He liked to present them as areas of thought or perhaps of specific research. But in his own mind they generally took the form of individual researchers. 'Ideas without men', he later wrote, 'don't excite me'. For Hancock, more than any other of his fellow Advisers, outstanding researchers were the foundations upon which the school would be built, and without which any paper plans would be worthless.

His discussion of staff arrangements led him to the question of relations with the Research School of Pacific Studies, and here he sounded a warning. As one school was based on mental disciplines and the other on geography, there would obviously be many points of overlap. It was therefore essential to have good relations between the schools and their directors. 'A bad school of Pacific Studies, under a bad head, would make life very difficult indeed for the School of Social Sciences.' But if Firth were in charge of Pacific Studies, all the potential problems would disappear in stimulating and fruitful collaboration. Working with him would be 'a delight'.

When Firth came to the job of drafting a blueprint, he found that others had been at the drawing board before him, especially Eggleston, who had put forward his own plans well before Firth had been enlisted as an Adviser. Eggleston wanted the emphasis to be on Asia, and would have preferred the title 'School of Pacific and Asiatic Studies'. He saw it as a means of remedying Australia's ignorance of the region and of responding to the major questions confronting Australia and its neighbours. He looked forward to visits from Chinese and Indian scholars, who could impart first-hand knowledge of Asiatic cultures. The school was also to have a vocational purpose: as a former diplomat he recognised an urgent need for training diplomatic cadets and colonial officials.

Firth, although aware of Eggleston's views, concluded (reasonably enough) that as the Interim Council had invited an anthropologist to advise them, they would be receptive to an emphasis on 'human studies' over politics. His anthropological perspective suggested that the major field of research should be the Pacific island territories for which Australia was responsible. Chinese and Japanese affairs should also be considered, but only in so far as conditions in these countries affected Australia and its Pacific island territories.

Eggleston had never been in favour of having an anthropologist as director, preferring someone with 'a broader approach', and specifically a geographer. Now he was confronted with 'a plan which concentrated somewhat narrowly on Anthropology in a limited area'. However, he and his fellow councillors concluded that any school which Firth directed would do distinguished work and therefore accepted the plan, with one major proviso: the school would also study the political problems of the Pacific, including the role of the major powers in the region and the development of new national communities. Thus the most significant element of what we might call the 'Pacific affairs approach', championed by Eggleston the diplomat, was tacked on to the 'Pacific studies approach', prepared by Firth the anthropologist.

In many respects the approaches were, almost literally, oceans apart. The differences came out strongly at the Easter conferences, especially during the discussion of how history should be covered in the school. Firth argued that the minutiae of the Pacific might prove to be 'the ultimate explanatory forces behind the history of the area', and Hancock, in his support, warned against synthesising in

Hancock addresses the conference on research in the social sciences, Easter 1948. Identifiable faces include, at the far left of the photograph and looking towards Hancock, R.M. Crawford (Professor of History, University of Melbourne); moving to his left, Herbert (Joe) Burton (Associate Professor of Economic History, Melbourne), E.H. Clark, R.G. Osborne, Hancock and Mills; at the centre of the far table, J.M. Ward (Challis Professor of History and later Vice-Chancellor, University of Sydney); to his right, Gordon Greenwood, Professor of History, University of Queensland) and two to his left, Richard Downing (Senior Lecturer in Economics, University of Melbourne, and later Chairman of the ABC); Firth is furthest to the right of the photograph; Eggleston is in the foreground, hand on forehead, and Paul Hasluck (Reader in History, University of Western Australia, and later Minister in the Menzies government and Governor-General) two to his right.
Australian Official Photograph, ANU Collection.

advance of sufficient detail. Eggleston, on the other hand, spoke of 'the stockbroker who spent his life making decisions on insufficient evidence and ended up by being a millionaire'. His concerns were immediate and urgent: what was needed was a good political history which would provide a sound basis for understanding the present.

Firth never got around to amending his plan to meet Council's wishes. Early in 1949, having reached the conclusion that he and his wife were culturally Europeans and that they would not be prepared to come permanently to Australia, he resigned from the Academic Advisory Committee. Eggleston at once seized the opportunity to do away with the 'microcosmic approach' and substituted a 'broader conception of the scope of the School'. In a revised plan which he worked out with Copland, the geographical boundaries were extended to Asia, including India, South-east Asia, China and Japan, and the emphasis of research was reoriented to practical questions facing Australia. Firth's three sections were replaced by seven major departments: Geography, Demography, Political Science, History, Anthropology, Economics and Linguistics. The Department of Demography would study overpopulation in the region and its effects on world tension; Political Science would analyse developments as the European powers withdrew from the region; and Anthropology would focus on the problems arising out of the clash of races, the political aspects of tribal organisation and the behaviour of peoples in various stages of development.

While the new blueprint supposedly drew on Firth's plan, in fact it owed much more to Eggleston. Firth's situation was therefore rather incongruous when, in mid-1949, he was persuaded to resume the role of Adviser and charged with giving effect to the plan over the next three years, one of which he would spend in Canberra. By this time, however, the selection and appointment of new staff had assumed priority. Theoretical points about the school's overall purpose and geographical scope were overtaken by the practicalities of getting on with the job.

The intended relationship between the Pacific Studies and Social Sciences schools remained ambiguous. During the Easter discussions, the economist (and future Vice-Chancellor) J.G. Crawford remarked that it would be almost impossible to differentiate between the work of the two schools, and the historian and diplomat (and future Governor-General) Paul Hasluck left the conference doubting whether Pacific Studies should exist at all. Eggleston, however, was confident that each school would rely on work done in the other, and overlapping would be avoided. Firth came closest to providing a resolution to the problem in his happy vision of 'a large building with two doors, one of which was labelled School of Social Sciences and the other School of Pacific Studies'. Although he elaborated the picture, probably none of the planners knew for certain how the researchers behind one door differed from those behind the other: except, of course, that one group enjoyed ocean views while the other had windows on the world.

There was an occasional hint that research in Pacific Studies might be more empirical than work in Social Sciences. Eggleston was no friend to what he called 'mere descriptive fact-finding'. But his own comments to the effect that Pacific Studies would be concerned with practical questions and Social Sciences with 'fundamental social truths' did, in the absence of any clearer definition, suggest a more empirical role for the Pacific Studies school. So too did his eagerness that the school should embark on the production of a Pacific atlas, intended as an indispensable research tool for scholars in both schools. Crawford, speaking about economics in Pacific Studies, was more explicit: fact-finding should play an important part, while the study of universals would have to be limited. The theorist, he argued, would probably be better placed in Social Sciences.

Was there any feature of the school that would bind it together, beyond its regional orientation? At the end of the Easter conferences, Firth remarked that several people seemed bothered about the apparent lack of theoretical unity. There was, however, general agreement that the school would have 'value and interest' as a focus. Firth also thought it would need a general theory of society as a background to all its activities. But what exactly he had in mind the school would never know.

Two gentlemen on a park bench

Hancock had left Australia after the Easter conferences fairly confident that he would be returning as a foundation director and generally pleased with how discussions had gone. At the second meeting with the Interim Council, he later wrote, everybody seemed to be in agreement with everybody else. With the benefit of hindsight he saw this as a bad omen.

There was, as Wright had predicted, 'a first class dust up'. Hancock made it famous several years later when, in his autobiographical work *Country and Calling*, he told just enough of the story to make everyone who read it want to know more. His account focused on a meeting between himself and the Vice-Chancellor on a bench in London's St James's Park; and, perhaps deliberately, he blurred the circumstances which preceded it. That meeting and its context reveal so much of where the University, and especially the Research School of Social Sciences, was headed that we should pause near the bench to compose a wider and sharper picture.

The exchange occurred a year after the Easter conferences. As soon as he arrived back in Oxford Hancock threw himself into the task of recruiting a group of senior colleagues, four or five men of first quality. Success in this endeavour was the key to his coming: if he could recruit the nucleus of a professoriate, he would come; if not, he would not. From his investigations while in Australia, he concluded that, with one exception, there was little chance of finding anyone there. He therefore searched diligently within Britain and came up with some esteemed names: Max Beloff of Oxford or Nicholas Mansergh of the Royal Institute of International Affairs for Political Science, R.M. Titmuss of the London School of Economics for Sociology. Their responses, for the most part, were politely unenthusiastic: 'The true pioneering spirit may be lacking', said Beloff. Hancock even looked across the Atlantic, but with no more success.

What he most wanted was an economist, preferably 'someone of experience and reputation, and middle age'. It appeared that such people were hard to come by, as opportunities for economists in various parts of the world were good. Perhaps Arthur Smithies, an Australian-born economist in the United States, might answer 'the call of the kookaburra', or at least give advice. But Smithies replied that he was quite at a loss to think of anyone in the United States who would be willing to go to Australia and whom he would recommend. There were plenty, he said, who would meet one of those conditions, but none who would meet both.

By the end of 1948, Hancock's recruiting efforts were becoming embarrassing, not just for himself but for other people who had the University's interests at heart. Trevor Swan, a colleague of Coombs attending a conference in Paris, wrote home that he had had lunch on three successive days with three different economists, each of whom confessed to a Canberra invitation. By February Hancock was prepared to scale down his requirements to 'just one good man' and decided to try Roland Wilson, another economist who had been recommended by Copland. If Wilson said no, he wrote, 'I shall feel close to the edge of failure'.

Just when Hancock's prospects seemed most gloomy, Firth made his decision to resign from the Academic Advisory Committee. Hancock was sorry to hear this: but, like Eggleston from another perspective, he immediately recognised the opportunity it offered. He had always had misgivings about the relationship between the two schools. Why not now give up the idea of a separate Research School of Pacific Studies and go for Social Sciences, allowing it to make the most of its Pacific opportunities? In a few years, a Pacific Studies school might grow out of this 'joint school'. This would solve the problem of recruitment: with the field of research thus widened, there should be no problem finding two or three professors very quickly. As luck would have it, he had just heard from his old friend W.R. Crocker, who was then Chief of the Africa Section in the Trusteeship Department of the United Nations in New York, and keen to return to Australia. Why not appoint him to a chair of International Organisation? Then there was J.W. Davidson, a young Cambridge man, whom Firth had already enlisted as Professor of Pacific History.

During the Easter 1948 conferences, Oliphant, Hancock and Florey take a break from proceedings at the nearby Institute of Anatomy to inspect the ANU site.

Oliphant Papers, Barr Smith Library, University of Adelaide.

After mulling over the idea for a couple of weeks, Hancock put it forward enthusiastically in a letter to Copland, but with a significant revision. Why not get both schools under way in conjunction under a single director, who would have responsibility for building them until such time as Council decided that each had grown sufficiently to be able to stand apart? So confident was he of getting his men that he told Copland that he would accept the position of director immediately, if Council agreed to his proposal.

But Council did not agree. While Mills and Copland might have been prepared to compromise, several other members were adamant—especially Eggleston, who had already prepared the memorandum designed to bend the Pacific school towards its original objectives. Leaving aside the question of what work the school might be expected to do, Eggleston was determined that it should remain an integral part of the University. After all, an emphasis on Pacific studies had helped persuade the government to accept the university proposal in the first place, and to make a fundamental change at this early stage might jeopardise the whole scheme. So Council determined to leave the immediate future of the school to Copland and Eggleston, and instructed Copland to tell Hancock firmly and politely that his idea was not acceptable.

This rebuttal was unexpected and unwelcome. Hancock, armed with a rejection from yet another economist, spelt out to Copland the dimensions of the problem as he saw it and warned Council that it was in danger of adopting ways and means which would cause the miscarriage of both schools. He also passed on a comment from Davidson that, now that Firth had withdrawn, he would be prepared to go to Canberra with Hancock but with nobody else, adding that other men were likely to make the same condition. This was a bad tactic, serving only to confirm Eggleston's view that Council should stand its ground. And the veiled threat was undermined when Davidson, in Canberra shortly after Hancock had approached him, said nothing about coming only if Hancock were appointed director.

In mid-April 1949, Copland set out on a visit to Britain and the United States that had been planned well before Hancock had broached his scheme for a single director. If he had any illusions about the import of his forthcoming negotiations, they were dispelled by a letter from John Foster who warned that Hancock was about to pull out and that, with two Advisers gone, the others were likely to follow suit. But Eggleston, having read the same letter, steeled Copland's hand: 'The matter', he told Copland, 'is personal to Hancock; he is unable to get a team in Social Studies and now wants to make a radical change in arrangements, a change which does not seem to be in consonance with our responsibilities under the Act'. As for the other members of the Committee, what reason could they possibly give for dropping out simply because Hancock refused the University's offer? 'I resent this ganging up very much', he added privately, 'and I would not mind if none of them came'. The University would succeed without them; he had never favoured Oliphant's concentration on nuclear physics, and it seemed now that Rivett and one or two others shared his misgivings—'so no irreparable damage would be done if they all refused'.

The careful planning was showing signs of turning into a muddle.

Arriving in London on Thursday 21 April, Copland seemed little weighed down by the responsibilities he was carrying. The next day he wrote a cheery note to 'My dear Keith', looking forward to the lunch they had arranged for next week, hoping he hadn't been unduly worried, and expressing confidence that all the problems could be satisfactorily solved. On Saturday he saw Oliphant, and Firth (who had already agreed to remain as Adviser until a successor could be found), and explained to them Council's point of view. Then, on Wednesday, came the meeting with Hancock, recalled so wistfully by Hancock in *Country and Calling*:

> The Vice-Chancellor has just arrived from Canberra and he and I are sitting together on a bench in Saint James's Park. He opens the talk and I follow.

> Within ten minutes everything is finished between the Australian National University and me. The Vice-Chancellor and I linger a little in the sunshine and chat amiably about this and that.
>
> My misery that day and for many days and weeks to come was great ...

Several months after the meeting he recounted it to Firth in similar terms. Copland, he said, had mentioned other workable schemes, but he was adamant that his own proposal would not be considered. 'When he told me that I felt sick. It happened in the first five minutes and we broke then.'

Did he mean 'we broke for lunch'? Or perhaps 'we broke to resume for a longer session later in the day'? Or if the rupture came so soon, did all later discussion seem to Hancock to be nothing more than amiable chat about this and that? For more discussion there certainly was, and almost certainly it took place on that same day. Copland, in a private letter to Mills the following Monday, recorded a discussion extending over four hours, which explored various options for getting the two schools under way. But Hancock, Copland reported, had apparently made up his mind that the two schools should be associated under him in their initial stages. That left no room for compromise. For his part, Hancock complained that Copland 'never really explored my mind' and concluded that Council, in its obtuseness, had condemned itself to many years of chasing shadows. A few days after the meeting on the park bench, the Academic Advisory Committee held a meeting at All Souls, with the Vice-Chancellor present, and Hancock formally submitted his resignation.

In the days that followed, Hancock continued to hope for some compromise; but Copland showed no sign of backing down, or even of seeking some resolution which would bring him back into the fold. So Hancock became, as he told Mills, 'very sore at the National University' and convinced that it would end up a second-rate show. Towards the end of Copland's month-long stay, Hancock invited him to his home for tea in what was presumably intended as a gesture of goodwill. It went badly, with Mrs Hancock telling Copland exactly what she thought of Australia, the University and its Vice-Chancellor, including a remark that he was a second-rate economist. But relations between the two men remained cordial: 'As chaps', Hancock told Mills, 'we got on very well and we parted excellent friends'. And Copland congratulated himself and Hancock on how they had managed to disagree with such affability.

In the meantime, Copland galloped ahead with his own and Council's plans for the two schools, spurred on now by a desire 'to show Hancock that we mean business'. Immediately after Hancock's resignation, the Vice-Chancellor approached K.C. Wheare and found him (by implicit contrast with Hancock) 'a very satisfactory person with whom to do business'. Wheare, another Australian at Oxford, where he was Gladstone Professor of Government and Public Administration and a Fellow of All Souls, had been mooted for some time as a substitute for Hancock should negotiations come unstuck; and now he agreed willingly to act as Adviser on the Social Sciences, making it clear that he had no intention of coming permanently to Australia. For the moment, a problem was solved. Copland solved another by talking again to

Firth, who gave indications that he might yet be prepared to continue as Adviser and take charge of the Research School of Pacific Studies during its first few years. He also met Florey who, despite his earlier prejudices about Copland's qualifications as a gentleman, appears to have enjoyed his company. 'We shall now be able to curse each other without any ill feeling', Copland told him, 'so when you feel like it just let yourself go'. Oliphant, though unhappy about Hancock's departure, was pleased that Copland had proven himself 'a man of action'.

So by the time he boarded the *Queen Mary* to cross the Atlantic, the Vice-Chancellor was pleased with himself, especially since Council, through Mills, had congratulated him for handling a difficult situation so well. The story, however, had an anticlimax which suggested that his diplomatic skills were better exercised in person than on paper. Hancock was anxious about the form in which his departure should be announced to the press, especially after he had been offered and had accepted a new appointment as Director of the Institute of Commonwealth Studies at the University of London. However, after coming up with a draft which Copland thought too explicit, he decided to trust the Vice-Chancellor to prepare a form of words which accurately represented the manner of his 'signing off'. Copland, showing little appreciation of Hancock's acute sensitivity on the matter, blundered in with a statement that could be taken to imply that he had abandoned Australia for a better job in London. This was exactly what Hancock had wanted to avoid. Having trusted Copland, he now felt betrayed, especially after receiving critical letters from 'a few fanatical fools'. But he remained silent, at least in public, until he told as much of the story as he cared to tell in *Country and Calling*.

In the months that followed, Hancock reflected unhappily on what might have been had he said to Copland: 'Dave, old man,' (he meant Doug), 'don't let us fling *ultimate* about. Let us give each other a week or two to think.' But he didn't, and was left to ponder how the separation had come about. While he tended to blame the Council, he also conceded that the negotiations had come for him at a bad time: he had just emerged from a battle with the British civil service over the official war histories and he was weighed down with worry about the health of his wife. Some close to him were inclined to blame Theaden Hancock for stampeding her husband into the wrong decision. Most, including Hancock's friends, thought he had made a mistake: though at least one fellow historian, his old friend Fred Alexander in Perth, congratulated him on a lucky escape.

Whatever immediate stresses may have influenced the final parting, problems in the relationship had been signalled long before. The issue that brought matters to a head was Hancock's proposal for starting the two social science schools under one director. Behind that lay the larger problem of recruitment, meaning who was recruited and how it was done. On both matters, Hancock and some members of the Council, especially Eggleston, were at opposite extremes. Hancock's concept of recruiting was based on personal relationships. The type of person he would be prepared to appoint would, of course, be an outstanding scholar; but he (or, just possibly, she) would also be able to work with him as a member of an integrated team which shared his own high ideals of scholarship. Hancock would probably know such people, at least by reputation. He did not approve of advertising for senior positions, arguing that crowds of mediocre people would apply while the good men held back. This was the Oxford way. In Australia, however, there was a distinct preference for advertising, or at least for conducting recruitment procedures in an impersonal manner. Eggleston complained to Copland that Hancock's activities were 'inconsistent with the impersonality which should attach to intellectual tasks' ... 'I have always disapproved of Hancock's excessively personal method of approach—will you go if I am Director?'

The matter was complicated by Hancock's status as *prospective* director. He wanted to be able to approach people with a 'firm offer' which would be contingent on his accepting the position of director. Council believed that only a confirmed director should be able to make a firm offer. Coombs managed to find a way around the dilemma, but only after irritation had risen high on both sides.

The question of who should be appointed was probably more vexing to Eggleston and his colleagues than to Hancock, who seemed largely impervious to his compatriots' sensitivities on the matter. Eggleston thought that, instead of pursuing an 'all star cast', he ought to be looking for young Australians. Copland urged him to think about the inspiration and satisfaction that comes with training relatively young men and creating a school with an international reputation. But Hancock had no wish to be, as he put it, 'King of the kids'; and while he was prepared to concede a slight preference for Australians if they were available, he understood that they were not, since if they were really outstanding they would be well known overseas. What eventually decided the argument was Hancock's evident failure to attract the sort of people he wanted. Reluctant to admit his failure, he wrote to Mills: 'If I could have got some chaps I could have made a start'. But then he removed a word and added a full-stop to convince both himself and Mills: 'I could have got some chaps. I could have made a start.'

There were still deeper divisions, which Hancock only became aware of through correspondence with Eggleston late in 1949. Eggleston in many respects was Hancock's antithesis. Steeped in the history of the Commonwealth and the experiences of wartime Britain, Hancock's perspective in the late 1940s was profoundly British. He wanted the Australian National University to be in the image of Oxford, and more precisely, of All Souls. Eggleston had never been to Oxford. He had not even been to university, except as a part-time law student at the University of Melbourne, which he described as 'lifeless and boring'. That did not stop him pursuing an outstanding career in politics, law and diplomacy. Between the wars he achieved some prominence as a public philosopher. Above all he was, in the words of his biographer, an 'Intellectual nationalist'. His view of the new University was shaped by Australia's wartime experience and the promises of post-war reconstruction.

The two men were most at odds about what Eggleston described as the intellectual objective of the school. Eggleston was unequivocal: the school should be concerned with 'fundamental social truths'. 'The faith of the social scientist', he later reflected, 'is that, if we can formulate reliable scientific conclusions, they will be a guide to human conduct and that informed conduct will increase the effectiveness of social life

& lead to a progressive solution to our problems'. At that moment, Eggleston believed, the social sciences were failing western civilisation by offering no systematic methodology, no definition of basic concepts, no synoptic view, and no understanding of their intrinsic unity. This was largely the fault of the British universities, such as Oxford and Cambridge, and their 'euphemistic concept' of the humanities as a loose group of independent studies.

> We want economists who are aware that their main decisions are political in character; political scientists who understand how dependent they are on law, and lawyers who understand how the law must give substance to political concepts; historians who are capable of showing how institutions work; and a philosophy which shows how knowledge and thought are articulated in institutions and conduct.

Hancock liked to call himself a craftsman. While not much concerned about nomenclature, he would have preferred the school to be called 'Social Studies' rather than 'Social Sciences'. He was suspicious of what he called 'the 'ologies', telling his colleagues at the Easter conferences that there was 'a good deal of nonsense in some of the enthusiastic demands made for research in the social sciences'. For example, he thought the school should have a good psychologist at some time, but at the moment he could not tell the difference between a good one and a bad one. The accent of the school should be heavily on the advancement (meaning the accumulation) of knowledge, for which the starting point should be empirical surveys: hence the urgent need for a Reader in the Sources of Australian History.

These different views extended to the way research should be planned and carried out. Eggleston demanded collaborative research from the outset, with clearly defined objectives. He was impatient with Hancock's notion of growing points, and wanted instead a comprehensive plan. Hancock's approach was evolutionary: cooperation could not be imposed; it could emerge only as selected scholars worked alongside one another in the appropriate intellectual environment. He wanted each scholar to be free to pursue his own interests; Eggleston expected researchers to work in teams.

So Eggleston lost no time grieving when Hancock departed and indeed welcomed his resignation as an opportunity to reshape Social Sciences as he and Copland were then recasting Pacific Studies. Although Wheare played a part as Adviser, Eggleston, more committed and determined, and with more time to spare, took the lead in drawing up a new plan; and on his advice the Interim Council concluded that four main chairs were necessary: in Political Science, Economics, Social Philosophy and Law. Readers in Demography and Statistics would probably be appointed within the Department of Economics, though a chair in Statistics might be established if a statistician with broad social interests happened to come along. The key ingredient was Social Philosophy, which Eggleston intended to cover 'the fundamental problems of the social sciences', such as community, social force, political authority, and the way communities make decisions and formulate policy. He also argued successfully for a chair of History which, so long as Hancock was the likely director, had not received much attention.

Sir Frederic Eggleston in the 1940s.

Australian News and Information Bureau, ANU Collection.

But Eggleston had neither the wish nor capacity, owing to old age and infirmity, to assume Hancock's role as prospective director. As there appeared to be no other likely candidate, the school was left to follow the course that had been set in 1946 when Council, having settled on the strategy of finding the right men to head each school, adopted a fallback position: where no outstanding man was available, the school should be established as a federation of departments. Hancock warned Eggleston that unless the Social Sciences and Pacific Studies schools had at least one full-time, first-rate director, the 'separate competitive specialisms' might fall apart exactly as Eggleston had feared. 'You run the risk of collecting a rabble of individualists.' But Eggleston wasn't much interested in advice from Hancock and responded curtly that if they were unable to find a director, they would certainly appoint people who were inspired by the idea of cooperation.

In the second half of 1949, three years after the ANU Act had passed through parliament, only one of the original four Advisers had signed up, one had signed off, and two were keeping their options open. Oliphant was enthusiastically wielding the maestro's baton (and occasionally using it to beat anyone who questioned his conducting style). Florey, with only one foot on the podium, was conducting more than one orchestra at the same time, but nobody wanted him to move aside. The situation in the social science schools was more confused. Eggleston's objectives, which had more in common with the original intentions of Coombs and his colleagues than with traditional models imported from England, appeared to have triumphed, and it now seemed that the research schools of Social Sciences and Pacific Studies would be directed towards meeting immediate national needs. Although Firth might still be an Adviser, he was administering what was partially at least someone else's plan. And Hancock had not merely gone, but Mills, Copland, Eggleston and Coombs were doing their best to forget him.

In the development of the social science schools, did the maestros have a long-term impact? Perhaps Conlon's term for the Advisers was misleading; at this stage there were no players in the social sciences for the maestros to conduct. Soon they would begin to arrive in Canberra: but it would be some years before anyone could say whether or not Firth and Hancock had left a significant mark.

Pioneers

Recruiting

With Hancock out of the way, Copland stepped into the job of recruiting officer for the Social Sciences school, sharing with Firth the task of recruiting for Pacific Studies. A day or two after the exchange on the park bench, he sat down in the same park with W.D. (Mick) Borrie, a demographer who was already on the University's books as a Social Science Research Fellow. Hancock had provided for a demographer in his plans for the school, and he had approached Borrie several months earlier. Copland now confirmed the invitation, and Borrie became the University's first appointment in the Social Sciences, with the title of Research Fellow. In the same park he also sounded out Geoffrey Sawer, Associate Professor at the University of Melbourne, about a position in law.

A fortnight later the Vice-Chancellor met S.F. (Siegfried Frederick) Nadel, who was Firth's suggestion for the chair of Anthropology in Pacific Studies. Born in Vienna in 1903, Nadel's early career had been devoted to music, including the publication of a biography of the Italian-German composer, Ferruccio Busoni. From musicology in German he passed quickly through ethnomusicology to anthropology in English. Moving to London in 1932, he immersed himself in the study of the Nupe people of central Nigeria and completed a University of London PhD on the subject a few years later. In the late 1930s he prepared a detailed comparative survey of the hill tribes in the Sudan, which led to a wartime post with the British Army in north Africa. Returning after the war to London, he taught for a while in Firth's department before moving to Newcastle as Reader in Anthropology at King's College in the University of Durham. By the time Copland met him in London, Siegfried had given way to Fred and he had become, as Firth put it, 'very British'. Firth regarded him as outstanding: he had been promised a chair in Newcastle and would probably be a candidate for one in Cambridge. Although he knew little about the Pacific, no doubt he would quickly learn.

Copland continued recruiting in the United States, where he met Hancock's friend Walter Russell Crocker. Born in 1902 as a fourth-generation South Australian, Crocker had lived what Hancock admiringly termed a 'life of action', first with the British Colonial Service in Nigeria, then with the International Labour Office, and during the war with the British Army in Africa, India and Britain. This had not prevented him writing several books, on the Japanese population problem, British colonial administration in Nigeria, and problems of colonial self-government. His interests were ideally suited to the school: he wanted to work on problems relating to international government in the Pacific area, and on how the United Nations and other international organisations might fit into the Pacific picture. Copland concluded, after visiting him in New York, that despite his reputation for being rather prickly, his interests and vigorous mind were exactly what the University needed.

Another of Firth's and Hancock's suggestions for Pacific Studies had already agreed to come to Canberra. James Davidson, a New Zealander in his mid-thirties, was an exception to Hancock's preference for recruiting to the senior positions proven men of middle age. After a doctorate from Cambridge he had served briefly in the New Zealand public service, then returned to England, where he had worked as a research assistant at Oxford before joining British Naval Intelligence. Since the end of the war he had been a Lecturer in Colonial History and Fellow of St John's College, Cambridge; and when Hancock approached him early in 1949 he was busy advising the New Zealand government on a new Constitution for Western Samoa.

These three appointments—Nadel, Crocker and Davidson—provided the nucleus of a professoriate in Pacific Studies. Two other senior positions in the school were created in 1949 and filled early in 1950. On Firth's recommendation, W.E.H. Stanner was appointed Reader in Comparative Social Institutions in the Department of Anthropology. A Sydney graduate with a PhD from the University of London, Stanner's research interests extended from east Africa, through northern and central Australia to New Guinea and the South-west Pacific. He had recently published a book entitled *The South Seas in Transition* and was currently working on the economics of Australian Aboriginal societies.

The other reader was C.P. FitzGerald, whose translation to Canberra was probably the only appointment in the history of the ANU that was foretold with the help of a horoscope—or, to be precise, the visit to Australia which immediately led to his appointment was accurately foretold. Born in London in 1902, FitzGerald had spent over half his adult life in China. After working in Britain on secret assignments during the war, he returned to China in 1946 as representative of the British Council, first in Nanjing and then in Beijing. In December 1948, on the very day that the siege of Beijing began, a Chinese fortune-teller told him that in the Chinese equivalent of July next year he would set out, without his family, on a long voyage to a country he had never visited before. Shortly afterwards Copland wrote a letter inviting him to undertake an extensive lecture tour of Australia for the ANU. The invitation reached him a few months later, after the blockade had been lifted, and in July he duly set out, without his family, for Australia. After travelling around the country for more than two months, delivering lectures on contemporary China, he returned to Beijing, followed soon after by a letter from Copland offering him a three-year appointment as Visiting Reader in Oriental Studies.

FitzGerald was Copland's nomination: they had got to know one another well when their families had lived close by in Nanjing. Firth too had met him before the war, and thought well of his writings on Chinese culture and history. Not so Eggleston, who was annoyed by FitzGerald's public advocacy of international recognition of the new regime in China when the situation in Eggleston's view was far from settled; and who wanted in any case to offer visiting positions to Chinese and Indian scholars who would bring their

PIONEERS

Sir Douglas Copland, Vice-Chancellor 1948–1953. This posthumous portrait shows him much as he was during his time as Vice-Chancellor. Oil by Bryan Westwood, about 1976.

own cultural perspectives to matters of importance to Australia. However, Copland argued that the revolution in China would prevent the University from getting the sort of indigenous Chinese scholar they wanted; and the quality of FitzGerald's lectures in Australia convinced the Vice-Chancellor that the University need look no further.

The earliest professorial appointments to the Social Sciences school were Geoffrey Sawer for law and Trevor Swan for economics. Sawer, who was approaching 40, had been born in Burma but had lived in Melbourne most of his life, where he had taught at the University, specialising in constitutional law. During the war he had been in charge of propaganda broadcasts to Japan and Japanese occupied territories. Wheare thought well of him, and Eggleston was pleased that he was likely to take an interest in 'the scientific aspects' of the law. Sawer, with a substantial work on Australian constitutional cases to his credit, as well as a popular paperback on Australian government, was regarded as a solid investment. In contrast, Swan was less remarkable for his solidity than for his outstanding intellect: in 1948 he was being eagerly sought by a leading economist in the European Economic Commission, who described him as 'exceptionally able and brilliant'. Except for a short stint as lecturer at the University of Sydney, most of his work to date had been in government departments. Coombs knew him well and supported him warmly; but Copland, who suspected he thought too highly of himself, remarked that he had not yet undertaken a sustained piece of work and thought he would benefit from a few years at a more junior level. Swan had initially applied for an advertised readership in economics. However, as Hancock had shown, the market was not teeming with economists; so, despite Copland's doubt, he was offered the chair.

Trevor Swan, the youngest professorial appointment, in the 1950s.

In addition to the two professorial appointments, three readers were appointed to Social Sciences. Where the chairs were filled by invitation, Council members thought it appropriate to advertise for readers, even though they might have someone in mind. Hancock's suggested readership in the Sources of Australian History was filled by Laurie Fitzhardinge; L.C. Webb, a New Zealander who had been in charge of price stabilisation in New Zealand during the war, was appointed Reader in Political Science; and H.P. Brown, Director of Research in the Commonwealth Bureau of Census and Statistics, joined Swan as Reader in Economic Statistics.

This amounted to ten senior appointments in Pacific Studies and Social Sciences during the first year of recruiting. (Borrie's post of Research Fellow was a junior academic position.) Eggleston, assuming that there would not be enough Australians available to staff the two schools, had hoped for a balance between Australian and overseas appointments, but as it turned out, five had been born in Australia, two in New Zealand, and one (Sawer) was as Australian as anyone could wish. Where Hancock had favoured experience and middle age, Copland and Eggleston leaned towards youth and promise. Perhaps the result fell between the two: the average age in 1950 was 41, with Swan at 32 the youngest, and Crocker and FitzGerald, the eldest, not yet 50.

No precise formula governed these early appointments. As might be expected for a research institution, Copland and his colleagues attached great weight to research experience, capacity and potential. While they were impressed by evidence of teaching experience, they were prepared to take promising candidates on trust. Fields of interest were important, especially for Pacific Studies, although Nadel was appointed without ever having written about the Pacific. Publications were also significant, and here Nadel, with three books and many articles, was one of several appointees who stood out. Swan, on the other hand, had exactly the right interests, but his capacity to publish was judged almost entirely on potential.

Formal qualifications were less important than reputation. In the days before doctorates became commonplace, there was no minimum qualification in the social sciences and humanities: many senior professors at the time, in Australia as well as Britain, had only Master degrees (which in the case of Oxford University were BAs elevated by the passage of time and the payment of a fee). Eight of the ten professors and readers had taken their first degrees from Australian universities or a college of what was then called the University of New Zealand; four of the eight had overseas postgraduate qualifications, from Oxford, Cambridge or London. There were no American degrees, though Crocker had spent two years studying at Stanford. Of the two who had not graduated in Australia or New Zealand, Nadel was laden with degrees from Vienna and London, while FitzGerald had no degree at all.

This was as remarkable then as it would be now. The Professor of Chinese at London's School of Oriental and African Studies told Firth, when he asked, that FitzGerald could not hope for a university post in Britain without a degree—but that if he had a degree, he would have had an appointment long ago. Firth was troubled by this advice, but not deterred; and Copland was confident of his man. Fortunately, the regional readerships were regarded as experimental, so his appointment could be labelled 'Visiting', meaning short term, without its seeming at all odd. Nevertheless, for a young university eager to make its name in the critical world of Academe, it was a brave decision and testimony to the Vice-Chancellor's 'spirit of adventure'.

Above all, Copland and his colleagues on the Interim Council wanted their early appointments, especially of the first professors, to be outstanding; and if this meant they were different from the sorts of people who were appointed to state universities, then so much the better. Conversely, they avoided the conventional: a geographer who currently held a chair in New Zealand was rejected because he was merely 'a capes and bays man'. Being outstanding implied being creative, able to design innovative research programs, and capable of leading the University in unfamiliar directions. Some of those first appointees seemed to fill these criteria to the letter; others, such as Brown and Fitzhardinge, had special qualities to offer—in their cases statistical and bibliographical skills. All were sympathetic to the ideals which Copland or Firth had put to them, and willing to act out the role of pioneers.

Wright warned that not all their appointments would be successful: the social science schools would undoubtedly attract academics who would 'collect tailored tweeds and discuss wines ... just like any other university'. But if they were careful they should be able to keep this group to a minimum.

Well before Copland and Firth were ready to recommend appointments to the social science schools, the first professors in the John Curtin School had been entered on the University's payroll. Recruitment, for Florey, was a straightforward business. What he was looking for was a small group of men who were masters of their own subjects and able to make discoveries themselves, while at the same time gathering around them research workers of high calibre and training students for PhDs. His self-imposed constraint was that recruiting for the ANU should not disadvantage other Australian institutions.

His first recruit was a biochemist from Melbourne, Hugh Ennor, who had come to his notice during the two years Ennor had recently spent in Oxford. In mid-1948, when Florey approached him about the chair of Biochemistry, he was 35 years of age. After completing a first degree from the University of Melbourne in 1937, he had worked at the Baker Institute for Medical Research in Melbourne, where his investigations into the metabolism of fat had won him a DSc. During the war he had conducted research on chemical warfare and served for a time as superintendent of a large group of scientific workers. Then, after the spell in Oxford, he had returned to the Commonwealth Serum Laboratories in Melbourne, where he was senior biochemist. According to Wright, Ennor in each of his roles had shown originality, sound judgement, and a capacity for leadership and organisation of 'a most unusually high level'. Privately he conceded that Ennor's achievements, while considerable, were not epoch making, and that the appointment was 'a bit of a gamble'. But everyone agreed that he was an open and engaging fellow, and such matters weighed heavily with Florey.

Ennor formally joined the University in August 1948 and before the year was out had delivered his inaugural lecture. In the meantime, Council appointed Adrien Albert to the chair of chemistry, the title of which was shortly changed to Medical Chemistry because Albert wanted to avoid 'pure organic chemistry', as well as allow for the formation of other chemistry departments in the future. Born and educated in Sydney, Albert had just turned 41. After serving as chemist to a firm of dyers, he had moved to London, where he completed a PhD in Medicine in 1937. Returning to the University of Sydney, he initiated a novel research program in chemotherapy and gathered around him a strong team of chemists who worked, in association with bacteriologists in Melbourne, on the relationship between chemical constitution and antibacterial activity. Since 1947 he had been back in London as a research fellow in the Wellcome Institute. According to Sydney Rubbo, head of the Bacteriology Department at the University of Melbourne, he was already generally regarded as one of the foremost chemists in the field of chemotherapy, and there was every indication that his reputation would be further enhanced. Florey was confident of his capacity, and Wright regarded him as 'well proven'—though privately he wondered whether his personality would cause problems.

Chemistry was a strong area and, had Albert not been attracted, there would have been other outstanding people to choose from. Florey's own field of experimental pathology presented more of a problem, as in his view there was nobody who was both suitable and available. Similarly, he held out little hope of making an immediate appointment to microbiology, where there were people who were up and coming but no-one who was yet ready to be taken away from full-time research. Florey handed the problem of microbiology to his colleagues in Australia, and was pleased when Bill Keogh of the Commonwealth Serum Laboratories and Macfarlane Burnet put forward the name of Frank Fenner at the Walter and Eliza Hall Institute, one of the young scientists whom Florey dared not poach, especially since he had heard that Burnet had him in mind to succeed him at the Hall Institute. Florey sought assurances from Burnet that Fenner, whom he had not met, had the qualities required in a head of department, and that there would be no future recriminations; and thus reassured, he invited Fenner in guarded terms to accept the chair, telling him that he was still young and that he should be devoting most of his time to research. Burnet, having offered Fenner, now made a half-hearted attempt to dissuade him; but he had already decided that, as the ANU was clearly here to stay, collaboration made more sense than resistance.

Fenner was formally appointed to the chair of Microbiology early in 1949, at the age of 34. Born in Ballarat, Victoria, he had graduated in medicine from the University of Adelaide. In the early years of the war he completed a Diploma in Tropical Medicine at the University of Sydney and an MD by thesis at the University of Adelaide. As a member of the Australian Army Medical Corps, he served in Australia, the Middle East, New Guinea and Borneo, first as a pathologist and then as a malariologist. Back in Australia, he joined the Hall Institute and conducted research on mousepox, which Burnet described as the most comprehensive study ever made of a virus disease in an experimental animal, with important implications for the study of smallpox in humans. 'I regard Fenner as the most accomplished investigator I have ever worked with', Burnet told Copland.

The chair of Physiology took longer to fill. After pondering whether his rule relating to poaching extended across the Tasman, and concluding with the help of the New Zealander Copland that it did not, Florey decided to try to tempt J.C. Eccles, who was then Professor of Physiology at the University of Otago, Dunedin. Born in Melbourne in 1903, Eccles had graduated MB BS from the University of Melbourne before winning a Rhodes Scholarship to Oxford, where he took out an MA and later a DPhil. After several years in the Physiology Department at Oxford, he returned to Australia to direct the Kanematsu Memorial Institute of Pathology at Sydney Hospital. He had taken up his position in Dunedin in 1944. Eccles' contributions to fundamental knowledge about the nervous system, presented in a long series of papers, had won him an international reputation, Florey describing him as 'one of the best living neurophysiologists'. That speciality was, in Florey's view, a slight drawback, as he considered that neurophysiologists tended to work in extremely narrow fields. Nevertheless, he was a brilliant catch.

So, by mid-1950, the John Curtin School had four professors (though the date of Eccles' appointment had yet to be settled). On Florey's advice, Council had appointed two established scientists with international reputations and in the two other cases had, in Wright's words, taken a bet on the youngsters. There were, as yet, no readers. Florey was pleased with his work, and sure that the University would have within a few years four first-class departments, which would constitute a solid basis for the future development of the school.

Oliphant was in no hurry to appoint professors or readers to the Physical Sciences school. What mattered most to him was having the building erected and the equipment installed so that he could get on with his own major research project. The most important people for this purpose were the technicians who had worked with him in Birmingham, especially Mick Cornick and Jimmy Edwards, who came out to Australia early in 1950 as an advance guard. Oliphant himself, and several others of the Birmingham team, arrived in August 1950.

By this time, Oliphant had made only one senior appointment, Ernest Titterton as Professor of Nuclear Physics. Titterton, now in his mid-thirties, had been Oliphant's first research student at Birmingham and, during the early years of the war, had worked with Oliphant on the development of radar. From 1943 to 1947 he worked on the Manhattan Project in the United States, where he got to know most of the western world's leading nuclear physicists and became convinced that nuclear weapons offered the best prospect for world peace. He contributed a major discovery which helped show that it was possible to produce a nuclear bomb; and on 16 July 1945 he was given the historic task of triggering the world's first nuclear test explosion in New Mexico. Returning to England, he joined the Atomic Energy Research Establishment at Harwell, and it was here that Oliphant approached him with the offer of a chair at the ANU. One referee remarked that he would make an able lieutenant, whose gifts lay in applying current knowledge to specific problems rather than breaking new ground.

The Research School of Physical Sciences also grew through the addition of a ready-made Department of Astronomy. Before Oliphant took up duty as Director, the Commonwealth Astronomer, Richard Woolley, had approached the University with a proposal that researchers in the Commonwealth Observatory should have their work recognised for the degree of PhD at the ANU. Oliphant, who had known Woolley from Cambridge, was happy to suggest that he be given the title Professor of Astronomy and that the Mount Stromlo Observatory be recognised as fulfilling the functions of a Department of Astronomy within the research school. Woolley duly became an 'Honorary Professor' in 1950, though it was a few years yet before Mount Stromlo was formally transferred from the Commonwealth government to the University.

By mid-1950, two years after recruitment had begun, the University had sixteen senior academic staff on its books (though not necessarily on its payroll). Eleven of these, including Oliphant but not Woolley, were professors, and five were readers. There were, in addition, ten or so 'junior' staff, most of whom were designated Research Fellow; although Borrie had been promoted to Senior Research Fellow, and D.J. Brown in Albert's Department of Medical Chemistry had been given permanency with the title 'Fellow'. Several technical officers, laboratory managers and research assistants were on the fringes, their status varying according to their official roles and personal capacities.

The pioneering staff were as diverse as might be expected of people with different academic interests and personal backgrounds: and some of their differences, political as well as professional, became obvious as they settled in. One thing they had in common: they were all men. This was so obvious that nobody at the time seemed to notice—or if they did, it was not something commented on, least of all by the men of the Interim Council. Occasionally a woman was considered for an academic appointment: Firth spoke to a senior female colleague about the chair of Anthropology, but concluded that she probably would not be interested; and Hancock knew a 'first rate' woman at Oxford who had worked with him on shipping history and who could pursue fundamental research on Australia's transport problems: 'Apart from her merits, I think it is a good thing to get a woman when she makes the grade'. But presumably they usually did not, or if they did no male was aware of it. So the ANU began as a male preserve, which made it little different from other Australian universities at the time, and no different at all from All Souls.

The lure of Canberra

'Yes, I'll come', Davidson told Hancock after the idea of coming to Canberra was put to him. 'The answer surprises me. I had no intention of coming to it three days ago; but I discovered it yesterday and felt thoroughly delighted with it.' Sawer, when Copland asked him the question, had to pinch himself to be sure the offer was true. Nadel, who was then visiting Illinois, reacted more soberly. He took a long walk along the shores of Lake Michigan before deciding to accept new challenges in Australia.

Why did they come? And what did they expect to find when they reached Canberra? On the face of it, the Australian National University around 1950 had little to offer. While salary levels remained higher than in other Australian universities, they were starting to lag behind those in Britain, so that the original objective of providing generous conditions of service to help reverse the brain drain was no longer relevant. The proposed conditions for research were intended to be of the highest world standard, and for many senior scholars the chance to pursue research full time was appealing. But to counter that, it was well known that Canberra as yet had little or nothing in the way of buildings, laboratories and library resources that made efficient

Florey relaxes during a day trip to the Brindabella Range, west of Canberra, in 1950. Like many other expatriates, he responded to the lure of the Australian landscape. The photograph was probably taken with his camera.

research possible. As Oliphant prepared to embark on the voyage to Australia, Florey warned him, in words that Oliphant would repeat many times in future years, that all he would find in Canberra was 'a hole in the ground and a lot of promises'.

Happily for the Interim Council, an ample budget and the absence of too many strict rules and regulations allowed it to offer unusually generous salaries and perquisites. Eccles asked for and received £500 above the stated professorial salary of £2000, setting a precedent for differential salaries to take account of exceptional qualifications. Many of the new appointees had special requirements and the University tried hard to oblige rather than risk losing them. Oliphant, reminding Copland of the sacrifices he and his wife were making in coming to Canberra, insisted on accommodation comparable with his 40-square, six-bedroom dwelling in Birmingham; and as the cost of building in Canberra placed such a house well beyond his means, he asked the University to build it and rent it back to him. This was a tall order; but the Interim Council, after initial hesitation, recognised that the University's flag was 'nailed to the Oliphant mast'. Mills approached the government for the extra money and Oliphant—after long building delays and some public criticism of the transaction—eventually moved into what was, by Canberra standards, a mansion.

The attractions of Canberra differed from one person to the next. Davidson was drawn by the prospect of working 'on the edge of the Pacific for the next five years or so'. Eccles, who might have commanded a chair in Britain or the United States, concluded that the ANU would give him 'exceptionally favourable opportunities' for pursuing his research interests and a release from his current burden of teaching at Otago. Fenner had reservations about moving to a position that would carry a significant administrative load, but knew that if he stayed at the Hall Institute he would remain in the shadow of Burnet. He chose independence over the security of the known. In contrast, FitzGerald came in part because he had nowhere else to go: confronted with the tumult of revolution in China, at odds with his current employers in the British Council, and barred from academic employment in Britain through the want of a degree, he was attracted by certainty and security, at least for the next three years.

For all the early appointees, the prospect of moving to Canberra was an adventure: but their enthusiasm for the adventure varied. Albert, set up comfortably at the Wellcome Institute, tried to postpone his departure as long as possible. In no time at all he had his own stationery printed, which was headed:

The Australian National University

CANBERRA

DEPARTMENT OF MEDICAL CHEMISTRY

EUSTON 4477.

183, EUSTON ROAD,
LONDON, N.W.1.

Copland thought this rather cheeky, but what could he do about it? When Copland and Wright arranged for Albert to be accommodated at the Munitions Supply Laboratories at Maribyrnong, ten kilometres from the centre of Melbourne, he protested that the laboratories were too isolated and primitive, and threatened to resign if he were forced to go there. He was wrong about the standard of the laboratories; but Florey supported him, so the Department of Medical Chemistry remained in Euston Road until the permanent laboratories were ready in Canberra.

Crocker, on the other hand, heard 'the call of the kookaburra'. Inspired perhaps by his South Australian ancestry, he expressed eloquently the enthusiasm of a pioneer. On the one hand, he wanted to escape from New York, which he loathed, as soon as possible; on the other, he was drawn by the physical environment: 'The sun, the healthy air, the space, the association with human beings most of whom are healthy and buoyant, and the beauty—and the varied beauty—of the Australian landscape ... It is better than the South of France, it is better than Arizona, it is better than Morocco.' He did not like 'the cult of excessive social security, of bets & beer, and all that'. But what really distinguished the Australian, he wrote, was hope. 'And living in such a favoured land he damned well ought to have hope.' Admittedly, he was trying by these words to persuade Hancock (too late, as it happened) to come to terms with the Interim Council. But he too was keen to come to Canberra, so much so that he was willing to accept a much lower salary than he had earned in New York.

W.R. Crocker, centre, listens to the Vice-Chancellor, Copland, explain this 'great intellectual adventure' to a radio interviewer. Photograph by L.J. Dwyer.

Crocker would soon be disappointed. Influenced by Hancock's vision of the University, he saw himself helping to recreate Oxford in the antipodes. He was the first professor to come—and the first to go.

Overseas scholars

Well before the first academic staff had started packing their trunks for Canberra, the University had begun sending its first scholars abroad. The idea of overseas research studentships had been suggested early in 1947 by a federal Labor backbencher, Kim Beazley, a former schoolteacher and university tutor, and later a long-term member of the University Council. A few months later Wright put forward a similar proposal which had the specific purpose of providing the ANU with a pool of potential employees.

Eager to provide signs of activity, the Interim Council approved the scheme without consulting the Academic Advisory Committee or laying down precise rules and regulations. From the outset it was never exactly clear what it was intended to achieve.

There was general agreement that the scholarships should be used to train students in research techniques; but was every student expected to take out a degree? If so, the scholarships' two-year tenure was scarcely sufficient to complete a PhD. What happened in practice was that students tended to have their scholarships extended or to be granted an additional stipend; but some did not feel impelled to enrol for a PhD at all.

Nor was there universal agreement about whether the scholarships should be used specifically to train ANU staff. Florey, who was most anxious to avoid charges of poaching, was the only member of the Academic Advisory Committee who favoured the scheme as a source of researchers for Canberra. The others were at best lukewarm, tending to argue that the money would be better spent in providing opportunities for people who had already gained substantial research experience. Certainly, nobody tried to force research scholars to come to Canberra at the end of their terms. Whether they should return to Australia was another matter. Although there was an understanding that they should, the University could hardly insist that scholars come home if Australia had no jobs to make use of the expertise they had spent two or three years acquiring.

The scholarships paid generously and were in high demand. For the first round in 1948 there were 186 applications, two-thirds of which came from Australia and the rest from Britain. Twenty-seven scholarships were awarded in that year, all but six to students applying from within Australia. Twelve were for Medical Research, seven for Social Sciences, five for Physical Sciences and three for Pacific Studies.

Recipients of ANU Overseas Scholarships were, theoretically, allowed to pursue their research in any appropriate institution. In practice, the dollar shortage meant that nearly everyone went to the United Kingdom, which in any case was probably where most people wanted to go. Of the 56 recipients from 1948 to 1950, 31 went to Oxford or Cambridge and 14 to London. Eight more were sprinkled around other parts of the United Kingdom, one travelled widely without enrolling for a degree, and only two enrolled at Harvard.

The character of the scheme differed significantly from one school to the next. Florey did his best to ensure that the scholars attached to the John Curtin School worked in areas relevant to its research interests, and tried to develop some sort of family spirit among them, inviting them as a group to the occasional dinner at Lincoln College and keeping an avuncular eye on their progress. He also encouraged them to return to Australia once their degrees were completed, except in his own field of experimental pathology, where Australia was not yet ready to receive them.

The social scientists, on the other hand, were given an almost free choice of what they wanted to study and where they wanted to go. This resulted in a wide diversity of research topics. R.A. Gollan, a Sydney graduate in History who won a scholarship in 1948, sought advice from Hancock and ended up with Harold Laski at the London School of Economics, studying the influence of British political thought on Australian politics in the nineteenth century. C.M. Williams, an Assistant Lecturer in History at Melbourne, chose Oxford to work on the English civil war. N.G. Butlin wanted to go to the United States to study the latest analytical techniques of economic history. With

Copland's help he obtained additional dollars through a Rockefeller Fellowship and enrolled at Harvard, only to find that working for a Harvard PhD would take him away from the research he so much wanted to do. Thumbing his nose at the PhD, he devoted himself to studying the relationship between public and private investment in nineteenth-century Australia and learning all he could from Harvard's Centre for Entrepreneurial History. The University let him go his way and had its investment repaid many times over. Occasionally, however, it was necessary to pull a scholar into line. In Pacific Studies, George Nadel (unrelated to Siegfried) set out to write a Harvard PhD on Australian intellectual history, but showed signs of not producing. He was sent a rocket and told to return immediately to Australia, where his book on *Australia's Colonial Culture* eventually appeared.

Although these were the first ANU scholars, they could hardly be described as the first ANU students, as their degrees were awarded by overseas institutions. In 1951, as the research schools prepared to take in their own students, the scholarship scheme was changed to provide for students enrolling in Canberra and to ensure that their research work was related to the work of the schools. An overseas scheme was maintained until 1953, but on a more modest scale.

It was hard to judge at the time whether or not the Overseas Scholarships Scheme, in old and new guises, was a success. Just over a quarter of the total number of scholars remained overseas at the expiration of their scholarships, and fewer than a quarter returned to take up positions at the ANU. These proportions improved, from the University's point of view, with the passage of time, as former scholars of some years' standing accepted posts in Canberra. The return on the investment received a larger boost from the remaining half of the scholars, who found places in other Australian universities. ANU scholars spread around Australia testified to the University's national credentials and strengthened the argument that the ANU would help rather than hinder the Australian university environment.

The full achievement could only be measured in decades to come. Out of a total of nearly ninety scholars, comprising participants in the Overseas Scholarships Scheme to 1950, and 'general scholars' and special cases to 1953, some forty had achieved by 1990 the status of professor or its equivalent in Australia or overseas. The overseas professors included Henry Harris, who succeeded Florey at the Dunn School; Peter Worsley, Sociology at Manchester; A.E. Beck, Geophysics at Western Ontario; Ken Burridge, Anthropology and Sociology at British Columbia. Richard Storry and Adrian Mayer each held research fellowships at the ANU before taking up the chairs, respectively, of Japanese History at Oxford and Asian Anthropology at the School of Oriental and African Studies in London.

Among the scientists who came to occupy chairs in Australia there were J.H. Bennett, Genetics at Adelaide; Stuart Butler, Theoretical Physics at Sydney; A.J.F. Boyle, Physics at Western Australia; J.T. Clifford, Botany at Queensland. The social scientists included the historians F.K. Crowley and J.D. Legge at New South Wales and Monash; A.F. Davies, Political Science at Melbourne; G.A. Wilkes, English and Australian Literature at Sydney; and three professors of Law at Sydney, W.L. Morison, D.G. Benjafield and R.W. Parsons.

Nine of the scholars became professors at the ANU: historians R.A. Gollan, K.S. Inglis and C.M. Williams; N.G. Butlin, Economic History; B.D. Cameron, Economics; D.J. Mulvaney, Prehistory; J.H. Carver, Physics; F.W.E. Gibson, Biochemistry; and I.G. Ross, Chemistry. Some of these we will meet later in their ANU careers.

Other scholars made distinguished contributions in universities, government, the Commonwealth Scientific and Industrial Research Organisation (CSIRO) and industry. But this list is long enough to show that, as an Australian contribution to the world of learning, the scheme was an unequivocal success.

A shed in a paddock

The business of building a university moved slowly. Early in 1950, as the first academic staff arrived to take up residence, there were no permanent structures to greet them. The *Sydney Morning Herald*'s comment that 'the National University is still a shed in a paddock' was close to the mark.

The paddock was an area of about 200 acres (80 hectares), which embraced the site Walter Burley Griffin had set aside for educational purposes in his 1912 plan. During the 1930s and early 1940s, diligent lobbying by the University College, along with the Canberra University Association, had protected the site and adjacent areas against encroachments, and had even managed to increase the designated area by half as much again. Not that the College gained any immediate benefit from its efforts: as soon as the ANU was established, it was taken for granted that the land would be vested in the University's name. The Interim Council, as one of its earliest tasks, began negotiations to lease the site from the Commonwealth government and the formal transfer was

Work starts on the temporary administration building, February 1948. The shortage of labour and materials in Canberra after the war made every building project a major undertaking. The old hospital buildings are at the left of the photograph, partly hidden by the trees. *Australian Official Photograph, ANU Collection.*

The 'shed': the first building erected on campus, photographed by Russell Mathews about 1950.
By courtesy of Russell Mathews.

effected in 1953. Meanwhile, planning for the erection of buildings went ahead on the assumption that the formalities would be completed, all in good time.

There were already structures on the paddock when the University came into being. Most had been erected in the few years after 1912, during which Griffin's prize-winning design had largely been ignored. They included four brick buildings: Canberra House, once the home of the Administrator of the Federal Capital Territory and now occupied by the British High Commissioner; two other residences; and a Department of Health laboratory. There were also various timber constructions: sixteen cottages, Acton Guest House (a hostel for single public servants), and the several buildings which had once comprised Canberra Community Hospital. All these structures were currently serving other uses, chiefly office and storage space for the government or residences for Commonwealth employees. Gradually the government would move out and the University would move in. But in the meantime, the University had to solve its accommodation problems in other ways. The Interim Council was shunted around from one venue to another: the Senate committee room in Parliament House, meeting rooms in the Department of Post-War Reconstruction or the Treasury, or the library in the Institute of Anatomy. Subcommittees met wherever they could, even in a quiet corner of the Hotel Canberra if nothing better offered.

The shed was a Royal Australian Air Force mess hut which was moved in sections from the country town of Cootamundra to the site at Acton, where it was reassembled and refurbished to accommodate a board room, offices and a kitchen. It was the first building the University could call its own. The Registrar, R.G. Osborne, looked forward to hanging a few pictures and adding some modest improvements 'to mitigate some of the asperities of Canberra' and impress visitors. The Interim Council met there for the first time at the end of 1949.

The first academic staff began to arrive early in 1950: Borrie from Sydney, then Crocker from New York by way of Britain and Europe. Within a few months Crocker had concluded that the asperities of Canberra were almost too much to bear. When he arrived there was no office for him, not even a desk or chair. After several weeks, he and Borrie were given rooms alongside the public servants who were about to vacate the old hospital building, but still no shelves, so that he could not unpack his books.

The front of the main old hospital building, 1954. This building survived long enough to achieve heritage status and the accompanying guarantee of preservation. In the 1990s it was part of the Research School of Earth Sciences.
Australian News and Information Bureau, ANU Collection.

Domestic accommodation was worse. Initially he was lodged in the Hotel Canberra, where he had to move rooms three times in ten days to make way for politicians, who were given priority. He escaped to the South Australian bush. On his return he was given a poky room, without a desk, in Lawley House, a relatively superior hostel for unmarried and mostly young public servants, where meals were at fixed times and there were community singsongs on Thursdays.

Little wonder that he wrote to Hancock about the woes of life in Canberra: the wholesome but dreary atmosphere created by civil service clerks, the primitive and expensive shops, the absence of restaurants, the need to book weeks ahead for a dental appointment. 'In short, the last $3\frac{1}{2}$ months have been lonely, dull and irritating.' And yet he would make the same mistake again, as he really liked Australians and the landscape was wonderful!

More academics took up duty over the next twelve months, mostly social scientists, including Swan, Davidson and Nadel—but also Oliphant, full of energy and enthusiasm for getting Physical Sciences under way. They too were given rooms in the old hospital building which was soon adorned with signs to show that this was in fact The Australian National University and not some government department. The medical scientists remained where they were until temporary laboratories were erected in 1952. By the end of the year, Fenner, Ennor and Eccles had moved in with much of their equipment and some of their staff.

The paddock—or a large part of it—had now become a construction site. Early in 1953, when Albert was visiting Canberra, the four medical professors arranged for photographs of changes on the site to be sent to Florey, who regarded photographs as the only proof that things were actually happening. Together they and the Laboratory

Manager, Bunker, arranged to pose alongside some 'very decrepit sheds' near the laboratories, brushing off flies and patting a starved-looking mongrel which had adopted them. But to Ennor's disappointment, the day before the photographer's arrival the contractor pulled down the sheds, depriving them of an opportunity to record for posterity their pioneering spirit.

Academics and architecture

New arrivals in Canberra—scholars as well as staff—were often welcomed at the railway station or airport by Ross Hohnen, who had succeeded Osborne as Registrar in 1949. They were then taken on a tour of the site, with Hohnen pointing out where future buildings were planned to be—the John Curtin School here, Physical Sciences there, and so on. Some were bemused: it took a fair stretch of the imagination to accept Hohnen's vision of a university in the paddock.

Nevertheless, it had been assumed from the outset that fine architecture and appropriate landscaping would be a feature of the University, as it was of most great universities. Even before the ANU Act was passed, Coombs was thinking about a grand design: he proposed an architectural competition, which would have been normal in such circumstances. But the Academic Advisers pressed for an architect to be appointed immediately; and Oliphant in particular made it clear that he regarded the provision of the simple buildings he required as a test of the Interim Council's capacity to get things done.

Brian Lewis, architectural drawings in hand, with Copland and the Registrar, R.G. Osborne, at the Easter conferences, 1948.
Australian Official Photograph, ANU Collection.

Lewis's site plan dated April 1948, after the Easter conferences. Details differ significantly from his sketch of the previous November, which is reproduced as the front endpaper. Deferring to the Academic Advisers, he has made the library, at the centre rear of the plan, significantly larger than the administrative building, which dominated the earlier sketch.

Existing buildings in 1948 include the Institute of Anatomy and Canberra High School, which later became the University's School of Art.

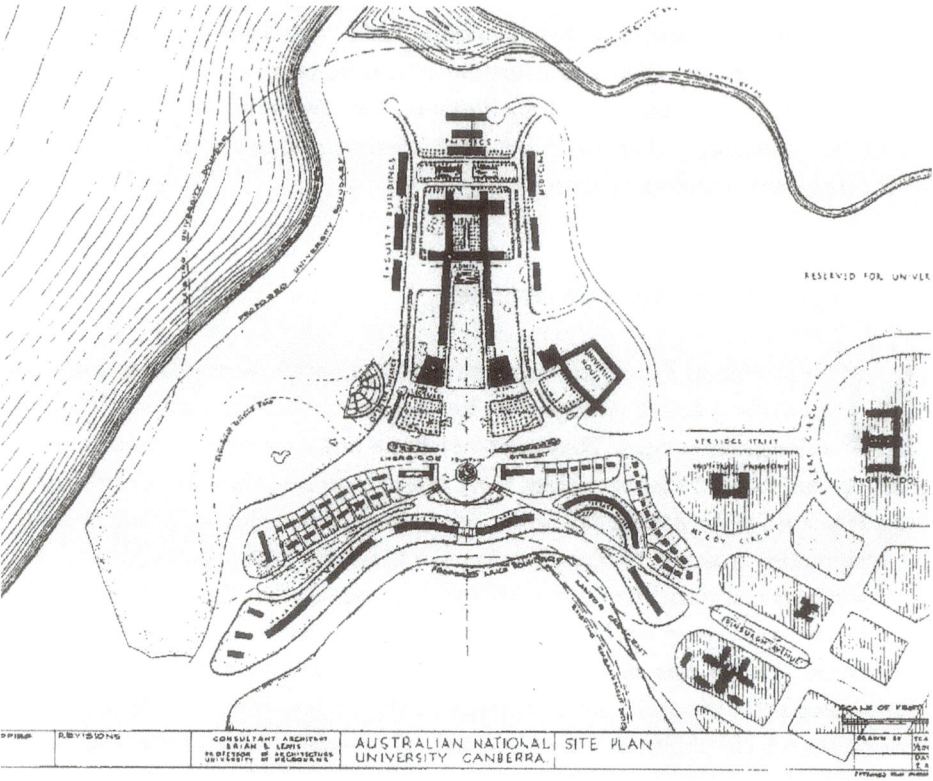

The Academic Advisers required that University House should be in 'a gracious and dignified style'. Lewis obliged with a design that won both their approval and the Sulman Medal for architecture.

Council decided to appoint a single architect to get on with the job, and on Wright's suggestion turned to Brian Lewis, Professor of Architecture at the University of Melbourne. Lewis had trained in Melbourne and practised there as an architect before moving to England, where he studied at the University of Liverpool, a hub of architectural innovation. In the late 1930s he worked in the architectural department of the Great Western Railway, designing stations, hotels and other railway buildings, and after war service returned to the railway in 1944 as its Chief Architect. Success in England led to his appointment in 1946 to the new Melbourne chair, where he immediately introduced the University's first full-time course in architecture and set about creating a school where one scarcely existed before. Lewis was an extrovert, quick-witted and short-tempered, a bit pompous, but with a touch of the larrikin. Like the members of the Academic Advisory Committee, he did not put up with any nonsense. Wright judged him a good fellow.

Lewis was appointed Consulting Architect late in 1947 and asked to produce an overall site plan, together with ideas for buildings for physical sciences and medical sciences; a combined building for the two social science schools, a residential hostel and the library; and residential housing, including flats. The combined building was Wright's idea: he saw it as a 'cross between All Souls and a rooming house'. Although the idea did not last long, it is a significant reminder of where he and his colleagues often looked for inspiration.

In sketching the site plan, Lewis drew inspiration from the landscape and from Griffin's 1912 design for the city. The dominant feature of the site was a well-defined ridge, running from the University's northwestern boundary near Sullivan's Creek, then steeply descending to its southwestern boundary on the shore of the proposed lake. Viewed from where the west basin of the central lake would one day be, this ridge led the eye towards Black Mountain, along the water axis which was integral to Griffin's original plan. Lewis arranged the University's buildings in rough symmetry along this axis, adding a great hall, public lecture theatres and faculty buildings to provide for growth. The medical and physical sciences buildings were at the Sullivan's Creek end of the axis, along with an eight-storey administrative block, which was to be the largest structure on the site. The other end was open, overlooking the lake: here the main feature was a tall tower (soon replaced by a fountain), flanked by 'community buildings' and, further out, by houses and flats stretching around the water. The proposed faculty club, described even in these early years as University House, was situated on a secondary ridge and looked towards the tower from an angle of just over 50 degrees to the axis. Lewis assumed that, with the exception of Canberra House and some of the other residences, the existing buildings on the site would be demolished as his plan was implemented: the old hospital buildings, which the axis bisected, could stay for a while, though eventually they would have to make way for the grand administrative building.

Most members of the Interim Council liked Lewis's plan. As the Academic Advisers had asked earlier in the year for an opportunity to consult with the architect as soon as he was appointed, Council obligingly despatched him to England. That was the first mistake. The Advisers, who were then in a testy mood about other matters, were annoyed that he had been sent without Council asking them first. Then, having assumed that he had come to discuss the physics and medical buildings, they were irritated when he produced sketches of the overall site. They objected vehemently to the provision of an eight-storey administrative building, on the ground that administration in any well-run university should be small and efficient, and should be seen to be so in the architectural layout. If there were to be a monumental building, it should be the library, 'a dignified building expressing the solidarity of the University and thus establishing an academic tradition dating from its foundation'. Florey declared that he did not want his medical building to be symmetrical with the other buildings, and so gave the impression that he did not want a site plan at all. The Advisers decided that, for all future plans, the architect would need to be given a comprehensive and exact description of what was required and a clear statement of what the building was for. Lewis and the Council were therefore told that any plans should be regarded as 'absolutely tentative'.

A sensitive person might have regarded this as a setback—but not Brian Lewis, who thought he had handled the Advisers well: 'they showed off to each other and were a bit bloody silly', he told Wright; 'I made myself a good fellow by saying what sods etc the Interim Council were'. Oliphant was not impressed. 'We were puzzled', he later remarked, 'by the fact that Lewis was able to show us no examples of his work beyond some rather conventional housing and some lavatories for the Great Western Railway'. John Foster was worried that Lewis, though thoroughly primed, did not seem to appreciate the need for showing complete deference to the Advisers' views.

Back in Australia, his plan met a more decisive obstacle in the form of the Canberra planning authorities, who did not like the amount of space given over to residential accommodation. While not rejecting the plan outright, they did not endorse it. Although this may not have seemed especially significant at the time, it left the design in limbo, with no more status than the various interested parties were prepared to give it. Midway through 1949, Council's Buildings and Grounds Committee declared that it was too early to consider the general site plan, deciding that the siting of any new buildings in the immediate future should be determined on an ad hoc basis.

Lewis had by now been appointed design architect for the immediate building program. This was to comprise just three buildings, Physical Sciences, Medical Research and University House, together with essential residential accommodation, including the vice-chancellor's residence. Wright's idea for a combined building was set aside, as the social science schools and the library could be housed initially in the old hospital buildings.

The requirements of the Academic Advisory Committee, as Lewis reported them after his visit to England, seemed clear enough: 'the character and construction of all buildings should be unpretentious' and 'good taste and reticence rather than extravagance should be expressed'. This was quite in keeping with the architect's own views. The tradition of Australian university architecture, in so far as there was one, was to try to recapture European university traditions through Gothic spires and grass quadrangles, and then allow less expensive and more functional buildings to grow up around the monumental centre. Lewis, who owed no allegiance to any particular architectural style, was content to design cheaper buildings better suited to Australian conditions and more in harmony with the local landscape. He was also ready to let each building have its own style, relying on other features to provide coherence: ponds and fountains, tree plantings (especially clusters of crab apples), the use of tinted common bricks, and the massing of buildings along the axis.

These ideas attracted a good deal of interest among architects and enthusiasm from the press. The *Sydney Morning Herald* welcomed Lewis's refusal to transplant Oxbridge concepts to an alien environment: his contemporary approach, remarked the writer, reflected the expected role of the new University 'which, with its emphasis on research into practical Australian problems, looks forward to a Pacific tomorrow rather than back to our European yesteryears'.

This could hardly be said of Lewis's design for University House. While the exterior might have been modern, in most other respects it looked to Oxbridge for inspiration. The concept was Hancock's, though his colleagues on the Academic Advisory Committee shared his enthusiasm for the project and were keen to give it priority, even ahead of the buildings for Physical Sciences and Medical Research. Along with first-class laboratories and a fine library, it was seen by the Advisers as an essential condition of their coming to Canberra, and as the surest way of softening their landings in the bush. Hancock portrayed it as fulfilling many of the functions of an Oxford or Cambridge college, serving as the centre of *'academic* social life' for all graduates within the University, and providing accommodation for single research workers and members of staff. It should also offer superior accommodation to distinguished visitors; and lastly, it should provide service facilities—meals, cleaning, household maintenance—to married members of staff and others who were not in residence, thereby helping solve the problem of having no servants. In Hancock's presentation, the faculty club function took precedence over providing accommodation for single scholars. Here, the 'wife factor', as Hancock called it, was at work. University House was, among other things, the most likely means of making Canberra tolerable for his wife, a consideration which also appealed to other members of the Academic Advisory Committee, in relation to their own wives.

So Hancock imagined University House with dining areas, recreation rooms, small rooms for informal discussions, quiet reading rooms, and perhaps a swimming pool and squash courts. Above all, it should follow the pattern of modern university colleges in Europe by providing a corner where ladies might be entertained, and where the female relatives of members of staff might receive their friends. He hoped that older traditions would be sustained at the University, permitting 'a certain amount of gracious living'—as an inspiration to first-rate work as well as an end in itself. 'What we want is the twentieth century equivalent of that medieval institution, the Oxford College', but 'freed from the tradition of medieval celibacy'.

University House today, except for some later additions, is much as Lewis planned it. The residential section, three storeys high, was built around three sides of a quadrilateral in what the historian of University House calls the shape of a truncated fan. The fourth side, a single-storey building containing the main foyer,

Right: University House in 1955, a year after its opening.

Below left: Scholars' study bedrooms, with elegant furnishings and heated floors, were luxurious by the standards of college accommodation in state universities.

Below right: The Dining Room was the main meeting place for academics and scholars from all schools and disciplines.

administrative rooms and some of the meeting and sitting rooms, curved gently around the rim of the fan, completing the quadrilateral. Additional buildings, including a three-storey high refectory or dining hall, projected from the two outer corners of the quadrilateral.

Various elements of the design recalled Oxbridge. Following the wishes of the Interim Council, the architect had the rooms and flats in the main residential wings open onto staircases rather than corridors, suggesting that the building was a college rather than a hostel. The dining hall, as Lewis described it, was conceived as the setting for 'those almost solemn ceremonial dinners which are a feature of collegiate life'. There was plenty to encourage gracious living: the spacious bedrooms, the generous balconies, the heated floors, the double-glazed windows to shield the sitting rooms from the Canberra cold, the ornamental pool which ran the length of the single-storey, communal wing; and Hancock's 'place for the ladies', discreetly isolated from the main residential wings. As the showpiece of the ANU, University House was expected to become 'something of a museum of contemporary Australian art'. Leading artists and designers, including the sculptor Lyndon Dadswell and the furniture designer Frederick Ward, were chosen to create or select suitable works of art, furnishings and fittings: all this to enhance the impression that University House was a repository of Australian culture, as well as European university tradition.

Luxury and tradition came at a price. Oliphant had suggested that the flats for distinguished visitors should be planned on a slightly extravagant scale, so that academics visiting the University would spread the news of efforts made for their comfort. In the event, the whole of University House was planned and executed on a scale that was more than slightly extravagant, so that constraints had to be introduced as building proceeded. It was by far the most expensive residential college on a cost per bed basis constructed in Australia to that date, and so it remained. What was worse, running costs proved to be much higher than expected, so that an institution which was initially intended to be self-sufficient soon became a burden on the University budget.

The foundations of University House were laid in 1950 and the building eventually opened in 1954. Leaving aside the financial problems, the completed structure was widely regarded as a success, not least by Hancock, who praised it in later years as convenient and beautiful. Even Oliphant and Florey, both of whom had no time for Lewis, thought it worked well. It won for Lewis Australia's most prestigious award for architecture, the Sulman Medal. On the other hand, the Prime Minister Robert Menzies told Oliphant that it looked like 'an institution or orphanage from some angles and a seaside block of flats from others', adding that Lewis (whom he knew from student days) had indulged in misguided and expensive tastes. But no architect could please everyone: and in relation to University House, Lewis came close to keeping his academic masters happy.

The same could not be said about the two other major buildings that were part of his commission. Both Oliphant and Florey had strong opinions about the type of construction needed for each of their schools, and insisted that their requirements be carried out to the letter. Oliphant wanted single-storey factory-style laboratories that

The Cockcroft Building, designed by Lewis more or less in accordance with Oliphant's specifications, was cheap and functional.

could be altered and added to quickly and cheaply in response to the changing needs of physics: their useful life should not be seen as exceeding fifteen years. To make sure that he got what he wanted, he commissioned his own architect in England to draw up preliminary plans.

But things went wrong in the execution, and before long Oliphant was cursing Lewis and the builders responsible for construction. The problems began when he arrived in Australia and discovered, instead of completed laboratories, a hole in the ground, which was exactly as Florey had predicted. Thenceforth, construction was painfully slow, owing chiefly to the acute shortage of building supplies but also, according to Oliphant, to Lewis's time-consuming and expensive mistakes. Lewis asserted that the building's specifications kept changing. Oliphant complained that Lewis refused to take instructions and was incapable of appreciating the technical requirements of a laboratory. It was an unhappy episode; and while the building, when eventually completed in 1953, corresponded generally with Oliphant's requirements, it was not exactly as he had wanted.

Florey too wanted simplicity in the design of the medical research school. Drawing inspiration from the new laboratories of the British National Institute of Medical Research at Mill Hill, he and his colleagues sketched a plan based on the letter H, with common services, including administrative offices, a tea room and a library, occupying the central spine, and laboratories at each of the extremities. Lewis complied and produced preliminary plans. But again problems arose as the plans were refined to cut costs and to meet the needs of the individual professors, each of whom had specific requirements for his own department. Before long Florey had concluded that Lewis was a disaster; and Copland and Hohnen, alarmed at the architect's mistakes and evident prevarication, decided that he had to go. Given a hefty push, he resigned in 1953 as architect for the John Curtin School, remaining somewhat ambiguously architect for the site plan which everybody else tended to ignore. University House and an elegant boiler house are his only enduring monuments on the ANU campus.

Lewis brought many of his problems on himself. In retrospect, he lacked the requisite technical skills and support capacity for the job; and his personality did not help relations with his fellow academics. Nevertheless, he had a forbidding task, dealing with academic clients who showed little respect for his professional judgement and who assumed that architects were there to do their bidding. As Florey put it in his inimitable style, he did not intend to be 'pushed around by an architect for architectural reasons'.

A genuine university

Copland dedicated himself to 'selling' the 'great intellectual adventure' of the ANU to anyone prepared to listen, especially people who could be useful to the new institution or might be prepared to join its staff. Much of his time was spent talking to small groups of academics and students in universities throughout Australia and addressing conferences, such as the 1949 conference of the Australian and New Zealand Association for the Advancement of Science, where he delivered a paper on 'The Place of the Australian National University in the Australian Academic Structure'. The title hints at one of his favourite themes, that the ANU would assist rather than threaten the state universities, and help bridge the distance between them. Through publicity and diplomacy he managed to remove much of the resentment that had been in evidence during the Easter 1948 conferences, and to convince the state universities that they had more to gain than lose from the presence of a well-endowed research institution in Canberra.

A tireless traveller, he made several overseas tours. While each had specific purposes, he also regarded them as 'propaganda missions'. In Oxford he addressed about a hundred members of the Australian Society, where he did his best to counter scepticism that such a well-conceived idea could be hatched in Australia, let alone in Canberra. In the United States and Canada he met academic leaders in several universities, drawing on them for information and ideas, while spreading the word about what the ANU had to offer.

Copland described himself as an incurable optimist, and his optimism infected those he worked with. Oskar Spate, who arrived in mid-1951 to take up the chair of Geography in Pacific Studies, later remembered him as a great encourager.

'Welcome to the ANU!' Ross Hohnen greets a visiting dignitary, 1957.
By courtesy of Ross Hohnen.

> You'd go to him with some idea and he'd say, 'Well, that's a jolly good idea. Might be very difficult to get any money from Treasury. For goodness sake, let's have a crack at it.' And you'd go away by no means certain that he'd live up to his words but feeling good.

His optimism also extended to the small band of administrative staff he gathered around him. Chief among these was the Registrar, Ross Hohnen. Born in Sydney and now in his early thirties, Hohnen had worked in a bank while studying economics as an evening student at the University of Sydney, where his seminar leader in fourth year had been Coombs. After war service in New Guinea and Borneo, he had joined New England University College in Armidale as its first Registrar, before joining the ANU in September 1948 as Assistant to the Registrar. Copland took to him immediately as 'an enterprising person with a real pioneer touch about him'. Like Copland, he was tall, upright, confident and a little brash. Like Copland, he thrived on the excitement of creating a new institution. He told a colleague how it was 'rather thrilling to see the pattern forming, with piece by piece falling in its place despite the obstacles which oppose us at every stage'.

Behind all the thinking of Copland and those who shared his vision was a determination to create a genuine university, not just in terms of material fabric, but in ambience and culture as well. Most universities were (and still are) defined as such largely through the presence of students, and the process of teaching and learning. But the ANU in its early years (as Geoffrey Sawer remarked in ironic verse) had few students and no undergraduate teaching. Nor was there yet much in the way of research, the other means by which a university might be deserving of its name.

University House, once built, would be best proof that the University was the genuine article. This would be home to a scholarly community, and the means of maintaining scholarly traditions. Accordingly, much thought was given to the position initially referred to as Warden (as at All Souls), but soon to be styled Master. This office was seen as one of the most senior in the University, next in status to that of the vice-chancellor. Oliphant believed that the warden, more than any other member of staff, would be responsible for the atmosphere and spirit of the University as a whole. Crocker wanted someone in the humanities, possibly a clerk in holy orders of the Oxbridge kind, who would be able to counterbalance the over-specialisation which would come with research. Both wanted someone who would give the University a soul.

The University also needed symbols. As early as 1947 Osborne raised the question of a motto and coat of arms, and people were soon thinking about the need for a distinctive academic dress. None of these came easily. In the case of the coat of arms, the collective effort put into the task might have produced a substantial thesis. The difficulty was to produce a design which was distinctive, recognisably Australian, free of clichés, consistent with the requirements of heraldry, and capable of being reproduced in black and white on a small scale. In 1949 the Interim Council's Advisory Committee on Art commissioned sketches from several Australian designers. None of them stimulated much excitement in Canberra; and somewhat to Hohnen's irritation, the Academic Advisers amused themselves in dissecting the one that was sent them, pointing out, for example, that the crowning edifice of the shield, though intended to represent enclosed university life, expressed with equal felicity the confines of a prison. But they could come up with nothing better.

Even at this early stage Hohnen was wondering whether the University could get away without a coat of arms; and Oliphant, referring to both the coat of arms and the motto, hoped that Australia had grown beyond 'such out-worn conventions'. However, some 'trade mark' seemed necessary to place on buildings, stationery and beer glasses; and before long other universities were asking for copies of the shield to adorn their own halls of learning. It was clearly something no university could be without.

LINES
WRITTEN BY A PROFESSOR OF THE AUSTRALIAN
NATIONAL UNIVERSITY
ON DISCOVERING
TWO SCRIBBLING STRANGERS
IN ATTENDANCE AT A JOINT SEMINAR.

Thou wretched, rash, intruding fools - you say
They're students, here by right? It cannot be.
Is teaching, dreadful trade, our destiny,
The profound hell to which we wend our way?

Then farewell, happy fields, where I did play
At donnish politics, and poesy,
Where dons spoke but to dons, and all were free
From worldly cares, except on budget day.

Yet all's not lost. Around me still there sit
Professors, Readers, Fellows—near a score
Of faithful friends. Let not this alien crew
Jeer at my doctrine, denigrate my wit,
Question my sources, call my logic poor;
Be humble, students; we outnumber you!

August 1952. G.S.

A selection of designs proposed for the University's coat of arms. The first three, from the left, are by professional designers, Paul Beadle, Gené Kellock and Allistair Morrison. The fourth is by the Professor of Law, Geoffrey Sawer, who incorporates a feature of the local landscape, Mount Tidbinbilla in the Brindabella Range, leaving space below for an open book.

Hohnen referred the problem to a dignitary of the College of Heralds, who obliged with a design that was obedient to heraldic traditions but, as Spate put it, 'too damned conventional for words'. The new professors wanted something distinctively Australian, perhaps with an Aboriginal motif. Having lost patience with the 'erstwhile Garter Principal King of Arms', Hohnen decided to leave it to them. Inspiration, however, was slow in coming, and it was not until late 1953 that Council was able to approve a design that everyone was more or less happy with. Ironically, it was Oliphant who saved the day, with a simple sketch incorporating waves (the Pacific), a boomerang and the Southern Cross. Spate, who preferred a much more complicated design of his own, thought this was 'rather thin heraldically'; but at least it was unambiguously Australian, and everyone understood it because there was so little to understand. He took solace in recounting the epic story of his own design in 29 stanzas of mock heroic verse, in the style of 'The Ballad of Sir Patrick Spens', which he called 'The Ballad of the Scutcheon'.

One concern about the coat of arms was that nothing in it suggested learning. Fortunately, this could be compensated for in the motto, which the academic board, known as the Board of Graduate Studies, discussed in detail once the coat of arms had been chosen. After considering a dozen or so proposals, most of them in Latin, the board expressed a preference for '*Rerum cognoscere causas*', from Virgil's *Georgics*. This had been suggested some years earlier by Leslie Allen, a Latin scholar at the University College. However, as Virgil's phrase was in fact an adaptation from his near-contemporary, the poet, philosopher and scientist Lucretius, who had written '*Naturam primum cognoscere rerum*', the board opted for the original version.

The meaning of the motto, as explained by Richard Johnson, a Professor of Classics in later years, is 'To study first the nature of all that is'. In *De Rerum Natura*, the poem from which it was taken, Lucretius aimed to dispel the fears and passions that disturbed mankind. He believed this could be achieved only by rational knowledge of the nature of men and the material universe. At the time, the preferred translation was 'First to learn the nature of things'. Though later subjected to erudite and exhaustive criticism (prompting a registrar to remark 'who would think translating four words could cause such trouble!'), this simple translation survived all challenges and remained the more or less approved version.

Thus equipped with arms and motto, the officers and troops were ready to be

The final choice: 'Per chevron Azure and Barry wavy of eight Argent and of the last a Boomerang chevronwise Or in sinister chief five Stars representing the Constellation of the Southern Cross also Argent.'

apparelled. Early in 1950, before either the Interim Council or the Academic Advisers had given much thought to the matter, Charles Franklyn, a physician who held the honorary office of Bedell of Convocation at the University of London and who had recently designed a set of gowns for the University of Malaya, offered to design for the University a complete system of academic dress. As Copland thought he was worth pursuing, Ernest Clark, who had been appointed representative of the University in London, visited him in Sussex, where he found him to be 'a very voluble gentleman', expert in the field, but eccentric and intense in his devotion to the subject. Before long Franklyn had come up with elaborate designs for every form of dress the University could ever expect to use, and many more besides. These were magnificent in their detail. Doctors in philosophy, for example, would be entitled to wear in full dress a robe of claret-coloured cloth similar to the London PhD, of the same shape as the Oxford DPhil in full dress, the bell-shaped sleeves being of 'peacock blue silk shot with green', which was to be the University's colour. The fronts were to be faced with five inches of the same silk, while on the yoke of the robe behind was to be a silk-covered button and twisted cord of the faculty colour in which the degree was taken.

This was all a bit much for Hohnen. 'Just now and again', he told Clark's successor Russell Mathews, 'introduce the idea that we are not so very determined to follow suit in matters of ceremonial'. Already some members of Council had suggested that there was no need for the University to have robes at all. What happened was, from the purist's point of view, even more shocking. Maurice Brown, Hohnen's second in command, took to Franklyn's dress regulations with a pair of scissors, having in mind the cost and availability of local materials. The mutilated garment was then referred to the Board of Graduate Studies, which did a little stitching and unstitching, so that the end result bore little resemblance to Franklyn's original. Franklyn's 'peacock blue silk shot with green' was replaced by a 'plain bright blue colour', the claret gown for the full dress PhD was abandoned in favour of black, and colour distinctions between faculties were cast aside. Franklyn, when he heard what had been done, was apoplectic, describing the destruction of his system as an act of 'unbelievable vandalism', and the substitute system as 'an appalling mess'. Hohnen was unrepentant, calmly explaining to Franklyn that the arrangements took into account 'the needs of a new University in this country as well as the precepts of tradition'.

Franklyn, before learning of the ravages of the philistines, had suggested that the University might acknowledge his efforts by awarding him an Honorary MA. Hohnen and his colleagues thought this a bit brazen: degrees, honorary as well as earned, were precious commodities which should be jealously guarded, especially in a young university. It might have been acceptable to have an academic dress that was less than *de rigueur*; but academic standards, symbolised in the award of degrees, had to be protected with rigour. Here there could be no compromise of tradition.

In relation to academic titles, however, tradition's primacy was less assured. Traditional universities in Britain and Australia had an established nomenclature for the academic hierarchy. The tenured grades were generally 'professor', 'reader' (or the American import 'associate professor'), 'senior lecturer' and 'lecturer'. Below the lecturer were the untenured positions of 'tutor' and 'research assistant'. After considering the matter in 1948, the Academic Advisers concluded that professor and reader should be retained as 'well-known and honoured' titles. However, lecturer (and senior lecturer) were considered unsuitable, partly because there was nobody to lecture to, but also because there was a risk of confusion with members of Canberra University College, who had lecturers and senior lecturers but not yet readers or professors. The Committee therefore favoured 'fellow' as the grade below reader, suggesting that it should be used in the same sense as in an Oxford college. Council accepted this title, and in due course divided it into senior fellow and fellow for permanent positions, and senior research fellow and research fellow for untenured staff. This was a useful means of proclaiming a unique identity for the staff of the ANU. But the distinction was not to be carried too far. When Davidson and Swan showed egalitarian tendencies by suggesting soon after their arrival that they should have 'Mr' rather than 'Professor' on their doors, Copland shut his own door on further discussion by declaring that 'the title of professor is a burden inseparably connected with the emoluments of their office'. And that was that.

Two ceremonies in the latter half of 1952 offered further testimony that the University had arrived as a prestigious scholarly institution. On 5 September Sir John Cockcroft, Nobel Laureate in Physics and Director of the British Atomic Energy Research Establishment at Harwell, opened the University's first permanent building, the laboratories for the Research School of Physical Sciences. The mood was optimistic. Coombs, as Deputy Chairman of Council, began the proceedings, describing the event as 'another step in what is probably the greatest adventure in the field of learning in the southern hemisphere'. The Prime Minister R.G. Menzies, whose conservative coalition had displaced Chifley's Labor government in 1949, declared his 'unlimited faith in the capacity of the scientist' to contribute to the well-being of mankind. Cockcroft anticipated that the new laboratories would do for Australia what the great Cavendish Laboratory had done for England. And Copland reminded the audience that the establishment of the ANU was a mark of great confidence in the future of Australia. He then ushered the guests inside the building to inspect the giant machine under construction, warning them, however, that they wouldn't 'understand any more than I do about it, so don't make any mistake about that!'. In the afternoon, Coombs conferred on Cockcroft the honorary degree of Doctor of Science, making him the University's second graduate, the first, Sir Robert Garran, having received the honorary degree of Doctor of Laws nine months earlier.

The opening ceremony looked to the future. A second function, held several weeks later, looked to the past. This was the installation of the University's first Chancellor, Stanley Melbourne Bruce, the Right Honourable Viscount Bruce of Melbourne, Prime Minister of Australia for much of the 1920s, High Commissioner to the United Kingdom for over a decade, and now retired and resident in London. On 22 October, the day before the installation was due to take place, representatives of some ninety other universities each presented to the new University greetings on behalf of their own institution, sometimes in the form of a parchment scroll and, in the case of

Page, Bruce and page boy uphold tradition at the opening of University House, February 1954. The Chancellor, Lord Bruce, talks to Sir Earle Page, Chairman of the Council of the University of New England, which has just acquired independent university status. Bruce is a former Prime Minister and Page his Deputy. The page boy, a little uncomfortable in lace and buckles, is Sir John Eccles' third son, John.

Oxford, written in Latin. The public installation ceremony the next morning was to have been held outdoors, but heavy rain made much of the campus a bog and forced the ceremony across the river to the Albert Hall. Amid continuing drizzle, almost all the academic and senior administrative staff of the University arrived, together with several hundred visitors: the Governor-General, politicians, diplomats, clergymen, representatives of the armed services, and other dignitaries, many of them dressed in ceremonial apparel. Leading the academic procession, the Registrar carried the University stave, a gift of the University of Oxford and an exact replica of the eighteenth-century stave which was carried by the Bedell of Arts at Oxford; then came the Vice-Chancellor, in the robes of a University of New Zealand DSc, and the Chancellor-elect, wearing Franklyn's robes which had been carefully fitted in London. The remaining academic staff followed, each in the apparel of a university from which he or she had graduated. The Vice-Chancellor then conferred on Bruce the honorary degree of Doctor of Laws, after which proceedings climaxed with the installation ceremony. It was, said Copland, a great event, especially for a town unused to such grandeur. Each ritual element and ceremonial flourish helped confirm the fledgling University as the inheritor of ancient tradition.

Crocker missed the installation. Several months earlier he had taken leave of absence to accept an appointment as Australian High Commissioner to India. Although marriage had helped smooth some of the jagged edges of life in Canberra, in his view the ANU still had far to go before it resembled the sort of university he had once thought he was joining. He formally relinquished the chair of International Relations in 1954 and continued to serve until 1970 as a high commissioner or ambassador in various parts of the world, from where he looked back to the ANU with critical interest and occasional regret that he was not still a part of it. His departure was a sad loss, from the point of view of his personal contribution as well as of maintaining appearances. If other senior academics were to leave so early, the University would be seriously weakened.

Everyone attending the installation ceremony knew by now that the University would shortly be losing its Vice-Chancellor. Copland was restless by nature, and ever since he had joined the ANU there was a chance that he would be tempted away by a political or diplomatic position. Now he was offered appointment as High Commissioner to Canada; and as his term as Vice-Chancellor was due to expire in April 1953, he decided to accept. Some believed he would have stayed on if Council had offered to extend the appointment. Sawer thought that, when he announced his decision to a meeting of the academic staff, he half expected—half hoped—that someone would leap to his feet and say 'No, no, don't go!' But nobody did, nor did Council make the necessary overtures. So Copland packed his bags and was gone early in the new year.

Many people in the University were sorry to see him go, including Ennor, Sawer, Hohnen and others who had worked closely with him. Oliphant was unperturbed, suggesting that the University would benefit from a change; and Florey, from a distance, complained as usual that he seemed to have left 'an intolerable mess' in the medical school. One reason why Council members might have thought twice about reappointing him was a report from the Commonwealth auditor (which we will look at more closely in another context) casting doubt on various aspects of the University's financial administration. Some critics argued that he spent too much time on matters outside the University, such as commenting on the state of the Australian economy, and that he allowed Hohnen and the growing administration too much influence.

A larger question mark related to his role in representing the ANU as a university of academic distinction. Crocker, a perceptive and acerbic critic, remarked in later years that he had little instinct for quality and that he contributed no ideas. But that was a harsh judgement; and his own earlier estimate, confided to Hancock early in 1952, comes closer to the mark. Copland's defects, wrote Crocker, were not concealed and they were very trying: he liked publicity; he was not 'a scholar and a gentleman' in the traditional sense; he loved 'robust and rather undistinguished lunch and dinner parties'; in some respects he lacked sensitivity. On the other hand, he had the courage of the lion, inexhaustible energy, extraordinary patience with his staff, and a better mind and more fineness of sentiment than he was usually credited with. Had he not been Vice-Chancellor over the last eighteen months, Crocker concluded, the University would have fizzled out. Writing again to Hancock, nearly a year later from New Delhi, Crocker expressed satisfaction that Copland was both well-placed and gone: he had made his contribution, and now the University needed a different kind of vice-chancellor and a new regime with more rigorous standards.

Copland was a publicist, an entrepreneur, a vigorous defender of the University and what he believed it stood for. Those qualities were exactly what the University needed in its early years. He was the man for the moment: but as his term neared an end, Crocker and others were beginning to ask whether his moment had passed.

A week or so before leaving Canberra, Copland organised a meeting with the Prime Minister to promote the interests of the University, and especially to combat doubts in Cabinet about the wisdom of proceeding with the medical school. After an amiable discussion between the old friends and colleagues, Menzies asked Copland to present his case to the Cabinet meeting scheduled for two days later. This interview with Cabinet lasted 45 minutes, during which the Vice-Chancellor was subjected to some sceptical questioning. Conceding that the early plans of the University might end up costing £15 million, he managed to explain why the high cost was necessary, and he warned that if the medical professors were not to work in Canberra they would be lost to Australian science. By this time his case was strengthened by significant research achievements. Perhaps with a glance at critical ministers from the Country Party, he mentioned work in the John Curtin School on myxomatosis, which was having a powerful impact in controlling the country's rabbit plague. 'It was my last working day in Canberra', he recorded in a private note:

> and I took advantage of every opportunity opened in the questions to reiterate the aims of the University, its place in the Australian academic structure and the interest that had been developed in it abroad ... when the Prime Minister asked if there were any further questions, one of the Ministers jocularly remarked that he thought Cabinet had had enough of an exercise in the arts of persuasion.

Copland was then asked to wait outside while Cabinet weighed the case before it. Before long, the Secretary to the Prime Minister's Department Allen Brown (himself a member of the University Council) emerged to say that Cabinet had been persuaded and that the extra funds needed for the medical school would be made available. It was a fitting end to Copland's regime.

The staff of the University had said farewell to their Vice-Chancellor several weeks earlier, at a function organised by Hohnen. For Copland, it was a moving occasion:

> So many came up to me at one stage or another during the evening that I felt that somehow or other we had all managed to achieve in so short a time an extra-ordinary spirit of community of interest in an exciting adventure. I must say that I had a feeling also that I was deserting a rather high-minded group of people ...

'A rather high-minded group of people': the administrative staff in 1950, two and a half years before Copland's departure. Seated on either side of Copland, from left to right, are Joan Morrish, his Secretary; Lois Bellingham, Assistant Accountant; Ross Hohnen, Registrar; Maurice Brown, Assistant Registrar; Bill Hamilton, Accountant; and Russell Mathews, Copland's Research Assistant and, many years later, Professor of Accounting and Public Finance.
Australian News and Information Bureau, ANU Collection.

Research begins

4

Opportunities

For those who were ready to imbibe Copland's pioneering spirit, the University in the 1950s offered opportunities in abundance. There was money, vastly more than academics in the state universities were used to; and although funds were reduced during the decade by high inflation and limits on government spending, there were still generous budgets for equipment, travel and new appointments to the academic and support staff. There was time, a luxury for most academics burdened with heavy teaching loads, but especially for those whose research activities had virtually ceased during the war. Freed from teaching responsibilities (except for the occasional PhD student), the professors, as Sawer remarked, lectured to one another. And there was the richest opportunity of all, the freedom to range across the vast tracts of uncharted intellectual territory and select a field of research for intensive cultivation. Sawer wrote what many others thought: 'Bliss was it in that dawn to be a Don ...'.

The planners had assumed that the new University should have research facilities as good as or better than any other research institution in the world. This implied that the staff should have ample opportunities for overseas travel, to keep abreast of developments in other countries and to establish the University's place in the international scholarly community. Professors were therefore given a 'sabbatical' leave entitlement of one year in four, significantly better than the usual one year in seven, along with generous travel allowances.

The first staff were encouraged to inspect relevant research centres in other countries. On his way to Australia, Crocker, at Copland's request, toured universities in the United States, Britain and Europe, and prepared a lengthy report on research in international relations. Wes Whitten, the Animal Veterinary Officer, was sent around the world to inspect animal houses and then design one suitable for Australian conditions. FitzGerald, on his way to Australia and with £3000 to spend, went shopping for books in Hong Kong and the United States, and assembled the basis of a library of some 25 000 volumes, mostly in Chinese and including many classical works which would soon become difficult to obtain. The Librarian, McDonald, spent several months in 1950 visiting libraries and booksellers in Britain and the United States.

The first University Librarian, A.L.G. McDonald, 1953.

McDonald had been appointed early in 1948, before any of the professors. This reflected the priority that the Interim Council gave to the Library. Initially he and several assistants were housed in Ormond College in the University of Melbourne, where they brought together some 40 000 volumes. At the end of 1950 these were transferred to Canberra where, despite cramped conditions in the old hospital building and nearby huts, the collection grew to 110 000 (excluding pamphlets) by the end of 1955 and 150 000 by the time of McDonald's retirement in 1960. McDonald fashioned the Library's acquisitions policy to meet the specific needs of the research schools, avoiding less directed purchasing which might lead to overlap with the holdings of the National Library, whose permanent building was destined to occupy a site just a few kilometres away. With large annual budgets, he was able to give the schools the books and periodicals they wanted: he was an academics' librarian, and he created a library well suited to their immediate needs. On the debit side, he wished upon the University the inaptly named and relatively untried Bliss system of classification, on the grounds that the widely used Dewey system was inadequate for science and the Library of Congress classification was too hard for the Library's inexperienced staff.

What Florey had said about medical research was true, and it could be applied with equal force to nearly all the other natural and social sciences: Australia had contributed little to the world of learning, except through its sons who had decided to live abroad. At the 1948 conference on the Social Sciences school, senior academics had given a mostly gloomy view of the research achievement in their disciplines. In economics, said S.J. Butlin from Sydney, university research was 'very narrowly limited in range and generally at a comparatively low level'. In constitutional law and economics, said G.W. Paton from Melbourne, there had been much scattered work on the fringes; but there was 'vast scope' for research, while the whole field of Australian legal history had been 'shockingly ignored'. At the Pacific Studies conference the Sydney anthropologist Ian Hogbin described Melanesia as 'virtually a *terra incognita*', while one of his Sydney colleagues remarked that the study of linguistics in the Pacific was in its infancy: 'to set out the problems that await research is therefore practically to set out all the possibilities of the field'. Oliphant's chosen area of nuclear physics was entirely new to Australia.

Postgraduate training scarcely existed before the war and it was not until 1945 that the PhD degree was introduced at the University of Melbourne, with the other state universities soon following. In 1950 there were still only a dozen PhD graduates from all Australian universities. In later decades, aspiring PhD students in many areas would have to search for a topic and ascertain whether or not it had been 'covered' already. But in the 1950s they could begin their explorations confident that no researchers in Australia had trodden that path before, or that if they had their journeys were well known.

The professors were free to follow research of their own choosing. Some continued the work they had been doing before joining the ANU; others branched out in new directions. The degree of freedom extended to non-professorial staff and students differed from one school and department to the next, depending on the nature of research being conducted and the plans of the head of department. But whether academics were working on their own or as part of a team, there was a prevailing sense of optimism. David Curtis, a young Research Fellow in the Department of Physiology, reflected as an Emeritus Professor in the 1990s that he was 'very privileged having gone through that period. Well, I'm still very privileged now, but that to me was the most exciting time of my life.' There was so much waiting to be discovered.

The John Curtin School of Medical Research

In the John Curtin School, Florey remained a dominant presence, even from the distance of Oxford. He corresponded regularly with the professors, offering encouragement and advice, and castigating anyone who in his view stood in the way of scientific research. Every year or two he visited Canberra, giving himself enough time to dissect an echidna (whose unique properties as a monotreme invited investigation) and, verbally at least, to take his scalpel to an architect or administrator. During these visits, the lights in Hugh Ennor's laboratory, visible from Florey's top floor flat in University House, burned late into the night. Yet while he served as an inspiration to research, Florey did not attempt to influence the work of the individual departments, except in relation to his own field of experimental pathology.

The formal arrangement was that Florey was Academic Adviser to the school. Early on he had suggested that Ennor might become 'Temporary Assistant Director for the whole school (without prejudice to later arrangements)'. Copland decided otherwise, and for its first few years the school remained without any head other than its Adviser. In 1953, after all the departments except Medical Chemistry had gathered in Canberra, Ennor was appointed Dean, a title then in use in the social science schools. As such, he was regarded as chairman of the professors and representative of the school for administrative purposes. His role was viewed, especially by his colleagues, as purely administrative. There could be no question of his exercising any form of intellectual leadership.

The research directions of each department were therefore set by the individual professors, which was what they wanted and what Florey had intended in his early plans for the school. Adrien Albert in particular was adamant that he should have free rein to run the department of Medical Chemistry as he thought best. As he insisted on remaining in London until the permanent building was ready for occupation, his

The four medical professors, meeting in Canberra in August 1950, study the plans for the proposed John Curtin School building. Left to right: John Eccles, Adrien Albert, Frank Fenner and Hugh Ennor.
Australian News and Information Bureau, ANU Collection.

department grew in isolation from the rest of the school. The move to Canberra eventually took place towards the end of 1956, when every piece of equipment, right down to the last beaker, was carefully packed and reassembled in the new laboratories.

Albert's work, and therefore the work of his department, focused mainly on exploring the chemical structure and physical properties of certain organic compounds, especially a group called the pteridines which had significant potential for the development of new drugs. This led to a fascination with heterocyclic compounds, which play a vital role in the metabolism of living cells. The department accumulated a mass of data on these substances and Albert devised a new classification system to describe them. This was classical organic chemistry, often pioneering and always of high quality, yet having no direct or necessary relationship to the rest of the school's activities. Given Albert's request at the time of his appointment that the department should be called *Medical* Chemistry, this research orientation was surprising.

Adrien Albert in the 1950s.

In many ways, Albert epitomised the dedicated scientific researcher: enthusiastic, meticulous and encyclopedic in his knowledge of the field. According to his long-term colleague, D.J. Brown, he operated on the simple principles that time was the most precious commodity in life and that, in scientific research, the work was infinitely more important than the worker. Lean and elongated, he spent long hours stooped over the bench, starting late in the morning (owing to a medical problem) but remaining there until midnight, often seven days a week. He demanded much of his staff and supervised his students closely, so closely in fact that some decided to pursue their careers elsewhere. But those who stayed with him comprised a cohesive and productive team.

The starting point for work in Biochemistry was Ennor's fascination with compounds containing phosphorus, especially their role in producing muscular energy. This relatively new area of research promised a better understanding of animal and human metabolism. Results were often unexpected, as when Harry Rosenberg, then a research scholar in the department, stumbled on a new method of estimating the presence of arginine, one of the amino acids which form an essential part of the human diet. His discovery became the standard method used in biochemical laboratories throughout the world.

Ennor relished the role of pioneer. Rather than purchasing (at high cost) certain compounds they needed from overseas, he and his colleagues would 'knock off a few rabbits' and spend a couple of days extracting what they needed. The school's own workshop built much of their equipment, such as a micromanipulator which, Ennor told Florey, had everything except the ashtray. On the other hand, facilities for meeting researchers' personal needs were to be Spartan, as befitted pioneers: Ennor insisted that the Biochemistry floors in the permanent building should be joined only by a goods lift, so that he and his colleagues would have to use the stairs.

In the early years, Ennor spent many hours at the laboratory bench, where he was, according to Rosenberg, 'full of vigour, excellent wit, and boundless energy'. He was a great encourager, taking an interest in everyone's work, but leaving each researcher free to do as he wanted. Relations in the laboratory were relaxed, even familiar: but Ennor was always addressed as 'Prof', never as Hugh. When an American visitor remarked that this seemed odd, given that Ennor was not much older than some of his colleagues, Rosenberg simply replied 'This is the way'. Gradually Ennor moved away from the bench, devoting more of his time to administration at school and University level, to lunches with Cabinet ministers or senior public servants, or attending high commissions and embassies on their countries' national days. He continued to read and encourage the work of his colleagues; but the initiative for research moved entirely to the non-professorial staff. In contrast to Albert, who was scrupulous in ensuring that research papers were accurately acknowledged, that did not stop him putting his name to papers which he played little part in generating, a practice familiar to scientific researchers. Rosenberg shrugged his shoulders: this too was the way.

Hugh Ennor describes recent research to members of the Department of Biochemistry, 1955.

Staff and students throughout the medical school often described their own work as 'fundamental' research, as distinct from 'applied' research, which they regarded as properly the province of the CSIRO. Rosenberg appreciated the relevance of the University's motto. 'In those days it was perfectly clear what we had to do', he reflected many years later: 'We had to ... find out the truth about nature'. Research was driven by curiosity: so long as they did good and inspired work, nothing else was asked of them. In Medical Chemistry, Albert frowned on applied research, even though much of the department's work had obvious biological implications. The job of the medical chemist, in his view, was to discover and explore the nature of compounds, leaving others to show how they might be used.

In practice, fundamental research was rarely as refined as it was made out to be. Florey argued that his own experiments were undertaken for their intrinsic biological interest, without practical objectives. Yet Henry Harris, his student as an ANU Overseas Scholar, noticed that nothing he did was far removed from some major human disease, and indeed that almost all his work related in some way to illnesses from which he or close members of his family actually suffered. Few if any medical scientists embarked on a project without some expectation or hope of practical applications, sooner or later. This meant that the ultimate goals of fundamental and applied research were often the same, differing only in their distance from the research itself and the clarity with which the researcher perceived them.

Whatever the stated objectives of a research project, results were best expressed in terms of practical applications. In the departments of Medical Chemistry and Biochemistry, the raw data of achievement, numerous papers published in prestigious journals and many lectures presented to international conferences—was impressive to fellow scientists. But there was little point in announcing to people who did not know the difference between a pteridine and a pterodactyl that the Department of Medical Chemistry had discovered, over the years, some hundreds of compounds. Although Florey had always warned against encouraging people outside the University to expect dramatic results, there was nevertheless an understanding that a research school which housed some of the nation's best scientific brains and which was using so much of the taxpayer's money should produce significant results, meaning results which contributed to the health of the people. Even Albert, looking back in later years on the work of his department, emphasised how discoveries in the broad field of medical chemistry had led to the design of new drugs, and how those drugs had contributed to advances in chemotherapy, and helped in the treatment of malaria, leukaemia, gout and so on, as well as facilitating organ transplants.

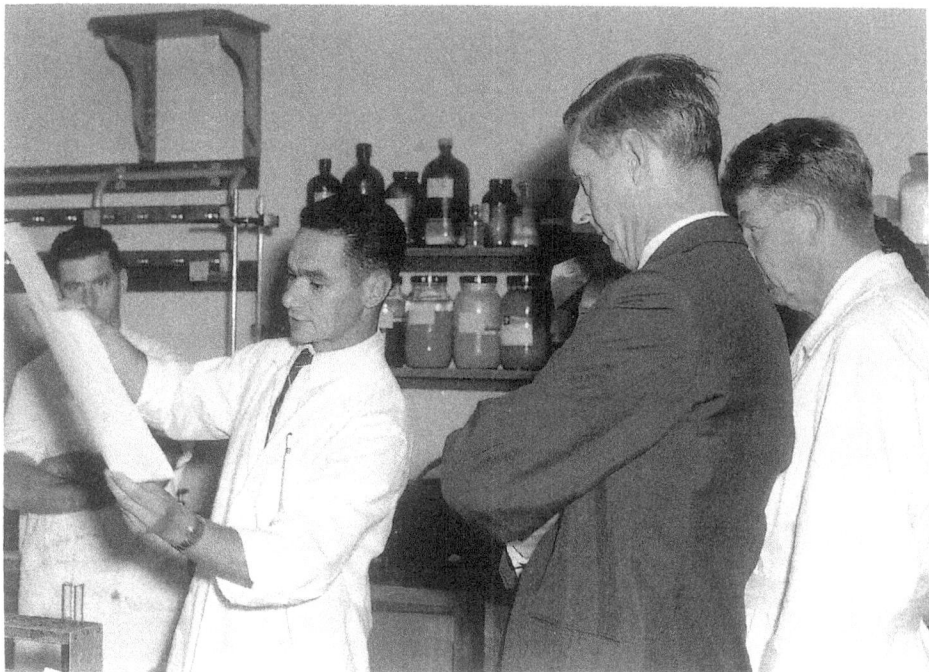

Harry Rosenberg explains work in the Biochemistry Department to Lord de L'Isle during a vice-regal visit in 1962. Ennor, partly hidden, escorts the Governor-General.

George Mackaness, who in Florey's absence ran the Department of Experimental Pathology, acknowledged that science had to appeal to the wider community. Experimental pathology, he told Florey, was better able than other departments to show visitors to the school what a quarter of a million pounds of their money was doing for them. He therefore urged that the person appointed to the chair should be engaged on work with human interest which could easily be interpreted to politicians and the press. This was 'a loathsome desideratum': but Mackaness contended that Australians were quick to judge, if often lacking in their judgement; and while teaching was recognised as a legitimate occupation, research was not. Research therefore had to be justified in terms that ordinary Australians could understand.

Mackaness went further than most of his colleagues in suggesting, in effect, that public appeal should influence research directions. But many people in different parts of the University well knew that the University had to communicate with the person in the street. After Copland, the consummate publicist, had left the University, Coombs thought more effort was needed in public relations, and suggested that the University approach members of parliament, leaders in commerce and industry, the press and trade unions. When the biochemists began to extract substances from crocodiles and, with the help of Trans-Australia Airlines, arranged a crocodile hunt in the Northern Territory, he saw the opportunity to draw a link between research and an adventure, which was much easier to communicate than what the biochemists were actually trying to do.

Frank Fenner's work in the Department of Microbiology showed how fundamental and applied research merged. After taking up duty with the University in 1949, he initially continued the bacteriological work he had been pursuing at the Rockefeller Institute; but he was keen to return to virology and was, as he put it, looking for a virus to work on. He found one early in 1951. During a stopover on a flight from his laboratory in Melbourne to a meeting in Canberra, he and Hugh Ward, Professor of Bacteriology at the University of Sydney and a member of the ANU Council, were shading themselves under the wing of a DC3 at Albury Airport. Not far away, along the Murray valley, an outbreak of myxomatosis was decimating the rabbit population. 'You ought to get into that', said Ward. Fenner took the hint, wondering why he had not seen the opportunity for himself, and immediately threw himself into studying the myxoma virus. A 'fortunate change has come over my circumstances', he told Florey. Myxomatosis was to occupy much of his time over the next fifteen years.

Rabbits had provided the stimulus for the beginnings of microbiology in Australia in the 1880s, when the New South Wales government offered, unsuccessfully, a large prize for the discovery of a biological means of controlling the rabbit plague. Prompted by the Melbourne paediatrician Jean MacNamara, the CSIR initiated experiments with myxomatosis in the 1930s, and again between May and December 1950. CSIRO scientists were about to give up when the infection took hold with astonishing effect in the warmth of the summer, especially along the waterways in Victoria and New South Wales. The obvious conclusion was that the virus was carried by mosquitoes.

What intrigued Fenner most of all were the theoretical aspects of the disease. This was an extraordinary natural experiment: a highly virulent parasite among a completely susceptible host. How, he asked himself, would the virus evolve? What would happen to the host animal, given that the virus was killing nearly all of the rabbits it infected? As he later recalled, 'it was a marvellous opportunity for somebody interested in the evolution of infectious diseases'. Paradoxically, perhaps, Fenner and his small team viewed the relevance of their research to the rabbit problem as a side benefit. They were well aware of the potential economic significance of their work and its value to the nation, not least because it ensured that they would always be well funded. And they were certainly keen to bring the rabbit problem under control. As the virulence of myxomatosis decreased, they were out in the field with CSIRO scientists, investigating ways of maintaining its strength. But from the virologist's perspective, the nature of the virus, and its implications for research into other viruses in animals and humans, were more deeply interesting.

In the event, science played little part in enhancing the success of the natural virus. As rabbits developed resistance, its influence steadily declined: though in the 1990s it still helped control the rabbit population. But the study of myxomatosis yielded rich results. As well as identifying the distinctive properties of the virus and its relationship to other viruses, Fenner and his colleagues were able to explain why the virulence of the disease declined rather than increased, as it usually did in laboratory experiments. And by monitoring the resistance of rabbits over several generations, they were able to show that this resistance had a genetic basis. This was a major discovery in virology, and it led Fenner to further explorations of animal virus genetics.

Frank Fenner, about 1958, titrates myxoma virus by inoculating developing eggs with tenfold dilutions of fluid containing the virus.

Experimental science rarely proceeds in a straight line, from one significant discovery to the next. Fenner, along with almost every other researcher in the John Curtin School, sometimes followed leads which turned out to be false, having then to abandon them and set out in other directions. Mackaness, after eighteen months in Canberra, told Florey that his research was progressing as it had done in Oxford: 'Many failures and partial success, followed by an era of productivity'. One of the tasks of the researcher, he wrote, was to distinguish between perseverance and stubbornness, 'for one grades imperceptibly into the other'. As his own research became ever more frustrating, Mackaness joined his colleague Leigh Dodson, whose research on the effects of pregnancy on hypertension (abnormally high blood pressure) was showing great promise. Through experiments on a large colony of hypertensive rats, Dodson showed that during the latter half of pregnancy their blood pressure returned to normal levels, sometimes quite abruptly. Then, within two hours of parturition, the blood pressure returned to its previous hypertensive levels. Dodson looked for an explanation: did foetal kidneys produce an anti-hypertensive agent? Or did it have something to do with hormonal balance during pregnancy?

After laborious research, Dodson and Mackaness stumbled unhappily on a more prosaic explanation: a laboratory technician, presumably inadequately supervised and quite unaware of the implications of what he was doing, had been adjusting the anaesthetic administered to produce normal blood pressure levels while the rat was under examination. Many months of work had been wasted; and the result was acutely embarrassing, especially since Ennor had brought the Vice-Chancellor to view this exciting research, just as the truth was revealed. The outcome was an example of the sheer bad luck that sometimes attends scientific research; but it also suggested that research could be skewed by the eagerness for results, especially when expectations were high. For Mackaness and Dodson, the incident was a major setback, although both went on, in different spheres, to pursue distinguished scientific careers.

Research in the Department of Physiology built on the neurophysiological work that J.C. Eccles had been pursuing at the University of Otago. Neurophysiology was one of the newer medical sciences, having taken shape as a discipline during the previous few decades under the guidance of Eccles' mentor at Oxford, the Nobel Prize winner Sir Charles Sherrington. The war gave it a hefty boost through the development of radar and other techniques which could be adapted to biological purposes. Now it was possible to use oscilloscopes (a rarity before the war) to provide visual images of electrical impulses from the brain, and cameras to record the images, frame by frame. In New Zealand Eccles had worked closely with a physicist and instrument designer, Jack Coombs, who transferred to the ANU in 1952, bringing with him across the Tasman the highly specialised equipment that he had designed and built in Dunedin. This included four electrical stimulating and recording units which were critical to Eccles' research during his fourteen years in Canberra and which continued to be used until the mid-1980s.

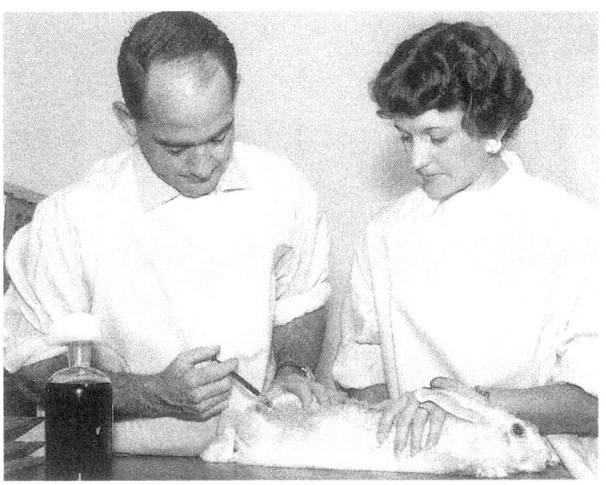

Ian Marshall, Research Fellow in Microbiology, assisted by Beverley Renfree, inoculates a rabbit with myxoma virus, 1958.

Eccles and his colleagues set out to explore the nature of the nervous system, and specifically how electrical messages or nerve impulses act across zones of close contact (synapses) between nerve cells. Previously, the nervous system had been analysed purely in terms of its output, by measuring reflexes. With the aid of Coombs's recording equipment, and by inserting into nerve cells extraordinarily fine glass tubes containing conducting solutions, Eccles was able to show how the cells related to one another. The breakthrough, achieved before the move to Canberra, was to distinguish the processes of excitation and inhibition of cells, and to demonstrate that inhibition was itself an active process in the function of the brain. That discovery meant investigation of the brain could be conducted on new levels.

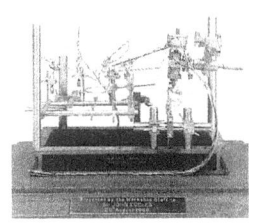

This model of the device used to conduct experiments on cats was constructed by workshop staff in the John Curtin School and presented to Eccles on his retirement in 1966.

Research on the nervous system demanded wide-ranging skills in physiology, pharmacology and electronics. Eccles sought the best people wherever he could find them, so that Physiology quickly became the most 'international' department in the University. In the first five years the team comprised, besides Eccles, three Americans, two Australians, two New Zealanders, two Swedes, and one each from Mexico, Canada and England. They worked in groups of three or four, a number dictated by the size of the laboratories.

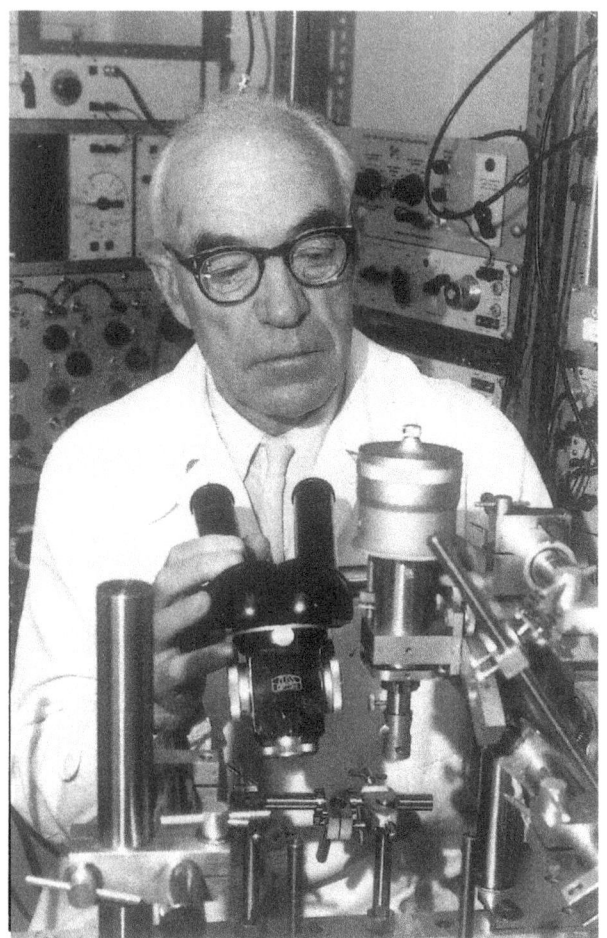

Sir John Eccles in the neurophysiology laboratory, 1963. This part of the laboratory bore some resemblance to the cockpit of an aeroplane.

Eccles was an inspiring and profoundly knowledgeable leader, who knew the literature of neurophysiology so well that he could quote relevant material by volume and page number. In his approach to experimental research, he had been influenced by the British philosopher, Karl Popper, whom he had come to know when Popper was in Christchurch. Popper advocated scientific enquiry through two stages of investigation: the development of a hypothesis using the creative imagination; and the attempt to falsify this hypothesis by challenging its most vulnerable aspects. Eccles subjected his own theories to this process of challenge, and urged his junior colleagues, if not to follow Popper to the letter, at least to pursue the most rigorous methods during experimental research.

The neurophysiologists did all their experiments on cats, which were convenient to work on, easy to obtain, and cheap, their only drawback being occasional protests from animal welfare groups or furious cat owners who charged that their pets had been stolen by the University. When an experiment was arranged to take place, a group would start work at 7.00 or 7.30 a.m. to prepare and anaesthetise the animal and prepare the equipment. By 5.00 or 6.00 p.m. everything was ready for the cat to be moved into one of the laboratories which were shielded against electrical interference. They would then work all night, going home briefly for a shower and breakfast, and returning to work on the cat throughout the next day and perhaps the day after that. Many hours were spent waiting for things to happen, thus allowing time for a nap or for keeping up with the literature in the nearby medical library.

'It was a time of intense discussion and a great interaction between people', David Curtis remembered in the 1990s. 'We used to work all the week. We were usually in Saturday morning till mid Saturday afternoon getting ready for experiments the following week. Sometimes you'd go in on Sunday nights to do things.' When a series of experiments was over, Eccles (if he had been involved in the project) usually wrote the first draft of a paper; then there was a seminar or two, often lively discussion, and preparation of a final draft which represented as close to agreement as the group was likely to come. This process led to a string of publications through the 1950s, some of which were of seminal significance. 'As I look back on those years', wrote Eccles in 1977, 'I can hardly imagine how we dared to attempt so much!'.

The Research School of Physical Sciences

Oliphant's overwhelming ambition when he arrived in Canberra in August 1950 was to build a machine to split the atom, a machine which was more powerful, yet cheaper, than anything comparable anywhere else in the world, and which would thrust Australia unequivocally into the nuclear age. Having played a part in creating the atomic bomb, and having seen its horrifying effects, he had determined to have nothing more to do with the development of nuclear power for military purposes; but he was convinced that the peaceful uses of atomic energy offered new hope to humanity. Once the energy was harnessed, he declared, the world would enjoy 'a period of unparalleled prosperity', with man's work 'reduced to a vanishing point'. As yet, little was known about the laws which governed nuclear energy: but 'We are passing through a similar period to that which preceded Sir Isaac Newton's formulation of the laws of gravity'. The sort of science he wanted to do, he once told Wright, was 'where we let our imaginations go and leave it to our wits to devise the experimental procedures'.

Oliphant's mentor, Lord Rutherford, had been first to split an atom in 1919; and in 1932 two of Oliphant's colleagues in the Cavendish Laboratory, John Cockcroft and Ernest Walton, built a particle accelerator which fired protons towards atoms at such high energies that the atoms disintegrated. Soon afterwards Oliphant himself had designed and built an accelerator which, though less powerful than the Cockcroft–Walton apparatus, produced many more particles and directed them in a fine beam towards their target, increasing the likelihood of the atoms being broken apart. The machine yielded a wealth of discoveries, including two new isotopes, and won Oliphant his Fellowship of the Royal Society. It also left him with a compelling question: what would happen if atoms were bombarded by particles from more powerful accelerators?

The move to Birmingham in 1937 gave him a chance to find out. Soon he was building a new type of accelerator called the cyclotron, modelled on one then nearing completion in the United States, and vastly more powerful than his machine at the Cavendish. It was to be the largest accelerator in Europe. But war intervened, Oliphant was diverted into other tasks, and not until 1950 did the cyclotron produce a beam of particles. In the meantime, Oliphant had started work at Birmingham on another new type of accelerator, the proton synchrotron. He had also accepted the job in Canberra, with the promise it held of building a still bigger and better machine in his own country.

Oliphant announced his plans for this new accelerator in *Nature* early in 1950, before he set out for Canberra. He called it the cyclo-synchrotron, as it combined elements of both the proton synchrotron and the cyclotron, and it was to produce a particle beam of one thousand million electron-volts (MeVs). The first version was a synchro-cyclotron producing 200 MeV protons, which were then to be injected into an air-cored magnet at the periphery of the synchro-cyclotron magnet to increase their energy fivefold. The source of power for the air-cored magnet was to be a homopolar generator, comprising a heavy metal disc spinning rapidly in the strong magnetic field of the synchro-cyclotron

The Research School of Physical Sciences about the time Oliphant arrived to take up duty in 1950. Florey had warned him to expect 'a hole in the ground and a lot of promises'.

magnet, and capable of delivering very large current pulses when stopped suddenly. He noted that the homopolar generator might also be useful for other applications.

Oliphant predicted that the cyclo-synchrotron would be working in two to three years. But by 1953 he and his team had come to realise that their design, as well as being exceedingly complex, would not represent the great advance they had hoped for on the Birmingham synchrotron and would not equal the output of accelerators now under construction in the United States. This was a major setback: Oliphant, however, turned it to advantage and decided to convert the magnet of the existing half-built accelerator into a larger homopolar generator as the power source for a new air-cored magnet of a proton synchrotron providing particle energy ten times greater than they had originally aimed for. With this enormous energy it would be possible (so theory suggested) to produce the anti-proton, the negative particle whose existence had been predicted in 1930.

There was a problem: for reasons of economy of design, Oliphant's new accelerator would produce a particle beam only once every ten minutes, which was slow by current standards and much slower than the rate of other machines then being built. That was the price Australia had to pay if it was to have its own accelerator. And the prospect of building a successful accelerator for a fraction of the cost of its rivals became part of the challenge. The team pressed on, borne along to a large extent by Oliphant's drive and enthusiasm. In his Bakerian Lecture, delivered to the Royal Society in 1955, he announced that the Canberra accelerator would probably be completed in 'about three years'.

Oliphant, Hancock told Florey, was the most optimistic man he had ever met. There were, of course, doubters, those who said an Australian accelerator would never be built, or that if it was it would never achieve the predicted results. Equally, there

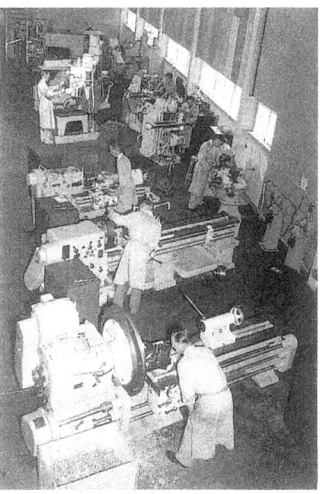

Left: At work on the homopolar generator, 1954.

Right: A by-product of the construction of Oliphant's 'big machine' was the creation of an outstanding workshop for the physical sciences. This photograph was taken in 1953.

were many who were convinced that the development of nuclear energy for peaceful purposes represented the way ahead. 'No one knows where this may lead', wrote one journalist: 'Possibly in 10 years' time scientists may look back on our present atom theories, atom bombs, and atomic energy machines as we look back on the first crude radio sets and theories of wireless waves.' In parliament there was bipartisan support. W.C. Wentworth, Liberal backbencher, predicted that the accelerator would enable man to create matter out of energy. Labor leader H.V. Evatt spoke of Oliphant as one of the two foremost scientists in the world: 'and in Oliphant, we have an Australian'.

Oliphant's optimism was the optimism of the times. Wentworth, one of the best informed of his supporters in the non-scientific community, recognised there was a chance that the machine might not work. But the prospect of a world with nuclear energy in the service of humankind and Australia at the forefront of nuclear technology was so enticing that he and others were prepared, like Oliphant himself, to set the risks aside. When Oliphant's spirits flagged, as they did from time to time, they were uplifted by the knowledge that so many Australians had confidence in him and keenly wanted him to succeed.

Was that confidence well placed? Apart from his colleagues in the world of nuclear physics, who was to say? Yet so much of the University's allocation of funds, and so much of its reputation, were invested in this one project that people associated with its administration could hardly fail to be anxious, especially after the school abandoned the cyclo-synchrotron. Copland, some months after leaving Canberra, sounded out the Nobel Prize winning physicist Patrick Blackett, who commended Oliphant's courage and said he was keeping his fingers crossed about whether his machine would work. 'I didn't ask him whether the Birmingham thing had worked', Copland told Hohnen. 'It was a bit stupid of me not to have found out.'

In the meantime, other sections of the school were forging ahead. After remaining at Harwell for the first eight months of his appointment, Titterton arrived in Canberra in May 1951, and immediately started building his department of Nuclear Physics. It was assumed that the department would make use of the cyclo-synchrotron, once it was completed. As an interim measure, the University imported a smaller accelerator of the Cockcroft – Walton type, allowing Titterton and his colleagues to get on with their research, which included photodisintegration studies, fast neutron experiments, and an intensive study of the energy level structure of an isotope of Beryllium. Early in 1952, the accelerator produced a nuclear reaction, stimulating great excitement within the University and among the press. The machine was in heavy demand, especially after the arrival of four PhD students in 1953, so the school decided to purchase another small accelerator, both as a source of spares for the larger machine and as a research tool in its own right. Titterton then acquired a third machine, an electron synchrotron which had been used at Harwell but was now surplus, as a gift from the British government to Australia. This supplied much more energy than the two existing machines, and gave the work of the department a powerful boost. Driven by Titterton's forceful (some said overbearing) personality, the department won acclaim for high productivity and turned out some outstanding students. Yet Titterton's reputation came in later years to rest more on his work outside the University, as an adviser to the British and Australian governments on atomic weapons testing.

Ernest Titterton, 1951.
Australian News and Information Bureau, ANU Collection.

Oliphant's third professorial appointment in the school was another former Cambridge man, John Conrad Jaeger, who came to the chair of Geophysics early in 1952. Geophysics was not on Oliphant's early list of priorities. A visit by the Canadian geophysicist J.T. Wilson excited his imagination as to what the area had to offer, and he determined to find someone to fill the chair, thus reversing the expectation often expressed by the Advisers that new fields should be opened up as men became available.

Geophysicists were in short supply, and Oliphant had two rejections before he approached Jaeger, who was not in fact a geophysicist at all. Rather he was, according to Oliphant, probably the finest applied mathematician in Australia. Born in Sydney in 1907, he had studied at the universities of Sydney and Cambridge before moving to the relative isolation of the University of Tasmania in 1936. His interests, spanning mathematics, theoretical physics and engineering, were unusually broad. While in Hobart he developed a highly productive collaboration with his former teacher Horatio Scot Carslaw, Professor of Pure and Applied Mathematics at Sydney for over thirty years, relating chiefly to operational methods in applied mathematics and the conduction of heat in solids. During the war he worked with CSIR scientists on aspects of radiophysics with direct implications for the war effort. At the time of his appointment to the ANU he was a hefty, bear-like man, with a large, round head and a genial but sometimes gruff manner. Although usually shy and retiring, he was a vigorous teacher and a forthright advocate of any cause he determined to pursue.

As this was the first chair of geophysics in an Australian university, Jaeger recognised a particular responsibility to develop the field. He saw geophysics as an extraordinarily wide subject, embracing the physics of the earth's atmosphere and its crust. In line with J.T. Wilson's recommendation, he decided to restrict work at the ANU to the crust and interior, leaving atmospheric research to the CSIRO and other institutions; but within that restriction he argued that, as the department was unique in the country, it should offer postgraduate training in all aspects of geophysics. Research should therefore embrace the core subjects relating to the behaviour of the earth and its materials, namely mathematics, physics, petrology and crystal physics. He also insisted, contrary to Wilson's advice, that research should extend outside the laboratory into the field, as there was no point in making physical measurements on rocks whose petrology and geological history were unknown.

The first research in the department grew out of Jaeger's interest in heat flow in the earth and related chiefly to the cooling of mines and bore-holes. His earliest appointments, Germaine Joplin and Mervyn Paterson, opened up the study of petrology and crystal physics, and within a few years he had moved the department into rock magnetism, seismology and geochemistry. By 1960 he could claim, with reasonable accuracy, that the department was the most productive, not merely in the school, but in the whole University. As well as a steady stream of significant papers, there were several major achievements: the first determination of the thickness of the crust in Australia, making use of the atomic tests at Maralinga in South Australia in 1956; the first conclusive demonstration of continental drift, using palaeomagnetic observations on Australian rocks; the organisation (in association with the Sydney Metropolitan Water Board and the Snowy Mountains Hydro-Electric Authority) of a network of seismological observatories, which promised important engineering and geological results; the construction of very high pressure apparatus for deforming rocks, which opened the way to research of international quality in this area.

John Conrad Jaeger, about 1970.
By courtesy of Ross Hohnen.

Most of these discoveries had prospects for practical applications. Jaeger was unashamedly an applied scientist, who turned the usual motivation for fundamental science on its head. He wanted to engage in 'pure' research in mathematics, physics and chemistry, in response to problems that arose in practice. He wanted to train geophysicists in fundamental science, but in areas directed towards later work in organisations such as the Bureau of Mineral Resources. He talked about 'exploration geophysics', meaning the study of the physical principles behind prospecting in the field. From the outset, he had his eye on 'a very large audience out there'—politicians, mining companies, prospectors—who were aware of the potential value of geophysical research for exploiting Australia's mineral resources. He also recognised that the department had the potential to attract external support, long before the quest for outside funding became part of the scientist's job.

Some members of the University winced at Jaeger's enthusiastic pursuit of practical applications. Oliphant, who held a purist's view of fundamental research, expressed discomfort about where the department was headed; and Jaeger complained that he stood in the way of any incursion into the exploration side, 'which in my view is the core of the subject and is the region where the money and the interest lie'. But he received plenty of encouragement from outside the University. H.G. Raggatt, Secretary of the Commonwealth Department of National Development, reassured him that research on the basic physics of the earth was essential if Australia was to discover new mineral reserves. What was wanted, he wrote, was fundamental knowledge about rocks and geological processes; there was no need to pursue economic objectives when conducting research, as economic results would certainly follow.

Academics often turn out to surprise those who appointed them. Oliphant had expected Jaeger to work on one or two fields of geophysics, and could scarcely have imagined his determination to develop geophysics as he did. Jaeger had the foresight to recognise the potential role of geophysical research in Australia and the determination to carry it forward. He also saw that geophysics, if it was to advance as he believed it should, had to eschew narrow specialism and bring together a range of disciplines. As early as 1955 he suggested that the department be regarded as 'an embryo School of Earth Sciences', and in so doing signalled the beginnings of a long and sometimes stormy campaign.

If Geophysics was an outstanding success, the Department of Radiochemistry was, in Oliphant's terms, a disaster. Frank Scarf, whom Oliphant imported from England to head the department at the level of Reader, found that his wife could not adjust to Canberra and was soon weighed down with health problems of his own. He produced nothing and gave no leadership; and although two or three of those nominally under him did good work, Radiochemistry as a department became an embarrassment. On Oliphant's initiative, Scarf was encouraged to retire and the department was closed down, its other members divided between Geophysics and Particle Physics. If nothing else, Radiochemistry showed that departments were not immortal.

With the creation of the Department of Astronomy in 1950, the University gained an association with Mount Stromlo's experienced and committed staff. Established in 1924, the Commonwealth Observatory antedated the University by many years, a point which later professors of astronomy were happy to make if ever the status of their department seemed under threat. Initially concerned with solar and geophysical work, Mount Stromlo had languished during the Depression. Woolley, who was appointed Commonwealth Astronomer and Director of the Observatory in 1939, promised to revive it and set it on a new course. Recognising the preponderance of observatories in the northern hemisphere and their scarcity in the south, he proposed to abandon the interests of the past and introduce stellar and galactic astrophysics. But war intervened, deflecting the astronomers towards designing and manufacturing precision optical instruments for the armed forces (which had the side benefits of increasing their number to about thirty and providing them with a well equipped workshop). The war over, Woolley turned Mount Stromlo towards the stars.

Woolley, who came from the classical British school of Cambridge and the Royal Observatory at Greenwich, was the first in a line of exceptional heads of the department. There was some dispute as to whether he was a great astronomer; but he was certainly a formidable presence, tall and imposing, with a sharp wit, plenty of style, and an extraordinary range of proficiencies, from folk-dancing to polo. He knew how to get things done, including extracting money and equipment from government and other sources. In 1948 he persuaded Chifley to part with £100 000 for the purchase of a 78-inch telescope. This was commissioned in 1955, and was at the time, along with a similar instrument in Pretoria, the largest telescope south of the equator.

Under Woolley's direction, the Observatory focused on the galaxies known as the

Magellanic Clouds and the southern portion of the Milky Way. S.C.B. (Ben) Gascoigne and Gerald Kron, joined later by a visitor to the Observatory, Olin Eggen, discovered that some of the star clusters in the Magellanic Clouds were much bluer, and therefore much younger, than stars in our own galaxy. This provided the first clue that the Clouds had evolved differently from the galaxy, and helped explain galactic evolution. A Research Fellow, Gerard De Vaucouleurs, was able to show through

Above: Richard van der Reit Woolley at the eyepiece of the transit telescope at Mount Stromlo, 1947.

Left: The administration building at Mount Stromlo in 1951, with the Farnham Telescope at the left and the Solar Telescope at the right.

small-scale photography that the Large Magellanic Cloud was a flat rotating system similar to the Milky Way. Most spectacular of all, a graduate student, Colin Gum, identified the remnant of the Vela supernova, which was named the Gum Nebula after its discoverer, who died too young to enjoy the fame due to his achievement.

Although the University's annual reports claimed Astronomy as a department, and although the department produced the University's first PhD graduate (Antoni Przybylski in 1954), the link was tenuous and dependent largely on Woolley's status as honorary professor. Woolley wanted integration: he thought that the University would be a more congenial home for a research organisation than the Commonwealth Department of the Interior; he also held strongly that research should go arm in arm with teaching. There was some resistance inside and outside the Observatory, but Woolley, making use of his cordial relations with the Prime Minister, managed to get his way. Menzies told the University to proceed with the appointment of a full professor of astronomy, and in 1957 Mount Stromlo formally became part of the ANU.

By this time Woolley had returned to England to take up the position of Astronomer Royal and in due course receive a knighthood. His successor, Bart J. Bok, inherited a department and observatory ready to capitalise on the coming boom in astrophysics.

The Research School of Social Sciences

Geoffrey Sawer, the newly appointed Professor of Law, hitched the caravan to the Vauxhall and the trailer to the Morris, and with his wife and two children set out in convoy on the two-day journey from Melbourne to Canberra. A lawyer needed no equipment, except books; and in Canberra he would be able to supplement his own library with the collections of the University Library, the National Library and the library in the Attorney-General's Department. Shortly after arrival he was able to resume where he had left off, in the study of Australian constitutional and administrative law.

Sawer's intellectual baggage contained the elements of both a practising and an academic lawyer. While a barrister he had tutored part time at Ormond College in the University of Melbourne; and in 1939 he joined the University as a Senior Lecturer, where he taught courses in legal theory which drew on American as well as British texts. During the 1930s he took a close interest in the process of constitutional change which was shifting power from the states to the Commonwealth, and the evolution of administrative law to protect the individual against the actions of government. Although he immersed himself in technical aspects of the law, he also took a broad view of political and constitutional issues. As a divergent member of the Round Table movement, which sought to maintain links within the British Commonwealth, he spoke as an Australian nationalist and argued for greater Australian autonomy. As a friend and confidant of H.V. Evatt, he moved towards a political stance which was radical yet moderate.

His interest in legal theory was never far removed from what was happening in the parliaments and courts of Australia: for example, the application of the Westminster system in Australian parliaments; the composition of the High Court and the influence of different sorts of judges; the balance of authority between the Commonwealth and the states. Arriving in Canberra, he set to work on a mammoth project to record and analyse the relationship between federal politics and the law during the first half century of the Australian Commonwealth. The results were published in two volumes, the first in 1956 and the second in 1963. At the same time, he revised extensively his book on *Australian Constitutional Cases*, and researched and wrote on legal and political issues, ranging from hire purchase agreements and penalties to Australia's role in the United Nations.

Like Sawer, Noel Butlin knew exactly what he wanted to do. Back in Canberra in 1951 after his term as an Overseas Scholar, he was appointed Senior Research Fellow in the Department of Economics, and immediately threw himself into studying the structure of the Australian economy from 1860 onwards. Using the analytical techniques and informed by theories he had learnt at Harvard, he started gathering statistical data which showed the relationship between public and private capital formation and economic change. Soon the floor of his room was covered with mountains of statistical registers, yearbooks and every source of economic statistics he could lay his hands on for all the colonies and the first few decades of the Commonwealth. Nothing like this, even on a small scale, had ever been attempted in

Australia. The result was a completely new interpretation of the structure of Australian economic history. After hearing Butlin outline his central thesis at a conference in 1957, Brian Fitzpatrick, one of an earlier generation of economic historians, commented that it was masterful and fascinating, though it made him feel like 'a pioneer who had survived to hear his own obituary'. After the publication of Butlin's two books on investment and national income in 1962 and 1964, Australian economic history would never again be the same.

Geoffrey Sawer, 1953.

In contrast to Sawer and Butlin, Laurie Fitzhardinge was unsure of what he ought to be doing. He had been appointed Reader in the Sources of Australian History, a position suggested by Hancock. But Hancock was not around to spell out what the position ought to entail, and nobody else—least of all Copland—was prepared to guide him. Left to his own devices, he planned a survey of Australian manuscript sources, organised a seminar program on methodology in Australian history, edited one of the 'First Fleet' diaries, and delivered a paper to the Royal Australian Historical Society on the early political career of William Morris Hughes. The Hughes paper set the course for his main work over the next two decades. Hughes, then approaching the age of 90, attended the lecture and liked what he heard; and when in due course he saw the paper in published form, he immediately telephoned Fitzhardinge to say 'You must drop everything you're doing ... and get on to my life'. The next thing Fitzhardinge knew was that Hughes had arranged with Copland for a contract to be signed by which Hughes provided the University with modest support for research assistance and the University agreed that Fitzhardinge should write his life. 'So that', Fitzhardinge recalled 40 years later, 'is how I got lumbered with Billy'.

Trained as a classicist and brought up in the tradition that history was one of the humanities, Fitzhardinge was never entirely comfortable in a school with the title 'Social Sciences'. Mick Borrie, on the other hand, found that the garments of the social scientist fitted well. Before joining the University, he had taught social history to social workers in the University of Sydney. Early in his career, he had developed an interest in population studies, which he pursued as a Social Science Research Fellow. When he became Research Fellow in Demography, he went straight on with work already well under way.

Demography was a relatively new discipline. While courses in the subject had been introduced in some British and American institutions in the 1930s, chiefly in response to declining fertility rates in the west, Hancock was thinking ahead when he suggested it as one of his half-dozen growing points. As an area of research, it could be approached from various directions: history, biology, genetics, mathematics, statistics, human geography. Borrie came to it as a social historian, without a clear conception of the nature of demography as a separate discipline, but with an understanding that he should be concerned with qualitative research rather than the

Noel Butlin in the 1950s.
By courtesy of Joan Butlin.

quantitative analysis of statistics, which would best be left to official statistical agencies. Soon he was joined by Charles Price, whose background in history was similar to his own, and Norma McArthur, whose training in mathematics and genetics provided the formal statistical capacity the department needed, though it remained essentially a department of social demography.

In view of the post-war boom in immigration, Australia was a likely place for demography to flourish as a discipline. But its success at the ANU also owed much to Borrie's ambition and achievement, and to the people he gathered around him. Demography proved to be a fine example of Hancock's concept of intellectual development through growing points. In 1952 it was formally designated a department (though it had been one, in all but name, from the outset), and Borrie was appointed Reader and head. This made it the first Department of Demography in the world; and when Borrie was elevated to a chair in 1957, he became the world's first Professor of Demography.

During its first decade, the department's work ranged widely to embrace the structure of the Australian family, ethnic minorities in the nineteenth century, and the effects of post-war immigration on Australian society and culture. McArthur completed pathbreaking surveys of the growth and structure of the populations of the Pacific islands, before leaving in 1956 to direct the first thorough census in Fiji. Borrie set himself the ambitious task of researching and writing a demographic history of Australia. *The European Peopling of Australasia* eventually appeared in 1994; in the meantime he and his colleagues created the discipline of demography in Australia.

The Department of Demography, about 1955. Left to right, front: Isabel Gooden (Secretary), Charles Price, W.D. (Mick) Borrie, Lillian Wilson; rear: David Packer, Kathleen Jupp, Norma McArthur, John McDonald.
By courtesy of W.D. Borrie.

Statistics, like demography, was a relatively new academic discipline, having been established first at University College, London, in the 1930s, and introduced as a separate department at several other universities, including some in Australia, after the war. When Hancock initially suggested that the school should include a statistician, he had in mind someone who would fulfil a service function for his colleagues, though he might also have a large research project of his own. Eggleston went further, suggesting that the discipline might become a separate department if someone with appropriate interests in social statistics were available to head it.

K.C. Wheare located such a person in Patrick Moran, a young Australian who had trained at Sydney, Cambridge and Oxford, and who was now a lecturer in mathematics at Oxford. Moran had begun his career as a pure mathematician and had turned to statistics during the war. Rather than devoting himself to a single highly specialised line of research, as many statisticians tended to do, he had ranged widely across the field, developing the work of others and working closely with researchers in other disciplines. Copland, after meeting him in Oxford, doubted that he would

Staff and scholars in the Research School of Social Sciences have a beer outside the tea room, about 1957. Left to right: Noel Butlin (supporting the verandah), Ross Martin (Political Science), Don Rawson (Political Science), David Packer (Demography), Warren Hogan (Economics), A.J. Catt (Economics) and Ted Hannan (Statistics). *By courtesy of Joan Butlin.*

simply provide a service function to other departments, but thought he would prove a stimulating and helpful colleague to anyone seeking statistical advice. According to the Vice-Chancellor, he was also 'highly suitable' on other grounds: he had taken a firm line on the debate about the Soviet scientist Trofim Lysenko (who advocated an extreme version of Lamarckian evolutionary theory), and 'seems to have got some pleasure in job[b]ing the left wing scientists about their devotion to a group or party that could perpetrate such intellectual rubbish'. Moran was duly appointed to a chair (statisticians being in a seller's market) and took up duty in Canberra in 1952.

Moran arrived with clear ideas about what he wanted to do. On the teaching side, he expected to give lectures to economists and other social scientists about statistical methods, such as the theory of sampling and sampling surveys. There should also be courses with a different emphasis for biologists and medical scientists. On the research side, he hoped to stimulate fundamental work in the theory of statistics. Within a short time, he and his colleague E.J. Hannan, appointed as a Research Fellow in 1953, were working on the prediction of sunspots, a general probability theory of dams and storage systems, trend and seasonal variations in the value of sales in Sydney clothing and drapery stores, and a remarkable range of other problems to which statistical methods might be applied.

Eggleston's plans for the school were taking shape. By early 1952 there were (if we include Demography) six departments, three of them (Economics, Law and Statistics) with chairs, and three (Demography, History and Political Science) headed by Readers. Council had also reached a decision about the keystone of Eggleston's edifice, the chair of Social Philosophy. The occupant of this position, as Copland explained it, was to explore the deeper problems of social structure, and to stimulate and guide his colleagues in the school, acting as 'a sort of elder statesman'.

Partly because of the significance attached to it, this chair proved to be exceedingly difficult to fill. Eccles caused no end of trouble by proposing his friend Karl Popper, who was now Professor of Logic and Scientific Method at the London School of Economics. Although Popper had declined offers of several chairs in Britain, the Continent and New Zealand, and had refused to allow his name to be put forward for Cambridge, Eccles persuaded him that the ANU would offer him the opportunity to write the books that were in his mind, without losing his contacts throughout the world. Eccles was a powerful advocate, pressing Popper's value as an integrating influence for the University as a whole. 'With Popper on the campus', he told Copland, 'there would be little danger of our university becoming an assemblage of isolated departments. We would realise how much we held in common in our quest into the unknown.'

Coombs, Sawer and Swan favoured the appointment, but others, including Wheare and Copland, were not so sure. Copland sought advice from all quarters, including some who knew Popper and his work and some who did not, and the more he heard, the more uncertain he became. The problem was that Popper was a controversialist, who attracted disciples and violent detractors wherever he went. Bertrand Russell, during a brief visit to Canberra, spoke highly of him, while some of Oxford's younger philosophers said that his appointment would put the ANU on the philosophical map. Eggleston, after initial concerns that he might be one of those philosophers who evaded the great issues confronting mankind and took refuge in techniques which debunked reason and meaning, read *The Open Society and its Enemies* and came out in his favour. Others condemned his work as unscholarly and hinted that he was a charlatan, or suggested that he was really a logician and therefore unsuited to a position in Social Philosophy. Florey, who tended not to like Jews unless he happened to know them, warned Wheare that such types should be avoided:

> ... I know absolutely nothing about him, though I have views about this sort of thing on general grounds. I have no doubt that he is of Central European origin, and I feel very strongly that it would be a thousand pities if the University is loaded up with these people, who tend to throw their weight about quite unnecessarily and, in a place that is growing and will undoubtedly have troubles, are likely to be intolerable nuisances.

This said much about Florey and nothing about Popper, and would be irrelevant except that Florey's prestige made his views, mediated through Wheare, inevitably influence the outcome. After six months' agonising, Council reached a compromise decision by which Popper would be invited to visit Canberra for six months, sufficient time to assess his suitability for a permanent appointment. In the event, Popper could not come for longer than three months, and Council seized the opportunity to let the offer lapse.

Copland was evidently relieved. It was all very well to be adventurous in making appointments, but Popper threatened more adventure than the University was ready for. First, there was a question mark hanging over his scholarship: if, as time passed, the most commonly heard answer to the question turned out to be 'no', the University's academic prestige would be compromised. Equally dangerous was the prospect of his becoming a focus of division. As John Passmore, an Australian who held the chair of Philosophy at Otago, told Hohnen, Popper lacked academic manners: one had to put up with being interrupted, misunderstood, prevented from getting a word in, and so on. Passmore thought this defect was compensated by the quality of what he had to say; but others thought him insufferable.

All in all, as the University was translated from paper to reality, it was not becoming easier to make appointments. There was now an additional criterion of selection: new appointments had to fit in with those who were already there. As Sawer put it, they had to be 'clubbable'. According to Wheare, Popper was a great success in Britain and the United States, where he could bombard people with his ideas. But would Canberra survive the onslaught? Those who were already there determined that, unless they were allowed an obligation-free trial, the risk was too great.

With the Popper diversion out of the way, and after tossing up whether the chair should be renamed simply 'Philosophy' but deciding to stay with Eggleston's title, Council went on to appoint P.H. Partridge. Now in his early forties, Partridge had studied and trained under John Anderson at the University of Sydney, where his chief interest had been in epistemology. From the late 1930s, he moved towards ethics and political theory and he was now Professor of Government and Public Administration at the University of Sydney. The blending of a philosophical background and current interests made him well suited to the role Eggleston had in mind. Another attraction was his reputation as an inspired teacher and outstanding administrator.

Partridge regarded Social Philosophy as akin to Political and Social Theory, as it was taught, for example, at Oxford. He defined the field as 'the examination of the more general and fundamental conceptions, the more general assumptions and principles, which are employed both in the several social sciences and in the thinking of ordinary men about the organization of political and social life'. If this was to be the main work of the department, he thought it needed to be buttressed by at least one philosopher who was thoroughly abreast with developments in the fundamental branches of philosophy, namely logic, epistemology, metaphysics, and the history of philosophy. Such a person was his former colleague and fellow Andersonian, John Passmore, who came across from Otago in 1955 as Reader in Philosophy.

Partridge and Passmore, along with their untenured staff and students, comprised as strong a team as was gathered anywhere in the University. Partridge began work on theories of freedom, with specific reference to recent history, and published 'think pieces' on such subjects as 'The rights of the citizen', 'The Australian universities and governments' and 'Value judgements in the social sciences'. Passmore, after almost a year in Oxford, arrived in Australia to complete what turned out to be a seminal work on *A Hundred Years of Philosophy*, published in 1957. In other papers, he considered historical and methodological themes as well as problems in modern philosophy. Before long the buttress of 'pure philosophy' was as strong as the social philosophy structure it was intended to support.

John Passmore, 1965.
Canberra Times.

The Research School of Pacific Studies

Patrick FitzGerald was preceded to Canberra by several crates of the books he had bought in Hong Kong. His first job was to unpack and arrange them on the shelves of his office in the old hospital building. Then he had to find staff with expertise in Chinese or Japanese history, which proved to be no easy task.

FitzGerald intended to range across nearly three millennia of East Asian history. The Far Eastern historian, he argued, had to be more of an all-round scholar than would be thought necessary in fields where workers were numerous and the sources easy to come by. In his own research, he moved with ease between classical Chinese history and the tumultuous events in the country he had just left. Soon after arriving in Canberra he published *Revolution in China*, which was later published in Penguin Books as *The Birth of Communist China*. Then came a biography of the seventh-century Empress Wu, followed by *Flood Tide in China*, which explored the first few years of the Maoist regime. In the early 1960s he was working on the origins and use of the chair, or 'barbarian bed', in China, as well as writing and presenting papers on contemporary Chinese politics and international relations. Both tasks were part of his mission to understand China and interpret the Chinese mind to western audiences, at a time when Australian government policy towards the People's Republic amounted to little more than wishing it would go away. In 1956 he led an eleven-member unofficial cultural delegation (including Partridge) to China, which improved the prospects for academic exchanges between the two countries.

Patrick FitzGerald receives his first degree, a DLitt, from the Vice-Chancellor, Sir John Crawford, in 1968.

Although the government remained suspicious of FitzGerald's political outlook, the University quickly acknowledged his attainments, especially after the School of Oriental and African Studies in London tried to tempt him away with the offer of an associate professorship. His 'Visiting' status was dropped, and he was asked to take charge of a separate Department of Far Eastern History, a name chosen in preference to 'Oriental history', but which yielded to tradition in locating China and Japan to the east of England. Soon he was appointed to a chair, which went most of the way towards removing any seeming illegitimacy implicit in his want of a degree; the award in 1968 (shortly after his retirement) of a DLitt, on the basis of published works, dissolved the stain entirely. By that time he had created, almost single-handed, Sinology in Australia.

Jim Davidson plunged into Pacific research with an enthusiasm that was comparable with FitzGerald's and which suggested a more than merely academic love for his subject matter. According to his long-term friend and departmental colleague Harry Maude, his initial interest was based on a frankly romantic attraction towards the South Seas, which his mother had instilled in him since childhood. During frequent field trips he developed an affinity with the peoples whose history he was studying: in Western Samoa, wrote Maude, 'he passed with honours his apprenticeship in the subtle nuances of island life and acquired a sensitive perception of the ethos of the islander which so many Europeans have sought and so few have gained'.

Davidson intended the Department of Pacific History (once FitzGerald and his colleagues had broken away) to cover the Pacific islands fairly comprehensively and to enter South-east Asia selectively, as opportunities for comparative research arose. By 1960 he and his colleagues had conducted research on Western Samoa, Fiji, Tonga, the Cook Islands, French Polynesia, New Guinea, Malaya and Indonesia. Davidson believed that the exact location of research did not much matter, so long as the work illuminated problems relating to the contact between western and indigenous cultures. Where previous researchers had tended to approach the Pacific from the perspective of imperial policy-makers, Davidson saw the islands through the eyes of the colonised as well as the colonisers. This approach led him into other disciplines—anthropology, sociology, linguistics—and it constituted his own and his department's special contribution to Pacific studies.

Jim Davidson, about 1955.
Australian News and Information Bureau, ANU Collection.

When he was not editing the journals of Captain Cook or following the exploits of the early nineteenth-century adventurer Peter Dillon, Davidson was engaged in a long-term study of how political institutions in Western Samoa had evolved since the coming of the Europeans. As the colony moved towards independence from Britain, his services were eagerly sought by the Western Samoan government, and between 1959 and 1961 he spent several months in Apia as Constitutional Adviser. In his view this was an appropriate extension of the work of a Pacific historian; but the Vice-Chancellor at the time, Sir Leslie Melville, was not so sure, commenting that 'While he is certainly taking part in the creation of history, such activities are perhaps marginal as academic activities of a History Professor'. In Melville's estimation, a professor's worth was measured by his publications; and Davidson's promised books were slow in coming. When *Samoa mo Samoa: the Emergence of the Independent State of Western Samoa*, eventually appeared in 1967, it offered convincing evidence of the historian's role as the link between past and present, and confirmed that his time in Apia had been well spent.

Oskar Spate, about 1955.
Australian News and Information Bureau, ANU Collection.

The Pacific Historians (or most of them) were linked by a theme. The Geographers, on the other hand, ranged widely across their discipline and were not even particularly obedient to regional constraints. Oskar Spate, who arrived as Professor of Geography in 1951, was a polymath whose interests knew no mental or geographical boundaries; and given that geography had made little headway in Australian universities (at the time he took up duty there was only one other chair), he thought the ANU department should try to develop as many facets of the discipline as possible. This implied striking a balance between the physical and human sides of the subject, pure and applied research, and systematic and regional studies.

A geography department above all ought to have been comfortable in a regional school. But there was a problem, which Spate expressed with characteristic whimsy: 'geography is the study of man and land in their relations, and there is not really much of either in the Pacific'. While it was hard to attract students to work on the Pacific islands, there were plenty of people eager to work on Australian geography and there was much important work to be done. So Spate adopted a frankly opportunistic policy of encouraging research on the mainland, while seizing every chance to work in the Pacific islands, South-east Asia, and especially New Guinea.

Like the Pacific Historians, the Geographers spent much of their time in the field. In the mid-1950s staff and students in the department were studying coastal geomorphology on King Island, tracing the steps of early European explorers along the Birdsville track, investigating irrigation geography along the Murray River, and conducting regional surveys in Samoa, the New Hebrides, New Guinea and Sumatra. Fieldwork was often arduous and often an adventure: the department's report for 1956 recorded, with nice understatement, that a student's research in central Sumatra 'was to some extent protracted by the unusual prevalence of tigers in her area, which made work away from the villages somewhat hazardous'.

Spate's own research interests, as they developed over the next few decades, extended from Burma (where he had lived before and during the war) to Chile. He brought with him to Canberra a near-complete manuscript of a geography of India and Pakistan, which was published in 1954 and soon became a standard work, in Russian as well as English. While maintaining an interest in the subcontinent, he embarked on a study of the Australian cultural landscape, made several forays into New Guinea and conducted, at the request of the Fijian government, an enquiry in 1958 into the economic problems of the ethnic Fijians. Although he maintained a steady stream of publications and presented many conference papers, he later described much of this early work as scholarship rather than research, as so much of his time was taken up in encouraging the work of others. His own greatest work was yet to come.

International Relations had troubled beginnings. When Crocker left for New Delhi in 1952, the small department was placed in the charge of Michael Lindsay, a Senior Research Fellow who was soon promoted to the permanent position of Senior Fellow. Lindsay, son of the distinguished Master of Balliol College, Lord Lindsay of Birker, was an expert on contemporary China, having taught in Beijing in the late 1930s and early 1940s. During the war he had served alongside Mao's armies against the Japanese occupation and had expressed strong support for the communist cause. This effectively disqualified him for a university job in Britain; so his father wrote to his old friend and student Crocker about finding him a job at the ANU. As it happened, by the time he arrived in Canberra Lindsay had reversed his previous opinions and had become a fervent critic of the Maoist regime.

On Crocker's resignation in 1954, Lindsay (now Lord Lindsay) applied unsuccessfully for the chair, which remained unfilled. As the University seemed reluctant to promote him even to the readership that he insisted had been promised, he came to see himself as the victim of an injustice and made his grievances publicly known, questioning the University's standards in social science research, as well as its appointment and promotion procedures.

In 1957 the department's problems looked as though they might be solved when Martin Wight, an outstanding scholar from the London School of Economics, accepted the chair and reached the stage of passing a medical examination. But Lindsay wrote to him in terms that scared him away. Soon the case was completely out of hand, with Lindsay writing scathing articles for the Sydney *Observer* and lambasting the University on ABC television. In the meantime, the department languished. While individual members, including Lindsay himself, continued to do valuable work, there was nothing and no-one to hold it together.

Anthropology, on the other hand, demonstrated a remarkable cohesion from the outset. Apart from the vibrancy of the discipline and the fact that four of its early staff, along with Firth, the Adviser to the school, were products of the London School of Economics, it owed much to Fred Nadel's intellectual leadership and his sense of urgency about all the jobs that needed to be done. Within a few weeks of his arrival in Canberra he had set out a detailed research program, comprising projects on social organisation in the New Guinea Highlands, social and cultural change in the Pacific islands (with emphasis on the appearance of the 'cargo cult'), a Pacific community responding to western influence, village communities in Indonesia or the subcontinent, and the process of assimilation among recent European immigrants to Australia. The last of these, he conceded, was not strictly 'anthropological' in the conventional sense of the word, but that did not matter: there was no sharp distinction between anthropology and sociology, and the anthropologist ought to be concerned with both 'primitive' and 'advanced' cultures. There was as yet no chair in Sociology in an Australian university, and Nadel was keen to stake a claim. At his request (and despite some mutterings about empire-building), the department was soon renamed to embrace both Anthropology and Sociology.

Where Spate allowed individual preferences to determine research directions, Nadel believed that the continuity of research and the extension of knowledge were best served by connected and well-planned programs. He favoured teamwork; and before long a group of students was hard at work on comparable studies of several communities in New Guinea and New Britain. This association of interests provided the basis for a lively seminar program.

The department also developed interests in Aboriginal anthropology, although for a decade Bill (W.E.H.) Stanner was the only staff member in the field, and only two of the first dozen students conducted research on Aboriginal themes. In the 1950s, Stanner returned to places in the Northern Territory that he had visited nearly twenty years earlier and recorded the drastic changes that had taken place there. His observations led him to question the adequacy of current anthropological theories: 'We have men in anthropology like those trees in whose shade nothing will grow. In a sense we should be glad of it. It gives a relish to radical thinking.' He

Bill Stanner, surrounded by books and Aboriginal paintings, in 1958. Working clothes include coat, tie and slippers.

Fred Nadel, early 1950s.
Australian News and Information Bureau, ANU Collection.

thought radically about continuity and change in Aboriginal societies, and wrote profoundly about Aboriginal religion, including that 'impalpable and subtle' concept, The Dreaming. Not many people, beyond his professional colleagues, listened. It was well into the 1960s before his work started to attract the attention it deserved.

Nadel's own work culminated early in 1956, when he posted to his publishers a major book on *The Theory of Social Structure*. A week later, suddenly and unexpectedly, he died of a heart attack, aged just 52. His colleague Derek Freeman wrote: 'By the tragic untimeliness of his death anthropology has lost incalculably'. But the department he created was already strong enough to withstand the blow.

The creative imagination

By 1953 there were sufficient senior academics on campus for the University to offer a public lecture series. The breadth of subject matter was impressive: Woolley on 'Ancient and modern theories of the universe', Borrie on 'The growth of populations', Sawer on 'Law as logic and common sense', Oliphant on 'The methods of modern physics', Nadel on 'National character', Davidson and Partridge debating 'The uses of history'. The University was taking shape as the intellectual community envisaged by its founders.

There was a sense of intimacy within the University, a result partly of its members being pioneers together, and partly of their numbers being small. As in Oxbridge colleges, people from different schools and disciplines were thrown into contact with one another, confirming the impression of a community of scholars. Moran in Statistics worked with Steven Fazekas de St Groth in Microbiology to develop a mathematical theory relating to host resistance to virus infection. Jaeger in Geophysics helped Eccles with his work on nerve cells. The Department of Social Philosophy conducted a seminar on methodology in the social sciences which was attended by staff and students from several departments in Pacific Studies and Social Sciences. The professors from all four schools met for a formal dinner three times a year. Staff who kept to themselves during working hours might well meet their colleagues at social gatherings or the shopping centre. Most staff lived within walking or pedalling distance of the campus, so the chances of casual contacts between the disciplines were high.

University House, when it opened in 1954, served, as Hancock intended it should, as a universal meeting place, especially at lunchtimes, when staff, scholars and visitors from all schools and the administration were thrown together indiscriminately in the hall. The first Master, Dale Trendall, was a New Zealander, aged 44, with a fine appreciation of Oxbridge (in his case, Trinity College, Cambridge) collegiate life. Coming to the ANU from the chairs of Greek and Archaeology at Sydney, where he had also occupied various senior administrative positions, Trendall was an urbane scholar, with cultivated tastes and a cutting wit. He was also an internationally acknowledged expert on South Italian Greek vases, which brought him dangerously close to Wright's collector of tailored tweeds, but fashioned him well for the integrating function the Master was expected to perform.

But despite all the favourable signs, some of those involved in setting up the framework of the University were starting to have doubts, especially in relation to the social science schools. Alf Conlon decided as early as October 1950 that these schools were 'irreparably stuft'. His opinion by this time did not matter, but Oliphant's did; and he, isolated as the only Director and frustrated by his building problems, was 'appalled' by his colleagues' lack of academic experience and appreciation of what a university ought to be about. In his view, the schools were developing as watertight compartments, each pursuing its own interests, without a common objective. The problem, he said, was acute in the social science schools, where too many staff had come from public service backgrounds, with the result that the University was starting to be run like a government department. His answer was to forget the past and appoint Hancock, who had the capacity to turn the place into 'a real university': an institution which embodied the traditional academic ideal of a group of men with a common aim and a common spirit.

Oliphant expressed these misgivings to Eggleston, who defended the social science schools on the grounds of their experimental nature, but nevertheless picked up the cue. Early in 1951, while still a member of the Interim Council, he warned in a testy memorandum that the social science schools were developing without a sense of direction: 'those who commence work in Canberra apparently take up the subject which, for the time being, appeals to them as appropriate'. There was no formal provision for cooperative research, with the result that academics could engage in 'an orgy of fact finding' in their own discrete disciplines. Renewing his correspondence with Hancock, he wrote that it was essential to forget the accidents of history and differences in methodology which kept the disciplines apart, to get away from 'narrow specialisation and academic evasion', and to encourage researchers to explore the fundamental problems of society. 'Apparently I was wrong to think that the schools of research at the National University could help in producing these men, but that was my dream.' Assuming Hancock received this letter, we can imagine him reflecting wryly on his earlier premonitions

Nobody in the social sciences took much notice of Eggleston's warnings. Sawer had just finished writing a report on the manuscript of his *Reflections of an Australian Liberal*, praising it sufficiently for publication, but denouncing it to himself as 'a shallow piece of pro-democratic propaganda masquerading as sociology ... I agree heartily with the objects of the propaganda, but detest the half-baked identification of wish with facts.' Swan, whom Eggleston had privately reproached for pursuing subjects of purely technical interest, argued (in another context) that the study of techniques was a legitimate object of research and appealed for funds to collect empirical data, since a school of social sciences which relied on published statistics would be severely handicapped.

This was Eggleston's last attempt to influence the way the University was headed. He did not seek membership of the new, permanent Council convened later that year, but continued to contemplate the University and the world with growing disillusionment from his wheelchair in Melbourne until his death in 1954. It seemed that Eggleston was yesterday's man; but in some senses, he was also tomorrow's.

Dale Trendall with research photographs of South Italian Greek vases, 1965.

Nevertheless, there were signs that some members of staff were aware of a loss of direction, especially in Pacific Studies. The school's Annual Report for 1953 remarked that interest in staff seminars, in which people from the two schools expounded their research, was waning, while enthusiasm for interdisciplinary training courses was more theoretical than practical. The report conceded that, while there was rapid expansion, there was as yet little trace of coordinated planning: 'rather, centrifugal tendencies predominated, concentrated attacks upon related problems giving way before diversity of research'.

Coombs, though similarly troubled, was more reticent than Eggleston in expressing his reservations. Publicly at least, he kept his peace until 1957, when he seized on continuing uncertainty in the Department of International Relations to press for a reexamination of the role of its school within the University. The present organisation of Pacific Studies, he told the Vice-Chancellor, does not take advantage of 'the unique opportunities for co-ordinated studies of problems which arise in the Pacific of importance to Australia'. In other words, the academics were concentrating too narrowly on problems within their own disciplines at the expense of a broader concern with meeting national needs. The school took this warning to heart, and undertook a broad review of where it was headed.

But Coombs knew better than to force the issue, remembering perhaps what Wright liked to call Conlon's 'law of social institutions': 'Every such institution comes to the level of the society in which it is and bears no essential relationship to the expressed ideals of the people who founded it'. Wright repeated this dictum from time to time with varying emphases and degrees of relish. But it was Coombs who refined the idea (perhaps it was as much his own as Conlon's) and gave it most forceful expression when he delivered over ABC Radio the Boyer Lectures for 1970, which he called 'The fragile pattern: institutions and man'. By now he was (almost) reconciled to what the ANU had become, 'a university of quality and distinction, but bearing little resemblance to the ante-natal image of its parents'. The concerns which he had shared with Wright and Conlon, Walker and Mills, and the rest of the post-war planners were not shared by the newly appointed staff.

> Scholars were disinclined to direct their labours to policy objectives, which they felt to be parochial and earthbound; the problems which excited their curiosity and imagination were intellectually rather than practically motivated; they were anxious to establish their identity with their colleagues in other places and in other times rather than with the eager re-builders of contemporary society.

This, said Coombs, was as it should be: the investigator 'can no more be guided or directed than can the artist.' The days of social engineering had passed, and the creative imagination had to be given free rein.

Ironically, as Coombs was well aware, the freedom assumed by scholars at the ANU to pursue their own research interests was one of the marks of a genuine university.

Academic freedom and leadership

The University and the government

The academics gathered in Canberra for the Easter conferences in 1948 needed reassuring. Would the Australian National University degenerate into an arm of the federal government and bureaucracy? Public servants had been prominent among its makers, and it owed its existence to an Act of the federal parliament. If the circumstances of its birth were not sufficient liability, growing up in such close proximity to politicians and public servants surely would be.

The issue seemed most urgent at the Pacific Studies conference, where Paul Hasluck warned that political pressures might influence research planning. The government, he argued, might insist that the school show something for its money: 'it would be essential to take care that no promises were made concerning the production of results'. Eggleston responded that the Interim Council was confident the University would not be used in this way, and that 'heads of Government departments would not be allowed to ask the National University questions'. J.G. Crawford thought the anxieties were something of a phobia, warning that the school might be so keen to avoid work of use to the government that it might end up with research so pure and rarified as to be altogether pointless. But he was in a minority: whenever someone spoke of the dangers of government interference, the response was generally earnest nods.

The banner was academic freedom, and Copland was just the man to carry it. Writing from Nanjing just after he had accepted appointment as Vice-Chancellor, he told Menzies how he hoped to help build up a tradition of academic freedom at the new University, adding that 'the establishment and maintenance of academic freedom is more important than the actual research and teaching done inside the walls of a university'. Surely he was exaggerating: yet it is worth noting that a couple of years later a fellow vice-chancellor, A.P. Rowe at the University of Adelaide, placed the preservation of independence from external control at the top of his list of suggested aims for his institution.

Freedom was a tradition at the heart of the university, as defined by Cardinal Newman and others. In Australia, where all universities were creations of the state, the tradition was fragile, partly because it was largely untested. Copland was determined to give it strength. After his visit to universities in Britain and the United States in 1949, he reported: 'The characteristic feature of a university is that its leading scholars become a corporate body with wide powers to determine academic policy and to promote the advancement of learning, but with the obligation to observe the responsibilities that attend the use of these powers'. A new institution should take the advice of more experienced centres of learning and allow its faculty to establish a sound tradition of academic freedom. This might lead to 'awkward incidents' and bring the University into controversy. But in the long run, it would be better to put up with controversy than to impose restrictions on the activities of the staff.

'Academic freedom', as Copland and others used the term, had two meanings: the freedom of the individual scholar to pursue his or her own research; and the freedom of the university to conduct its own affairs without external interference, especially by government. Often the two meanings merged into one: but we will keep them apart, saving the liberty of the individual academic for later in this chapter, and focusing for the moment on the vexed issue of the University's relationship with the government which paid its bills.

John Dedman, Minister for Post-War Reconstruction, having just affirmed his commitment to university autonomy, lays the foundation stone of University House. Photograph by J. Lazern, 1949.
Australian Official Photograph, ANU Collection.

Copland was optimistic. He thought the constitution of the ANU—meaning the Act which had created the institution and which gave the Council sole control over its affairs—was very liberal, and that the provision of a statutory grant, which might be reviewed and increased every three to four years, was the right way to go. In October 1949, at a ceremony to mark the laying of foundation stones for the John Curtin School, the Physical Sciences school and University House, he had reason to feel secure as he listened to John Dedman affirming his commitment to university autonomy. The University, Dedman declared, should be responsible for its own internal administration; there should be no intrusion of party politics; and there should be no strings attached to its income, apart from the one which outlined its purposes in broad terms. As the Minister sat down, Copland leaned across to the Prime Minister to say what a good speech it was. Yes, Chifley replied: 'but the trouble is that he really believes in it'.

Chifley nevertheless helped establish the principle of autonomy in response to a question from Jack Lang, the former New South Wales Labor Premier and now a truculent member of the House of Representatives. Lang attacked Copland for writing an article which he interpreted as critical of the working man. Was the Vice-Chancellor entitled to accept jobs writing for newspapers? Chifley replied that the matter was entirely between the Vice-Chancellor and the Interim Council, and thereafter the precedent was set: if politicians asked questions about the University, they would be told it was the University's business.

Menzies, elected to office soon afterwards, accepted this convention. Like Dedman, he was committed to university tradition and, having been uplifted by Oxford's dreaming spires, was probably more aware than Dedman of what that tradition meant. The new

Prime Minister, who had once declared that 'the University must be a custodian of mental liberty, and the unfettered search for truth', won a reputation as a defender of academic freedom, a reputation somewhat enhanced by comparison with the illiberal stands taken by a few of his colleagues. Two ministers in particular, Richard Casey and Wilfred Kent Hughes, made no secret of the fact that they regarded the ANU as a waste of government money and did their best to pull it into line. The social science schools were, by their origins and nature, as well as some of the people who inhabited them, apt to arouse conservative suspicions. And the very name of the John Curtin School of Medical Research was an affront, partly (so they said) because you could not have a medical *school* which did not train medical practitioners, but more because of the person whom the title remembered.

Menzies enjoyed playing honest broker between the academics demanding more and his Cabinet colleagues arguing for less. Under Copland, the academics generally seemed to get the better of the contest, as Sawer recorded in verse: 'when all other grants received a slash, Doug, and his A.N.U. were showered with cash'. When Labor supporters of the ANU attacked the government for parsimony, the Prime Minister was able to respond, correctly, that the Labor government's original estimates had fallen far short of what was needed and that his own government was giving vastly more to higher education than had ever been given before.

With Copland vigilant and Menzies benign, the University remained fairly safe from ill-disposed politicians. A more formidable challenge to autonomy came from Commonwealth public servants and the bureaucratic structure they inhabited. Copland had not been six months in office when he noticed the public service encroaching on what he took to be the University's domain. The offence occurred very close to home, as it related to the University's provision of his own superannuation. Copland had put a proposition to the Interim Council, but this was resisted by H.J. Goodes, who was Assistant Secretary at the Treasury. When the Interim Council's Finance Committee prepared an alternative proposal, Goodes submitted it to the acting head of his department.

Copland was incensed, complaining to Mills that Goodes tended to regard himself as representative of the Treasury on the Interim Council. This was a matter of principle: if Goodes were allowed to get his way, it would suggest that, contrary to the Act of Parliament, the Council was not independent of outside control. On this occasion, Goodes did appear to get his way: Copland failed to get the superannuation arrangements he was after, and the principle remained unconfirmed.

Alarm bells rang again in 1950 when Goodes asked that an item on Council's agenda be deferred until he had discussed it with the Treasurer. Copland protested to Mills, who tried to reassure him: Goodes had always been a warm friend to the University and had smoothed its relations with government; and as the University had been created by the government and was sustained by an annual grant, some measure of Treasury control was perhaps an inevitable growing pain. But Copland received support for his stand from another quarter. Rivett, lamenting a loss of autonomy at his old stamping ground (now called the CSIRO), urged him to stand firm against Treasury people who might mean well but whose machinery and techniques were simply inappropriate for universities and scientific bodies: 'Whatever happens we must keep the A.N.U. out of their clutches. In the atmosphere of Canberra, this means a big job—especially for the VC.'

There could be no avoiding the fact that the University was accountable to the taxpayer. While the Act may have affirmed the Council's independence, it provided that the University's finances should be audited in such a manner as the Commonwealth Treasurer should direct. So from the outset the Auditor-General was involved in the University's affairs, and the Registrar and his staff tried to organise the University's accounts to meet his requirements. These efforts ran directly counter to the more relaxed accounting procedures that Florey and Oliphant were used to in the older English universities. Oliphant, who was purchasing equipment and materials on a grand scale, thought all transactions could be covered by 'two sheets of paper', and objected vigorously to having to run to a clerk (meaning the Registrar) in order to get things done. Given these internal tensions, it is not surprising that the University's financial arrangements attracted outside notice.

But nobody within the University expected the Auditor-General, James Brophy, to drop a bombshell. Late in 1953, without warning, he refused to certify as correct the balance sheet for the previous year, reporting to parliament that Council had failed to keep satisfactory stock and plant records or carry out regular stocktakings. There were other charges: that contracts for building were let in an unsatisfactory manner, that the University allowed staff to rent premises it owned on privileged terms. Although there was no suggestion of wrongdoing, the report gave the impression that the University's accounting procedures were sloppy and that, relative to other members of the Canberra community, its staff were looked after rather well.

Hohnen, as the officer formally responsible, was dismayed, and suggested that there was malice behind some of the Auditor-General's comments. The University closed ranks to argue that everything was in order; and Hohnen and his staff set about implementing a stores system apparently more elaborate (and expensive) than that of any other university in the country.

While the controversy soon evaporated, it left a residue of wariness among members of the University who had anything to do with financial matters. They would have to watch their steps.

'No Melville, no money'

By this time the University had a new vice-chancellor. The search for a successor to Copland had begun a year earlier, when Council had appointed a committee to scour the English-speaking academic world. So much depended on finding the right man. As Florey had told Oliphant at the time, 'If you make a mistake the place has had it'.

As in 1947, no one candidate stood out. Oliphant and Crocker pushed hard for Hancock, but Coombs was cool on the grounds that he had shown himself to be 'an exceedingly difficult person'. The committee set its sights on Sir John Cockcroft at

Harwell, whose work on atomic energy made him especially appealing to the Menzies government. The Prime Minister, in company with two of the government's nominees on Council, Allen Brown and Roland Wilson, wooed him, but to no avail. Oliphant then urged Coombs to take on the job and restore the vision of the founders, but he still said firmly no.

After much agonising, the committee was left with two front-runners. Coombs nominated Leslie Melville, as he had done at the time of Copland's appointment. Melville, now an Executive Director of the International Monetary Fund in Washington, was well known, at least by reputation, to everyone involved in making the appointment. The other contender was a complete outsider: Basil Schonland, a geophysicist from the University of Witwatersrand, Johannesburg, whom Wright had discovered through a South African colleague in Melbourne and Oliphant remembered from Cambridge days. Oliphant and Wright decided that Schonland was their man. Coombs, who was shortly due to leave for England, thought it would be worth flying him to London, where he and the Chancellor, Lord Bruce, who had already agreed to help with the selection process, could interview him and report back to the committee.

The interview took place over lunch and was a great success. Bruce was won over entirely, concluding that Schonland was 'a gift from Heaven'. Coombs, initially sceptical about appointing an outsider, found him much more suitable than he had expected: quiet and pleasant, genuinely keen on the project, interested in the social as well as the natural sciences, and likely to fit in well. But the recommendation that Coombs sent back to Canberra on his own and Bruce's behalf was equivocal. While he personally expressed 'a slight preference for Melville', he emphasised that Schonland would be very good; and while the Chancellor (in Bruce's own words) 'feels strongly Schonland is the man we are looking for', he stressed that Melville, whom he had known many years earlier, might now be equally good.

This advice polarised the committee. Oliphant, supported by Wright and the Solicitor-General, K.H. Bailey, seized on it as endorsing their own view that Schonland should be appointed. Wilson, who strongly believed the University needed an administrator rather than an academic in the top job, put a brake on proceedings by insisting that Bruce be given the opportunity to talk to Melville before expressing a final preference. 'The ball is now in your court', Wilson warned Coombs. 'I fear Oliphant's machine will prevail unless you and Bruce can agree on L.G. Melville.' We may wonder if Wilson intended 'machine' to have a double meaning.

Melville was duly flown across the Atlantic for the meeting with Bruce, who agreed that he had developed well since he had known him in the early 1930s, while holding to his view that Schonland was the better candidate. But this was not the advice received in Canberra nearly a fortnight later. Coombs, in a cable drafted in a Stockholm hotel and approved by Bruce in London, reiterated his personal preference for Melville before expressing Bruce's considered conclusion: 'the Chancellor wishes me to say that taking all aspects of the question into account he would concur with me in a joint recommendation for Melville's appointment'.

This was enough for Wilson and the supporters of Melville to win the day, but only just: at the next Council meeting, eight members voted for Melville and seven for Schonland. Oliphant accepted the decision with good grace, though he complained to Coombs that the 'official' members (meaning those nominated by government) had lined up against the 'academic' members to get their way.

What had caused Bruce to change his mind, in those days between the interview with Melville and the cable from Stockholm? The answer lies in a long and confidential cable that he received shortly after his interview with Melville. Though its author was probably Wilson, the sender was the Prime Minister himself. Menzies urged Bruce to consider the benefits of appointing an Australian citizen of Melville's quality over 'the supposed advantage' of having an academic in the 'high administrative position' of vice-chancellor.

> I feel strongly that the Institution's interests would best be served by Melville particularly having in mind some opposition to National University expenditure in Cabinet circles. I need hardly add that a unanimous recommendation from yourself and Coombs would make Melville selection much more easy for the University Council.

The Prime Minister's meaning was utterly clear. Nevertheless Bruce, with a confidence reminding us that as well as being Chancellor he had also been a Prime Minister, declined to take the hint, and cabled back for elaboration. Schonland, he told Menzies, was still the better man. But was the Prime Minister's cable saying that, in the interests of the University, there were matters other than personal qualifications that had to be taken into account? If so, he would be prepared to yield and join with Coombs in a joint recommendation of Melville.

Menzies didn't bother to reply. After waiting ten days for a response, Bruce gave in, leaving Coombs to draft the faintly equivocal despatch which came out in favour of Melville, while hinting that neither of them would be at all offended if Council opted for Schonland.

Bruce thought he had been blackmailed. (Although he did not use the word, he made it clear to Florey that he would have liked to.) It was a case, he told Hancock, of 'No Melville, no money'. As Chancellor of the University with the interests of the University at heart, what else could he do? As he explained to Florey, if he were faced with choosing the best vice-chancellor in the world with the government refusing to provide finance, or a lesser vice-chancellor with a generous government, the latter would seem the better option.

Sympathising with Bruce's predicament, Florey told Oliphant *'in greatest confidence'* that there had been direct political interference, of the sort that they had always feared. But only a few people (apart from the perpetrators) knew about it, and they were not telling: so the University's reputation as an autonomous body remained intact—and Menzies remained the honest broker.

Sober administration

Oliphant thought two economists in a row would be two too many. But he need not have worried: Copland and Melville were chalk and cheese. Where Copland was confident, self-important (in an amiable sort of way), and fond (perhaps to excess) of the high life, Melville was cautious, modest and abstemious. Copland got on easily with almost everyone; Melville often seemed anxious. Copland, who had a long chat with his successor in New York before he set out for Australia, commended his intellectual integrity, courage and honesty: 'perhaps [he] is apt to be more suspicious than I would be, but he will think more before coming to a decision. Is that good or bad?'

Everyone agreed that Melville would be careful about money. His arrival in Canberra in November 1953, soon after the Auditor-General had submitted his critical report, helped reassure the government and diminish the report's adverse impact. 'I have some fear that the Auditor-General may wish the University to be run like a Government Department', he told Bruce. Council might resist, though personally he would be prepared to go some distance to accommodate Brophy.

Coombs was especially pleased to see how things were falling into place under the new Vice-Chancellor. Copland's seemingly careless administrative style and his fondness for delegation had worried him and, what was more, it had worried the government. It was important, he told Florey, that the government should have confidence not merely in the University's scientific and professional capacity, but also in the soberness of its administration. Melville, he thought, was just the man to bring trust and certainty to the relationship. Eighteen months after Melville had taken office, Coombs was happier about the University's future than at any time since the legislation that created it was first passed.

Leslie Melville during his term as Vice-Chancellor, 1953 – 1960.
Australian News and Information Bureau, ANU Collection.

Oliphant, on the other hand, was becoming increasingly angry about what he took to be interference by Cabinet and the Treasury. In his view, the University was becoming 'just a very minor government department', ruled in effect by the public service members of Council, Brown, Goodes and Wilson, who were able to get their way by means of innuendo: all they had to do was hint at what the government wanted, and other Council members fell over backwards to oblige. As for Melville, Oliphant thought him earnest and decent, but more like a bank clerk than a Vice-Chancellor, even saying on one occasion that the University had to abide by the rules, like any other government department. Relations became strained: Oliphant accused Melville of calling him a liar, and thought about resigning.

There was now an understanding with the government relating to financial matters. Soon after Melville's arrival, he and Coombs had held a meeting with the Prime Minister, which was also attended by Goodes as representative of the Treasury. In the course of discussion it was pointed out that the University's running costs, originally set at £325 000 a year, had now more than doubled, and that they were likely to be nearly three times that amount by the 1955–56 financial year. Even allowing for high inflation, expenditure appeared to be out of hand. Menzies proposed that the University put a stop on further increases in spending. Coombs and Melville responded that a complete halt to expansion would lead to a badly balanced structure. By the end of the meeting, the two parties had reached a compromise: the government would provide sufficient funds over the next few years to allow for modest expansion within the existing structure; and the University would consider the period as one of consolidation, embarking on no new projects, and aiming to demonstrate effectiveness within its original fields of research.

This understanding contributed to at least one lost opportunity. In 1954 Arthur Birch, Professor of Organic Chemistry at the University of Sydney and widely recognised as one of Australia's foremost scientists, decided that he had had enough of having to beg for Bunsen burners and test tubes and set his sights abroad. Oliphant intervened, and suggested that there might be a place for him in the Research School of Physical Sciences. After all, if part of the purpose of the ANU was to attract Australian scholars back home, it was equally important to try to hold onto those who were still here. Birch was ready to come, and Melville was keen to have him. But the timing was wrong: Melville and Coombs decided that, however much the University might benefit from this new venture, it would benefit more from demonstrating financial discretion. Birch accepted a chair at Manchester, and was there five years later when the ANU, in more affluent times, began to think about a research school of chemistry.

Freedom with discretion

Cold war politics gave a sharp edge to relations between University and government. As early as 1946, when the bill to create the University was before parliament, a Country Party member warned against including a school of social sciences which was likely to be 'fairly red'; and, even before the first academics arrived, Holmes was treading carefully to avoid 'the Opposition zeal for witch-hunting'. Soon the Opposition became the Government, China fell to the Communists, war erupted on the Korean peninsula, and Senator Joseph McCarthy tried to purge the United States administration of alleged communists and fellow travellers. In Australia too, anti-communists looked for a fifth column.

Some thought they had found evidence of one at the ANU. Richard Casey remarked privately that the social science schools were full of long-haired communists. In parliament the Chief Government Whip, Henry ('Jo') Gullett, suggested that the University was becoming more famous for its left-wing politics than its research and made pointed comments about taxpayers having to pay the salaries of communist sympathisers. From the Opposition benches, S.M. Keon, one of the Victorian right-wingers who would soon split from Labor to form the Democratic Labor Party, declared that the ANU had become, according to a planned scheme, a nest of communists who were dedicated to destroying the country's institutions.

Allegations usually took the form of questions. From Gullett:

1. How many members of the professorial or administrative staff of the Australian National University or the Canberra University College are known to have or to have had Communist affiliations?
2. Who are they?
3. How many of these were the subjects of adverse security reports from their countries of origin?

And again:

1. What are Lord Lindsay's duties at the Australian National University?
2. Was he previously an officer in the Chinese Communist Army?
3. Is it considered that he is a person capable of giving to Australian students a disinterested picture of affairs in China?

Gullett had the wrong target. Although Lindsay had accompanied Mao Zedong on the Long March and had once been a committed Marxist, he was now, according to Copland, no more a communist than he was. But however misinformed such allegations may have been, their tenor, from the University's point of view, was disturbing. At least the Prime Minister's position was reassuring. In response to questions about the appointment or employment of academic staff, he consistently replied that such matters were the University's business.

While Menzies took the high ground, in the suburbs of Canberra academic freedom lived more precariously. Officers of the Australian Security Intelligence Organisation (ASIO) kept a close watch on staff and students with alleged communist sympathies, such as R.A. Gollan, whom we met as an ANU Overseas Scholar and who was appointed a Research Fellow in History in 1953. ASIO officers correctly described him as 'one of the leading Communists in Canberra' and therefore kept his house in O'Connor under surveillance. The Gollans and their friends were aware of this and not much disturbed, drawing some amusement from ASIO's excessive diligence, which led on one occasion to the Solicitor-General's allegiances being called into question after his son had driven to a party at the Gollans' in his father's car.

In later years, Gollan reflected that the activities of the political right had no significant effect on his work as an ANU academic (although later it stood in the way of his appointment to a chair at the University of New South Wales). He continued to pursue his chosen research on radical and working-class movements in nineteenth-

MHR hits out at leftism at National University

Melbourne Herald, 28 August 1952.

"RED" AUTHORS AND PROFESSORS
Lively Debate In House

Sydney Morning Herald, 29 August 1952.

century Australia, allowing Marxist theory to inform his approach. Yet, for those academics and students with past or present left-wing allegiances, it was hard to escape the knowledge that while anti-communism did not at the moment stand in the way of their research or career prospects, it might one day do so.

Members of the Research School of Pacific Studies had most to fear. In 1952 Spate, who had carried the communist card in Cambridge many years earlier, had a bitter taste of McCarthyism when Casey, after a security check, stopped his projected appointment as First Commissioner of the South Pacific Commission. What worried Spate most was that Paul Hasluck, who was now Minister for Territories, might prevent him from pursuing his research interests in Papua and New Guinea. Hasluck reassured him, but there was no room for complacency. Just a few months earlier Hasluck had refused entry to Papua and New Guinea to a research student in Anthropology, Peter Worsley, who intended to study social systems in the Highlands. The reason Hasluck gave in parliament was Worsley's 'political affiliations'. Exactly what that meant was never made clear, but it was sufficient to enable Gullett to ask threatening questions. The ANU Students' Association took up the case on Worsley's behalf, arguing that the Minister's action was a serious threat to academic freedom. Hasluck responded that his decision was based on principles which would apply to anyone wishing to enter the Territory, and that academic freedom had nothing to do with the case. Copland agreed: the University could not claim special privileges for its own members. Hasluck refused to budge, the students remained unhappy, and Worsley shifted his research interests to Groote Eylandt.

Within the University, opinions differed widely on how questions relating to academic freedom and communism should be handled. At least in regard to academic appointments, the issue should have been straightforward: either you took into account a person's political, religious and ideological beliefs or you did not. But it was rarely so simple. The first awkward staff question arose in 1951, when Oliphant wanted to appoint Ken Inall, who had been a key member of his team in Birmingham, to the position of Research Fellow. Inall was not a member of the British Communist Party, but he was known to have strong left-wing sympathies. As a member of the Department of Nuclear Physics, he would be working on a project with defence and security implications. Copland wondered whether the University should take the risk. Crocker, who leaned to the right, urged caution: why buy into this sort of trouble, especially in Physics? Sawer, who leaned to the left, agreed: 'An ignoble policy', he told his diary, 'but I'm afraid the only possible one'. The problem was solved with a compromise: Inall was placed on one year's probation and required to give an assurance that he would have nothing to do with politics. Copland, currently in

England, was relieved, though he expected 'some backchat among the comrades here'.

That was part of the problem: the University's policy-makers and appointment committee members knew they were being watched from quite different perspectives by the nearby government and by the academic world outside Australia. Certainly Florey was quick to notice an alleged incursion on academic freedom at the University of Tasmania (the Orr case), and to warn Oliphant of the sort of publicity Australian universities could get if they put a foot wrong. From the vantage point of Canberra, Oxford and Cambridge set absolute standards of academic freedom. But the government paid the bills; and, however much Menzies might defend academic freedom against parliamentary snipers, in the midst of the Cold War there was not much doubt that, if put to the test, the government's definition of freedom would be measured.

Two proposed appointments in 1955 tested the University's mettle. In March Council was asked to confirm the appointment of an American scholar, Sigmund Diamond, as Research Fellow in History. Nobody disputed Diamond's credentials; but one of his referees had let slip that he was 'one of the victims of McCarthyism in American academic life'. Further inquiry revealed that he had been a member of the Communist Party until 1950, though he was no longer associated with the left. The debate on Council was stormy. Two members, the Queensland Liberal Donald Cameron (appointed by the House of Representatives) and the Victorian retail mogul Sir Frank Richardson (appointed by the Governor-General) objected fiercely to the University taking on communists or ex-communists and pressed for an official security check. But other members stood firm on the principle of academic freedom, and Diamond's appointment was confirmed. Melville supported the decision but was fearful of the consequences: not without cause, since Cameron and Richardson took their case to the Acting Prime Minister, Arthur Fadden. Coombs smoothed things over and the government declined to intervene: but a few members of the University were left wondering what would happen next time. In the event, Diamond stayed in the United States, becoming in due course a professor of history and sociology at the Columbia University and a long-term editor of the *Political Science Quarterly*.

The next controversy was already brewing in the John Curtin School. Since 1953 Stephen Mason had been a Research Fellow in the Department of Medical Chemistry, where Albert considered him an outstanding success. With the department's impending move from London to Canberra, Albert proposed that he be given security by promoting him, in effect, to the position of Fellow.

There was a problem. Word had got around that Mason had been and probably still was a communist, and according to the Vice-Chancellor at Oxford University, he showed a tendency to allow his political opinions to flow into his university work. Melville and Hohnen, anticipating trouble on Council, tried to find out more. 'This is a proper concern with standards', said Hohnen, 'and not to be misinterpreted as a security check'. The evidence they gathered was conflicting. Mason's referees were uniformly supportive, pointing out that while he had once shown left-wing sympathies, he was now a conscientious scholar of unquestionable integrity. Albert was convinced that he was not and had never been a member of the Communist

Party. On the other hand he had written a book on the history of science which had provoked some controversy over what one reviewer called his 'unusually lenient views of Marxism and Soviet science'. Melville was told by 'a very responsible academic source' that there was little doubt that Mason was still a communist, and that he had recently attended at least two conferences that were communist-inspired.

Albert remained unconvinced and pressed for action; Florey warned that the University was doing itself great harm; even Ennor, who was certainly no friend to left-wingers, decided to stand firm on principle. But Melville, with Sir Frank Richardson telling him 'the risks are too great' and the government seeming to watch his every move, continued to agonise and delayed matters until a forthcoming visit to Britain, where he would be able to gather information in person.

Patrick Moran, about 1955.

It was becoming clear that Mason had enemies. Gradually it emerged who they were. His offence was not so much sympathising with communism as speaking against Catholicism during his time at Oxford, where he had fallen foul of an organisation called 'The Sword of the Spirit', whose members were dedicated to opposing anti-Catholicism. Their agent on the Board of Graduate Studies was Patrick Moran, who had resisted Mason's original appointment as a Research Fellow and who remained implacably opposed to his appointment to the permanent staff. At Oxford Moran had crossed swords with Mason at meetings of student societies, notably the Socratic Club under the presidency of C.S. Lewis, and Moran was alleged to have kept a black-list of left-wing academics who should not be appointed to the ANU. Here was Melville's 'very responsible academic source'. After visiting Oxford, the Vice-Chancellor yielded to the majority opinion that Mason's political views were above reproach, and the appointment was allowed to proceed. Albert was relieved: it was good to know that the ANU was not to be 'a McCarthy university' after all.

But the Board's decision came too late. Mason, having been told by Florey that political considerations were involved in his appointment, decided what the ANU could do with its position and accepted instead a tenured appointment at Exeter. Time showed that the University had lost heavily: Mason became an eminent physical chemist, ending his career as Professor of Chemistry at King's College, London.

The other main ingredient in the debate on academic freedom was the right of academics to express opinions that might be contrary to government policy. In 1954 Jim Davidson and Patrick FitzGerald, along with Manning Clark from the Canberra University College and Anglican Bishop Burgmann, had upset the conservative side of politics by referring to the nationalist origins of the Viet Minh movement in Vietnam and suggesting that the Australian government should think twice before following American policy in Indochina. That debate was interrupted by Menzies' dramatic announcement that a Soviet diplomat and spy, Vladimir Petrov, had defected to Australia, bringing with him evidence of systematic espionage and subversive activities.

A year later FitzGerald came under fire for attending a conference of Afro-Asian nations at Bandung in Indonesia and issuing a statement jointly with John Burton, head of External Affairs under Evatt in the previous government and a particular source of irritation to the current one. The content of their statement seemed, by later standards, completely innocuous: Australia, they said, was a part of Asia, and should be represented at such conferences. But Menzies, led on and misled by a journalist, reacted sharply, denouncing the comments as 'an impertinence of the first order' and referring caustically to 'an itch for political pronouncements in academic circles'.

FitzGerald, having made his point, might have been prepared to leave it at that; but not Davidson, who responded immediately by defending the duty of academics and other citizens to express their views, telling Menzies in effect to mind his own business, and adding for good measure a few words critical of government policy.

The issue split the University. Hugh Ennor and Ernest Titterton (who was then Acting Head of Physical Sciences) thought FitzGerald was undermining their negotiations for more money, and urged the Vice-Chancellor to take him in hand. Melville responded by calling a special meeting of the Board of Graduate Studies. Eccles framed a motion to censure Davidson and FitzGerald. Davidson, eager for battle, prepared to put 'the enemy' to rout: 'At the moment, I hope to beat Melville by frightening him', he told his friend Brian Fitzpatrick. 'That is I have said publicly that I shan't budge an inch. FitzGerald also intends to do the same.' If Melville resisted there would be a public scandal, and he would be doing himself and the University harm.

Davidson, while no doubt committed to the principle he was defending, revelled in the game. Over thirty years later Spate remembered the ensuing meeting for the most brilliant display of tactics he had ever seen. But there was no outright winner. Melville made his point that older universities such as Oxford and Cambridge were protected by centuries of tradition (not to mention large independent funds), and that what was possible there might not be so in Canberra; and he hinted that the government might withhold funds for salary increases. Davidson made *his* point that the acceptance of restrictions could lead to further restrictions. Moran said the real question was about academic responsibility, not academic freedom; and Spate warned against a heresy hunt. Most agreed that there had been errors of judgement and that Davidson had overplayed his hand. But the final resolution censured no-one, merely confirming the right of University members to freedom of expression on any matter of public interest, while urging them to take account of the University's interests. Everyone present could agree to this without having to change their opinions, so matters remained much as they were before. If nothing else, the debate demonstrated that academic freedom meant different things to different people.

PERSONAL.

MINISTER FOR EXTERNAL AFFAIRS
Parliament House,
CANBERRA. A.C.T.

20th April, 1955.

My dear Bob –

The Professorship of International Relations in the Canberra National University is vacant – by the resignation of Crocker. They have advertised the post and applications close at the end of April. I telephoned Melville today and he tells me that they have received a number of applications – largely from overseas, although a few from within Australia. He has agreed privately to let me know those that they believe are in the running. I have stressed with him the importance of qualifications other than professional.

I know you appreciate the importance of getting the right *type* of man. I think a word from you to Melville and to others concerned, would be useful.

The Rt. Hon. R.G. Menzies, C.H., Q.C., M.P.,
Prime Minister,
Parliament House,
CANBERRA. A.C.T.

Richard Casey, Minister for External Affairs, offers the Prime Minister a private word of advice regarding academic appointments.
Australian Archives.

Melville remained anxious, reminding Florey that the University would have to keep the government on side if it wanted more money: 'I am not at all happy about the way we are going about this at the moment'. Or as Sawer had wryly put it after the previous year's run-in with the government:

> ... The A.N.U. must prosper and get fat—
> Unless its Dons insist on staying thin
> By writing notes in praise of Ho Chi Minh.

Return of the native

Melville thought the University might have been spared most of these embarrassments if firm hands were in charge of the social science schools. Although administration by deans seemed to be working well enough, these arrangements had always been regarded as interim. Only directors could provide the prestige, protection and inspiration (not to mention the discipline)—in short, the leadership—that the schools appeared to need.

For a long time Copland and some other members of the Council clung to the hope that Firth would come permanently to Canberra, an impression confirmed by his frequent visits to Australia and participation in University field trips. Eventually, having decided once and for all that his heart lay in Europe, he resigned as Adviser and Acting Director of the Pacific Studies school in 1952. As there was no obvious candidate for the position of director, Nadel was then appointed Dean. Although he was widely regarded as intellectually preeminent, he was also seen as something of a martinet; and while the staff of the school might be prepared to work with him as dean, there was no way they would have him as director. After his death and an interregnum, he was succeeded by Davidson, who brought quite different qualities to the deanship. But Davidson was considered unsuitable to fill the office of director, even if he had wanted it.

Life was easier in the Social Sciences school. The (provisional) faculty, at one of its earliest meetings, discussed whether the school should have a director and decided it would be best to wait. Sawer recorded the gist of the debate in verse:

> *The (Acting) Chairman.*
>
> Let's get us a Director,
> Who'll hark to people's woes;
> Someone the Vice can hector,
> Someone to fight our foes.
>
> *The (Provisional) Faculty.*
>
> A Director? Don't be crazy;
> The bastards cost a lot,
> They're a waste of dough if lazy,
> And a menace if they're not.

Chairman.

But have you no respect
For the wishes of the Founders
Who said someone must direct
You anarchic lot of bounders? ...

Once a formal faculty structure had been set up, Sawer was appointed dean and filled the office more or less to everyone's satisfaction.

Whenever anyone spoke of a director for Social Sciences, there was a strong chance that Hancock's name would be mentioned. If Hancock was in bad odour with several members of Council, he also had strong supporters, especially Crocker and Oliphant, who tried their hardest to persuade him to join them, and the rest of the University to have him. First they put his name forward as warden of University House, and then as vice-chancellor, but neither proposal made much headway. On being told that the warden's position had been filled when he thought he was still in the running, Hancock urged his friends (through the historian John La Nauze in Melbourne) not to bother him with hypothetical approaches:

When I played cricket, there were grounds which I felt put a hoodoo on me; I was certain to make a duck there. And I have always made a duck on the Canberra ground. But then, there have always been grubbers bowled to me! It seems to me most unlikely that I shall ever bat at Canberra.

Nevertheless, some friends remained confident that he would respond to the captain's call.

Hancock at this time was writing *Country and Calling*, which was published late in 1954. Like any autobiography, the work had many objectives. One of them, inspired by his falling out with Copland and the ANU, was to set the record straight about where his loyalties lay, and to deny any suggestion that his conduct had been in some way 'un-Australian'. Wright mischievously suggested another, joking to Coombs that the book was the longest job application ever written. Whatever might have been Hancock's intentions, *Country and Calling* certainly attracted plenty of attention in Australia and, in relation to the episode on the park bench, managed to convey the impression that he had been hard done by.

Who Froze Out This Brilliant Australian?

CANBERRA LOST A BRILLIANT BRAIN

NO JOB HERE FOR THIS HISTORIAN

Copland, in Canada, damned the account as misleading, grossly unfair to the ANU and unjust to himself. But Hancock's version of events made the headlines: the craftsman had had the final say.

About the time *Country and Calling* appeared, Melville received messages from England that Hancock might now be receptive to an invitation to come to Canberra. Melville had already decided that the Social Sciences school needed Hancock as director. The University, conceded its Vice-Chancellor, had problems of standards and staffing. Somehow these managed to be resolved, but more as a result of divergent forces than through conscious policy. Hancock, he thought, could change this in the Social Sciences school through guidance and persuasion. Casey, writing to Hancock, gave another reason: 'Although there are a number of good people there, there are a number of others who create considerable apprehension in my mind. I know that Melville is quite aware of this—and it is no doubt for this reason that he is making efforts to get you.'

Now, given the hint that Hancock might be willing, Melville wanted to make an offer without delay. But some members of Council had long memories and were not at all charmed by *Country and Calling*, Wilson going so far as to describe the relevant passages as unwise, mischievous and childish. To counter the expected opposition, Melville prepared a long and confidential memorandum which set out what he knew of the University's relationship with Hancock and suggested that he would no longer give the University trouble. His case was balanced and perceptive, although Florey, fulminating in Oxford, said it read like 'an eminent headmaster dealing with a sixth form boy who has developed surprisingly well during the last few years'. But it did the trick: after a stormy meeting, Council approved the match and Melville posted an offer the next day.

Hancock was delighted to receive it; but it was not within him to give a quick response. Rather there followed a long period of agonising over whether people in the University still wanted him, whether his own research and writing would suffer, whether the University was genuinely free of government interference, and above all whether his wife, who was still susceptible to depression, would be able to cope. At his request, Melville flew to London at the end of 1955 and, over four days extending into the new year, the two men approached the question from every conceivable angle. Towards the end of February a letter of acceptance was in the post. But before it had time to reach Australia, he got cold feet and sent a cable to Melville asking him to put his acceptance on hold. He had received new evidence, relating to a case at the University of Technology (now the University of New South Wales) in Sydney, that McCarthyism might be rife in Australia, and he wanted to be reassured about the outcome of the Mason case. Also Theaden, who had lately suffered a relapse, was now recovered enough to discuss the decision. Several cables passed between Canberra and London before he was satisfied there was nothing sinister in the Mason affair and felt he could safely cable Melville 'Ready if you are ...'. 'I'm hired', he wrote exuberantly to Florey. The decision, once made, came as an enormous relief.

And not just to Hancock. John La Nauze told Melville that he 'must have been caused almost as much trouble over the negotiations with a single person as with the whole Medical School'. As we will shortly discover, that was not quite true; but certainly the protracted negotiations with Hancock suggested how much the University, through its Vice-Chancellor, was prepared to invest in the potential contribution of an individual scholar, and how much weight it assigned to academic leadership. Hancock might not have been seen as representing the social sciences' salvation (though Oliphant and some of the natural scientists saw him as nothing less than a saviour) but he was universally seen as showing the way ahead.

Melville deserved congratulations and he got them. The *Sydney Morning Herald* announced the decision in an article headed 'The return of the native' (which Hancock liked and used to describe his homecoming in a later book), and reported that 'Mr Melville has succeeded where Sir Douglas Copland failed'. And within the University there was a widespread sense of elation. When the Vice-Chancellor announced the appointment to a meeting of the Research School of Social Sciences, everyone stood and burst into spontaneous applause—everyone, that is, except Noel Butlin who, having looked to America rather than England for inspiration, didn't know much about Hancock, hadn't liked the little of his work he had read, and didn't know what all the fuss was about. Yet Butlin's abstention did not detract from what was for Melville a rare moment of popularity and triumph.

Melville achieved another coup in 1960 when he recruited J.G. Crawford, by now Sir John Crawford, to head the Research School of Pacific Studies, as Professor of Economics. Aged 50, Crawford was one of Australia's best-known and highly esteemed economists, enjoying the respect of both sides of politics. Educated in Sydney, he had taught rural economics at the University of Sydney from 1934 to 1941, before joining the Commonwealth public service, where he rose to prominence, alongside Coombs, as one of Arthur Fadden's 'seven dwarfs'. As Director of Research in the Department of Post-War Reconstruction, he had participated in discussions about the ANU when the original legislation was being drafted; then, as head of the Bureau of Agricultural Economics, he had attended the Easter conferences in 1948. At the time of his appointment to the ANU he had reached what he regarded as the pinnacle of his public service career as Secretary of the Department of Trade. Now he required, as he later put it, 'new fields to conquer'.

Had Eggleston been alive, he would have rejoiced at the appointment. Crawford was his kind of academic, someone who believed that scholars should help understand and overcome the urgent problems confronting the world. He was well acquainted with the Pacific region, especially Japan, and had wide contacts among academics and practising economists in other Commonwealth countries and the United States. As a bonus, his close relations with government promised to serve the University well. With Crawford in charge of Pacific Studies and Hancock of Social Sciences, the futures of both schools seemed assured.

Hancock at the crease

'I am grooming myself as a Father figure', Hancock told Florey shortly after his arrival in Canberra in March 1957. Soon he was hard at work pulling his 'rabble' into shape, applying himself with an intellectual and physical energy that belied his 59 years. In his own department, he encouraged (by what means nobody ever knew) Laurie Fitzhardinge, who had a reputation for what he called 'frittering, pottering and gadding', to get a move on with his biography of Billy Hughes: the first volume, *That Fiery Particle*, covering Hughes's life to 1914, was published in 1964 to widespread acclaim. Aware of Manning Clark's sensitivities, he brought together the historians in the University and the College into what he called 'The History Consortium'. Contemptuous of parochialism in historical research, he appointed Anthony Low to open up the field of South Asian history: the result was a series of lively seminars, known as the 'Sepoy seminar', and a steady flow of publications. He wanted to do the same for the Americas, but Melville said no.

Sir Keith Hancock bowls the first ball at the opening of the University's 'No. 1 Oval', 30 November 1962.

One of his main aims was to get people from different disciplines talking to one another. He achieved this through what became known as 'The Wool Seminar', which was one of the first major multidisciplinary undertakings in the University. Every fortnight during term for three years people met to talk about the development of the wool industry in Australia. About half came from the social sciences and half from the natural sciences, including a significant representation from CSIRO. The eventual outcome was a book of essays, edited by Alan Barnard in the Department of Economic History, entitled *The Simple Fleece*. Hancock encouraged Ann Mozley (later Moyal) to talk to people in the Academy of Science: she did, and became in due course a pioneering historian of Australian science.

Aside from his own publications, his greatest achievement at the ANU was the foundation of the *Australian Dictionary of Biography*. The idea for such an enterprise was not new: Percival Serle had published a two-volume dictionary in 1949, and there were many overseas models. Fitzhardinge was already compiling a card index of names, with brief biographical details, which he saw as laying the foundations for a future dictionary on a grand scale. Hancock took up the idea as a project immensely valuable in itself and appropriate to the University's national status. With Ross Hohnen's help, he convinced the University to fund it, and at a conference he convened soon after his arrival, he persuaded historians throughout Australia to support it. Before long working parties in every state were nominating people for inclusion, and in 1962 Douglas Pike, who held the chair of History at the University of Tasmania, was appointed foundation General Editor. The first volume, published in 1966, was enthusiastically received.

In relations with students, whether in his own department or others, Hancock was a great encourager, always stimulating, always concerned. His comments in seminars were searching, demanding, constructive. He drove himself, and others followed his example. Often he could be seen with a 'pupil' or staff member pacing backwards and forwards on the lawns in front of the old hospital building, a substitute perhaps for the Great Quadrangle at All Souls. When occasion demanded it, he took a turn around the racecourse, then situated in the valley west of Acton ridge and now immersed beneath the lake. He nurtured a genuine community of scholars, many of whom later found themselves in senior academic positions throughout Australia, where they applied the Hancock brand of intellectual rigour to their own teaching and research.

With a puckish, self-deprecating sense of humour, he sought to bridge the gulf between Oxford (or more recently, London) and Canberra. Cricket offered metaphors for communication with people high and low. Late in 1958, as the cricket season was getting under way, he wrote jovially to the Prime Minister, a famous cricket-lover, proposing the formation of a Department of the History of the Art of Cricket, with Jack Fingleton, former test batsman and journalist, as professor and Menzies and Hancock as readers. 'The expense will be enormous, since all three members of staff will be expected to pursue continuous field work in the Australian States, the English Counties, the South African Provinces, the West Indian Islands and elsewhere.' The Prime Minister responded with equal good humour, rebuking Hancock for listing as recreations in Who's Who 'swimming, walking, fishing' where he himself had proudly proclaimed a commitment to 'watching first-class cricket'. Menzies later arranged Hancock's elevation to the rank of KBE.

Douglas Pike, foundation General Editor of the *Australian Dictionary of Biography*, with volume 4, published in 1972. Photograph by Gabe Carpay, 1973.

One day in the early 1960s Bill Gammage, one of Manning Clark's bright young history students, was having a hit at the University nets with several other undergraduates when Hancock, in company with a new lecturer in Clark's department, Bruce Kent, strolled across the oval towards them. Instead of pausing at a respectful distance to watch the play, Hancock walked up to Gammage and took the bat from him, saying 'Here, let me show you how it's done'. 'Who's this old coot?' thought Gammage. Hancock then proceeded to face half a dozen balls, calling each one in his pukka (to Australian standards) English accent, 'york-er!' (with an upward inflection), or such as the ball demanded. Gammage and his mates decided that the 'old coot' knew his cricket. Despite Hancock's earlier predictions, there could be no doubt that he had come to bat in Canberra, and that he was captain of the team.

Hancock was at his best when everybody played the game as it should be played. He believed that the university world, in Canberra as well as Oxford and London, was indeed a community of scholars, inhabited by 'chaps' who shared a commitment to learning. Although in London he had warned Adrien Albert against the risks of appointing a communist to his department, he now learned from Gollan, for whom he had great affection and respect, that a communist could be a competent and trustworthy academic colleague.

'Chapdom', said Clark, was Hancock's 'great delusion'. He believed that if the circumstances of a particular issue were fully and honestly presented to intelligent people, then reason would prevail. He failed to realise until it was too late that not everybody reasoned as he did. There were 'wreckers' in the academy, most of whom were 'careerists, pedants or idiots'.

Malcolm Ellis was a wrecker from outside the academy, which was part of his problem. A journalist by profession, he had written lively and acclaimed biographies of three leading figures in the early history of New South Wales: Governor Lachlan Macquarie, the ex-convict architect Francis Greenway and the pastoralist and entrepreneur John Macarthur. He was widely acknowledged (and he regarded himself) as an expert on sources in the Mitchell Library. It was therefore reasonable that Hancock should approach him to be a member of the national committee to set up the proposed dictionary of biography.

Everybody who knew anything of Ellis warned Hancock to stay clear of him. As well as being an extreme individualist, he was prominent as a Cold War warrior, ready to rush into battle at the least provocation. When he realised that he would be sharing the limelight with Manning Clark, whom he regarded as an emissary of Stalin, he attacked him personally and seemed about to sabotage the whole project. There were heated arguments, generally in the form of Ellis versus the rest, about the choice of publisher and who was to do what. Hancock tried to save the situation and Ellis, after 'resigning' no fewer than six times, eventually withdrew, publicly denouncing the project as 'an amateur effort'. The dictionary survived the turmoil, but it was a close run thing. 'I judge myself severely for the immense mistakes I made with Ellis', Hancock later confided to Ann Mozley, the Research Fellow who kept the project going while the battle raged. '... and I have little excuse, for I had made similar mistakes a little earlier in my dealings with a similar person: too much optimism and tolerance at the beginning leading to head-on conflict at the end.'

Malcolm Ellis in the 1950s.
Harper Collins Publishers and the State Library of New South Wales.

The 'similar person' was Lord Lindsay. When Hancock arrived in Canberra, he found Lindsay agitated about the impending appointment of Martin Wight as Professor of International Relations. Assuming that he was troubled about how Wight would regard the type of research he was undertaking, Hancock encouraged him to write to Wight setting out his concerns. Lindsay took the advice and wrote the letter which convinced Wight that he would do better to remain in London.

By this time, Hancock had concluded that Lindsay was mentally unbalanced and that he considered the chair his by right. Hancock was equally certain that he was neither qualified for the chair nor entitled to it. As Lindsay spread his grievances far and wide, Hancock determined to save him from himself. 'If I were not so sorry for Lindsay', he told Wight, 'I should enjoy the whole affair as a little and quite amusing comedy'. When Lindsay demanded a full inquiry, Hancock discouraged him, suggesting that everything would turn out for the best if he played by the rules. But Lindsay became increasingly testy, especially after Hancock arranged for International Relations to be subsumed under Political Science in his own school and postponed further consideration of the chair. Eventually Hancock agreed to investigate his grievances, but it was too late.

By mid-1959 the case was being reported at length in the press and beamed to every household with a television receiver. Lindsay now announced that he had accepted the offer of a full chair by the American University in Washington, which seemed to confirm that the ANU had made a bad mistake. Before he left in September, he delivered the University a parting insult in the form of a cheque for one penny, which he deemed sufficient compensation for his not giving the standard six months' notice of impending resignation. The University duly banked it and hoped the saga was at an end.

But Lindsay continued to agitate from abroad. Two years later a draft of a book arrived from Washington, entitled 'A study of academic standards', which detailed the ways in which he thought he had been unjustly treated and argued that the ANU was destined to become a second-rate institution. The University might have chosen to ignore the draft had it not been for the Orr case in Tasmania a few years earlier (involving the dismissal of a professor of philosophy for improper conduct towards a female student), which showed how much trouble a university could get into if it failed to follow correct procedures. So Council set up a committee of seven chaired by Coombs to enquire into the case. Two of its members, Gollan and Swan, drafted a 50-page report which analysed Lindsay's charges, leaned wherever they could in his favour, but concluded that no significant injustice had been done.

Then, to make absolutely sure it was on safe ground, Council asked John Anderson, recently retired as Professor of Philosophy at Sydney University, to go over the committee's work as an independent adviser. Suggested by Swan, this was a brilliant stratagem, as Anderson was famous as a champion of the underdog and of liberty. His conclusion was emphatic: there was no charge for the ANU to answer. In fact, wrote Anderson, the University had been *too* conciliatory towards Lindsay, and 'it would be unworthy of the University to yield another inch to his pressure tactics'.

Lord Lindsay, about 1955.
Australian News and Information Bureau, ANU Collection.

Lindsay would have presented a formidable challenge to the most capable administrator. Whether in relation to Mao's China or the University administration, he knew no shades of grey. Nevertheless, Hancock had exacerbated the problem, first by encouraging him, and then by refusing to enquire into his grievances. Overall he gave the impression of inconsistency: it was little wonder that Lindsay christened him 'Sir Fox', or that Coombs and Anderson blamed him in part for Wight's withdrawal. After a great deal of anguish and effort, the University's reputation was saved. J.D.B. Miller was appointed to the vacant chair, and under his guidance International Relations became a department of distinction. Lindsay failed to find a publisher for his book and his case receded in the corporate memory, though it served as a reminder, when comparable cases arose in later years, of how an individual could undermine the orderly procedures of academic life.

Hancock regarded the Lindsay problem as part of larger troubles with the Research School of Pacific Studies, whose existence had been an irritant ever since Copland and the Interim Council had refused his offer to act initially as director of both schools. When he arrived in Canberra he found that the two schools were linked by joint faculty meetings. Within a few weeks he decided that his 'rabble' had become a 'band of brothers', and that the 'Pacificos' were the rabble. He therefore abruptly severed the connection, in a manner he later had cause to regret; though he described the act of separation as 'in every way liberating'.

The schools remained linked by physical proximity in the old hospital building

Architect's model of Coombs Building, about 1961. Three more sides were added later, at the rear, to constitute a third hexagon.

which, by the end of the decade, had become uncomfortably crowded. A new building was in prospect: but planning was complicated by the need to satisfy both schools, including their respective Director and Dean. In order to obtain 'a design of distinction', the University approached several architects. The specifications required rooms where users could enjoy 'scholarly seclusion' and places where they could discuss their problems with colleagues or hold small classes. 'At all cost the feeling of traversing interminable corridors should be avoided …' The architects were provided with exact details of the sizes of rooms for every category of staff, from professors to secretaries, and the numbers of each type of room required by each department. If the academic structure of the schools was not already fixed in concrete, these specifications ensured that they soon would be.

In assessing the designs, the selectors were to consider 'convenience, economy and delight' (a phrase which could only have come from Hancock). Davidson, a noted aesthete, had no doubts about what he wanted. His friend Roy Grounds sketched a series of buildings which reflected (literally, in a lagoon) an Asian-Pacific theme. Hancock favoured a design by Mockridge, Stahle and Mitchell based on three hexagons connected by covered ways. At first it seemed that Davidson had won the day; but Hancock, who could be ruthless when he wanted to be, undermined his case at a Council meeting and got the hexagonal plan accepted. Economy, though, was the final victor: as the plan proved to be too expensive, the architects introduced major changes, including joining the hexagon together like Siamese triplets, reducing the size of the stair halls, situating rooms on both sides of the corridors and making the corridors narrower. Later visitors, disorientated by enclosed corridors which changed direction every twenty or so metres, might well have wondered if the corridors were indeed interminable.

The first two hexagons were opened in 1962 and named after Coombs, a departure from the previous policy of naming buildings only after the deceased. Coombs was uncomfortable about the honour, but thought it would be churlish not to accept. It was, of course, quite appropriate that the person who had done more than anybody else to bring the schools into being should be honoured by having the building named after him. On the other hand, as he later implied, the H.C. Coombs Building, with its many small rooms facing outwards towards lawns and shrubbery, contradicted the original conception of the schools. 'Scholarly seclusion' was far removed from the university of the post-war reconstructionists, as far removed, in fact, as Oxford. The building for Social Sciences and Pacific Studies may have carried Coombs's name, but it was Hancock's building.

By the time of the opening, Hancock had also imposed much of his personality on his own school. He liked to see it as having evolved from the 'growing points' he had talked about in 1948. In fact, for most of the 1950s the departments had simply grown, without significant reference to his earlier ideas. But his coming imposed on the school a sort of retrospective coherence and gave the impression that it was now as he and others had always intended it to be.

After the death of his wife from cancer in 1960, Hancock handed over the office of Director to P.H. Partridge. He remained Professor of History until 1965, when on retirement he was created the first University Fellow. Although his time at the crease was shorter than most people expected, it was an impressive innings, distinguished by some powerful straight drives and elegant glances: but he never did learn to play the googlies.

Florey's decision

Administrative arrangements in the John Curtin School continued as they had been from 1953, with Ennor as Dean and Florey as Adviser, though Florey was often regarded and sometimes described as 'de facto absentee director'. So long as the two men remained on friendly terms and retained confidence in one another, the system worked well enough. They corresponded frequently, sometimes two or three times a week, Ennor addressing Florey deferentially as 'Dear Sir Howard', and Florey responding in a paternal, occasionally admonitory tone, 'My dear Ennor'. They also shouted at one another by means of Emidicta cylinders, a precursor to tape recordings, which allowed Florey in particular to let off the powerful head of steam he built up in his study at Oxford whenever he thought about the ANU.

Many people in the University still hoped that one day Florey would come to Canberra permanently to lead the school he had founded. He was the obvious director, and nobody else in Britain or Australia seemed an appropriate substitute. Better to have Florey as 'Potential Director' than someone inferior as the real thing. Within the school he was a source of inspiration and guidance; outside the University, his name could be invoked to command respect. Yet his status was ambiguous: while the University's decision-makers were keen to cite him as Adviser, they did not invariably heed his advice, partly because they realised, in Copland's words, that it was impossible to administer the medical school from Oxford, but also because his advice often seemed wide of the mark.

Florey remained torn. He felt the pull of his own country and a desire to contribute to its scientific development, and perhaps he looked forward to being fêted as a favourite son. Yet Oxford had been good to him; and he enjoyed his place as a respected and influential member of the British scientific establishment. As for the John Curtin School, he was eager to nurture his creation and he felt a responsibility, if not to the University, then at least to the people he had encouraged to go there. On the other hand, he wanted to break with what he once described as 'Florey's Folly'. As Copland shrewdly perceived, he wanted a distinctive monument to his own enterprise, and this made him suspicious of change. All this was complicated by domestic concerns quite different from but almost as powerful as those which sustained Hancock's indecision.

This inner turmoil led to a barrage of complaints, most fired privately to Ennor and Oliphant: about architects who couldn't design and builders who wouldn't get on and build; about interfering politicians; about a University Council which had no understanding of the needs of medical scientists; about vice-chancellors who would not do what they were supposed to do; about social scientists who were not worth a crumpet; and above all, about narrow-minded administrators, who should have been there, unseen, to do the scientists' bidding but who were constantly getting in the way. His outlook improved each time he came to visit Canberra; but then distance, Oxford gossip and disheartened letters from Canberra helped keep his wrath warm. At times he seemed to be itching for a brawl: after detecting in Melville 'a slight resistance' to his visiting Canberra in 1954, he told Oliphant to let him know if the Vice-Chancellor wanted to sack him 'so that I can give him a damn good excuse to do so'.

In late 1955 Florey finally decided that he had had enough and submitted his resignation as Adviser, offering the formal reason that he could no longer shoulder the burden of running a large department in Oxford while taking a close interest in the ANU. This was no doubt true, although it was equally true that he had come to recognise that he could no longer do what he had originally set out to do. For the benefit of his friends, he gave a subsidiary reason: that the institution had lost its way.

According to the experimental pathologist George Mackaness, a member of Council, this news had 'a horrifying effect' on councillors, who regarded it as the biggest blow the University had ever sustained. Melville, genuinely dismayed, urged Florey to set out 'with the greatest frankness' his concerns about the University. Florey accepted the challenge and, encouraged by Oliphant and Ennor, set about preparing a long memorandum which amounted to a forthright and sometimes angry criticism of how he had been treated and how the University was going about its business. His own school, he claimed, had achieved the highest standards of research. The University, however, had sunk into an administrative morass. Some of his complaints were specific: the failure to retain the services of his protégé Bunker, the laboratory manager whom he regarded as crucial in building the school; the cumbersome stores system (part of the Auditor-General's legacy); Copland's attitude that departments were 'like sausage machines, spewing out graduates in a steady stream'. Then there was the problem of 'political and civil service considerations' influencing University appointments, by which he meant Melville's appointment and the case of Stephen Mason, which was a subject of high table gossip just as Florey was preparing his brief. In a separate memorandum intended for the Prime Minister, he recommended that the Council be restructured to get rid of the public service influence, and that the University be reorganised to give the research schools more or less complete autonomy.

All this was delivered with the attitude he expressed to Ennor: 'I don't care whether I am right or wrong'. He told Hancock that he was letting people in Canberra know that he did not want to be worried any more about the ANU after December 31st 1955, midnight!

Melville had got more than he had bargained for. But Florey achieved less than he had intended, partly because his document included errors that were obvious to people on the spot; partly because it dealt unfairly with matters that were patently trivial; but mostly because Melville was able to show that he was asking for things which were inconsistent, such as a rapidly expanding budget but no government influence, and a move towards autonomous research institutes while retaining the freedoms normally associated only with universities.

Wright concluded that there was a campaign on Council to demonstrate that the document was inaccurate. But a campaign was hardly necessary. When Oliphant told Florey that he might have got the Bunker story wrong, he responded, 'I am really not in a position to judge', without seeming to realise that this admission could have been applied to the whole document.

Accuracy aside, the report might have done the University considerable harm had anyone leaked it to the press. Although Wright and Oliphant tried to keep it on Council's agenda, it was effectively suppressed until a Director of the John Curtin School resurrected and made use of it for his own purposes some 25 years later.

When it became clear that Florey was intent on going, the members of the school started thinking about what life would be like without him. The four professors, along with Mackaness, decided that the school should develop along the lines set down by Florey, with some minor recasting in relation to Experimental Pathology. After pondering briefly whether they should look for a director, they decided to continue with Ennor as Dean; and on Melville's suggestion, the meeting of heads of departments was formally constituted into what was called the School Committee.

Before this committee had a chance to meet, Florey dropped a hint that he might yet be willing to come as Director. This was less than nine months after he had submitted his damning report. What could have caused this sudden change of heart? Had he never really lost the desire to come? Did preparing the report purge him of his irritations? Or was he influenced, as Wright suggested, by a letter from the relevant authorities in Oxford notifying him that his house was to be demolished to make way for a highway? Whatever the reasons, he seemed keener to come than at any time since those early discussions with Wright and Conlon. And despite some feeling about his memorandum, Melville and his colleagues were keen to have him, especially since Menzies expressed delight at the prospect and promised to support a substantial development of the school.

Inevitably there were complications. In order to maintain his research momentum, Florey expected to bring with him a small team from the Dunn School. The University and the government were agreeable, but Florey's colleagues turned out to be not as enthusiastic as he was about coming to Australia. He therefore suggested that he should come as Acting Director on a trial basis, along with those of his team who wished to accompany him. From the University's point of view, this was a far less appealing proposition, as the increased government funding was conditional on his coming as permanent Director. Several members of Council and the school began to

Florey's building about the time of its completion in 1957. The old hospital buildings are to the left and the Physical Sciences buildings to the right. Part of the racecourse, later to be submerged by Lake Burley Griffin, is visible top right.

have second thoughts. Eccles stated bluntly that Florey had 'ratted' on his previous proposal, and that the school could not put up with another year of uncertainty. Ennor suggested that he simply could not make up his mind whether or not to come, and that he would be in no better position to do so after twelve months as Acting Director. Behind these views lay the assumption that the school had now established its own strong credentials, and so did not need Florey as it had done in the past.

Council decided to put an end to Florey's indecision. It concluded that he should be offered once again the position of Director, and that if he said no, he and his team should be invited to visit Australia for a year, with the ANU paying most of the costs. But the position would not be left open for him: on the offer of the directorship, Council wanted 'an immediate decision'. Ennor, as Dean, was sent to Oxford with instructions to explain to Florey why Council could not leave the position open indefinitely and to urge him to make up his mind about a long-term commitment.

Ennor's visit to Oxford became a talking point at the Lamb & Flag, the pub just down the road from the Dunn School, for many months afterwards. In delivering Council's message, he managed over several days to give Florey the impression that he and his team were definitely not wanted. He allowed Florey no room for manoeuvre and made it clear that, if he came, he would not be allowed to interfere in the management of the school. In pub chat with other members of the Dunn School, he let slip that the great man was wanted only as a figurehead and a source of funds, and inferred that he was scientifically finished. All this was reported back to Florey, word for word. Henry Harris, another Australian in the Dunn School who, until now, had intended to come to Canberra as part of the team, suspected that Ennor wanted the director's position for himself. That might not have been true, though it is likely that he was keen to retain the deanship, and that his fellow professors in the John Curtin School were happy to leave things as they were.

Whatever his private intentions, Ennor had handled the negotiations badly. Although he was a capable administrator, he had a tendency, as Coombs put it, to rush fences, and his loud and self-important manner was the last thing Florey needed during a period of personal anguish. On the other hand, if not in the spirit, at least in the substance, Ennor had followed Council's instructions. And for his part, Florey had tested the patience of Council and the John Curtin School once too often. He had also given Ennor rough treatment, failing to recognise that he could no longer be regarded as 'Temporary Assistant Director'. Ennor, he told Wright, was like a faithful watchdog that had turned on its master. Perhaps he should have realised long before that Ennor had outgrown watchdog status.

Henry Harris told Wright that he had never seen Florey more desperate or upset. Oliphant, who was visiting Oxford at the time, noticed tears in Florey's eyes and said he himself could have murdered Ennor. Florey, after his initial feeling of rejection, was angry, complaining to Wright that Ennor's 'knowledge of medicine is nil & his ideas on the future of J.C.S. left me aghast because of their inadequacy'.

On his return to Canberra, Ennor reported to Council that the discussions had been conducted on the most friendly basis, and that he had made various offers to Florey, none of which proved workable. Prompted by Titterton, he conceded that the school had doubts about Florey's coming: 'Nobody wants someone who cannot make up his mind'. Coombs, reading between the lines of Ennor's blow by blow report, concluded that it was a distressing story. But Ennor had at least forced the issue, and there was now no prospect that Florey would ever come as Director.

Nevertheless, his influence on the ANU and the medical school persisted long after this altercation. Relieved of his uncertainty, he came to view the school more benignly and continued to offer advice as it was sought. A year after the final breach he visited

Lord Florey, 'Honorary Doctor of Bush Week', at the time of his installation as Chancellor, July 1966.

Canberra to open the building for the John Curtin School, where he expressed appreciation of the roles played by various people, including Ennor and (with more enthusiasm) Bunker. On that occasion he delivered an exhortation to excellence that was repeated often in later years: the John Curtin School 'need not only to be good but it must be superlatively good'. In 1965 his election to the office of Chancellor served as due recognition of his role in the early years of the University and the school, as well as a balm to heal past wounds entirely. Even after his death in 1968 he remained a sort of posthumous patron, whose name could be invoked when the interests of the school or the University were under threat.

His influence could also be seen in the shape and culture of the John Curtin School. The departmental structure which he had set out in the late 1940s proved as sturdy as the building he had helped design; and largely as a result of his own ideas about the role of directors and heads of departments, and his own prolonged indecision, the departments emerged as he had warned that they would: as 'independent little kingdoms', resistant to change and jealous of their own autonomy. The structure he built sustained conservatism; and as a result, John Curtin remained Florey's school for many years to come.

Two cultures?

'I repudiate the much publicised theory of The Two Cultures', wrote Hancock in 1976: no university which accepted that notion was worthy of its name. Oliphant shared this opinion, telling an audience at the University of Melbourne in 1970 that the natural scientist and the social scientist should work together, each drawing strength from the other.

The idea that members of these two groups held opposing world views was centuries old. In the late 1950s it was given new currency by the English physicist and novelist C.P. Snow, who coined the term 'Two Cultures' to describe what he called the 'gulf of mutual incomprehension' between literary intellectuals and scientists, especially physical scientists. 'They have a curious distorted view of one another', Snow told an audience at Cambridge. 'Their attitudes are so different that, even on the level of emotion, they can't find much common ground.'

The ANU had been conceived as one university with one culture. Coombs, Wright, Conlon and their colleagues had expected that it would be bound together by the single purpose of serving national needs. The Academic Advisory Committee had expected that natural and social scientists would meet freely to exchange ideas and draw insights from each other's research, just as they did (or were supposed to do) in the senior common rooms at Oxbridge. Firth, at the Easter 1948 conferences, imagined the two social science schools linked to the medical research school by a covered way, along which medical men would come to collect maps and talk with the social scientists. Oliphant, expressing the supreme confidence of post-war science, declared that physics, as 'the most highly developed of all the sciences', could help bring order to 'the less highly

Sir Mark Oliphant in 1959, the year he was created KBE. The artist, Noel Counihan, captures the confident image of post-war Science.

organised sciences'. Florey thought the medical school would benefit through association with the other schools as part of an intellectual community.

Nevertheless, from the outset there was a tacit understanding that the natural and social scientists had different interests, which had to be balanced, on Council for example, or in the selection of vice-chancellors, so that neither group was seen to have the upper hand. There were irritations; and within a few years these had grown to an extent that Florey, in his caustic report to the Council, could point to a deep schism which threatened academic life in the new institution.

Although distance, as usual, magnified the problem, it was certainly there, especially among Florey's chief informants, Oliphant and Ennor. Oliphant himself personified the 'scientific culture' as depicted by Snow, his old friend from Cavendish days: 'expansive, not restrictive, confident at the roots ..., certain that history is on its side, impatient, intolerant, creative rather than critical, good-natured and brash'. And if Snow wanted extra evidence to support this side of his proposition, he need only have listened to Oliphant railing about the unbelievable irresponsibility and immaturity of many (not all) of the social scientists and lamenting his own sense of isolation:

> Outside my own School I find that I cannot even communicate with colleagues other than Eccles and Ennor (Fenner is just not interested in anything but his work), Trendall & Stanner. All others live in a strange world in which I have no part & with which I can find no point of contact.

Best therefore to keep them at a distance: when it was suggested that some social scientists might move into the new medical building, Oliphant warned Florey against it 'unless you have the most complete safeguards & the power to throw them out at any moment, without notice'. On the other side of Snow's dichotomy, the social scientists were not defensive or hostile, as Snow would have them, though occasionally they seemed faintly contemptuous of their scientific colleagues and sceptical of their naivety.

Part of the problem was money. At the time when the government was urging restraint, the natural scientists in particular tended to see 'the Schools on the hill' as competitors. What was worse, the behaviour of some social scientists—Davidson and FitzGerald in particular—was seen as turning the government against the University as a whole and standing in the way of additional funding. Ennor sought to compensate by forming close associations with Menzies and other ministers (a task which he found congenial) and persuading them that the University was not full of reds. But many of the natural scientists remained fearful of guilt by association.

The natural sciences, said Florey, were different: their ultimate authority was the experiment, and this clearly distinguished them from other disciplines. Too few people at the ANU, he argued, understood the outlook of scientific researchers or the means of achieving results. And the natural sciences were being burdened with administrative arrangements which might have worked for the social sciences, but which were quite inappropriate for experimental research. 'The Natural Scientist', he declared, 'is usually loath to spend his time on University matters not directly concerned with research.

When he does have to give up time, better spent in research, he becomes irritated.'

Oliphant came close to proposing that the natural science schools secede and set themselves up as independent research institutes. Yet he was reluctant to forgo the association with a university or to surrender the traditional advantages of being part of an academic community. He told Hancock: 'we are a collection of technicians without the guidance of or the atmosphere created by the true humanities in a full university'. That was Oliphant's dilemma: he recognised that the University was dependent on the social scientists to be worthy of its name; but at the same time, he thought the behaviour of the social scientists was dragging the ANU down.

That was why Hancock had so much to offer. Appalled by the stories he was hearing from Oliphant and Florey, Hancock thought he could heal the 'accursed feud' between the two cultures; and in his short period as Director of Research School of Social Sciences he helped bring the two sides of the University closer than they had been since research work had begun in the early 1950s. Part of his contribution was to identify areas of interest to natural and social scientists alike, especially through the Wool Seminar. But equally significant was his capacity to reassure the natural scientists that representatives of 'the literary culture' could comprehend and appreciate their endeavours, and to demonstrate to the University as a whole that they could work in common pursuit of knowledge and understanding. In Oliphant's terms, Hancock's leadership helped give the University a soul.

6 The College

'A University College for pass men'

As the first staff of the new University arrived to take up their appointments in 1950, Canberra University College was entering its third decade. The first two had been less than glorious. Despite the optimistic predictions of Sir Robert Garran and other members of the University Association, the College had to struggle from the outset. The timing of its birth had been unlucky: the modest budget of £3000 which provided for the appointment of the first staff scraped through Cabinet just a few weeks before Wall Street collapsed, and the ordinance which brought it into being was passed not long after the crash. Within two years the annual grant had been chopped in half, threatening its very survival. When the three full-time staff members had their appointments renewed for three years in 1934, they were warned that 'if, during that period, the College ceases to exist, the engagement shall thereupon terminate'.

The College continued to exist because it was there, and because it met the needs of public servants based in Canberra who would otherwise have no satisfactory way of completing or improving their qualifications. Student enrolments started out at 34 in 1930 (though rather more attended lectures) and had grown to 163 by 1939, when the war put a halt to further increases. Most were public servants, and all were part-timers. They attended lectures dutifully, if often sleepily, between 5.00 and 9.00 pm, wherever the College was situated at the time: Telopea Park School and the Physics Laboratory at the Royal Military College, the Institute of Anatomy, the Hotel Acton, and then from 1948 in the Melbourne Building in the centre of Civic, none of which ever resembled a permanent home.

The staff too were mostly part-timers, drawn from the local population. They included some distinguished names: Laurie Fitzhardinge (who taught Ancient History), the Acting Commonwealth Statistician L.F. Giblin (Public Administration and Finance), and the Commonwealth Crown Solicitor H.F.E. Whitlam (Commercial Law), whose son Edward Gough appeared on the College's books as a scholarship holder, though he was never actually enrolled for courses in Canberra. The pillars of the College were two full-time lecturers, J.F.M. Haydon (French and German) and L.H. Allen (English and Latin), whose joint contribution is remembered in the Haydon-Allen Building on the ANU campus.

The students enrolled for a range of courses in Arts, Commerce, Law and (infrequently) Science, including traditional university subjects along with courses directed towards the needs of public servants. Many found the going tough, and failure rates were high. English A was notoriously demanding: of the six students enrolled in 1935, three sat for the examination and only one passed (in a supplementary). Economics I, the most popular subject in that year, had seventeen enrolments and seven examinees, of whom only three passed.

Students who managed to pass the requisite number of courses were awarded degrees or diplomas of the University of Melbourne. While the College had in most respects an independent existence, the ordinance which created it required that its courses be recognised by either of the well-established institutions in Sydney and Melbourne. The College Council opted for Melbourne, whose requirements for attendance at lectures in certain courses were less rigid than those of Sydney. Melbourne responded by passing a temporary regulation which recognised College courses for the purposes of examination. In return, the University received a fee of one guinea for each student examined in a particular subject. The regulation was approved initially for three years; then the College requested an extension for five, and was grudgingly granted two, followed next time by five.

Neither institution found this arrangement very satisfactory. The College, aware that it could not survive on its own, was never certain how long Melbourne's grace and favour would last; and Melbourne sometimes doubted that its grace and favour were deserved. Technically, the University of Melbourne reserved the right to vet all teaching appointments, and each faculty was entitled to visit the College and investigate the courses it had approved. But in practice the College was left to develop with minimal supervision, a notable exception being when one College lecturer was himself required to take the first year practical examination for the course he taught.

Pillars of Canberra University College during the 1930s and 1940s, L.H. Allen and J.F.M. Haydon, photographed in the early 1950s.

In 1940, faced with a request for yet another extension, the relevant professors in Melbourne put their heads together and concluded that the courses were of mixed quality. The professor of French thought Haydon's students were doing outstanding work. The professor of Mathematics considered that work in his subject was mediocre, and that the lecturers were leaning too heavily on his department for help. The professor of English drew a general lesson (that might have been relevant in later decades) that 'any Subordinate College is bound in time to become a nuisance to its Parent'. Overall, the professors decided that it would be unwise to convert the temporary regulation to anything more permanent; but they were reluctant to force the College onto its own resources.

Again the regulation was extended, this time until the end of the year following the end of the war, on the understanding that both parties would seek closer cooperation. This was in fact achieved, with better reporting by the College and more frequent liaison with the departments in Melbourne; so that when Garran begged for a further extension in 1947, Melbourne's Vice-Chancellor, J.D.G. Medley, jovially replied 'We would not for the world cast you off after so many years'.

That was no doubt reassuring (although Melbourne's magnanimity amounted in practice to an extension for just one year); but it was small recompense for the efforts of Garran, Haydon, Allen and others who had worked so hard to make the College a success. Despite their dedication, there was no disguising the College's invidious situation, or the fact that it was generally held in low esteem. The *Canberra Times* in 1945 referred pointedly to the success of New England University College in Armidale, remarking that Canberra University College had made no significant impression at all.

Apart from the practical problems of insufficient funding, inadequate accommodation and an uncertain future, the College suffered ignominy on three separate counts. First, it prepared students for external examination, which (according to one of the Melbourne professors) invariably injured the true university spirit and retarded its growth. Second, it was an institution intended chiefly for public servants, whose main object (according to another professor) was to improve their chances of promotion. But worst of all, the students, whoever they might be, were part-timers, and that was generally considered inimical to what 'a real university' was all about: they were there for the wrong reasons. Allen looked forward to a time when the students would attend the College primarily for cultural rather than practical reasons. Garran admitted that the College lacked the academic leadership to attract undergraduates who sought 'the highest plane of University education, namely a search after knowledge for the sake of knowledge itself'.

The students themselves were well aware that they were missing out on something. 'Only the hectic anti-social side of university life remains for us', wrote one of them in 1937. 'We cannot distinguish ourselves in winning scholarships and prizes, nor do we go in much for organised sport.' There was an absence of any corporate spirit, which Allen blamed on the predominance of part-time staff. In 1944 the introduction of a course in Diplomatic Studies brought an infusion of students and money, but it did nothing to bring the College closer to university status. Nor did the sharp increase in student numbers which followed the end of the war and pushed staff and accommodation to breaking point.

In this gloomy context, the decision to establish a National University offered the brightest hope since the College's inception. The College Council, staff and students had every reason for optimism, especially after they read in the Act that 'the University may provide for the incorporation in the University of the Canberra University College' and learnt that £20 000 had been set aside for the purpose.

They soon realised, however, that the Act placed the College in a new relationship of dependency, as it said nothing about when incorporation should take place and gave no guarantees that it should take place at all. And the University's Interim Council (even though two of its members, Garran and Daley, were also members of the College Council) showed no signs of taking up what was for them no more than an option. On the contrary, the University's responses to the College's overtures were distinctly coy. The Academic Advisers, who had received negative reports about the College from Coombs, Wright, Rivett and others, were implacably opposed to incorporation, and they made it clear that they would consider coming only if the Interim Council stood firm on the issue. Oliphant was opposed to any form of undergraduate teaching in the foreseeable future. Hancock was more accommodating, acknowledging that the link between research and undergraduate teaching at the highest level was a good thing, and that there might be a natural coming together of the two, perhaps in fifteen years' time. But in the meantime, it would be ruinous to the chances of a genuine research university to be associated with 'a University College for pass men'. Copland, anticipating trouble, decided to use the views of the Advisers to resist the local pressure for incorporation; but he concluded that, in the long term, some form of association would evolve that would leave the University's research activities 'uncontaminated' by the work of the College.

Garran was deeply disappointed, telling the crowd assembled at the Commencement Ceremony for 1948 that 'Instead of being the parent of the University, the College finds itself, for the time being, a sort of poor relation'. Ironically, confirmation of its inferior status provided unexpected opportunities. As prospects of an immediate association with the University receded, the College's Council seized the initiative and approached the government for increased funding, on the understanding that money was available for the purpose and that the College had to get itself into shape for eventual incorporation. What was now needed, Garran told the Minister, was a principal and professor with outstanding academic qualifications and sufficient status to attract and hold other staff members; and eight additional lecturing appointments, to open up new fields and handle a student population which now numbered well over three hundred.

Determined lobbying paid off. The government increased the College's grant to the £20 000 it had asked for, and Garran and his colleagues set about planning for the future. Hancock during his 1948 visit offered some detailed advice about what a real university looked like and came up with some possible names for the position of principal. Soon the College had recruited one of them, Herbert Burton, who took up duty early in January 1949.

Burton's appointment as Principal and Professor of Economic History pleased everybody, except perhaps a few friends who wondered what he had let himself in for. Now approaching 50, he was short in stature, with a genial, striking face and an engaging manner. Everyone seemed to know him by the name his wife had given him, 'Joe'. A Queenslander by birth and affection, he had distinguished himself as a rugby footballer and Rhodes scholar. At Oxford he had spent time with Hancock, and the two had become close friends in Adelaide in the late 1920s. For nearly twenty years, he was Senior Lecturer, then Associate Professor, at the University of Melbourne, where he pioneered the teaching of Economic History in Australia. For much of that time he had served under Copland, whose association with the ANU he regarded as one of the attractions of the Canberra job. Burton brought to his new position astuteness, sensitivity and integrity. His appointment made the office of principal immediately respectable; and his insider's knowledge of the University of Melbourne turned out to be of great value to the College when it came to getting things done.

Herbert 'Joe' Burton, soon after his arrival in Canberra in 1949. Photograph by Fred Bareham.

The Principal's first task was to recruit new members of staff. These were initially to be lecturerships, but the College Council, unable to find suitable people and buoyed by the promise of Burton's arrival, asserted itself in defiance of Treasury and advertised for chairs. The first to be appointed (after the Council had assured itself through ASIO that he was not a communist) was a Melbourne historian, Charles Manning Hope Clark. Then came L.F. Crisp to a chair of Political Science, H.W. Arndt to Economics, and A.D. Hope to English. Burton regarded these four as the 'foundation professors'. Together they gave the College a new beginning.

As for the University, if anyone asked at the time whether the College would ever be a part of it, the answer was likely to be 'yes, but not yet'.

College types

Manning Clark came from Melbourne to Canberra on 29 September 1949 to take up the chair of History. The date stuck in his memory. Melbourne had made him, but now its intellectual self-confidence seemed to stultify, and he had to escape the temptations of the Carlton bars. Canberra offered uncertainty, but also the opportunity to make a new start on his grand project to write a history of Australia.

Clark later remembered those early years at the College as some of the most rewarding of his career. Canberra may have lacked tradition, but there was no shortage of intellectual stimulation: from his fellow professors, Arndt, Crisp, and Hope; from other members of the History Department, Don Baker and Laurie Gardiner; from Murray Todd in English, Alan Donagan in Philosophy, Burgess Cameron in Economics and Brian Beddie in Political Science; and from others outside the College, especially the grazier poet David Campbell who shared Clark's thirst for meaning and lust for life. While Crocker was recoiling from the horrors of the Hotel Canberra, Clark quickly found that the Hotel Civic, just across the road from the Melbourne Building in which the College was then located, was no less alluring than the watering holes he had left in Melbourne.

Heinz Arndt (with pipe), Manning Clark and Joe Burton (at right), outside the Childers Street Building in 1954 with diplomatic cadets from Malaya.

The whole staff, clerical as well as academic, congregated each morning and afternoon in their tea room, where they functioned as a lively community. Two or three times a year the Staff Association organised a dinner for the academic staff and their wives (there were as yet no husbands), at which various of the company let their hair down and Fin Crisp organised party games, including 'pass the orange'. At Easter 1953 a fire in the Melbourne Building left the College homeless, and hastened its move into a disused workers' hostel in Childers Street, a few hundred metres away, where it remained for almost a decade. This accommodation, although primitive, encouraged the sense of intimacy and solidarity which already existed among the College staff. So too did awareness of the University, with its relatively luxurious buildings and sanguine prospects, over on the hill.

Members of the College and the University ran into one another at committee meetings or social gatherings. Although Canberra's population more than doubled during the 1950s (reaching 56 000 by 1961), it remained a small town, with all the benefits and drawbacks that small towns tend to offer. R.F. Brissenden, who joined the College in 1953 as a Temporary Lecturer in English, recorded his misgivings in 'The Canberra Blues':

> Go east or west in this fair city, of one thing you may be sure:
> You'll see the same damned faces that you saw the day before.

There was a busy round of parties, often beginning at 8.00 p.m. and ending with a large supper around 11.00. Sawer recorded in his diary boisterous evenings at the Clarks', including one where a student in the Diplomatic Studies course told bawdy stories and Sawer shocked one of the ladies with the song 'A soldier told me before he died'. Academics from the two institutions came together for film nights and concerts in private homes, attended dances in the Albert Hall, and performed on the stage of the Canberra Repertory. On weekdays their wives met and talked at the local shops, perhaps about the local school or the housing problem, and on weekends their families shared picnic spots at Weston Park or along the Murrumbidgee River.

Nevertheless, despite many pleasant social and intellectual contacts, there was an uncomfortable sense of difference between people in the University and the 'College types', as Sawer called them. At the installation of Lord Bruce as Chancellor in 1952, when rain forced the ceremony inside the Albert Hall, someone omitted to reserve seats for members of the College. This left some College academics fulminating for years about 'A.N. bloody U.'. Everybody knew that the University, collectively, regarded the College as 'on trial', and that some of the natural scientists in particular were dismissive of the inhabitants of Childers Street, irrespective of their individual merits.

Condescension was just one of many burdens members of the College had to bear. Another was the relationship with the University of Melbourne, which in 1951 was extended for two years, then for three, and year by year after that. Burton spoke warmly of relations between the two; but it remained frustrating for College professors and lecturers to have to teach courses which had been developed elsewhere and to seek approval for their own courses from a higher authority. Then there was the extra workload, including the annual visits to Melbourne to share the marking of examination papers from Canberra and Melbourne candidates and ensure that standards were much the same. From the point of view of the Professorial Board in Melbourne, the association was a nuisance, as it had been in the past, entailing extra work for no obvious benefit.

Hope and Arndt complained that the College was failing to attract good students. In 1950 there were just under 350 students in all, and in 1957 over 450. The admission of the first full-timers in 1954 was cause for celebration, though by 1957 they still comprised fewer than 10 per cent of the overall student population.

One solution to the part-time problem was to make the College residential. In 1950 it took over 'Gungahlin', an old two-storey homestead beyond the northern outskirts of town. This provided accommodation for eighteen men, most of them cadets in the Department of External Affairs who were enrolled in the Diplomatic Studies course.

'Gungahlin' acquired a corporate spirit of its own and a place in College and

University folklore one night in 1951, when the staid Warden happened to be out of town. Jim Davidson, who was then a resident, was celebrating with three cadets the appointment of one of them, Richard Woolcott, to a diplomatic posting in Moscow. After an evening on the town, they rolled up in front of the homestead about midnight in Davidson's Riley tourer, continued their revels in the common room with much din and bawdy songs, and brought proceedings to a climax around 1.00 a.m. by chopping down

Alec Hope leads an English tutorial.

the flagpole at the front of the building with the evident intention of using it as a battering ram. The Warden, returning from Sydney, was livid; Davidson, unrepentant, was asked to find accommodation elsewhere; Woolcott made amends with an apology and £5 towards the cost of a new flagpole, before setting out the next day for Melbourne on his way overseas to begin a distinguished career which culminated 37 years later in his appointment as head of the Department of Foreign Affairs and Trade. He was one of several students in the Diplomatic Studies course, including Murray Bourchier, Peter Henderson and Nicholas Parkinson, who achieved later distinction. 'Gungahlin', too small and distant, was abandoned as a residential college in 1954. Students were then accommodated in Turner Hostel, Narellan House and, later, Lennox House, all within walking distance of Childers Street.

The diplomatic cadets were exposed to teachers of remarkable talent. Over forty years later Sir Nicholas Parkinson remembered especially Arndt's seminars on international economics, always challenging and often developing into a row; and Clark, with 'enormous personal charm, ... infuriating and stimulating', and sounding

College students outside 'Gungahlin' in 1950. Left to right: John Robinson, Geoff Mannall and Jim Gibbney. Gibbney later became one of the mainstays of the *Australian Dictionary of Biography* in the Research School of Social Sciences.

'an outrageous raspberry at life'. While Clark's approach to history offered much to disagree with, Parkinson welcomed the change from the aridity of the History Department at the University of Sydney, where he had earlier been a student. The College showed what a real university ought to be like.

The course in Diplomatic Studies came to an end in 1953, after the government decided it was no longer required. Later students showed little sign of a communal feeling, except perhaps at the revues which were usually held each year from 1955, and which gave students the opportunity to get their own back at their lecturers and members of the College Council. From 1949 the Students' Association published a cyclostyled newssheet, which in 1952 changed its name to *Woroni*, an Aboriginal word meaning 'mouthpiece'. The Association boasted in 1956 that this included 'intelligent and controversial articles and abusive but provoking attacks on authority in general'. Under the guidance of a few dedicated editors, *Woroni* grew by the end of the decade into a twelve-page publication. Several clubs and societies emerged during these years, including the Canberra University Dramatic Society, the Student Christian Movement, and the Law Society, whose members (*Woroni* claimed) considered themselves a cut above the rest.

Diplomatic Cadets Phil Peters, Bill Morrison, Dick Woolcott and Tony Powell participate in a bushfire drill in the grounds of 'Gungahlin' in 1950.

By courtesy of Geoff Mannall.

Despite Burton's efforts to breathe life into the student body, most undergraduates remained weighed down by an earnestness of purpose. The staff kept the College vibrant. By 1957 there were 40 full-time academics, spread across a dozen disciplines in the humanities and social sciences. Except for a course in Zoology, offered to meet the needs of the CSIRO, there was no longer any teaching in the natural sciences.

Many staff members were leaders in their respective fields. Apart from Arndt and Clark, there was Crisp, working on his biography of Ben Chifley, which was published in 1961, and Hope, whose first collection of poems, *The Wandering Islands*, was published in 1955. John Fleming, who joined the staff in 1949 and served as Robert Garran Professor of Law from 1955 to 1960, went on to a chair at the University of California at Berkeley. Hans Bielenstein, appointed Professor of Oriental Languages in 1952 on C.P. FitzGerald's recommendation, later accepted a chair at Columbia University.

The College grew in strength and reputation. In 1957 the Committee on Australian Universities, chaired by the head of the British Universities Grants Committee, Sir Keith Murray, remarked that it was now 'a mature institution' with 'a highly qualified and enthusiastic staff', and recommended that it be given independence from Melbourne and allowed to expand. As a result its annual grant grew from £259 000 in 1958 to £440 000 the following year. The professoriate grew from twelve to eighteen, with new chairs in Botany, Chemistry, Geology, Physics, Zoology and Statistics. For the first time, the departments were organised into faculties of Arts, Economics, Law and Science. The committee also recommended that the College be allocated a permanent site close to the ANU. This was promptly implemented with a grant of 138 acres, 40 of which were

The Canberra University College Commencement Ceremony in Albert Hall, 27 March 1952. *Above*: Sir Robert Garran confers the degrees; the Vice-Chancellor of the new University, Copland, sits immediately to his right. *Right*: the graduands wait to receive their degrees. The photograph depicts the approximate enrolment ratio of over eight men to one woman. Photographs by L.J. Dwyer.

National Library of Australia.

extracted from the original grant to the University. Before long a site consultant had been appointed and plans were on the drawing board for the College's first permanent building, which was to house the Faculty of Arts.

In their discussions with representatives of the College and the University, Murray and his colleagues asked searching questions about what sort of relationship should exist between the two institutions. In both places some staff were alarmed. But Murray stopped short of recommending amalgamation, suggesting instead that the matter be given 'very serious consideration' and pointing out that the establishment of two universities in a city as small as Canberra should not be lightly undertaken. Nor did he comment on the form amalgamation might take, except by saying that 'it should not pass the wit of man to devise constitutional arrangements which might suit the situation in Canberra in a manner which would be acceptable to all concerned'. That remark resounded around campus meeting rooms for many years to come.

Amalgamation

When Murray delivered his report to the government in September 1957, men had already been applying their wits to the problem for several years. So far they had made little progress towards amalgamation, and if anything had moved in the opposite direction.

So long as the Australian National University Act continued to provide for the possible incorporation of the College, the relationship between the two institutions would be open to debate. Burton wanted some form of amalgamation, and most of his staff agreed. But when the College initiated discussion in the early 1950s, the University was inclined to play for time, suggesting that for the next few years at least the relationship should be, in Oliphant's phrase, 'spiritual rather than physical'. For the College, looking forward to increasing numbers of students and with nowhere to house them, the issue was urgent. If it was not to join the ANU, it wanted to develop into a fully-fledged and independent university.

Within the University, opinions were divided. Some, including Davidson and Sawer, argued that teaching and research went hand in hand, that University staff could only benefit by exposure to undergraduates, and vice versa. Hancock, when he arrived, made sympathetic noises about a closer association, and gave practical evidence of cooperation through his 'History Consortium'. Apart from the academic reasons for amalgamation, proponents offered arguments about sharing resources, especially library facilities.

But for every argument in favour, there seemed to be half a dozen against. Butlin and Passmore, deeply committed to their own demanding research projects, denied that there was an essential link between teaching and research. Partridge suggested that incorporation would lead other universities to conclude that the ANU experiment had failed. Many feared that the University's national character would inevitably be diminished. With the notable exception of Woolley, the natural scientists tended to see incorporation as a threat to research, with undergraduates competing for bench space in the laboratories. Most of these arguments were presented as matters of principle; but some staff openly voiced their concerns about the quality of the College relative to the University and of College staff relative to themselves. Before the College introduced undergraduate courses in science, Oliphant anticipated that it would attract only inferior staff who, in the event of amalgamation, would be foisted on the University. And once the Science Faculty had been formed, he remarked privately that most College staff would not qualify as research fellows at the ANU. This was an overstatement of the kind to which Oliphant was prone; but it reflected a feeling widespread among his colleagues that the University had little to gain from union and much to lose.

Besides the two institutions there were other interested parties, including residents of Canberra represented through the local press, politicians who asked the occasional question in parliament, various departments of government, and most important of all, Prime Minister Menzies, who kept a close watch on the debate. When it appeared in 1954 that the matter was about to come before Cabinet, the University suggested to the College that they jointly convene a working party to advise on future arrangements. After balancing the arguments for and against incorporation, the working party recommended that the two institutions should be associated for a trial period of five years, which would allow the College time to mature, and give both parties time to determine whether or not a 'permanent and organic union' was likely to work.

This was a cautious proposal; yet its immediate effect was to galvanise opinion among staff in the University against any form of association. At a joint meeting of the social science schools, the two faculties came down decisively against incorporation, resolving instead to encourage the College in its bid for independence. The Board of Graduate Studies then declared that a decision to incorporate would require complete unanimity in the academic community: in other words, that the question should be indefinitely postponed. This left the College, whose arrangement with the University of Melbourne was about to expire, stranded, and its staff perplexed.

Wise heads urged circumspection. Sawer warned his colleagues that they should try to avoid sounding 'snobbish, pharisaical, condescending or impertinent' (while suggesting that this was exactly how they had sounded to date). Coombs, a strong advocate of incorporation, tried to arrange a compromise based on some form of minimal association which would at least ensure that the ANU retained a say in how the College developed, warning his senior colleagues in the University that, if the institutions were unable to resolve their difficulties, the problem would probably be solved at a political level. But opponents of amalgamation within the University stood firm; and many College staff, responding to what could reasonably be interpreted as a snub, abandoned their own support for amalgamation to emphasise the problems the College was likely to encounter from association with the University. Now the College pointed out that its undergraduates would be regarded as second-class citizens; that in periods of financial stringency the research schools would have the lion's share of the budget; and that, all in all, it too had much to lose.

Coombs was right. If the academics were unable to reach agreement on some form of association, the Prime Minister was ready to do the job for them, especially after Murray had made it clear that something could and should be done. Early in 1958 Menzies summoned representatives of the two institutions, along with the Minister for the Interior and three senior public servants (two of whom, Sir Allen Brown and Professor K.H. Bailey, were members of both Councils), to a round table discussion about their future relationship. Menzies at the outset drew the bottom line: 'There is a very wide-spread feeling in Australia, rightly or wrongly—I do not sit in judgment on it—that Canberra is a spoilt darling; that if you have a national university, the sky is the limit; but a university in another place must battle for itself'. How, therefore, could a second university be justified? His guests were less inclined to confront this political problem than to show the Prime Minister that amalgamation would be wrong in principle and practice. After a long day, the meeting adjourned without reaching any firm conclusions, Menzies merely commenting that he and the Minister for the

Interior would think about what had been said and that he had not had such an enjoyable day for quite some time. The academics might not have come away so pleased: if it had not been clear in the past that their future would be influenced by political considerations, it certainly should have been now.

But the political considerations were not entirely straightforward. Menzies, having to decide between disappointing academic Canberra and offending the rest of Australia, and confronted with a Cabinet divided on the issue, took his time. For nearly two years the issue was left undecided, during which the proponents of independence won additional recruits. Even Coombs, lobbied on the golf course by his friend Crisp, conceded that the government should grant the College independence, and urged the Prime Minister to take into account its recent progress. Menzies, on a visit to England, also discussed the matter with Sir Keith Murray, who confirmed his earlier view that two universities in Canberra could not be justified; and the new Australian Universities Commission, a body created as a result of the Murray Report, concluded unanimously that there should be just one institution.

So when Menzies made his long-expected announcement a week before Christmas in 1959, the outcome was hardly surprising: 'We have decided in favour of association'. The government, he explained, could not justify two universities in a small town at a time when other cities with larger populations had more pressing demands; and if Canberra University College were given independence, it would either remain a second-rate institution or provide costly facilities for research which would duplicate those of the ANU. There were also the academic benefits of amalgamation for researchers and students alike.

Crisp, anticipating the decision two months earlier, denounced it as a shotgun wedding; but it could better be described as an arranged marriage between dissenting parties. The main element of surprise was the extent to which the government had shown itself to be the final arbiter in matters affecting the two institutions. Academics might think what they liked; the decision was clearly non-negotiable.

The same applied to the timetable. Menzies told the parties that he wanted to introduce legislation into parliament the following year so that the amalgamated body could come into being from the beginning of 1961. To achieve this the University and the College would need to agree on ways and means by mid-March, just three months from the date of his announcement. The government's requirements were general: one university with a single governing body, with common degrees conferred by a common authority, and as far as possible, a common administration. Other than this, the details of association were for the institutions themselves to determine; and if they were unable to reach agreement on specific issues, Menzies himself would be happy to decide.

Whatever the long-term outcome of the ultimatum, the Prime Minister had certainly put a dampener on the Christmas and New Year holidays of several academics and administrators. There was a flurry of activity, with meetings and report writing starting just before Christmas and continuing through to mid-February.

The challenge was formidable: to forge a link that would work in theory and practice between two institutions that differed significantly in functions and size. At the beginning of January 1960, the University had a total of 682 staff, 177 of whom were academics or senior administrators; the comparable numbers for the College were 164 and 94. The ANU had 111 PhD candidates and no undergraduates; the College had 665 undergraduate enrolments (133 of whom were full-timers), 29 Masters' candidates and none for the degree of PhD. The annual running expenditure for the University was approaching four times that of the College. Yet Menzies had spoken of 'association' rather than 'incorporation', and this gave the College, theoretically at least, equal status at the negotiating table. This appalled Oliphant, who had assumed that the University would be the dominant party, 'lifting the poor sister institution, academically speaking, into its auspices'.

The University approached the negotiations on the premise, as agreed by the Board of Graduate Studies, that 'whatever form the academic structure took, it was essential that the fundamental principle, that the integrity and independence of research which had been provided for in this University and was Australia's only original adventure in the university field, be preserved'. The safest way of achieving this was to ensure that the research schools maintained the maximum degree of independence, within the limits defined by the Prime Minister's statement. The College approached the negotiations determined above all to ensure that association did not mean subordination. This too could be avoided through independence. In other words, the newlyweds, as Laurie Fitzhardinge put it, decided to occupy separate rooms.

The University's anxieties were evident during discussions about the role of the proposed professorial board. In most universities the board was the supreme academic body, comprising the professorial staff and responsible for high academic policy. Tradition suggested that there should be such a body at the ANU. But if the College continued to grow at its current rate, the College professors would eventually be able, as Oliphant put it, 'to outvote the interests of the Research Schools'. Best therefore to have two academic boards, one for each part of the University, and each reporting directly to Council. The College readily agreed. The negotiators also agreed that there should also be a professorial board for the whole University to resolve possible conflicts on academic matters; but it would meet rarely and have no prescribed policy-making role.

John Fleming, Professor of Law in the College, warned that this arrangement was risky: if there was no dominant academic body, important academic matters might well be determined by the Council and the executive. Later years proved him right: the ANU Council often seemed more powerful and assertive than councils and senates in other universities. Oliphant and his colleagues, by splitting academic policy-making in two, had protected the research schools from anticipated domination by the teaching professors; but in so doing they had opened the way for a non-academic body to fill a policy-making void.

As happens when constitutions are being made, matters of terminology assumed large importance. The University was determined to maintain the identity of the research schools by giving them a collective name. The term 'institute', commonly used to describe research organisations in Australia, such as the highly respected

Walter and Eliza Hall Institute in Melbourne, immediately suggested itself and won general approval. The Princeton Institute for Advanced Study inspired the rest of the title, so that the research schools, while retaining their individual names, would now be identified as the Institute of Advanced Studies (the plural having overtaken the singular) in the ANU.

This much was easy. But what about the teaching faculties? The College representatives at the negotiating table preferred to call them simply 'The Faculties', without assigning a collective name. The University representatives realised that this would not do: if the research schools were identified as the Institute while the faculties had no collective name, Canberra University College would become 'The University', while the Institute would be pushed to the periphery. The University insisted and the College reluctantly gave in. Burton wanted to retain the name College, but nobody agreed. Instead, his colleagues suggested that their part of the University be titled 'The School of General Studies'. It was an unhappy choice, reminiscent of generalist courses in humanities then being offered to technology and science students at the University of New South Wales; and although members of the research schools had not chosen the term, it was they who in future years tended to get the blame.

One of the most difficult issues was what to do about the library. The University Library, which currently housed some 150 000 volumes including the extensive Oriental Studies collection, had been assembled to serve the specific needs of the research schools. The College Library had about 50 000 volumes, selected chiefly to serve the needs of undergraduates. The University Library was catalogued under the Bliss system; the College Library followed Dewey. Both collections were housed inadequately in temporary accommodation, and both were bursting at the seams. Two new buildings were planned; and in the case of the University, funds had already been allocated and a contract let for a building with plenty of room for books but limited accommodation for readers, and certainly insufficient to seat large numbers of undergraduates.

University and College representatives agreed that (administratively at least) there should be a single University Library under one University Librarian; but they differed as to the physical form it should take. Crisp was adamant: undergraduates should have free run of a large, well-stocked library, comparable with the best national collections, and located in the teaching part of the campus. The University, however, was reluctant to abandon its claim to a separate research library, which was after all a bird in the hand. It therefore submitted a proposal for two separate libraries, one (as planned) for research, especially in the social sciences; the other for undergraduate work, with a limited collection of books but plenty of room for readers. Burton was angry, telling the Prime Minister that the University's scheme discriminated against undergraduates and contradicted the government's picture of an institution of national standing.

The parties were also unable to agree on who should be responsible for the award of PhDs and higher doctorates. Representatives of the University argued that doctorates were one of the main ways in which the quality of the institution would be judged, and that therefore the Institute should retain sole control. College negotiators, while accepting Institute responsibility in the short term, anticipated a time when the School of General Studies would award at least as many doctorates as the Institute, at which point the degree should become the responsibility of a joint body. The University wanted its powers enshrined in the new Act of Parliament; the College wanted the matter to be determined by statute, which could readily be changed. Both parties refused to budge.

Yet despite these and other points of conflict, negotiations proceeded with remarkable harmony and speed. Manning Clark gave credit to Melville: 'In a subject where passion, prejudice and vested interest could have caused ship-wreck your work helped greatly to avoid such a disaster'. Burton too was a voice for moderation, while other senior academics and administrators helped smooth the way. Within two months of Menzies making his announcement a joint submission was ready to present to government. This provided for a single Council, with 36 to 38 members, and a Chancellor, Pro-Chancellor, Vice-Chancellor, Deputy Vice-Chancellor and Registrar, who would have responsibility for the University as a whole. Below them, the University would be in two parts, the Institute of Advanced Studies and the School of General Studies, each with its own board and administrative structure. Burton would retain his title of Principal of the School. The Vice-Chancellor, his Deputy and the Principal would all be members of both academic boards. The Board of the Institute of Advanced Studies (which quickly became known by its unhappy acronym, BIAS) would also comprise the heads of the research schools, the heads of departments and three members of the School of General Studies. The Board of the School (BSGS) would consist of all its professors, along with three members of the Institute. In this way, each Board would be kept in touch with the work of the other.

Menzies settled the outstanding issues peremptorily. On the matter of doctoral degrees, he prescribed a compromise, giving the Institute legislative responsibility for the next decade, after which the question would be dealt with by University statute. With regard to the library, he determined that for reasons of time and money the plans to build a research library close to the social science schools should proceed, thereby implying that an undergraduate library would eventually be built near the School of General Studies. Obviously, the Prime Minister's motives in forcing amalgamation were not chiefly economic: two libraries would cost in the long term much more than one.

The arrangements proposed in the submission, along with the Prime Minister's additions, were promptly approved by government and passed through the parliament with little dissent. Gough Whitlam, the newly elected Deputy Leader of the Labor Party, lamented the demise of a purely research institution, and his colleague Kim Beazley protested that the measure conflicted with the wishes of both institutions. This, of course, was true. But given that amalgamation was inevitable, at least the University and the College were given the constitution they had asked for, incorporating the key feature of independence from one another.

How well the arrangements would work remained to be seen. Would the School of

General Studies, as Oliphant predicted, grow to swallow up the available money, leaving the research schools to die? Would the old College, as the CUC Students' Association anticipated, become an unwanted lean-to of the ANU? There were also optimists, who saw the potential for informal cooperation among schools, faculties and departments, and who looked forward to the University achieving a national status in teaching as well as research.

The University in 1960

An aerial view of the campus, looking towards Black Mountain, about 1960.

Students

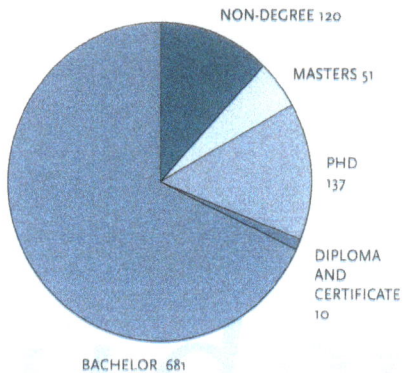

- NON-DEGREE 120
- MASTERS 51
- PHD 137
- DIPLOMA AND CERTIFICATE 10
- BACHELOR 681

Undergraduates by Faculty and Gender

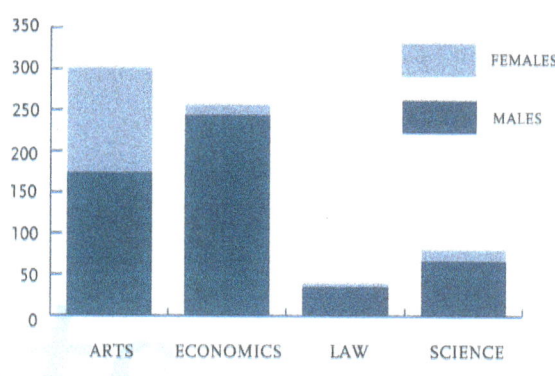

Origins of Postgraduate Students

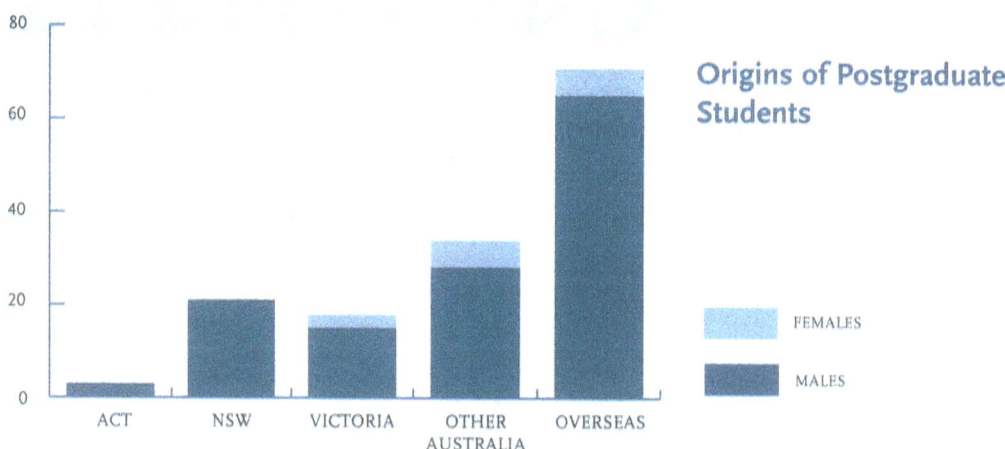

Staff

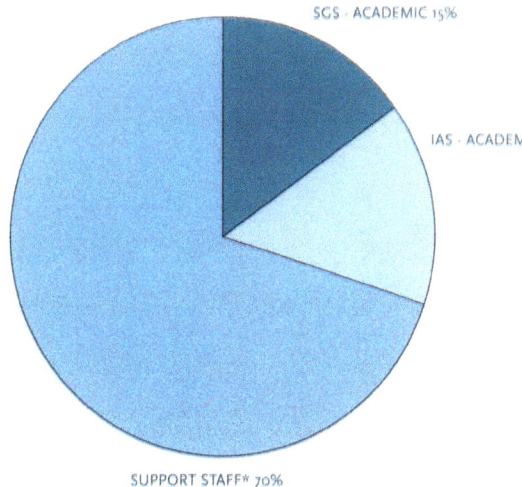

* Includes administration, library, maintenance, laboratory staff, research and departmental assistants

IAS Academic Staff*

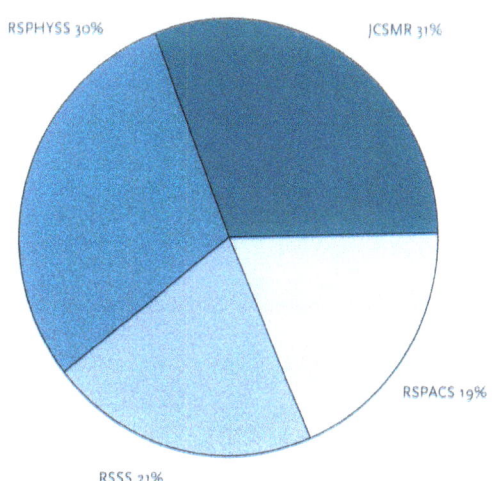

* Excludes research assistants

SOURCE: COMMONWEALTH BUREAU OF CENSUS AND STATISTICS *UNIVERSITY STATISTICS*, 1960.

COUNCIL

Professorial Board

ADMINISTRATION

Board of the Institute of Advanced Studies

Board of the School of General Studies

Research Schools

John Curtin School of Medical Research
Research School of Physical Sciences
Research School of Social Sciences
Research School of Pacific Studies

Faculties

Arts
Economics
Law
Science

University Library
Hall of Residence
University House

From 1960 to the mid–1970s

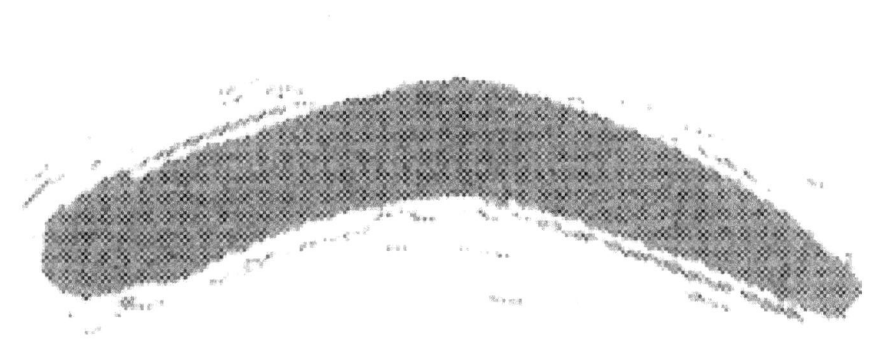

Setting directions

7

'There can be no end to the building of a university'

In May 1960, several months before amalgamation, Sir Leslie Melville, as he was now called, addressed the University's seventh annual conferring of degrees ceremony, held as usual in the Albert Hall. This time twenty graduates took out the degree of PhD, many more than in any previous year. Eleven of them were present, along with most members of the academic and administrative staff.

'We have come to the end of a beginning', said Melville, 'for this is the last time we shall meet as a purely research university'. He spoke confidently of achievements to date, mentioning specific successes in each of the four schools, the increasing numbers of publications and students, and the growing reputation of the ANU in the world of learning. He spoke too of the buildings already erected and planned for the future. With amalgamation the campus was set to expand from 193 to 331 acres: but this, said Melville, was unlikely to be enough. To provide for future growth the University was seeking an additional 100 acres of neighbouring land. As he told his audience, 'There can be no end to the building of a University'.

Leonard Huxley, Vice-Chancellor from 1960 to 1967.

This was Melville's last graduation ceremony. After seven years as Vice-Chancellor, he retired on the eve of amalgamation to become Chairman of the Tariff Board, where he was free of Oliphant's badgering. To succeed him, Oliphant, supported by Eccles, nominated Leonard Huxley, who satisfied Oliphant's essential criterion of *not* being an economist. A former Rhodes Scholar for Tasmania, Huxley had been with Oliphant in Birmingham and was now Elder Professor of Physics at the University of Adelaide. As a member of Council from 1956 to 1959, he was well known and well liked at the ANU and his appointment went through with less anguish than had accompanied that of his two predecessors. Oliphant assumed that, having spent many years in England, Huxley would understand what a real university was all about, and that as a fellow scientist he would have a proper appreciation of the capital requirements of pioneering research in nuclear physics. But if he had expected

The campus in 1963, a year before the filling of Lake Burley Griffin. Clearing for the lake is evident at the top left and centre. The Childers Street buildings inherited from Canberra University College are at the bottom left, and the CSIRO complex is at the right. The numbers show some of the major buildings, several of them recently completed or under construction:

1 Haydon-Allen;
2 General Studies Library (later the J.B. Chifley Building);
3 H.C. Coombs;
4 Oriental Studies;
5 R.G. Menzies;
6 University House;
7 Cockcroft;
8 JCSMR;
9 Bruce Hall;
10 Physics (SGS);
11 Chemistry;
12 Geology.

Australian News and Information Bureau, ANU Collection.

him to favour one part of the University over the others, he would have been wrong: Huxley was impartial from the outset.

Like Melville, Huxley was a shy man, with absolute integrity and little taste for academic wheeling and dealing. Formal in manner, he never removed his coat, even on the hottest Canberra days. He preferred one to one discussions rather than large meetings, and got on well with the staff he worked with regularly. Occasionally he lost his temper, glowering with large, fierce eyebrows at academics who made a nuisance of themselves at committee meetings. Although he worked hard, some saw him as a reluctant Vice-Chancellor, too fond of delegation, and more interested in birdwatching or some problem in cloud physics than in University policy and administration. Where Melville had a detailed understanding of the University's finances, Huxley had neither interest nor capacity in financial affairs. When forced to consider some budgetary matter his eyes tended to glaze over, wandering perhaps towards a pair of gang-gang cockatoos consorting in the gum tree outside his office. Within eighteen months of his appointment, he and other senior members of the University agreed that someone else should take overall financial responsibility; so Crawford, only just settled into the headship of Pacific Studies, accepted an honorary appointment as Fiscal Adviser. Oliphant might not have appreciated the irony: while he had made sure the Vice-Chancellor was not an economist, his own nominee turned out to be so little interested in budgetary matters that financial power fell into the hands of an outstanding economist from the social science schools.

Taking up duty on 30 September 1960, the day before the amalgamated University came into being, Huxley anticipated that his main job over the coming years would be to make amalgamation work. This proved to be a demanding task. On the other hand, he had the good fortune to preside over the University when the country was affluent and the government prepared to endow generous funding for tertiary education. His seven years in office were, as he later recalled, honeymoon years between the universities and the government, when it sometimes seemed necessary only to ask in order to receive.

From the date of amalgamation until Huxley's retirement at the end of 1967, undergraduate numbers quadrupled, from about 800 to 3200. Postgraduate numbers increased at an even greater rate, from 120 to 500. Total expenditure on the University increased from $5.5 million to $17.5 million. The most obvious evidence of expansion was the changing appearance of the campus, where buildings sprang up like mushrooms where real mushrooms used to be.

Builders were always at work on two or three sites at the one time. When Huxley came, the only 'permanent' buildings were University House, the Cockcroft Building for the Physical Sciences, the John Curtin School building and the boiler house, together with the recently opened Haydon-Allen Building in the School of General Studies. When he left, these had been joined by the Coombs Building for Social Sciences and Pacific Studies, buildings for Geophysics, Mathematics and Chemistry; and in the School of General Studies, new buildings or groups of buildings for Geology, Botany, Zoology, Chemistry, Law, Oriental Studies and Economics. There were two libraries, an administrative building known as the Chancelry, and a students' union (later converted to an administrative building). The first of the halls of residence, Bruce Hall, which opened soon after Huxley arrived, was followed by Burton Hall and Garran Hall, while plans for colleges run by religious denominations were well advanced. The site now looked like a university.

Where was the University headed? Despite Melville's confident predictions, this rate of growth could not continue forever. In 1962, after the University had set forth its program for the next three years under the government's new system of triennial funding, Partridge raised the question in relation to the Institute of Advanced Studies. Besides being Director of the Research School of Social Sciences and Deputy Chairman (de facto Chairman) of the Institute, Partridge was an astute observer of the overall framework of tertiary education in Australia. Assuming the role of 'internal philosopher' to the University, he suggested to his colleagues that, after twelve years of development and planning, they should have some firm ideas about the Institute's 'final form'. 'Until now', he wrote, 'we have never taken the trouble to ask ourselves concerning the Institute what the machine will be like when it is finished, and how it will work'. They had moved forward on the principle that it was better to travel than to arrive; and if there was any philosophy behind the Institute's current plans, it seemed to be one of 'galloping, permanent expansion'.

P.H. (Perc) Partridge, about the time of his retirement as Professor of Philosophy, RSSS, in 1975.

Partridge thus introduced the notion of 'completion' to Institute planning and started a discussion which continued until the 1970s, when a new era of financial constraint made it no longer relevant. Various questions were open to debate. How large should the Institute be, both on its own account and in relation to the School of General Studies? What should be the total number of research schools, and how large should each school be? What was the optimum size of a department? What influences should be allowed to determine the rate of growth? These questions raised others about how widely the Institute should cast its academic net and how many disciplines it should try to cover.

Partridge's own view was that the Institute should not simply be another university which happened to specialise in research and postgraduate teaching, but a 'relatively small, compact and concentrated' research institution. In choosing subjects for research, it should be 'extremely selective': 'we should go for quality, and for intensity and solidity of work rather than for width or range'. His colleagues agreed, sketching 'a picture of an Institute of limited size, containing at most six Schools, each containing a number of rather small departments which could change with time'. They also agreed that any attempt to make the Institute 'complete' by including all the disciplines normally found in a university would be disastrous. On the other hand, there was also a feeling that it should eventually contain schools representing 'the basic divisions of knowledge', including Mathematics, Physical Sciences, Chemical Sciences, Medical and Biological Sciences together, and the two existing social science schools. These principles found their way into a policy document which, in broad terms, set the course of development during the next decade. The document avoided difficult questions about the proper nature of Institute research, simply concluding that there was no formal limit on the branches of learning the Institute could encompass.

Everyone agreed that the Institute should not be allowed to become too big, partly because it would be impossible to continue to recruit staff of the highest calibre, but also because a large Institute would lose its identity and coherence. But how large was too large? The medical scientists were happy to remain within the walls of their already substantial building. Ennor reinforced the case for restraint by suggesting that when medical science departments grew much beyond ten members they tended to become amorphous and moribund. The physical scientists, on the other hand, argued for departments of up to thirty, since expensive equipment demanded more staff to make use of it. The outcome avoided placing a numerical limit on schools or on the Institute as a whole, settling instead for a statement of general principle: 'if there is not a ready and free interchange of ideas and healthy criticism both between and within Schools, then the Institute of Advanced Studies would surely have become too large'.

Apart from restricting the size of departments in normal circumstances to twelve members, this policy left the Institute to develop as Partridge had described the social science schools growing in previous years, 'as our academic interests pull us'. Nobody seemed willing to come to terms with numbers. This was understandable: academic organisations should be measured for size as intellectual rather than administrative entities. And while the optimum size of departments could be determined on the basis of experience in other institutions, the research schools were entirely new. Who could say what numbers would function best? In the meantime, the Institute continued to expand. By the end of the decade, two new schools, covering the fields of Chemistry and Biological Sciences, had been added to the original four; and within Physical Sciences, the Department of Geophysics and Geochemistry was starting to resemble a school within a school.

By now the University had a new Vice-Chancellor. Huxley was succeeded at the end of 1967 by Crawford, whose years as Fiscal Adviser made him well aware of the problem of size. In 1972 he decided it was time 'once and for all' to make a definitive statement about the size of the research schools. Using the John Curtin School with a target of 100 academic staff as a benchmark, he suggested a limit of 120 for each of the three other original schools. Geophysics and Geochemistry were excluded from the Physical Sciences total, in anticipation of the formation of a new school of Earth Sciences. The new schools of Chemistry and Biological Sciences were assigned a limit of 85 and 80 respectively, bringing the Institute total to 625, plus a yet unspecified allocation for Earth Sciences.

It proved easier to set limits than to enforce them. By the mid-1970s three schools were well in excess of their allocation, with Social Sciences reaching 174 full-time academic staff in 1975, including appointments on outside funds, and Pacific Studies just one behind. So long as money, buildings and staff were available, and ideas for research were plentiful, pressure for growth would be hard to resist.

The size of the Institute was discussed chiefly in terms of academic staff numbers; for the School of General Studies the measure was students. With fewer than a thousand undergraduates in 1960, any problem relating to ultimate size may have seemed remote. But as the School, unlike the Institute, had other universities to look to as models, and as size seemed to be an issue everywhere, the question came up for discussion soon after amalgamation.

There was no single accepted view of the optimum size of a university. In 1960, Australian universities (excluding the ANU) ranged from 1300 students at the University of Tasmania to over 11 000 at each of Sydney and Melbourne. By the end of the decade, the largest universities had student numbers approaching 17 000. In 1964 a Commonwealth government Committee of Inquiry into the Future of Tertiary Education in Australia (the Martin Committee) suggested that, in Australian conditions, universities of fewer than 4000 students might be considered too small, while those with more than 10 000 might be too large.

The School of General Studies had already expressed a preference for remaining small. Members of staff who had been part of the School in its former life were keen to retain the sense of intimacy that had been associated with the College. The universities of Sydney and Melbourne, which appeared to lack unity and to overwhelm the individual student, were not attractive models. J.E. Richardson, Dean of the Faculty of Law, commented on 'the impersonal and deleterious atmosphere' associated with the large law schools and urged that his faculty restrict itself to the equivalent of 400 undergraduates. Huxley believed that universities underwent a change of character once they exceeded 4000 students, and boasted that ANU students enjoyed a privileged relationship with their professors and lecturers compared with their counterparts in the larger institutions.

But as in the Institute, there were formidable pressures for growth. At the time of amalgamation, the Prime Minister had made it clear that the University's rate of development must be related in some degree to the growth of Canberra. During the early 1960s, Canberra was transformed by an infusion of public servants from Melbourne and Sydney, the construction of numerous public buildings, the opening of new suburbs in the Woden Valley, and the filling of Lake Burley Griffin, all of which helped confirm that the idea of the national capital was something more than a previous generation's folly. Between 1958 and 1965 the population more than doubled to nearly 87 000, and the city's planners expected it to reach a quarter of a million by 1980. With such projections, the figure of 4000 soon seemed inadequate.

At the same time, this was the *National* University, and as such it had an obligation, implied in the ANU Act, to cater for students from other parts of the country. While there was no prescribed ratio for 'local' to 'national' intake, it was generally understood that one group of students should not overwhelm the other. At the moment it was possible to admit everyone who matriculated and wanted a place. But how long would the University be able to meet both local and national demands? At some stage, admission standards more rigorous than bare matriculation would surely have to be imposed.

Leaving aside the question of demand for places, there were many within the University who insisted that departments and faculties must grow in order to flourish. In an age of increasing specialisation, so the argument went, large departments were essential to 'cover the field', as well as to provide room for new developments. Richard Johnson, Professor of Classics, was convinced that at least 8000 undergraduates were needed if the School of General Studies was to become anything more than 'a competent, run-of-the-mill undergraduate college, with a very limited range of disciplines'. Where Classics departments in some universities had concentrations of expertise in specific areas, in his own department a permanent staff of six had to cover languages, history, philosophy, art and archaeology, poetry and rhetoric, and education. With resources spread so thinly, said Johnson, the department could never achieve an international reputation.

Against these pressures, the optimum number of undergraduate enrolments never seemed fixed. In 1964 it was increased to 5700; but later in the decade, the Faculty of Arts was looking to 3000 Arts students alone, though this figure was later reduced to 2200. In 1969 C.A. (Cec) Gibb brought the issue to a head, arguing that the time had come to decide on the ultimate size of the School. As Deputy Chairman of the Board of the School, Gibb occupied the position equivalent to that of Partridge in the Institute in earlier years, and he shared with Partridge a broad interest in institutional structures and educational philosophy. Before joining Canberra University College as foundation Professor of Psychology in 1955, he had spent several years in the United States, first as a doctoral student at the huge University of Illinois and later as a visiting lecturer at the small college of Dartmouth in New Hampshire. He was therefore familiar with the relative merits of large and small institutions. His reflections on the size of the School were also informed by his interests as a psychologist in leadership and group dynamics.

C.A. (Cec) Gibb, Professor of Psychology and Deputy Chairman of the Board of the School of General Studies, about 1970.
Canberra Times.

There was no real way, said Gibb, to establish an optimum size for universities generally, or for any one institution. There were, however, several considerations which might be used to set a maximum size for the undergraduate population of the ANU. He placed at the top of his list 'a sense of community', quoting a comment of the Duke of Edinburgh at the University of Hull: 'Don't grow beyond 4,000. Remember tribalism is important.' A sense of community, said Gibb, meant that students and staff identified themselves with the university rather than a specific part of it, and that there were opportunities for interaction across disciplinary lines as far apart as Chemistry and Hindi. Other criteria included the freedom to communicate on a personal basis between staff and students, which meant that classes should remain small; the capacity of policy-making bodies to represent and respond to the views of the University community; and the ability of the institution to accommodate the bright dreams of future years.

Gibb offered no formula and came up with no new figures, though he calculated that the University's present target was about right. This accorded with Crawford's view that the ANU should remain a small and select institution which aimed to teach a limited range of disciplines very well indeed. Council agreed, and in 1970 imposed a limit of 5900 undergraduate enrolments, with the expectation that this number would be reached in a decade. As it turned out, enrolments in 1981 were about a thousand short of that mark, owing in part to the increasing availability of tertiary places throughout Australia.

Maintaining the difference

It had always been intended that the ANU should be different. Until 1960, that had been easy enough to achieve. As well as being unique in having no undergraduates, it was the only university funded entirely by the Commonwealth; and it was funded far more generously than any of the state universities. While it could lay claim to some of the traditional characteristics of a university, especially autonomy and academic freedom, further parallels with the state universities seemed remote.

From the 1960s onwards this sense of difference, much valued by many members of the University, came increasingly under challenge, as a result of changes both on and off the ANU campus. Amalgamation brought the most obvious change in the form of undergraduate students, the main distinguishing feature of state universities. And just as the ANU was accepting its first undergraduates, the state universities were devoting more of their efforts to postgraduate training. This new concern with postgraduates was illustrated graphically by the increasing numbers of graduates taking out the degree of Doctor of Philosophy from all Australian universities: from a dozen in 1950 to 117 a decade later. (Granted, the ANU accounted for twenty of these, and the number of higher doctorates had diminished: but the increase was still impressive.)

The third sweeping change which had a profound effect on the ANU was the growing involvement of the Commonwealth government in higher education. The Murray Report in 1957 signalled the beginnings of what the Adelaide historian Hugh Stretton called at the time a 'noble revolution' in the universities. To the surprise of many, the Menzies government accepted the report's recommendations in their entirety, and unprecedented grants for capital works and recurrent costs poured into the existing universities and provided the foundations of new ones. Shortly afterwards, the New South Wales University of Technology widened its functions and changed its name to the University of New South Wales, and Monash University was founded in Melbourne. Then, in the mid-1960s, both Sydney and Melbourne were given third universities, Adelaide a second, and the college in Newcastle was elevated to University status. Student numbers increased dramatically: from 37 000 when Murray delivered his report, to 53 000 in 1960 and 83 000 in 1965.

Apart from encouraging the government to open its coffers, the Murray Report recommended the formation of a committee to advise the states and the Commonwealth on how the money should be spent and to formulate policy towards the universities at a national level. The result was the Australian Universities Commission (AUC), which was charged with the task of implementing the Murray proposals and promoting (in the words of the legislation which created it) 'the balanced development of universities so that their resources could be used to the greatest possible advantage of Australia'.

This was a momentous initiative. In the past, the Commonwealth had supported the universities through the states while avoiding direct involvement in university affairs. Now it was appointing a more or less independent body, chaired by the Melbourne physicist Sir Leslie Martin, to oversee the system. While each state government continued to have responsibility for its own university or universities, the

In the temporary administration building, members of the Australian Universities Commission meet senior members of the University (and prospective founders of a research school of chemistry) in 1962. The Vice-Chancellor, Huxley, is at the far end of the table, in front of the door, and the Chairman of the AUC, Sir Leslie Martin, six to his right. Much of the discussion is about building projects: plans line the right hand wall, and a model of the proposed building for the Social Sciences and Pacific Studies schools is in the centre.

Australian Universities Commission quickly assumed a major role in determining how each university and the system as a whole should be allowed to develop and in demanding levels of accountability. This was a revolution in central planning, more in keeping with the activities of the post-war Labor governments than with the restrained rule of Menzies and his colleagues. Until a decade ago, said Stretton in 1964, there was only micro-analysis, or rather micro-impressionism, of university problems: 'People in universities knew what they were like, and had various ideas of what they needed'. Now there were foundations for planning, both rational and national. 'We can count the customers, compare the costs, predict the breakdowns.' It was becoming possible to make an informed choice about how much of the national effort should go to the universities, and about the most economical distribution of resources among them. In short, where the individual universities had once stood in tenuous relationship to one another and to the Commonwealth government, the creation of the AUC signalled the beginnings of a university *system*.

Astute commentators at the time, such as Stretton and Partridge, noted that these changes entailed risks. There was a tendency, wrote Partridge, to regard universities as public institutions, giving effect to important aspects of public policy, and therefore being accountable for the way in which they carried out their public functions. He wondered what this would mean for traditional ideas about academic autonomy. Would universities in the future, he asked, be less independent, more conformist, more utilitarian, more fully professionalised? Universities, once fairly well insulated from their host society, would now be obliged to have carefully prepared policies that could be defended before such bodies as the AUC.

What did the changes mean for the ANU? Initially there was some doubt whether the University would be part of the system at all. The AUC Act, which referred explicitly to 'universities established by the Commonwealth', made it clear that it would. But in early meetings between members of the Commission and the University, both parties were unsure what the exact nature of the relationship should be. The Commission decided to assess the needs of the ANU alongside those of the state universities, while acknowledging that the ANU was free to approach the Commonwealth government for any development request, without referring to the Commission. Crawford, however, in his capacity as Fiscal Adviser, concluded that the government was unlikely to support any ANU proposal unless it had AUC support: safest to be in the system rather than out of it. So the University embraced the AUC with guarded optimism, and started to think and plan in terms of the AUC's triennial calendar.

In its submissions to the Commission, the University emphasised, first, that it was quite different in character from the state universities and, second, that each of its two major sections had to maintain its own function. The Commission readily accepted the second premise, which the government took a step further by preventing the transfer of funds from one section to the other. But with regard to the first, the AUC did not take long to decide that the School of General Studies could be compared with any other Australian university. Nor did the University take long to realise that such comparisons might not be to its advantage. Although the system was well endowed, the demand for funds invariably exceeded the supply. For example, submissions from all universities for the triennium beginning in 1967 totalled £103 million compared with £41 million for the triennium then current. In such circumstances, all the universities, the School included, would have to exercise restraint.

People elsewhere in the system were on the watch for signs of favouritism. When the Commission visited the ANU in 1962, Martin warned that he and his fellow commissioners would have to look critically at building projects, since other universities sometimes felt that the ANU received special treatment from the AUC. Another of the commissioners (the retailer and philanthropist K.B. Myer) remarked pointedly that the University was proposing an extensive program for relatively few students. Crawford drew the conclusion, obvious only in retrospect, that the Commission was inclined to make comparisons between universities in terms of costs per student. This policy, as part of an increasing tendency to make statistical data the basis of policy decisions, had implications for the debate on the size of the School: the ANU might wish to restrict undergraduate numbers, but would it be allowed to do so? As Stretton remarked, 'objective' planning almost invariably made a case for big universities. On matters such as academic salaries and student to staff ratios, the School of General Studies found itself (sometimes reluctantly) pulled into line.

Having decided that the Institute was unique, the AUC continued to treat it as a special case with needs over and above those of ordinary universities. Australia could afford only one such organisation, said Martin, so it had to be a good one. Funds were therefore granted to the Institute without specific reference to submissions from other universities. The Commission accepted that members of the Institute should

Charles Bastable, a designer in the Buildings and Grounds division and occasional cartoonist for ANU publications, depicts the AUC as a source of munificence, about 1971.

receive higher salaries than their counterparts in state universities and the School of General Studies, and encouraged them to assert their identity, advising for example that all grades of subprofessorial staff should have distinctive titles. So, at the Commission's suggestion, Readers in the Institute became 'Professorial Fellows', a title unique to the ANU which not too subtly disguised the salary differential.

The Institute was said to be unique, not just in its form and functions, but also in the quality of its research. 'Our constant aim must be excellence', declared an Institute policy paper in 1962; and for many years, until the word lost meaning through overusage, 'excellence', whether aimed for or achieved, was proclaimed as a distinguishing feature.

As the University told the AUC, the Institute was not in competition with the state universities. In fact, the research schools set themselves apart by deliberately avoiding research in areas which state universities claimed as their own. This policy led the Institute to define its role as conducting outstanding research and training in a limited range of subject areas where it had what the economists referred to as a 'comparative advantage'. This could take several forms: the location of Canberra (relevant for Astronomy), the availability of outstanding equipment (such as accelerators in Physical Sciences and the purpose-built instruments in Neurophysiology), and the presence at the ANU of academics whose brilliance was reason in itself for promoting particular areas of research. More often than not, the work of the research schools was justified by a combination of such advantages which placed the Institute in a league of its own, or at least in a position of leadership.

The School of General Studies seemed to challenge the University's claim to uniqueness. During an early visit to the ANU, Martin remarked that the University's main problem was to reach some understanding about the School's role and suggested that if it was to play its true part in a national university it must have a stature and character different from the universities in the states. This was easier said than done. Crawford, when he became Vice-Chancellor, conceded that the School had not departed much from the traditional mould and urged fresh thinking to avoid conformity. Oliphant, with characteristic bluntness, expressed widely held fears that the threat to the University's uniqueness came from within: 'The more that formal undergraduate training is allowed to dominate the University, the more certainly we shall become just another Australian university'.

'Poor relations'

Melville set the tone of relations between the two parts of the University in his 1960 graduation address. 'Nothing would be more tragic', he declared, 'than if a great teaching university grew up at the expense of a great research institution'. The whole University, said Melville, must advance evenly: 'but the pace must be set by the Institute'.

Menzies may have intended that Canberra should have only one university, but in many respects there continued to be two, albeit sharing the one name and the one campus. Between the two there was a good deal of cooperation, as there had been before amalgamation. This differed greatly from one subject area to the next, and changed as each part of the University took on new areas of teaching or research. In the early years, members of the John Curtin School, for example, had virtually nothing to do with SGS (the School of General Studies), where there was nobody with similar research interests. Oliphant complained that he had offered to give lectures in the School at any level, but had been brushed off. On the other hand, social scientists from several departments strolled across the campus to give the occasional lecture or participate in a joint seminar.

The dual structure had significant administrative and academic costs, the most obvious of which were seen in the Library. The University's foundation Librarian, A.L.G. McDonald retired at the time of amalgamation, and was succeeded by his deputy, J.J. Graneek, who had the formidable task of seeking to achieve, as he put it, 'a measure of unity in diversity'. Unity at first existed only in name. While there was a University Library and a University Librarian, there were two collections, each administered by an associate librarian, each with a cataloguing system incompatible with the other, and each housed in its own building. New buildings were opened in 1963 for each collection. The building for the Institute collection was named after R.G. Menzies, to honour the universities' current and prospective benefactor. The SGS building was initially called the General Studies Library until Crisp and others urged that it be given comparable status with the Menzies by calling it the J.B. Chifley Building, to remember the Prime Minister at the time the ANU was founded, and at the same time maintain the University's bipartisan spirit. To complicate matters, the natural science schools already had their own small libraries, while separate collections were planned for other areas, including Oriental Studies and Law.

Undergraduates in the reference section of the Chifley Library, 1960s.
National Library of Australia.

With the two main collections growing side by side within a limited overall budget, the Librarian had no chance of pleasing everyone. Each side of the campus suggested that the other was being favoured. People in the Institute complained about delays in cataloguing, insufficient opening times, and the absurdity of having to use the Chifley Building as external borrowers. Their colleagues in SGS insisted that undergraduates should have access to the whole University collection. As Crisp concluded in 1968, the original decision to divide the Library into two had been 'administratively and financially disastrous'. By that time the Library housed half a million books, and was growing at a faster rate than the architects of amalgamation had ever foreseen.

Graneek worked hard to rationalise the administration and the collections, abandoning the system of associate librarians in charge of each collection in favour of librarians responsible for subject areas. He proposed that the two buildings should be known as the research and undergraduate collections, serving the needs of the University as a whole. And he replaced the inadequate Bliss classification system, as

Two professors of History with contrasting views of the world: *above*, Manning Clark in the School of General Studies, 1969; *below*, John La Nauze in the Institute of Advanced Studies, about the same time.

well as the less unsatisfactory Dewey, by a single Library of Congress catalogue. By the time of his retirement in 1972, computer technology was offering new opportunities for remedying the mistakes of the past.

Practical problems aside, the University in two parts created an environment which encouraged disharmony. At the outset, the mood of the Institute was uncompromising, even on seemingly trivial matters of nomenclature. When the College asked on the eve of amalgamation if the academic bodies in the research schools could be renamed so that the term 'faculty' was used only in relation to the School of General Studies, the new Board of the Institute snubbed the proposal, declaring that the two parts of the University were quite separate and that the change would be too much trouble. Members of the School wanted the first residential hall for undergraduate students to be named after the first Principal of SGS, Burton, but their colleagues in the Institute preferred to honour the retiring Chancellor, Bruce, perhaps in the hope (in due course realised) that he would remember the University in his will. The advocates of Bruce got their way, and Burton had to wait. Among members of the School the mood was resentful. Huxley tended to be dismissive of their grievances, remarking on his retirement that many of them 'chose to assume the role of poor relations'.

The mutual antipathy was nowhere more evident than between the heads of the History departments in the School of General Studies and the Research School of Social Sciences (RSSS). Manning Clark in SGS never took kindly to rivals; but so long as Hancock was in charge of History in RSSS his resentments were largely suppressed.

Hancock was succeeded on his retirement in 1965 by John La Nauze, who came from the Ernest Scott Chair of History at the University of Melbourne. La Nauze and Clark were poles apart, both in their personalities and in their approaches to their discipline. Clark by this time had published *A Short History of Australia* and the first volume of his projected multi-volume history, which offered a grand vision of Australia's past and established his reputation as the nation's most controversial historian. La Nauze had just published, in two volumes, a penetrating and elegantly written biography of the federationist and early Prime Minister Alfred Deakin, which promised to set the standard for Australian biographical writing. Where Clark saw himself as an artist who wanted 'to paint the human heart in all its complexity', La Nauze's main commitment was to rigorous professionalism in historical inquiry. Where Clark looked for the mystery at the heart of things, La Nauze looked for technical perfection in books, articles and theses. La Nauze was a fierce rationalist: when a Catholic historian had asked at a conference of historians some years earlier whether he could cite God as a cause in history, La Nauze had passed around a blank sheet of paper with a footnote '1. God'. With a cutting tongue, sharpened at high tables at Oxford and Cambridge, he had no time for what he saw as Clark's sloppiness and flamboyant behaviour. Clark in turn regarded him as a 'fact-finder' from the company of 'Historical Industries Proprietary Limited'.

Clark and La Nauze would have been opposites in any context. But the structure of the University widened the distance between them. After Clark's death in 1991, his publisher Peter Ryan remembered an occasion when Clark made 'a long, bitchy and very witty verbal assault on the Institute of Advanced Studies, all it stood for, and all who worked there'. As they strolled in the sun outside the Haydon-Allen Building, Ryan tried to placate him.

> He turned and seized my arm with almost ferocious bitterness: 'Let me put it in terms which you might understand. How would *you* feel if it were an Institute of Advanced *Fucking*, and you were left down below with all the General Fuckers?'

'You're the star of this campus, on any terms', Ryan told Clark. Whether or not this was true, it seemed that the School was starting to set the pace. While the Institute continued to be responsible for admitting and examining doctoral students, the School became increasingly involved in PhD supervision. The University's proposals for the 1964–66 triennium acknowledged SGS initiatives by arguing that there should be considerable development of postgraduate teaching and research in the School; and in 1964 the heads of the research schools decided that the Institute needed to have 'clear and firm policy and ideas to match the increasing vigour of the School'.

Wise heads in the Institute saw the future in cooperation rather than competition. Partridge suggested that the separate development of postgraduate teaching would lead to a waste of resources which would be hard to defend. Why not make all the resources of the whole University available for postgraduate training and set up a committee to oversee informal collaboration? The natural scientists tended to see such moves as the beginning of the end. Jaeger, now Dean of Physical Sciences, pronounced that it was 'absurd and impracticable' for one part of the University to attempt to control the degrees of the other: 'we seem to be involved in the obvious processes of confrontation by the S.G.S. and what seems to be a growing philosophy of appeasement by the Institute'. Oliphant urged Huxley to enforce a 'complete separation, administratively, of Institute and School' and to avoid compromises, which would inevitably weaken the Institute. The symbols of difference must also be maintained, including the salary differential which, according to the physicists, was 'a clear indication of the difference between the School and the Institute and the policy of excellence in the latter'.

In the last years of Huxley's administration, relations between the two parts of the

L.F. (Fin) Crisp, Professor of Political Science, SGS, since 1950, prepares to vacate his office in the Childers Street buildings. A determined opponent of amalgamation, he remained in the old Canberra University College quarters until 1972, when the department moved to the Haydon-Allen Building. Photograph by Gabe Carpay.

University reached their nadir. Crawford, when he assumed office as Vice-Chancellor, aimed to heal the breach, signalling at once his intention to get rid of the offensive name 'School of General Studies'. The task ahead, he said, was to blend the work of the Institute and the School, so that while there was a spectrum ranging from an emphasis on research in the Institute to an emphasis on undergraduate teaching in the School, there would now be far more common ground in which research and teaching at all levels were shared. He promised to promote the unity of the University; but at the same time he undertook to maintain the structure created by the 1960 legislation, so that the identity of the research schools and the uniqueness of the Institute would not be impaired. Much of Crawford's formidable energy was directed towards meeting these contending aims.

Governing the University

Although the ANU was unique, the broad structure of its government was the same as other Australian universities, which in turn had drawn on British models. Its key elements, as defined in the 1946 legislation and refined in the 1960 amendments, had served the University well.

At the peak of the structure was the Council, described in the legislation as the University's 'governing authority'. The Act gave Council 'the entire control and management of the affairs and concerns of the University', while allowing it to delegate to any member or committee any or all of its powers, excepting the power to delegate and to make statutes. Like its counterparts in the state universities, Council comprised a mix of academic and lay members, some nominated, some elected and some coopted. The nominated members enabled the Commonwealth government, formally through the governor-general, to have a significant influence in University affairs. The elected members represented each house of federal parliament; the University staff; the students; and convocation, which was in turn made up of past and present members of Council, graduates of the University, and anyone else Council chose to admit through its statutes.

In the absence of a powerful professorial board, the non-academic members of Council continued to play a prominent part in the affairs of the University, probably more so than did their counterparts in any of the state institutions. This was also a legacy of the Interim Council's influence in shaping the University over so many years. Every so often one of the academic boards complained that Council was ignoring the wishes of the academics; and Oliphant thought it objectionable in principle that non-academics should have a say in academic matters. But he, when the mood took him, was just as likely to applaud the contribution of the non-academic Coombs.

The effectiveness of Council depended more on the people who sat on it than its formal composition. The ANU was lucky to have among the non-academic members people with specific expertise or privileged access to government who could be brought into the University's service. H.J. Goodes, for example, notwithstanding his earlier contretemps with Copland, proved a loyal friend to the University and provided a direct line to Treasury. He served on Council (initially the Interim Council) for over twenty years. John Ewens, the Commonwealth Parliamentary Draftsman, transferred from the College Council in 1960 and remained until 1973. As well as giving expert advice on legislation, he was one of the Council workhorses, carrying the burden of demanding jobs that nobody else wanted to do. The longest-serving member, longer (by a few months) even than Coombs, was Pansy Wright who, as Sir Douglas Wright, retired in 1976, 30 years after joining the Interim Council. He remained throughout a staunch defender of the University's interests and a forthright critic of anyone inside who failed to measure up or outside who tried to put it down.

As well as creating the Council and specifying its powers, the 1946 Act named the University's two most senior officers, the chancellor and the vice-chancellor. The chancellor's position was honorary and his most important functions were symbolic. A chancellor was like a coat of arms and a motto: every university had to have one.

There was symbolic significance in the fact that the first three Chancellors were based in England. The first, Lord Bruce, served for a decade, representing the University at ceremonial functions in Britain, helping out in relation to senior appointments, and occasionally visiting Canberra, where he lent status and antiquity (if not too much in the way of refinement) to the chancellor's office. He was hard to replace: but as he approached 80 and became increasingly deaf, Council set out in earnest to identify a successor. Unable to find someone suitable in Australia, Council elected the physicist Sir John Cockcroft, who had previously been considered as a potential vice-chancellor and who was now Master of Churchill College, Cambridge. Under a new policy, Cockcroft served for the maximum four years, in two-year terms. He proved a valuable acquisition, visiting Australia regularly and helping out in Britain, especially in relation to the formation of the Research School of Chemistry. On Cockcroft's retirement in 1965, Florey, now Lord Florey and no longer a potential director of the John Curtin School of Medical Research (JCSMR), was an obvious successor. He served diligently into the second of his two-year terms, but died in office in 1968.

Sir John Cockcroft, Chancellor from 1961 to 1965.

Local functions of successive chancellors were performed in their absence by Coombs, first as Deputy Chairman of Council, then as Pro-Chancellor, a position created especially for him in 1959. The most important of these functions, apart from the ceremonial, was presiding at Council meetings. Coombs had other jobs which were more than 'full-time': he was Governor of the central bank, known as the Commonwealth Bank until 1960 and then as the Reserve Bank. But he continued to involve himself closely in University affairs, including major policy issues and appointments, and the development of the social science schools. Although his manner of speaking tended to be flat and uninspiring, he could see ahead of others to the essence of an issue, make sense of the most involved debates, and through force of argument and the information at his disposal persuade fellow councillors of the wisdom of pursuing a specific course of action. 'He really was', as Sawer later put it, 'an intellectual eminence'.

On Florey's death, Council elected Coombs to be the fourth Chancellor. The appointment coincided with his impending retirement from the Reserve Bank, and justly acknowledged his previous role as de facto resident Chancellor over so many

Sir John Crawford, Director of the Research School of Pacific Studies from 1960 to 1967, Vice-Chancellor from 1968 to 1973, and Chancellor from 1976 to 1984. Oil by Bryan Westwood, 1973.

years. As with previous chancellors, his election was symbolic. The University, more confident of its own status in the academic and political world, had less cause to seek patronage from abroad. Coombs, the local boy who had more than once declined imperial honours, carried all the prestige and influence the University needed.

From Copland's time onwards, the most powerful officer in the University, in terms of formal status, was the vice-chancellor, who was nominated in the Acts and Statutes as the University's executive officer, responsible to Council for the academic and financial administration of the University. He was ex-officio a member of every faculty, board and committee, and Chairman of the Standing Committee of Council and the Professorial Board. He was formally Chairman of the boards of Graduate Studies (to 1960) and the Institute and School (from 1960), although Huxley and his successors left these responsibilities to the deputy chairmen.

The vice-chancellor's duties evolved as the University changed, so that Crawford's job in a University with four thousand students was vastly different from Copland's in an institution with (initially) none. The office also adjusted to the style and personal interests of its incumbents. While every vice-chancellor could rely to an extent on the formal definition of his power and the general understanding that he was the most senior individual in the University, his real influence depended as much on personal capacity and academic prestige.

Crawford had an abundance of both. As Fiscal Adviser he had been, as he privately called himself, the University's 'principal "inside" rescuer', with Coombs filling a comparable position on the 'outside'. He accepted the appointment as Vice-Chancellor, in preference to other tempting positions, on the understanding that he was no longer to carry the main theme from the second fiddle's chair.

Like Coombs, he was short, unassuming in manner but vastly impressive for his depth of knowledge, understanding of issues and diplomatic skills. Russell Mathews, whom we met in London in the early 1950s and who in Crawford's time occupied various senior positions including Dean of the Faculty of Economics, listed his qualities as 'authority, persuasiveness, reason, fairness, humanity, integrity, stubbornness, fiscal acumen, a background of scholarship and public service, academic vision and administrative capacity'. He was most impressive when taking a submission to government or the AUC for more funding, or in meetings with staff and students, where he was able to listen to all sides of a debate, sum up the feeling of the meeting, and put his own stamp on the outcome. He knew how to get the most out of people and made extensive use of the creative talent around him. He was innovative, but with a keen appreciation that innovation was subject to financial and institutional constraints. He was, to use a word just then coming into popular usage, a workaholic.

If Crawford had a fault, it was his willingness to take on too much. He was in heavy demand, especially from government and international organisations, including the World Bank. Aware of his own capacity, he insisted, both as Director of the Research School of Pacific Studies (RSPacS) and Vice-Chancellor, on his right to decide for himself how many outside activities he could handle. He was perpetually overextended, and the senior administrators often found themselves squeezed in at

Two bastions of the administration: *above*, Bill Hamilton, Accountant, 1950–1956, Bursar, 1956–1974, and Registrar, 1974–1978, photographed in 1974; and *below*, David Hodgkin, Registrar, IAS, 1961–1968, and Registrar, 1968–1974, photographed in 1968. With Ross Hohnen, they were sometimes called 'the three H's'.

the end of a long day when he was unable to give his best. Capable of extraordinary bursts of concentration, he might achieve more in an hour than others did in a day: but those who worked with him sometimes wished he would learn how to say 'no'.

The administrative staff had always played a major part in the development of the University. When Crawford became Vice-Chancellor in 1968, Hohnen had been on the staff for nearly twenty years, all but one of them as Registrar. Hamilton, now styled the Bursar, who had been with Copland in China, was not far behind. Many others had been at either the University or the College well before amalgamation and were destined to remain at the ANU for most of their working lives. Where many academics tended to come and go, long-serving administrators developed a strong sense of loyalty to the institution, which Hohnen in particular worked hard to encourage. They also, through knowledge of procedures and precedents, went a fair way towards making themselves indispensable.

Hohnen shared Copland's vision of a great national institution, whose objectives had been outlined by Dedman in his second reading speech on the ANU bill and whose design had been formulated in the first half dozen or so years of its existence. He pursued this vision energetically, almost relentlessly. Forthright in speech and occasionally overbearing in manner, he was (to borrow a phrase he used of Copland) 'a boots and spurs man'. At the same time, he perceived the University as a close-knit family, in which the administration played a paternal role, as much concerned with the domestic welfare of staff and students as with their academic needs. He believed that administrators should do everything they could to create an appropriate environment for productive research (which was not the same as Florey's notion of administrators as the academics' unseen and obedient servants). His door in the old Administrative Building and later in the Chancelry (a term which he borrowed for the purpose) was always open, and he, Hamilton and other senior administrators were often seen talking with academic staff in other buildings across the campus.

There is always a fine line between the creation of policies and their execution. The bald description of the Registrar as secretary to Council and head of the University's administrative structure might suggest that he was a mere functionary, without a significant creative role. In fact, Hohnen assumed responsibilities which gave himself and those directly under him a major part in the making of the University. He was largely responsible for the University's housing scheme, without which it would have been impossible in the early years to attract and retain staff. He recruited the furniture designer Frederick Ward, whose designs lent dignity and elegance to University House. He contributed to major academic initiatives, including the Australian Dictionary of Biography and the Research School of Chemistry.

Hohnen's influence varied according to his working relationship with successive vice-chancellors. He and Copland worked as one, united in their understanding of the University's objectives and how to achieve them. By contrast, Melville's restrained approach was somewhat inhibiting and more to the liking of the Bursar, Hamilton, who admired his overall command of the University's finances, his shrewdness and humanity. Huxley, more inclined to delegate than his predecessor and with more occasion to do so, made the Registrar formally responsible for correspondence on administrative and policy matters, and for negotiations with government and the AUC.

When Crawford became Vice-Chancellor, the University's administrative culture changed significantly, partly as a result of the continuing growth in staff and student numbers and partly because he believed the vice-chancellor should retain firm control over all aspects of administration. His years as Fiscal Adviser and Director of RSPacS had given him a clear view of how the administration worked; and in the months before he took office as Vice-Chancellor, he worked with Hohnen to plan major administrative changes. These were part of his larger efforts to bring about a greater sense of unity in the University. The old positions of Registrar of the Institute and Registrar of the School of General Studies were abandoned in favour of a single structure, with the duties of senior officers being determined by their administrative function rather than by their responsibility to one of the University's two academic divisions.

The other major ingredient of these changes was a clearer distinction between academic and administrative activities. To assist him on the academic side (and at the same time enhance the status of SGS), Crawford asked Council to appoint a full-time Deputy Vice-Chancellor in place of the part-time deputies of previous years. Noel Dunbar, Professor of Physics in SGS, was appointed to this position and acted for Crawford during his frequent absences from Canberra. Crawford strengthened the administrative side by extending Hohnen's responsibility under the vice-chancellor for the whole administrative structure, while distancing himself from day to day administrative routines. At the same time he specified that the senior administrative officer, now styled Secretary to the University, should have no responsibility for policy formulation in relation to teaching and research. That was a job for the academics.

Noel Dunbar, Professor of Physics, SGS, and Deputy Vice-Chancellor, in 1969.

Outside the Chancelry, the academic government of the University took place at the faculty, research school and departmental level. The structure of the School of General Studies resembled that of most of the state universities, where the main academic divisions were faculties and departments. At amalgamation, the University inherited from the College four faculties—Arts, Economics, Law and Science—plus a School of Oriental Studies, which soon became a faculty. The faculties or elected faculty boards had responsibilities relating to staff appointments, student admissions, degree structures, and other policy and administrative matters. Each faculty was chaired by an elected dean, who executed policies determined by faculty or faculty board and represented the faculty on School and University boards and committees. The powers of a dean in SGS were modest, especially in contrast to their counterparts in some of the new state universities, where deans controlled large portions of the university budget.

Much real power in SGS resided in the departments. The main formal recognition of the department was in the conditions of appointment of professors, which referred to their responsibilities as departmental heads. A head of department was expected to exercise leadership in relation to research and teaching, but the nature of that leadership was rarely defined. Whether a department was authoritarian or democratic in its workings depended largely on the personality of the professor who ran it. In the mid-1960s the Staff Association was questioning whether professors should remain heads indefinitely and suggesting that there should occasionally be departmental meetings. But for some time yet, until students started to insist on a say in university affairs, the head of department could play God, if he had a mind to do so.

Departmental autonomy was also a common ingredient in the government of the four original research schools. (The new Research School of Chemistry put into practice the revolutionary notion of having no departments.) Beyond that they differed significantly, especially between the social science and natural science schools. The social scientists, with their faculties and faculty boards, enjoyed a degree of democracy which the early deans and directors upheld. In the natural science schools, the professors successfully resisted the formation of faculty structures, retaining power in their own hands and exercising it through school committees, comprising only the director or dean and themselves.

Oliphant continued as Director of the Research School of Physical Sciences (RSPhysS) until 1963 when, weary of the administrative burden and weighed down by problems with his own projects, he withdrew to the back bench as a professor in the school. In the early years he had resisted any suggestion of sharing power: when there was talk of recruiting the distinguished physicist Harrie Massey in the late 1940s, he offered to resign rather than contemplate any possible weakening of the Director's authority. But the men whom Oliphant appointed to the first chairs—Titterton and Jaeger—were no shrinking violets, and nor was Woolley; and when Oliphant attempted to influence research directions in departments other than his own, as he did in the case of Geophysics, they were inclined to resist. Like it or not, Oliphant saw his powers receding in favour of an oligarchy, in which he was acknowledged with mixed enthusiasm as the most senior member.

Oliphant's resignation as Director introduced a period of prolonged uncertainty about the headship of the Physical Sciences school. After consulting Oliphant, Coombs and a small group of fellow councillors concluded that in view of the diverse nature of research in RSPhysS and the strong sense of departmental identity, there was little chance of finding a person who would be able to exercise intellectual leadership. Best, therefore, to appoint a dean, as in the other schools, and to emphasise the administrative responsibilities of the position. Jaeger was asked to fulfil this role, which he did reluctantly and on the understanding that he should not interfere in the work of individual departments.

As RSPhysS grew, so its unity diminished. By 1965 Coombs and his colleagues were alarmed that it was swallowing 40 per cent of the Institute's overall budget and growing at the expense of the other schools. At the same time Jaeger was referring ominously to 'an unwieldy complex of departments which were frustrated because they could not expand' and pressing, as he had done for some years, for a separate school of earth sciences. Reversing an earlier decision, Coombs and his committee now decided that the school needed a permanent director, appointed from outside the University, who would plan and direct the work of the school over a period of at least seven years. As nobody could be found, and as Jaeger made it clear that he had had enough, Council decided that Titterton should be appointed for three years as Dean.

Even the most astute administrator (which Titterton wasn't) would have found the growing tensions within the school hard to manage. As pressure for resources increased, departments became 'pot-bound', as Jaeger put it, and more competitive with one another. There were fissiparous tendencies, in the form of continuing pressure from the geophysicists, the mathematicians and the astronomers to break away from Physical Sciences and create new schools of their own. Then there was pressure from staff, many of them quite senior, who were becoming increasingly frustrated that they played no part in school decision-making. Democracy asserted itself in 1967 when the academic staff met to express their 'genuine and deep dissatisfaction' with the RSPhysS school committee and some heads of departments, and to ask the Vice-Chancellor to do something about the school's administrative structure. Ironically Oliphant, no longer a head of department but still the school's most senior member of staff, consented to chair the meeting and carry the people's demands to the Vice-Chancellor. One way or another, something had to give: the only question was when.

The story was similar in the John Curtin School, where the notion of God Professor extended beyond Olympian heights. From time to time after Florey's resignation as Adviser to the school, the professors discussed the chances of importing a distinguished scientist to direct them. On each occasion they concluded that nobody of sufficient distinction would be attracted to a position which offered, now that the school was well established, so little room for opening up new areas of research. Within the school, Eccles was acknowledged as the outstanding scientist; but he had neither the desire nor the administrative capacity to run it. So Ennor remained as Dean, willingly accepted for his skills as an administrator, but only on the understanding that he did not try to tell the others what to do. After a series of temporary appointments, in 1962 he was offered the deanship on a more or less permanent basis.

Departments were regarded as sancrosanct, a perception encouraged by the shape of the John Curtin School building. When Eccles complained to his colleagues that a member of another department had brought strangers into his wing without first asking permission, there were nods of agreement that this should not happen again. Albert worked hard to convert his kingdom of Medical Chemistry into an empire, inhabiting what Ennor and Eccles called a 'palace' that was vastly larger than Florey ever intended. He fiercely resisted encroachments, specifically by a nominee of Wright, Frank Dwyer, whose research in biological inorganic chemistry was proving embarrassingly successful.

Research in the departments continued to thrive, but the school as a whole began to suffer from a lack of long-term planning. By the mid-1960s most of the departments were reaching their complement of staff and the school's building was full. There was little room for variations on the existing pattern. With the impending retirement of some of the senior professors, Wright warned Florey that the school was running down. This was unduly alarmist: but increasingly members of staff were wondering where the school was headed.

As in the Physical Sciences school, there were rumblings among the 'other ranks'. Through the Staff Association and at meetings convened for the purpose, they pressed for regular departmental meetings and the creation of a faculty structure, with appropriate representation for all academic staff. Ennor, supported by most of the school committee for JCSMR, firmly resisted, arguing that there was no problem of government that existing arrangements could not handle.

Ennor was now Deputy Vice-Chancellor; and as Huxley approached retirement, he set his sights on the top job. But there was growing resistance among academic staff to what they perceived to be his autocratic style. As the selection committee prepared to meet, with Florey (on his first visit as Chancellor) in the chair, a group of social scientists organised a petition to draft Coombs to the position, partly as a means of keeping Ennor out. Petition in hand, Bob Gollan strolled over to the John Curtin School, where he explained the move to half a dozen or so of the most senior staff and asked what they thought of Ennor. After a long pause, Bede Morris, a Professorial Fellow in Experimental Pathology, replied in words that cannot be printed. 'Have you told Florey that?' asked Gollan. Morris replied that he had, in the same words.

Coombs declined to stand, but Florey helped persuade Crawford to let his name go forward. This left the selection committee with three strong candidates, Ennor, Crawford and an outsider from Melbourne. Ennor was liked by politicians and would no doubt serve the University well in its relations with government; but Coombs reminded his five colleagues on the committee that they also had to satisfy another 'electorate', the academic body, which might not respect Ennor's judgement. The two medical scientists on the committee were more blunt. Wright dismissed Ennor on the grounds that he had given up his science and that he believed in regulating the academic community through the rule of law. Florey remarked that few of Ennor's colleagues would speak well of him and that there would be a good deal of resistance to his nomination. These comments alone might not have kept Ennor out of the vice-chancellorship, but they certainly helped tip the balance in Crawford's favour.

According to the *Sydney Morning Herald* (12 January 1967), RSSS under Partridge was referred to jocularly as an Athenian democracy, RSPacS under Crawford as a guided democracy, and JCSMR under Ennor as an Oriental despotism. Hence this invitation to his farewell dinner.

We can only guess how much Florey was influenced by Bede Morris's unprintable opinion of Ennor, or by Florey's own experiences in Oxford nearly a decade earlier. What is clear is that the staff of the University were demanding a voice in its government and that, more obviously than before, the vice-chancellor would have to possess their confidence. Ennor had no time for consultation and showed little respect for contrary opinions. His administrative style was characterised by a comment he had once made to Florey about one of the University architects: 'at times one must pick up the first weapon that lies at hand in the hope that somebody may be beaten down into a submissive state'. In the early years of the ANU, when the main task was to get things done, this uncompromising approach had much value. But by the time he was a candidate for the vice-chancellor's position, confrontation had no place as an instrument of University government.

Several months after Council announced Crawford's appointment, Ennor suffered another blow when a meeting of the academic staff in the John Curtin School voted, against his express wishes, in favour of a faculty structure and asked him to convey the resolution to Council. Turned down for the vice-chancellorship and now defied in his own school, Ennor 'got the huff', as Wright put it, 'and sought comfort in the bosom of John Gorton', the Minister for Education and Science. Gorton appointed him to head his new department, where a later Science minister, Labor's Bill Morrison, dubbed him

'Sir Huge Error', for reasons that may find a place in someone else's history.

In response to the revolt in JCSMR, Huxley, as one of his last acts as Vice-Chancellor, proposed a formal inquiry into the government of the school. Crawford followed through, appointing a committee chaired by an 'outsider', David Bensusan-Butt, an economist from Pacific Studies and former British civil servant, who had a keen appreciation of how institutions work. Butt and his colleagues did a thorough job, looking closely into existing arrangements in JCSMR, and making recommendations which related to all the research schools. They knew, as Ennor evidently did not, that 'Academics share the normal human characteristics of disliking having decisions affecting themselves taken over their heads ... They like to have a right to have their say (whether they use it or not), and to be consulted (even though sometimes they may have little to offer).' Endorsing the 'ancient ideal of a University as a self-governing community of scholars', the committee proposed that the John Curtin School immediately introduce a faculty structure, comprising a faculty and faculty board. The faculty, which would meet at least once a term, would offer a forum for all members of the academic staff to air their views and hear about policy developments throughout the school and the University. The faculty board, comprising the head of school, the heads of departments and a limited number of staff representatives, would make decisions about general matters of academic policy, as well as appointments, promotions and financial management. It would be small enough to avoid becoming 'infested by chatterboxes' (a problem which might overtake faculty as a whole), yet large enough to avoid 'a detestable feeling of professors versus plebs'.

The committee concluded that the head of school should continue to have wide-ranging powers, including final responsibility for the school budget, the opportunity for independent confidential discussion with the vice-chancellor on any school or Institute matter, and the right to determine issues that were too urgent or personal to present to faculty board. These should give the holder of the office 'ample scope for creative leadership', provided that it was exercised by persuasion and consultation rather than command.

Members of JCSMR welcomed the report, almost with a sense of relief that past troubles were now behind them. The faculty structure was adopted, and after an interregnum, Frank Fenner was appointed head of school, the first to hold the title Director. Although he had never shown much enthusiasm for administration, Fenner's academic credentials were outstanding. He knew the school and its problems, and having been a member of the Butt committee, he knew what the staff expected in a head. Enjoying their confidence, as well as that of the new Vice-Chancellor, he looked forward to offering firm and creative leadership within the new faculty structure.

In Physical Sciences, too, the Butt report was greeted enthusiastically by the other ranks. Titterton thought it was an excellent report, full of sound commonsense, and moved immediately to give it effect. Not everyone was happy: Jaeger and Olin Eggen, the head of Mount Stromlo, strongly resisted enlarging the present school committee, and tried to have the matter deferred. But Titterton had support from above and below, so the diehards were dragged reluctantly into the new era of democracy.

Lost vistas: although Denis Winston and Grenfell Rudduck changed much of Brian Lewis's plan for the University, they retained his emphasis on the ceremonial point at the front of University House, overlooking the lake. These views from the early 1960s capture something of Lewis's original vision.

A new orientation

Brian Lewis, the University's first architect, was gone. Even before he fell out with the University in 1953, his grand plan had been left to languish, never quite accepted and never entirely rejected. Temporary structures remained along the Acton ridge, and were added to without reference to his plan, so that his favoured site increasingly resembled an odd assortment of disconnected buildings.

In his place, the University appointed another academic architect, Denis Winston, Professor of Town and Country Planning at the University of Sydney, and Grenfell Rudduck, a senior member of the Commonwealth Department of National Development, whose association with the University dated from 1947 when he was appointed a Social Science Research Fellow. Winston and Rudduck were pragmatic planners, more concerned with the functional requirements of buildings and the relationships between them than with the aesthetic composition of buildings and landscape. They also held that existing developments of value (which presumably included some of the old hospital buildings) should be retained wherever practicable. Rather than focusing, as Lewis had done, on the overall site plan, they emphasised the needs of the individual research schools, arguing that each group of buildings should have plenty of room to expand 'without having to conform rigidly to a pre-conceived architectural scheme for the whole University'. Where Lewis had arranged the University along a dominant geographical feature and had sketched in less than half the available acreage, they looked towards developing the whole site. This left them free to consider locating the library and the social science buildings off the ridge, behind and to the side of University House, and to imagine new developments stretching towards University Avenue. While they retained a concentration of buildings along the ridge, they abandoned Lewis's symmetry. But they restated his emphasis on the high, southeastern end of the axis, where they placed a tower, a great hall, an art gallery and a theatre, all commanding a splendid vista over the west basin of the proposed lake.

So well before amalgamation, the University on paper had started moving down the hill towards University Avenue and the site assigned to Canberra University College. Amalgamation confirmed the process. At the time of the merger, Winston was the University's only site consultant, Rudduck having resigned some years earlier. Winston was also site consultant for the College, the first elements of which were starting to appear on the landscape. Now the two plans were brought together, and Winston was given a fresh commission to prepare a site plan for the new, expanded campus. As his earlier plans for the College were quite in keeping with his ideas for the University, the architectural merger proceeded a good deal more harmoniously than the academic one.

Winston's composite plan guided the University during most of the 1960s and fixed the location of over a dozen major buildings, including the Chancelry, the SGS library, the (old) student Union, the residential college, and buildings for most of the teaching faculties. As there was still plenty of room for growth, and as Winston made generous provision for each academic and administrative centre, members of the University tended to accept his ideas uncritically and focus on their specific building needs. The main challenges to the site plan came from the authority responsible for the planning of Canberra, the National Capital Development Commission (NCDC), which engaged in a process referred to by a University administrator as 'filching University land' to provide more room for business growth in the city centre and allow for arterial road developments. Under intense pressure to negotiate a new perpetual lease, Council yielded the equivalent of several blocks facing the city near University Avenue. But it stood firm against proposals for a western distributor, which threatened under one proposal to cut a swathe between the social sciences building, then under construction, and Canberra High School (later the Canberra School of Art). From these prolonged and sometimes heated exchanges with the NCDC, the University administration learnt that a 'lease in perpetuity' was only as perpetual as successive governments were prepared to concede and the University was determined to defend.

By the late 1960s the ANU was growing at a pace which seemed to be leaving Winston's plans some distance behind. The main problems related to the School of General Studies, where he had adopted much the same approach as he had done for the Institute by giving precedence to the parts over the whole. Rudduck, his erstwhile collaborator and now an Associate Commissioner with the NCDC and a member of Council's Buildings and Grounds Committee, warned in 1961 that a teaching institution, unlike the research schools, needed to be compact. By contrast, Winston's dispersed approach was likely to produce 'one of the most inconvenient Universities in Australia', with students having to drive from their halls of residence to the Union or library, and from one lecture to the next. Those fears were perhaps exaggerated. Yet traffic and parking problems would soon take priority over matters relating to the overall appearance of the campus.

Unlike some of the newer universities, such as Macquarie, Flinders and La Trobe, the buildings at the ANU did not conform to a single architectural style. Florey and Oliphant had set the pattern of divergence when they insisted that the functional needs of each research school should take precedence over any architect's grand notions. As the University grew, the demands of research continued to influence the shape of buildings and the overall appearance of the campus, most obviously at the western extremity of the Acton ridge, where a tower to accommodate a new nuclear accelerator ('Titterton's tower', jovially known at the time as 'Ernie's erection') rose several storeys above the other physics buildings nearby.

Even where the functional requirements of buildings were fairly straightforward, academics often played a major part in planning their design. The contest between Davidson and Hancock over the shape of the H.C. Coombs Building had little to do with the overall design of the ANU. So long as the social scientists were located opposite the library, larger planning questions rarely concerned them. In common with their colleagues across the campus, their approach to building design was parochial. While in the Coombs Building they achieved a building of distinction (or, at least, a distinctive one), it did nothing to help portray the University as a single entity with a single culture.

Architectural diversity was also encouraged by official policy. In the late 1950s Council's Buildings and Grounds committee was chaired by Warren McDonald, a leading figure in the construction industry, who proposed that the University, as a public body, should give as many architectural firms as possible the opportunity to compete for commissions. As a result, nearly every new construction project through to the late 1960s had a new architect, each with his own style and each keen to produce something distinctive.

The combined effect of these influences for diversity was incoherence, to the extent that the distinguished architect and architectural critic Robin Boyd (who himself designed with others the Zoology building, opened in 1964) described the campus as Disneyland and discussed it in a chapter entitled 'The descent into chaos' in his book *The Australian Ugliness*. On the other hand, the ANU avoided the New Brutalism in architecture which characterised at least one other Australian campus (Macquarie) established during the 1960s. In the absence of a unifying architectural theme, the University looked to landscape design to provide coherence. Guided by the Professor of Botany, Lindsay Pryor, gardeners planted trees and shrubs across the campus, adding to the existing stock of exotics but emphasising natives against the backdrop of Black Mountain. Their success was such that, notwithstanding Boyd, the ANU became widely regarded as one of the most attractive campuses in Australia.

While the trees were growing, Council's Buildings and Grounds Committee decided in 1967 that something had to be done to restore order and unity to the site plan. To achieve this the University appointed a full-time site planner, Roy Simpson of Yuncken Freeman Architects, who was noted for his capacity to bring 'aesthetically exciting solutions' to practical planning needs.

In his preliminary assessment of the University's character, Simpson tactfully acknowledged that its better parts were a 'highly attractive recording of the University's evolution in a way that is uniquely Australian'. But he also observed that its less attractive parts highlighted the dangers of a 'permissive and adaptive' planning approach which, if pursued further, could lead to a dull and inefficient suburban scatter, lacking the visionary qualities expected of a National University. Obviously, existing buildings could not be swept aside. The task now was to conserve and integrate the University's assets of character and capital investment.

Simpson's solutions were decisive. First, halt the scatter, concentrating new buildings in four functional groups (the School of General Studies; undergraduate residences; the Institute of Advanced Studies and the ceremonial group) and seeking aesthetic cohesion within each group and significant connections between the groups. Next, maximise the open spaces between the groups, remove (temporary) buildings and roads that impede the contrast between the groups, and improve the road pattern to segregate vehicles and pedestrians. Finally, integrate the internal road system and points of entry with adjacent civic traffic arrangements. While acknowledging claims for individual creativity and freedom of architectural expression, Simpson argued for overall discipline: 'site planning is one of the areas in which a University should speak with one voice'.

In one dramatic gesture, Simpson recognised the University's shifting centre of gravity and confirmed the movement to the north. In the existing plan, the proposed ceremonial group looked over the lake in 'monumental isolation', removed from the

University's day to day activities. Simpson proposed relocating the main elements of this group, including an auditorium, exhibition building and other public entertainment areas, to the eastern end of University Avenue, which would be developed as a pedestrian precinct and 'the main spine of undergraduate activities'. Here, near the centre of undergraduate activity and where the University faced the city, the ceremonial group would provide 'a striking and appropriate theme for the main gateway to the University, merging town and gown with considerable drama'.

And what should happen to Acton ridge? Simpson agreed with his predecessors that the eastern end demanded special treatment: but the place of the ridge in the geometry of the national capital was so important that underdevelopment would be worse than no development at all. As there was no obvious building waiting to occupy the site, best to tidy it up as parkland and leave it to later generations to build on, as and when they should see fit. He conceded that the relocation was a great sacrifice:

> I would be tempted to sell my soul for the commission for a really monumental complex poised on this lovely ridge, amidst great sweeps of idealised landscape stepping up from the lake's edge. Consequently, my advocacy of another possibility has been no emotional whim, but has grown out of serious doubts as to whether the great vision is an attainable one. So often one gets caught in tides of enthusiasm, only to find the dreams left stranded amongst the kelp and the painful realisation that great splendour cannot be achieved through inadequate resources.
>
> ... This country is littered with the pathetic evidence of impoverished attempts at grandeur. We talk bravely of Versailles—and achieve suburbia. I would like to protect the University from such a result.

So Simpson looked for and found a site where magnificent scale was not obligatory, and where quality could be achieved at reasonable cost.

Few people seem to have appreciated the full significance of the relocation. One who did was Frank Fenner, who asked the planner why he had sited the Great Hall in the heart of the undergraduate area and as far as possible from the main mass of the Institute, which gave the ANU its distinctive quality.

'Where is the "main mass"?' Simpson replied. The Institute was already creeping in towards University Avenue. In any case, did the question matter? The Vice-Chancellor, Crawford, was keen to express the unity of the University as a whole; hence the Great Hall should be situated where it was likely to enhance the campus as a whole, both functionally and aesthetically. The issue was clear cut: 'Is the Great Hall to be built to the glory of advanced research, or as one of the refinements of higher education?'

So Simpson put the Institute in its place as part of 'a transcendent unity' and gave the University a new orientation. Or did he merely give architectural expression to shifts in direction, both physical and philosophical, that had already taken place? The University in 1970, when Council accepted the essence of his proposals, was quite different from the one imagined by Lewis and the planners of the 1940s. Lewis had

Architect Roy Simpson explains to David Dexter, Registrar (Property and Plans), elements of his site plan, 1974. Photograph by Gabe Carpay.

planned for four research schools and an academic population of 400 in an institution dedicated to research and postgraduate training. When Simpson started work, there were some eight hundred research and teaching staff, and over four thousand students, five-sixths of whom were undergraduates. The University was in two parts, but the Vice-Chancellor's declared objective was to make it one.

Simpson also assimilated and expressed changing perspectives about the University's identity in relation to the outside world. At the time of its foundation and for many years thereafter, the University had looked abroad for guidance and inspiration, and specifically to Oxford and Cambridge, which stood out in the world of learning much as the Australian National University was intended to dominate Acton ridge, obediently to Walter Burley Griffin's grand design but largely oblivious to the neighbouring community. Simpson turned the University towards the city centre, creating a significant point of arrival which served both the University and the people of Canberra.

But if he translated the University's new orientation to architectural sketches, Simpson also recognised that it might again change direction, requiring corresponding adjustments to the development plan. 'Growth and time', he pointed out in his report, 'bring changes of physical needs and philosophical approach'. Just as Coombs was reflecting in 1970 on how institutions could deviate from the intentions of their founders (leaving some at least of their dreams 'stranded amongst the kelp'), the site planner was warning that nobody could accurately predict all the University's needs in future years. His plans were plans for the time, which had to allow for future adaptation. Council took the hint, accepting the essence of his proposals as the development plan 'for the foreseeable future', but introducing at his suggestion the notion of continuous planning. Henceforth the site plan would be subject to revision, perhaps at triennial intervals.

The University's shifts in direction left some casualties. One was the relationship to Griffin's water axis and the opportunity to develop the commanding position looking over the lake. Simpson appreciated the potential, imagining a complex of buildings arranged in the manner (but not the style) of a medieval fortification. But as there was no urgent practical need to develop the site, he left it to an uncertain future. At least the vista along University Avenue towards City Hill acknowledged a significant element of Griffin's original design.

At the other end of the ridge, the Physical Sciences and Medical Research schools were becoming increasingly remote from the rest of the campus. They were some ten minutes' walk from the SGS library, which Simpson calculated to be the centre of gravity for undergraduate teaching, and even further from the proposed Great Hall and entrance plaza. As members of both these schools tended more than their colleagues in the social sciences to keep to themselves, they were not too concerned about their growing isolation. What suffered was not so much the individual schools as the understanding that the University was, or ought to be, a single entity.

The main casualty was University House. The world of Oxford and Cambridge that Hancock, Trendall and others had sought to evoke seemed increasingly irrelevant to where the University was headed. Trendall, as he approached retirement in 1968, told his old friend Crocker, who was now Australian Ambassador in Rome, that he felt sad at heart about what was happening to the ANU. His hopes for a university where mature scholars might pursue their research in peace and freedom from the chores that beset 'the ordinary professors' and where they might influence young minds had long since evaporated; and the pressure for integration of the School and the Institute threatened to destroy the University's distinctive character. Now he saw declining standards among the professoriate and a relentless pursuit of mediocrity: 'it is noticeable that not one of the present hierarchy from the Chancellor himself down to the Registrar has either an Oxford or a Cambridge degree'.

University House was having financial problems. As it received a large University subsidy for services to the campus as a whole, Crawford asked questions about value for money, pointing out that there was now an external observer, the Australian Universities Commission, that had to be satisfied as well. Trendall was told how much more revenue the House could get by developing the bar trade, opening a bistro beneath the hall, and 'generally vamping the place up', without any consideration of what it might lose. The opponents of high table and the traditions it represented were becoming increasingly vocal. Trendall knew several people who expected the present 'stuffy' regime to be replaced by something more in keeping with modern trends. The time had come, he told Crocker, for him to go.

The role of University House on the changing campus had to be redefined. This task was left to Trendall's successor, Sir Rutherford Robertson, and his fellow members of the governing body who, as they strolled across from other parts of the campus to discuss the future of the House, were likely to approach from the side or the rear: for University House, which once looked towards Lewis's fountain at the gateway of the University, was now facing the wrong direction.

Students

Who were the students?

People in the Institute who saw the School of General Studies as a threat must have been alarmed by the growth of undergraduate numbers in the years following amalgamation. In 1961 there were 948 undergraduates, comprising 497 inherited from Canberra University College and 451 new students. By 1965 total undergraduate enrolments had swelled to 2387, 977 of whom were new enrolments. These figures gave the University an undergraduate growth rate about three times the national average.

Over the next decade, numbers continued to rise steadily, though not so sharply. By 1976 they had reached 5058, more than double the 1965 figure. Thereafter they continued to hover around, and usually under, 5000 until the beginnings of a national boom in student enrolments in the late 1980s. The peak of 1976 is an appropriate year to break our discussion of students, as we can also identify about that time some significant changes in student culture.

The most obvious feature of undergraduate enrolments in 1961 was the large proportion of part-time students, who outnumbered the full-timers two to one. Burton and his colleagues regarded 1965, when for the first time full-timers outnumbered part-timers, as a watershed and an indication that the School of General Studies had come of age. By 1976 the ratio had reversed, so that there were two full-time students for every part-timer.

Men outnumbered women throughout the sixteen-year period, with the proportion of women increasing steadily, in line with the national trend. In 1961, the ratio for Bachelor degree enrolments (which offer the most convenient set of figures) was three males to one female. By 1976 the gap had narrowed to three to two, which corresponded with the average for all Australian universities.

Gradually the students became younger (and not just through the eyes of their ageing teachers). This can readily be explained by the decreasing percentage of part-timers, who were often in their early to mid-thirties. Most of the full-timers were aged between 17 and 21, as they were in other Australian universities. A small proportion were in their thirties, with a few aged 40 and above. The most distinguished of the 'senior' students was John Dedman, the same Dedman who had presented the ANU bill to parliament in 1946. After losing his parliamentary seat when Ben Chifley's Labor government was thrown out of office in 1949, he had worked as a farmer and then as an administrator for the World Council of Churches before retiring to Canberra in 1962. As his previous efforts to take a degree had been interrupted, he now enrolled for a BA with a major in Political Science. Seated in the middle of the second row amid a large class of undergraduates, he listened attentively as Fin Crisp lectured, a little uncomfortably, on the role and working of the Curtin Cabinet in which Dedman had been a Minister. Although the University decided to award him an honorary doctorate of laws, he persevered to complete a creditable degree in the minimum time, graduating in 1966 as he approached his seventieth birthday.

Where did the students come from? Despite hopes that the ANU should function, in the School of General Studies as well as the Institute, as a truly national university, the undergraduates came predominantly from Canberra and the surrounding region. Of the new full-time enrolments in 1961, nearly half came from Canberra and the nearby town of Queanbeyan. Another 30 per cent or more came from more distant New South Wales, including Sydney, Wollongong and a pattern of country towns stretching south to Albury, west to Hay and north to the Blue Mountains, with a sprinkling beyond. Eight per cent came from Victoria, and 5 per cent from all the other states put together. Eight per cent came from overseas. If we add part-timers, who were by definition local, the bias leaned heavily towards Canberra.

In 1976 students from the Canberra region and (mostly southern) New South Wales still made up some three-quarters of the full-time undergraduate population. With the addition of part-timers, the figure rises above 80 per cent. Although the other states were contributing just a few percentage points more than in 1961, in the larger University there were now sufficient interstate students to be noticed, including, for example, 121 Queenslanders and 95 Tasmanians. There were also 191 undergraduates from overseas, including 30 from Vietnam and 24 from Malaysia, with New Guinea, Japan, Thailand and the United States also reaching double figures.

By telling us where most of the undergraduates came from, the statistics also suggest *why* they came to the ANU. The main attraction was geographical proximity. Just as undergraduates in other cities and states looked for a university close to home, so too the ANU came to be viewed as the 'local' University for residents of the Australian Capital Territory and southern New South Wales. This view was encouraged by members of the academic staff, who had been visiting schools throughout the region since the days of Canberra University College. Students wishing to pursue courses in medicine, engineering and other faculties not offered by the ANU were obliged to enrol in Sydney or Melbourne. But many aspiring undergraduates in Cooma, Griffith, Wagga Wagga and Wollongong looked to the ANU as their university of first choice.

Students from Sydney and outside New South Wales came for a variety of reasons. One was the pressure on places in the old universities of Sydney and Melbourne, which imposed quotas in most faculties in the early 1960s. Some academics worried that the ANU, which was open to anyone who matriculated, would be left with the dregs. From the early 1970s, quotas were imposed in several faculties, starting with Law, with the incidental effect of raising admission standards. But in 1976, it was still easier to enrol at the ANU than at Sydney, Melbourne or Monash universities, prompting the Pro Vice-Chancellor, Ian Ross, to acknowledge that 'our admission standards, for faculties other than Law, hardly give evidence that ANU is seen as a particularly worthy university to come to'.

After the conferring ceremony in 1957, new doctors of philosophy pose outside University House with the Vice-Chancellor and Pro-Chancellor. Left to right: Harold Fallding (RSPacS), Ronald Hieser (RSSS), Melville, Russel Ward (RSSS), Alan Barnard (RSSS), Coombs, David Curtis (JCSMR) and Bernard Smith (RSPacS). Five more doctorates (two from JCSMR and one from each of the other schools) were conferred in absentia.

On the other hand, the University attracted some of the best students from all over the country through National Undergraduate Scholarships which offered generous stipends to ten or twelve new students each year. Introduced in 1962, the scheme justified itself with some outstanding graduates, including John Coates, who became a Professor of Mathematics at the Sorbonne; Philip Eliason, Director of the Real Estate Institute of Australia; Alan Knight, Professor of Chemistry at Griffith University, Brisbane; Rod McDonald, Dean of Education at the University of Technology, Sydney; and Marlene Spiegler, a Professor of English at Columbia University. It also significantly enhanced the University's national complexion.

The University benefited through the introduction in 1970 of an early admissions scheme, which enabled students to enter on the basis of their school performance, before they had sat for their final examinations. It also allowed intending older students, whose school results now had little relevance, to enrol on the strength of more recent qualifications which might have been gained inside or outside the state educational systems. The scheme owed much to C.A. Gibb's experience with comparable procedures in the United States. A study in 1974 suggested that students admitted under this system had a higher survival rate than their colleagues. Although it was abandoned in 1977, when changes in assessment procedures in secondary schools made it redundant, before that time it succeeded in attracting a range of good students who might otherwise have gone elsewhere.

For most of the period, around 40 per cent of undergraduates received some form of assistance, including Commonwealth government scholarships, state government scholarships (from 1968), National Undergraduate Scholarships, and other forms of support offered by the University. In 1974, when Gough Whitlam's Labor government abolished tertiary tuition fees, the figure dropped to 16 per cent and then to 8 per cent in 1976. These figures were close to the national pattern.

Although the statistics tell us little about the sociological composition of the student body, there was a widespread perception that ANU students were different. Given that so many of them came from Canberra and that the social composition of the national capital was and is so different from the rest of Australia, some differences would not be surprising. Added to that, private schools were well represented among the National Undergraduate Scholars. There seemed to be a high proportion of sons and daughters of senior public servants: or was it just that these students, along with the children of other professionals, tended to be more vocal and hence more noticeable than those with less distinguished backgrounds?

The postgraduate students were always a distinctive group in the academic and social life of the University. From the early 1950s, when PhD scholars first enrolled with the expectation of taking out degrees from the ANU rather than an overseas institution, numbers grew steadily, reaching 136 at the time of amalgamation. By 1976 there was a total of 524 students researching for a PhD, comprising 8.5 per cent of the total student population. This proportion was more than double that of any other Australian university.

The School of General Studies was responsible for most of the Master's degree students, who numbered 327 in 1976. From the late 1960s onwards, the School also accounted for at least one in three PhD students. The gulf between the Institute and the School was reflected among the postgraduates. Apart from the fact that Institute scholars generally enjoyed better research conditions than their counterparts in the School, they were drawn from different sources. From the 1950s, about half the scholars in the research schools came from overseas, and most of the remainder from other parts of Australia. Postgraduates in the School, on the other hand, came chiefly from the Canberra region, which implied that many had previously been ANU undergraduates. In 1976, over 60 per cent of postgraduates in the School were locals, compared with under 20 per cent in the Institute.

The University in its early years included a number of scholars who enrolled in their mid to late thirties. Notable examples were Russel Ward and Bernard Smith, whose revised PhD theses later became the seminal works *The Australian Legend*, first published in 1958, and *European Vision and the South Pacific 1768–1850*, 1960. Most postgraduates, however, were in their late twenties; in 1976 their average age was 27. In that year men outnumbered women by four to one, though in previous years the ratio had sometimes been closer to nine to one. For most of the 1950s the two social science schools accounted for about two-thirds of all PhD students. By the mid-1970s their share had fallen to well under a half. Enrolments were subject to numerous variables. Changes in fashion partly account for the Research School of Biological Sciences doubling its numbers between 1970 and 1976, while Physical Sciences and Chemistry together fell by almost the same extent.

ANU PhDs graduating in 1960 represented 17 per cent of the Australian total. In 1964, the peak year, this figure rose to over 25 per cent. Then the ANU's proportion gradually declined, as the old state universities became more active in research and postgraduate training, and new universities entered the field. In 1976, ANU PhD graduates made up just under 12 per cent of the total. This was no cause for alarm. On the contrary, the ANU could take much credit for training many of the staff who took up positions in other universities and for stimulating research endeavour throughout Australia, just as it had always been intended to do.

'Welcome to the ANU!'

First-year undergraduates were introduced to the University during Orientation Week, which preceded the start of lectures in first term. In accordance with long-established tradition, it gave new students the chance to find out from staff and seasoned undergraduates what the next few years had in store for them, academically, socially and culturally. Although its tone changed markedly between the early 1960s and the mid-1970s, the orientation theme remained much the same: as the 1968 program declared, 'The essential point about Orientation Week, and university life generally, is that it will be only as good as you are prepared to make it'.

Orientation Week in the early 1960s was a staid affair. Highlights of the 1963 program included an Official Welcome by Trendall, Burton and the President of the Students' Association, Don Brewster; a cricket match between the township of Bungendore and the A.N.U.S.G.S. team on the University Oval; and on Saturday night the Orientation Week Dance in Childers Street Hall. Each faculty presented lectures on its various courses, Graneek spoke about Canberra's libraries, and Gibb gave advice on How to Study. The program also introduced a dozen students (ten men and two women) who were prominent around the campus: Chris Higgins, 'a big wheel in the economics society'; Bill Gammage, who had the most extensive collection of souvenired signs in Bruce Hall and who was 'in his spare time' a student of history; Tony Whitlam, 'an embryo lawyer' and 'one of the most loquacious and eloquent people around the place'; and John Yocklunn, a part-timer who represented the students on Council. Higgins later became head of the Commonwealth Treasury, Gammage a leading academic historian, Whitlam a judge of the Federal Court of Australia, and Sir John Yocklunn a senior public servant in Papua New Guinea.

If new arrivals in 1963 often found themselves at a loose end, their successors in 1969 were not allowed to be. The main aim of Orientation Week, said its director Ron Colman, was 'to get you into the habit of giving everything you've got, of developing all sides of your character and making this university the vital, lively place it should be'. The intensity of the program suggested that it already was. While there were the usual 'introducing your courses' sessions, tours of the Library, and informal gatherings where students could meet their teachers, the main focus was on political involvement. There were talks and debates on 'Tanks and freedom' (in Czechoslovakia), 'Student revolt ... why and why now?', 'The Republic of New Guinea?', 'Non-violent action', and 'To march or not to march'. Aboriginal and Torres Strait Islander leaders Faith Bandler and Harry Penrith asked 'Is Australia racist?' Laurie Aarons from the Communist Party debated with conservative journalist Peter Samuel 'That Australia should support revolutionary guerila wars in Asia'. Malcolm Fraser, federal Minister for Education and Science, explained the government's education policy; Jim Cairns, Labor frontbencher, presented the case for a revolutionary education system. Throughout the week there was a sense of urgency and immediacy. The program for Thursday included course introductions: but 'If the Berlin Crisis blows up this week, the 3.00–4.00 time slot will be used for an expert talk or debate on this topic'.

Entrants in the 'Miss University Quest', 1963, line up for judgement in Bruce Hall. Left to right: Helen Sutherland (sponsored by Bruce Hall), Margaret Ochiltree (Faculty of Law), Beverley Male (International Club), Lynne Murphy (basketball team), Marie Geissler (Science Society), Dawn Kohlhagen (Faculty of Arts), Bernadette Western (Newman Society), Olwyn Grant (hockey team) and Judith Summerhayes (Faculty of Economics). The winner received a week's skiing holiday.
Canberra Times.

In any university, participation in clubs and societies was generally seen as one way in which students could make the most of their undergraduate years. At the ANU in 1963 there were just a few of them, including the Newman Society, the Law Society and the ALP Club, together with the Students' Representative Council, which offered aspiring student politicians the best opportunity to be involved. By 1969 there were over fifty student organisations, academic, political, social, cultural, sporting and others that catered for specific interests and needs; and if students found that there were no clubs to suit them, it was easy enough to form another. During Orientation Week, each group hawked its wares on the lawns in front of the Chifley Library: the Labor Club, not formally affiliated with the ALP, which (according to the *Orientation Handbook*) could be counted on to oppose almost every aspect of the status quo; the Liberal Club, likewise unaffiliated with the Party and professing 'small-l liberalism'; the Student Christian Movement, probably the most lively of the several religious clubs on campus; the Debating Society; the Choral Society; the Folk Music Society; the Chess Club; the Beethoven Music Lovers of Garran Hall, and a range of others equally esoteric. Abschol, an inter-university group aimed at providing scholarships for Aboriginal students, attracted a large membership. The Overseas Students Association now embraced a cluster of subsidiary clubs representing students of various nationalities. There was also a Part-Time Students Association, a reminder that this group was now a clear minority.

By the end of Orientation Week students had to decide what they wanted to study. Most had settled on their preferred faculty; but each Bachelor's degree offered a range of subjects and units. They made their choices on the basis of personal interest, relevance to future career, or perhaps the reputation of a course and its teachers. Full-time students in all faculties usually took four units in their first year, and a total of eight (for Science) or ten (for Arts and Economics) over the minimum three years of a pass course. Law students had to complete 21 courses over a minimum of four years. In each faculty, honours entailed an extra year's study.

As the School of General Studies grew, so did the choice of subjects. Students enrolling in 1961 who wanted to major in Psychology for a pass degree in Arts or Science were presented with a straightforward curriculum: Psychology I (General Introductory Course); Psychology II (Personality); Psychology III (Social Psychology). In 1976 there was still a common first year, either in Psychology or Human Biology; but after that students were offered a supermarket full of half-year courses: Learning and Motivation, Neuropsychology, Environmental Psychology, Psychological Statistics, Human Information Processing. This explosion of courses reflected the increasing specialisation of knowledge in western societies. It also followed the trend in other Australian universities, with which the ANU was obliged to compete.

In several areas, the ANU was keen to innovate. At the time of amalgamation, the Faculty of Arts abandoned the University of Melbourne's system of grouping subjects, which gave students a broad education but often forced them to take subjects in which they had no interest. Arts students at the ANU now had an unsurpassed freedom of choice. The Faculty of Economics also broke away from a Melbourne pattern by requiring one or more units of Political Science in the Economics degree. This recognised different local circumstances: where in Melbourne it was appropriate to prepare Commerce graduates for the commercial world, in Canberra there was more purpose in training people for jobs in government.

Similarly, the Faculty of Law recognised that its graduates were destined either for private practice or for the public service, and fashioned its offerings accordingly. The ANU LLB was unusual in gaining recognition in three jurisdictions (Victoria, New South Wales and the Australian Capital Territory). Law had to respond to the needs of a profession; as a result it was perhaps the most innovative faculty on campus. A course in Air and Space Law, introduced in 1964, was unique in Australia. The Legal Workshop, introduced in 1971, offered a novel alternative to taking articles as a means of entering the profession. This six-month course was widely supported in the various branches of the profession, and other institutions soon followed the ANU's lead.

But the School of General Studies as a whole was not much different from other universities in Australia. Many of the staff thought it should be, and came up with various stratagems for making the ANU unique in undergraduate teaching. Several members of the Faculty of Arts proposed in the late 1960s a standard three-year Honours degree for undergraduates, together with an additional 'super-honours' four-year course, involving seminars and postgraduate research for the top 1 per cent of students. The other faculties were sceptical, opposing the concept in principle or arguing that their exceptional students were already well catered for. So the School of General Studies remained obedient to tradition.

Life on campus

The other big decision confronting students new to Canberra was where to live. In the early years, unmarried doctoral students had no choice: they were required to reside at University House. True to Hancock's vision, residence among a community of scholars was considered an integral part of postgraduate training. At the official opening of the House in 1954, the Duke of Edinburgh commended the University for choosing 'to follow the ancient pattern, and build a house where your learned men and women, young and old, may live as a household and enjoy in dignity and relaxation the company of each other'. Trendall worked hard to shape the House into the intellectual and social centre of the University, where young scholars could mingle freely with eminent professors, including many famous visitors from overseas. Every evening, in keeping with Oxbridge tradition, the Master led a procession of gowned academic staff and guests to high table, where he began dinner with a Latin grace which he had composed, occasionally adorning it, for the benefit of those with a classical education, with a humorous pun appropriate to the name of a distinguished visitor.

This was not everyone's cup of tea. Many scholars found the atmosphere of the House repressive, and some disturbed the calm in spectacular fashion. In February 1957, when a group of Anglican bishops was in residence for a conference, several students returned late one night from a party in a nearby suburb and continued their drunken revels in one of their rooms, spilling over into the courtyard. Sober residents (presumably including the bishops) were awakened by bellowing and banging on doors. Some of them tried to put a stop to it, only to be abused in foul language by one of the ringleaders, R.J.L. Hawke. One of the young women was reduced to tears. A student of Sawer's and former Rhodes scholar, Hawke, as a married scholar with a newborn child, lived in one of the University flats off campus. Already he was well known as a student representative on Council, and for his drunken escapades. The debauching culminated when one of the revellers stripped naked, jumped into the ornamental lily pond and swam the length of the pool, with Hawke and others offering loud and ribald encouragement. By three in the morning, the party had run its course and the stayers staggered off to bed.

High table at University House, mid-1960s. Master Trendall sits sixth from the right.

Retribution followed swiftly. Stanner, a Fellow of the House who had confronted Hawke on the rampage, wanted to 'put them all on a train tonight and send them away'. Trendall, who had been absent that evening, proposed throwing Hawke out of the University. But Hawke apologised promising to give no cause for future complaint. And Sawer, who regarded him as an outstanding student, argued 'on academic grounds' that he should not be sent down, defending him as one who had 'suffered of adolescence perpetuated by [the] Oxford system'. Hawke and the other chief offender were each fined £15 and debarred from the House, and Hawke took a broad hint, resigning his place on Council. In the event, he never completed his PhD, becoming instead a trade unions advocate and eventual prime minister.

Residence in University House ceased to be compulsory in 1964, partly because the House was unable to accommodate all the single doctoral scholars. While some chose to remain there, increasing numbers preferred to live in privately rented accommodation off campus, often in groups of two or three students. Instead of extending University House, as had long been expected, the University built flats for married scholars and then a postgraduate residence within walking distance of the campus. Opened in 1971, the new postgraduate hall, known as Graduate House, provided self-catered accommodation for students, and had nothing of the collegiate ambience which was now, in any case, starting to fade from University House.

Although undergraduates were not required to live on campus, in the early years after amalgamation newcomers to Canberra had little choice. The rental market was such that only a few students had the opportunity to set up for themselves in private 'digs'. In any case, that was not the fashion. Living on campus was still the thing to do, generally regarded by students and staff as part of the university experience.

Bruce Hall, opened in 1961, provided accommodation for 165 students. Two years later this number was increased by 45, and supplemented by 100 or so places in Lennox House and another 25 in a nearby motel purchased by the University. Being able to offer a large number of residential places was essential if the ANU was to be truly national, so the University set itself a target of having at least half the undergraduate population in residence. Burton Hall and Garran Hall, linked by shared dining and common rooms and providing places for a total of 480 students, were opened in the middle of the decade.

Bruce Hall, about the time of its opening in 1961.
National Library.

One means of meeting the demand for accommodation was to invite religious denominations to build and run alternative accommodation on campus. In line with Murray Report usage, these were referred to as 'affiliated colleges', to distinguish them from 'halls' run by the University. Although religious colleges had been a feature of Australian university campuses since the beginnings of Sydney and Melbourne universities in the 1850s, the prospect was immediately controversial. For many staff and students, they challenged the notion of a liberal university education, whose hallmarks were the free pursuit of knowledge and truth. Opponents argued that denominational colleges encouraged 'adherence to dogma, inculcation of religious doctrine and segregation of students according to religion'; that, as universities in Australia were government-funded, religious colleges denied the principle of separation of church and state; that colleges run by outsiders would be unresponsive to the wishes of residents. Supporters suggested that the University, as well as providing for individual liberty, should allow individual beliefs to have 'a corporate life'; that denominational colleges contributed variety to the intellectual life of universities; and that many parents wanted their students to attend religious colleges, so why should the ANU deny them?

In the event, the decision was effectively made off campus when Senator John Gorton, Minister for Works, with responsibility for education and research, came out strongly in favour of denominational colleges, hinting at the same time that the University would not get all the accommodation it asked for if it opted only for halls. Council approved two developments, one sponsored jointly by the Ursulines and the Dominicans, and the other by the Anglicans, Baptists, Congregationalists, Methodists, Presbyterians and (a little later) the Churches of Christ. In 1967 the Dominicans started operating their college, John XXIII, in Lennox House, pending the completion of their new building two years later; Ursula College opened in 1969; and Burgmann, the 'interdenominational' college (which in this context meant Protestant), took its first students in 1971. All colleges were open to students of all faiths or of none. Together, the affiliated colleges accommodated some 750 students and enabled the University to exceed its target of half the full-time undergraduates living on campus.

The argument about whether or not to admit religious colleges took place in the context of a general understanding that the student residences on campus were integral parts of academic life. At its inception, Bruce Hall introduced a system of College Fellows, comprising University staff, CSIRO scientists and other friends of the College, all of whom were appointed on the advice of the Vice-Chancellor. The Fellows, informally known as 'moral tutors', each had responsibility for ten students. This system was replicated in Burton and Garran halls; and the affiliated colleges too were required to introduce a tutorial system aimed at looking after the academic as well as the social welfare of their students.

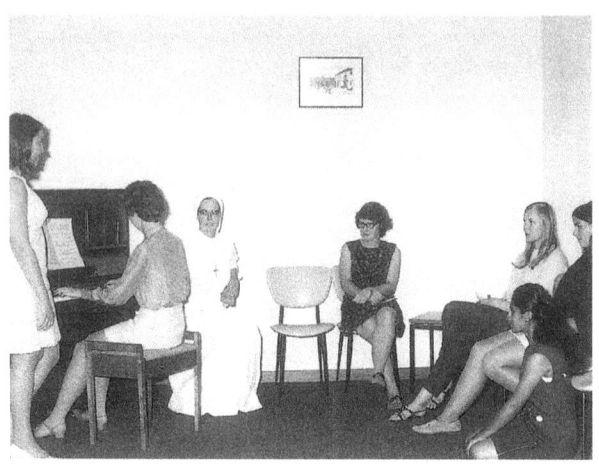

Evening entertainment at Ursula College, 1969.

Burton described the halls of residence as something intermediate between an Oxbridge college and an American dormitory. Gradually the links between the halls and colleges and the academic departments weakened, as the student residences became just that: places to live, with a more or less structured communal life of their own, but on the periphery of the larger academic community. A fourth hall of residence, opened in 1974 with accommodation for nearly 240 students, did away with communal dining arrangements and provided instead for groups of ten students of at least one year's standing, each with an individual study bedroom, sharing a common kitchen, bathroom and lounge. The students, lacking reverence for the tradition of naming the halls after the University's great men, christened the new building Toad Hall, owing to its proximity to Sullivan's Creek and its willows. The name stuck, and Toad Hall became Australia's first self-catering hall of residence.

Toad Hall pointed the way. By 1976, the other halls and colleges were having trouble filling their beds, while Toad had a waiting list. This was partly due to relative costs, the self-catering arrangements being much cheaper than the catered and serviced accommodation provided elsewhere. In addition, students were tending to resist the regimentation of college life, however gentle it may have been, opting instead for shared housing in the nearby suburbs of Turner, O'Connor, Braddon or Ainslie.

Each hall and college assumed over time its own characteristics. Bruce Hall enjoyed special status as the University's first purpose-built hall of residence. Moreover, it was better equipped (and more expensive) than halls and colleges constructed in other universities around that time, as the National Capital Development Commission, which paid for the building, wanted something imposing at the end of University Avenue. Even when there were several halls and colleges to choose from, Bruce Hall continued to attract a disproportionate number of students who were academically outstanding or socially privileged. The National Undergraduate Scholars were sent there as a group, and the non-Catholic private schools were well represented.

Bruce Hall also distinguished itself as the first hall or college in Australia with accommodation for both men and women. The reason for this initiative was economic: the University had to provide for both sexes and it could not afford two colleges. Although some members of staff, including the Vice-Chancellor, Huxley, feared moral degradation, the experiment won general approval from staff and students. At the time of his retirement, Huxley withdrew his earlier reservations and quoted approvingly the views of a warden of one of the halls that 'The young women become less giggly and the men better mannered'. Bill Packard, who came as Warden in 1961 and remained for 25 years, administered and relaxed the rules in response to changing attitudes among students and the wider community. At the outset, visitors of the opposite sex were excluded between 10 p.m. and 9 a.m. These limits were gradually whittled away and in 1970 abandoned entirely. Initially the men and women were housed in separate wings, but in response to student demand the whole hall was rearranged on a mixed-gender basis in 1971.

Bill Packard in 1970.
By courtesy of Bill Packard.

Burton and Garran halls followed Bruce's lead by offering co-residential accommodation. According to the *Orientation Handbook* for 1968, Burton saw itself as 'the swinging, sparkling, spontaneous hall', in contrast to the more conservative Bruce; while Garran catered for all tastes. The University specified that the affiliated colleges should provide for both men and women, though the Catholics were able to meet this requirement by building one college for men and one for women. Ursula's, under the sharp eye but gentle hand of the Ursuline sisters, projected an image of harmony and scholarship. John XXIII, governed in more authoritarian fashion by the Dominican brothers, soon achieved a 'rugger-bugger' image which it confirmed on and off the football field and took many years to live down.

Undergraduate lives were ruled by the rhythms of the academic year. After Orientation Week, students settled into first term, which usually ran for ten weeks. A three-week vacation was followed by a nine-week second term, a further four-week vacation, and a final fourteen-week term, which included a short study vacation and a three-week examination period.

The routines of study were broken in second term by Bush Week, which began as a week's activities but soon contracted to one or two days. The ANU lacked any single day that might offer an excuse for a special occasion comparable with Foundation Day or Commemoration Day in other universities. Bush Week, although conceived in the early 1960s as a way of taking the city to the bush and soaking up some of the bush ethos, was soon commandeered by the Students' Representative Council. As the orientation program for 1963 admitted, it served ostensibly to raise funds for charity while providing 'the perfect excuse for student hilarity' and giving them something to do during winter.

Bush Week activities were often boisterous. A regular event in the early years was a raid on the Royal Military College, Duntroon, a few miles away. The 1963 raiders painted a hopscotch square on the military parade ground, hoisted a swastika and an umbrella to the top of the flagpole, and woke the cadets and officers with a fake reveille at 5 a.m. The cadets responded by capturing twenty students, cutting their hair short, and throwing some of them into an icy fountain in the middle of town. A procession of floats became a regular event, during which students challenged with varying degrees of creativity and wit some commonly held values. Many Catholics were offended when a student frocked in priestly habit handed out mock contraceptive pills, and another, dressed as a pregnant woman, danced before a crucifix. Burton complained that Bush Week 'gave an opportunity to the exhibitionist and the hooligan under the hypocritical facade of raising money for charity', and tried to pull the offenders into line. But other staff members saw it as an appropriate outlet for adolescent exuberance. Perhaps there was sympathy for the student leader who argued plaintively that Bush Week was 'the only tradition the A.N.U. has'.

Scavenger hunt, Bush Week, 1973. Photograph by Huw Price.

The students of the ANU were well looked after. Soon after amalgamation, when it was possible to buy a pie or soft drink on campus, but not much else, Fin Crisp and Colin Plowman, Registrar of the School of General Studies, started moves which led to the formation of a Union. Although they had intended it to serve the needs of both students and staff, it evolved as an organisation chiefly managed by students for students, providing a refectory and coffee lounge, entertainment rooms and, after winning the right to serve liquor in 1970, a bar. As originally conceived, the Union was also to have something in common with its Oxbridge counterparts, arranging debates, holding dinners with guest speakers, and generally contributing to the intellectual life of the University. But its main contribution to campus life was as a meeting place, where students could exchange ideas and lecture notes, gossip about their lecturers, argue about social and political issues, and when the time came, plan to change the University and the world.

Teaching and learning

Staff in the School of General Studies took their teaching duties seriously. This may have owed something to the proximity of the Institute of Advanced Studies and the implicit pressure on the School to excel in its appointed field. Manning Clark in the Department of History told his staff that they were there first to teach and second to do research. Russell Mathews, the University's agent in London in the early 1950s and now Professor of Accounting and Public Finance, sat in on lectures given by members of his department, vetted their examination questions, and generally made sure they were all doing their job as he thought they should. There were, of course, some teachers who were lazy or indifferent, provoking criticisms from the Students' Association. But they were the exceptions, frowned upon by most of their colleagues. By and large, the teachers of the ANU were dedicated and the quality of their teaching was high.

Arthur Hambly, the Professor of Chemistry impressed on his colleagues the distinction between teaching and 'just lecturing', and urged them to see teaching and learning as a two-way process. Hambly was unusual, especially among the scientists, in that he had trained as a teacher. Most of his colleagues were, as they perceived it, thrown in at the deep end. Ian Ross, a former ANU Overseas Scholar who joined Hambly's department as a professor in 1968, had no formal training; but he had, as a Master's student in Sydney, attended dramatic classes, from which he had learnt how to project his voice and how to make lectures lively. He had also spent some fifteen years at the University of Sydney teaching large classes, which made the relatively intimate classes in Canberra a pleasant change. Like most of his scientific colleagues, he lectured from detailed notes, often distributing specially prepared explanatory material. Another member of that department, Ben Selinger, thought deeply about presenting chemistry as a subject with immediate practical importance for everyday life. This led him to prepare a laboratory handbook which ran, under the title *Chemistry in the Market Place*, to several editions and opened up new areas of environmental and consumer chemistry.

Ian Ross at the time of his appointment in 1968.

Paul Lyneham, later prominent as a political journalist, remembered the mid-1960s as the golden time of the ANU. As an Arts student, he was taught Economics by Heinz Arndt, Australian History by Manning Clark, Political Science by Fin Crisp and Australian Literature by Alec Hope: 'you tell me what period of Australian academic life you've had more talented first-class people together in one campus than that ...' Clark in turn reflected on the students: Alastair Davidson, 'a young man with a lively mind and a fire in the belly'; Philippa Weeks, 'one of the silent members ... who put what was in their mind into essays rather than into frivolous tutorial discussion'; Iain McCalman, who was 'such a born teacher that he began to teach me in class—to my great benefit'. For Clark, like Lyneham, these were golden years.

Undergraduate students were taught through a combination of lectures and tutorials, which in the natural sciences often translated to demonstrations in the laboratory. Where the University of Sydney placed heavy reliance on formal lectures, Melbourne had a tradition of tutorials in which the teacher exchanged thoughts with a small group of students, often in smoke-filled studies, on the prescribed topic. Canberra University College inherited the Melbourne system and allowed it to develop during the 1950s, when student numbers were small. The system encouraged rapport between students and their teachers, and fostered a sense of belonging to the departmental family.

Approaches to teaching differed. Students in Clark's tutorials in Australian history were invited to explore 'the mystery at the heart of things', to seek answers to the great questions confronting humankind. 'We, teachers and students, were all looking for those answers', Clark later wrote. The student engaged in that process of discovery need not have worried about formal course requirements. When other members of the faculty urged that late essays should be penalised, Clark resisted.

In contrast, Gibb argued for efficiency in teaching, urging his colleagues to establish 'stable standards' and to review their teaching and examining policies and procedures. Inspired by American examples, he attempted to quantify student motives, ambitions, abilities and performances, and urged the University to undertake 'institutional research'. In Clark's language, Gibb was a 'measurer', whose pronouncements he dismissed as 'Gibberish'. Gibb's Department of Psychology was one of the first areas to experiment with continuous assessment, which involved playing down the significance of the annual examination and relying instead on the regular evaluation of class work throughout the year, such as essays, exercises and periodical tests. Students, like their teachers, were expected to be efficient, to submit their assignments on time or accept appropriate penalties.

Manning Clark takes a History honours seminar, about 1968.

Gibb and Clark were at opposite extremes on fundamental issues about the nature of teaching and learning, and the concept of a university education. The two world views came into direct conflict when Gibb, whose department straddled the faculties of Arts and Science, urged his colleagues in Arts to follow the lead of Science (and a trend in other universities) by replacing terms with semesters. For the scientists, semesters meant flexibility; for members of the Arts Faculty, they suggested that knowledge and understanding could be delivered in segmented blocks. The scientists won: in the early 1970s, terms were abandoned in favour of two fifteen-week semesters, separated by a five-week break, each with a one or two-week teaching break in the middle. Students now took one or two-semester units. Most worked harder and (if Clark was right) thought and understood less.

Were teachers born or made? The question, as old as institutional learning, was debated at the ANU, as it no doubt was in every other university in the country. Gibb, who believed that teaching skills could be taught, proposed in the early 1970s the formation of the Office for Research on Academic Methods, which he modelled on a research bureau in Michigan. Opened in 1975, ORAM's functions included gathering data about teaching and encouraging staff to improve their teaching skills.

Clark knew teachers could learn, but whether they could be taught was another matter. In 1969, when Henry Mayer, Professor of Government at the University of Sydney, suggested that he take on Humphrey McQueen as a tutor, Clark's first question was 'Is he a Catholic and a Communist?'. Mayer said, yes, he was. Then Clark asked: 'Has he taught fourth form boys?'. Mayer replied that he had, Clark replied, 'Oh good, then we'll have him'. Given that McQueen had published two significant articles and that he had a book, entitled *A New Britannia*, nearly finished, he was evidently a highly suitable appointment.

McQueen may have had no problem with the fourth form boys at Glen Waverley

High; but lecturing and tutoring at university demanded different skills. Clark was not much help: he warned his colleagues that, when giving essays back, they should always do so in a room with two windows, so that the reflected eyes of teacher and student need not meet, which (if the student was crying) was apt to be a painful experience. More useful advice came from Don Baker and Eric Fry, two old hands in the department (Baker having arrived in Canberra a few days before Clark, and Fry, a former ANU scholar, a decade later). Fry offered to mark the essays of McQueen's students while McQueen could mark his; and when the process was over, Fry explained to him gently and humorously where he had been too severe and where his comments might have been more helpful.

Humphrey McQueen declaims at a seminar on unionism in 1972.
Canberra Times.

Baker was never a 'natural' lecturer. To counter the anxiety of performing in front of a class, he prepared his lectures thoroughly, coming into the department each Sunday to write them out in full. As a result he became over the years one of the faculty's finest lecturers. Clark knew all this, so he asked Baker in a staff meeting to explain his success. Baker responded with a list of points: write out the lecture in full; in 50 minutes you can read four and a half thousand words; if you mention anyone by name, then the name should be important enough to write on the blackboard; if anything is worth quoting, you should repeat it; and so on. This was basic but valuable advice. McQueen took it, becoming what Clark later described as 'a brilliant teacher'. But he found the academic system too constrictive and left early in 1975 to write books, one of which, *Australia's Media Monopolies*, he dedicated to his old mentors, Baker and Fry, 'for showing me how to teach, and more'.

The degree of independence accorded to individual teachers to teach what and how they wanted varied across the campus. Some Faculty of Science departments, in particular, were hierarchical in structure, with the professor and two or three of his senior colleagues setting out the overall course structure and allocating staff to particular classes. The lowly tutor or demonstrator, generally employed on a one-year contract, did what he or she was told. The Faculty of Arts tended to be more democratic, allocating responsibilities in a collegiate fashion and allowing at least the permanent staff to develop and teach such courses as they chose. Arts professors wielded considerable power and influence, but they were less likely than their counterparts in other faculties to play god.

The courses in History ranged over the centuries and the continents, much as in other Australian universities. Clark would no more expect to interfere in the teaching of, say, Indian history or the rise and spread of Christianity than he would expect one of his colleagues to question his own approach to teaching Australia's past. So when McQueen, as a newcomer to the department, asked innocent questions about Clark's grand plans for an Australian history major, such as how methodological approaches might differ from one year to the next, the atmosphere in the meeting room suddenly cooled. McQueen persisted until Clark said 'There comes a time when one must distinguish between the general will and the popular will'. And that was that.

Just as teachers differed in their teaching methods, so students varied widely in the ways they learnt. A senior undergraduate in the 1968 *Orientation Handbook* earnestly advised first-years to study moderately and consistently throughout the year. Alongside students who heeded this advice were many others who idled away their time or threw themselves into extracurricular activities, leaving themselves with a frantic rush to catch up in the third term.

Staff throughout the School of General Studies were perpetually alarmed by the large number of students who failed or dropped out. The Murray Report had remarked in 1958 that failure rates were appalling throughout Australia, and that this was largely due to inadequate teaching. While wastage was also a problem everywhere, at the ANU it seemed to be especially serious. In 1963 nearly 20 per cent of students fell by the wayside, most of them during their first year of study. This figure declined as the number of full-timers increased and, during the 1970s, as admission standards were raised. By the mid-1970s, the wastage rate had fallen to under 10 per cent, significantly lower than the national average. In the meantime, staff agonised about matriculation standards, the quality and motivation of students and the adequacy of their own teaching, which could no longer be (if it ever had been) taken for granted.

'Make love not war'

Time, 28 October 1966.
AAP Photos.

Megan Stoyles, a second-year Arts student, became famous during President Lyndon Johnson's visit to Australia in 1966, when news photographers took a fancy to the slogan on the bosom of her T-shirt. She stood out among the large crowd who demonstrated outside the Canberra Rex Hotel (where Johnson was staying) against the Vietnam war and Australia's support for United States policy.

For the moment her views were well in advance of those of most of her fellow students. Undergraduate life at the ANU, wrote an anonymous commentator in a *Current Affairs Bulletin* in 1967, 'is distinguished by its apathy, conservatism and indifference to national causes'. The writer, as many people knew, was Richard Walsh, a prominent student leader at the University of New South Wales. While he was generally scathing about the lack of student activity on campuses throughout Australia, the ANU deserved special mention since, owing to its location among the nation's decision-makers, 'it might well have been expected to prove the most dynamic and involved campus in the country'.

Among the few students who were politically inclined, his comments hit a raw nerve. But what could they say? The evidence of apathy was there, in reluctance to join political societies, in the conservatism of the Students' Association, and in published student opinions about the large issues of the day. A survey of attitudes to the Vietnam war, conscription and the voting age, conducted by the Students' Association in 1966, revealed what most people expected: that students at the ANU held views similar to the rest of society.

Apart from these specific issues of national policy, there was a continuing debate about whether the Students' Representative Council, as the elected representatives of the Students' Association, should take a political stand. Ross Garnaut, an Arts/Law student (and later an ANU Professor of Economics), tried hard in 1965 to get the SRC to pass a motion condemning the commitment of regular troops to Vietnam, but was defeated by the argument that the SRC was not a competent body to issue dictums on student opinion. Two years later the SRC passed a motion denying itself the right to make political comments, except on matters relating to the ANU and education, and others on which majority student opinion could be ascertained. After heated debate and several resignations from the SRC, a general meeting of the Students' Association, attended by some four hundred students, confirmed that the Council should remain 'apolitical'. But just in case students in other universities should think they were apathetic, they went on to vote in favour of Aboriginal rights, increased academic freedom, and the readmission of Boris Pasternak to the Soviet Union of Writers.

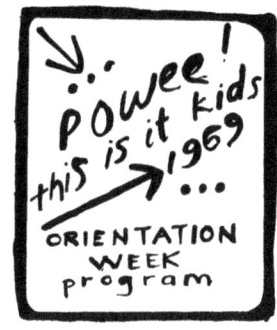

Cover of the Orientation Week Program, 1969.

Those who thought the ANU should be at the forefront of political activism wondered why it was not. Some accepted Walsh's view that the halls and colleges were to blame, by fragmenting potential campus unity and absorbing the students in internal affairs and parochial competition. Others drew attention to the high proportion of students from wealthy or 'established' backgrounds who were content with things as they were. John Iremonger, a Master's student in History, suggested that the material conditions on campus, including plentiful library seats and staff/student ratios which were the envy of students in other universities, left ANU students with little to protest about. Or was it that the ANU, like other small campuses around Australia, simply had too few students to generate a politically active community? Bruce McFarlane, a Senior Lecturer in Political Science and one of the few outspoken Marxists on campus, was resigned: 'The number of students who are going to be interested in unorthodox ideas is quite small and the number of students who are interested in the degree shop idea is very large, and that's a fact of life'.

McFarlane was speaking at a 'teach-in' in September 1968. The *Canberra Times* reported that only 100 students attended, suggesting that 'Students at ANU shun reform'. Six months later the campus was throbbing with political activity. In retrospect, it was possible to trace a gradually increasing political awareness, as conversations in the Union moved from football to Vietnam, Aborigines, feminism and apartheid. But at the time it seemed as if the ANU had moved from apathy to activism almost overnight. Students started speaking the language of revolution, about imperialist oppression, civil disobedience and direct action. Words changed meaning: in 1968 a 'rort' was a party; two years later it was a demonstration.

ANU students became part of the revolutionary movement that was sweeping across the western world. In mid-1968 students in Paris were erecting barricades and tearing up paving stones to hurl at the *gendarmerie*. In Australia, Monash University students were showing the way towards participatory democracy, with strident talk and sometimes violent action against authority inside and outside the University. The ANU followed, never at the forefront of revolutionary activity, but never far behind

Left: Over 5000 people attended the Aquarius Festival of University Arts at the ANU in May 1971. An appreciative crowd listens to a rock group from Melbourne University on the lawns in front of the Chifley Library.

Right: The Canadian Prime Minister, Pierre Trudeau, responds to questions from students and staff in a packed Coombs Lecture Theatre, May 1970.
Canberra Times.

The *Bulletin*, in a survey of student activism in Australian universities in 1969 which categorised campuses from 'hot' to 'frigid', described the ANU as 'simmering steadily'. That description remained apt for the next few years.

Perhaps there was a sense that in student radicalism, as in other things, the University had to live up to its national status. Certainly, those involved in the turmoil believed that the ANU was where it was all happening; and in some respects it was. There was never much difficulty in luring a politician across the lake to address a lunchtime crowd, gathered on the lawn between the Union and the Chifley Library. And prominent national and international figures gave talks at various campus venues: Pierre Trudeau, the Canadian Prime Minister; Benjamin Spock, the guru of parenting and opponent of the Vietnam war; Don Dunstan, the South Australian Premier who seemed to promise a new era in Australian politics; and the communist novelist Frank Hardy, who castigated his student audience for their unconcern with the plight of the Aborigines. All contributed to make the campus a focus for vibrant intellectual and political debate. Students were optimistic about their capacity to bring about change: it seemed that there was nothing they could not do.

Protest was associated with an assertion of freedom. Mark O'Connor, a PhD student in English, defied conventional morality by posing naked with his girlfriend Rigmor Helene Borg for the 1974 edition of the *Orientation Handbook*. He later won fame as a poet. Students experimented with drugs, and for a time Lennox House was known as a place where heroin was freely available. Many students accepted hard drugs as a legitimate part of an alternative lifestyle. When the doctor in charge of the University Health Service, Bryan Furness, warned new students about the likely dangers of experimenting with LSD, a student defended 'acid' as 'a means of providing an alternative insight into the environment'. At least one student died from a drug overdose. Nevertheless, apart from alcohol, sustained drug use never extended beyond a small minority, so that Crawford could tell Council in 1972 that there was no evidence of a serious drug problem at the ANU.

'We were all committed', wrote Alan Gould, then an English honours student and later a poet and novelist. 'We were up to our eyebrows in Commitment.' But the reasons for their commitment and the way they expressed it varied from one student to the next.

Chris Swinbank stood out among the angry young men on campus. The son of a Melbourne scientist with left-wing sympathies, he came, like many of the most determined radicals, from a private school. In 1967 he had spent a year with his parents in Hawaii, where he had witnessed the growing protest movement against the Vietnam war. A National Undergraduate Scholarship brought him next year to Canberra, where he played Australian Rules Football for Bruce Hall and embraced a succession of social and political causes. First he became a supporter of Abschol, which was now an assertive voice for Aboriginal rights. Then he threw himself into the anti-Vietnam movement. In Bush Week 1968 he and some cronies donned stolen military uniforms and dismantled an Army careers booth in the middle of Civic, removing it to the safety of the campus. In the early 1970s he was marching in the front cohort during the Vietnam moratorium campaigns, resisting the police when they came to tear down the Aboriginal embassy in front of Parliament House, and leading the local opposition to apartheid in South Africa, especially during the Australian tour of the all-white Springbok rugby team.

Swinbank belonged to no political party. Some of the hard-line Marxists, Trotskyites and Maoists berated him as ideologically unsound. In retrospect he described himself as 'a political ratbag'. He saw the answer to all forms of social injustice in direct action. This took the form of distributing anti-apartheid leaflets, demonstrating in the streets of Civic, and maintaining a 24-hour vigil in front of the South African embassy. As self-styled urban guerillas, he and his colleagues spray-painted anti-racist messages on the embassy gates, which became thicker as they were painted over, resprayed and repainted time and time again. They often conducted their exploits with a sense of adventure, but always with the conviction that what they were doing was necessary and right.

March 1971: ANU students left their mark in front of the South African embassy after a demonstration against the projected Springbok rugby tour. Photograph by courtesy of one of the perpetrators, Chris Swinbank.

Effective protest demanded efficient organisation. Much of it took place in Bruce Hall, which Gould, in a later novella, translated to Beasley College (an evident play on the local car sales firm, Beazley & Bruce). 'Here, in its narrow rooms, with a dozen or so people sitting on an unmade bed, a littered desk, or the floor, with curtains drawn resolutely against any daylight, meetings simply happened spontaneously and action flowed directly from them.' The other meeting place was a four-bedroom brick and fibro house in Canning Street, Ainslie, three kilometres from the campus on the other side of Civic, which the ANU Labor Club occupied from 1969. 'Canning Street' rocked and throbbed to endless meetings about strategy and tactics, debates about the rights and wrongs of this action or that, and the comings and goings of volunteers for writing letters, distributing leaflets, creating silk-screens, producing banners and megaphones.

ANU students and other demonstrators confront police at Manuka Oval during the Springbok tour, July 1971. Jack Waterford, second year Economics/Law student (and later editor of the *Canberra Times*), stands with right arm raised. *Canberra Times.*

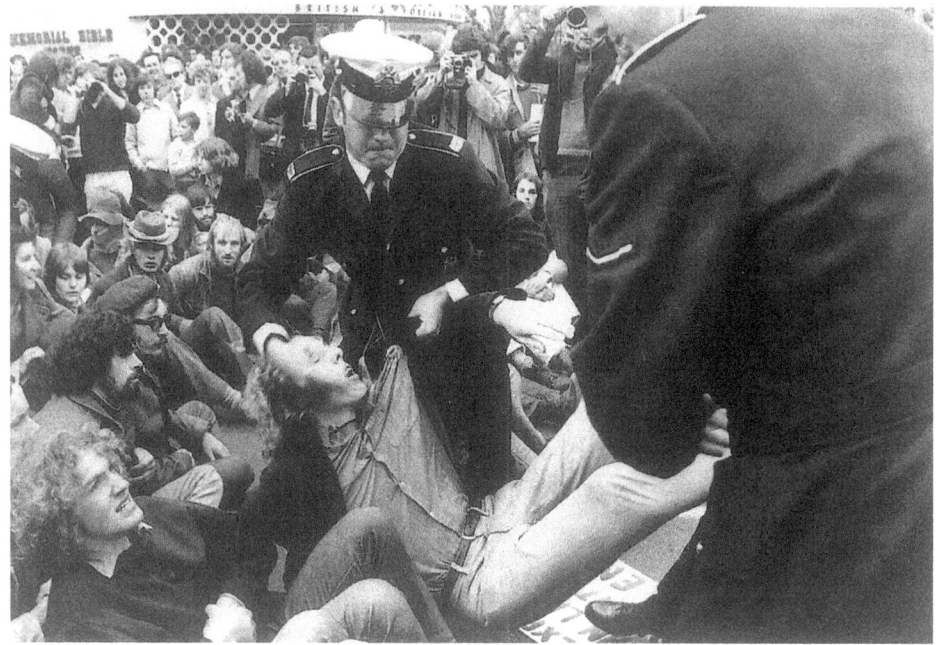

On the 'Day of Rage', 21 May 1971, over 2000 anti-war demonstrators staged a sit-in in Civic. Police arrested nearly 200 of them, including this ANU student.
Canberra Times.

June 1972: a march on the courthouse to support draft resister Steve Padgham.
Canberra Times.

Stephen Padgham, who enrolled as a Law student in 1968, was the ANU draft resister best known to students, staff and the police. In contrast to Swinbank, he was an erudite revolutionary, having read and absorbed the thoughts of Marx, Hegel, Marcuse, Mao Zedong and other writers whose works were fashionable. Having turned eighteen, the age when all Australian males were required to register for national service, and having decided that the Vietnam war was immoral, he became involved in a battle with the courts and the police which extended over the next few years. Twice he went to gaol, for seven days each time; and twice he went underground, causing a good deal of interest and excitement on campus. On the second occasion he remained inconspicuous for two months until he was sighted on campus by two plain-clothes police. Emulating the famous swagman, he jumped into Sullivan's Creek, ice cold in the middle of winter, only to be dragged out by his pursuers and lodged safely in the watch-house. Several weeks later, to the accompaniment of chants and protests outside the courthouse (which was conveniently located at the city end of University Avenue) he was sentenced to eighteen months' hard labour. But while he was still out on bail pending an appeal, the conservative coalition was replaced by Whitlam's Labor government, one of whose first acts was to abolish conscription and lift the burden from those who had resisted the draft.

For every protester who was willing to stand up to authority and face possible arrest, a dozen or so were keen to stay out of trouble. Nevertheless, Swinbank, Padgham and their colleagues regarded the campus as a sympathetic environment and believed that the

University community, from the Chancellor and Vice-Chancellor down, was on their side. When Swinbank sought help for his campaign against apartheid, he received $2 and $10 donations from many of the senior staff, along with letters of encouragement. Padgham, with the help of his girlfriend, found refuge in the all-female Ursula College; and when his girlfriend moved out, the Principal, Sister Angela, asked maternally: 'And who's going to look after Stevie now?'. Colin Plowman, now the Academic Registrar, and Diana Riddell, the Secretary of the Students' Association, kept a money box to bail students out of gaol, should occasion arise.

The Students' Association, administered by Di Riddell, provided coordinated support for protesters. Photograph by Gabe Carpay.

Protest was becoming respectable. Sir Keith Hancock, now in his mid-seventies and still hard at work as an Emeritus Professor in his old school, took a stand on the issue of a telecommunications tower for Black Mountain, the tree-covered backdrop to the University and a critical point in Griffin's design for Canberra. Early in 1973 he addressed a protest meeting of 700–800 people; and over the next two years, as a member of the Committee to Save Black Mountain, he devoted almost all his time and energy to the issue. When the battle seemed all but lost, some of the students wanted to put sand in the bulldozers' fuel tanks, but in deference to the old man refrained. Hancock and the committee chose to fight through the courts, and when they were defeated and the tower was erected his disappointment was profound. But at least the campaign had allowed him to relive the complementary roles of professional historian and active citizen, and had brought him into touch with the spirit of the times.

The Troubles

There was no obvious moment when the students turned their attention inwards, away from the problems of larger society and towards the University and how it was governed. Certainly the advent of Whitlam's Labor government removed some of the main causes of protest and gave the impression that many of the students' aspirations were about to be realised. Such protests as there were in the Whitlam years, on Aboriginal land rights, abortion, the mining of uranium or French nuclear testing, were moderate by comparison with what had taken place before.

Widespread interest in what was happening off campus was reawakened in late 1975 after the sacking of Whitlam's government by the man who had once been considered as a potential head of the Research School of Pacific Studies and who was now the Governor-General, Sir John Kerr. When Kerr attended a function at Bruce Hall in 1976, a noisy crowd of demonstrators from inside and outside the University protested loudly and alarmed the police. But this and later incidents were merely short-lived interruptions to a life on campus that was otherwise calm.

Concern with internal issues had been evident from the time students had begun speaking the language of revolution. Initially, the key question was the level of student participation on decision-making bodies. When in 1968 the students sought a larger say in University affairs, Council gave them most of what they wanted: an undergraduate representative on Council, and representation on various Council committees, faculties and departments (but not on the Board of the School). These concessions did not put an end to student protests. But, especially by comparison with turbulent universities such as Monash and La Trobe, where it seemed that undergraduates were about to erect the barricades, student complaints at the ANU took the form of grumbling—about semesters, the examination system, the quality of teaching, and so on—often ill-mannered, but rarely seriously threatening. Such grievances tended to be subsumed by the larger protest movement. Occasionally internal and external issues merged, as in relation to the moves in the Research School of Pacific Studies to set up a Centre for Strategic and Defence Studies along what were seen as ideologically unsound lines. But more often than not the administration and staff were seen as allies rather than enemies.

All that changed in 1974, when the undergraduates—or a vocal minority of them—sought a much greater say in the way the University conducted its business, especially in relation to the content of courses and modes of examination. They demanded more than most of the staff were prepared to give. The events of that year, which extended somewhat half-heartedly into the next, were described at the time and in retrospect as 'The Troubles', as they were on other campuses. For some staff, the term signified a passing inconvenience which interrupted their normal activities of teaching and research; for others it was a bitter euphemism for a movement which threatened the core of what a university was or ought to be about.

Coombs and Crawford had always seemed to be one step ahead of student opinion. Apart from the wisdom which came with experience, they enjoyed the great advantage of information, often gleaned directly during their overseas travels. Coombs happened to be in Paris in 1968 when students were disrupting the life of the city. He visited university campuses and talked to academics who were trying to understand and respond to the revolt, and others who were a part of it. At the University of Nanterre one slogan among many plastered on the walls caught his attention: 'They think therefore I am', a bitter parody of Descartes' *'Cogito ergo sum'*. This set him thinking about the sense of alienation among young people, and about how members of a university might seek to understand and devise ways of resisting the depersonalised quality in contemporary life. With the help of Partridge, who was then reflecting on the turmoil while on leave in London, he prepared his inaugural speech as Chancellor, in which he urged his colleagues to heed student opinion and not to let universities become too much a part of the 'Establishment'.

> A society, to remain vigorous requires inbuilt sources of regeneration—and the university is, by its traditions and the quality of its members, well equipped to provide one such source; the more so since through its

membership flows the ablest of our youth—those who come to our society with a fresh and innocent vision.

Students, he said, should not be ground into professionalism too soon; rather they should have time to wonder and time 'for a certain irresponsibility'.

After the speech someone wrote anonymously to tell him he was talking nonsense and accuse him of being 'a middle aged adolescent delinquent'. It was a description that he subsequently treasured.

Crawford too was interested in what was happening in other parts of the world. After listening to an American college president outline the elaborate precautions on his campus should demonstrations get out of hand, he expressed relief that 'The need for this type of preparation calls for no additional comment, other than one of sympathy'. (Nevertheless, at Hohnen's request one of the Chancelry staff devised a series of tactical responses to any organised campaign to 'D and D', demonstrate and disrupt.) At the beginning of 1969, when student leaders were announcing a 'year of protest' throughout Australia, Crawford anticipated the course of unrest: initially, he wrote, the protests would centre on national and international events rather than university policies, but the two might end up being linked.

To forestall action directed against the University, he proposed changes to its formal structures. He also wanted to facilitate, as he put it, 'close personal relations between faculty and students; mutual respect; proper attention to constructive criticism about university policy from staff and students alike; academic freedom but not disruption'. At the vice-chancellorial level he practised this policy by making himself available to the leaders of student opinion, always listening attentively to their grievances, giving the impression that they were participating in the decision-making process, but at the same time keeping himself at just the right distance to maintain their slightly deferential respect. Colin Plowman, the Academic Registrar, served as his able lieutenant, mixing freely with the troops and reporting on changes of mood in the mess. There was no secret about Plowman's role as an intermediary: he welcomed it, and so did the students.

The Vice-Chancellor, Crawford, addresses students on student participation in university government, July 1969. Photograph by Charlie Dickins.

It was all very well for some of the more radical students to see in Crawford the skilled manipulator of opinion, and to accuse the administration of 'repressive tolerance' as defined by Marcuse. The problem was that, except in theoretical terms, the University's leaders were hard to criticise. Crawford exuded reason and understanding, especially by comparison with vice-chancellors in some of the other universities; and Plowman, always accessible over a bottle of red in the Union bar, always ready to listen and argue, never appearing to 'talk down' to undergraduates, was everybody's conception of 'a good bloke'.

Colin Plowman with friends, at a dinner to mark his resignation as Academic Registrar in 1974. Left to right: Martin Attridge (student), Di Riddell (Secretary of the Students' Association), Plowman, Richard Refshauge (student and later a member of Council) and Joanne Langenbert (student).

The rest of the staff followed the Chancellor's and Vice-Chancellor's lead, some eagerly, others with deep misgivings. Geoffrey Brennan, a Lecturer in the Department of Accounting and Public Finance, and typical of many younger members of staff, argued strongly in favour of student participation, partly to forestall unrest, partly to improve decision-making, but most of all to contribute to the undergraduates' education by drawing them into the academic environment. Crisp, then President of the Staff Association, was one of the old school, who regarded formal representation as an unjustified admission that informal contacts had failed. But Gibb, as chair of BSGS, saw the way the wind was blowing, and warned his colleagues that if the Board did not make recommendations for student participation, then Crawford certainly would. 'This is what worries me', said Crisp. 'The Vice-Chancellors will sell us down the river.' Gibb agreed: 'Our Vice-Chancellor will not be in the rear of this movement. We may be stuck with something we do not want.' After much agonising the Board agreed to various levels of representation, perhaps not as much as Crawford thought desirable, but still more generous than in any other Australian university, and sufficient to ensure that any unrest was nipped in the bud.

How far would Coombs and Crawford accede to student demands? For Coombs, encouragement of student participation was an article of faith. In the Boyer Lectures for 1970 he urged his listeners to look to the young as the hope of the future, and specifically to those who were demanding a say in decisions affecting their own lives and the world they would inherit. Their willingness to accept responsibility provided 'a bridge between us and them'. 'I would plunge heavily on giving them that responsibility.'

Crawford's liberality was perhaps more restrained; but then, it was put to an acid test. In late 1970 two former Monash students and well-known revolutionaries, Albert and Kerry Langer, applied to enrol as undergraduates. Albert Langer made no secret of his intention to undermine university administrations whenever the opportunity presented itself. Crawford was confronted with an unhappy dilemma. 'A university', he told the Admissions Committee, 'cannot be closed to ideas no matter how destructive'. But here was a case where a potential student, on the basis of his past record, might disrupt the whole campus.

There was a way out: the Langers had submitted their applications late and could be rejected for that reason. Crawford did not like this option. But he also believed that the University stood to lose more by letting Albert Langer in than by keeping him out. Having said that, he left the matter to the committee which, after much soul-searching, rejected the applications on the grounds of lateness. At least one member lamented that the University had suffered a moral loss by departing from the principle of academic quality as the basis of admission. Crawford remained uneasy; but whether his uneasiness derived more from the sacrifice of principle or a fear of repercussions, we will never know.

Robert Williams at a buffet luncheon given by the Students' Association in June 1972, soon after his appointment as Vice-Chancellor had been announced. He served as Vice-Chancellor from March 1973 to January 1975.

Crawford's policy of involving students in the government of the University worked, at least up to a point. The problem was that it was one thing to give students formal status on decision-making bodies, but quite another to ensure that they had significant impact. So much depended on the confidence and capacity of individual students, and the receptiveness of senior academic staff. Plowman's individual efforts to involve students in University affairs probably contributed more to mutual understanding and harmony between staff and students than formal student representation on a dozen committees.

By 1974 both Plowman and Crawford had gone. Crawford had retired in April 1973, having served over a year longer than he had originally intended. He was succeeded by R.M. Williams, formerly Vice-Chancellor at the University of Otago, who had been recommended by his fellow New Zealander, Mick Borrie. Plowman had moved later in the same year, first to the Australian Council for the Arts, then to the University of New South Wales as Academic Registrar. His place at the Union bar remained empty. Their departure might not have prevented the ensuing Troubles; but certainly the University's response would have been quite different and probably much more effective had they been there. Suddenly, for many of the more vocal students, the staff had become the enemy.

What had caused the change? Were the students' protests a residue of the momentum which had built up against Vietnam, conscription and the Springbok tour, and which now wanted direction? Did they reflect a sense of disillusionment with a government whose achievements seemed to be falling short of its promises? Staff members unsympathetic to the students suggested that they were merely imitating their brothers and sisters on other campuses.

But there were also causes closer to home. In the latter half of 1973 a few of the students were starting to realise that, despite all the talk of participation and representation, they really had little influence and no power. The Board of the School of General Studies made that clear by insisting that the student members who were proposed to be added to the Board were to be regarded as participants from the student body and not as representatives of the Students' Association. This was directly contrary to the Association's policy, and was interpreted by the students as a deliberate snub.

The sense of powerlessness was felt most acutely in relation to the content of courses and methods of assessment. There were specific problems in the Faculty of Arts, where students could hardly fail to notice significant differences from one department to the next. In the History Department, McQueen in particular encouraged student participation, offering his third-year class the opportunity to influence the lecture program and replacing the much despised end of year examination with a long essay. (At the same time, he maintained firm control over where the course was headed.) Psychology appeared by contrast conservative and intransigent. According to Julius Roe, the Chairman of the Students' Association Education Committee, Psychology students were expected 'to regurgitate textbooks, their initiative was stifled and they were assessed like the reflexive rats they were studying'. Students began to ask: if History could give them what they wanted, why not other departments? When staff resisted, they were branded authoritarian and reactionary.

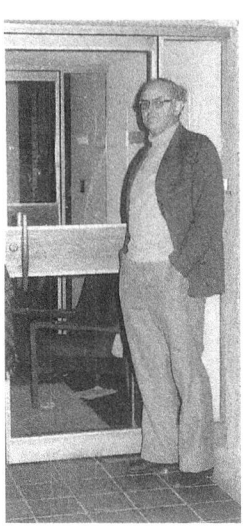

Locked out! Ross Hohnen during an occupation of the Chancelry by students in 1974.

Students such as Michael Dunn, a steely Maoist who was President of the Students' Association in 1974, and Roe, his equally committed but rather more humorous successor, saw the contest within the University as part of the struggle for 'a self-managed socialist society'. 'For students', wrote Roe, 'the struggle must be to bring the university into society as a whole and its struggles against racism, sexism, and exploitation but it must also be to end this injustice within the university. Neither struggle can succeed without the other.' They wanted 'relevance'. Gibb, and many academics who shared his views, was dismissive: students, he wrote, like industrial workers, were 'concerned to know how little they might do for how much'. Roe responded that students, in fighting the University, were fighting the capitalist system.

The simmering discontent exploded into direct action a few weeks after Orientation in 1974. After a lunchtime meeting in the Union Court to discuss educational issues, about a hundred students adjourned to the Mills Room on the top floor of the Chancelry, where Council meetings were usually held. As night fell, most of them left the building; but thirty or so staged an overnight sit-in. When Council members convened for their scheduled meeting the next morning, the students presented them with a series of demands: for control of course content to be equally shared by staff and students; for students to be able to choose their own means of assessment; for an end to overcrowded classes by the repetition of lectures and tutorials; and for the establishment of a Women's Studies course, whose content was to be decided by the women of the University: a new proposal which signified that women's voices were starting to be heard in the precincts of the Union.

The Board of SGS, in a tense meeting in Melville Hall with some three hundred students, accepted these demands as 'desirable objectives' and set up a committee comprising equal numbers of staff and students—the '10/10 Committee'—to decide how they might be implemented. Negotiations then dragged on for several months, as the committee's proposals were referred back to the faculties and departments. There were compromises and signs of progress, but also of resistance from various parts of the campus. Fearing they might lose the gains they had already made, the student activists became increasingly frustrated.

The crunch came in August. The Board, meeting in the Mills Room to consider the report of the 10/10 Committee, overturned its previous decision and the principle of equal voting by staff and students on course content and methods of assessment. As the meeting continued, a group of students marched on the Chancelry, only to find the doors locked and the Acting Registrar, the diminutive Helen Cumpston, barring their way. They then moved across to the Chancelry Annexe (the old Union Building), where Patricia White, the Assistant Registrar in charge of student records, had taken the precaution of placing the current files under lock and key. In the meantime, a small group, inspired no doubt by revolutionary practice abroad, targeted the centre of communications and raided the University telephone exchange, located in the gatehouse at University House.

The Chancellor, Coombs, in the foreground at the far left, leads negotiations with students during the occupation of the Mills Room in April 1974.
Canberra Times.

For Noel Dunbar, the Deputy Vice-Chancellor who witnessed the proceedings, this was the limit: without adequate communications the University was at risk, especially if an emergency should occur in one of the science laboratories. After consultation with colleagues, he took the unprecedented step of calling in the police. Twenty-seven students were carted off to the watch-house, which was what some of them had presumably hoped for; and the shaken switchboard operators were left to resume their duties as best they could.

A month later, after another Chancelry sit-in, Williams announced that he had accepted a senior position in the New Zealand public service and would therefore be leaving Canberra in February, less than two years after taking office as Vice-Chancellor. A journalist remarked that he was leaving with obvious relief. At Otago he had been an energetic and resourceful vice-chancellor, with a firm grasp on administrative and financial issues, and popular among staff and students. But the placid students of Dunedin had given him no indication of what to expect in Canberra and no experience of how to handle recalcitrant undergraduates. Cheery and well-meaning, he was no politician: and that in those years was what a vice-chancellor most needed to be.

For Williams, the ANU represented an unhappy interlude in an otherwise distinguished career. On other members of the University, the Troubles left deeper scars. White, like Plowman and many other members of the administrative staff, was almost maternal in her relations with students and had always enjoyed friendly contact with them. But confrontations with her erstwhile friends, now cold and sometimes threatening, was a distressing experience which left her with a bitter taste for many years to come. Clark was deeply pained by the events, especially since several of the leading revolutionaries, including Dunn and Roe, came from his own department, in seeming defiance of the humane, liberal values that he had always espoused. The confrontation hastened his retirement

Nobody reacted more bitterly than Crisp, the old Labor man, biographer of Ben Chifley and staunch defender of the university as a bastion of freedom. In October 1974, two months after the raid on the telephone exchange, he delivered the annual John Curtin Lecture, taking as his text Dedman's comments back in 1949 about the need to cherish academic freedom. Now, he declared, there were new 'gravediggers of academic freedom', who challenged the crucial freedom of all academics to determine the content of their own courses and research programs, and their methods of teaching and assessment. These were the 'Marxists with Grammar School accents', the 'hard-core campus ideologists, a self-consciously "alienated" small sect of frequently affluent and privileged middle-class youth born into a generation of conspicuously full employment'. These 'disaffected darlings' had nothing to complain about, yet were out to destroy the University; and the University, seemingly ignorant of the lessons from overseas, was bent on surrender, its Chancellor even appearing to offer the militants encouragement. Crisp had had enough.

Throughout the tussles of 1974, Coombs was never far from centre stage. As chairman of Council during the sit-ins, he found himself playing a mediating role between staff and students. Rather than resisting the protests, he welcomed them as a rejuvenating force, shaking the University from its innate conservatism. Just as the ANU had been founded in the belief that society should be transformed, so the current generation was questioning underlying social values. The University, he told Council members and students crowded together in the Mills Room, had failed to take sufficient account of student opinion. He had no intrinsic objection to sit-ins: while it would have been pleasanter if the students had asked to be invited, some reprehensible behaviour was a small price to pay to ensure the University was revitalised by healthy debate. Impolite activism was always preferable to apathy.

'I believe in controversy within the university', he told a student forum during Orientation Week in 1975; although he conceded that he was perhaps a little remote from its effects. In fact, Coombs probably had a better understanding of the protest movement than anyone else in the University, and more reason to fear where it was headed. By the time he eventually retired as Chancellor in 1976, there were already signs that it had run its course.

By mid-1975 Richard Johnson, the Professor of Classics and Dean of Students who had spent much of the previous year trying to steer between the Scylla and Charybdis of staff and student demands, was cautiously optimistic. Students were becoming increasingly involved in discussions on course content, and in nearly every unit assessment procedures were under review. The staff seemed more accommodating and the students more subdued, still firm on the subject of examinations, but now equally anxious on issues relating to housing and undergraduate stipends.

On the face of it, the students seemed to have got what they were after. But on closer inspection, the changes fell far short of their demands. Certainly, students were well represented on this committee and that; but staff maintained effective control of course content and methods of teaching. It was one thing to gain a voice on various committees, but quite another to make that voice effective, especially since the students were themselves by no means clear on what if anything they wanted, beyond the right to have a say.

Examinations were giving way to various forms of continuous assessment, as the students had wished; but continuous assessment did not necessarily mean that each student was able to choose *how* he or she was to be assessed. Ironically, the need to produce a steady stream of papers and perform well in tutorials imposed more restraints on undergraduates than the end of year examination had ever done. Bright students who in past years might have devoted the first two terms to politics or socialising were now bound to their desks soon after Orientation Week. They had little time to organise protest meetings, and still less to attend the innumerable meetings of which the academics seemed inordinately fond. Students in the latter half of the decade faced the added pressures imposed by a deteriorating job market. No longer did a degree guarantee suitable employment; now it paid to do well.

University was becoming a serious business. Coombs no doubt lamented the change, as he had regretted the demise of post-war optimism. Many academics welcomed the restoration of staff 'prerogatives', not noticing, perhaps, that they had never really lost them. Diana Riddell, who had served as Administrative Secretary to the Students' Association since 1965, remained in that office until 1985 when she decided to move to another part of the University, having concluded that student politics had lost their zest.

Graduation

Sir Robert Menzies, recently retired as Prime Minister, attended the Conferring of Degrees ceremony in 1966, held in the new Canberra Theatre, to receive the degree of honorary Doctor of Laws and deliver the graduation address. As he described it to his successor, Harold Holt, the occasion was something of a trial:

> By the time I got to my feet (long, long after processing began) I was nearly blind. The lighting was really fierce. For a break I would turn my back on my next door neighbour, Hugh Ennor, who appeared to be suffering no discomfort whatever, and concentrate on poor Nugget Coombs who manfully doffed the headgear five hundred times; smiled about five hundred times; presented a Roll about five hundred times. After I reached the rostrum it took me a minute or so to pick out the audience. All in all, you were lucky to be out of it.

Former Prime Minister Sir Robert Menzies addresses the congregation after receiving the honorary degree of Doctor of Laws, May 1966.
Canberra Times.

As this was Menzies' twentieth honorary doctorate, his lack of enthusiasm may be forgiven. But to most of the other new graduates, including John Dedman, who was adding the earned degree to his honorary one, the ceremony meant a great deal.

Although the numbers of PhDs produced by Australian universities were increasing rapidly each year, they were still a rarity and therefore much in demand, especially within the rapidly expanding tertiary education system. New PhD graduates could assume that they would be offered jobs that related fairly directly to the sorts of research they had just completed. Many had been offered appointments long before graduation, and were eagerly snatched up the moment they submitted their theses.

Bastable reflects in the early 1970s on what all the credentials mean.

Some went on to make research their careers, usually in the universities or the CSIRO, occasionally in industry. A few entered the middle levels of the public service, where they were generally headed for quick promotion, or joined commerce and industry at salaries which acknowledged the letters after their names.

The Bachelor graduates, too, had no trouble finding jobs. We do not know where the 1966 graduates were headed; but a 1969 survey suggested that all who graduated that year soon had a job, unless they were continuing their studies or training to be a teacher. Over a quarter of the graduates went into the Commonwealth public service. As the survey showed, ANU students were fortunate in having the nation's largest employer of graduates on the University's doorstep.

Many of the 1976 graduates, whether they wore a Bachelor's mortarboard or a Doctor's cap, were not so lucky. A national survey of first degree graduates from all Australian universities showed that 8 per cent of ANU students who had qualified in the previous year were still seeking full-time employment about the time of their graduation. This was a little higher than the national average, and more than double the 1969 figure. Doctoral graduates generally found themselves a job, but whether it was the job they wanted was quite another matter, varying sharply from one discipline to the next.

A university education meant more than a meal ticket; but exactly how much more depended on the individual, and in any case seemed to be changing over time. In 1968 Partridge, reflecting with Coombs on the nature of student protest, lamented the growing tendency to think of universities as training for economic and other social vocations. 'The production of professional competence in a specialised academic discipline has become increasingly the central goal of university teaching ... Educationally I believe this to be disastrous.' There was, he argued, too much grading and ticketing, which was mainly for the sake of filtering students into their proper niche in society. He wanted more informality in university education, which 'would no doubt produce more inefficiency from the point of social employment, but also perhaps, greater spontaneity and intellectual independence and initiative in the people we educate'.

Bettina Arndt BSc, with her parents Ruth and Heinz Arndt, Professor of Economics in RSPacS, in September 1971. Photograph by Gabe Carpay.

Partridge was conservative, in that he wanted to restore some of the traditional values of university education. He wanted above all to give students the freedom to think. In the same sense, the protesters of 1974 were conservative. They were also revolutionary in that, having lost confidence in their teachers' power to restore traditional values, they demanded a larger say in their own education.

In 1974 the nature of a university degree was the burning issue. Under the title 'Just a piece of paper?', the *ANU News* devoted its November edition to exploring the relevance of the degree in the outside world, presenting articles by eight graduates from various parts of the University. Bettina Arndt, who graduated in 1971 as a Bachelor of Science majoring in Psychology, and then took out a Master's degree from the University of New South Wales before becoming a professional psychologist specialising in sex therapy, thought her years as a student gave her little preparation for the outside world. So much of her time was spent in 'a competitive mark-grabbing scramble for distinction' that she forgot to enjoy learning. 'In the race through units that is essential to degree-acquisition there is little time for questioning, for innovation and curiosity.'

Andrew Bain, who graduated BA in 1972, likewise doubted whether his degree in Political Science contributed much to his current employment as an administrator at the fledgling Murdoch University, though he conceded that it might have helped him develop his capacity for critical thinking. He was more positive about his experiences outside the curriculum. As a prominent student politician, he developed skills in public speaking, debate and decision making. 'Those years increased my political awareness, enhanced my ability and willingness to question the accepted, and greatly expanded the breadth of my personal and intellectual horizons.' Twenty years later he was Deputy Registrar at Murdoch University.

Susan Ryan, a Sydney graduate who took out an MA from the ANU in 1973, was more positive: she believed her study of English literature was an appropriate preparation for her role as an education lobbyist. She later became Minister for Education in a Labor government, before embarking on a career in private enterprise.

Each response was illuminating. Overall they tended to reflect the critical spirit of the times. A decade earlier they would have been different; but then, presumably, nobody would have asked the question. Two decades later, they might be different

The graduation ceremony in Llewellyn Hall, 1976. Photograph by Bob Cooper.

again. And the same students might change their view of the University over time. Penny Chapman, who took out an Honours degree in Arts in 1972 and later became a leading television producer and director, acknowledged a debt to the University, remarking in 1994 that 'The influence of ANU on my student days grows more significant with each passing year'.

Stephen Padgham and Chris Swinbank likewise reflected on their student years with affection and a touch of nostalgia. Padgham had spent ten years in Britain as a teacher and part-time reviewer of dramatic productions before returning to Australia to teach at a Canberra high school. Swinbank had lived in the United States, where he played professional football and made money from dealing in stamps; in 1995 he was the affluent proprietor of a Canberra business specialising in used government furniture. Both confirmed the repeated claims of the *Orientation Handbook* that students benefited from their university years in proportion to what they put into them.

Signing the Graduation Register, April 1976.

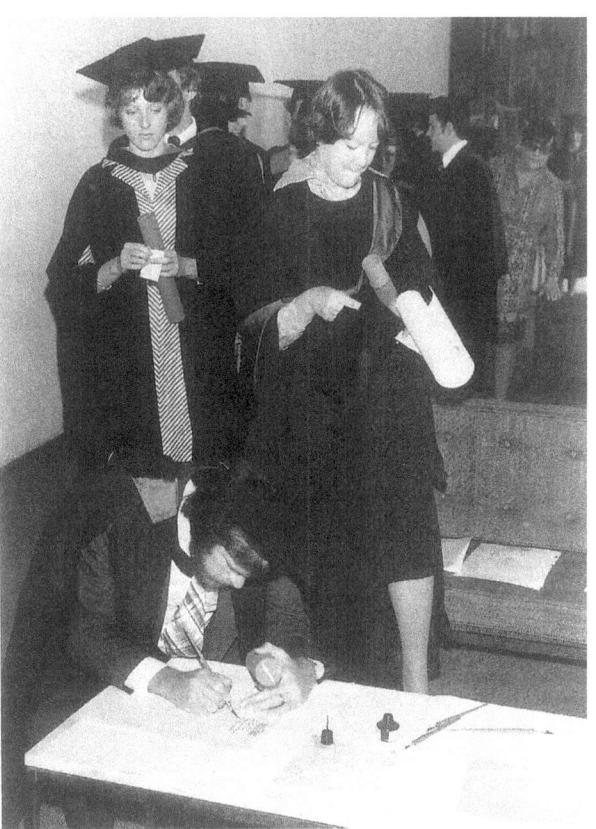

New initiatives

'Project C'

In the heady days of the early 1960s, when the Vice-Chancellor and the heads of schools were contemplating the future of the Institute, several ideas were put forward for new research schools. The makers had always intended that there should be more than four schools, though they did not say how many more, or exactly how, when and why they should be founded. Now, with the original schools well staffed and securely funded, and the government smiling on tertiary education, the time seemed ripe for expansion.

Two proposed schools received consistent support: chemistry and biological sciences. Whenever these were discussed, John Jaeger revived his arguments for a separate research school of earth sciences. All three were established by the early 1970s, each for different reasons and in different ways. One grew out of the ANU's existing research activities; another showed the University embarking on a new field of endeavour; the third was created chiefly because outstanding scientists were available. Together they suggest how the Institute evolved, both then and in later decades: not in response to carefully laid out plans, but rather as opportunities presented themselves in varying guises. Once established, the schools took different shapes and developed in contrasting ways.

Chemistry came first. Although there were strong academic reasons for pressing ahead with the biological sciences, the proposed chemistry school had a great advantage: there were men available to head it. This gave the University a persuasive argument to put to the Australian Universities Commission and the government. It seemed an opportunity too good to miss.

The idea for a research school of chemistry had been around at least since the mid-1950s, when there had been talk of recruiting Arthur Birch to a chair in one of the existing schools. It was revived in University House (where many grand ideas were hatched) one afternoon towards the end of the decade, when Frank Dwyer from the John Curtin School remarked to Hugh Ennor that there were several Australian chemists in Britain who ought to be back home contributing to Australian science. Ennor seized the idea and ran with it, first to his colleagues in the University, who offered enthusiastic support; and then to the expatriate chemists in Britain. This was just the job for a boots and spurs man. Once on his mount, he set out relentlessly in pursuit of his quarry.

Dwyer had in mind four chemists who had made a name for themselves in Britain. Birch, Professor of Organic Chemistry at Manchester, we have already met. The others were John Cornforth, also an organic chemist, who was at the National Medical Research Institute; and Ronald Nyholm and David Craig, who held chairs in inorganic and physical chemistry at University College, London. In 1961, when Ennor first approached them, they were all in their early to mid-forties, with Birch, the eldest, separated from Craig, the youngest, by a little over four years. Three of them had been born in Sydney and the fourth, Nyholm, in Broken Hill. All had been undergraduates at the University of Sydney before pursuing postgraduate research in Oxford or London. While Cornforth had spent nearly all of his career in Britain, the others had been together in Sydney in the early 1950s, Birch and Craig at the University of Sydney and Nyholm at the New South Wales University of Technology. By 1956 all four were back in Britain. Rarely had such an array of Australian talent in a single discipline been gathered overseas at any one time.

The first Craig heard of the ANU proposal was in the Express Dairy Café, not far from his department in University College, but out of sight and hearing of prying eyes and ears. There Ennor expounded in glowing terms the prospects of the new school, depicting (as Craig later remembered) 'a kind of chemical palace ... which would house every piece of equipment, instrument or device known to the subject at that time. Liquid helium, piped to every lab, would flow at the turn of a tap.' Craig was a little dubious, not least because he was already well equipped in his London laboratory. The others, approached separately by Ennor, expressed interest in the project, with varying levels of enthusiasm—sufficient, though, for Ennor to be able to return to Canberra confident that the project would go ahead.

Cornforth dropped out early. (Remaining in Britain, he went on to share the Nobel Prize for Chemistry in 1975.) The remaining three nevertheless covered the field. Nyholm seemed keenest to return to Canberra. Flamboyant and extroverted, he was the model academic administrator and entrepreneur, with an assertive Australian manner and a reputation for getting things done. Birch, though more formal and reserved, also had rough Australian edges, strong opinions and a forthright manner. Craig, the only one of the three with a private school education, was urbane, moderate in tone, and a sobering influence on his colleagues.

Taking matters in hand, Nyholm drafted a submission for the Vice-Chancellor, which suggested that he and his colleagues be styled 'Advisers' on the development of the school. This arrangement, willingly accepted by Council, gave the project the necessary impetus. At the same time, it more or less bound the University to move at the speed set by the Advisers and accept their recommendations. History was about to repeat itself, in more ways than one.

Money was not a problem. During a visit to Canberra in October 1962, the three Advisers spoke forcefully about the proposed school as 'a centre of excellence' for chemical research and training (using a term that only later came into vogue). Borne along especially by Nyholm's eloquence, the AUC was entirely won over; and early next year Cabinet gave the project the go ahead, subject to two of the three Advisers agreeing to accept chairs. Shortly afterwards, the University issued invitations to Nyholm, Birch and Craig to accept chairs in Inorganic, Organic, and Theoretical and Physical Chemistry. Hohnen, as the University's agent, embarked on an epic exercise of persuasion, visiting Britain to assure the Advisers that the University would give them everything they asked for. Building plans were set in motion and Hohnen, with characteristic determination to let nothing stand in the way of success, installed the architects for a time in London so that they could give immediate expression to the Advisers' requirements.

All this proceeded, over a period of two or three years, in secrecy: or rather the pretence of secrecy, since every time one of the prospective professors was seen talking to Hohnen, perhaps at an airport, the meeting was reported in Chemistry tea rooms throughout Australia. The proposed school was referred to as 'Project C', which fooled nobody, but at least reminded everybody that there was some distance to go before it became a reality.

Birch initially had many misgivings about coming to Canberra, and Ennor thought him the least likely of the three to commit himself. But encouraged by Hohnen, he started to think about the advantages the ANU had to offer, and before long he had accepted the invitation. Craig, more cautious by nature, was concerned about Australia's capacity to produce sufficient scholars to work with him in theoretical chemistry. Confronted with illness in the family, he withdrew from the project, but rejoined a few months later when his problems seemed resolved.

In the meantime, Nyholm was having second thoughts, suggesting when Craig dropped out that the project be deferred for three or four years. Hohnen complained to Coombs that he was fed up with this change of front. Craig's return promised to save the situation. But then the head of the Chemistry Department at University College suddenly died, causing Nyholm to ask for another postponement. Now everybody had had enough. Ennor warned Hohnen that Nyholm was 'very jittery and hard to pin down though if he did pull out now or later he could only do so by losing everyone's confidence and respect'.

Ennor provided the denouement, in circumstances which recalled the exchange with Florey eight years earlier. This time the confrontation took place at London's Tavistock Hotel, with Birch as witness and participant. Birch urged Nyholm to make up his mind, asking caustically if he intended to postpone accepting the University's invitation until it was time to retire in the sun. Then Ennor went at him 'quite mercilessly': 'A firm date, if necessary in a few years, or I report to the ANU that your attitude amounts to a refusal'. Nyholm, now quite distraught, replied that Ennor should do what he thought he had to do.

Nyholm was not normally indecisive. But on the large question of whether to remain in Britain or return to his native land he was, like Florey and many other expatriate academics before and since, almost constitutionally incapable of making up his mind. Even after Ennor forced the issue, he desperately wanted to return to Australia and looked forward to applying for a chair some time in the future. But Britain held him in its grip. As well as the need to pay what he saw as a debt to University College, he took deep pleasure from his place in the British chemical world. Here was 'the boy from Broken Hill', as Birch remembered him, with the prospect of a knighthood and the presidency of the Chemical Society before him. He achieved both before his premature death in a car accident in 1971.

The incident at the Tavistock put an end to Nyholm's association with the new research school. Nevertheless, he deserves to be remembered as a driving force behind the project and as a creative hand in giving the school its shape. Shortly after what Huxley referred to as Nyholm's 'defection', Birch and Craig formally accepted the University's invitation and 'Project C' was revealed to the world as the fifth research school.

From the time they first started thinking about the proposed school, Nyholm, Birch and Craig had expected it to be different from its predecessors. Doing most of their planning in Britain made it easier to depart from established forms. While members of the University were sometimes troubled by this spirit of free-thinking, they were hardly likely to put obstacles in the way of success.

The new school was planned to be novel in three major ways. First, on Nyholm's initiative, the Advisers decided that there should be no departments. Chemistry presented a special case for a non-departmental structure, since in recent decades the discipline had changed so much that traditional divisions were no longer especially relevant. While there was benefit in having professors with expertise in the traditional areas of organic, inorganic and physical chemistry, new research tended to straddle these fields. The structure of the school should therefore allow for complete flexibility, achieved through 'research groups' which would work under the direction of an outstanding, and not necessarily senior, researcher, and would come and go as projects ran their course and new opportunities appeared. The group structure, moreover, would allow the facilities of the school to be available to all, avoiding the constriction of historical budgeting which seemed endemic in departmental systems. The Advisers also put much thought into planning a building to allow for flexibility. While each of the three main branches of chemistry would have its own floor, this was to make best use of equipment and infrastructure rather than to impose artificial limits on fields of research.

The second innovation was that the school should have no director. The original schools had been administered by deans chiefly because no director was available; now the chemists suggested that a system of short-term deans was inherently better than having a long-term director. Given that the three prospective professors were of similar age and standing in the scientific community, the notion of one of them 'directing' the work of the others seemed particularly inappropriate; and none of them wished to sacrifice science for administration, as Ennor had done. The Advisers also identified a structural reason for preferring short-term deans over a long-term director. In a non-departmental school, where resources were subject to frequent reallocation from one research group to another, the head would be more powerful than in a departmental school, where financial control resided in the departments. It was therefore more than usually necessary that the head should enjoy the trust of his or her colleagues; and the Advisers, well aware of how universities worked, understood that a head of school had a much better chance of winning that trust if his or her term of office was strictly limited to three years. With some misgivings, the Board of the Institute agreed to a system of three-year appointments; and when the Research School of Chemistry (RSC) was inaugurated in 1967, Birch was installed as foundation Dean.

These initiatives were radical enough: the third presented a philosophical and physical challenge to the structure of the University. One of the Advisers' concerns before they committed themselves to Canberra was that there should be enough junior staff and students to allow them to pursue their research. Where students in the social sciences tended to work on individual topics, often isolated from the work of others in their department or school, natural science students usually formed part of a team with other students and staff members. Chemistry was one of those areas where research was labour-intensive; and if there were too few bright scholars to conduct experiments, the larger projects could not be done.

So a good supply of postgraduates was essential. Although the state universities might supply some, the Advisers knew that young Australians continuing to a second degree tended (more than their overseas counterparts) to remain at their alma mater, or at least in the same city. The solution for the proposed research school was to have an exceptional undergraduate school nearby. An undergraduate school already existed in the Faculty of Science, where Arthur Hambly had rapidly built up a strong teaching Department of Chemistry. Why not, the Advisers asked, integrate the department and the proposed school? As this seemed too radical, they suggested a close association, with staff in the research school participating in teaching and examining in the department, and staff and students in the department having access to the excellent facilities in the school.

Arthur Hambly, Professor of Chemistry in the School of General Studies, 1963.

It was all very well for the Advisers to say (and no doubt mean) that this arrangement was intended to be mutually beneficial. From Hambly's point of view, their comments, especially those of Nyholm, could be interpreted in more ways than one. He could be forgiven for being suspicious, especially as there were people in the Institute who were ready to ride roughshod over the School of General Studies. Would his department become merely a nursery for the school? Worse still, would it lose its entitlement to postgraduate students, whose departure would sound its death knell? The Advisers worked hard to allay his fears, and eventually both parties reached an agreement which spelt out the relationship between the department and the school. Hambly remained wary, but he promised to try to make it work.

For members of the University administration, the proposed relationship between the school and the department was both exciting and worrying: exciting because it promised to thrust chemistry at the ANU to the forefront of teaching as well as research; worrying because it threatened the uniqueness of the Institute, and potentially the basis of its separate funding. The Advisers offered another challenge by proposing that the building for the research school be located adjacent to the Department of Chemistry, which had its own building facing University Avenue, in the heart of the School of General Studies. Some members of the Institute objected, urging that Chemistry should be placed near the other natural science schools along Acton ridge. But the Advisers stood firm; and when staff of the John Curtin and Physical Sciences schools set out to attend the official opening of the Chemistry building in 1968, they had to allow themselves time for a five to ten minutes walk. Within a few years the department and the school were physically linked by a chain of new laboratories. The location of the school may have undermined the geographical integrity of the Institute; but it also held out the prospect of helping to bring the University together as a whole.

As had always been intended, the school was open to research in any field of chemistry. The first research subjects were chosen, as Birch wrote in his initial report, primarily because they were 'lively, challenging and difficult topics, of fundamental interest in the strict sense of the term'. That meant that they were not inspired by the prospect of short-term practical benefits; though Birch was careful to add that many of

David Craig (left) and Arthur Birch at the opening of the Research School of Chemistry, September 1968.

the projects had potential long-term applications in the Australian environment. While he and Craig remained jealous of their right to pursue fundamental research, they also recognised that chemists were expected to produce results that were useful. There was therefore a broad understanding within the school that about a tenth of its work would be directed towards national needs, relating perhaps to agriculture, industry or mining, so as to demonstrate visibly and convincingly that the school was 'paying its way'.

Within a decade of the opening, research in several areas suggested that the school would realise the high hopes of its founders. Alan Sargeson, an experimental inorganic chemist, discovered a means of trapping metals in molecular 'cages', which promised many practical applications. Lew Mander, who joined the ANU in 1975, led investigations into a group of natural compounds call gibberillins, which have profound and varied effects on plant growth. While Mander had begun this research many years earlier at the University of Adelaide, the research school gave him the time and resources to bring it to fruition. Before long, he and his team were producing synthetic or modified gibberillins to order, with large potential benefits for agriculture and side-benefits for other areas of applied chemical research.

Biological Sciences

At times, when the problems of luring the chemists to Canberra seemed insoluble, some senior members of the University suggested deferring the proposed chemistry school and promoting a school of biological sciences instead.

Sir David Rivett of the CSIR had argued for a biological science school as early as 1946, but Coombs had overruled him on the grounds that it was safer to get the four original schools well established before introducing new ones. The idea was raised again in 1961 by the Australian Academy of Science. The Academy, founded in 1954, was itself largely the creation of ANU and CSIRO scientists. Lately ensconced in an igloo-shaped building just outside the campus, it enjoyed a symbiotic relationship with the University, giving ANU academics who were also members of the Academy an opportunity to play a prominent part off campus in scientific initiatives which might have a direct impact on the ANU. At the time the school of biological sciences was being discussed, Frank Fenner was the Secretary (Biological Sciences) in the Academy, and therefore well placed to exert the necessary pressure.

The main argument for a school of biological sciences was simply expressed in a letter to Fenner from several biological Fellows: while astronomy and space research were receiving large sums of money, Australia's flora and fauna were being grossly neglected. The Academy responded by setting up a Flora and Fauna Committee, whose members included Fenner, Ennor and Huxley; and as a result of its report Fenner drafted a letter for the President of the Academy to write to the Vice-Chancellor, Huxley, urging the creation of a research school of biological sciences and pointing out that Australia's flora and fauna were 'unique, to a greater degree even than the southern heavens'. Fenner then handed the letter to Huxley, who was at this time his opposite number in the Academy, as Secretary (Physical Sciences). Huxley quietly put it into his top drawer lest it get in the way of the chemistry proposal, an object lesson in the dangers of not sending mail through official channels.

But there was sufficient enthusiasm for the initiative, especially among the professors of the John Curtin School, to keep it alive. In order to develop a detailed plan, Fenner, now on leave in Cambridge, approached David Catcheside, Professor of Microbiology at the University of Birmingham, who had lately been considered as a likely prospect for a proposed chair of Genetics in JCSMR. In 1963 Catcheside accepted the chair, along with the formal title of Adviser of the projected school. Unlike the earlier Advisers and the three chemists, he was not Australian or New Zealand born, but four years in Adelaide as Professor of Genetics had established his Australian credentials. He was also older than the other Advisers at the time of their appointments, although he looked and sounded younger than his 54 years. While some regarded his work as a little old-fashioned, meaning that he was not directly engaged in DNA research, he was enthusiastic about his subject and had shown no signs of decreasing productivity.

Over many years, Catcheside had become convinced of the need for an integrated approach to the biological sciences, based on genetics as the core discipline. Although his Birmingham chair was in microbiology, its purpose was to bring together genetics (especially microbial genetics) and biochemistry in what could later be seen as a sort of precursor to the study of molecular biology. The function of biology, he said, was 'to explain the nature of life'. Traditionally, biologists had approached this task in diverse ways, and often quite independently of one another. They were concerned with animals, plants or microbes, with emphasis on particular groups or activities. They focused on individual organisms or whole populations. They employed different methodologies, broadly categorised as descriptive, biochemical, biophysical and genetical. As a result of this diversity, biology was divided into many separate and largely independent specialisms, such as embryology, anatomy, ethology and taxonomy, and others that were defined by the organisms that were the object of their study.

David Catcheside at the time of the inauguration of the Research School of Biological Sciences in 1967.

Yet biologists were coming to realise that they all had a great deal in common. 'Living organisms', said Catcheside, 'consist of a limited range of special molecules, especially large ones such as proteins and nucleic acids, which are built up from a limited number of small basic molecules which are strung together in various orders... The whole range from molecules to population is a continuum, which it is the purpose of biology to understand as a whole.' He therefore argued that the new school should abandon the traditional specialisms in favour of an integrated attack on four specific problems, each of which needed to be developed in Australia: the relation between molecular structure and function, with special reference to proteins and nucleic acids; the mechanisms of development and differentiation; the dynamics of populations; and animal behaviour. The first two of these were at one end of the biological science spectrum, the second two at the other. As with the Research School of Chemistry, the school would have no departments and no boundaries, permitting easy adaptation to new research interests. Catcheside delivered a warning: the success of the integrated school would depend on staff and students in the various areas taking a lively interest in one another's work.

Compared with the Chemistry school, the Research School of Biological Sciences (RSBS) progressed smoothly to a subdued inauguration in 1967. Catcheside, with most of his department, moved across from the John Curtin School as Professor of Genetics and first Director of the school, and professors were promptly appointed with expertise relating to two of the four selected fields: Ralph Slatyer, who was Chief Research Scientist in the Division of Land Research at the CSIRO, accepted a chair in Environmental and Population Biology; and Dennis Carr, Professor of Botany at Queen's University, Belfast, came to a chair in Cellular and Developmental Biology.

Ralph Slatyer, Professor of Environmental and Population Biology.

Within a year it was clear that, while the idea of an integrated school might be sound in theory, it was extremely difficult to put into practice. Each of the new professors had his own research program, which bore no necessary relationship to what was happening in other parts of the school. And each was determined to see that his research area received its fair share of the available resources. Carr argued that differences in terminology and methodology among the various branches stood in the way of adequate communication, making integration all but impossible.

These problems were compounded by accommodation arrangements. Where the chemists had insisted on the need for a single building at the outset, Catcheside thought the building could wait. As a result, the staff were scattered—Slatyer in RSC, Carr in a timber block near JCSMR, Catcheside and his own small group in another part of the timber building, and the rest of Genetics in JCSMR—and people from distant groups rarely had the chance to talk to one another, even if they had wanted to.

Catcheside tried to forestall the inevitable, arguing that it was easier to create a departmental structure than to break it down. But less than two years after the school's inception, he had to accept that the existing informal divisions were departments in all but name, and that therefore they might as well be given the same degree of budgetary autonomy that departments enjoyed in other schools. So the four original research 'problems' were converted to departments of Genetics, Developmental Biology, Environmental Biology and Behavioural Biology, supplemented by two units (a term recently introduced in other parts of the University) of Molecular Biology and Taxonomy. Before long, two new departments were added, in Neurobiology and Population Biology. Catcheside continued to argue that integration was the way of the future; but by the time of his retirement in 1972, the departments and units were well entrenched. Although a new Director, the former Master of University House, Sir Rutherford Robertson, and a new permanent building, mostly occupied by 1973, helped in different ways to bring it together, a later review committee described the school as a set of watertight compartments, some with imperial and separatist heads.

Why had Biological Sciences failed as an integrated school where Chemistry had evidently succeeded? Part of the answer lay in the nature of the respective disciplines, the one relatively coherent, the other divided into any number of sections and subsections which had evolved over many decades. Then there was the practical matter of dispersed accommodation. But most of all, Biological Sciences suffered from the structural weakness that the Chemists had avoided, of having a director of a non-departmental school. Catcheside's job was almost impossible. And he was not the person for an impossible job. Birch and Craig, though very different from one another in manner and style, were as one on the things that really mattered, and together they made a formidable team. Catcheside, while strong in his opinions about the benefits of integration, lacked the assertiveness and leadership skills to give them effect, especially in the face of determined opposition from one of his professors.

Sir Rutherford (Bob) Robertson, second Master of University House and second Director of RSBS.

Although Catcheside lamented the failure of his integrated structure, the respective departments were achieving a great deal. By 1975 the school had 65 academic staff and 50 research students, working on living matter ranging from the smallest organisms to humans. The report for that year described major achievements in all departments, referring to 'the exciting atmosphere in which advances in much of our knowledge are made'. The Department of Neurobiology was working on problems of vision and hearing in insects and crustaceans, which had relevance throughout the animal world. The Environmental Biologists were conducting research into the process of photosynthesis. The Behavioural Biologists, exploring the mechanism of memory, had discovered a class of biochemical inhibitors which blocked a specific process in brain cells and in so doing blocked short-term memory in fish, chickens and humans. The Geneticists were investigating how nitrogen is brought by bacteria from the air into the soil. The Developmental Biologists were using an electron microscope to analyse the fine structure of plant cells, while the Molecular Biologists were seeking to understand the mechanism of protein synthesis. The Department of Population Biology, although mostly concerned with the dynamics and genetics of insect populations, was beginning an analysis of a large sample of medical records from Sydney in order to study the inheritance of susceptibility to certain diseases in humans. All this was fundamental research, aimed at understanding biological principles, but often within easy reach of practical applications.

Earth Sciences

In the Research School of Physical Sciences, John Jaeger's Department of Geophysics had gone from strength to strength. A succession of notable appointments enhanced its geochemical capacity, and in 1964 it was renamed the Department of Geophysics and Geochemistry to acknowledge its wider ambit. As well as being the largest department in the school, it remained the most productive in terms of the total output of research papers.

Its work continued to concentrate on the earth's crust and interior, often with practical applications. The most extensive program, conducted in collaboration with the

Commonwealth Bureau of Mineral Resources, studied the ages and isotopic compositions of rocks in Australia, India, Ceylon, New Guinea and the Pacific islands, providing further support for the theory of continental drift and constructing the essential framework for large-scale mineral exploration. Convincing evidence of the department's growing international reputation came in 1969, when several members were chosen by the United States National Aeronautics and Space Agency (NASA) to carry out research on lunar rock samples brought back by the Apollo space missions. This participation in lunar research was greater than that of any other institution outside the United States.

Each new achievement seemed to reinforce, in the eyes of its members, the department's case for independence. In the late 1960s it moved into its own building, which strengthened its integrity while distancing it even further from the rest of the school. Jaeger, looking forward to retirement in 1972, started a new campaign for a research school of earth sciences with a hefty push, then left it to his protégé Ted Ringwood, who had joined the department in 1959 and was now Professor of Geochemistry, to keep up the momentum. Ringwood and his departmental colleagues offered some persuasive arguments, based chiefly on the potential of a separate school to develop new areas of research which were of vital social and economic significance to Australia but were currently inadequately catered for. These included environmental geochemistry and the sciences involved with the formation and nature of mineral deposits.

The case for earth sciences was quite different from earlier arguments in favour of the other new schools. Chemistry and Biological Sciences were entirely new initiatives, each opening up areas that the University had so far largely ignored (except, perhaps, through the departments of Medical Chemistry and Genetics). A school of earth sciences would be created from something that was already there and would involve breaking off part of an original school. Fission, as the Physical Scientists liked to call it, threatened not only their school but the structure of the Institute as a whole.

Staff in RSPhysS became increasingly divided on the issue, with Titterton, encouraged by Oliphant, leading a determined opposition. The critical question was: where would it all end? Would other parts of Physical Sciences—astronomy, engineering, mathematics, nuclear physics—be hived off in the same way? Why incur the administrative cost of setting up a new school for research that could just as well be accommodated by existing arrangements? Oskar Spate, a relatively disinterested observer, assumed that the opposition had, at least for the time being, won the day:

> ... I fear
> Jack Jaeger's grand and sacred mission
> to propagate himself by fission
> goes by default, to tamely shift
> into mere Continental Drift ...

But the Vice-Chancellor, Crawford, was determined that the proposal should be given a fair hearing, especially since Titterton, notwithstanding his position as Director, was so obviously a fierce partisan. At a tense Council meeting late in 1971, Ringwood and

Left: Ted Ringwood, Professor of Geochemistry, in 1969. Photograph by Gabe Carpay.

Right: Ernest Titterton, with the tandem accelerator in the Department of Nuclear Physics, 1969. Photograph by Gabe Carpay.

Titterton were summoned to present the cases for and against. Ringwood spoke first, with numerous bullish references to the importance of geology in the mining boom and the national need for geoscientists. What he did not do was to establish a convincing case for a new school. Ian Ross, attending his first Council meeting as representative of the deans of the faculties, concluded that all Titterton had to do was to say that the case was not proven, and offer to answer questions. But that, Ross remembered, was not the Titterton way: 'with all the subtlety of a pit bull terrier he went on the attack, a bitter attack on Ringwood and his colleagues'.

The protagonists withdrew, leaving most councillors with no doubts as to why the earth scientists wanted to be and had to be in control of their own destiny. The question was put to the vote and the new school was approved on the voices. 'In fifteen dramatic minutes', said Ross, 'Ernest Titterton had created a new Research School'. The 'unconscious midwife', Spate recorded, had given Earth Sciences the kiss of life.

Titterton was not finished yet. After the decision went against him, he wrote to senior earth scientists in various parts of the world, including prospective applicants for Jaeger's chair, telling them (in words that were, at best, disingenuous) that the school had been created against the wishes of his own school, the heads of the other schools and a majority on the Board of the Institute, and supported only by members of Jaeger's old department and 'a small, but vocal, group on Council'. 'If you have any views on the matter', he wrote, 'I would be very glad to hear them and if you would be interested to read it I would happily send you, in confidence, detailed information on the problem'. The appeal to professional colleagues outside the institution was a tactic familiar to anybody associated with any university. Titterton's blatant use of it got him nowhere.

The Research School of Earth Sciences (RSES) was formally created in mid-1973 and Anton Hales, a South African who was Director of the Institute of Geological Sciences at the University of Texas, was recruited to head it. Rather than breaking into separate departments, the school inherited the structure of the old Department of Geophysics and Geochemistry, with groups that varied in size and number. Its work was extended to cover the motions and dynamics of the sea and atmosphere, and soon there were new appointments in Geophysical Fluid Dynamics and Economic Geology. Staff maintained such a high and steadily increasing rate of productivity that before long the proponents of a separate school could claim that their case had been justified.

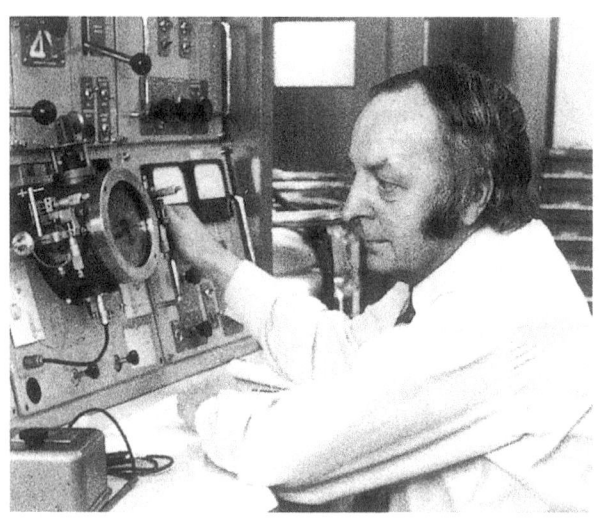

Ross Taylor in the new Research School of Earth Sciences examines in 1975 samples of rock from the moon. Photograph by Patrick Power.

Spate had feared that the creation of Earth Sciences might lead to Balkanisation of the Institute. It did not; but it did contribute to Titterton's undoing. In 1968 he had been appointed Director of RSPhysS for a period of five years on the understanding that, unless grave difficulties stood in the way, his appointment would be renewed. In the ensuing years, Titterton alienated Crawford and various members of Council, while his conduct within the school (notwithstanding his earlier support for a more democratic faculty structure) was so tyrannical that many staff rebelled openly. A reappointment committee concluded in 1973 that the unity of the school demanded that he must go.

The faculty of RSPhysS decided that it was not enough that he should cease to be Director: 'it is our conviction that the attainment of harmony within the School ... will be difficult, if not impossible, unless Sir Ernest Titterton's continued presence in the University is accompanied by measures designed to ensure that he is effectively isolated from the affairs of the School'. The Vice-Chancellor, Williams, obliged by setting him up in a separate unit, which denied him membership of decision-making bodies. Titterton protested that these measures were 'unnecessarily harsh, legalistic and restrictive', adding ironically that after 22 years devoted service he hoped the Vice-Chancellor was not expecting him to break out into some 'wild excesses of an irresponsible nature'. That was exactly what Williams and his colleagues did expect. The ANU, like most other universities in the British tradition, was a very tolerant institution. Titterton proved that its tolerance had limits.

New teaching departments

The School of General Studies inherited from Canberra University College many of the core disciplines in Arts, Science, Economics and Law that were part of a traditional university, together with a traditional structure that located disciplines in departments. The exception was Law, which had a range of courses in specific subject areas, but no departments. Oriental Studies achieved faculty status in 1961 (and changed its name to Asian Studies in 1970).

While some of the newer universities, such as Macquarie and Flinders, were introducing multidisciplinary schools without departments, SGS staff generally opposed experimenting with what some regarded as 'gimmickry'. On the other hand, the University allowed students an unusually wide choice of degree structures.

The usual way of opening up a teaching area was by creating a department within an existing faculty. During the 1960s new departments were established in traditional disciplines, such as Classics, Geography, Theoretical Physics and German, and in newer teaching fields such as Sociology, Indonesian Languages and Literature, and South Asian and Buddhist Studies. By the early 1970s, the faculties covered most of the traditional disciplines and a few more. The AUC now decided that the departments had proliferated quite enough, and forced the University to make hard decisions about the optional extras. As a result, Prehistory was chosen in preference to Religion, and Fine Arts to Music.

Departments were created for various reasons: to split an existing large department, such as Mathematics, into its component parts; to meet an anticipated student demand; to cover a subject area which it seemed that any university, or the ANU in particular, *ought* to cover at a departmental level. As in the Institute, a department was sometimes formed when opportunity offered, perhaps when somebody especially suitable was available to head it.

The Department of Prehistory grew out of the remarkable work in Australian, South-east Asian and Melanesian prehistory that had been conducted in RSPacS, first in the Department of Anthropology and Sociology and from 1970 in a separate Department of Prehistory. The name Prehistory was chosen to suggest links with history comparable with classical archaeology's links with the classics: in other words, to confirm the credentials of a new area of study. It drew together threads of various disciplines and subdisciplines—archaeology, anthropology, ethnography, geomorphology—into an integrated study of the distant past.

During the 1960s archaeological fieldwork, much of it conducted by members of RSPacS, had transformed understandings of Aboriginal Australia, dispelling myths associated with the 'stone age' and revealing a society much richer and older than most people had previously thought. John Mulvaney, who had attended Cambridge as an ANU Overseas Scholar in the early 1950s, joined the school as Senior Fellow in Prehistory in 1965; and Jack Golson, who had been a member of the school from 1962, was appointed Australia's first Professor of Prehistory in 1970.

That year was described in the University's annual report as an *annus mirabilis* for the prehistorians: F.J. Allen, who had studied the archaeological remains of early European visits to tropical Australia, became the first entirely Australian-trained archaeologist to receive a doctorate; Mulvaney and an Indonesian archaeologist, R.P. Soejono, led a joint Indonesian–Australian expedition to Sulawesi; Mulvaney published *The Prehistory of Australia*, a landmark work in the history of Australian archaeology; and Jim Bowler in the Department of Biogeography and Geomorphology discovered on the shores of former Lake Mungo in western New South Wales a human cremation site, calculated by

John Mulvaney, 1965, sorts archaeological materials from Kenniff Cave in the Great Dividing Range, Queensland, which was discovered to have been occupied by humans 19 000 years ago.

radiocarbon dating to be around 26 000 years old, so continuing the process by which Aboriginal antiquity was thrust back by successive millennia.

Mulvaney was keen to develop Prehistory as a teaching discipline, and Crawford, having witnessed the flowering of the Prehistorians in RSPacS, recognised its potential. As the AUC would not permit the creation of a new department, the Vice-Chancellor circumvented the problem by appointing him to a third chair in the Department of History, where he received a fraternal welcome. Students enrolled in the new courses in large numbers, helping to give Prehistory a distinct identity; and by 1973, AUC rules had been relaxed sufficiently to allow the formation of a new department. Crawford wanted it to include Anthropology, which he considered to be an essential university discipline: so with Mulvaney's agreement the department was named Prehistory and Anthropology, thereby admitting another new discipline by the side door.

Both sections of the department thrived, Prehistory under Mulvaney and Anthropology under Anthony Forge, a Cambridge graduate who had worked with Firth at the University of London. Mulvaney interpreted Prehistory widely. The breadth of his interests was reflected in the work of research students: Aboriginal bark paintings in Arnhem Land; the history of anthropology; industrial archaeology and land settlement in New England, New South Wales; the role of women in gathering shellfish in a north Australian coastal community.

Prehistory took its place alongside the traditional academic disciplines (though Mulvaney would insist that much of the department's teaching and research had immediate implications, especially for Aborigines and their relationships with other Australians). Other new departments leaned more towards professional or vocational training. Although Canberra University College had been set up partly to serve the professional needs of public servants, during the 1950s professional studies (except for Law) had tended to be overshadowed by the traditional academic disciplines. After amalgamation the University developed new areas of professional training which helped restore the balance.

Forestry was one of the first, and it opened up large questions about the place of professional courses in a university. The Australian School of Forestry had been in Canberra since 1927 (as long as the federal parliament), just a few kilometres from the ANU in the suburb of Yarralumla. By an arrangement with most state universities, students pursuing forestry careers took two years of a university science course, two years of professional training at the School of Forestry, and were awarded degrees from their own universities. By the 1960s this arrangement had become unsatisfactory, both from the point of view of the school, which was unable to offer its graduates opportunities for postgraduate research, and of the universities, which were granting

Above: Derrick Ovington, Professor of Forestry, with students in an ACT forest 1968. Photograph by Mick Tanton.

Left: Forestry students in the laboratory in the late 1960s. Photograph by Mick Tanton.

degrees for work over which they had little control. The school needed a home on a university campus, and the ANU, with its national status and nearby location, obviously had strong appeal. So just after the government announced that Canberra University College would shortly amalgamate with the ANU, the school approached the University suggesting some sort of association that would lead to the creation of a first-class centre for forestry research and education. In due course, the government gave its backing and promised the necessary funding, and incorporation seemed set to proceed.

There were problems. One was the school's desire to retain the Board of Higher Forestry Education, which comprised the Principal of the School of Forestry and representatives of the state universities and forestry services. From the University's perspective, this would allow outside bodies an influence in matters over which its own academic bodies should have sole control. (It might well have seemed ominous that the current Chairman of the Board, who was also a member of the University Council, was the Managing Director of the Australian Newsprint Mills.) The difficulty was resolved by replacing the Board with an Advisory Committee, similar to the Board in composition and function but able to give advice only through the Faculty of Science. This placed solid academic protection between the new Department of Forestry and any potential and possibly improper external pressure.

The other problem was less readily solved. In the eyes of many members of the University, especially staff of the Institute already resentful about amalgamation with Canberra University College, a large question mark hung over the School of Forestry. Although forestry occupied an honourable place in many universities in Europe and the United States, they wondered whether it was a genuine university discipline. After all, the school made no secret of the fact that its main function was to train the professional practitioner, and that its purposes in seeking to join the University were both to give intellectual depth to its courses and to achieve the enhanced status which membership of a university would confer. In fact the school wanted more than mere membership of the ANU, arguing strongly for faculty status, which would lift the standing and autonomy of Australian forestry education in the eyes of other professions and forestry scholars in other parts of the world.

The dichotomy was not simply between 'pure' or 'basic' and 'applied' science,

Oliphant drew a distinction between teaching 'creative applied scientists', which was an appropriate role for a university, and training the 'run-of-the-mill technologists' required by industry, which should be conducted by improved technical colleges. While he was willing in principle to welcome forestry into the fold, he thought that the School of Forestry staff were not yet ready to become part of the University and that the infant Faculty of Science was not yet ready to receive them. Crisp, on the other hand, wanted to let them in now: 'I do not share the view I have heard sniffily put at meetings over the past eighteen months by one or two of our leading Institute colleagues that we should not sully ourselves with practical and technological work'.

While most members of the University involved in the issue conceded that what the school did it did well, Lindsay Pryor, who as Professor of Botany in SGS and with a first degree in forestry was well placed to judge, remarked that the curriculum, influenced by non-academic advisers to meet the needs of the major forestry employers, 'tends to develop too little the component of far-sightedness and intellectual inspiration desirable in a first-class academic course'. That was perhaps as good a description as any of what distinguished a university course from professional training; but it left plenty of room for debate in this and other cases.

Incorporation of the School of Forestry nevertheless went ahead, not as a separate faculty, but as a department in the Faculty of Science, which gave the University firm control over curriculum and academic standards. While there were academic arguments for and against, government support and money made it hard for the University to say no. J.D. Ovington, formerly Head of the Woodland Section of the British Nature Conservancy, was appointed foundation professor; and from 1965 the University offered a BSc (Forestry) degree, teaching initially from the Yarralumla premises and temporary accommodation on campus. Three years later the Department of Forestry moved into its own new building, which featured elegant timber panelling donated by forestry and industrial organisations from various parts of Australia and the world. This was nicely symbolic, not just of the subject matter, but also of the department's links with the profession which provided jobs for its graduates and the main reason for its being.

The Department of Forestry grew rapidly, from an intake of 40 students in 1965 to over 80 a decade later. At that time, staff members defined their main objective as training professional foresters in 'a multidisciplinary approach to the study and practical application of multiple use principles in the integrated management of forest resources', with the subsidiary aim of catering for students in other areas who needed to know something about forest resource management. Teaching and research focused on environmental aspects of forestry, and reflected society's increasing concern with renewable resources. As well as maintaining a strong association with forestry authorities in Australia, staff provided advice and technical aid to several developing countries in South-east Asia. By the end of the decade, Forestry was one of the largest departments in the Faculty of Science, with many postgraduate students, and well enough entrenched to ignore any lingering doubts about its status as a professional discipline.

If Prehistory was 'academic' and Forestry 'professional', the Department of

Accounting and Public Finance occupied the grey area between. Accountancy had been among the inaugural courses offered by Canberra University College when it began teaching in 1930, and Public Finance was introduced later in the decade to meet the needs of public servants. Both courses included a theoretical component, although Accountancy was chiefly concerned with nuts and bolts, such as the preparation, presentation and analysis of accounting reports, external audits, and the ethics of the profession.

Following amalgamation, Burton and other senior members of the School of General Studies wanted to develop Accounting (as they preferred to call it) to the status of a full university discipline and to offer an Accounting major, in close association with Economics and Political Science. While the new course would introduce students to basic accounting techniques, the emphasis would be on problems of accounting theory which interested economists, and problems of government and public authority accounting. This was a tall order, as there were few academic accountants in Australia, and fewer still with the necessary interests in public finance. But Burton had someone in mind, Copland's former assistant and the University's agent in London during the early 1950s, Russell Mathews.

Since leaving the ANU's service, Mathews had been successively Reader and Professor in the Faculty of Economics at the University of Adelaide, where he had published a textbook *Accounting for Economists* and conducted research on areas including accountancy theory, taxation and income measurement. He was just completing a book on public investment which, when published in 1967, became the first systematic study of public policy issues on the expenditure side of public finance. Tall and imposing, but softly-spoken and unassuming in manner, Mathews knew as much about public sector accounting as anybody in Australia. He was just the right person to transform the course into a discipline.

Russell Mathews in 1981.
By courtesy of Russell Mathews.

Mathews took up the chair of Accounting and Public Finance in 1965, in a new department of the same name. The courses were rigorous, and first-year failure rates were alarmingly high, partly because the content was often not what students expected. Teaching leaned heavily towards the theoretical, emphasising conceptual and analytical frameworks rather than technical forms and procedures, even omitting some areas normally part of professional training, such as bankruptcy law and practice and income tax law and practice. This could have been a problem for the many students who looked to Accounting to provide a meal ticket, and in retrospect Mathews thought the professional institutes were sometimes generous in accrediting ANU courses. His successor as head of department, Allan Barton, conceded that the utilitarian role of Accounting could lead to 'goal conflict'; but he, like Mathews, insisted that in Accounting, as in all university disciplines, the primary function should be to train students to think analytically, and that they should not expect to achieve full professional competence by the time of graduation.

Women's Studies

In the early 1970s there was little interest on campus in women's issues. Although a branch of Women's Liberation had been set up in Canberra in 1970 by a group of women meeting at the student house in Canning Street, and although some staff and students were active in the movement and the Women's Electoral Lobby, formed two years later, the links between the University and the women's movement were tenuous. If successive issues of *Woroni* were anything to judge by, the campus was a hotbed of male chauvinism (though probably no more so than other Australian universities); and while student organisations gave material support to women's activities, the Union bar was often inhospitable to women who, inspired by the flood of (mainly American) literature on women's issues, were seeking to find their own identities. Women's issues were largely missing from the academic curriculum, except for occasional lectures and seminars in Classics, History, Political Science and Sociology.

Liz O'Brien, right, explains the proposed course in women's studies to fellow students, 1974. Photograph by Ian Mackay.
Australian Archives.

The women's movement on campus became suddenly vigorous in 1974. At the beginning of the year a group of students published a women's handbook. Then Liz O'Brien, a radical feminist and former part-time student who had lately returned to full-time study in Arts, introduced the idea of a course in women's studies. Assertive and voluble, with clear ideas of where the women's movement ought to be headed, O'Brien had attended a conference in Melbourne on feminism and socialism, where there had been discussion of courses devoted to women, including a women's studies program that had been set up at Flinders University the preceding year. Returning to Canberra, she presented a forceful case in favour of a women's studies course at the ANU to the mass meeting of students in the Union forecourt which signalled the beginnings of the Troubles. The proposal went to Council, along with the demands relating to assessment, overcrowded classes and the control of courses. By comparison with these other demands it seemed fairly innocuous, and easily cleared the first hurdles.

Thelma Hunter in the 1970s.
By courtesy of Thelma Hunter.

Several months of lively debate followed. In the Faculty of Arts, discussion of the issue was brought forward when Thelma Hunter, a diminutive Scot and Senior Lecturer in Political Science, cheekily asked for permission to speak on the subject before the effects of her Valium wore off. Manning Clark told faculty that he wished there had been such a course when he was an undergraduate so that he might now understand what went on in the heart of a woman. Several members argued that women's studies were not and could not be a serious academic pursuit, and at least one professor portrayed the proposed course as a threat to family values.

The sharpest disagreements took place among those who supported the principle of women's studies, but were deeply divided as to how and where they should be taught.

O'Brien demanded a multidisciplinary course dedicated to women's studies: 'Women are not a minority group—their role must be examined in an integrative manner, not piecemeal'. Hunter, who had already demonstrated her commitment to studying women through her lectures and seminars in Political Science, feared that such an approach would be self-defeating, reinforcing the segregation of the sexes within the University and leading to a course 'about women, for women and by women' which would become marginal to the mainstream curriculum. She wanted women's studies to permeate the existing disciplines, so that teachers in existing departments, women and men alike, were obliged to read and teach the relevant literature. The radical feminists hoped for this outcome too, but were convinced that without a dedicated course they would never achieve it.

Ann Curthoys, Coordinator of the Women's Studies course, 1976. Photograph by Bob Cooper.

The debate, in terms of feminist theory at the time, was between revolutionaries and reformists. The reformists, mostly staff members, conceived women's studies in the context of traditional academic disciplines, whose emphasis they sought to change. The content of women's studies courses should be decided not by the women of the University, but by members of staff, irrespective of their sex, who had expertise in the area of study. The revolutionaries,—mostly students but also a respected Lecturer in History, Daphne Gollan—viewed women's studies as a manifestation of the women's movement and a means of challenging existing social and political structures. Unless it had a continuing link with the movement, women's studies risked a descent into 'arid and incestuous scholasticism'.

The revolutionaries won. After extended and often heated discussion, a separate women's studies program was approved for introduction in 1976. A historian, Ann Curthoys, was appointed to run it, and she developed a course which was both academically rigorous and adventurous in incorporating current feminist thinking.

The course, offered only to students who had successfully completed a full first-year unit in a relevant Arts department or the interdisciplinary program in Human Sciences, ranged widely across issues and disciplines, exploring for example women and literature, women in developing countries, and sex differences and psychological processes. It quickly proved popular, especially among female mature-age students, and attracted strong student loyalty. A second course was added in 1978. Susan Magarey, who succeeded Curthoys that year, described her first year as coordinator as 'an electrifying experience'. 'Students were enrolled not merely because they wanted another unit towards a degree, but rather because they wanted to read and discuss the rapidly expanding literature that the Women's Movement was producing.' No other course so comprehensively blended personal and academic interests. The program also explored new methods of teaching and assessment, and new ways of transfusing the disciplines.

Susan Magarey (left), who succeeded Curthoys as Coordinator of Women's Studies, with students Sue Waddell-Wood (centre) and Maryanne Mooney, 1979. Photograph by Stephen Berry.

Yet in one important respect the reformists had been right. Within the University, the program was widely regarded as marginal. While Magarey worked hard, with some success, to introduce women's studies into other departments, she lamented that few colleagues consulted her about how to integrate what were now being referred to as gender issues into their curriculums. Program staff, whose first allegiance was to the women's movement, developed strong links with women in the public service and other institutions, and gave the program a high national visibility. But within the University, Women's Studies could easily be ignored.

Building bridges

In addition to departments, the University's academic structure included centres and units, sometimes referred to as a 'third dimension'. These were mostly located within one of the research schools, although there were some within SGS or straddling both sides of the University. Most served specific research needs not well covered by existing departments or disciplines; a few, such as the Computer Centre (established in 1964) and the Office for Research in Academic Methods (1973) performed service functions. Apart from adding to the University's already generous supply of acronyms, the units and centres encouraged flexibility and helped break down departmental barriers.

There were nearly as many reasons for their establishment as there were centres and units: the History of Ideas Unit (1967) acknowledged the outstanding work and entrepreneurial zeal of Eugene Kamenka in the Department of Philosophy, RSSS; the Electron and Ion Diffusion Unit (1961) enabled Huxley to maintain his research interests while Vice-Chancellor; the Urban Research Unit (RSSS, 1965) and the Contemporary China Centre (RSPacS, 1970) provided a focus on contemporary issues for existing staff members within their respective schools. In 1973, when there were about twenty such units and centres, one professor remarked that they were 'mushrooming all over the place'.

Two of the largest and most successful were the Centre for Resource and Environmental Studies (CRES) and the Humanities Research Centre (HRC). CRES, which was chiefly Crawford's creation, owed much to growing national and international concerns about the deterioration of the environment. In 1966 a committee recommended against the University embarking on undergraduate teaching in agriculture, which had been mooted for some time, proposing instead the establishment of a centre or school devoted to research and training in natural resources and environmental problems. Following AUC approval of revised plans, the Centre for Resource and Environmental Studies was established in 1972 and the following year Frank Fenner, now in his sixth year as Director of the John Curtin School, was appointed Professor of Environmental Studies and its first Director.

Fenner's interest in environmental issues grew out of his work as a virologist, including research on the ecology of myxomatosis and later work on viral diseases in human populations. In recent years he had contributed to various national and international committees, including the Standing Committee on the Environment in the Academy of Science, the national UNESCO Committee on Man and the Biosphere, and the international Scientific Committee on Problems of the Environment; at the time of his appointment he was Vice-President of the Australian Conservation Foundation. Presenting the case for a natural resources centre at the ANU, he wrote of the need to find a balance between economic development and human demands: 'The rational utilisation of natural resources in a way which is biologically, culturally and economically acceptable to man requires the skills and understanding of integrated groups of people of different disciplines brought together with the common commitment to seek solutions to the practical problems of natural resource management'. CRES would go part of the way towards meeting this need.

Like CRES, the Humanities Research Centre was intended to develop fields of research that were not well covered by other parts of the University. The humanities were an obvious gap in the structure of the Institute, which Hancock and his colleagues in RSSS had proposed to fill by renaming their school the 'Research School of Humanities and Social Sciences'. The idea lapsed, as did later proposals for a humanities school comparable with the existing research schools. The decisive initiative came in the late 1960s when Richard Johnson in the Faculty of Arts proposed a school or research group in the humanities as a part of SGS. The idea won favour with the AUC, which recognised a large gap in humanities research in Australia. The result was the Humanities Research Centre, which started work in earnest in 1974 when Ian Donaldson, Professor of English in the Faculty of Arts and an expert in Elizabethan literature, was appointed foundation Director.

The staff of the Humanities Research Centre in 1987. The Director, Ian Donaldson, is third from the left. Operating with a small core staff, the centre attracted visitors from many countries.

Unlike the research schools, the HRC was to have a core academic staff of only two or three people, who were to attract visitors, arrange lectures, conferences and exhibitions, and generally encourage work in the humanities at the ANU and throughout Australia in the broad field of 'European thought and culture and their influence overseas'. In 1975 the HRC was host to a dozen visiting fellows, four from within Australia and eight from overseas, who worked for several weeks or months in various areas of European history, philosophy, literature, music and fine arts. A conference on 'Problems of contemporary biography' was attended by 40 people, and another on 'Cultural developments in Australia in the 1890s' by over sixty.

CRES and the HRC were independent entities, structurally separate from both the Institute and the School. Although they were not created specifically for this purpose, Crawford saw them as 'bridges of great importance to the unity of ANU'. So they turned out to be: the HRC seminars regularly drew large audiences from the Institute as well as the School, and the CRES staff maintained close links with various parts of the campus. They helped counter suggestions that the ANU was two universities and deflect the barbs of resentment of Clark and others in the School.

Nevertheless, their independent existence was tenuous. A committee on centres and units in 1976 argued that, for the purposes of resource allocation and peer assessment, both centres should be affiliated with either the Institute or the School. CRES resisted and maintained its autonomy; but the HRC, while keeping its separate budget, became affiliated with the Faculty of Arts. The twofold structure of the University resisted change.

Why were bridges necessary? Why not blend the two parts of the University into one, as individual staff members often suggested? For example, Germaine Joplin, a Senior Fellow in Geophysics, deploring the lack of cohesion between the Institute and the School, argued for a major restructuring by which the teaching departments would be incorporated into existing and new research schools. This, she said, would maintain the original concept of a research University while allowing a limited number of carefully selected undergraduates to work with senior staff in the existing schools, to their mutual benefit. Arthur Birch often argued for closer ties between the Institute and SGS, sufficient at least to permit Institute staff to contribute to an elite honours school.

But Crawford was adamant: 'To face our future by concentrating on structural change as a means of providing greater unity in the University is to start at the wrong end'. Above all, he was determined to preserve the integrity of the Institute, for reasons that were both academic and pragmatic. While convinced that the concept of the Institute, as originally conceived, was worth preserving, he also knew that the University would surrender its claim to special treatment by the AUC and the government if the Institute lost its unique status. The challenge for the Vice-Chancellor was to ensure that the University as a whole benefited from the Institute's singularity.

This demanded a deft political hand. In the University's 1968 submission to the AUC, Crawford emphasised the common use of administrative, library and other resources by both Institute and School, arguing that the financial arrangements for the two parts of the University were so closely interwoven that they could not be unravelled. This was a risky strategy: the AUC concluded that University policy was to merge its component parts, and Crawford had to step in quickly to set the Commission straight. But the strategy worked. For the 1970–72 triennium, the ANU received a 37 per cent increase in funding compared with a 30 per cent increase for the combined state universities.

Despite the constraints of structure, Crawford's initiatives—and other initiatives that he encouraged—went a long way towards promoting the intellectual unity of the University. At the time of his retirement in 1973, CRES and the HRC were pointing the way ahead, while a Graduate Degrees Committee had brought together coordination and innovation of postgraduate matters 'without the slightest suggestion of political division between the IAS and the SGS'.

One objective had eluded him: he had been unable to find a satisfactory term to replace the offensive 'School of General Studies'. This was achieved soon after his retirement in 1973 when the Deputy Vice-Chancellor, Noel Dunbar, suggested that the School be renamed 'The Faculties', as they were often described in common usage. The research schools, no longer jealous of their use of the term in relation to their own faculties, offered no resistance, allowing the name to be introduced formally when the ANU Act was next amended in 1979. While it may have seemed trivial, this simple change represented a major step towards making the University one.

The ends of research

10

The Prize

'It can be claimed', wrote Eccles in 1970, several years after his retirement from the ANU, 'that in our civilization science represents the highest creativity of man, and it provides our best hope of winning through to a deeper understanding of the nature and meaning of existence'. He sought that understanding by exploring the brain, and its relationship with the conscious mind. Yet as a Catholic he believed his search would take him only so far. Scientists could come close to truth, but the ultimate mystery lay beyond their reach. 'Cannot life be lived as a challenging and wonderful adventure that has meaning to be discovered?'

This was Eccles' great ambition: to come as close as any human might come to understanding the meaning of life. At the same time, he sought and gained earthly rewards. In 1958 he was knighted; then Cambridge awarded him an Honorary ScD and Exeter College Oxford made him an Honorary Fellow. He was awarded the Baly Medal of the Royal College of Physicians and the Royal Medal of the Royal Society; he was elected a Foreign Honorary Member of the American Academy of Arts and Sciences; and he became the first Australian to be elected as an Academician of the Pontifical Academy of Science and as a Member of the German Academy of Science.

As the significance of his discoveries permeated the scientific world, he increasingly came to be spoken of as a potential winner of the highest accolade for the natural scientist, the Nobel Prize. Since its foundation in 1901, only three Australians had won it: the father and son physicists William and Lawrence Bragg in 1915 (the former being Australian by adoption) and Florey in 1945, all of whom had conducted most of their prize-winning research in Britain. The selection process had become highly politicised, and the chance of an Australian winning the award for work conducted in Australia and New Zealand seemed slim; but then again, there was no doubt that Eccles' research was of Nobel Prize calibre.

The Prize became Eccles' goal, and he drove himself towards it relentlessly. For a brief moment in 1960 it seemed that it was within his grasp. Such was the level of secrecy surrounding the awards that the recipients were not supposed to be aware of their success until it was announced to the world. In 1960, as the time for the annual announcement approached, rumours circulated that an Australian scientist was among the winners. At 9.00 p.m. on 20 October the ABC broadcast that the winners included Sir John Eccles, jointly with an American scientist, Magoun (pronounced M'goon). Eccles immediately organised an impromptu party in the laboratory, and set up a cat for the expected television cameras. The mood was euphoric, not least because Eccles had triumphed over Macfarlane Burnet, his rival at the Hall Institute, which he referred to as 'that fowl pen in Melbourne', an allusion to Burnet's research on chickens. Then came the late news: 'The Nobel Prize for Medicine for 1960 has been shared by an Australian medical scientist, Sir Frank Macfarlane Burnet. He shares the prize with an Englishman, Professor Brian Medawar, of University College, London. ... An earlier message from London tonight incorrectly reported that the prize had been won by Sir John Eccles of the Australian National University.'

Someone had played a cruel hoax, evidently inspired by the character Eccles in 'The Goon Show'. The party stopped; Eccles put the cat down and left. But he was back in the laboratory the next morning, in determined pursuit of understanding as well as acclamation.

Eccles was out of the country three years later when a cable arrived from the Australian legation at Stockholm announcing that he would share the award 'with two Englishmen' (his colleagues A.L. Hodgkin of Cambridge and A.F. Huxley of London). In his absence, the University rejoiced, and following his return a fortnight later held a jubilant celebration at University House to which politicians, public servants, diplomats and other dignitaries were invited. The award was a triumph for Eccles, but also for the ANU. Politicians and academics in other universities who doubted the University's value would have to think again.

The Australian Academy of Science, about the time of its opening in 1958.

By courtesy of Adrian Young.

Few scientists could hope to win a Nobel Prize. A more realistic ambition was to become a Fellow of the Royal Society of London (FRS), Britain's oldest scientific society. Each year the current members of the Royal Society elected some thirty fellows, after rigorous inquiry into the quality of their scientific achievement. This number did not leave much room for Australians. In 1951 Oliphant and D.F. Martyn, a radiophysicist in the CSIRO, initiated moves to form an Australian academy of science, modelled on the Royal Society. Formally inaugurated in 1954, the Academy initially comprised eleven fellows of the Royal Society who were resident in Australia (one FRS declined to be involved) together with twelve other leading scientists, all drawn from various universities, institutes and the CSIRO. The foundation fellows promptly elected 41 additional fellows, and then increased their number normally by six each year to 1970, then nine to 1992, after which the prescribed number was increased to twelve. Fellowship of the Academy was restricted to those who were 'eminent by reason of their scientific attainments and their researches in natural science'. Fellows were entitled to place the letters FAA after their names; and while fellowship of the local academy never attained the same kudos as membership of the Royal Society, the letters FAA became a mark of genuine scientific distinction.

As the ANU grew, its staff made up a growing proportion of fellows of the Royal Society and the Australian Academy. By 1975 there were (excluding Sir Robert

Menzies) a total of 36 fellows of the Royal Society resident in Australia, of whom 13 were or had been attached to the ANU and 12 to all the other universities put together. The remainder were associated with the CSIRO or other institutions. There were more FRSs in the ANU than in any other university outside Britain, and only 6 of the 48 British universities had a larger number. The links between the University and the Australian Academy were close from the Academy's inception. Apart from Oliphant's involvement, the University provided office accommodation for the Academy until its own building was opened nearby in 1959. From 1964 onwards the annual list of new fellows included at least one, and sometimes up to four, from the ANU. Of the 161 living fellows in 1975, 29 were present or past members of the ANU, many more than of any other university. This high proportion owed something to the quality of the ANU staff, the proximity of the University to the Academy, and the tendency of existing fellows to elect their colleagues.

Sir John Eccles, winner of the Nobel Prize. Photograph by Neville Whitmarsh in the *Daily Mirror*, 16 February 1966.
News Ltd.

Not everyone shared Eccles' enthusiasm for honours and awards (although it is unlikely that the academies and prize-giving bodies were overburdened with refusals). Arthur Birch, who during a lifetime devoted to science accumulated a swag of medals, honours and prizes, including the Royal Society's Davy Medal, Foreign Membership of the Academy of Sciences of the USSR, the prestigious Tetrahedron Award for creativity in organic chemistry, a CMG and an AC, had mixed views about the value of awards. 'I rather like medals myself: they are artistically attractive although normally useless ... They reinforce feelings of personal worth and perhaps stimulate further endeavours for public recognition through public good.' But major awards with large money prizes, including the Nobel Prize (for which Birch had been nominated many times), often depended on politics and momentary fashion, and tended to 'distort scientific programs and warp fallible personalities'. The sooner they were abolished the better.

Nevertheless, awards could be of immense value to institutions as proof of achievement. Although few people outside the University might have understood that Eccles and his colleagues had been honoured, in the words of the citation, for their discoveries 'concerning the ionic mechanisms involved in excitation and inhibition in the peripheral and central portions of the nerve cell membrane', the two words 'Nobel Prize' shone out for everyone to see.

◠ The homopolar generator

John Carver returned to Australia in 1953, after four years at the Cavendish Laboratory as an ANU Overseas Scholar, to take up duty as a Research Fellow in the Department of Nuclear Physics. He remembered the laboratory as an exciting place: 'we were going to do some quick experiments in nuclear physics, and Oliphant and his team were going to build the proton synchrotron with which we would all win Nobel prizes by discovering the antiproton ...'.

By the time Eccles received his Nobel Prize a decade later, all such hopes had faded. Carver himself had gone to a chair in Adelaide; those who remained, including Oliphant, were struggling to salvage all they could of what was threatening to become a financial and political disaster for the whole University.

The homopolar generator (HPG) was a much more modest project than the cyclo-synchrotron that Oliphant had originally intended, and the proton synchrotron that had first taken its place. Yet it was beset with problems; and Oliphant's predictions of how much it would cost and how long it would take to complete proved to be well wide of the mark. He sought and received nearly £40 000 from the Australian Atomic Energy Commission. Melville, on his behalf, asked the government for an additional £14 000 a year. When the government said no, Oliphant threatened to drop the project entirely, despite the money so far invested. In 1957 Menzies obliged with £30 000 over two years, urging as he had done in the past that the machine be completed as soon as possible. But the money was never enough, and as the years rolled by people inside and outside the University wondered if the end would ever come. In the meantime, accelerator projects in the Soviet Union and the United States had left the proposed proton synchrotron far behind.

From the outset, Oliphant had had his critics. The most forthright was Harry Messel, an ebullient, cigar-puffing Canadian who had taken up the chair of Physics at the University of Sydney in 1952 and who shared Oliphant's flair for publicity. Messel declared that Oliphant's approach to science was fundamentally wrong: Australia could not compete with other countries in the big machine field and should avoid projects requiring massive money and manpower. Instead it should concentrate on smaller activities depending for their success on ingenuity, such as his own work on cosmic radiation. Accelerators, he said, were a waste of money. Oliphant remarked privately that Messel was destroying science in Australia. Publicly he was conciliatory, inviting the Sydney team to Canberra for a conference in 1955, where he spoke frankly about the design problems the project was facing and appealed for a 'fair go'. He also announced that his team was setting aside work on the proton synchrotron and concentrating on the HPG. This blunted Messel's attack: while he did not wish to appear defeatist, he also

Oliphant (right) discusses work on the homopolar generator with Senior Technical Officer Jimmy Edwards in 1955.

Australian Official Photograph, ANU Collection.

conceded that the HPG had potential uses, especially in the field of astrophysics. Henceforth, in public at least, Oliphant's most forceful critic was silent.

There was little further public criticism until 1961, when the *Bulletin* published a long article entitled 'The white Oliphant?' (an allusion in part to Oliphant's abundant head of hair). This told the story of the project to date, detailing some of the problems it had encountered and narrating the earlier exchanges between the Canberra and Sydney physicists. The article was fair, well informed, and deeply damaging. Some of Oliphant's colleagues saw Messel's hand behind the story, although Messel vehemently denied any part in it. Critics were quoted as saying that nearly £1 million had been squandered, plans had been changed several times, and the machine was not yet complete and might never be.

Oliphant was angry and distressed, but determined to persevere. At last, in June 1962, the HPG was put through a series of successful tests, during which it delivered nearly two million amperes, well over the design limit. Oliphant was jubilant, and his team's morale rose enormously.

The triumph was short-lived. On 3 July Ken Inall, a Senior Research Engineer, and four technicians were filling a tank in the HPG with NaK, an alloy of sodium and potassium which was used to extract electrical currents from the generator's rotating disc. The procedure was known to be hazardous, as NaK was highly combustible and fires had often occurred in the past. Suddenly there was an explosion, filling the air with burning NaK particles and throwing the group against the wall or to the floor. Four of the men were burnt, and one, George Lagos, lost the sight of both eyes.

Although the HPG suffered little damage, the harm to the project was immense. One of the team was quoted in the press as saying it was madness to continue with the use of NaK, and newspapers accused Oliphant of irresponsibility. Many staff members, inside and outside RSPhysS, were uneasy. Trevor Swan reminded Huxley that the Physics Store, which housed the combustible alloy, was just 25 yards from the statistician Patrick Moran's room and 50 yards from Hancock's in the old hospital building.

The Standing Committee of Council immediately convened a committee of inquiry, which concluded that all safety procedures had been followed and absolved Oliphant from blame. Although it did not prohibit the future use of NaK, it recommended additional safety measures. Their cost was such that Oliphant eventually decided to abandon NaK and look for an alternative. Now there was lively debate among the team, with Oliphant pressing for mercury and threatening to resign if he did not get his way. But the engineers argued for a system of metal brushes lubricated with graphite, which proved to be 'a perfect success' at its first trial. 'It was all too much for poor old "Olly"', one of them later told Oliphant's biographers. 'He walked out of the control room without saying a word. At that moment the HPG ceased to be "his" machine.'

Oliphant, now in his early sixties, wondered what to do next. In mid-June 1963 he approached a senior physicist in Britain about the possibility of taking over the Department of Particle Physics so that he could concentrate on being director of RSPhysS. Less than a fortnight later he wrote to the Vice-Chancellor submitting his resignation as director and asking to be replaced as head of department, so that he could return to research. A week later, following discussion with his colleagues, he asked to be allowed to

ACP Publishing Pty Limited.

TESTS ARE MADNESS, WARNS SCIENTIST

Adelaide News, 5 July 1962.

remain as head of department until all the problems relating to the HPG had been solved, which he now anticipated would be at least two years away. But by this stage even Oliphant realised that he had little to offer the project. In June 1964 he retired as head of department and withdrew from further involvement with the HPG, an unhappy and disappointed man. By that time the project had cost at least £1.25 million, a vast sum in relation to the allocation of resources to scientific research in Australian universities (though small by comparison with the amounts spent on similar projects overseas).

What had gone wrong? When asked to explain the high cost and long delays, Oliphant referred to the challenges of building a machine unique in the world, together with the problems associated with mounting such an ambitious project in Australia, where it was always so hard to get anything done. The country lacked money, labour and materials, but the main problem was one of attitude: 'my principal quarrel with Australians', he had complained to Wright back in 1950, 'is that they have no fire in their bellies & prefer to carry out the experiment to see whether sitting beneath a gum tree does or does not produce piles rather than get on with the job'.

As one setback followed another, Oliphant always accepted responsibility, yet managed to convey the impression that Australia was somehow to blame. 'All my planning was based on British experience', he told Melville in 1954, when applying for extra funds. 'I did not bargain for the even slower tempo of all such work in Australia.' This in itself was an extraordinary admission: but it was difficult to call Oliphant to account without accepting, as nobody wanted to do, that Australia was incapable of rising to the challenge. When criticised in the *Bulletin*, he responded to its proprietor, Sir Frank Packer, that the proton synchrotron might well have been beyond the resources of Australia, but at least it was 'a product of our own brains', and not something imported from the United States. 'If we fail, we will, at any rate, have made a good try with an Australian concept ...' There were moments of self-awareness, as in 1955 when he told Florey that 'Perhaps I have lost my punch and many of my difficulties are of my own making'. But mostly, by shifting—or, at least, diluting—the blame, he managed to portray himself as a victim of his own misjudged but well-intentioned optimism, and of his compatriots' failure to share his commitment and vision.

By such means Oliphant disarmed potential critics (and seduced his gentle biographers). He was also protected by the armour of Science. Having proven their worth in wartime, scientists in the 1950s were as powerful as they had ever been, confident of their own capacity to change the world, and dismissive of those who stood in their way. When a journalist from the Melbourne *Age* asked the University some carefully considered questions about the cost of the project and how it was managed, Oliphant responded haughtily to the Vice-Chancellor that 'these reporters and others' did not know the profound difference between buying equipment off the shelf and developing it from basic principles, and that 'such folk prefer Australia ... to be a mere follower of leads given by others'. The tone was characteristic of Oliphant and all he stood for: ordinary people should learn to trust the scientist. He was also able to refer to famous scientists from overseas, including Sir John Cockcroft, who supported the project. The mere mention of such names was a powerful weapon for beating off the critics.

The same protection worked within the University. When Melville tried to contain costs, Oliphant complained to Florey that the Vice-Chancellor had 'no understanding of or sympathy with science or the conditions under which it can be pursued'. Although Huxley could scarcely be tarred with the same brush, he was reluctant to interfere with the work of a fellow physicist. Moreover, Oliphant enjoyed special status, not merely as a Director, but as the only one of the original Advisers who had committed himself to the University at its inception. The University in turn was committed to Oliphant, and its reputation was bound up with his success.

So the project escaped close scrutiny, and serious errors of judgement were allowed to pass almost unnoticed. By the mid-1950s those errors had dug the University into a deeper hole than Oliphant had found on his arrival. With the decision to set aside the proton synchrotron and focus on the homopolar generator, the particle physics project became an engineering one, for which Oliphant and his colleagues were underqualified and ill equipped. Certainly, the team included some experienced and talented engineers, and Oliphant himself solved some challenging engineering problems; but it was not primarily an engineering team, with the concentrated expertise necessary for a massive project of this nature. Oliphant had high regard for a few specific engineers, but he considered engineers in general to be overcautious impediments to adventurous physics. The project was therefore organised, as Jaeger put it in 1964 when Dean of RSPhysS, 'on an amateur basis'. This meant that progress was slow. Furthermore, the overriding object was to get the machine built, so that the unprecedented difficulties encountered along the way were not explored as fundamental problems in engineering research, as they would have been if engineers had been in charge. From the engineering point of view, it was an opportunity wasted.

As soon as Oliphant retired as Director, Coombs, Huxley and other members of Council took matters into their own hands and decided to seek outside engineering advice, in relation both to specific aspects of the machine and to its overall potential. Oliphant, while accepting the need for advice, protested that the consultants should be reporting to him rather than Council, and that the University was improperly intervening in departmental affairs. But his advice had ceased to matter.

Early in 1964 a representative of a Californian engineering firm visited Canberra with a wide brief to assess the project as a whole, including whether or not it was worth completing. He concluded that it was, in that the cost of completion would be less than acquiring a comparable source of energy, but pointed out that the value of pursuing the project depended on its intended use. While the machine was now 'hopelessly inadequate' as a source of energy for a particle accelerator, he listed half a dozen other potential uses, including plasma physics (the area of physics concerned with gases that carry electric currents), which was favoured by Oliphant. With the report before them, Huxley and his advisers, including Jaeger, Titterton and Cockcroft (as physicist as well as Chancellor), enlisted the help of Gordon Newstead, Professor of Electrical Engineering at the University of Tasmania, whose experience included the large engineering projects associated with Tasmania's hydro-electric power scheme, to tell them whether the HPG could be finished and used as a reliable

Gordon Newstead about the time of his appointment in 1965.

research tool and how much it would cost. Newstead concluded that, if the project had cost only a few thousand pounds, it would be worth starting afresh, but as so much money and effort had been expended, the machine, with some modifications, could be put to valuable use. He also suggested that the department responsible for the HPG jettison the title Particle Physics, which had only ever been appropriate as an aspiration, in favour of Engineering Physics, and concentrate on such areas as high magnetic fields, current interruption, and the control of large currents.

In 1965 Newstead was appointed to the new chair and given the task of acting on his own recommendations. Soon the HPG was operating and the department was producing numerous papers relating chiefly to engineering aspects of the project. As Newstead described it, the HPG was probably the largest and certainly the most unusual electric generating machine in the world. Its main feature was two enormous contra-rotating discs, each weighing some 40 tonnes and spinning at their outer rims at half the speed of sound. These generated and stored vast amounts of energy which were released in a single pulse sufficient to bring a Boeing 707 aircraft travelling at about 240 kilometres per hour to a halt in one second. Sparks often flew as the discs reached high speeds, and there was always an element of risk.

The HPG became a powerful tool for a variety of research projects, including arc experiments, an electromagnetic rail gun which achieved projectile speeds of about six kilometres per second, a high magnetic field facility, and circuit breaker experiments associated with flash tubes. After Newstead's retirement in 1970, the University decided that the Department of Engineering Physics should base its research on utilisation of the HPG. But in 1976 a review committee enquiring into the work of the school concluded that this 'optimistically contrived arrangement' had not resulted in the effective exploitation of the capabilities of the machine, which had merely been used, in the words of one assessor, as a wall socket. After considering whether or not the HPG should be closed down, the committee decided that it should henceforth be used exclusively to power a thermonuclear reactor used in plasma physics. Although the machine would be 'grossly under-utilized', the plasma research appeared to be 'the only way in which all the expenditure of time and money which has gone into the development of the facility can be at least partly recompensed'.

When the plasma project came to an end in 1985 there was no further use for the HPG, so John Carver, who had returned to the ANU from Adelaide in 1978 as Director of RSPhysS, announced to Council that the machine would be decommissioned 'after nearly a quarter a century of valuable service'. The service was indeed valuable, and the process of building it created the outstanding workshops and equipment that made later achievements possible. But it was equally certain that the HPG had failed to justify the amount of money and human effort that had been spent in constructing and running it (not to mention the physical injury that had occurred in 1962).

Oliphant's plans for world-shattering discoveries had ended with a whimper. Ironically, this limited the damage to the reputation of the school and the University. And there were sufficient achievements in the physical sciences and other areas to neutralise the failure. The demise of the HPG also challenged the authority of

Science; but scientists throughout the western world in the 1980s no longer stood on their 1950s pedestal, so any specific damage caused by the HPG was slight.

The HPG project held out many lessons for those who were willing to learn. Oliphant, contemplating the understandably low morale of the team just as he was about to leave it, concluded that the efforts of a department should never be devoted to a single, large project, as the failure to produce results along the way could be just as soul-destroying as the failure to finish the overall project. Newstead remarked that a university was not the best place to conduct such projects, since traditional academic organisation made it hard to allocate tasks and fix specific responsibilities. While nearly everyone working on the HPG was, according to Newstead, personally willing and able, together they functioned as individuals pursuing an ill-defined policy. The project also showed how large undertakings can command attention to the detriment of other worthwhile activities. While the machine was being built, the HPG team had little time for training students, whom Oliphant regarded as an unwarranted intrusion on his main job; and once completed, the machine influenced research directions by demanding that researchers make use of it.

Other large questions are evident in hindsight. In a university committed to recognising the value of creativity, how much latitude should be allowed individual researchers and research teams? How far should governments rely on the reputation and promise of individual scientists when funding research projects? The answers are elusive. As Titterton reflected in 1975 when supporting a proposal that Oliphant be awarded the Nobel Prize, if his original gamble had come off and his machine had been used to produce the first anti-protons, 'it would have been a fantastic achievement, very much in the Rutherford tradition'. On the other hand, had anyone in the University or in government enquired closely, they would have learnt that Oliphant's Birmingham accelerator had been labelled 'the white Oliphant' in the early 1950s, before his Australian plans started to come unstuck. According to Freeman Dyson, who was at Birmingham at the time and who later became a professor of Physics at the Princeton Institute for Advanced Study, the Birmingham synchrotron never did any important experiments and was 'a textbook example of how not to do particle physics'. Referring to both Birmingham and Canberra, Dyson reflected that 'A high-visibility accelerator project, driven by political prestige rather than by scientific need, usually sets back the progress of particle physics in a country by about ten years'.

Following the dismantling of the HPG (a massive task in itself), some of its parts, including one of the giant rotors, were erected outside the Cockcroft Building as a piece of abstract art, intended as a reminder of a machine that had played so large a part in the history of the school and the University. We may also see it as a rusting monument to science that required little more justification than a fire in the belly.

~ Exploring the universe

Bart J. Bok exploded in Australian skies like a supernova. In 1957 he succeeded Richard Woolley as Director of the Mount Stromlo Observatory and became, as a result of the Act of Parliament that formally linked the Observatory with the ANU, the University's first full professor of Astronomy.

Born in the Netherlands in 1906, Bok had spent most of his adult life in the United States, where he had been an assistant director at the Harvard Observatory and one of America's best-known astronomers. His decision to resign from Harvard for a position at half the salary in what must have seemed a remote backwater raised some eyebrows. But Bok had watched at close hand the work of the House Committee on Un-American Activities, which had hounded the director of the Harvard Observatory and questioned his own liberal politics. By the time the offer came from Canberra, he wanted 'to get the hell out'. So for reasons similar to those that had lost the chemist Stephen Mason to the ANU, Harvard lost Bok to Canberra. Also Bok and his wife, Priscilla Fairfield Bok, had a passion for the Milky Way, about which they had written the definitive work to that time; and the Milky Way was best viewed from south of the equator.

Bart J. Bok, about 1963.
By courtesy of A.W. Rodgers.

Few Australians had encountered the likes of Bok, and those who did never forgot him. Short in stature, he was nevertheless a dominating presence, with boundless energy, a booming voice and an ebullient manner. Many people found him instantly engaging; others were embarrassed in his presence, especially when he marched in for breakfast at University House and greeted them with a bellowing 'Hello there, so-and-so', causing them to look hard at their plates.

The professional astronomer has four major roles: as an observer (whether through optical or radio telescopes), as an interpreter of what he or she sees, as an expert in the technology needed to make observations, and as a publicist for the discipline. Bok was highly competent in the first three, and brilliant at the last. Among politicians, teachers, students and the general public, he had a remarkable talent for generating interest in astronomy and support for astronomical activities at the ANU. Granted, he was sometimes lucky: seven months after he took over as head of Mount Stromlo, the Soviet Union launched the first Sputnik into space, throwing much of the free world into confusion and giving Australians a new interest in the night skies. Bok engineered an invitation to address members of parliament during their dinner adjournment about the implications of the new technology, and although he was no expert on satellites, he instantly became one. By the end of the evening, and after he had escorted a committee of six members outside the House to gaze skywards at the appointed time, he had the politicians eating out of his hand. Visits to Parliament House by Bok, accompanied by students who worked a slide projector, became regular events in the parliamentary calendar. He also developed a close relationship with the Prime Minister, Menzies: so close that on one occasion after the President of the Academy of Science had accused Bok of offending 'the establishment', Menzies acknowledged his delinquency at an official function at the ANU by poking him hard in the belly and whispering, 'You are a bad, bad boy!' This was not the Menzies most people knew.

 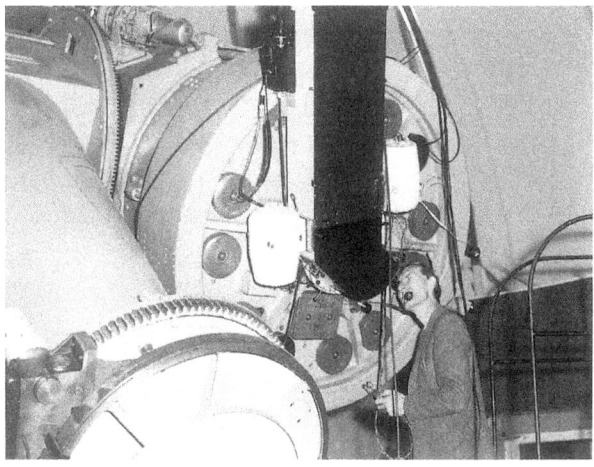

Under Bok, Mount Stromlo moved decisively into astrophysics, the branch of astronomy concerned with the physical and chemical properties of astronomical phenomena, including the structure, evolution and dynamics of stars and stellar systems. The Observatory made significant advances in two major areas: the Magellanic Clouds and the structure of the Milky Way. The Magellanic Clouds, which are two galaxies close to one another and the earth's own galaxy, have been described as 'the Rosetta Stones of astronomy', since they offer unique opportunities to decipher galactic evolution. Mount Stromlo's discoveries about these galaxies helped confirm its prominent place in the world of astronomy.

Despite Woolley's enthusiasm for teaching, by the time Bok arrived at the ANU only three students had taken PhD degrees in astronomy. Because astronomy was not taught as an undergraduate subject at any Australian university, there was no supply of graduates necessary for building a graduate school. Bok set out to remedy the situation, first by instituting a scheme of summer vacation scholarships, which enabled promising mathematics and physics undergraduates to spend two months at the Observatory and opened up for them the prospect of a career in astronomy. Then he made frequent visits to the state universities, delivering public lectures and selling astronomy to students who were nearing graduation. In other disciplines, this practice might have been frowned on as poaching, but Bok managed to do his recruiting without giving offence and won admiration for his work in promoting astronomy throughout the university system. Finally, he achieved notable success in recruiting students from abroad.

By the time Bok left the ANU in 1966, to take up the directorship of the Steward Observatory at the University of Arizona, Mount Stromlo had a lively graduate program, with fourteen scholars enrolled for the degree of PhD. During his nine years as Director, nearly thirty postgraduate students had been attracted to the Observatory. Many of them went on to hold senior positions in astronomy, at the ANU and throughout the world.

Astronomers at Mount Stromlo had once enjoyed, on moonless and cloudless nights, a view of the sky that few observatories anywhere could rival. By the 1960s, however, the lights of Canberra were threatening to get in the way. Bok used his good relations with Menzies to have thousands of hectares around the mountain reserved as forest areas. But

Left: Vacation scholars at Mount Stromlo, December 1960 to February 1961, with astronomers Arthur Hogg, Bart J. Bok and S.C.B. (Ben) Gascoigne. Four of this group later occupied senior positions in astronomy, astrophysics or physics in Australian universities. One of the four, Ken Freeman (at the far left in the back row), became a professor at Mount Stromlo.

By courtesy of A.W. Rodgers.

Right: Astronomer at work: Alex Rodgers, Research Fellow (and later Director of the Observatories), at the 50-inch Great Melbourne telescope at Mount Stromlo, about 1965. In the 1990s this telescope was given a new life in the MACHO project, noticed in chapter 15.

By courtesy of A.W. Rodgers.

still there was an evident need for a new observation point, far away from the polluting lights of any town or city. In 1957 the search began for a permanent field station. Several years later, after many nights spent in remote parts of the continent and lively debate among the astronomers about the relative merits of various sites, the University selected Siding Spring Mountain in the Warrumbungle Range, 30 kilometres by road from the nearest township of Coonabarabran and 660 kilometres due north of Mount Stromlo.

A 40-inch telescope winds its way to the University's new observatory at Siding Spring in 1964.

Bok knew before the site was chosen that it might one day become the location of a telescope much larger than any of the existing instruments at Mount Stromlo. The largest of these had an aperture of 74 inches, small by comparison with the 200-inch instrument at Mount Palomar in California and with more modern types, such as the 120-inch telescope mounted at the Lick Observatory, also in California, in 1959.

Australia could not contemplate financing, building and installing such an instrument alone: international collaboration was essential. As early as 1955, Woolley and Oliphant had proposed a joint project to establish a British Commonwealth Southern Observatory, with a 200-inch telescope at Mount Stromlo. Bok took up the cause enthusiastically; but some of the biological scientists in the Academy of Science were not so keen, arguing that 'gigantic' expenditure on a telescope would divert funds from other deserving areas of science. So the project moved slowly, and not until 1963 did serious discussions between scientists in Britain and Australia begin. In Britain, Woolley (as Director of the Royal Greenwich Observatory and Astronomer Royal) helped convince his fellow scientists and the government that the project was worth pursuing, and in 1966 the British government formally proposed a collaborative venture. After some anxious moments for the astronomers, the Australian government signalled that it was willing to join Britain as an equal partner in building and operating a large optical telescope, sharing the observation time, the capital costs (estimated at $11 million) and the annual running costs (estimated at $450 000), as well as responsibility for running it. Detailed negotiations followed, and the Anglo-Australian Telescope Agreement was signed in 1969.

ANU scientists had been prominent throughout the project's evolution. Woolley and Oliphant had conceived it, Bok had promoted it, and Huxley, wearing his Vice-Chancellor's hat, had lobbied the government at a crucial time. The University's proven expertise in astronomy provided the foundations for genuine scientific collaboration. The 1969 Agreement strengthened the University's stake in the project by providing that the new telescope should be located at Siding Spring, and that the ANU should share its existing and future facilities at Siding Spring and Mount Stromlo with the

Anglo-Australian Telescope. The terms of use were to be negotiated directly between the AAT Board and the University. So began the University's first major experience of collaboration. A challenging and sobering experience it turned out to be.

By now the two observatories had a new Director, Olin Jeuck Eggen, an American-born astronomer of mixed European descent who had already spent some time at Mount Stromlo as a visitor in the 1950s. Born in 1919, Eggen rapidly completed his schooling and enrolled at university at the age of fourteen. He then worked his way through a degree by earning money as a waiter, pianist and bartender at a nightclub in Madison, Wisconsin. During the war he had an unlikely career as a courier for the Office of Strategic Services, the predecessor of the Central Intelligence Agency, posing in Europe as a Swedish ball-bearing salesman. Then, after taking out the University of Wisconsin's first PhD in astronomy, he had held senior positions with Woolley at the Royal Observatory in Britain and various American observatories including, most recently, Mount Palomar.

Olin Eggen, 1969.

In many respects, Eggen was Bok's antithesis. Vast and unkempt, resembling (as one colleague put it) an unmade double bed, his manner was sometimes engaging but more often gruff. Eschewing any form of family life, he was, according to another Mount Stromlo Professor of Astronomy Ben Gascoigne, 'a compulsive observer', who 'must have spent more time at the telescope than almost any other astronomer this century'. His output was prodigious: during eleven years as Director of Mount Stromlo he produced 99 papers. Astronomy for Eggen meant gradually extending the boundaries of the known universe by observing meticulously with the aid of powerful telescopes and examining the photographic records of observations. He believed that the best form of astronomy was optical astronomy, and that the best way of pursuing optical astronomy was by small groups of astronomers spending long nights in cold domes. Large-scale collaboration was not his forte.

Problems began soon after the Anglo-Australian Telescope Agreement had been signed. While the Agreement created a Board to have overall control of the operation, it made no provision for who was to run the telescope on a day to day basis. The government had earlier given the impression that the ANU would be in charge. Eggen reasonably assumed that, as the ANU owned the mountain and all the facilities on it, and as he and his colleagues were the local experts, the University should be contracted to do everything. Crawford, Hohnen and the Council, keen to maintain the University's leadership, agreed. Some of the British participants in the project were not so sure; and the more it appeared that Eggen might have charge of the operation, the more uneasy they became. Eggen was famous for his absolute dedication to what he considered the best interests of astronomy, and notorious for his intolerance of anyone or anything that got in the way. A master of the studied insult, his negotiating style was sometimes flippant and dismissive. During discussions on the Joint Policy Committee about formulas for allocating telescope time, he made his point by taking some facetious examples of prospective users: Harry Messel wanted a week near Christmas to look for the Star of Bethlehem; and Fred Hoyle, an eminent British scientist and member of the AAT Board, needed 16 nights between March and July, excepting three nights when he had to appear on the David Frost Hour on television, and a fortnight in June during an opera premiere. Some members of the Joint Policy Committee were not amused.

The British negotiators were also sceptical about the University's claims to technical expertise. Astronomy at the time was experiencing a 'back end revolution', 'back end' meaning the end of the telescope where the photographic plates which had traditionally been used to record information were now being replaced by electronic devices. Eggen, owing to the nature of his research, wanted a superior type of conventional telescope, comparable with the instruments he had been used to at Mount Palomar and elsewhere. He was less interested in technological change, and doubtful of what computer innovations had to offer. 'More than anything else', wrote Hoyle, 'it was Eggen's almost complete lack of interest in the technical aspects of the telescope that prompted our initial stand against the ANU', especially in contrast with the strong technical support from CSIRO scientists.

By 1972 there was so much antagonism between the British and Australian camps that the project appeared to be headed for disaster. The showdown came when the six members of the AAT Joint Policy Committee, including Eggen, met on neutral territory in California. More than one seasoned member remarked that it was the roughest meeting they had ever attended. The outcome was a divorce. By a vote of four to two, the Joint Policy Committee determined that the AAT should be established with its own director and supporting staff, who would be responsible only to the Board.

The ANU took the decision badly, and tried to mount a rearguard action. But this served only to increase opposition among other Australian astronomers, who were anxious that the AAT should be seen as a national rather than an ANU facility. To complicate matters, there was resistance to the official ANU view from within the University, especially from Titterton, who argued as Director of RSPhysS that if the ANU was made responsible for the telescope and the management of the project failed, the University would get the blame. The alignment of interests was fast becoming the ANU (or most of it) versus the rest. The Minister for Education and Science, Malcolm Fraser, concerned that the ANU's loss was also a loss for the nation, confronted his British counterpart, Margaret Thatcher, on the issue: that got him nowhere. Then, after the federal election late in 1972, Coombs and Crawford lobbied the new Prime Minister to restore the ANU's position. Whitlam was supportive, but the wording of the AAT Agreement enabled the Board to do as it wished.

So the University watched powerless as the Board proceeded to choose a director and scientific staff and set up its scientific headquarters adjacent to the CSIRO Division of Radiophysics in Sydney. In Eggen's view, these arrangements were creating government astronomy at the expense of university astronomy. Then the Board bestowed on its facilities the title 'Anglo-Australian Observatory', provoking loud protests from the University that the AAT Agreement provided only for a telescope, not an observatory. But by now nobody was listening.

The ANU, having long seen itself as the prospective operator of the telescope, had been relegated to the status of landlord and user. How had it come to this? The AAT Agreement provided little guidance as to how the telescope should be run. Moreover, there were so many interested parties: the two governments, the University, dissenters within the University, and various groups of astronomers in Britain and Australia. In such circumstances, negotiations would inevitably be difficult. But there is also no doubt that the University negotiators, holding most of the best cards, played them badly. They made the mistake of assuming that, for reasons of economy and scientific expertise, the operation of the AAT ought to be the University's by right. For Eggen, convinced that nobody else could run the telescope, the issue became one of promoting, then protecting, the ANU's leadership in astronomy. Crawford insisted that the University was prepared to negotiate, but not before much damage had been done. There was a lesson here for the whole University. While the ANU should offer leadership where it was equipped to do so, it must studiously avoid giving any impression that it aimed to dominate.

Siding Spring in the early 1980s. The Anglo-Australian Telescope is in the large dome at the right of the photograph.

So when the Anglo-Australian Telescope was commissioned by Prince Charles in 1974, it was, as its historians remark, 'famous throughout the astronomical world for a long and bitter dispute about how it would be run'. Even at the ceremony, Eggen attempted to assert the ANU's ascendancy by raising the University flag, in defiance of protocol, to the same level as the Prince's standard. He was intercepted at the third attempt and the flag remained at the prescribed level. He did, however, by making sure that accommodation was not available, manage to thwart the AAT Board's invitation to the Prince to return to Siding Spring after dark for an astronomer's view of the stars.

During the ceremony, held beneath the AAT's massive dome, Prime Minister Whitlam gave eloquent endorsement to the value of astronomy:

> ... the true glory of astronomy lies in the value it places on knowledge for its own sake—knowledge of an absolute and fundamental kind. No civilisation can remain indifferent to the origins of the earth or its place in the cosmos.

He also warmly praised the telescope and all who had designed and built it. Despite all the problems over management, the ANU deserved a large share of that praise, especially through the work of several of its scientists and engineers who had been seconded to the enterprise.

The new telescope quickly proved itself an outstanding success, especially when it was equipped with a control system that vastly increased its efficiency compared with conventional instruments. Now a research team could extract sufficient data from a night's viewing to keep it hard at work for months analysing the information. ANU astronomers were given about half the Australian share of telescope time, amounting to some eighty nights a year.

Eggen continued to provide some tense moments until he left the ANU in 1977 for the Cerro Telolo Inter-American Observatory in Chile, where he continued to pursue an outstanding scientific career. Long before his departure the management issue had largely ceased to matter, as most astronomers revelled in new ways of exploring the universe, oblivious to concerns about who was in charge of what.

The publishing imperative

Some titles from the Australian National University Press.

Like the natural scientists, academics in the humanities and social sciences could look forward to the occasional prize or other form of public recognition. But such distinctions generally meant less to them than to their scientific colleagues. There were fewer specialist prizes comparable, for example, with Arthur Birch's Tetrahedron Award in organic chemistry. And while ANU economists, poets and historians shared in imperial honours and memberships of the Order of Australia (from 1975), and honorary degrees from other universities, these rarely constituted a motivation for research activity, as they did in the case of Eccles and the Nobel Prize, or a measure for judgement by their peers.

The same applied to membership of the learned academies. Although by 1975 four Australians, three of whom were members of the ANU, had been admitted to the British Academy, the social sciences equivalent of the Royal Society, the initials FBA were less widely recognised than FRS as a mark of high academic distinction in an Australian context. The local Academy of Science had its equivalents in the Australian Academy of the Humanities (founded in 1969) and the Academy of the Social Sciences in Australia (1971), both of which were based in Canberra and, like the Academy of Science, enjoyed close links with the ANU; but while they 'massaged the minds', as one member of both academies put it, of prospective fellows, organised conferences and seminars, and occasionally tried to influence government policy, neither functioned in parallel with the Science Academy as gatekeeper to an academic elite.

The most widely accepted measure of a social scientist's or humanist's academic worth was his or her publications. Where natural scientists looked to scientific discoveries as the ends of their research, sought to communicate those discoveries through publications, and welcomed such awards and acclamation as those discoveries might bring, the social scientists and humanists often saw publications as ends in themselves. Publications based on original research distinguished academics from teachers. They brought their own rewards, in the form of internal promotion and public recognition.

The makers of the University assumed that, if academics were expected to publish, the University should assist them to do so. Oxford, Cambridge and the great American universities each had its own press, and so therefore should the ANU. Although the natural scientists, who communicated most of their findings through specialist journals or international scientific serials such as *Nature*, were not much interested, the social scientists were keen.

The first works published under an ANU imprint appeared in the early 1950s: a series of Social Science Monographs, humbly and laboriously produced using a varityper machine, and beginning with a review of the literature on genetic twinning by Norma McArthur in Demography, followed by the first of Noel Butlin's detailed analyses of Australian economic history in the late nineteenth century. The University also arranged with other publishers to produce in more elegant format the works of its staff and students. Several major titles appeared under a joint imprint, including Leicester Webb's study of the 1951 anti-communist referendum in Australia (with the publisher F.W. Cheshire) and Robin Gollan's *Radical and Working Class Politics* (with Melbourne University Press), which became standard reading for students of Australian history. As research output from the social science schools increased in the early 1960s, the University began publishing hardbacks in its own name. Then in 1966, following an enthusiastic report by a Canadian publisher, Council formally established the Australian National University Press.

Operated by a small and dedicated staff, the ANU Press became quickly, but briefly, one of Australia's largest academic publishers. Over two years from mid-1970, 53 titles appeared with its imprint. This was exceeded only by the University of Queensland Press with 59 titles, a figure which included over 20 volumes of poetry and departmental papers. A large majority of works published by the Press originated within the University, so that its editorial committee could claim accurately (at least in relation to the social sciences and humanities) that the Press significantly reflected the University's contribution to scholarship. This, according to the committee, was what it was there for: to extend the research function by making the results of that research readily available to an informed public. The University in turn drew benefit from 'the lustre shed by its publications'.

Lustre was expensive. The editorial committee correctly argued that almost any scholarly publishing involved deficit budgeting. As finances became tighter, and as the annual subsidy began to exceed six figures, how much was the University prepared to pay? While publication could be seen as an additional research cost, such costs also had their limits. Should those limits be influenced by commercial considerations? At the opposite extreme, some people associated with the Press argued that it should be run entirely along commercial lines in order to give the University some return for its investment.

The issue of cost was central to the sorts of books the Press published and how it was run. Should titles be selected solely on the basis of their academic merit or also on their potential for making a profit? Should the Press confine itself to works published by ANU staff and students or look anywhere for authors who would sell? Should decisions about publishing policy and specific publications be made by academics or publishers? There was room for compromise. But before anyone got around to finding and implementing one that worked, the Press foundered, partly on the large dilemmas inherent in academic publishing, including the pressure from academics to print large runs of books that sold few copies. In addition, the Press had no exclusive right to publish the works of University authors, many of whom regarded it as just another publisher. Free to choose publishers best suited to their specific needs, they often looked elsewhere. Many already had links that they wished to maintain with other publishers; some, seeking international readers, preferred to publish overseas; others were attracted by the well-established Melbourne University Press or increasingly entrepreneurial publishing houses outside the academy.

Following the closure of the ANU Press in 1984, the University tried to maintain formal links with scholarly publishing, first through an arrangement with Pergamon Press (which went overboard with the British entrepreneur Robert Maxwell) and then in the 1990s with Oxford University Press. Many academics regretted that the University had ceased to be its own publisher, while recognising that there was no longer much need for it to be so. Titles that were likely to sell usually found their way into print, while others reached their selected markets through desktop publishing or other forms of communication made possible by the computer revolution. All that was missing was an imprint which advertised the University's research output and promoted its name.

With or without the ANU Press imprint, staff and students of the University contributed enormously to the Australian scholarly output in the social sciences and humanities. The list of publications from 1960 to the mid-1970s included a few best-sellers and many more titles that opened up new fields of inquiry. Apart from those we have already noticed, there were Sol Encel's *Cabinet Government in Australia* (1962), Charles A. Price's *Southern Europeans in Australia* (1963), Manning Clark's *Short History of Australia* (1963), W.S. Ramson's *Australian English* (1966), Norma McArthur's *Island Populations of the Pacific* (1967), T.B. Millar's *Australia's Foreign Policy* (1968), John La Nauze's *The Making of the Australian Constitution* (1972), John Passmore's *Man's Responsibility for Nature* (1974), the first volume in the *New Guinea Languages and Language Study*, edited by Stephen Wurm: and so we might go on to fill many shelves. There were also journals and monograph series initiated and published by departments, such as the *Journal of Pacific History*, the *Federal Law Review*, the *Australian and New Zealand Journal of Sociology* and *Contemporary China Papers*.

In the complete list of publications from the late 1940s to the mid-1970s, some names figured prominently, some consistently, some irregularly and some scarcely at all. Irregular publication was not necessarily a problem: in the course of long careers, many academics had peaks and troughs of productivity as the creative spirit blessed or deserted them, or outside influences, including their domestic lives, intervened. As John Passmore observed, 'Annual production is not the best test of efficiency—whether what is in question is a farm or a professor'. But consistently low productivity *was* a cause for alarm, especially in the research schools, whose very existence was premised on maintaining an output higher than that of teaching universities. The 'non-producer' took one or both of two forms: first there were those in whom, as a distinguished British visitor to the ANU in 1959 delicately phrased it, 'the zest for research' had failed, including those who were just plain lazy; then there were those who were unable for one reason or another to transform their research into print.

Trevor Swan fell tragically into the second category. Early in his career, some people had seen him as a successor to Keynes. In 1953 he was invited to give the Marshall Lectures at Cambridge, one of the highest honours available to an economist. Coombs continued to regard him as among the most brilliant economists Australia had ever produced. From 1975 to 1985 he was a member of the Reserve Bank Board. Yet he seemed unable to publish. No draft was ever good enough; there were always figures to be questioned, paragraphs to be tidied up, final work to be done. His colleagues waited eagerly, then anxiously, as the years slipped by and virtually nothing appeared under his name. By the late 1970s successive directors of RSSS were urging him to take early retirement. Refusing to be pushed, he retired in 1983 at the age of 65, and died five years later.

What had gone wrong? Coombs thought he had suffered over the long term from an illness contracted in India in the late 1950s. This may have diminished his output; but it is also likely that Swan's mental capacities were ill suited to meeting the demands of publishing in a university environment. During his wartime and post-war careers in the public service he had been a problem solver, and so he remained. With an extraordinary capacity to apply theoretical models to the real world, he was at his best when set to solve an immediate problem in economic policy. When writing for his academic colleagues, he could never attain the standards he set himself.

Swan's career, and the careers of other non-producers, raised questions to which there were no easy answers. Should academics be appointed to the permanent staff only after they had proven themselves as researchers and writers, by which time they would presumably be middle aged? Should all appointments to research positions be for fixed terms? But if such restrictions had applied when Swan was appointed, the academic market suggested that some fields in the social sciences would not have been adequately covered. On the other hand, many young researchers appointed to permanent positions turned out to be some of the University's most productive members of staff.

Had the social science schools evolved as Coombs and his wartime colleagues originally intended, working closely with government on issues of immediate importance to Australian society, Swan might well have been at home. But in the more traditional university environment that the social science schools became, few doubted that academics should obey the publishing imperative.

Papua and New Guinea

The University's work in Papua and New Guinea showed, on the other hand, that publications were certainly not the only ends of research in the social sciences. Members of the Research School of Pacific Studies, along with a few of their colleagues from Social Sciences, had been active in New Guinea research almost from the moment they had arrived in Canberra. For anthropologists in particular, the Territory of Papua and New Guinea was a laboratory where it was possible to study peoples who had scarcely been touched by the outside world. At the same time, it offered opportunities for scholars to contribute to social, political and economic changes in a developing country which was then directly under Australian control. In 1951, at the request of Paul Hasluck, who was now Minister for Territories in the Menzies government, Oskar Spate, Trevor Swan and Cyril Belshaw, a Research Fellow in

Anthropology, looked into different aspects of economic development in the Territory and in due course produced a report which Hasluck later described as 'a basic document in any study of the post-war economic policy in Papua and New Guinea'.

Some of the outcomes of research were often quite different from its initial objectives. In 1966 two linguists in RSPacS, Stephen Wurm, a Professorial Fellow, and Clemens Voorhoeve, a Research Fellow, visited the Upper Strickland region in the Western District of Papua to investigate various language groups, including that of the Biami people, whose previous contacts with the outside world had been almost entirely hostile. The language of the Biami was quite unknown, and there were no interpreters, so attempts to communicate had invariably failed.

At the request of the District Commissioner, Wurm and Voorhoeve persuaded a group of Biami to stay at the local patrol post for several days, during which the researchers gained the rudiments of the language and managed to break down the initial communications barrier. Voorhoeve then remained in the area for nine months to make a thorough study of the language family, which resulted in linguistic discoveries. He was also able to report that the Biami people were gradually losing their reserve towards the local government and showing an increased interest in government activities.

Stephen Wurm, Professor of Linguistics in RSPacS, records a Kamano-Kafe speaker, Hesingne Naremeng, in the Papua New Guinea Highlands, about 1980.

During the 1960s and early 1970s, much of the University's research effort was conducted under the umbrella of the New Guinea Research Unit, comprising a small group of academics and support staff based in Canberra and New Guinea. The Unit provided accommodation, motor vehicles and local assistance for ANU staff and students as they arrived in Port Moresby and set out for the remote parts of the Territory. But it was much more than a base for visiting scholars. It originated as a response to Coombs's concerns in 1957 that RSPacS was not making the best use of its opportunities to engage in coordinated studies. The Unit was intended to encourage interdisciplinary exchanges among existing research programs, to initiate research in various areas, including social change, urban sociology and economic anthropology, and to carry out scientific inquiries that would have practical implications for the Territory. Coombs contributed toward this practical and humanitarian orientation. Wearing his Commonwealth Bank hat, he made it clear to Melville that he was enthusiastic for results and ready to help with funds: 'I am particularly anxious to ensure that worthwhile schemes for the material improvement of the natives should not be held up for the want of finance that could be reasonably provided by the Bank'. With the Bank's support, the Unit developed research into subsistence farming and cash cropping.

The Unit started work in 1961 and soon began publishing in humble format a bulletin which suggested a busy and diverse program. By 1975, when the bulletin ceased publication, 63 papers had appeared on such subjects as inter-tribal relations, land tenure, village industries, the economic effects of road construction, and esoteric sound instruments and their role in male–female relations.

As catalysts in a country undergoing rapid change, ANU academics often had cause to consider whether their academic independence was at risk. Nowhere were the risks greater than on the island of Bougainville, where the University conducted research on behalf of Bougainville Copper Pty Ltd, a subsidiary of the multinational company Conzinc Rio Tinto. Large deposits of copper ore had been discovered on Bougainville in 1965. As Oskar Spate pointed out several years later, the development of this new source of wealth would clearly have profound effects on the political life of the country, and on the social life of Bougainville itself.

In 1969 Bougainville Copper approached Crawford with proposals for grants approaching $30 000 for research on the economic and social problems of Papua and New Guinea, with special but not exclusive reference to Bougainville and the effects of the company's activities on the island and the Territory as a whole. After some agonising on the faculty of RSPacS, the grant was unanimously accepted, on the understanding that any report or publication arising from the study should be made publicly available and that there should be no confidential report to Bougainville Copper. Most of the money was to be used to undertake an intensive study of the Nasioi people of Bougainville. To lead the research, the University appointed Eugene Ogan, an American anthropologist with extensive experience among the Nasioi people, anticipating that the final results of his work would be of value to all parties, academics, administrators, indigenous Bougainville leaders and Bougainville Copper Pty Ltd.

Spate, now Director of RSPacS, conceded that the 'question of subsidised research must always be a delicate one'. But economic development would clearly have such shattering effects on Bougainville society that intensive research was 'absolutely essential' to try to mitigate them. If Big Business was prepared to fund independent studies, argued Spate, so much the better, so long as the independence was assured. He also thought that Bougainville Copper had acted 'with far more solicitude for the welfare of those its operations must inevitably affect than is the normal practice of great companies'. But not everyone was convinced. Some critics suggested that the University had in effect conspired with the company to force the acquiescence of the Bougainville people. The question remained open, and became increasingly complicated in later years as the Bougainville people demanded their independence from Papua New Guinea.

Apart from the issue of subsidised research, there were inevitable risks when academics from a developed nation conducted research in a dependent territory. Spate, together with Ron Crocombe, the Executive Director of the New Guinea Research Unit from 1965 to 1969, warned that there were more ways of despoiling a country than by simply taking its mineral resources, and urged their colleagues to ensure that the results of their research were made available to the people they had studied. Borrowing terms used by an Asian studies scholar, they divided researchers into 'miners', who dug their spoil and made off with it, and 'planters', who ensured that their research would be as fully and usefully available as possible in the researched country. Academics, they wrote, were under a moral obligation to give some tangible returns for the raw material from which they drew their livings, and to avoid anything which might look like 'an exploitative cultural imperialism'.

Spate obeyed his own homily, contributing immensely to the development of the Territory over 25 years. Perhaps his most lasting contribution was towards the establishment, against the odds, of the University of Papua and New Guinea. In 1963, at Hasluck's request, he joined Sir George Currie, who had been Vice-Chancellor at the universities of Western Australia and New Zealand, and John Gunther, the Assistant Administrator of Papua and New Guinea, in a commission to report and advise on higher education in the Territory. After taking evidence from over four hundred people and visiting 22 places in the Territory, the commission submitted a detailed report with 172 recommendations. Spate claimed responsibility for about one-third of its content and all of its text.

Oskar Spate, after receiving an honorary degree from the University of Papua New Guinea in recognition of his part in its creation.

University of Papua New Guinea.

The new University accepted its first, preliminary-year students in 1966. Like the ANU, it began with an interim council and an academic advisory committee. Spate, as the only member common to both, continued to visit Port Moresby at least twice a year until 1972, when the University awarded him an honorary LLD in recognition of his services in bringing it into being.

As the University of Papua and New Guinea grew, links with the ANU remained close. Apart from the fact that the New Guinea Research Unit was situated adjacent to the new campus, many staff at one time or another served both institutions. K.S. Inglis left his chair in History in the School of General Studies to become foundation Professor of History and then second Vice-Chancellor (succeeding John Gunther) at UPNG, before returning to RSSS. R.G. Ward came (on Spate's recommendation) from University College, London, to the foundation chair of Geography at Port Moresby and was later appointed to RSPacS, where he subsequently became Director. Friendships formed in Port Moresby were transported to Canberra, where memories of challenging and happy years in the tropics remained strong in the 1990s.

However beneficial the ANU's involvement in Papua and New Guinea might have been, the relationship, especially as it was symbolised through the New Guinea Research Unit, was essentially colonial. By 1973 the Territory was moving rapidly towards independence. Anthony Low, the Director of RSPacS and a member of Hancock's History Department many years earlier, recognised from his experience as a young academic in east Africa in the 1950s that 'decolonisation' of the Unit was inevitable, and that it was important that it should take place at the right time, neither precipitately nor allowing the University to outstay its welcome. Accordingly, the Unit was handed over to the newly established and autonomous Papua New Guinea Institute of Applied Social and Economic Research at the time the Territory won independence as Papua New Guinea in 1975. Some of the expatriate staff then crossed the Torres Strait to Darwin, where the ANU acted on yet another of Coombs's ideas and set up a North Australia Research Unit, which made good use of the administrative experience gained in Papua and New Guinea.

In 1979 Michael Somare, Papua New Guinea's first Prime Minister, told an ANU graduation ceremony that:

> the wealth of knowledge about the nature of both traditional and modern Papua New Guinea is due, in no small measure, to the influence and activities of this great institution.

Michael Somare, Prime Minister of Papua New Guinea, thanks the ANU for its contribution to research on his country.

The public professor

In November 1972, shortly before the federal election that was to sweep Labor into power after 23 years in opposition, sixteen distinguished Australians signed a letter to the Melbourne *Age* expressing the view that the time had come for a change in government. The names included three senior ANU academics—Manning Clark, Frank Fenner and Hedley Bull (Professor of International Relations)—along with Walter Crocker, now retired from the diplomatic service and living in Adelaide, and Sir Keith Hancock, still a Visiting Fellow in RSSS. The letter explained that, while none of them was a member of a political party, they all believed that a change in government would benefit both the major parties, 'on which the vitality of our political system depends'. 'The ultimate beneficiary will be the Australian nation and its people.'

The declaration was a significant reminder that university people were part of the wider social and political environment and that they were prepared to take a stand on the issues of the day. That had not always been the case. A decade earlier, P.H. Partridge had commented that in the past Australian universities had been well insulated against 'the vulgar noises and strivings of the outside world', and that those scholars who had 'made a stir in the political and social affairs of the state', such as the Sydney historian George Arnold Wood and the philosopher John Anderson, had not received support from most of their colleagues. Academics, said Partridge, had attempted to avoid public controversy, seeming to feel that this compromised the respectability of the university, perhaps endangering their own security and peace. He sensed that things were changing: but in 1963 he could scarcely have guessed how quickly those changes would happen.

Individual ANU academics had contributed to public policy and public debate from the University's inception, as Coombs and his colleagues in the Department of Post-War Reconstruction had expected them to do. Copland had certainly not let the office of vice-chancellor interfere with his right to comment on contemporary economic issues; FitzGerald and Davidson, as we have seen, had weighed into discussions on international affairs, including matters directly relevant to Australian foreign policy; Sawer had made regular radio broadcasts and written newspaper articles on diverse subjects; and Swan, Spate, Borrie and others had contributed to government inquiries. The natural scientists, too, had often participated in public debate, most notably Oliphant as an opponent of nuclear weapons, and Titterton as an advocate of any and every use of nuclear energy.

Academics contributed to public affairs in three major ways. First, they generated the raw material, both empirical and interpretative, on which others could draw: the data that enabled people in government and elsewhere to make informed policy decisions. Second, they offered their own informed opinions, sometimes solicited and sometimes not, about contemporary events and issues. Lastly, they participated directly in policy-making activities, as members of government boards and inquiries or as policy advisers and consultants. Crawford in particular warmly supported this kind of 'public service' as something the universities could offer as one response to the liberal community support for their work. In each of these roles (which tended to merge with one another) they wore the mantle of 'public professor', with responsibilities to the wider community as well as to their own institution.

The ANU had no formal policy on staff participation in public affairs, except to ensure that the amount of outside earnings and the time spent on outside activities did not in particular cases get out of hand, and to uphold the individual scholar's freedom to speak as he or she thought fit. Support for the right to speak did not necessarily mean encouragement, and often senior members of the University would have preferred their colleagues to remain silent. This was especially so when their comments offended the government of the day, as in the cases of FitzGerald and Davidson in the mid-1950s.

Bruce Miller, Professor of International Relations, RSPacS, from 1962 to 1987, photographed in 1969.

On the other hand, Titterton showed that overzealous support for government policy could also cause discomfort. In 1952, a year after his arrival in Canberra, the British government sought his release from the University to join its atomic testing team at Monte Bello Island in Western Australia. Thereafter, the Australian government urged his continued participation in the atomic program and appointed him to various committees relating to atomic testing, nuclear energy and defence. Together these placed him at the centre of government policy-making relating to atomic energy. As his participation in such activities increased, Council expressed concern that they would impede his own and the research school's productivity. And when the Prime Minister proposed that he be appointed to the National Radiation Advisory Committee, Oliphant suggested blocking the appointment on the grounds that the University would suffer, adding privately that Titterton, in view of his links with government policy, was an inappropriate appointment to a committee which should be able to provide an independent assessment of whether atomic testing was hazardous to Australia. But Titterton could argue that his outside activities had conferred significant benefits on the University, including the British gift of the electron synchrotron valued at £60 000 and the continuing goodwill of the federal government. He was appointed to the Radiation Advisory Committee and continued to figure prominently as one of the government's key advisers.

The growing conflict over Vietnam and conscription in the late 1960s and early 1970s brought the role of public professor into sharp focus. At the 28th International Congress of Orientalists held at the ANU in 1971, Sir Paul Hasluck, now Governor-General, raised the issue in his opening address when he urged the assembled scholars of Asia to 'remain high above topical controversy'. Academics should never attempt to influence government policy or descend to 'the lesser, lighter and more popular task of academic journalism'. This view was promptly challenged by the 'Concerned Asian Scholars of Australia and New Zealand', who had convened at the ANU several months previously and who now included some distinguished overseas members of the congress. CASAN urged all Asian scholars to signify their commitment on political and social issues, and become involved in current affairs.

Some academics welcomed the role of public professor or accepted it as a duty; others were unwillingly thrust into it owing to the nature of their research and its relationship to contemporary issues. J.D.B. Miller, head of International Relations in RSPacS, tried hard to stay out of controversy, fearing that if his department was too strident in opposing the Vietnam war, it would be 'snuffed out': 'my role', he later conceded, 'was a cowardly one. Keep your head down and try to avoid any interferences with the Australian National University.' Whatever his motives, Miller's silence could be interpreted as implying consent for government policies. The nature of research in international relations inevitably drew his department into controversy. In 1970 Gregory Clark, Tokyo correspondent for the *Australian* newspaper and formerly a postgraduate student in Economics, RSPacS, questioned the department's motives in organising three years earlier a conference on relations between India, Japan and Australia at a time when the government was toying with the idea of the three countries joining in an anti-communist alliance. 'It is doubtful', he wrote, 'whether the university has the right to divert research funds and lend its name for such obviously political ends'.

Established disciplines offered academics a protective shield against attacks on their independence or questions about their integrity. By contrast, some of the newer disciplines, such as International Relations, were vulnerable. This especially applied to centres and units which were created specifically to conduct research relating to contemporary issues.

The Strategic and Defence Studies Centre, set up in RSPacS in 1966 as an affiliate of the Department of International Relations, was controversial from the start. Its purpose was to coordinate and conduct research on strategic problems and other security questions in the Indian and Pacific oceans and Asian regions, and to provide facilities for strategic analysis outside the confines of government departments. While much of its work was to be 'purely military' in character, it was also intended to encompass such matters as peace-making, regional associations, and the relevance of international aid to national and international political stability.

The centre declared at the outset that it would not sponsor any particular policies or promote a particular viewpoint. It nevertheless attracted strong criticism, partly because its progenitors, A.L. Burns from Political Science in RSSS and T.B. Millar from

Arthur Burns, Professor of Political Science, RSSS, centre, leads in a game of chance and skill relating to the mathematics of nuclear proliferation, about 1968.

International Relations in RSPacS, were perceived as supporters of the political right. Nor did the presence of Titterton on its advisory committee help its public image. Opponents also suggested that the centre was wrong in principle, arguing that strategists, who took for granted the existence of military force, suffered from intellectual blindness which inclined them towards a hawkish posture; that they were mere technicians, unconcerned with the morality of the situations under analysis; that they collaborated with the establishment instead of using their knowledge to argue on matters of conscience. During the student protests of 1970, the centre took the precaution of restricting the numbers who could attend seminars, and so encouraged the view that staff were closing their doors to those who did not share their political outlook.

Robert O'Neill, a former Rhodes Scholar, officer in the regular army, Vietnam veteran Mentioned in Despatches, and head of the centre during the 1970s, conceded that some approaches to strategic studies were questionable, but argued that the field was nevertheless a legitimate area for scholarly inquiry. At the time of his appointment in 1971, he suggested that it might take a generation for strategic studies to win acceptance comparable with the traditional disciplines. 'Much will depend, of course, on the degree of responsibility and scholarship with which academic strategists pursue their calling.' Acceptance also depended on the political climate. By 1982, when O'Neill left the centre to become Director of the International Institute for Strategic Studies in London, Strategic Studies at the ANU had almost become an accepted feature of the scholarly landscape. Now scholars were asking questions about the even newer field of peace research: whether it was a legitimate area for study and whether it could be conducted independently of the government of the day.

Although it attracted less attention outside the University than the Strategic and Defence Studies Centre, the Centre for Research on Federal Financial Relations raised larger questions about the relationship between the University and the government. This centre grew out of Russell Mathews' work in the Department of Accounting and Public Finance relating to the allocation of taxing powers and financial

Robert O'Neill, Head of the Strategic and Defence Studies Centre, RSPacS, from 1971 to 1982, photographed in 1979.

responsibilities between the Commonwealth and the states. Mathews demonstrated that the states deserved a better deal from the Commonwealth than they were currently getting and developed a formula which in due course became the basis for the distribution of funds by the Commonwealth Grants Commission.

In 1970 the Academy of Social Sciences held a conference at the ANU, organised by Mathews, on Intergovernmental Relations in Australia, with the expectation that it might lead to permanent organisation devoted to research in this area. Academics from various disciplines attended, along with some senior politicians, including the Leader of the Opposition, Gough Whitlam, and the Minister for Civil Aviation, Senator Robert Cotton. As the final session was nearing an end, Cotton proposed the formation of a research organisation on intergovernmental relations, to be funded by the federal government. The conference agreed (with Whitlam expressing keen support); and before many people in the University realised what was happening, the Prime Minister, William McMahon, announced that the government would provide funds for the ANU to establish a federalism centre.

Mathews then put together a program for interdisciplinary research on intergovernmental financial relations in five main areas: expenditure functions, intergovernmental cooperation, taxation and loan finance, grants, and constitutional issues affecting financial relationships. The centre would provide information and analysis which governments might use as a basis for policy decisions. This, said Mathews, was a proper role for universities. At the same time, the centre would be explicitly excluded from making political statements, and it would not attempt to resolve political issues.

But some members of the University thought that the centre was compromised from the outset and that the government was using the ANU to serve its own political ends. There were grounds for suspicion: with an election in sight, the initiative showed the Liberal-National coalition government to advantage in attempting to deal with a thorny problem. The main difficulty for the University related to the issue of separate funding. Crawford, who warmly supported the proposal, insisted on a separate grant so that the centre would not become a burden on University finances; but this arrangement implied a separate line in the Commonwealth budget, and this in turn opened a specific aspect of research to political scrutiny. There was a fundamental difference, said Gordon Reid, Professor of Political Science in the Faculty of Arts (and later Governor of Western Australia), between an omnibus grant to the University from the Department of Education, allocated as members of the University thought fit, and a specific purpose grant from the Prime Minister's Department. Trevor Swan, who fought the proposal at every opportunity through various committees, warned his colleagues against 'Greeks bearing gifts' and urged them to remember that the ANU was especially vulnerable to interference. 'Governments, Ministers, Monarchs change: we cannot spread our academic cloak impartially in the mud before each of them.'

Despite the protests, the centre was established with dedicated Commonwealth funding in mid-1972. Mathews was appointed half-time Director, a position he retained until his retirement in 1986. The centre flourished around him, with a small staff, a lively visitors' program, and a prolific publishing output. Although many of its publications were critical of current government policies, Mathews in later years was unable to recall any instance of political interference. Governments from both sides of politics looked to the centre as a source of advice, especially valuable because of its independence, and implemented many of its recommendations, relating for example to the taxation system and federal fiscal arrangements. Mathews also served on various government commissions and inquiries, and as a member of the Commonwealth Grants Commission from 1973 until well after his retirement. In each of these capacities he performed with finesse the role of public professor.

Stephen FitzGerald, on leave from the Department of Far Eastern History, RSPacS, meets Chinese Premier Zhou Enlai in 1973, after taking office as Australia's first Ambassador to the People's Republic of China.

In December 1972, six months after the formation of the Centre for Research on Federal Financial Relations, those who had called for a change of government could celebrate the Labor Party's victory at the polls. The result had a profound impact on the higher education system, as it did on so many areas of Australian life. One change was the abolition of student fees. Another was the vastly increased use of academics as policy advisers and consultants to government, accompanied by an expectation on the part of government that the universities would make their skills available to the wider community.

Prime Minister Whitlam, in a speech on 'Universities and governments' delivered in Sydney in mid-1973 and reported at length in ANU publications, was explicit: 'I would like to see Australian universities participate more readily in the solution of current problems, and seek a more relevant and contemporary role as organs of public service'. Whitlam listed approvingly the names of 23 academics who were currently contributing to his government's program, five of whom came from the ANU: Russell Mathews who, as well as directing the Centre for Federal Financial Relations, served on an inquiry into urban land tenure; the demographers W.D. Borrie and J.C. Caldwell, who were key members of a national population inquiry (commissioned by the previous government); the lawyer Patrick Atiyah, a member of the national compensation inquiry; and P.H. Partridge, who was on a committee investigating the prospects for an Australian open university. As the *ANU News* pointed out, the Prime Minister had 'barely scratched the surface of contemporary ANU involvement with government'. Among other major contributors were the environmental biologist R.O. Slatyer, who chaired the Australian National Committee for UNESCO's 'Man and the Biosphere' program, as well as serving on the National Capital Planning Committee; the economist F.H. Gruen, adviser to the Department of the Prime Minister and Cabinet on economic issues; and Stephen FitzGerald (no relation of Patrick), who took leave from the Department of Far Eastern History to become Australia's first ambassador to the People's Republic of China.

The universities, said Whitlam, could no longer be 'the sequestered retreats of an intellectual or cultivated elite'. And the communities that maintained them could not afford to let them remain apart:

> None of this means that universities must sacrifice any part of their independence. I merely suggest that, where strength lay in isolation, it lies now in participation, in a process of organic involvement with the needs and aspirations of society.

Research, in other words, should be driven by new imperatives. If universities were to survive into the twenty-first century, they would not exist as 'cloistered retreats for the privileged few', but rather as 'man's chief ally in the struggle to preserve our freedom, and our species, from destruction'.

Whitlam's comments could be read as a challenge or a warning. Either way, universities, as he put it, could no longer assume that their future was secure.

The University in 1975

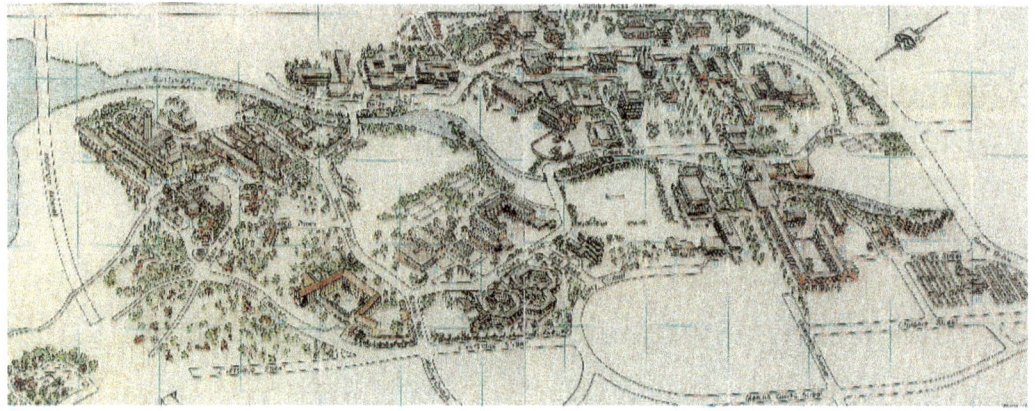

Students

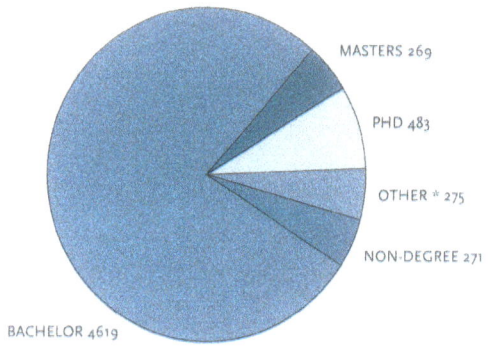

MASTERS 269
PHD 483
OTHER * 275
NON-DEGREE 271
BACHELOR 4619

* Includes Masters qualifying, Legal Workshop and special courses.

Origins of Undergraduate Students

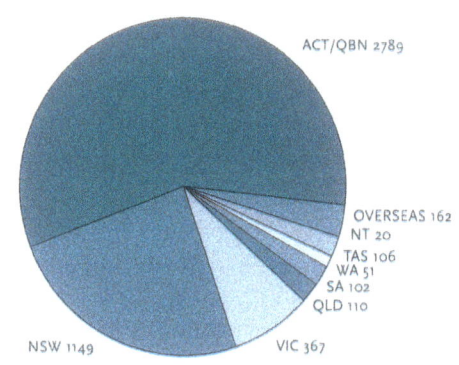

ACT/QBN 2789
OVERSEAS 162
NT 20
TAS 106
WA 51
SA 102
QLD 110
VIC 367
NSW 1149

QBN denotes Queanbeyan.

Undergraduate Students by Faculty

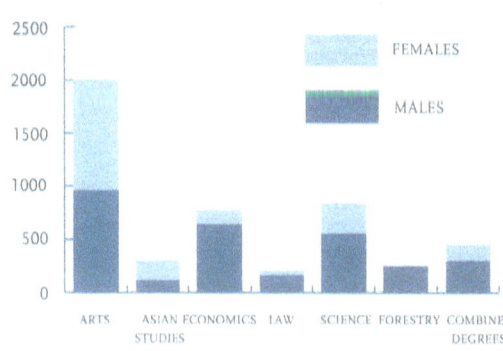

FEMALES
MALES

ARTS, ASIAN STUDIES, ECONOMICS, LAW, SCIENCE, FORESTRY, COMBINED DEGREES

Origins of Postgraduate Students

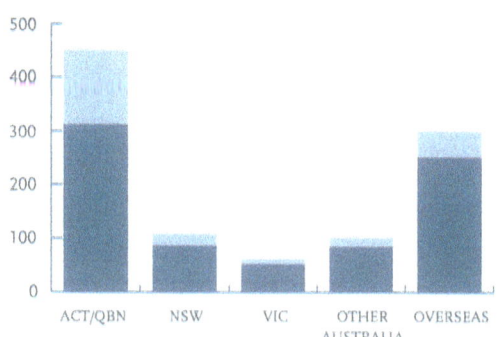

ACT/QBN, NSW, VIC, OTHER AUSTRALIA, OVERSEAS

Staff

- CENTRES/UNITS ACADEMIC 1%
- SGS - ACADEMIC 11%
- IAS - ACADEMIC 16%
- SUPPORT STAFF* 72%

* Includes administration, library maintenance and laboratory staff, research assistants and research officers.

IAS Academic Staff*

- RSES 3%
- RSC 11%
- RSBS 12%
- RSSS 20%
- RSPHYSS 17%
- RSPACS 22%
- JCSMR 15%

* Excludes research assistants and research officers.

SOURCE: ANU *STATISTICAL HANDBOOK*, 1975

COUNCIL

Professorial Board

Board of the Institute of Advanced Studies

Board of the School of General Studies

ADMINISTRATION

Research Schools

John Curtin School of Medical Research
Physical Sciences
Social Sciences
Pacific Studies
Chemistry
Biological Sciences
Earth Sciences

Faculties

Arts
Asian Studies
Economics
Law
Science

University Centres *
University Library
Residential Halls and Affiliated Colleges

* Centre for Resource and Environmental Studies, Humanities Research Centre, North Australian Research Unit and Survey Research Centre, all associated with the Institute of Advanced Studies for resource allocation purposes. Other centres and activities include: Computer Centre, Centre for Continuing Education, Office for Research in Academic Methods, Instructional Resources Unit, Counselling Centre, Health Service and ANU Press.

From the mid–1970s to the mid–1990s

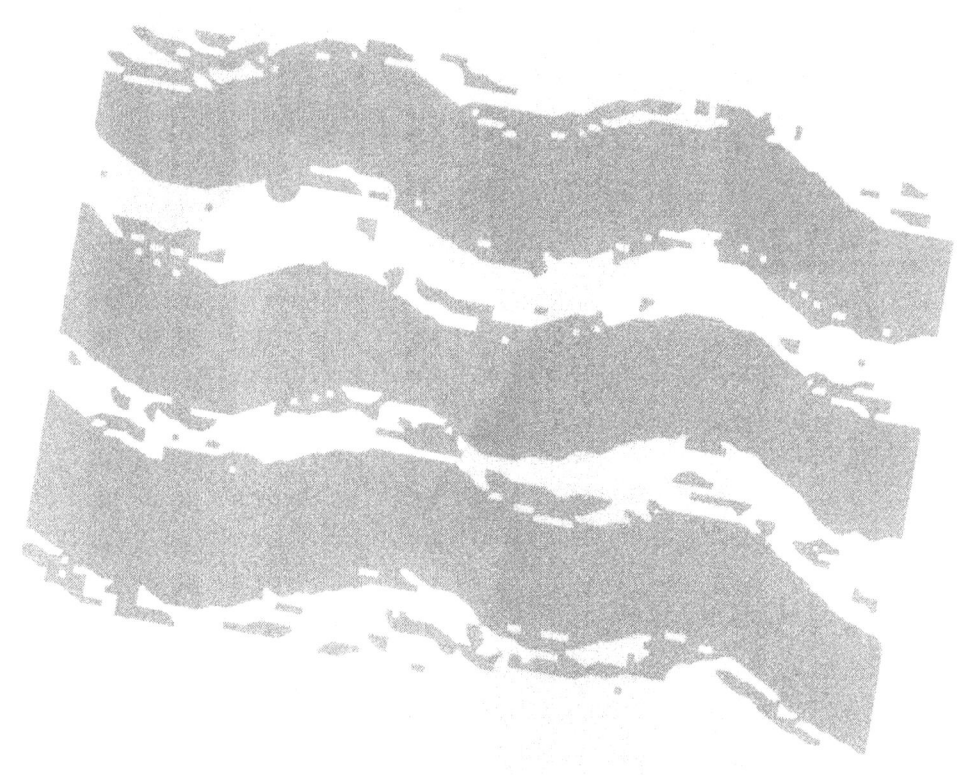

Anthony Low, Vice-Chancellor from 1975 to 1983, in the year of his appointment. Photograph by Gabe Carpay.

A new era

Low at the helm

The sudden departure of Robert Williams for New Zealand early in 1975 left the University without a vice-chancellor or an obvious successor. After a bumpy electoral process, during which each day's deliberations of the electoral committee mysteriously found their way into the following morning's *Canberra Times*, Council invited Anthony Low, Director of the Research School of Pacific Studies, to take on the job.

Low had two large assets. First, he was a known quantity. Although he had been in RSPacS for just two years, he had proven himself a capable and popular Director, and had managed to overcome some initial discomfort within the school that he had been appointed without sufficient consultation and that his research interests were some distance from the Pacific. Second, his reputation and perspective were truly international. Born in India, he had read Modern History at Oxford before going to Makerere College in the University College of East Africa in 1951. After nine years in Uganda, during which he was East African correspondent for the London *Times* and the *Round Table*, he joined the ANU, where we met him as a member of Hancock's Department of History in RSSS. In 1964 he was appointed to a chair at the University of Sussex, where he set up the School of African and Asian Studies and later took charge of graduate education in Arts and Social Sciences. After a year at Clare Hall, Cambridge, he returned to Canberra in 1973. When he took up the vice-chancellorship in May 1975, he was nearly 48 years of age.

If Hancock could be seen as captain of a cricket team, Low can be imagined standing confidently at the helm of an ocean liner, moving sedately between countries and continents (especially England, East Africa, India and Australia). Tall and upright, with an urbane and engaging manner, he spent many hours at the captain's table educating key politicians and public servants about the ANU's contribution to the nation. Where Hancock made a virtue of his research school and department remaining small, Low was comfortable with a large and diverse crew. Hancock was most at home in the seminar; Low, while equally confident in that setting, welcomed the opportunity to address the whole University, either at graduation ceremonies, or at open meetings of staff and students. Five times during his seven-year term, he delivered 'Reports to the University' in the H.C. Coombs Lecture Theatre, where he spoke proudly (for external as well as internal consumption) of the University's recent achievements, expounded his vision of where it was headed, and pointed to obstacles in its path. Like Hancock, Low had a way with words, both orally and on paper, including dextrous use of the telling phrase or metaphor. He had the historian's skill of creating order out of chaos, and his reports to the University were masterly syntheses. They were also reports for posterity: no other vice-chancellor, before or since, has so eloquently summed up the University during his tenure or so persuasively presented his part in its history.

Addressing a graduation ceremony in September 1975, Low declared that the University was at the start of a new era. The years of expansion were over, and now universities generally looked forward to a period of limited growth. No longer, he said, could the ANU meet so many of its problems, as it had lately tended to do, by making allocations from new resources. Now it would be necessary to trim, cut and even delete: but it would also be essential to take new initiatives and to avoid any slump in morale. The culture of the institution had to change, and Low was confident that with positive and imaginative thinking it could do so.

Apart from alerting the University to its changing circumstances, there were advantages (which Low did not mention) in distancing the institution from its recent past. The truncated term of Williams as Vice-Chancellor had been the least happy in the University's experience, characterised by student assaults on the Chancelry and a general impression on and off campus that the administration did not know where it was headed. Low wanted a new beginning, in which the Vice-Chancellor would be 'making the running'. That meant that he should 'climb the next hill, and point up the contours of some of the things I see in the middle distance', and plot the route ahead (though he emphasised that he would not be giving the University its marching orders). It also meant that he would not be yielding precedence to the old guard of Coombs and Crawford, either or both of whom had been a dominant presence ever since the days of Copland. Shortly after taking up duty, he steeled himself for a private lunch with Coombs at which he politely conveyed the firm message that he intended from time to time to consult him in his position as Chancellor, but that he as Vice-Chancellor was the University's chief executive officer and that he did not wish Coombs to go over his head, as he had done with Williams. The injunction was probably unnecessary, as Coombs never intervened unless there was need. But Low was pleased to have set the rules, and pleased too that he and the Chancellor remained good friends.

In 1976 Coombs retired as Chancellor, ending nearly 24 years of continuous service as the local representative of chancellors or as Chancellor himself, and was succeeded by Crawford. With Crawford too, Low was careful to retain the initiative, always ensuring that he called on the Chancellor to discuss any issue, rather than having the Chancellor call on him. Crawford remained influential, both through the value people attached to his opinions and by chairing meetings of Council (often an onerous task); yet although at least once in coming years his role was decisive, the functions of chancellor were henceforth, as in most other universities, chiefly confined to presiding at Council and at graduation ceremonies.

Changes within the higher education system also suggested the beginnings of a new era. In 1974 the Labor government assumed full financial responsibility for higher education. While the ANU remained the only university established by an Act of the federal parliament, now it was just one of nineteen universities (including Deakin, inaugurated in that year) funded by the Commonwealth. Henceforth, it would have to take its place in the queue. It also became part of a wider higher education system administered by the Commonwealth. The Whitlam government set up three commissions responsible for funding the three sectors of post-secondary education: the universities, the colleges of advanced education and the colleges of technical and further education. Then the Fraser government constituted a single Tertiary Education Commission, responsible for all three areas. Under both governments there were in effect three queues, all competing for limited resources.

Owing to the unique status of the Institute, the ANU received the most funding; but how long would that last? As old universities became increasingly involved in postgraduate training, and new universities created as a result of the Murray Report joined them, the ANU's proportion of postgraduate students declined, so that where in the early 1960s it produced over 20 per cent of PhD graduates, reaching a peak of 27.5 per cent in 1964, by the late 1970s the figure had fallen to around 15 per cent. The trend was especially evident in the social sciences and humanities, where the ANU's share fell during the same period from over 50 per cent to around 20 per cent. Increasingly, the University looked to new ways of asserting its uniqueness and demonstrating that it paid its way.

When Low took office, students were already less strident than they had been, the great causes of representation and continuous assessment having given way to demands, equally urgent but more mundane, for cheaper accommodation. Low, who had first-hand experience of student turbulence in England, took no chances: recognising that Colin Plowman had 'the best antennae in the business', he retrieved him from the University of New South Wales as Assistant Vice-Chancellor, with a brief to look after the students. Owing partly to Plowman's presence, but more to the larger changes affecting them, student unrest quickly ceased to be a major problem.

But the Troubles had left their mark. Within the University they bequeathed distrust between staff and students, hard to define but nevertheless palpable. And they helped diminish the status of the University in the wider community. This trend was by no means confined to the ANU, or even to Australia. Returning from a congress of Commonwealth vice-chancellors held in New Zealand early in 1976, Low reported on growing public hostility towards universities, especially in Britain and Canada, and predicted that Australia would not be far behind. Nor was it limited to the teaching functions of universities: about the same time, Arthur Birch was commenting on the 'public disenchantment with research'.

Then in 1977 a conservative journalist, Peter Samuel, launched a scathing attack in the *Bulletin* on 'The scandal of our universities', in which he denounced the 'tertiary education industry' as an 'appalling waste of taxpayers' money'. Occasionally, he said, the universities did some excellent work, but by and large they were 'drab, unproductive institutions', populated by 'drones and parasites', characterised by 'internal intrigue and vicious-infighting', and susceptible to takeover by 'intolerant, illiberal, irrational minorities'. While the colleges of advanced education received the most severe drubbing, Samuel also cited some of the more arcane examples of research at the ANU as instances of overspecialisation, which, he suggested, implied a tendency to award promotions within the confines of a tiny clique rather than on the basis of scholarly excellence.

Whatever the rights or wrongs of Samuel's comments (and some of them were wild), they signalled that the universities, once largely immune from public criticism, would henceforth be fair game.

The change of government did not help. Academics and students responded fervently to Whitlam's appeal to 'maintain the rage' over his sacking, and protested, sometimes violently, whenever his successor, Malcolm Fraser, stepped onto a university campus. The coalition government regarded the universities as broadly unsympathetic, and showed signs of wanting to bring them into line.

As usual, the ANU, close at hand and federally funded, was vulnerable, especially since so many of its staff were prominent supporters of the previous government and outspoken critics of the new one. Low himself was angry about the Whitlam government's dismissal. A television camera caught him among the crowd protesting outside Parliament House, which was probably unfortunate for the University's relations with the incoming government, and his own relations with those people on campus who welcomed Whitlam's sacking; but Low, always his own man, was unrepentant. One of the University's most forthright and best-known protesters was Manning Clark, who had an unsurpassed talent for getting up conservative nostrils. Writing for *Meanjin* magazine, Clark dismissed the Fraser government as 'a group of men who had the moral values of a troop of Boy Scouts, and the economic and social values which were rapidly disappearing off the face of the earth', and suggested that future historians might deal harshly with the Governor-General who had dismissed Whitlam. When a government Senator, after mangling the comment about the Governor-General, implied that Clark was unfit to sit on University appointment committees or examine theses, and the Minister for Education, Senator John Carrick, joined in the attack, Low politely but firmly accused the Minister of impugning Clark's scholarly integrity. The University and academic freedom were well defended, but the risks of government interference remained great.

Ross Hohnen, retiring in 1975 after 27 years at the ANU, receives from the Chancellor, Coombs, 'a complicated but sincere symbol of our appreciation'.

The prospect became an unpleasant reality in 1979 when the government, responding to pressure from Liberal students, attempted to ensure that none of the income from the General Services Fee, which was paid by every student, reached left-wing student organisations, specifically the Australian Union of Students. Council prepared a statute to deal with the matter. The government rejected it, as had never before happened to a statute, and proposed instead to amend the ANU Act so as to abolish all compulsory fees. Low decided it was time to bring Crawford into the battle; and after a vigorous public debate, the government agreed to a strategy whereby the fee would remain compulsory, but students could choose whether or not to join local organisations including the Students' Association, and the money could be directed only to organisations approved by the government. The specific issue ceased to be important, as the question of government interference dominated Council debates. From the point of view of the University, the result was better than it might have been; nevertheless, the exchange was an indication that the relationship between the government and the University was no longer cosy.

Within the institution, too, things were changing. As Low was moving into the vice-chancellor's office, Hohnen was seriously ill in hospital, and it seemed certain that he would be forced to take an early and reluctant retirement. For many people he was 'Mr ANU'. Having served the University for nearly 27 years, he not only knew *how* the institution worked, but in many respects he had *made* it work. Coombs, at a presentation ceremony held during a Council luncheon in March 1975, remarked: 'Each job he has taken on he has so built up that he can always do it better than anyone else'.

The University was unprepared for his departure. For he and his colleagues had created structures and procedures around themselves. In the early 1970s efficient administration continued to depend, as it had done in the past, on personal knowledge, influence and networks. While the system had served the institution well, it could not last forever. So much information resided in a few grey or greying heads. David Hodgkin, who had succeeded to the title of Registrar of the University when Hohnen had become Secretary in 1968, had already retired. Bill Hamilton, the Bursar, succeeded him, but retired within four years owing to ill health.

The pressures for change were there already. Low himself, as a director of a research school, had felt left out of the budget-making process. As he saw it, the directors and deans were summoned to meetings in the Chancelry to be told how much of the cake they were to receive. Waiting their turn to be ushered into the vice-chancellor's office, the academic heads of the University were becoming restless: but so long as the cake was large and generously iced, it would have seemed churlish to complain.

Low changed all this by establishing a Vice-Chancellor's Advisory Group, comprising representatives of the directors and deans, who now had a genuine say in how the money was allocated. Rather than creating another 'administrative supremo', he transferred power away from specific individuals and into the hands of office-holders and committees. He also deprived the administrators of some of their influence and gave the academics a larger role in running the University.

Hohnen's retirement also symbolised the loss of corporate memory that comes to any institution when the first generation of its makers departs. Like Coombs, he was a direct link with the past. More than anyone else, he carried forward Copland's sense of participating in a 'great intellectual adventure'. He had a clear vision of what the University was or ought to be about, and he imparted that vision to all who worked with him. A few of his close colleagues, including the Assistant Registrars Molly Bouquet and Patricia White and the Academic Registrar, George Dicker, remained custodians of the memory into the 1980s (and in White's case, the early 1990s). But most of their colleagues had either forgotten the past or assumed that it was no longer relevant.

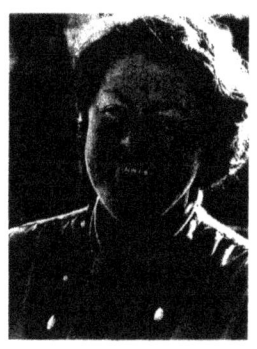

Pat White and George Dicker spanned the old and new eras. White, photographed in 1983, came as a Graduate Assistant in 1962 and retired as an Assistant Registrar (acting as Registrar) in 1991. Dicker, photographed in 1979, came as an Assistant Registrar in 1966 and retired as Registrar in 1985.

The most apt symbol of change was the disappearance with Hohnen's retirement of what many people referred to as his 'capacious pouch'. With Hohnen in the Chancelry, there always seemed to be money available to get things done, not just a few hundred dollars to provide for an expensive overseas visitor, but tens of thousands of dollars to buy a costly item of equipment or extend a building. The source of the funds often seemed a mystery. (In fact, he managed to juggle savings accrued from one year to the next.) But while his colleagues might have wondered where the money came from, one thing was certain: when Hohnen left, his capacious pouch simply could not be found.

'A tighter ship'

The new era was one of uncertainty, especially about money. The signs that times would get tougher were there during Whitlam's administration. Crawford, while still Vice-Chancellor, had proposed (rather cheekily) to the AUC that the growth of the Institute should be linked to the gross national product. The Chairman of the AUC, Peter Karmel, responded during a visit to the University that the rate of growth should be geared to the national economic situation, which implied slower growth than the University proposed.

Then, in 1975, the government's turbulent last year, the three education commissions presented demands for funding which together far exceeded the nation's capacity to pay. This led to, among other things, an immediate suspension of triennial funding for higher education and the introduction of financial guidelines for the education commissions. 'Guidelines' was nicely euphemistic: if it did not mean so already, it certainly came to mean 'controls'. As Coombs put it during his valedictory address as Chancellor in 1976, 'we may be moving towards a period when the terms of our dependence with honour will need to be negotiated'.

That year the Fraser government reintroduced triennial funding, but on a rolling basis, so that the universities were at least guaranteed minimal funding for the coming three years. It also promised to maintain a modest level of growth of 2 per cent a year in real terms. But government grants failed to keep pace with rising costs, so that by 1977, when there was a prospect of a 4 per cent decline in funding for the coming year, Council was complaining that the government had abrogated its previous assurances. The Minister's response left little room for further protest: economic recovery must have overall priority. This undermined the University's capacity for forward planning and led many members of staff to conclude that the government could not be trusted.

In various ways the University became enveloped in financial crisis. Some problems emerged gradually, such as 'incremental creep', the increasing cost of paying staff whose salary rates were increasing as they became older and more senior. Others came suddenly, such as the realisation that the University would have to increase greatly its contributions to staff superannuation funds in order to comply with Commonwealth legislation and ensure that staff in different schemes received equal benefits. As salaries made up 80 per cent or more of the overall budget, every percentage point increase in salary-related costs forced cuts to staff numbers or to non-salary expenditure. Then there was the fuel crisis, beginning in 1973 but extending throughout the decade, so that, even with expensive conversions from oil heating to electricity, especially relevant to the ANU because of Canberra's cold winters, the University's fuel bill more than doubled from 1978 to 1979. Finally, the ANU, in common with other universities, was unprepared for the levelling out in student numbers and the resulting loss of anticipated extra income.

All this had harsh effects on teaching and research. First tutorships, then chairs, were left unfilled, equipment purchases postponed, budgets for field trips curtailed and library orders cancelled. Both the faculties and the research schools were forced to trim their sails. Frank Gibson, Director of the John Curtin School, warned that while his school had advertised for two extra chairs, he doubted that it could fund them, and that in any case the school would have trouble attracting good people owing to its deteriorating conditions for research. Gibson expressed the view held widely around the campus that the 'ANU's reputation as a centre of excellence was under threat'.

At first Low's public comments about the financial situation were restrained. In 1980, however, he decided that the time had come, as he put it, to press the alarm button. Without an injection of funds for the coming triennium, the work of the University, especially in the area of fundamental research, would be seriously jeopardised. Although the ANU had 'patently tightened ship', its budget, which had declined in real terms by 10 to 12 per cent from 1975 to 1981, was becoming too small to run a university of its range and size.

Low responded to the crisis by urging the government to increase its funds and his colleagues to reduce their spending. What was needed, he said, was 'a tighter, trimmer ship, fore and aft, port and starboard, up in the mizzen, down in the hold'. But the University, having evolved during years of relatively generous government grants, was ill equipped to cope with hard times. This especially applied to the Institute. Where in the faculties student numbers provided the natural basis for distributing funds, the research schools' budgets were determined on historical lines. Historical budgeting worked so long as there was growth. But in a period of contraction, the main object of each school was to maintain its slice of the cake relative to the others. The Vice-Chancellor, without access to any budgetary surplus, had no room to manoeuvre.

Yet a research institution had to be able to accommodate new endeavours. In concert with Ian Ross, now Deputy Vice-Chancellor, Low devised a scheme by which each school would be taxed by 1 per cent of its budget to provide a sum which would be assigned competitively to new projects. Although the percentage was modest, some directors were outraged by what they saw as an invasion of their traditional rights. Nevertheless, the scheme went ahead in 1980 and led to several valuable initiatives, including a research group in RSES in environmental geochemistry, a study in RSBS of the development and function of the cerebral cortex, and a centre in RSSS for economic policy research.

Besides having to handle contraction, Low and his senior advisers had to guard the University's integrity. Dangers lurked within the public service. As well as cutting funds, the Treasury tried to impose restrictions on how they were spent, suggesting that the University's budget should be subject to line by line approval. Low enlisted the help of Crawford and appealed to Alan Carmody, the head of the Department of the Prime Minister and Cabinet, and a former member of the Department of Trade and Industry, where he had been, as Low later put it, 'one of Crawford's young men'. The two of them prevailed, Treasury was overruled, and at least for the time being the University could distribute its depleted resources as it thought best.

Low tells an unhappy audience about cuts in government funding, June 1977.
Canberra Times.

Low was adamant, as others had been, that the University should not be treated as a government department. The problem was that being a government department had its benefits. Until the early 1970s, the University had taken it for granted that the government would meet unexpected contingencies and make up major budgeting shortfalls. Now it was on its own. This was illustrated by the Whitlam government's response when Cyclone Tracy, which devastated Darwin in late 1974, wrecked the buildings of the North Australia Research Unit, scattering books and papers far and wide. The ANU, by direction of the Treasury, was not insured, relying instead on the Commonwealth coffers to cover any such disaster. But now the government said no, and the University was left to finance its own rebuilding.

'So bit by bit...', recalled Ross (who seemed to have picked up Low's partiality to a nautical metaphor), 'the government cut the painter'.

≋ The University community

Low began his first report to the University by talking about the '10,000 of us', the 6 000 students and 4 000 staff who made up the ANU community. All 10 000, he said, were a part of the University, whether they were 'busily engaged in laboratories, ... going to the library to find a book or an article, ... paying bills, typing letters, checking inventories, or seeing that the buildings, the electric power, the university grounds, are properly provided for'. Low tried to visit as many departments and sections as he could, knowing how important it was that everyone should share a commitment to the institution and, so far as possible, a common understanding of its functions and purposes.

The concept of universities as communities of scholars was as old as universities themselves. As they had grown, the communities had been extended to include supporting non-academic staff who, in recent times, usually outnumbered the academics. Thus the fabric of Oxbridge colleges included porters and scouts as well as masters and wardens. Notwithstanding their distance apart in a well-defined hierarchy, all were expected to give the college their allegiance.

The ANU had inherited this tradition of community. It had also inherited, though not in the rarefied forms evident at Oxford or Cambridge, some of the traditional divisions within a university, especially between the academic and non-academic staff. While Hohnen might define 'academic' to include administrators who had a highly developed perception of 'what the University is all about', most ANU people acknowledged a gulf that was sometimes difficult to bridge, narrow in the early years, but steadily widening as the institution grew in size. Also, within the categories 'academic' and 'non-academic', there were hierarchies, defined by titles, salaries and spatial arrangements, so that in some buildings the status of a member of staff could be measured by the number of square feet or metres he or she occupied. This did not always apply: Noel Butlin, perversely egalitarian, insisted as a professor of Economic History on a small room, just large enough to accommodate (in chaotic fashion) the shelves and piles of books and documents he happened to be using at the time.

Many members of the academic and general staff spent most of their working lives at the University. Peter Darling, photographed at the time of his retirement in 1991, spent 40 years as a craftsman carpenter and cabinet maker in RSRhysS. Photograph by Andrew Campbell.
Canberra Times.

Vertical and horizontal divisions notwithstanding, the sense of community remained strong, at least until the 1970s. Various formal and informal structures helped bind the community together. In the early years, Hohnen and his wife Phyllis took the lead in ensuring that not only the staff but also their spouses and children were integrated into the larger University 'family'. A Women's Club, founded in 1961 by Huxley's wife, Molly, provided practical help for new arrivals and initiated a range of social activities for female spouses and staff, including bridge, tennis, French conversation, discussion groups on poetry and politics and, as fashions changed, birdwatching, bushwalking and spinning. Many staff and their spouses founded or joined clubs and societies devoted to music, film, poetry, drama and or some other cultural activity.

Sport likewise bridged the gaps between staff and students, academics and administrators, and one faculty, school or department and another. Cricket was as much a social as a sporting activity. The ANU Cricket Club, established in 1952 with Butlin as first President, organised some memorable matches, such as Men v. Women and Academics v. Administration, in which the players wore colourful outfits better suited to gardening or sunbathing than batting or fielding. In one of the earliest games between academic and administrative staff, the academics batted 26 and fielded 17 while the administrators batted 16 and fielded 13´ (Copland having left early). The academics won. Staff v. Student matches were played annually from the mid-1960s, and usually won by the students, a notable exception being the 1971 match when Deane Terrell, a Lecturer in Econometrics, carried the staff to glorious victory. He later became Vice-Chancellor.

Annual Town v. Gown matches, introduced in 1989, became great social and political events, capriciously favoured by the weather.

Certain sports joined specific parts of the University in friendly rivalry: the Central Administration v. The Faculties golf tournaments; the Bent End Inter-School Darts Championship, a competition between JCSMR, RSC and RSBS; the Purple Shin Inter-Departmental Soccer Competition. In the 1990s the Meninga Club, named after a

Above: Members of the ANU Club for Women on a bushwalking expedition in 1979.

Right: Members of the Vice-Chancellor's XI celebrate their victory over Justice Gallop's XI in the inaugural Town v. Gown match in 1989. Vice-Chancellor Laurie Nichol, in striped shirt, stands beside the trophy. Photograph by Darren Boyd.

Canberra-based football hero, gave administrators and academics who might otherwise have had little in common the chance to share their enthusiasm for Rugby League.

Staff associations (a more apt term than trades unions) were a part of the University from the earliest years. In 1953 four social scientists, Mick Borrie, Noel Butlin, Bob Gollan and Trevor Swan, initiated moves to form the ANU Staff Association, which was open to academics and other graduate members of staff. Its purpose was to provide a formal mechanism for discussing salaries and conditions of service with the administration, and to play a social role in bringing staff together. In relation to salaries and conditions, Association members for a long time had little to complain about. Under the ANU Act, Council had 'entire control and management' of the University, which included relations with its staff. Hohnen argued that the National University should take the lead in such matters, and circumvented any immediate problems by dipping into his pouch. Such negotiations as were necessary on specific issues were usually conducted by the Association executive at regular lunches with the vice-chancellor and other senior officers at University House. For many years there was rarely a cross word.

By the mid-1970s, however, conditions for academics were becoming tougher. As the University lost the capacity to buy itself out of trouble, the Association defended members' interests with increasing vigour, while nevertheless insisting that it had no wish to set up an adversarial relationship between employer and employee. At the same time, industrial relations within the University were becoming subject to control by outside bodies. The creation in 1974 of an Academic Salaries Tribunal, responsible for determining salaries across the system, removed one wide area of dispute, but others remained. Superannuation became a major source of controversy, with the Association seeking to win equal benefits for all its members, who had been appointed when different schemes were in operation, and the University having to watch every dollar. Then, as tenured jobs became harder to get throughout the tertiary system, the Association concerned itself with the conditions of untenured staff.

Dwindling opportunities for aspiring academics outside or on the edge of the system put increasing pressure on staff who already enjoyed job security, especially on those who were perceived as failing to carry their weight. A series of reviews of the research schools in the late 1970s and early 1980s identified, in confidence, a small number of senior academics who needed to be shown the spurs or put out to pasture. On individual cases, senior members of the Association executive worked closely with the Vice-Chancellor and the relevant Director to find a solution which balanced the interests of the staff member with that of the University at large. Solutions were rarely easy, partly because the University was unfamiliar with dealing with problems of this nature and partly because the problems were often intractable. When Low, acting on the advice of a confidential report on RSSS, initiated in 1980 moves to compulsorily retire Arthur Burns, Professor of International Relations, who had ceased to be a productive member of the school, he began a protracted dispute which extended over fourteen years. Burns, although forced on medical grounds to retire, sued the University. The case was eventually settled out of court.

The University environment was becoming more litigious, mirroring the rest of Australian society. John Molony, Professor of History in The Faculties and President of the Staff Association for six years, predicted when he stepped down in 1981 that, as the ANU had ceased to be master of its own affairs, the role of the Association was set to change, from a body which sought to avoid confrontation and litigation to a more militant organisation akin to a trade union. In the years that followed, industrial relations between the administration and academic staff continued to move gradually away from the gentlemanly dealings characteristic of a collegiate environment towards hard-headed negotiations whose norms were set by the wider community.

Yet the transition was not, and probably would never be complete. While the Association attracted between one-third and one-half of full-time eligible staff (the proportions varying greatly from one part of the University to the next), the executive could never claim to speak for all its members on a particular issue. That was in the nature of a university. Most academics were pleased to have a union to represent their interests, but only so long as it did not deny them the right to express their own opinions on industrial and other matters.

As the academics had laid claim to the title 'Staff Association', the general staff were represented by the ANU General Staff Association. Founded in 1954, the

Academics, administrators and footballers gather at University House in 1993 to celebrate the success of the Canberra Raiders. Left to right: Ricky Stuart (Canberra Raiders), Mal Meninga (Raiders Captain), Sue Cameron (Department of Commerce, Faculty of Economics and Commerce), Russell Craig (Professor of Commerce), Amanda Hart (Secretary's Office), Paul Osborne (Raiders), Geoffrey Caldwell (Director, Continuing Education) and Peter Green (Business Manager, Central Areas).

ANUGSA was intended to protect its members and to advance the interests of the University generally. Although the Association never registered as a union, it negotiated with the administration over salaries and conditions, and worked hard to improve community facilities for non-academic staff. From the late 1960s it yielded some of its industrial relations functions to a number of unions, including the Health and Research Employees Association, which sought to bring the University within the ambit of the conciliation and arbitration system. Senior staff in the Chancelry thought this was a mistake: the general staff would do better to discuss their difficulties 'as colleagues in the University community' than as claimants conducting their disputes in front of an arbitrator. Nevertheless, the trend was towards unionisation. In 1972 the ANU Administrative and Allied Officers Association (AAOA), representing middle managers and some professional staff, became the first association in Australia made up entirely of university staff to achieve federal registration as a union.

So long as there was little to argue about, the unions functioned harmoniously alongside the traditional collegiate patterns of government. But as finances became tighter and outside pressures more insistent, relations became strained. In 1977 they reached breaking point during a sharp conflict with the AAOA. Under the pugnacious leadership of Peter Grimshaw, an ex-boxer, old Papua New Guinea hand and from 1964 Business Manager in RSSS and RSPacS, AAOA members argued that their salaries lagged behind those of administrators in comparable positions in government, and fought hard to increase their salaries while retaining existing superior conditions. The University appointed an external consultant, who recommended a new salary scale. Then, when the government introduced wage fixation guidelines intended to put an end to 'sweetheart' deals between employer and employee, the ANU was obliged to set the consultant's recommendations aside. The union reacted angrily. Several years passed before the issue was resolved.

The troubles between the University and the AAOA suggested a new era in industrial relations. So did the appointment as Industrial Officer in 1980 of a former industrial relations executive with a large mining company, and the registration about the same time of the ANU Academic Staff Association, as an 'organisation of employees', comparable, as the Personnel Officer David Gill put it, with the Waterside Workers' Federation and the Painters and Dockers Union. Gill was untroubled by the trend: 'What we have witnessed at ANU', he remarked, 'is no more than a slightly accelerated catching up with the realities of modern life'.

A series of events in 1982 suggested that the University had caught up entirely. As part of a campaign for the introduction of a 38-hour week for building and metals trades unionists, the ACT Trades and Labour Council demanded that members of its affiliated unions on campus be given one leisure day in twenty. The University, with a reduced budget and a new determination to resist future wage claims, said no, whereupon the unions called members out on strike and set up pickets at the entrances to the campus.

This was the ANU's first direct experience of strike action. Many staff found it distasteful. As pickets extended into a second week, some complained that the strikers were interfering with mail deliveries, the supply of chemicals, or provisions for laboratory animals. Others argued that the University was confrontational in its approach to the unions. Most simply wanted to get on with their business. The University's Industrial Officer was burnt in effigy outside the Chancelry. Eventually, after two and a half weeks of pickets, the University yielded the 38-hour week to members of the building unions and the strikers went back to work.

At the next Council meeting, over one hundred members of three of the major general staff unions mounted a protest against the University's industrial relations policy by holding a silent vigil outside the Chancelry. Perhaps they were right to protest: the University was making heavy weather of its relations with the unions. On the other hand, the problems were large and unfamiliar. Having once had almost complete charge of negotiations with its staff, the University now faced the prospect of being entirely subservient to outside forces, the unions on the one hand, and government regulations and the arbitration tribunals on the other. Uncertain of their own role, the University's negotiators moved shakily from one crisis to another. To complicate matters, University employees were members of over twenty unions, each with its own agenda.

There was also the unresolved question about the role of unions in a collegiate system of governance. Unions, in a traditional industrial relations environment, existed to serve the interests of their members, who were expected to show loyalty to the unions in return; yet a traditional collegiate university demanded the allegiance of the university community. Were collegiality and industrial processes in conflict with one another?

Following the turbulence of the early 1980s, relations between the administration and the unions were more harmonious, as they were in the nation at large. The administration grew more adept at handling industrial issues, while the unions became less belligerent in pursuing their claims. There were also fewer unions for the administration to deal with: several amalgamations culminated in the formation in the 1990s of the National Tertiary Education Union, which embraced both academic and general staff; though whether it would help sustain the notion of the University as a single community remained to be seen.

≋ Mixed reviews

After Titterton had been prised out of the headship of the Research School of Physical Sciences, an acting director occupied the position for a year while an electoral committee searched the world for a suitable successor. They found one in Robert Street, who had been appointed in 1960 foundation Professor and Chairman of the Department of Physics at Monash University. There he had put together an outstanding team of physicists, specialising in solid state and low temperature physics, and had built up a strong graduate school which had produced over seventy PhDs in a dozen or so years. He was also prominent on national committees relating to science, technology and education, especially the Australian Research Grants Committee, of which he had been Chairman since 1972.

Arriving in Canberra in 1974, Street was the first 'outsider' to head the Physical Sciences school. His appointment suggests one of the many ways in which the ANU benefited from the revolution in higher education following the Murray Report: the new universities and the expanded old ones provided a source of talent within Australia that had not been available in the late 1940s.

A gently-spoken and wickedly-humoured Yorkshireman, Street understood universities well. But he soon found that RSPhysS presented problems to challenge the most profound understanding. His first report to Council identified a malaise: 'For a variety of historical reasons the School had developed as a collection of independent, generally non-interacting departments, regarding themselves as largely autonomous'. The departments, he explained, had widely different philosophical bases, ranging from Engineering Physics, which had as its main objective the use of the homopolar generator, to theoretically oriented departments in which the activities of individuals were of prime concern. Student numbers were declining and the staff were getting older. There was a need for new blood and new ideas: but 'the great inertia of existing institutions' was likely to stand in the way.

To get things moving, Street persuaded the faculty board to advertise several senior appointments in any area of the school's activities. This in itself was quite a coup, breaking down traditional departmental allegiances. Then he managed to win the board's support for asking the electoral committee, which was made up partly of senior scientists from outside the University, to help in the assessment and evaluation of the school's activities: in other words, to review its work. This was a revolution, not merely for the ANU but for the higher education system generally. There had been reviews before, including an assessment of RSSS by a distinguished visitor in 1959 in 1959; and since 1973 there had been internal reviews in The Faculties each time a head of department had retired or resigned: but none had been as intensive and wide-ranging as the one Street now set in train. And so far, no university or part of a university had submitted itself to a full-scale review with a significant number of external reviewers.

Some outside members of the electoral committee had serious misgivings about what Street was asking them to do. 'The idea of a Faculty enquiring into the "intrinsic value of lines of research" and the "relative importance of various programmes in the context of

Robert Street, about the time of his appointment as Director of RSPhysS in 1974.

international research effort" fills me with dismay', wrote the Deputy Vice-Chancellor of the University of Adelaide. And the Vice-Chancellor at Newcastle wondered 'if members of the Faculty Board would be pleased to have outsiders stomping around and making gratuitous comments about their work. If so, they are very enlightened ...'

No sooner had the committee begun its review than the University experienced sharp cuts to its funding. So instead of choosing new areas for development, the committee could do no more than recommend the best use of existing resources. With the help of 56 outside assessors, many unsparing in their criticisms, it worked through each of the ten departments and units, weighing the quality of specific research programs and looking at the work of individual staff. Its conclusions varied markedly from one department or unit to the next, ranging from high praise for Applied Mathematics, which had 'an excellent record of achievement', tackled worthwhile problems and functioned as a team; to pointed criticism of Engineering Physics, which cost too much, spread its resources too thinly, and produced too little. According to the committee, some sections of the school appeared to have no clear idea of how their long-term objectives related to fundamental scientific questions; there was a preoccupation with the development of equipment and facilities for their own sake; and there was little enthusiasm for new and exciting areas of physics and mathematics.

The committee recommended remedies. Some activities should be terminated and others encouraged. Rigid departmental structures should be broken down and replaced by groups pursuing specific research activities. Resources should be allocated on the basis of academic merit and fulfilment of the school's role as a national centre of research excellence. Together the recommendations gave the Director the licence he wanted for wholesale reform.

But Street made two serious errors. First, rather than ensuring that the committee derive its powers of review from outside the school, he sought the approval of the faculty board for the evaluation process. What the board had given it could just as easily take away: as the official initiator of the review, it could control the outcome.

Second, he chaired the committee. This meant that staff members who did not like what the report had to say saw him as one of 'them' rather than one of 'us'. Many also assumed that he was the author of the report. This was untrue: in fact, the external members set the tone of the comments. Nevertheless, as chairman he was invariably associated with the committee's report; and if the report should fail, his own status and ambitions for the school would surely be compromised.

When the report reached the faculty board, reactions ranged from delight to outrage. Those who believed that the school was due for a shake-up looked forward to immediate action; others refused to accept the report as an accurate portrayal of the their activities and scientific worth, suggesting that Street himself was ill informed about the work of some departments. Titterton, still a professor in Nuclear Physics, told one of his overseas colleagues that the committee had been made up of 'inappropriate personnel' including competitors within the University for funds, 'a declared enemy of the School through his activities in fighting for Earth Sciences', a theoretical chemist, and two scientists who were not even members of the Academy!

'So I suppose one should not be too surprised that the report is as bad as it is.'

Street, said his colleague Barry Ninham, Professor of Applied Mathematics and one of the school's Young Turks, numbered among his attributes 'patience, decency, loyalty and a firm belief in the ultimate reasonableness of men'. These were feeble weapons against inertia, especially when buttressed by tradition. Confronted by the prospect of radical change, the faculty board went through the motions of approving new guidelines for the allocation of resources but stalled when the time came to implement them. Ninham, fearing that the review would come to nothing, appealed to Low to intervene: 'I plead, urge and beg you to exhibit your firmness quickly. Something must be seen to be done.' But what could be done? The professors and other senior staff who made up the faculty board were tenured and therefore almost invulnerable; and they were used to having their own way. Low, at Street's request, had already approved some additional appointments to bring in new blood. Beyond that, Street had little room to manoeuvre. But the ferment injected by his review was working and the school would never be the same again.

Early in 1978 Street left the ANU to become Vice-Chancellor at the University of Western Australia. After another interregnum, he was replaced by John Carver, who found it easier in harder times to bring about many of the changes that the review had foreshadowed.

If the immediate impact of Street's review was limited, its effects on the whole system of higher education were profound, in ways that Street himself could scarcely have imagined. As the review was taking place, Low recognised that the process offered opportunities for bringing about change in the new era, and decided to introduce a system of reviews for the whole Institute of Advanced Studies. 'As I see it', he told the University in his 1976 report, 'the essential purpose of any review is to help a School, a Department, or whatever, however good it may be already, to be better yet'. The fact that the older schools were now over 25 years old was sufficient reason, he said, to have a close look at them. He anticipated that reviews would in due course become 'part of our academic culture'.

So, one by one, all the research schools were reviewed, Social Sciences, Pacific Studies and the John Curtin School in 1978, Biological Sciences in 1979, Chemistry in 1982 and Earth Sciences in 1983. In the RSPhysS review, members of the University had been in the majority. The new reviews were each conducted by a panel of four or five members, not more than one of whom was a member of the University. The system was promptly extended to faculties, centres and units throughout the University, which were subjected to scrutiny by a panel which included at least one outsider.

Among the research schools, John Curtin came first and set a pattern. The committee of four, two from Britain, one from France and one from the United States, chaired by the Director of the National Institute of Medical Research in London, Sir Arnold Burgen, spent thirteen working days in Canberra, during which they talked with the Vice-Chancellor, the Director of the school and other senior members of the University, visited every department and unit, absorbed reports from numerous referees, and wrote a ten-page report, along with a confidential annex on specific departments and individuals. Later reports were sometimes longer: the Earth

Sciences report was over fifty pages. But generally they reflected a similar degree of intensive effort by a small team of academics eminent in their disciplines.

While the committees' conclusions and recommendations inevitably differed from one to the next, the similarities were also striking. Each commented on the achievements of the relevant school to date, with varying degrees of enthusiasm. The panel for Earth Sciences declared unequivocally that the school was 'an international leader in its field' and that some of its members had made contributions of worldwide influence. The John Curtin committee concluded that the school had greatly enhanced the development of medical sciences in Australia and given the country an enviable reputation in its field, while the Pacific Studies reviewers acknowledged the great measure of success the school had achieved, especially in relation to Papua New Guinea and the Pacific islands. The Biological Sciences and Chemistry reviewers were complimentary, but more reserved, while the Social Sciences panel found it easier to praise certain individuals and parts than to offer encomiums on the whole. On balance, the reviewers concluded that the schools were good, sometimes very good, but no better than they ought to have been in a well-funded environment devoted wholly to research.

Looking for means of improvement, the committees tended to focus on problems relating to their objectives, leadership and structure. The Social Scientists were reminded that the appropriate role of the school could hardly be the same as it was 30 years ago, when there was little postgraduate work in the social sciences in other Australian universities and The Faculties did not exist. There should now be less emphasis on training, more stimulation of research effort throughout Australia, fewer tenured appointments, and more collaborative research, especially on Australian topics. Similarly, the Chemists were told that they needed to sharpen their research objectives, while members of RSPacS were urged to identify priorities within a more precise definition of 'the Pacific'.

Leadership was seen to be a problem in the Research School of Chemistry. The panel challenged the system of changing deans every three years, which was a tenet of the founders. Where Birch, Craig and Nyholm had seen movement at the top as a means of encouraging flexibility, the committee judged that the system inhibited change, since it gave control over resources to the faculty board, which distributed funds on 'an egalitarian rather than a scientific basis'. What was needed, said the committee, was a leader, appointed perhaps from outside the University, who would be there long enough to give the school a clearer sense of direction.

The John Curtin reviewers concluded that the heads of departments had too much power and the director too little. Perhaps recalling Florey's warning 30 years earlier about the dangers of departments developing into 'independent little kingdoms', the committee referred to a 'regal interpretation of the prerogatives of professors'. Departmental barriers were high, and departmental integrity, space, equipment and staffing were jealously defended. There was little concern for research priorities. To prove its point, the committee cited the Department of Medical Chemistry, which had been slowly declining in the previous decade. Medical Chemistry under Adrien Albert had never been exactly at home in the school; and when the Research School of Chemistry and the Department of Chemistry in SGS developed, his department became largely redundant. In 1968, with the retirement of Albert and several other senior staff members forthcoming, the school decided to wind the department down. But the situation was 'allowed to fester', and a decade later Medical Chemistry still consumed what the committee called 'an entirely inappropriate proportion' of school resources.

So the reviewers proposed radical changes, including the total abolition of the departmental structure and its replacement by flexible groups, similar to those in RSC. They also concluded that the office of director was central to the well-being of the school and that its authority should be strengthened. There should be provision for the director to be creative and to realise 'some of his dreams of a finer institution'.

The Biological Sciences reviewers likewise focused on problems of structure; and while they did not go so far as to recommend that the school revert to its original structure based on groups, they did urge departmental heads to try to identify with the school's 'larger objectives'. The Social Sciences reviewers remarked that their school had calcified into departments, and that 'once a departmental structure is established it is remarkably resistant to change of any sort'. Their answer was to abolish departments, set up three divisions under associate directors, and introduce flexible groups.

The review process was not necessarily a pleasant one, with reactions varying from willing acceptance of some of the comments to outright opposition. Some recommendations were promptly implemented, others, such as the proposed restructuring of RSSS, vigorously resisted or quietly ignored. The impact of the report on RSBS was diminished by what the school's Director, Bernard John, called its 'highly emotive language'; and the inclusion in several reports of confidential sections relating to specific departments and staff opened sores that rankled in some cases, such as that of Arthur Burns, for many years to come.

Whatever their effects in specific areas, the reviews forced members of the University to look hard at the overall objectives of the research schools, individually and collectively; to consider large issues, such as the relationship between academic structures and research creativity and productivity; and above all, to see themselves as part of a wider higher education system in which the place of the Institute was not absolutely certain. What *was* certain was that the review process, having once been set in motion, was irreversible. Low had warned: 'we have to be careful that we do not overdo all of this'. But who was to say when enough was enough?

Because the Institute was unique, reviews of the research schools almost inevitably opened up basic questions about their nature and purpose. By contrast, reviews of the faculties, and of specific departments within them, whose teaching and research objectives were clearly understood, ought to have been straightforward. They usually were. Occasionally, however, a review panel pointed a faculty or department in a new direction, and made other suggestions which significantly changed the shape of the University. For example, the 1982 report of the Faculty of Economics review committee recommended the creation of a new degree, the Bachelor of Commerce, to provide more suitable courses for students who wished to pursue a career in accounting and who were deterred by the extremely demanding and heavily theoretical courses then on offer.

Asian Studies was the one faculty in the University unique in Australia, and like the research schools it posed some unique and testing problems for reviewers. The faculty was the direct descendant of the School of Oriental Languages, which had been established in Canberra University College in 1952 to provide language training for diplomats and other federal public servants. The first language courses were in modern and classical Chinese, followed by modern and classical Japanese, and Bahasa Indonesia and Malay. There were also courses which introduced students to the 'history and civilization' of Asian countries. Hans Bielenstein, the first professor of Oriental Languages, wanted the school to be seen as providing more than mere language teaching, and at his request its name was changed to Oriental Studies. Following amalgamation, it was given the status of a faculty. Bielenstein left for Columbia University in 1961 and was succeeded (as Professor of Chinese) by another distinguished Swede, N.G.D. Malmqvist, who became the faculty's first Dean. While these early professors gave Oriental Studies strong beginnings, they also tended to make the faculty perceive Asia through European rather than Australian eyes.

Arthur Basham in the 1970s. Photograph by Chi Chi Beaton.

Over the next two decades the faculty won a reputation for profound scholarship in various areas. At one time or another, several eminent people occupied chairs: Liu Ts'un-yan in the Department of Chinese, J.W. de Jong in South Asian and Buddhist Studies, and A.L. Basham, a guru of South Asian history who personified the otherwise intangible notion of Oriental Civilizations. The University Library, in stubborn competition with the National Library of Australia, built up one of the finest Asian collections in the world. In 1971 the faculty hosted and Basham presided over the world's foremost conference of researchers on Asia, the International Congress of Orientalists, which was attended by some 1200 people and, despite the contretemps mentioned in chapter 10 about whether or not academics should speak out on political issues, won for the faculty worldwide acclaim.

Liu Ts'un-yan in 1972 with a Buddhist shrine, part of the Lyttleton-Taylor gift to the University.

In teaching too, the faculty was a marked success, attracting large numbers of students. In 1968, a boom year, total enrolments nearly doubled, creating a need for repeat lectures in Asian Civilizations. Enrolments in Indonesian outnumbered those in French, which had traditionally been the most popular foreign language course. Then in 1972 new enrolments increased by over 30 per cent, especially in Chinese, which the Dean, Liu Ts'un-yan, attributed in part to President Nixon's 'ping-pong' diplomacy with the People's Republic of China. The faculty also extended its language course offerings to include Hindi and Thai, and the AUC accorded the University special status, with additional funding, for teaching 'languages in lesser demand'.

In 1970 the name of the faculty was changed to Asian Studies. At the Board of the School of General Studies, Basham explained on behalf of the faculty that the term 'Oriental Studies' was now inappropriate, because 'Oriental', as well as being geographically vague, literally meant 'eastern', which Asia in relation to Australia certainly was not. Also, the term had 'an exotic flavour of mystery and chinoiserie'. Yet

Bastions of the Faculty of Asian Studies: Luise Hercus and J.T.F. (Jos) Jordens present J.W. de Jong (centre) with a volume on Indological and Buddhist Studies, published in honour of Professor de Jong on his sixtieth birthday in 1982. Photograph by Dave Paterson.

Basham himself was associated with that mysterious view of Asia, or at least part of it, having published in 1954 (well before coming to Canberra) *The Wonder that was India*, an encyclopedic survey of the subcontinent before the coming of the Muslims in the sixteenth century, which ranged in subject matter across languages, literature, religions, government and the arts. Courses in the Department of Asian Civilizations, as it had now become, continued to reflect grand visions of Asian history, institutions and thought, but rarely ventured into the present. So while students studied languages both classical and modern, their non-language courses offered little sense of relevance to Australia's growing involvement with Asia, and still less to their possible future careers.

In the meantime several other universities, including Sydney, Melbourne and Monash, had developed Asian studies courses (often staffed by ANU graduates) which offered strong competition to Asian Studies at the ANU. While the faculty continued to house a wider range of studies relating to Asian languages and cultures than anywhere else in Australia, it was not, as the Dean, A.H. Johns conceded in 1976, a national beacon attracting the best students from throughout the country. About this time, enrolments in Asian studies were declining everywhere. Bound by tradition and starved of resources to embark on new initiatives, members of the faculty looked to the future with a sense of impending crisis.

In this context, Low appointed a review committee, chaired by himself and comprising a dozen other members from inside and outside the faculty, including the Director of the School of Oriental and African Studies in the University of London. As the committee recognised, the faculty had to confront the key question: 'How should Asia be studied?'. Implicit in this was a conflict, faced by every institution which sought to teach or organise knowledge along regional lines, between regional approaches and traditional disciplinary structures. There were also what the committee called 'perennial controversies', including the place of language training and the relative emphasis given to classical and modern studies.

The reviewers remarked that the faculty was not well situated to address these issues, and suggested changes to make it so, especially doing away with departments, which they saw as barriers to flexibility and creative thinking. They also did some creative thinking of their own. After deciding that the faculty should be retained as a separate entity, on the grounds that no other Australian university offered this distinct approach to Asian studies, they recommended a sharp change in direction. While the undergraduate teaching program should remain securely anchored in an Asian language, students should also be given a strong background in one of the disciplines relating to Asia, which would be offered by departments in other faculties. They would thus receive a more broadly based degree; and the faculty, now at the periphery of teaching in the humanities, would be brought into the mainstream, with programs to which the University as a whole would contribute. Within the faculty, departments should be abolished and replaced by centres based on area studies. By these means, Asian Studies would achieve 'a new kind of stature' within the University.

Many of the committee's suggestions were implemented in the early 1980s, and for a time the future seemed promising. But things began to go wrong. Although centres were introduced in 1983, against forthright opposition from some departments, before long the faculty was drifting again into separate compartments, mostly speaking (sometimes literally) their own languages, and unable to present a collective front to the rest of the University or the outside world. The committee failed to ensure that departments in other faculties were obliged to teach courses relating to Asia; and when representatives of the disciplines did teach such courses, they were often perceived as doing so from a western vantage point, without adequate consideration of historical and cultural contexts. Student numbers continued to decline; retiring staff were not replaced; and when from the mid-1980s enrolments began to rise, again in line with a national trend, the depleted staff were scarcely able to handle the load. In 1993, when another review committee applied itself to the faculty's problems, Asian Studies was once again facing an uncertain future.

Low's seven-year term as Vice-Chancellor ended in 1982. He would have liked to remain at least a little longer, but there was no precedent for extending a vice-chancellor's appointment beyond its original term; and in any case, many people in the University thought he had stayed long enough. Like every vice-chancellor before and after, he too had been reviewed on an almost daily basis by members of the University community; and the reviews he had received were noticeably mixed.

On the one hand, many praised his efforts to get out into the faculties, schools and departments, to bring people from diverse disciplines and sections together, to represent the University boldly in public forums, to vigorously defend the institution when it was under attack. On the other, many were critical of some of his appointments, offended by what somebody referred to as his 'episcopal style', and alarmed by his introduction of a 'new era' when they were quite happy with the old one, especially when the new era brought with it a potentially destructive system of reviews. Others were alarmed by the University's deteriorating relations with government and dismayed by his evident failure to halt the trend.

Low was 'a university man', a stout upholder of university traditions, with a tendency to see the university as self-contained. It was appropriate that his next appointment after leaving Canberra was as Smuts Professor of the History of the British Commonwealth and a Fellow of Churchill College, Cambridge, and that in due course he became President of Clare Hall, Cambridge. The problem was that university traditions, if not directly under attack, were becoming less relevant in Australia during the early 1980s. Also, Low's international perspective and networks were less valuable than they might have been in earlier decades, when the University was seeking to make its mark in the academic world. Now it was more important to know how the system worked in nearby government departments and in Parliament House on the other side of the lake.

Low also had the misfortune to be in charge of the University at a time when its financial situation was getting rapidly worse. No doubt there had to be a tighter ship; yet Low believed, like Copland in more affluent times, that a vice-chancellor's instinct should be to say 'yes' whenever an academic came to him with a good idea. (Other vice-chancellors have reflected that the art of being a successful vice-chancellor was knowing how to say 'no'.) So, as his term neared an end, Low could still be seen setting a course at the helm, encouraging the crew, or presiding at the captain's table. Unfortunately, many of his crew feared that the ship was making little headway in a choppy sea.

Crawford for one had decided it was time for a change. As Low's term neared an end he approached Peter Karmel, currently Chairman of the Commonwealth Tertiary Education Commission (successor to the three peak higher education bodies, including the AUC), a former Vice-Chancellor of Flinders University in Adelaide, and Australia's best-known tertiary administrator, who knew better than anybody the ins and outs of government and higher education. Many hoped that under Karmel's guidance the University would enter another new era.

Change without growth   12

Managing

Karmel's appointment was indeed a coup. Announcing his acceptance, Crawford described him without exaggeration as 'the leading figure in Australian tertiary education'. Educated at Melbourne and Cambridge universities, he had lectured in Economics at Melbourne before being appointed in 1950, at the age of 28, to a chair of Economics at Adelaide, where he remained until 1962. During the 1960s he was Principal-Designate, then foundation Vice-Chancellor of the Flinders University of South Australia, as well as Chairman of the Interim Council of the University of Papua and New Guinea and then its first Chancellor. He had contributed to numerous government commissions and agencies, more often than not as chairman. Most significantly, he had been chairman of the Australian Universities Commission and its successor, the Commonwealth Tertiary Education Commission, since 1971, which suggested, as well as exceptional competence, a rapport with governments of both persuasions. His one drawback was that he was approaching 60, and so could give the University only five and a half years.

Karmel was of medium height, portly and bespectacled, with grey curly hair, an interesting asymmetrical face resulting from surgery years before, and a secret penchant for sweet biscuits. Quintessentially Australian, he had an irreverent sense of humour and a total lack of pretence or pomposity. His style was spare: metaphors, ornate or otherwise, seldom passed his lips. In committees he had a rare capacity for putting people at their ease and drawing out what they had to offer. Don Aitkin, Professor of Political Science in RSSS and Chairman of the Board of the Institute of Advanced Studies from 1984, who sat with him through many meetings, likened him to Uncle Wattleberry in Norman Lindsay's *The Magic Pudding*:

> His prevailing good temper, quickness of mind and grasp of the whole made him a pleasure to work with, but like Uncle Wattleberry he was capable of 'bounding and plunging' with rage when someone pushed him too far. A few Institute academics had a rare facility for inducing his rage.

Gregarious by nature, he nevertheless spent most of his time inside the Chancelry, provoking occasional grumbles from the provinces that the Vice-Chancellor was invisible.

His association with the ANU dated back to the war years, when he was based in Canberra as a research officer in the Commonwealth Bureau of Census and Statistics, and lectured part time at Canberra University College to students in Diplomatic Studies. Many years later, in the 1970s, he was approached twice about the prospect of becoming Vice-Chancellor. Then he said no; but by 1982, having watched senior colleagues in the public service change abruptly on retirement 'from rooster to feather duster', he decided that the University would be a better place to retire from, and that the ANU offered a fitting end to his formal career.

Coming directly from the Tertiary Education Commission, Karmel viewed the ANU as part of a larger system. That gave him a well-informed appreciation of its strengths in teaching and research, and a clear recognition of its weaknesses. In the early 1970s he had listened, somewhat bemused, as Ross Hohnen had justified the University's shorter working hours for general staff on the grounds that the National University should take the lead in working conditions. Ten years later he thought that, although the ANU had suffered from budget cuts, it was still a very well funded operation compared with the state universities. He also thought that affluence had given rise to some bad habits, especially the tendency to seek more money for any proposed innovation. In the harsh new environment of scarce resources, the University had to mend its ways. He was convinced that change without growth was possible: the ANU could continue to be innovative, but only if it made better use of what it already had.

When Low had tried to deliver the same message, albeit gently through his 1 per cent levy on the research schools, many of his listeners had tried not to hear. Karmel, however, commanded attention with an authority derived from outside the University. Also, after seven years of attrition, staff were starting to accept that constraint might be a permanent affliction they would have to learn to live with. Perhaps Karmel the economist would be able to tell them how.

Signals from government made his task easier. At the election of March 1983, less than a year after Karmel had moved into the Chancelry, the conservative Fraser government was replaced by a Labor administration led by R.J.L. Hawke, who 26 years earlier had made his presence known beside the ornamental pond at University House. While education and research were not election issues, many hoped with Manning Clark that 'the days of unleavened bread' were over. They were soon disappointed. The new ministers were anxious above all to portray themselves as sound economic managers. The education sector was expected to provide 'value for money', which could be measured chiefly through its contribution to employment and the economy. Hawke's Minister for Education and Youth Affairs (and ANU graduate), Susan Ryan, began to talk about the universities as 'bastions of privilege'. Efficiency and effectiveness became the buzz words of the era.

Before Labor took office, Karmel had already begun a series of management reforms. Shortly after his arrival he noticed that, although the University had an academic Department of Accounting and Public Finance, its own accounting procedures were primitive: computerised record systems that had been progressively installed (and corrupted) since the 1960s were mostly inadequate and unreliable, financial reporting to parliament was a year behind schedule, and substantial special purpose funds scattered around the campus defied satisfactory management. While the ANU's arrangements may have been superior to those of many other Australian universities, they were far behind 'best practice' (a term that was yet to enter the politicians' lexicon) in large private enterprises or government. So he appointed Allan Barton, Professor of Accounting and

Peter Karmel, Vice-Chancellor from 1982 to 1987. Photograph by Bob Cooper.

an old colleague from Adelaide days, to take control of the finances as Treasurer. Barton proceeded over a period of some years to bring the system into line with modern management and accounting principles. The University's investments were consolidated and enhanced. Just in time, the ANU was equipped to meet increasing demands by government for information and analyses covering its finances and operations.

Karmel faced a more formidable challenge in the need to reform the University's decision-making procedures, especially as they related to the allocation of resources. Most members of the University, if asked to define in a word its form of government, would probably have responded that it was 'collegial', the term traditionally associated with the government of universities. Yet collegiality, of the kind often associated with Oxbridge colleges, where the master and fellows agreed to agree or disagree over a glass of sherry, was much diluted in Australia in the 1980s. Size had got in the way. So had diminishing resources: it was easier to apply collegial procedures when everybody's needs were more or less satisfied.

Collegiality was, in any case, located chiefly among the professors and other senior academics, whose authority, based on academic distinction, filtered through the university. They in turn were receptive to influence from more junior staff, who therefore saw themselves as part of the collegial system. During 'the Troubles' of the late 1960s and early 1970s, many professors, including Fin Crisp and Manning Clark, when confronted with demands for democracy had tended to yield their leadership and decision-making roles, sometimes even resigning in preference to sharing their powers. The influence of the college of professors was thus eroded, leaving no one system of government in its place.

At the ANU when Karmel arrived collegiality existed alongside almost every other known form of government, from autocracy to democracy, with a dash of anarchy. Owing to the dual nature of the University, its patterns of government were more complicated than those of its counterparts in the states. There were two academic boards (not including the Professorial Board, which rarely met), as there had been since amalgamation in 1960. The research schools were administered by appointed directors, the faculties by elected deans. Patterns of leadership varied from one school or faculty to the next, depending on its historical origins and the personalities in office at a particular time. At the departmental level, variations were even more extreme, ranging from highly democratic structures with significant student representation to feudal baronies, the vestiges of an earlier era.

The result was a system ill suited to setting priorities and planning for change. Karmel recognised that the University had to be managed, which implied a hierarchy of responsibility from the vice-chancellor down. He also understood that its system of government had to retain elements of the collegial model by taking account of the collective views of the teachers and researchers who embodied the University's intellectual resources and creative energy. As he later reflected, the old and new models of governance did not blend naturally together: 'tension between collegial and managerial styles is bound to be chronic'.

Karmel sought to improve management procedures on both sides of the campus. In The Faculties, he tried to replace the system of elected deans by one in which they were appointed by Council, and therefore responsible to it. When this proved too hard, he encouraged the deans to see themselves as part of a larger system, accountable to the vice-chancellor and committed to the welfare of the whole. In the research schools, he supported a new breed of directors who were committed to reform.

The Institute presented the largest management challenge. Its main problem, wrote Aitkin, who chaired its Board from 1984 to 1987, was that it had no corporate identity: 'the seven research schools were the reality, while the Institute was simply a name used to group them'. As had been the case since the University's inception, the individual research schools were all-powerful. There was no adequate mechanism for assessing priorities or redistributing resources, which were therefore allocated on historical lines. Within the schools, too, one year's budget chiefly determined the shape of the next. Karmel expressed the problem succinctly: 'History is very powerful'.

Pressure from outside provided the immediate occasion for a thorough review of resource allocation procedures. In 1984 the Commonwealth Tertiary Education Commission, sensing the changing mood in government about the value and direction of research, asked each university to review its current practices for managing research resources, 'with a view to establishing a strategy aimed at achieving the most effective use of funds at present available'. Karmel responded by setting up two committees, one for The Faculties and one for the Institute.

To conduct the inquiry in the Institute, he chose three younger members of the senior staff with high reputations who were known to be impatient with the existing system and keen to promote change: Peter Doherty from the John Curtin School, Jacob Israelachvili from Physical Sciences, and Don Aitkin who, as Chairman of the Board of the Institute, was asked to take the chair. Aitkin in particular knew the Institute well. In the 1960s and early 1970s he had been a PhD scholar and member of staff in Political Science, RSSS; and in 1980, after eight years as a professor at Macquarie University, he returned to a chair in his old department. He was also a member of the Australian Research Grants Committee, which gave him a good view of the Institute from outside. Youthful in appearance, and fluent in speech and on paper, he was regarded as an iconoclast, partly because he wrote an opinionated weekly column for a national newspaper. Journalism was always a risky undertaking for an academic, and Aitkin heightened the risk by writing in a style that almost every reader could understand.

Don Aitkin, newly appointed Professor of Political Science, RSSS, in 1980. Photograph by Vladimir Stojanovic.

Aitkin and his colleagues prepared a report which pulled no punches. Observing that these were 'testing times', they suggested a range of reforms to help the Institute survive in the harsher climate, including the reallocation of resources across schools, a mechanism for strategic planning, and a more hard-headed approach to poor performance by departments and individuals. They recommended that heads of schools should have more power and heads of departments less, that departments be replaced where appropriate by research groups, that the numbers of tenured staff be substantially reduced, that academics become less dependent on 'battalions of technical and other support staff'.

These were fighting words, which provoked a fierce reaction, especially in the natural science schools. At a meeting to discuss the report in the John Curtin School, one senior academic remarked that there would be plenty of money for research if the administrators 'got their snouts out of the trough'; in Physical Sciences, another accused the three reformers, along with Karmel and the Deputy Vice-Chancellor, Ian Ross, of being themselves poor performers: 'Your job is to provide money for *physics*, and you've *failed*!'. Others who might in previous years have resisted the recommendations resigned themselves to them, for there was general agreement with the committee that things would get worse before they got better.

Karmel accepted nearly all the recommendations. Even before the committee had submitted its report, he had initiated a program of strategic planning aimed at giving the University as a whole a new sense of direction. Strategic planning was, in his view, a means of releasing the University from the grip of its past. Hitherto, it had moved forward in accordance with historical precedents or ad hoc decisions. Strategic planning, he said, would promote the evolution of a pattern based on decisions taken deliberately, in the light of University-wide objectives. It would also enable the ANU to set out clearly what made it different from other institutions.

The notion of strategic planning was new in a university, and met with much indifference and some resistance. Teachers in The Faculties, their minds focused on the next lecture or tutorial, wondered what purpose it would serve. A few researchers, reminiscent of Hancock in the early years of planning, questioned whether the concept was inimical to creative and curiosity-driven research which, by its very nature, might lead in directions quite different from those originally planned.

Yet Karmel steered the plan firmly through the academic boards, eliciting contributions from each school, faculty and other section, and bringing them together into a coherent and compact whole. Published in late 1987, shortly before Karmel's retirement, it looked to the next five years, which he thought was as far as it was possible to plan in a university. Now that the structures for planning were in place, he anticipated that the process would be revisited annually, on a rolling basis. As well as giving expression to the Aitkin committee's recommendations, the plan acknowledged the Commonwealth Tertiary Education Commission's recent 'Review of efficiency and effectiveness in higher education', prepared by a committee which included Karmel and which emphasised, among other things, the importance of a managerial mode of operation. It was as up to date as anybody inside or outside the University could reasonably expect.

The plan specified goals for the University as a whole and its various parts, and outlined the ways those goals were to be achieved. For the first time since Coombs had proposed an exhortatory preamble to the original Act of Parliament, it set out in three dot points the University's 'broad objectives':

- the undertaking of research and scholarship which are at the highest levels by international standards, with emphasis on fundamental research and with provision for work on subjects of national importance to Australia;
- the provision of formal undergraduate and graduate courses which are at the forefront of those offered by Australian universities;
- the encouragement of links which make the research and scholarship of the University and the expertise of its members available to the Australian community.

Each point could be seen as dating from a different period in the University's history, the 1940s, the 1960s and the 1980s. Together they summarised implicitly how the University had evolved over the preceding 40 years.

But the focus of the plan was on the future; and here its authors were keen to emphasise 'flexibility and responsiveness', and the University's determination, through such means as strategic planning, to surmount the barriers to change, which they frankly acknowledged. Resources would be reallocated to activities which capitalised on existing strengths. Management processes would be streamlined. All in all, the plan fairly reflected its title, which the Vice-Chancellor had suggested, 'Commitment to change'.

Karmel regarded the development and publication of the Strategic Plan, the first produced by any Australian university, as his most satisfying achievement as Vice-Chancellor. Largely as a result of his foresight and perseverance, the ANU was better prepared than any of its counterparts to cope with anticipated changes in the external environment. Yet even Karmel, with his renowned ability to see around corners, could scarcely have imagined when he set out along the path of strategic planning, how tumultuous those changes would be.

Integration

In the early 1980s the ANU was still in two parts: some staff went so far as to suggest that it was two universities masquerading as one. To be sure, there was a central administration and other sections which served the University as a whole; and there were Crawford's 'bridges', the Centre for Resource and Environmental Studies and the Humanities Research Centre. Granted, too, many academics from the Institute contributed courses or individual lectures to departments in The Faculties; and, less frequently, academics from the two parts of the campus collaborated in research projects. But, taken together, these fell far short of academic integration.

Outsiders often found these arrangements perplexing. A review committee of the Faculty of Arts in 1982, comprising four external professors and the Dean, expressed astonishment at the overlap and sometimes duplication of academic interests between the faculty and the social science schools: 'To the "outside" members of the Committee, the present situation where a relatively impoverished Faculty exists cheek by jowl with relatively affluent Research Schools, especially where they have in many areas identical scholarly concerns and interest, seems rather bizarre'.

Ian Ross, acting as Vice-Chancellor after Low had stepped down, reflected that, now that amalgamation had 'come of age', the time had come to take a fresh look at the relationship between the Institute and The Faculties; so he set up an 'Interface Committee' to look into the matter. His own view was that the University had been oversensitive about pooling its resources in order to achieve common goals.

Yet there were sturdy barriers keeping them apart. One was the formula by which the teaching departments were staffed, which was based on student numbers. In Ross's view, the faculties were overzealous in allocating staff 'strictly on the basis of bottoms on chairs'. With departments diligently watching one another to see that none received more than its share, there was a fear that any department which benefited through help from the Institute might be penalised. Hence cooperative teaching arrangements were, according to Ross, 'scattered, irregular and even furtive'. Even the Chemists, their buildings physically linked, defied the plans of the founders of the research school and tended to keep to themselves. Collaboration on research was likewise impeded by the different government funding arrangements for each part of the University which made it difficult for staff from the Institute and The Faculties to seek support jointly for the one project.

On top of these structural problems, the resentments of the 1960s had not entirely evaporated. Manning Clark, now retired from his chair in the Faculty of Arts but much a part of the University, first as a Library Fellow and then as a Visiting Fellow, could still refer with heavy irony to those 'great minds' in the Institute. And young lecturers, struggling to maintain their output of publications against the burden of increased teaching loads, looked enviously to their colleagues in the research schools, who still enjoyed superior conditions.

At the same time, there were compelling reasons for bringing the Institute and The Faculties closer together. The academic arguments were obvious. The structural divisions of the University, along with the growing segmentation of knowledge, meant that some disciplines appeared in many different shapes and forms across the campus. Economics, for example, was represented in the departments of Economics, Economic History and Statistics (Econometrics), and the Centre for Research in Federal Financial Relations, in the Faculty of Economics; Economics, Economic History and the Urban Research Unit, RSSS; and Economics, the Centre for Development Studies, the Australia–Japan Centre and the North Australia Research Unit, RSPacS. Such complicated arrangements invited the question: was the University making best use of its human resources?

The same question could be asked about material resources, especially in relation to the Library. In the early 1980s there was still, as there had been since amalgamation, a single University Library, located in several different buildings. While all users were allowed access to the whole collection, which now comprised over one million volumes, 'the Chifley' was widely perceived as the undergraduate library and 'the Menzies' as the research library, where undergraduates were not especially welcome. There were also specific purpose collections, including those located in the John Curtin School and the Faculty of Law, and the new Life Sciences Library, which served the needs of researchers and undergraduates alike.

As well as being inconvenient for users, the system was uneconomic. As book prices rose and academics were forced to make hard decisions about maintaining subscriptions to expensive journals, there was no room for duplication. Fortuitously, computer technology was opening the way to integration. In 1982 a review committee chaired by Ross recommended that the Library's holdings be rationalised, so that collections of similar materials would be located together without regard to their likely use for teaching or research. This was effected over the 1984–85 summer vacation, when truckloads of books and journals were carted from one building to another.

Many academics, unable to find books in the familiar places, cursed the changes; but they might better have cursed R.G. Menzies' decision over twenty years earlier to allow the plans for a dedicated research library to proceed.

Integration of the two parts of the University was also suggested by political considerations. Ross drew a lesson from the CSIRO which, since the time of the Whitlam government, had been having trouble maintaining its integrity, even though it was cherished as a national treasure. He concluded that, in view of the growing disposition to question the value to the nation of research for its own sake, the Institute was at considerable risk. The Faculties, on the other hand, their purpose guaranteed by the presence of students, were not. So far the Institute had found the University label to be a safe shelter: but, warned Ross, that might not always be so.

This was not the occasion to illustrate again the other horn of the dilemma: if the Institute, through a process of integration with The Faculties, were to lose its separate identity, then its claim to separate funding would disappear. Without the Institute, the ANU would become what Oliphant and others had always feared, 'just another university', funded chiefly in proportion to student numbers. That could mean the end of the ANU. The task therefore was to achieve as much academic integration as political realities would allow.

Graduate students offered an apparent means towards this end. By the early 1980s The Faculties had many more graduate students (including part-timers) than the Institute. While all of them were regulated by a single Graduate Degrees Committee, students in the same discipline but from opposite sides of the campus often had little to do with one another, unless they happened to meet at University House or through the Research Students' Association. There was no cohesive body of graduate students, and so no cohesive body of higher degree graduates who might promote the University in the wider world.

Midway through his vice-chancellorship, Low, who had created a graduate school at Sussex, initiated a review of graduate education. Chaired by Wang Gungwu, Professor of Far Eastern History and Low's successor as Director of the Research School of Pacific Studies, the committee analysed graduate education across the campus, drawing on an expanding body of literature on the subject from other parts of the world. Having initially supposed that only minor changes to the present system would be necessary, Wang and his colleagues decided that the system needed a complete overhaul, and proposed the creation of a graduate school. Graduate education would be reorganised around a number of fields, such as Anthropology, Computer Science, Forestry, and Modern European Languages and Literature, each of which would bring together under a coordinator relevant staff from all parts of the University. The academic benefits, said Wang, were substantial: a graduate school would offer more flexible programs; instead of competing for students, departments would work together to attract the best graduates within and outside Australia; students would have access to the most appropriate supervisors and advisers from any part of the campus; and they would have much increased opportunities for meeting with their peers.

The report was thorough and challenging, too challenging for most of the faculties and schools. Wang urged the University to accept the proposals as a whole, which enabled various committees to reject the whole by identifying weaknesses in its parts.

Among the faculties, Asian Studies and Science offered wholehearted support; Arts and Economics approved in principle but forecast problems in practice; Law, generally a law unto itself (like Law schools and faculties in most universities), was ready for the other parts of the University to do as they wished, so long as it was allowed to go its own way.

Opposition in the Institute was stronger still. Even in Wang's own school of Pacific Studies, the reaction to his report was at best mixed, the main concern of his colleagues being that the proposed graduate fields would make it more difficult for departments to choose students to fit in with their own research programs. The Physical Scientists remarked that the review put too much emphasis on course work and was too much influenced by vocational concerns; the Biological Scientists forecast decreased flexibility; the Chemists warned of an increased administrative load. All were concerned with a potential loss of autonomy, at school or departmental level. Behind most responses were fears that the proposed graduate school put the Institute at risk. Ted Ringwood, Professor of Geochemistry and soon to become Director of the Earth Sciences school, was explicit in early discussions with the committee: 'The Institute should remain true to the Centre of Excellence concept on which it was founded. This is as essential to Australia now as it was thirty years ago. Policies on graduate education should remain subservient to this objective.'

So while several of the committee's specific proposals were implemented, for example those relating to arrangements for graduate supervision, the report went the way of most reports that propose changes ahead of their time.

Several years later, its time appeared to come. In 1985 Aitkin's Resources Review Committee revived the concept of a graduate school, and in due course Karmel incorporated it in the University's first Strategic Plan. Where the Wang report had conceived the school chiefly as a means of providing improved facilities for students and making better use of the University's resources, the Strategic Plan presented it as an opportunity both to enrich the experience of graduate students and to 'mesh together the two halves of the University'. The graduate school would take its place alongside the Institute and The Faculties, allowing the ANU to emerge as an integrated organisation. This third stage of the University's development was a 'vision of the future'; and according to the Strategic Plan, it could be attained in the 1990s.

Council set the school rolling and by 1989 the Graduate School was ready to take in its first students. The school was organised much as Wang and his colleagues had intended, with graduate programs based on disciplines and drawing staff from across the University. Ray Spear, a burly, taciturn Nuclear Physicist, was appointed the first Dean, and he committed himself to making the school a success.

By now there was a new political environment, even more pressure on resources, and vigorous competition among the universities for graduate students. More than in previous years, the Institute seemed vulnerable to government interference. All this helped Spear achieve levels of cooperation that a decade earlier had seemed far beyond reach. Nevertheless, many parts of the University continued to resist the Graduate School as a challenge to local academic autonomy. The school remained a test of the University's determination and capacity to act as one.

Dean of the Graduate School, Ray Spear, in 1991. Photograph by Gavin Gilman.

Change and resistance in the John Curtin School

Change came harder in the John Curtin School than anywhere else on campus. Since Ennor's unhappy departure in 1967, three men had occupied successively the office of director. First there was Frank Fenner, who had taken on the job hoping to promote the intellectual coherence of the school. By the time he left over five years later to take up the headship of the Centre for Resource and Environmental Studies, he had decided that there was little a director could do to provide academic leadership, and that the most important positions in the school were the heads of departments. His successor, the Professor of Experimental Pathology Colin Courtice, who was nearing retirement, was generally regarded, and regarded himself, as a holding appointment. Frank Gibson, Professor of Biochemistry, accepted the job in 1977, more out of duty than enthusiasm, and administered the school wisely while spending as much time as possible in the laboratory. Both Courtice and Gibson were appointed from within the school, which helped sustain its members' understanding that directors should not direct.

The 1978 Review Committee challenged this assumption by suggesting that the school should have a creative director. When the time came shortly afterwards to replace Gibson (who had signified his wish not to continue), the University—through its electoral committee—took the hint and decided that, other things being equal, it would be better to recruit an outsider who was not committed to the status quo. The new director should have vitality, and a capacity to redirect the school's research emphasis and do something about its public image.

Sir Gustav Nossal, Macfarlane Burnet's successor as Director of the Walter and Eliza Hall Institute in Melbourne, was the committee's first choice, but he said no. On his recommendation, the committee approached Robert Porter, who had been Professor of Physiology at Monash University since 1967 and whose research interests were in the mechanisms by which the brain controls human movement. Aged in his late forties, Porter, like Florey, had been trained at Adelaide and Oxford. As a medical student on a Rhodes Scholarship, he had attended Florey's lectures on general pathology in the mid-1950s. A few years later in the Dunn School, he had worked in a laboratory adjacent to Florey's, and had engaged in occasional tea room conversation with the great man. Nossal described him as an extremely able all-rounder, who would provide 'dynamic, driving leadership to the whole enterprise'. Invited to an interview, Porter emphasised the need to promote the work of the school within Australia and to attract more students. The director, he said, should be able to persuade the faculty board to adopt new ideas and to lead the school in new directions, restoring it to the forefront of medical research in Australia. He stressed the need to infuse the work of the school with clinical relevance. Committee members liked what they heard and decided to offer him the job.

'May I say "yippee"!' said Porter, when told the news. Arriving in Canberra early in 1980, he embarked on his new duties with energy and enthusiasm, and a large measure of support from his colleagues. Encouraged first by Low, then by Karmel, he

Robert Porter at the time of his appointment as Director of JCSMR in 1980. Photograph by Stuart Butterworth.

introduced changes, including the appointment of an Advisory Board comprising medical knights and captains of industry who might help attract outside endowments that could be kept out of the hands of individual professors. He worked hard to draw the attention of politicians and the general public to the school's achievements. New appointments helped shift the balance towards clinical medicine. William Doe, a gastroenterologist who had graduated in medicine from Sydney and worked in the Hammersmith Hospital in London and the Scripps Clinic in California, was appointed Professor of Medicine and Clinical Science. Doe, who specialised in the study of inflammatory bowel disease, colon cancer and the basic mechanisms of tissue injury, was given the task of redeveloping the department in laboratories at Canberra's main hospital in the Woden Valley. Peter Doherty, who had trained at the universities of Queensland and Edinburgh and been a member of the school in the early 1970s, was appointed to the chair of Experimental Pathology, which had been vacant since Courtice had stood down to become Director in 1973. His main interests were in the experimental pathology of virus infections and immunopathology, including cancer research and work on diseases of the nervous system, such as multiple sclerosis. Doherty, who like Doe was recruited from the United States, was credited with one of the most important discoveries in immunology during the preceding decade, and was awarded (jointly) the Paul Ehrlich and Ludwig Darmstaedter Prize for 1983, the highest international award in immunology other than the Nobel Prize. Porter regarded the recruitment of Doherty as the single most important action of his first term as Director.

William Doe, Professor of Medicine and Clinical Science, JCSMR. Photograph by Julie Macklin.

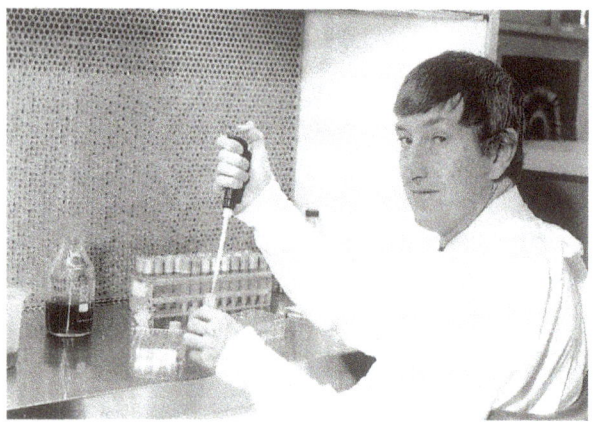

Peter Doherty, Professor of Experimental Pathology, JCSMR, in 1984.

While these and other appointments did much to revivify the school, Porter found the task hard going. In 1984 he lamented that, although he had been Director for four years, the burden of day to day administrative work had prevented him from formulating long-range plans. He also discovered that there were 'real administrative, industrial, social and human limitations to change'. Before his arrival, a working party of the faculty board had flatly rejected the review committee's notion of a creative director; and the faculty had passed a motion approving the spirit and recommendations of the Butt report of over a decade earlier, which had vested substantial powers in the faculty board. Although Porter succeeded in having this structural impediment removed, thereby strengthening his own powers, many staff members remained wary of any attempts to interfere with their traditional notions of departmental autonomy.

The school was firmly in the grip of the past, which also seemed to take hold of its new Director. Porter, who was also styled Howard Florey Professor of Medical Research, looked to the past for understanding and inspiration, which he found in the words of Florey. As he wrote in his first Annual Report, 'A new projection of the attitudes of the School to its future must take into account the role that was defined for the School at its inception and a realization of the objectives that were set out at that time'. He went on to quote long extracts from Florey's 1956 report to Council, which had been declassified at his request, selecting those parts that publicised the worth and needs of the school, and managing to disguise the fact that the report, when first received in Canberra, had caused several cases of near apoplexy. In another Annual Report four years later, Porter again invoked the founder's comments about the purposes of the school. 'These objects', he said, 'are still appropriate in 1984'.

By 1986, however, he had changed his mind entirely. Over the past 40 years, he told the faculty, the school's situation had been transformed: where it had once served an essential function in stimulating medical research and encouraging scientists to remain in Australia, now there were opportunities for research in all states, and the National Health and Medical Research Council was the major organisation engaged in encouraging postgraduate study. The school should therefore 'put aside the historical objectives that were defined at its Foundation and develop objectives appropriate for the 1980's and 1990's'. It should define (and, by implication, limit) future fields of study; it should move more towards clinical medicine; and it should accept some responsibility for undergraduate teaching. While Florey again featured in the 1986 report, now he was quoted to lend support to the case for the school to develop a corporate identity and to be accountable to the wider community. The message was clear: the school should escape the past and embrace the future.

Porter's recommendations read almost as a catharsis. They owed a lot to the University's new emphasis on strategic planning and to the need to come to terms with shrinking budgets. His proposals were also the outcome of a personal wrestling with the past, which somebody had to undertake if the school was to move forward.

The JCSMR section of the University's first Strategic Plan included the key elements of this rethinking: a new statement of objectives, provision for increased flexibility through fewer tenured posts, and the replacement of the departmental structure by five divisions, each comprising a number of groups. This divisional structure was introduced at the beginning of 1988, just as the school was preparing for the second major external review, due to be held ten years after the first.

In the meantime, the school had become increasingly fragmented and resentful. The fragmentation resulted partly from the 1978 recommendations, but was also partly Porter's doing: in order to break away from the rigid departmental structure or to circumvent personality problems (of which there were many), he approved and sometimes encouraged the formation of groups or units, which became so numerous, someone remarked wryly, that every individual would shortly become a group. The resentments derived chiefly from insufficient money, but the Director bore the brunt of them. Many staff regarded him as dogmatic and overbearing in his pursuit of change. Others complained that change was proceeding too slowly. Behind him, medical scientists from all sides were sharpening their scalpels.

Bede Morris was first to turn against him. The two men had been friends and colleagues at Oxford, where Morris was a research student in the Dunn School under Florey. There he had won a well-deserved reputation as a prodigious worker and a wild

Australian. Returning to Australia, he had joined the Department of Experimental Pathology in 1958, and in 1970 had been elected foundation Professor of Immunology. A veterinary scientist and part-time grazier, whose experiments involved surgical intervention on cattle and sheep, he was a brilliant and outrageous raconteur. He also had a powerful capacity to attract trouble and to cause it. Well known inside and outside the University, he contributed much to scientific relations between France and Australia, and was retained by the French government to advise on cattle production. The French honoured him by an appointment as Chevalier dans l'Ordre Nationale du Mérite: he died tragically in a car accident near Paris before the award could be bestowed.

Morris had played a major part in bringing Porter to the ANU; but by the mid-1980s he was grumbling that Porter had assumed more power than Ennor had ever dared to exercise, and that the school would be better off without him. Having inherited Florey's conviction that the experiment was the thing, he argued that the only way to achieve outstanding results was to create an academic environment conducive to the best original research and, within that environment, to promote bold ideas and adventurous experiments. (Research at the ANU, he said, should shine 'like a diamond in a slagheap'.) In a paper addressed to Porter and intended also for Karmel, he set out his philosophy:

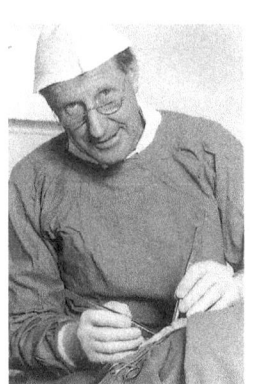

Bede Morris, Professor of Immunology, 1980.

> The nature of original, innovative research is its unpredictability, the high likelihood of failure and its potential for gaining new insights into areas of science whose boundaries remain undefined until the research is done. The most certain way of ensuring mediocrity in science is to do experiments whose outcome is predictable in terms of 5 to 10 year programmes.

The AIDS virus, Morris declared, showed that there was no way of knowing what research would become important in the future. Research could not be planned. By implication, there was no merit in the proposals for strategic planning. Nor, said Morris, was there room for ill-defined notions of 'accountability' or 'relevance' in laboratory-based medical research. The only way of restoring research effectiveness was to provide the departments with adequate funds and let them get on with their work as they had done in the past, without outside interference. Morris charged Porter with mismanagement, and many agreed: morale was crumbling, funds were lacking, and the Director was chiefly to blame. Others, including Peter Doherty, blamed Porter for not introducing changes fast enough.

Again the root of the problem was money. Unlike medical scientists in other universities, JCSMR staff had since the school's inception been disqualified from seeking support from the National Health and Medical Research Council, the main national funding body for medical research. So long as the school was well funded, this prohibition did not matter. But with the onset of hard times for the University generally, the school's position relative to other universities significantly declined, so that where in 1973 the total research funds distributed by the NH&MRC were roughly the same as the total budget for JCSMR (which included running costs not normally categorised as part of research funds), by 1984 NH&MRC grants had more than trebled in real terms, while the JCSMR budget had slightly declined.

For Doherty and several other outspoken members of the school, including the new Professor of Physiology, Peter Gage, the restriction on access to NH&MRC grants was intolerable. Porter and Karmel agreed, and urged the NH&MRC to relax its policies. In 1985 the NH&MRC opened the door a fraction by agreeing to consider a limited number of outstanding applications put forward by the school; and then slammed it shut by rejecting all of them and telling the school to reconsider its funding priorities. Porter was furious. Gage wrote angrily to the Secretary of the NH&MRC to complain about the Council's lack of objectivity.

Doherty in the meantime was becoming increasingly frustrated by what he saw as the school's failure to get its own house in order. In his view, certain 'low-key' members of staff were holding tenured positions at the expense of active young people, while scarce funds were being squandered on outmoded research. As there was apparently no prospect of getting extra money from the NH&MRC under current arrangements, he proposed transferring to the NH&MRC entire responsibility for funding the school's research. This would ensure that his own and other outstanding projects would receive, through the Council's normal processes of peer review, the funding they deserved, while unworthy projects would get nothing. Porter sympathised with Doherty's diagnosis of the problem but doubted that the NH&MRC offered the cure. Doherty, increasingly isolated within the school, wrote angrily to Karmel about what he saw as Porter's lack of leadership. In 1988 he returned to the United States to become head of the Department of Immunology at St Jude's Children's Research Hospital in Memphis, Tennessee, remarking as he left that his experience at the ANU made it unlikely that he would ever work in a university again.

Porter, too, had been contemplating his own future for some time. In 1986, as his seven-year appointment neared an end, he wrote to Karmel about his efforts to introduce change and the obstacles placed in the way. During his term, he had been 'undermined, discredited, compromised and almost totally incapacitated by the hostile resistance of a very few members of senior staff whose only concern seems to be the defence of their perceived privileged positions'. The director, he said, should have the powers of a chief executive. He should also enjoy the genuine cooperation of the heads of department, without which 'the job is frankly impossible'.

With the advice of a liaison committee chosen by the school, Council concluded that he had as good a chance as anybody of giving JCSMR some direction, and offered him a second term. In the ensuing weeks, his opponents mustered against him. The faculty board debated a paper prepared by Morris which effectively charged him with mismanagement. Another senior member of staff reminded him that he and others had removed Ennor from office nearly twenty years previously, and that Ennor was a tougher man than he was. Porter was nevertheless tough enough to accept reappointment in the face of such criticism. But the sniping continued; and by September 1988, following the circulation of an anonymous letter attacking his administration, he decided that life would be more pleasant and productive at his old university, and returned to Monash to become Dean of the Faculty of Medicine.

Earlier that year the school had been scrutinised by its second external review panel, chaired by Paul Korner, Director of the Baker Medical Research Institute in Melbourne, and comprising six other distinguished scientists from Australia, Britain and the United States. Like the review committee a decade earlier, the panel found much to praise; but it was even blunter than the earlier committee in its criticisms, especially the 'undue fragmentation of scientific effort' and the absence of adequate procedures for external peer review. Change was essential: 'the original scientific organisation of JCSMR that was so successful in the 1950's and the 1960's is no longer appropriate for the 1980's and 1990's'; and the ways to achieve it included external peer review (though not through closer association with the NH&MRC), a higher ratio of untenured to tenured staff, provision for early retirement and redundancy, and a strong director, who would provide scientific leadership, recruit new leaders, point the school in new directions, and eschew fragmentation made as a sacrifice at the 'the altar of scientific "independence"'. Where the 1978 panel had concluded that the director could rule only through consultation and persuasion, the 1988 reviewers emphasised that he should have 'considerable power', with the clear implication that consultation and persuasion might not be enough.

On Porter's role, the reviewers were equivocal, acknowledging the difficulties he had faced as a newcomer and approving his efforts to create a more flexible scientific organisation, but implying that he had not fostered 'the collegiate atmosphere that was such a feature of many of the great research institutions'. They gave little guidance as to how a collegiate atmosphere might be achieved; nor did they ask whether such a concept was at variance with their insistence on a strong director.

Why had change proved so hard to achieve? Much of the trouble went back to Florey, the structure he had created, and the way it had evolved over the past forty or so years to confirm the powers of the senior professors and the subservience of the director. Almost from the time of the school's inception, the parts had been considered more important than the whole; and as the parts became more numerous and money more scarce, small groups and individuals insisted on their rights to autonomy and funding, seemingly oblivious of the collective interests of the University or the school. Medical researchers, convinced that their work was uniquely beneficial to the future of the nation or of humankind, might well resist anybody whom they saw as getting in the way. Yet, according to the 1988 committee, in an organisation such as JCSMR it was essential that all members of the scientific staff should have a feeling for the institution, apart from an interest in their own area of science. Some staff, in expressing dissatisfaction about how the school was run, had 'transgressed reasonable limits of academic behaviour and standards of discussion' and had harmed the school. They had behaved as if they had nothing to lose. It would take another review, this time of the Institute as a whole, to convince them that they did.

Equal opportunity?

The ANU in the early 1980s was dominated by men.

Although women made up nearly 45 per cent of total student numbers in 1983 and nearly 40 per cent of the total staff, men occupied almost all the top positions. Of the 250 or so highest salary earners, only four were women. Women were much more likely than men to be employed on the general rather than the academic staff, to be part time rather than full time, and to be temporary rather than permanent or tenured members of staff. Among the academic staff, women were spread unevenly across the disciplines, being well represented in some areas, especially the humanities, and totally unrepresented in others. The proportion of women on the academic staff of The Faculties was more than twice as high as the proportion in the Institute, where total academic staff numbers were substantially greater. Only 2 per cent of tenured staff in the Institute were women, a figure which, according to the 1984 report from which all these figures are taken, was often described as 'grotesque'. A table reproduced in that report showed that, owing chiefly to the low numbers of women in the Institute, the proportion of women in the University as a whole dragged far behind the figure for all Australian universities.

WOMEN ON THE ACADEMIC STAFF
expressed as equivalent full-time numbers

Academic staff IAS and centres (excluding visitors) at 30 April 1983			
Male	Female	Total	% Female
544	38	582	6.53
Academic staff The Faculties (excluding visitors) at 30 April 1983			
Male	Female	Total	% Female
311	63	374	16.84
Total academic staff ANU (excluding visitors) at 30 April 1983			
Male	Female	Total	% Female
855	101	956	10.56
Academic staff Australian universities at 30 April 1983			
Male	Female	Total	% Female
10 272	2358	12 630	18.67

Male domination of the ANU, or of universities generally, was not new. Universities had begun as male preserves and had remained so for many centuries. Only in the later nineteenth century had women's colleges been founded at Oxford and Cambridge, and in the United States, followed by universities in the Australian colonies. By the 1950s women made up about a fifth of students in all Australian universities; but few of those who graduated went on to follow academic careers, and those who did so normally fell into teaching roles, the assumption being that, apart from a few exceptional cases, only men had the inclination towards and the capacity for creative research. So the ANU, as a research university, not merely followed, but exaggerated a well-established pattern.

Yet in its policies and practices towards the employment of women, the ANU was and is something of a paradox. For while its statistics for female employment continued to lag behind other universities, the recommendations of its committees and reviews were often ahead of them and of Australian society generally. Those recommendations related to the conditions of service for women, and the numbers and functions of women within the University.

Questions relating to women's conditions of service, including their salaries and benefits, came first. In Australia during the 1950s, rates of pay in most areas of employment were governed by the principle of the basic wage, a system of wage determination based on the assumed needs of the employee rather than the nature of work. Thus the basic wage was higher for a man than for a woman, on the assumption that the man had a family to support while a woman had only to look after herself or had a husband to support her. Benefits such as superannuation were similarly linked to the perceived roles of men and women. Although the universities were ahead of most other employers, including the Commonwealth and state public services, in acknowledging the principle of equal pay for equal work, the principle did not in practice extend far beyond academic and senior general staff, and was not taken to imply the uniform application of equal benefits.

From the vantage point of the 1990s, the inequities may be obvious. In the 1960s, however, people were just starting to notice there was a problem. At the ANU, as often happens in the process of institutional change, a specific anomaly gave rise to wider questioning. Max Corden, a Senior Research Fellow in Economics, RSPacS, was troubled that a research assistant in his department was ineligible for superannuation because she was married, while unmarried research assistants, both female and male, and female members of the academic staff, were all eligible. As her husband was nearing retiring age, the research assistant presumably needed the superannuation benefit. Corden wondered if an exception could be made or the rules changed.

Hohnen concluded that 'the climate might be right to propose to Council some further steps towards what is so facilely described as "equality"'. He then recruited David Bensusan-Butt, the economist from RSPacS whom we met in Chapter 7 when he was conducting an inquiry into JCSMR, to chair a Committee on Conditions of Service for Female Staff. Butt's committee enquired minutely into salaries, superannuation, leave entitlements, housing assistance and other conditions of service for every category of female staff, arduously teased out the principles, and proposed a series of policy changes intended to remove sex discrimination in the University.

Hohnen referred to the inquiry as Butt's 'quaint duty', suggesting (at the least) the extraordinary nature of the exercise. In so far as it was explicitly confronting questions relating to women in its workforce, the University was ahead of the times. Hohnen, Butt and others thought this was as it ought to be: the National University had a duty to set the lead as a good employer. The anthropologist W.E.H. Stanner in RSPacS, himself much concerned with discrimination against Aboriginal people, urged the University to make, adopt and publicise an explicit rule that there should be no discrimination on the grounds of sex. While he was not aware of instances of discrimination, he considered it 'a proper exercise of the University's social function' to give the lead in such matters and not merely follow the trend. The astronomer Bart Bok was equally adamant: 'conditions of service should be exactly the same for *all* staff, male or female, married or unmarried', and the ANU should show the rest of Australia the way.

These were heady arguments for 1964, and more than the committee could cope with. Butt and his colleagues, two men and two women, one of whom was the University's only female professor, the mathematician Hanna Neumann, endorsed without question the principle of equal pay for equal work; but they were reluctant to abandon the notion that the University, as a good employer, should assist married members of staff who had financial dependants. The important thing was that married women should be treated in the same way as married men. They were also constrained by political considerations: could the University introduce equal pay to all categories of staff without causing large repercussions outside the University, including the public service, and thereby offending the Commonwealth government? So while the work of the committee represented a bold attempt to confront awkward questions and encourage equity, its report stopped short of recommending equal pay and conditions for all University staff. Nor did it tackle some difficult problems, such as whether research and technical assistants who had chosen to make the University their career should be given the same degree of permanency accorded to senior academic staff, on the one hand, and secretaries on the other.

The University's first female professor, Hanna Neumann, at the time of her appointment as Professor of Mathematics in SGS, 1964.
Australian News and Information Bureau, ANU Collection.

Above all, the committee did little to confront the widespread assumptions about the role of women that were the basis of discrimination. These were nicely epitomised a few years after the Butt inquiry by one of the University's business managers who, troubled by having to decide whether or not a young research assistant was eligible for superannuation, minuted that she 'being a married woman would undoubtedly not wish to make the University a career as eventually she will have family responsibilities'. Adrien Albert, Professor of Medical Chemistry in JCSMR, was uncomfortable in the presence of women and, according to his biographer, clearly believed that their place was in the home or in service positions. Manning Clark, Professor of History in the Faculty of Arts, sometimes appointed women to lectureships, but invariably chose women as his research assistants. Ann Moyal, Assistant Editor of the *Australian Dictionary of Biography* in the late 1950s and early 1960s and a member of its National Committee and Editorial Board, recalled many years later that most of the men she worked with wished to consign her to a secretarial role. 'Academic men', she wrote, '—with rare exceptions—were adroit at marginalising women colleagues and devaluing their work'.

The committee counted the numbers of academic staff in 1964: there were 337 men and 32 women. Apart from Neumann, only five women occupied positions senior to that of lecturer or fellow. While nine out of ten men on the academic staff were married, the numbers of married and unmarried women were about evenly split. Nine of the seventeen married women were married to members of the ANU staff.

These figures might have led to some interesting questions about the role of women in the University; but that was beyond the committee's brief.

A few academics recognised wider issues. Bart Bok, well acquainted with developments in the United States, including President Kennedy's Commission on the Status of Women, and influenced perhaps by his wife Priscilla, also an outstanding astronomer, insisted in public lectures that there must be equality of opportunity for men and women, and that Australia was the loser by not making use of its 'Woman-Power'. But such views were exceptional. It was another decade before the role of women became a matter for serious debate at the ANU.

That debate took place in the context of wider concerns about women in society and at the same time that ANU students were demanding a course on Women's Studies. Coombs, with his unique capacity to force the University to look at itself, detonated the issue in 1974, when he was quoted as saying that the lack of women professors at the ANU was the result of conservative and male chauvinist views throughout the

Melbourne Herald,
19 June 1959

"SCIENCE IS NOT FOR MEN ONLY"

University. This caused consternation on the Board of the School of General Studies, which pointed out that only five out of 350 applications for chairs in the School over the last decade had come from women. Coombs explained that he had been misquoted: but what he then said to the Board and Council hit home.

> My intention in referring to the University was to emphasise that, even in institutions in which formal discrimination does not exist and in which there is often sympathy with women's aspirations, male domination tends in fact to be the practical outcome.

While the explanation lay deep within society and the difficulty of bringing about fundamental changes in social relationships, the fact was that women played 'a really inadequate role' in the ANU, as well as in most other universities, and that the University was the poorer because of it.

To combat the problem, Coombs suggested that Council set up a study of the role of women at the ANU and consider ways in which women might be enabled to make a contribution 'more consonant with their numbers and their potential'. Accordingly, the Acting Vice-Chancellor invited Marion Ward, a former head of the New Guinea Research Unit, to undertake a study of the role of women in the ANU and other universities and to suggest ways of correcting the imbalance in the proportion of men and women employed by the University. Gwenda Bramley, a chemistry graduate who had lately completed an ANU degree in psychology, was appointed Research Assistant to the project and finished it when Ward left to work on overseas projects.

Drawing on statistical data, responses to questionnaires, and group interviews, Bramley and Ward documented the scarcity of women in academic life, their uneven distribution across the faculties, and their absence from decision-making bodies. The low number of women in senior academic positions they attributed to the tendency of women to drop out of the academic hierarchy at junior levels in order to fulfil their socially acceptable role of full-time wife and mother. While Bramley and Ward avoided mentioning names, there were plenty of specific examples to choose from. Thelma Hunter, the Senior Lecturer in Political Science whom we met earlier when she was opposing the dedicated course in Women's Studies, described in the national staff association journal how she had attempted to combine an academic career with marriage, motherhood and family life. She set out the difficulties, among them assumptions about the natural or proper role of academic women: 'The academic community is predominantly male in structure and ethos. Women who have sought to make a reality of their formal equality are still essentially in conflict with existing role expectations and norms.'

Bramley and Ward proposed institutional changes to take account of women's work life cycles, including more flexible arrangements for employment which would allow both men and women to reshape their work and family roles. They recommended that Council consider the introduction of fractional full-time staff appointments, along with measures to assist women to leave and re-enter the workforce so that they might fulfil family responsibilities while maintaining their careers. Other recommendations included the appointment of a Women's Adviser to the Vice-Chancellor, and the initiation of a detailed study of student attitudes in an effort to explain why so few of them proceeded to higher degrees. They complimented the University on its support for child care facilities, which had been introduced as early as 1968, well ahead of most other universities and public service departments.

The Bramley–Ward Report was a pioneering study, not just in the ANU, but in Australian universities generally. In retrospect, it seems moderate in tone and cautious in its recommendations. 'In no way', the report declared, 'do we seek to encourage the situation in which women are antagonistic to men and seek to improve their status at the expense of men'. It explicitly rejected 'the introduction of a quota system or even an affirmation system for women'.

Nevertheless, it encountered some vocal resistance. Oliphant, now Governor of South Australia, after reading about the recommendations in the *ANU Reporter*, wrote to say that 'if women demand equality with men they must prove themselves to be equal ... Special treatment of women ... cannot be countenanced if the ANU is to remain outstanding academically.' Many people on campus agreed. There was also widespread indifference to the report, attributable mostly perhaps to lack of interest in the issues it raised, but also to cynicism about whether it would have significant effects. Apart from those who were specifically invited to respond, few staff took the trouble to comment. Those who did tended to be critical. Some questioned its methodologies. Others detected an inappropriate feminist bias. The proposal for fractional appointments was resisted on the grounds that part-time employees did not necessarily conduct the best research. General staff were dismayed that the report devoted little attention to them.

Without Coombs (now retired as Chancellor) or any senior member of the administration determined to give it effect, the report languished. Although Council eventually accepted most of the recommendations, some were diluted in committee, while others, such as the proposal for fractional appointments, failed to have the effects their authors had anticipated. The report omitted to set a timetable for implementing reforms or targets against which their effectiveness could be measured; and there was no pressure from inside or outside the University to ensure that the recommendations would be followed through.

Overall, the report failed because most people, men and women alike, were either indifferent or passively opposed to what it had to say. It also failed because of its own limitations. Marie Reay, a Senior Fellow in Anthropology, RSPacS, who had studied as a doctoral student in the department in the early 1950s and joined its staff in 1959, declared that, while the report was 'a very good study of the working conditions of wives and mothers', it was not a report on the role of women in the University. One deficiency, in her view, was that it did not deal with sex discrimination. The problem was that in 1975 few members of the University, male or female, acknowledged that sex discrimination existed, and those who did found it hard to define.

By the time Karmel became Vice-Chancellor seven years later, growing community support for the concept of equal opportunity suggested that the University should not merely formulate new policies, but should also carry them out; and when the Hawke Labor government took office in March 1983, with a strong commitment to women's issues and a vocal feminist, Susan Ryan, as Minister for Education and Youth Affairs, it became clear that if the University did not initiate and implement reforms the government certainly would. Karmel, together with the Assistant Vice-Chancellor, Colin Plowman, and the Secretary, Warwick Williams, anticipated the direction of future policy and instigated a new investigation by Marian Sawer, a forthright political scientist from outside the University, giving her a free hand to elaborate her own terms of reference.

Sawer's report, completed in 1984, built on the findings of Bramley and Ward and carried them further, taking care to cover issues relating to general as well as academic staff. She concluded that there had been no overall improvement in the status of women since the publication of the previous report; and that while Bramley and Ward had opened the way for the ANU to play a pioneering role in relation to what was now generally described as equal employment opportunity, the level of EEO awareness had not changed in the intervening eight or so years. Having lost its early lead, the ANU was now well behind other institutions in such matters as promulgating EEO guidelines and issuing a statement relating to sexual harassment.

Marian Sawer, consultant on equal opportunity for women.

Sawer was blunt about the cause: the University suffered from 'systemic discrimination'. One element of this, the failure to adopt work patterns and career structures to accommodate family responsibilities, had already been identified by Bramley and Ward. Sawer, with a new body of feminist literature to draw on, described others, including linguistic discrimination, homosocial reproduction (or 'recruitment in one's own image') and informal networking (of a kind perhaps that her ex-father-in-law,

Geoffrey Sawer, had identified 30 years earlier when he worried that Karl Popper might not be 'clubbable'). The cumulative effect of this systemic discrimination was that women were disadvantaged in all areas and at all levels of the ANU workforce.

Sawer presented 82 recommendations, ranging from broad policy initiatives to detailed adjustments to parts of the workforce. Her report urged the University to introduce objective selection criteria for all appointments; to ensure that women were represented on major decision-making bodies; to adopt guidelines for non-sexist language; to provide bridging finance to increase the number of women academics in the Institute; to encourage the appointment of women cleaners to supervisory roles; to refer in all job advertisements to the fact that 'The ANU is an Equal Opportunity Employer'. Not all the recommendations related exclusively to women. One enjoined selection committees not to regard qualifications achieved overseas as automatically superior (a tilt perhaps at the residual deference to Oxbridge in some parts of the University). Another encouraged the appointment of Aboriginal men and women to the University staff.

Where the Bramley–Ward proposals had existed (relatively speaking) in a political vacuum, Sawer had a formidable and well-organised constituency behind her. Soon after she began work, a group of 80 women organised themselves into an Association of Women Employees, circularised all women staff, assembled data which Sawer was able to draw on, and presented their own report which complemented her findings. By the time the two reports were ready for publication, the government had confirmed its commitment to equal opportunity by introducing anti-discrimination legislation into parliament and foreshadowing measures which would oblige tertiary institutions (among others) to implement affirmative action policies.

Karmel, the father of five daughters, committed himself to the proposals and steered them deftly through Council, proposing or accepting amendments, additions and omissions, but ensuring that their essence and spirit were maintained. With the appointment of an Equal Opportunity Officer, the University was well placed to respond to government initiatives, including affirmative action legislation passed in 1986 which required the University, along with other large employers, to submit annual reports detailing the ways in which it was applying equal opportunity policies.

Not everyone was entirely comfortable with these measures or the premises on which they were based. Beryl Rawson, a Reader in Classics and Dean of the Faculty of Arts, who had risen near the top of the academic hierarchy with family responsibilities along the way (and who was soon to become a professor), questioned the report's assertion that women with child-rearing experience were effectively excluded from senior decision-making and its recommendation that 'childrearing experience be regarded in a positive light' when assessing job candidates and appointments to decision-making roles. Other parts of the report failed to resonate with her own experience of the academic world. She reminded Sawer that 'all types of experience have their own validity and none should be denigrated'. Helen Hughes, an economist in Pacific Studies in the 1960s who had rejoined the School in 1983 after fourteen years in the World Bank, had little time for what she saw as special pleading. Ability alone had taken her to the top of her profession, and now, as Professor of Economics

The Vice-Chancellor, centre, with the Heads of Research Schools, senior administrators and other senior members of the University in 1982.

Helen Hughes, Professor of Economics and Executive Director of the National Centre for Development Studies, RSPacS, in 1984.
Canberra Times.

and Head of the National Centre for Development Studies, she held her own against the most formidable of her male colleagues. A decade later, in retirement, she expressed no regret at not having made it on to the lists of prominent Australian women (even though she had). 'I think that's an accolade', she told the journalist (and ANU graduate) Bettina Arndt. 'I am not a woman, I'm a professional economist.'

But, at least in terms of rhetoric, Sawer was more in tune with the times. With a few exceptions, those who had reservations about the assumptions behind her report tended to utter them softly, behind closed doors, where their resistance was often telling.

By the early 1990s the EEO Committee was able to report steady progress in implementing the Sawer recommendations, as endorsed by Council, that equal opportunity was widely understood and that practices were well integrated. There were now well-defined procedures for ensuring equal opportunity in academic appointments and promotions, guidelines on non-sexist language, safeguards against sexual harassment, and measures to make it easier for women and men to combine family responsibilities with academic careers. The results of affirmative action were evident in senior administrative appointments. Susan Bambrick, an economist, became Master of University House (a title that she chose to retain) in 1987. Karmel appointed Rosalind Dubs, a young chemist turned administrator, to the position of Registrar in 1985. By 1994 both Deputy Vice-Chancellors, the most senior positions after the Vice-Chancellor, were women.

Yet in 1995 there was still no female head of a research school (though one had acted in that position in JCSMR); and despite the various measures to bring about equal opportunity, the academic 'gender balance', as it was now called, remained heavily weighted towards men. The figures spoke for themselves. In 1989 there were a total of 245 tenured academics in the Institute, of whom only 6 were women, and 223 untenured staff, of whom 42 were women. Various committees wondered why. In the natural science schools, the imbalance could be explained by the paucity of applications from women: the problem could only be solved by changes to society at large. In some schools, too, there was continuing resistance to fractional appointments, a cornerstone of equal opportunity. And Susan Serjeantson, Professor of Human Genetics in JCSMR and soon to become the University's first female Deputy Vice-Chancellor, noticed that women who applied for appointments and promotions tended to be more reticent than men in putting themselves forward.

The imbalance in RSSS and RSPacS presented a larger problem. Here it was impossible to argue that women were not interested in the social sciences, since women had traditionally been attracted to these areas, and there were many female social scientists in The Faculties and in other universities. The two schools therefore tried hard to encourage women to apply for advertised vacancies, and with notable success. In RSSS, for example, the numbers of women applying for jobs increased from 11 per cent between 1986 and 1988 to 25 per cent between 1988 and 1994; and of the 93 appointments offered during the latter period, 42 per cent were offered to females, suggesting on the face of it that it was now a good deal easier for a woman to win an appointment than it was for a man.

Rosalind Dubs, appointed Registrar in 1985. Photograph by Bob Cooper.

The problem was that most of the openings were junior and untenured, since most of the tenured positions were occupied by men who had been appointed before gender balance had become a pressing issue, and the overall proportion of non-tenured staff was increasing. When senior positions did fall vacant, they tended to go to men, often within the two schools. In 1994 there was no tenured woman in the Research School of Social Sciences and only one in the Research School of Pacific Studies; no woman had ever occupied a chair in the RSSS, and only one, Hughes, had been a professor in RSPacS. The staff profiles of both schools provoked acerbic comments from The Faculties and from outside the University about 'glass ceilings' and 'hidden agendas'.

In both schools, faculty boards agonised about what could be done to increase the numbers of tenured women without deviating from the standard rule that all appointments should be made on the basis of merit. The History Program Review Committee tried to solve the problem by suggesting that jobs be advertised in areas of scholarship where women were known to be well represented, such as women's history or cultural studies. But this was risky. Apart from offering no guarantee of success, it could only work in those disciplines where women had laid claim to specific fields of research.

Faced with the prospect of continuing criticism from inside and outside the University, both schools advertised for tenured positions reserved exclusively for women. This was a bold initiative, unprecedented in any Australian university, and bringing an entirely new dimension to existing understandings of affirmative action. Many staff, including some who had warmly supported the Sawer proposals, reacted uneasily. Some saw it as a far-sighted attempt to correct the inequities of the past and introduce a change of culture, others as a misguided effort to solve an image problem that apparently could not be remedied by other means.

Either way, the advertisements affirmed that the research schools meant business in attempting to improve their gender balance. Had the University sacrificed something in the process? Was it an accident that the advertisement for these positions in what was now called the Research School of Pacific and Asian Studies omitted, contrary to the University's equal opportunity policy, the statement: 'The ANU is an equal opportunity employer'?

Innovation

In teaching and research, the 1980s were years of innovation, as Low and Karmel said they had to be. New initiatives, now relabelled 'innovative activities' to escape a tautology, spread across the campus and took many different forms: for example, the Centre for Recombinant DNA Research in RSBS; limited term projects in RSSS on Ageing and the Family, the Law and Politics of Industrial Relations, and Social Justice in Australia, each drawing on resources from across the school; a Bachelor of Commerce degree, which allowed students to gain professional accounting qualifications in three years rather than four; a Department of Art History in the Faculty of Arts. Encouraged by government policy, members of the University also embarked on collaborative research ventures—many more than in previous years—especially with members of CSIRO and other universities in Australia and overseas.

Despite the constraints on growth, some innovations were made possible by new money. In 1982, for example, the University received funding under the Commonwealth Special Research Centres (often called 'centres of excellence') program to set up a Centre for Mathematical Analysis in The Faculties. Other changes resulted from restructuring and redistributing resources within the University: thus the creation in 1989 of a School of Mathematical Sciences, which brought together mathematicians and statisticians from RSPhysS, RSSS and The Faculties, including the Centre for Mathematical Analysis (shortly to be renamed the Centre for Mathematics and its Applications). The new school enabled the University to harness individual strengths into a powerful team for teaching and research, while maintaining the necessary distinctions for funding purposes between the Institute and Faculties components.

The formation of the Peace Research Centre in RSPacS tested the University's readiness to accept money with strings attached. Peace research had emerged as a new interdisciplinary area in the 1960s, in response to public anxieties about the dangers of nuclear war. Australia was slow to enter the field; but in the early 1980s, a group of academics, public servants and representatives of voluntary organisations advocated the creation of a peace research institute, perhaps along the lines of existing institutions in Stockholm and Oslo. The idea won support within the Labor Party; and following Labor's victory in the 1983 election, the new Minister for Foreign Affairs, Bill Hayden, moved quickly to give it effect as part of a wider policy of emphasising Australia's commitment to disarmament.

Where should the centre be placed? The government's first choice was not to create a new institution, but to increase funding to the Strategic and Defence Studies Centre in RSPacS for studies relating specifically to peace issues. But this met with fierce resistance from advocates of peace research, who suggested that the Strategic and

Defence Studies Centre was more concerned with war than peace, and from the centre itself, whose Advisory Committee refused to change its name to accommodate the change in emphasis. The government looked elsewhere. Some proponents argued that the new centre should be located well away from Canberra so as to reduce the risks of interference by the Commonwealth government and the bureaucracy. On the other hand, if the centre was to have any influence on policy, Canberra was obviously the place to be; and Canberra, especially the ANU, offered unrivalled resources for research. So the government invited the University to establish a 'self-contained centre for peace studies', which would be funded by the Department of Foreign Affairs.

The proposal for a centre devoted to the study of peace caused more than its share of conflict. According to Andrew Mack, who became the centre's first head, peace research, though hard to define, is characterised in part by 'a commitment to certain values and to policy-oriented research intended to realise those values'. That made it unpalatable to those who did not share those values or who were committed to what they called 'value-free' research. The strongest opposition came from T.B. Millar, head of the Strategic and Defence Studies Centre, who questioned the 'academic merit and standing' of peace studies, just as the earlier opponents of his own centre had doubted the legitimacy of strategic and defence studies. And he warned that two centres concerned with similar issues, albeit from different perspectives, would lead to the duplication of research effort and competition for funds. Millar also protested that the University was giving way to government pressure, an argument reminiscent of objections a decade before to the Centre for Research in Federal Financial Relations.

Nevertheless, the University accepted the government's invitation and the Peace Research Centre was established in 1984, with the stated aim of carrying out research and providing training on 'topics relating to the conditions for establishing and maintaining peace on national, regional, and global scales'. Millar resigned in protest as head of the Centre for Strategic and Defence Studies.

The Peace Research Centre was certainly vulnerable. Its budget was open to parliamentary scrutiny and the government could close it down at one year's notice. Yet according to Mack in 1989 there had never been 'the *slightest* hint' of interference by the government or the bureaucracy. On the other hand, although staff in the centre were prepared to criticise government policies and did so, Mack conceded that 'self-censorship of a subtle kind is a near inevitable consequence of insecure funding'. As he wryly put it, the situation of being directly dependent on the government was 'highly instructive and enhances appreciation of the academic freedom which normal university life still offers'.

About the time that the Peace Research Centre was opened, the Mount Stromlo and Siding Spring Observatories celebrated a major innovation in the form of a 2.3 metre telescope at Siding Spring. This originated in the vision of Don Mathewson, who had succeeded Olin Eggen as Director of the Observatories in 1979. Mathewson insisted that if the ANU was to remain at the forefront of astronomical research it would need a new, superior telescope, the cost of which, if purchased, would certainly be beyond the University's means. His entrepreneurial solution involved ingenuity, expertise and risk.

The opportunity to build a new kind of telescope presented itself in the form of a massive slab of astronomical, low expansion glass, 90 inches (nearly 2.3 metres) in diameter, which had become available in Ohio. This could be used as the mirror in an advanced technology telescope, more versatile than conventional telescopes and operated by computers, which would allow stars to be tracked with meticulous accuracy. The glass was on the market at a bargain price of about $250 000.

There was a catch: the glass was too thick for its intended use and would have to be sliced in two. This was a hazardous undertaking. Moreover, as it was pitch black, there was no way of telling if it was cracked beneath the surface, which would make it unusable for astronomical purposes.

The gamble paid off. As Mount Stromlo held its breath, the glass was cut to order in the United States and discovered to be unflawed. The surplus half was sold at a price equal to the cost of the original purchase, so that the University had in effect acquired the glass for nothing. The remainder of the telescope was designed and constructed largely in-house, drawing on astronomical, engineering and computing skills in MSSSO and other parts of RSPhysS, with the result that the total cost was a fraction of what it might otherwise have been. The completed instrument won a national award for engineering excellence and is widely regarded as occupying a significant place in the evolution of the modern telescope.

During the 1980s, the ANU took several major initiatives in the related fields of engineering and information technology. The broad field of information, said Low in 1981, was clearly the way of the future and a subject of national importance in which the ANU had a role to play. Yet it was also 'a glaring omission' in the Institute's range of activities. Now there was an opportunity to make 'a small number of powerful appointments' in the field of systems engineering. In particular, Brian Anderson, Professor of Electrical Engineering at the University of Newcastle (NSW) and one of Australia's most talented engineers, had indicated he might be prepared to move to Canberra. Despite some resistance from those in the Institute who thought that enough money had gone to areas relating to the physical sciences, Low won the debate and Anderson was duly appointed to head a new Department of Systems Engineering in RSPhysS. Before long, the department was doing major work relating to adaptive control, signal processing and system identification. In 1991 it became the first section of the University to participate in the Commonwealth government's new program of Cooperative Research Centres when a CRC for Robust and Adaptive Systems was established in partnership with CSIRO, the Commonwealth's Defence Science and Technology Organisation and Australia's largest company, BHP.

The ANU's association with computers extended back to 1962, when it acquired an IBM 1620. This was housed in the Department of Theoretical Physics, RSPhysS, but members of the University from outside the department were encouraged to use it for research and some teaching. With the introduction of a 'state of the art' IBM 360/50 three years later, the University joined the computer revolution. Astronomers, physicists, psychologists, economists, linguists were soon vying for computer time and adjusting their research activities to exploit the opportunities the new technology offered. By 1968 the computer facility had evolved into a Computer Centre, independent of RSPhysS, and

Left: Don Mathewson in 1979, with a model of the 2.3 metre telescope he hoped to build at Siding Spring. *Below*: the telescope at the time of its opening in 1984, housed in a cuboid building which rotates on its base. The Anglo-Australian Telescope is in the background. Photograph by Bob Cooper.

An advanced calculating machine, an IBM 620, purchased for the Mount Stromlo Observatory in 1960 and photographed here with Huxley (centre) and Oliphant (right) in 1962. As the machine could not store a program, it did not qualify as a genuine computer.
Australian News and Information Bureau, ANU Collection.

intended to serve the whole campus. The centre, later renamed the Computer Services Centre, combined research and service functions, an arrangement typical of the early days of computing in universities, but later universally abandoned.

Over the next decade, the University's mainframe computer was upgraded, individual departments acquired their own facilities, and the various components were linked into a network. By the late 1970s, the University's total annual expenditure on computing equipment and programming staff exceeded expenditure on book and journal acquisitions and staff in the library system. Personal computers, introduced in the early 1980s, heralded the second phase of the revolution. By the mid-1990s most researchers, whether staff or graduate students, had their own computers and access to electronic communication.

The University also entered the new world of supercomputers. During the 1980s, the demand for computing power throughout the Australian university system was fast outstripping the capabilities of conventional computers, leading to talk about establishing a national supercomputer facility. As the national approach was making little progress, the ANU took the plunge with the purchase in 1987 of a Fujitsu FACOM VP50 vector processor, and the creation of the ANU Supercomputer Facility.

About the same time, the University formed a Centre for Information Science Research (CISR), which drew together relevant sections of the Institute of Advanced Studies and The Faculties, and also included the CSIRO's Division of Information Technology, which was soon to move onto the ANU campus to ensure close collaboration. CISR's purpose was to support innovative work relating to computer applications and telecommunications, and to develop collaborative ventures with the computer industry. Michael McRobbie, a logician from the Department of Philosophy in RSSS who had moved into the field of automated reasoning, was appointed Executive Director, and became an energetic entrepreneur.

Through CISR, the University entered into a wide variety of research and development contracts with the Fujitsu company, by now its principal supplier of mainframe computers. Fujitsu supplied without charge, before delivery to any other site, a prototype computer employing the new technology of parallel processing so that algorithms could be developed for its use. From this base, the centre and its departmental members, in collaboration with CSIRO, Fujitsu and numerous other industry partners, secured funding for a CRC for Advanced Computing Systems, and in further collaboration with universities and Telecom Australia (later Telstra) for a share in a Research Data Network CRC.

Teaching in computing had begun modestly in 1962 in the Department of Statistics in the Faculty of Economics. A separate Department of Computer Sciences was not established in The Faculties until the late 1970s, when Richard Brent, who had been a member of the Computer Services Centre, was appointed foundation professor. Brent helped show that the University was already rich in resources relating to research in computing; and John Carver, Director of RSPhysS, saw the potential to create a small research department with Brent, who was being wooed by other institutions, as its head. So in 1985 the Computer Sciences Laboratory was established, initially in the old Department of Engineering Physics.

Where some directors, most memorably Titterton, were determined to maintain the integrity of their research schools, Carver believed the University would benefit by the creation of new schools out of parts of the old. For many years the astronomers, still formally a part of RSPhysS, had been straining at the leash. Carver supported their claims for complete independence, so that in 1986 the Mount Stromlo and Siding Spring Observatories were established as an autonomous centre within the University. He encouraged the formation of a School of Mathematical Sciences, and he recognised that the Department of Systems Engineering and the Computer Sciences Laboratory, riding the wave of technological progress, had the potential to become a dynamic new school. This was achieved in 1994 with the creation of the Research School of Information Sciences and Engineering (RSISE).

A third major innovation in RSPhysS occurred in 1988 when the school received special funding for a Department of Electronic Materials Engineering, and lured Jim Williams from the Royal Melbourne Institute of Technology to head it. The new department aimed to redress the University's weakness in semiconductor science, and Australia's lack of capacity to compete in developing the solid-state electronic devices which are at the heart of computing and communications. This development provided the stimulus for RSPhysS to change its name in 1991 to the Research School of Physical Sciences and Engineering (RSPhysSE). As well as reflecting a gradual shift in emphasis, the change in name helped signal that over the preceding decade the school had been largely rebuilt.

Moves to introduce undergraduate teaching in engineering began in the 1970s. Ian Ross, one of the proposal's strong advocates, imagined a completely new kind of engineering degree, which emphasised the management and social aspects of the discipline. He was given to saying that the engineering graduate of the future would be a woman who knew how to design the Black Mountain tower (then under construction) and who also knew and understood why it should not be built. Apart from its intrinsic merits, engineering would enable the ANU to increase its range of offerings which, when compared with metropolitan universities which had the traditional faculties of medicine and dentistry, sometimes seemed narrow. On the other hand, just as forestry and accounting had met with resistance in the 1960s, engineering was suspect to those academics who regarded professional courses with disdain. There was also doubt whether sufficient students would be attracted to make

In 1989 the Pro Vice-Chancellor, Ian Ross, left, shakes hands with the President of Fujitsu Laboratories, Masaka Ogi, after signing a contract joining the ANU and Fujitsu in research and development projects in artificial vision systems and parallel computing.

Computers revolutionised access to the Library and began to transform its collections. Colin Steele, University Librarian from 1980, poses with a book on disc in 1992. Photograph by Peter Wells. *Canberra Times.*

Communicating science: Michael Gore, a senior lecturer in Physics in the Faculty of Science, developed a novel way of explaining science to secondary school students through simple but stimulating exhibits of scientific and technological principles. With an innovative teaching grant from the Commonwealth government and voluntary help, he created 'Questacon' in the former infants building of a local school. Questacon opened in 1980 and was an outstanding success. It became the basis for the National Science and Technology Centre, established in 1988 with Gore as Director.

the courses worthwhile. In the event, the Institute of Engineers, the professional body responsible for accrediting engineering courses, was unresponsive; and more decisively, the AUC, under Peter Karmel, declined requests for funding. So the proposals lapsed.

They were revived in the late 1980s, again with Ross at the fore. By now, new engineering courses were appearing in various institutions, including the Canberra College of Advanced Education. For a time it seemed that the University and the College might offer a joint engineering degree. But negotiations became submerged beneath a wider debate (discussed in the next chapter) about whether the two institutions should amalgamate.

In the meantime, Robin Stanton, Brent's successor in the Computer Sciences chair in the Faculty of Science, took the lead in devising a scheme for an engineering program that would start small and grow steadily into a faculty. In 1990 Darrell Williamson was appointed to head an Interdisciplinary Engineering Program in the Faculty of Science. This immediately proved successful in attracting high quality students and outside money for research. In 1993 the program joined with the Department of Computer Science in the Faculty of Science to form a new Faculty of Engineering and Information Technology. So, by the mid-1990s, the large field of engineering, having been neglected in the University's early years, now figured in the titles of two research schools and one faculty.

These are just a few of the areas where members of the University seized opportunities as they arose and created new ones. The common ingredients of innovation were ingenuity and leadership, augmented by the occasional infusion of new money. Gradually members of the University adjusted to hard times and learnt that it was possible to introduce change without growth.

A new generation of planners

13

 The Dawkins revolution

In July 1987, nearly six months before Karmel was due to retire as Vice-Chancellor, the Hawke Labor government was re-elected for a third term. The new government proceeded to reorganise the public service into a smaller number of 'mega-departments', each presided over by a Cabinet minister. The former Department of Education was subsumed within a new Department of Employment, Education and Training (DEET), a name which in itself suggested a major element of government policy: education policies should be closely linked with the restructuring of the workforce.

The Minister for Employment, Education and Training was John Dawkins, a 40-year-old Western Australian who had previously served as Minister for Finance and Minister for Trade. Dawkins had been educated at Roseworthy Agricultural College in South Australia and the University of Western Australia, and he was scornful of the teaching standards he had encountered. He believed that the higher education system was desperately in need of change; and while he as yet had no detailed plan for bringing change about, he was determined, as he put it, 'to shake the tree vigorously'.

John Dawkins, Minister for Employment, Education and Training, in 1989.
Department of Employment, Education and Training.

Few people at the ANU knew much about what Dawkins had in store. One of the first to find out was Don Aitkin, who had by chance delivered a speech on 'Education and national needs' a few days after the new ministry had been announced. The address, appropriately called the Copland Memorial Lecture and delivered at Copland College, one of Canberra's senior high schools, was prescient. Aitkin urged the universities to seize the initiative and begin to determine their own future. 'They have the intellectual resources to do it, and no-one else will do it as well. Moreover, if they do not take the opportunity now they will not only miss the possibilities for growth that are coming, but they risk having an exasperated government doing some bush surgery on them.'

Shortly afterwards, Aitkin met Dawkins, supposedly to discuss the Australian Research Grants Committee of which he was chairman. Dawkins wanted to talk about the speech, and he outlined some of his own ideas for higher education and research. Aitkin, subjected to an 'inquisitorial session' such as he had never encountered before, was impressed. Dawkins was 'informed and opinionated' about higher education, 'self-confident, and gifted with an excellent intellect and great powers of concentration'. He was also, like Aitkin, impatient for change. The system needed radical surgery.

Dawkins' reform proposals were developed quickly and set out in a Green (discussion) Paper in December 1987 and a White (policy) Paper the following July. According to Peter Karmel, the government's strategy encompassed 'the most drastic changes to arrangements for higher education that have occurred in the 140 years since the foundation of Australia's first university'. Key features included the abolition of the binary system of universities and colleges of advanced education that had been introduced in the 1960s, and its replacement by a 'unified national system', comprising fewer institutions, each with a minimum number of students; and the introduction of 'educational profiles', which required each institution to provide the government with details of its teaching and research objectives and activities in order to justify continued funding. By these and other means, Dawkins aimed to give higher education a clear sense of direction, to reshape it as an instrument of government economic policy, to increase access, and to make the universities more open, more accountable for the huge sums of public money invested in them, and more receptive to the marketplace and to national needs.

The emphasis on national needs recalled the purposes for which the ANU had been founded. That much Dawkins had in common with Coombs and his colleagues in the mid-1940s. He also shared with the earlier generation of planners an understanding that central government could play a creative role in formulating institutional structures for higher education. Beyond that, the differences were more substantial than the similarities. Dawkins conceived national needs in economic terms, largely ignoring the cultural role that had traditionally been associated with universities. Where the post-war planners had sought to build on centuries of tradition, and had looked to overseas universities to show them the way, Dawkins seemed to prefer demolition and building anew. As Karmel put it, the Green and White Papers showed 'limited understanding of the institutions and no great respect for them, their staff or their work'.

Some academics, especially in the colleges of advanced education, welcomed the proposed changes as promising to revitalise what they saw as a moribund system. Many more were hostile, rejecting as Orwellian the whole notion of a unified national system. Some remarked that the reforms were 'right on diagnosis' but 'wrong on remedy'. The most intensive public discussion of the Green Paper took place at a seminar convened by the Research School of Social Sciences and the Academy of Social Sciences, where the overall tone of comments was severely critical (with Aitkin lamenting that his colleagues had got it wrong).

In the eyes of their opponents, the most offensive element of the proposals was the threat to university autonomy. While the White Paper talked about educational profiles as 'a mechanism to balance the freedom of institutions to manage their own affairs with the need for improved public accountability', the Minister, by his statements and actions, left no doubt that he intended an unprecedented degree of intervention in the day to day affairs of universities. Shortly before the Green Paper appeared, Dawkins abolished the Commonwealth Tertiary Education Commission which, together with its predecessor the Australian Universities Commission, had kept governments at arm's length for 30 years. The body that replaced it, the National Board of Employment, Education and Training, was strictly advisory. This left the formulation and implementation of policy in the hands of Dawkins, who remained in charge of the portfolio until 1991; Peter Baldwin, the junior Minister in charge of Higher Education from 1990; and their departmental officials.

Although the White Paper denied that government had a role in dictating management structures to institutions, it rode roughshod over traditional concepts of collegial government, drawing links between universities and large businesses and urging them to achieve 'strong managerial modes of operation'. Governing bodies were to be smaller; and they were to delegate 'clear responsibility and authority to their Chief Executive Officers to implement agreements reached with the Commonwealth, and to hold them responsible for that implementation'. This hastened the movement towards a system of industrial relations where vice-chancellors and senior administrators were perceived as 'management', and academics as 'staff'.

Karmel had urged better management and stronger leadership, but this was going much further than he had ever intended. In any case, he was now retired as Vice-Chancellor, although he remained prominent in several other organisations and as an astute and constructive critic of the government's education policies. His successor was Laurie Nichol, whose appointment was formally announced in July 1987, the day before Australians voted to return the Hawke government to office.

The choice of Nichol may be seen as an assertion by the University, through its selection committee, that the tradition of collegial government should be upheld. Born in Adelaide, educated at Adelaide University, and now in his early fifties, Nichol had been a member of the John Curtin School for many years, as a research fellow in the mid-1960s, then as Professor of Physical Biochemistry from 1971 to 1985. During that time he had been active on University committees, especially the Board of the Institute (BIAS), where he had won a reputation as an able chairman, mild mannered and gently spoken, with a fine grasp of detail and a commitment to fair play. When he was asked whether he was prepared to be considered for the position of vice-chancellor, he was currently Vice-Chancellor of the University of New England in Armidale, NSW.

Laurie Nichol, Vice-Chancellor from 1988 to 1993, in 1990. Photograph by Stuart Hay.

One of the other candidates was Aitkin, who had succeeded him as chair of BIAS and whose views and style were well known. Where Nichol was a successful exponent of collegial government, Aitkin was an unabashed supporter of structures that were more managerial and a firm believer in decisive leadership. Members of BIAS had become increasingly restive as he led them along paths they were reluctant to take. Nichol was safe; Aitkin was risky, with a style that was perhaps too slick for some of his colleagues' tastes. Aitkin interpreted the choice as a decisive rejection of his own analysis of the University's problems and his proposals for the future: 'My reading of the decision was that a significant group within the Council, as well as within the University, seemed unconvinced that real change was necessary'. Looking elsewhere for challenges, he soon found them when Dawkins asked him to chair the new Australian Research Council, which replaced the

Australian Research Grants Committee. He later became Vice-Chancellor of the University of Canberra, several kilometres out of town, where he reflected with frequent astonishment on his old University while working to create a new one.

In the meantime, Nichol had to lead the ANU through what was perhaps the most difficult period of its career. Dawkins and Baldwin inflicted pain throughout the University and left scars that would take many years to heal. In the short term, the deepest wounds were caused by the abortive attempt to force a merger with the Canberra College of Advanced Education (the future University of Canberra). Then there was a review of the Institute which recommended that responsibility for funding the John Curtin School should be transferred to the National Health and Medical Research Council. This was followed by another review which recommended that The Faculties should be separated from the ANU and merged with the University of Canberra.

As academics throughout Australia realised the implications of the revolution, their responses became more strident. ANU staff were often at the forefront of the public opposition. In August 1988, Eugene Kamenka, John Mulvaney and senior colleagues in the humanities throughout the country wrote to the press deploring the Green Paper's view of higher education as 'a commodity that can be produced and made to order and sold'. In 1991 Barry Rolfe, Professor of Plant Molecular Biology in the Research School of Biological Sciences, organised a national advertising campaign severely critical of Dawkins' reforms and galvanising support among the academic community at large. Barry Ninham, Professor of Applied Mathematics in the Research School of Physical Sciences and Engineering, fulminated in the press about 'the damage caused by the idiotic policies of feral bureausaurs ... masquerading as so-called rational economists'.

The changes initiated by Dawkins gradually altered the shape and ethos of the University. A new Act of Parliament, passed in 1991, reduced the size of Council from 44 to 23, with fewer representatives of the University community. The administration became more overtly managerial, and more subject to externally initiated reviews of its efficiency and more susceptible to internal disaffection. The Faculties became more competitive in seeking students and more determined to make best use of their depleted resources. Staff found themselves teaching larger classes for longer hours, and many complained that they had little time to pursue research. The research schools doubled their efforts to show how they were contributing to national needs, looked for new links with industry and commerce, and sought strategic allegiances with other institutions. Staff on both sides of the campus responded to urgent demands that they perform, and present reports to prove that they were performing.

Oskar Spate, now many years retired, produced a sketch of 'Dawkins' dream', comprising 22 large volumes with titles such as 'Questionnaire on research', 'Significance of research', 'Significance of research on research', 'Organisation of research', 'Assessment of research' and 'Reorganisation of assessed research', accompanied by one tiny volume entitled 'Resultant actual research'. Many agreed that planning and reporting had become ends in themselves. But the new system was here to stay.

Amalgamation revisited

In mid-July 1988, shortly before the expected release of the government's White Paper, Nichol was invited to a meeting with Minister Dawkins. Also present were Peter Karmel, in his capacity as Executive Chairman of the Canberra Institute of the Arts, a part-time position to which he had been appointed soon after his retirement from the ANU; and Roger Scott, the Principal of the Canberra College of Advanced Education. The meeting was short. Dawkins told the representatives of the three institutions that the University, the College and the Institute should amalgamate.

The earlier Green Paper had identified three benchmarks for membership of the unified national system. To participate in the system and be eligible for government funding, an institution had to have a minimum of 2000 equivalent full-time student units, or EFTSUs; to support efficiently a 'comprehensive teaching program' with some research, it should have 5000 EFTSUs; to provide, in addition to this, a 'comprehensive research infrastructure', it needed 8000 EFTSUs. Institutions which failed to reach an appropriate benchmark were urged to 'consolidate' in order to achieve anticipated efficiencies and economies of scale.

Each benchmark was relevant to one of the institutions in the Australian Capital Territory. The Canberra Institute of the Arts (CITA), itself a recent amalgam of the Canberra School of Music and the Canberra School of Art, had under 600 EFTSUs with no desire to reach the necessary 2000 and no prospect of doing so; the Canberra College of Advanced Education (CCAE), with 4836 EFTSUs, was approaching the 5000 considered appropriate for a teaching university; and the ANU, with 5362 EFTSUs, fell way short of the 8000 which would enable The Faculties to be funded for both teaching and a comprehensive research structure.

The figures were clear. Nevertheless, because they were accustomed to regarding their institution as a special case, ANU academics and administrators wondered whether the amalgamation arrangements were intended to apply to them. Dawkins' meeting with Nichol, and his formal announcement after the release of the White Paper, left no doubt that they were. Moreover, where most state institutions would be able to choose their own forms of consolidation, the institutions in the ACT, governed by Commonwealth legislation, were given no choice but to amalgamate.

'With quavering boots', as he later remembered, Nichol called a meeting of all staff to tell the University what the Minister had in store. The immediate reaction was more of bewilderment than horror, as people across the campus tried to guess what the future held. Dawkins promptly appointed a steering committee to plan the merger; staff were told that CCAE and CITA staff should henceforth be regarded as internal applicants for positions in the University; and in October the government appointed an interim council to take charge of the amalgamated institution.

In the meantime, as people within the University gave thought to exactly what the merger would mean to them, there developed a solid body of opposition. The prospect of amalgamation with the Canberra Institute of the Arts, whose two main buildings were located adjacent to the ANU campus, was accepted with equanimity. A merger with the

Canberra College of Advanced Education, however, was seen by many people as presenting major problems. Established in 1967 in the new town of Belconnen, the College was a product of the Martin Committee's recommendations a few years previously to create a binary system of higher education, comprising universities, with their traditional emphasis on research and the pursuit of knowledge for its own sake, and colleges of advanced education, with a strong vocational orientation. The colleges would teach technical subjects, business and administration, as well as a component of general education. They were to offer diplomas rather than degrees; and they were explicitly urged to resist the temptation to copy 'the educational processes and curricula of universities'.

This prescription proved impossible to enforce. The colleges expanded rapidly, drawing strength from rising student entry standards and growing numbers of well-qualified staff, who might in former times have been welcomed into the universities. These staff continued to see research and publication as offering the best routes to advancement within the tertiary system. Before long the colleges were awarding degrees and adopting the ritual and forms of traditional universities, and some of their staff were engaging in research comparable with that of their university colleagues.

The Canberra College of Advanced Education was widely regarded as one of the more successful in the system; and given that it was only five minutes by car from the ANU, a merger seemed more feasible than some of the other amalgamations being negotiated at the time between campuses that were long distances apart. Nevertheless, on both campuses the opposition to the merger, once it gained momentum, was fierce. Opinion among academic staff at the ANU split roughly in two, though not along obvious structural lines. The faculties, which together expected to be most affected by amalgamation, were opposed, except for the Faculty of Science. The research schools were about evenly divided, with Social Sciences, for example, voting one way, and Pacific Studies the other. Both the Students' Association and the Staff Association voiced strong disapproval.

Some supporters saw significant academic advantages in the merger. Compared with the large state universities, the ANU's range of degrees and courses was limited. The College, with well-established schools of Applied Science, Communication, Education, Environmental Design, Information Sciences and Engineering, and Management, could be seen as complementing and extending the ANU's offerings, and so enhancing its capacity to attract students in an increasingly competitive environment. Links between the ANU's Science Faculty and the College's School of Applied Science seemed promising.

That pragmatic administrator Ian Ross, now Pro Vice-Chancellor, doubted whether the ANU had a choice. Responding to a letter in the *Canberra Times* from Bob Dixon, Professor of Linguistics in the Faculty of Arts and an outspoken opponent of amalgamation, he conceded that life would be easier if the merger were not to proceed. But the University had to look to the future; and the prospects of 'an unamalgamated ANU' ten years ahead were bleak. Until now, The Faculties had been well funded relative to other universities. There was little chance of this continuing under the new system, which would no doubt distribute funds more precisely on the basis of student numbers. So a merger with the CCAE, while uncomfortable in the short term, offered long-term financial security.

The opposition case rested chiefly on the inherent differences between the two institutions and the absence of convincing evidence that amalgamation would yield significant academic or administrative gains. Although parts of the College had become more like the University, many ANU people perceived a gulf that was impossible to bridge, chiefly because the two sides were at different levels of objective and achievement. There could be no denying that by various measures the University rated far above the College: where the ANU still had the largest number of representatives of any university on the Australian academies of Science, Social Sciences and the Humanities, the College had none; where the ANU, even if the Institute of Advanced Studies was excluded, could boast a formidable research output, the CCAE's publications were modest; ANU academics had proportionately many more PhDs in total than their College counterparts. Although its emphasis on teaching might have allowed the College to narrow the gap, teaching was rarely given the same recognition as research as a measure of academic achievement.

Amalgamation, said its opponents in the University, would mean lower standards. The Faculty of Economics and Commerce at the ANU engaged in acrimonious debate with equivalent sections in the College over the quality of their courses, with one head of department accusing another of 'blatant distortions'. John Pitchford, Professor of Economics since 1965, warned Nichol that 'a group of departments of world standing could be rapidly dissipated unless something is done to ensure their continuance'. Emotions ran high. At a meeting attended by about six hundred staff, John Molony, the Manning Clark Professor of History in the Faculty of Arts, urged his colleagues to defend 'the university we love, the community we have worked within, the ideals we have striven for, the traditions we have fostered'. Bob Dixon told Ross that the battle could be won: 'Maybe we'll lose in the end. But we'll go down fighting for what we believe in. And we will not bow before political intimidation.'

Opinions at the College were likewise divided, but united in the understanding that, if the merger were to proceed, it would be on terms agreeable to both parties, and not simply an ANU takeover. Hence there were suggestions that the new institutions should be renamed, with several possibilities being put forward, including the University of

Above: Nichol outlines developments relating to the proposed amalgamation with Canberra College of Advanced Education to a meeting of staff in Melville Hall, April 1989. Other members of the panel are, left to right, Deane Terrell (Acting Dean of the Faculty of Economics and Commerce), Derek Robinson (Chairman of the Board of the Institute of Advanced Studies), Eric Bachelard (Chairman of the Board of The Faculties) and, missing from the photograph, Chris Bryant (Dean of the Faculty of Science).
Above left: Staff members listen, many with evident scepticism. John Molony, one of the most vocal opponents of amalgamation, is third from the left in the front row. Photographs by Richard Briggs.
Canberra Times.

Canberra, Chifley University and the National University of Australia. Such talk stiffened resistance at the ANU. Taking matters into its own hands, the College Council conferred the titles of professor on its College Fellows and associate professor on its principal lecturers, astonishing and infuriating many people in the University, where the title of professor was jealously guarded by demanding appointment and promotion criteria.

Politics delayed proceedings. Towards the end of 1988 Dawkins introduced his bill to create a new university, intending it to come into being midway through the following year. The bill encountered resistance in parliament, where it faced the prospect of rejection in the Senate, and in the ACT Legislative Assembly, which expected to have a say in how the new or restructured institutions would be run. As the time originally scheduled for the merger passed, Dawkins asked the three institutions for their 'final, formal advice'. The ANU Council, which had hitherto wavered, now came out narrowly in opposition. Confronted with this decision, the CCAE Council agreed that amalgamation was unattainable. On both campuses, opponents of the merger were delighted.

Nichol, while welcoming an end to the uncertainty, anticipated battles ahead. But the threat of amalgamation quickly passed. The College negotiated an improbable 'sponsorship' agreement with Monash University far away in Melbourne, under which it achieved university status at the beginning of 1990 as the University of Canberra. The government introduced new formulae which provided funding on the basis of institutional profiles and supplanted the notion of arbitrary benchmarks based solely on student numbers.

Thirty years earlier, when Prime Minister Menzies had announced that the ANU and Canberra University College would be associated, there had been no doubt that it would happen. In 1988 and 1989, when a large part of the University community waged a battle against another government decision in favour of amalgamation, the Minister was obliged by a hostile Senate to let them have their way. Yet the victory probably had as much to do with the pace of political change in the late 1980s as with any weakening of political resolve. Between the time Dawkins announced his intention to amalgamate and the decision of the University Council to resist, amalgamations had occurred throughout Australia (excepting Dawkins' home state of Western Australia), the unified national system had taken shape, and the merger of specific institutions, even if located in the Commonwealth's own backyard, had ceased to be a pressing issue.

Few people engaged in the battles of the 1980s gave thought to the earlier debate or reflected on similarities and differences between the two attempted amalgamations. The past seemed remote. On the face of it, the two institutions that Dawkins aimed to merge bore little resemblance to the ANU and Canberra University College in 1960. Yet similarities between the events were striking. Both attempted amalgamations, the one fulfilled, the other abandoned, arose from considerations that had as much to do with politics as with education. Both took place in the context of sweeping changes to the higher education system, one instigated by the Murray Report in 1957, the other by Dawkins' Green Paper in 1987. Both confirmed the power of the Commonwealth government to do as it wished with tertiary institutions in the ACT, subject only to the power of parliament. Both sought to merge institutions that had different histories, with little concern for how those histories might influence the outcomes.

Immediate reactions were likewise similar: the divisions of opinion within each of the institutions; the anxieties in the larger institution about having its standards lowered and, in the smaller, about being overwhelmed; the arguments about nomenclature; the determined resistance within the University as the smaller institution demanded equal status at the negotiating table. Had the second amalgamation gone ahead, the long-term results were also likely to have been similar. By mid-1989, the opposing troops had settled into the trenches. If the previous experience was any guide, the sniping would have continued for many years.

Already the battle had resulted in at least one casualty. Ever since Dawkins had announced his plan, Nichol had been caught in crossfire between the Minister, who expected him to act as chief executive and implement the government's decisions, and the University community, which demanded that he represent the collegiate will. For a time he was in the invidious position of not knowing whether he would be head of the merged institution. Urging his colleagues to acknowledge that 'external pressures are a reality', he accepted amalgamation in principle while working to ensure that negotiations on large questions, such as the name of the new institution, went the ANU's way. His own views were ambivalent: while he envisaged long-term benefits in what he referred to as a 'multi-stranded university', comparable with some of the best institutions in the United States, he knew that amalgamation would cause 'a lot of heartache' in the short term. Nevertheless, he was widely perceived as a keen supporter of the merger and therefore an appropriate target for criticism. Then Dawkins was forced to abandon the cause, which suggested that the opponents had been strategically right to stand their ground. The Vice-Chancellor, his judgement and capacity for leadership called into question, found that the ground had moved beneath him.

Music and art

In marked contrast with the turmoil that accompanied the University's relations with the College of Advanced Education, the merger with the Institute of the Arts slipped through almost unnoticed. At the time, the Institute was not much more than a name on a letterhead, though its component parts, the Canberra School of Art and the Canberra School of Music, both had reputations far beyond the local community.

The School of Art had grown from humble beginnings as part of the Canberra Technical College, a conglomeration of huts behind a bus depot in the suburb of Kingston. Art classes were introduced after the war, under the auspices of the National Art School in Sydney and the New South Wales Department of Technical Education. In 1969 the art teachers moved to the elegant art deco building alongside the University, recently vacated by Canberra High School; and in 1976, when a separate system of technical and further education was established in the ACT, the College's Art School was reconstituted as the Canberra School of Art, with its own Director and Council.

The School flourished under its first Director, Udo Sellbach, who had previously been head of the Tasmanian School of Art. Sellbach, a printmaker, had a vision of a

Photograph by Julie Macklin.

community based School which drew on the national links that Canberra was able to offer. He brought cohesion to what had previously been largely unrelated courses, giving equal emphasis to crafts and fine arts. The School ventured into new areas: Klaus Moje set up the first glass workshop in an Australian art school, while Ragnar Hansen did the same for gold and silversmithing. Jörg Schmeisser enhanced the School's reputation in printmaking.

The Canberra School of Music opened in 1965, in modest premises in the suburb of Manuka. Like the Art School, it owed its creation to pressure from local community leaders, including Ross Hohnen from the University and Arthur Shakespeare, the Chairman of the Federal Capital Press, publisher of the *Canberra Times*. Unlike the Art School, it began life as a separate institution. Seeking a foundation director, the School benefited from an ill wind that had recently separated Ernest Llewellyn from the Sydney Symphony Orchestra, where he had been concertmaster for fifteen years. Llewellyn welcomed the challenge to create a new school in Canberra and insisted that it should aim for standards comparable with the ANU. Within a year he had gathered around him some outstanding teachers and performers, including the violinist Vincent Edwards, the tenor William Herbert, the cellist Laurie Kennedy and the pianist and composer Larry Sitsky.

Ernest Llewellyn, Director of the Canberra School of Music from 1965 to 1980.

Llewellyn remained Director for fifteen years, creating a school that ranked among the best in Australia. In 1976 it moved from Manuka to a new building in the grounds of the old Canberra High School, and hence adjacent to the School of Art and a short stroll from the University. The new building incorporated a concert theatre, later named Llewellyn Hall, which seated up to 1500 people and became the main venue in Canberra for concerts by local and visiting orchestras and artists, as well as the new location for the University's graduation ceremonies.

Even before Dawkins issued his general directive to amalgamate or perish, the independence of small institutions was becoming precarious. Sensing the threat, the schools of Art and Music decided they would be better placed to protect their integrity under a single banner, and initiated steps towards a merger. Early in 1988 they came together as an autonomous statutory authority known as the Canberra Institute of the Arts, governed by a Board comprising Peter Karmel as part-time Executive Chairman, and the directors of the two schools.

No sooner had that happened than Dawkins signalled his intention that the Institute should be part of the three-way merger with the University and the Canberra CAE. The Institute quickly arranged an affiliation agreement with the University, followed in 1992 by complete amalgamation. The event was celebrated by 'open house' at the two schools and an evening concert by the Canberra School of Music Symphony Orchestra in Llewellyn Hall, where works by Rossini, Mozart and Schubert appropriately symbolised the harmonious merging.

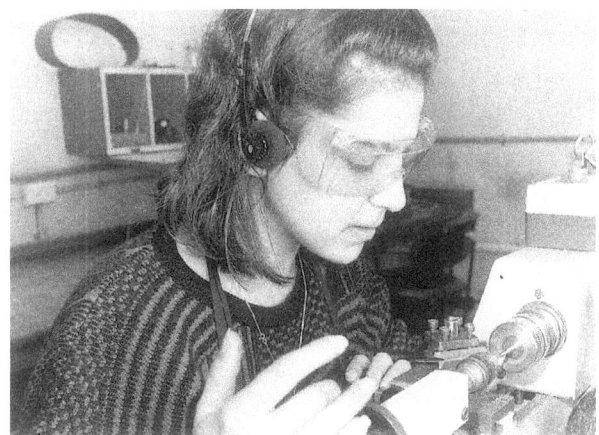 

Left: School of Art student Marica Barisic at the lathe in the Gold and Silversmithing Workshop, 1992. Photograph by Neal McCracken.

Right: Ceramic artist Bernt Weise, foreground, with students in the community arts program conducted by the School of Art, 1995. Photograph by David Paterson.

Amalgamation offered the Institute security in uncertain times. While Karmel and the directors of the two schools welcomed the merger, they also recognised that Dawkins' directive gave them little choice. Changes throughout the system added to the pressure: in other parts of Australia, similar schools and conservatoriums were joining universities and winning the right to award university degrees, which suggested that the Institute could not afford to be left out. At the same time, the form of amalgamation gave the Institute a degree of autonomy like that of a research school, allowed the schools to preserve their separate identities, and recognised that the Institute and the University applied different criteria in matters such as the appointment and promotion of staff and the admission and assessment of students.

From the point of view of the University, the two small schools were respected for their achievements and offered no significant threat to standards. There was little overlap between Institute and University courses and hence no occasion for conflict about their relative merits or the quality of staff. At the same time, there were numerous informal connections, as University staff attended concerts in Llewellyn Hall or members of their families enrolled for classes in the School of Art. Karmel's position as Executive Chairman provided another informal link, as well as confirming the Institute's academic standing. Physical contiguity strengthened the case in favour. And the Institute, which received a large proportion of its funding from the ACT government, offered opportunities for developing closer ties with the local community. Finally, amalgamation made sense on academic grounds. Music and Art promised to extend the range of courses in a University which, lacking some of the usual faculties, including medicine, dentistry and education, had less to offer than some of the large state institutions. All in all, Nichol and others who argued in favour of the merger were able to present a persuasive case.

Amalgamation nevertheless presented formidable challenges to both institutions. The University had long cultivated the creative arts, through the purchase and display of paintings, sculptures and fine furniture and through a Creative Arts Fellowship Scheme. Displaying works of art and having artists and musicians creating and performing on campus helped confirm the ANU as a genuine university. But there was less certainty about whether a university that measured itself chiefly through its

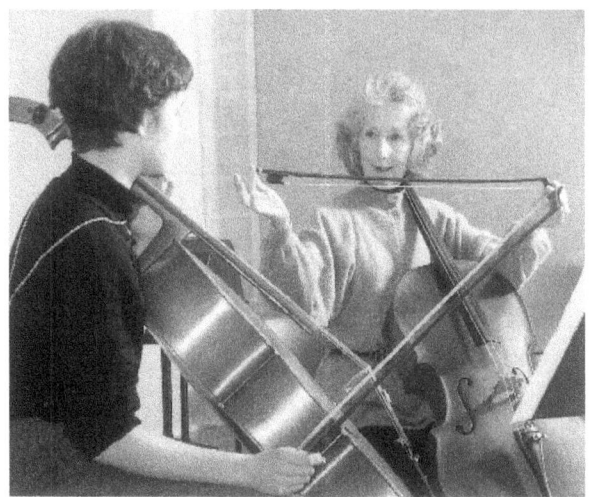

Lois Simpson, from the String Department in the School of Music, gives a cello masterclass in 1992. Photograph by John Tucker.

research achievement should incorporate schools committed to performance and for which, except in certain areas such as musicology, traditional research was incidental and even irrelevant. It was easy to overlook the fact that performance had always been a central part of the University's activities: A.D. Hope, for example, was better known as a poet than a researcher, and the writing of poetry is more comfortably defined as performance than research; and John Passmore was as much the practising or 'performing' philosopher as he was the researcher in the discipline called philosophy. Tradition had subsumed such activities under the research umbrella. Blowing a trombone and weaving a rug represented, for the ANU, unfamiliar forms of academic achievement. If amalgamation was really to work, the University would need to acknowledge new measures which gave such activities the same status as research.

The challenge for the Institute of the Arts, on the other hand, was to maintain its commitment to performance without yielding to traditional University expectations relating to research and publications. Would staff of the Institute continue to devote themselves to the quality of their performance, or would they be distracted by the demands of obtaining a higher degree? The PhD had often dulled the creative spirit in the humanities and social sciences. Would it have a similar effect in the creative arts? Or would the University's criteria for the award of PhDs adjust to accommodate outstanding performance? Would students seeking admission to the Institute be expected to conform to entry requirements for the University as a whole? 'Would

Visiting artist from Cuba, Juan Jacinto Herrera, in a masterclass with percussion student Alison Low Choy at the School of Music in 1994. Photograph by John Tucker.

Mozart get into Cambridge?' asked Don Aitkin, one of the few people to raise these issues. 'Would it have mattered?'

Such questions seemed remote as the University looked forward to its fiftieth anniversary celebrations, enhanced by creative presentations from staff and students in the Institute of the Arts. The future of the Institute as an integral part of the University seemed bright. Although the merger had so far brought few of the cost efficiencies forecast by the government, in other respects it was widely acknowledged to be one of the happier outcomes of Dawkins' reforms.

John Curtin under siege

No sooner had the University put the CCAE amalgamation crisis behind it than it was confronted with another.

Early in 1987 the Australian Science and Technology Council, in a paper which assessed the overall direction of Australian research funding, had suggested that the Institute of Advanced Studies as a whole should be reviewed. Karmel was suspicious: the proposed review seemed to imply that the future of the Institute was 'up for grabs', and that its resources would be distributed among the state universities. The proposal also suggested a significant change in the nature of reviews. The early reviews of the research schools, beginning with Robert Street's review of Physical Sciences, had been conceived as internal mechanisms for change. This new review could be seen as a means of enforcing external accountability.

Characteristically, Karmel decided that if a review was inevitable, the University should seize the initiative and make sure that the inquiry demonstrated the Institute's contribution to the national research effort. Nichol followed through, telling the Minister that the system of higher education had so changed since the foundation of the University that the role of the Institute deserved to be carefully explored, preferably by an external review, conducted under the auspices of government. The initiative was a pre-emptive strike. It was a risky undertaking, all the more so because Karmel was no longer there to see that matters did not get out of hand.

In consultation with the University, the government appointed a committee of eight, chaired by the highly respected former Governor-General, Sir Ninian Stephen, and including five other members who were resident in Australia, one Australian who was research director of a large biotechnology company in California, and one of America's most eminent social scientists. Unlike all the later reviews of individual research schools, there was no member appointed from within the University. The terms of reference were wider than originally intended, requiring the committee to enquire into the standing as well as the role of the Institute, the respective roles of the Institute and other Australian research and higher education institutions, its role in specific areas, and the ways in which it was funded.

Senior members of the University recognised that in the context of Dawkins' reforms the reviewers were likely to ask hard questions. The most pressing one related to funding: should the Institute seek to retain its separate research funding, comprising about 13 per cent of the total funding for higher education research in Australia, or should it seek to compete with other universities for some of its resources? While many research projects, well able to withstand the scrutiny of peer review, might benefit from access to Australian Research Council and National Health and Medical Research Council funds, the continuation of guaranteed funding provided opportunities, rare in the Australian research environment, to develop long-term projects and to pursue 'fundamental research' wherever it should lead.

Whichever way the University chose to argue, there was an element of risk. The Board of the Institute decided that the status quo was the safer bet, and determined to defend it vigorously by pressing not merely for a continuation of separate base funding, but for an increase. A presentation of almost three hundred pages showed, with the help of 'some standard and some novel bibliometric measures of success', how much the Institute was contributing to Australian research and in particular the impact of that research, and described how Australia benefited from a diversity of approaches to research funding.

The review committee was persuaded, and recommended that the non-competitive mode of funding should continue, with the qualification that a portion of the budget should be allocated on the basis of postgraduate student numbers. This gave renewed emphasis to the Institute's training role, about which there had been some doubt ever since the state universities had begun turning out large numbers of PhD graduates. The reviewers stated explicitly that 'the Institute should retain its distinctive character as part of a university, with all the benefits that brings, not only to the Institute but also to The Faculties'. At the same time they proposed a clearer distinction between the two parts of the University, with the current system of funding by a single parliamentary vote being replaced by two votes. This reversed the trend that Crawford had set in train twenty years earlier of using budgetary strategies to bring the two parts closer together.

Most of the other recommendations were uncontentious: the appointment of a director of the Institute to improve overall strategic management, a consultative committee to strengthen links with the rest of the higher education system, and advisory committees for each school; steps to forge closer connections with other Australian universities and to make the Institute a resource for the whole research community; the continuing encouragement of the Graduate School; determined efforts to recruit suitable women, especially at senior levels. The committee also recommended the total abolition of tenure in the Institute. Here the University demurred, arguing that a substantial core of traditional continuing appointments was necessary to make best use of the Institute's resources.

There was plenty of comfort in the committee's findings, especially in its broad conclusion that in most respects the Institute had met its charter 'outstandingly well'. The report gave specific endorsement to 'strategic research', which combines 'a search for fundamental understanding with a concern for significant use', commenting that the work of the research schools and centres was replete with examples of research that was guided by these complementary goals. By recommending a mechanism of funding by a block grant in the parliamentary estimates, the committee acknowledged the role of the Institute as 'a distinctive part of Australia's academic research system'.

Those inside and outside the University who had advocated radical change were disappointed. Aitkin, watching the proceedings as chair of the Australian Research Council, thought the University, by arguing defensively, had missed an opportunity for real change, and that the Institute would gradually run down, becoming more remote from the rest of the higher education system. Another member of the ARC dismissed the report as 'a bit of a squib'.

Yet in one area the committee's recommendations were revolutionary. In the John Curtin School, the reviewers found 'special problems' not shared by other parts of the Institute. 'What has particularly concerned the present Committee is not simply the existence of problems—all institutions have them—but rather the persistence of a set of particular problems identified in two successive decennial reviews and obviously still largely present in 1990.' The committee proposed 'drastic and immediate action': the transfer of some activities, the termination of others, and the continuation of the remainder in a smaller but more coherent institute situated within the ANU but funded for research by the National Health and Medical Research Council.

For most members of the school, this was an appalling and totally unanticipated prospect. Yet for anybody who had read the 1978 and 1988 reviews of the school, absorbed the various submissions to the committee, and listened to some of the public sniping, the recommendations should not have been surprising.

What *was* surprising was the committee's failure to demonstrate convincingly that it was pointing the school in the right direction. JCSMR staff asked why their school and no other was subjected to detailed performance evaluation, and charged that they had not been adequately consulted. Critics could point to the reviewers' failure to appreciate recent changes that had taken place under Robert Porter's successor, David Curtis, now one of the longest-serving and most widely respected members of the school, who had agreed to act as a caretaker director for the few years preceding his retirement. Curtis had been working cautiously to implement the recommendations of the 1988 committee and had made considerable progress towards healing the school's bruised morale.

David Curtis, Director of JCSMR from 1989 to 1992, in 1994. Photograph by Stuart Butterworth.

The school responded to the Stephen report with more cohesion than it had known for years. Although some staff welcomed the prospective changes, most rallied behind Curtis to oppose government intervention. The issue spread across and beyond the campus. If government could take responsibility for funding one research school away from the University, could it do the same with the others? Was this the beginning of dismemberment of the whole institution? Were there implications for the autonomy of universities generally?

Yet the government seemed determined to see that the recommendations were put into effect. Nichol decided to accept what appeared to be the inevitable and negotiate to ensure that the University, if no longer in charge of the money, would at least retain control over the directions and management of research. Opinions on Council were divided. Some members wanted to stand firm; others feared that, if the University did not accept the government's wishes, worse might follow.

In November 1991, after several months of discussions, Council voted by a narrow margin to allow negotiations with the NH&MRC to continue, as the least unpalatable of the options open to it. This was widely perceived as a surrender, and it brought matters to a head. The Board of the Institute urged Council to rescind the resolution, declaring that it represented a denial of the University's authority to manage its own affairs. The heads of schools, after agonising over how the University would cope if support for JCSMR was cut, nevertheless decided that the University must resist intrusions into its autonomy. The next day some five hundred members of the academic and general staff packed into the H.C. Coombs Lecture Theatre to send a message to Council members that their previous decision was 'wrong, divisive and irresponsible', and to urge them to think again.

That lunchtime rally was one of the most emotionally charged in the University's history. Although a majority of those present were staff and students of the John Curtin School, people came from all parts of the University. Oliphant and Coombs were present by invitation. A few held up banners for the television cameras, proclaiming among other things 'DAWKINS DIRTY DEEDS'. Barry Osmond, Director of the Research School of Biological Sciences, took the chair and attacked the proposal to transfer funding as 'a clearly orchestrated invasion of academic freedom'. Other speakers outlined the achievements of the school, exposed the Stephen committee's proceedings as 'a travesty' and warned that all Australian universities were at risk. Then came the climax as Oliphant, now aged 90, rose shakily to his feet to denounce the government and repeat a threat that he had earlier delivered to the Vice-Chancellor to return his Honorary Doctorate of Science should the University yield any control over JCSMR. Coombs, over four years younger and more sprightly than Oliphant, then explained (in the theatre named after him) why, after fifteen years of silence on University matters, he had decided to speak out against the threats to university autonomy and academic freedom. The audience gave the two old men a standing ovation. The chair invited everyone present 'to join a university reborn', and the rally passed motions bringing pressure on Council to stand firm against the government's 'destructive policy'.

Two days later Council, meeting for the last time in the form that it had been constituted in 1951, reconsidered the various arguments and rescinded its earlier motion, effectively putting an end to further negotiations with the NH&MRC. The government responded by announcing that the $16 million that had been set aside for JCSMR would now be administered by the Department of Health, Housing and Community Services, under arrangements to be worked out between the department and the University. In the short term, the University appeared to have lost the battle, in that JCSMR would continue to be funded as a separate part of the Institute; but at least the threat of being 'swallowed' by the NH&MRC had been removed.

Soon after the Stephen committee delivered its recommendations, a report to the Federal government by Ian Chubb, Chairman of the Higher Education Council, proposed that The Faculties amalgamate with the University of Canberra. The Vice-Chancellor, Nichol, and the Council vigorously and successfully opposed the move, which they said would dismember the ANU. Here, in early 1991, staff and students rally to the cause. Photograph by Darren Boyd.

Control of the John Curtin School now became a political issue in the Senate, where the Liberal-National Coalition, with minor party and independent support, had the numbers. In the early months of 1992 a Senate committee braved the unfamiliar territory of academic politics and tried to make sense of the contending issues. After considering over one hundred submissions and receiving oral evidence from nearly thirty witnesses, including Sir Ninian Stephen and three other members of his committee, the Minister for Higher Education, the Vice-Chancellor and many other members of the University, the Senate committee concluded that the school had been hardly done by, in that Stephen and his colleagues had failed to take account of changes that had taken place since the 1988 review and had not shown that their solution would overcome the problems that were said to persist. The Senators acknowledged that the school had faced a 'myriad of difficulties', and made a fair attempt to enumerate some of them; but was the situation grave enough to justify outside intervention? On the question of funding, the Senators divided along political lines, so that there was no unanimous conclusion.

At the rally in December 1991 to 'save the JCSMR', the audience gives Coombs and Oliphant a standing ovation. In the foreground, left, Tim McCombe, President of the Vietnam Veterans Association of Australia and a warm friend of the research school, and right, David Curtis. *Canberra Times.*

Later in 1992 the Senate passed a bill intended to force the government to return the school to the old form of funding as part of the University's grant through the Department of Employment, Education and Training. But the government rejected it in the House of Representatives, so that the school continued to be funded separately and therefore remained uniquely vulnerable to government intervention.

The Senate inquiry turned out to be a valuable exercise for the University and the school. There was some benefit gained from the Stephen committee's discomfiture, especially in the long term. Drawing on evidence provided chiefly by members of the school, the Senators were unanimous in criticising the committee's processes in relation to JCSMR and in urging that future reviews should follow more clearly defined procedures. It seemed now that even the most eminent reviewers were themselves not above being reviewed. Certainly, the second review of the Institute would have to be more careful and thorough than the first.

The inquiry also helped bring the school's problems into the open. Everybody had been given the opportunity to come forward with grievances, and nobody could now claim to have been ignored. Once exposed, the difficulties had a better chance of being resolved. And future directors would find their hands strengthened by an increased awareness among staff that internal dissent was a luxury they could not afford.

Nor was it possible to rely on notions of university autonomy to protect the University or the school from outside intervention. With disarming candour, the Senate committee remarked that the question of autonomy had been debated 'ad nauseam', an expression which suggested that the concept meant more to academics than it did to politicians. The committee concluded, implicitly, that government intervention in the affairs of a university could be justified if the circumstances were sufficiently grave, but divided along political lines about whether or not the Minister had undermined the autonomy of the ANU. The division suggested that autonomy was negotiable on political grounds, which was as it always had been.

Once again, the Vice-Chancellor had been caught in the midst of a conflict not of his making. While personally opposed to any suggestion that a part of the University should be funded differently from the rest, Nichol had concluded that it was safer to negotiate with the government than to resist. Yet many people on campus believed that there was no room for compromise, and that anybody who attempted to do so was betraying the University. As happened during the conflict over amalgamation, many academics were looking for strategic leadership which the Vice-Chancellor seemed unwilling or unable to give. Gradually he became marginalised within the University community. Some senior professors, chiefly from the natural science schools, urged him to step aside. With another review of the Institute scheduled for 1995, the year in which his seven-year appointment was due to end, Nichol decided to give his successor time to prepare for the review and submitted his resignation, to date from the end of 1993. It was a hard time to be a vice-chancellor.

The University in the marketplace

The Dawkins revolution thrust the ANU, along with the rest of the higher education system, into the marketplace. In the mid-1940s the University's planners had talked vaguely about links between research and industry. Academics would pursue basic science, and industry would develop their discoveries for the benefit of the whole nation. Few people gave thought to how exactly this might be achieved, other than supposing that industry would seize eagerly on whatever researchers had to offer.

This was wishful thinking. Unlike the United States and Western European countries, Australia had no tradition of universities and industry working together, or of industry supporting university research. People in industry, if they gave any thought at all to academics, tended to dismiss them as inhabitants of ivory towers, who had little or nothing to contribute to practical affairs. Academics, in return, were often suspicious of industry, judging that the profit motive was alien to pure research, the results of which should be freely available to all. The result was a stand-off, in which the nation was the loser.

So the situation remained well into the 1960s. From midway through that decade, however, a number of people on campus argued that the ANU should take the initiative in developing commercial applications; and if industry were not interested the University should do the job itself. Arthur Birch, as Dean of the Research School of Chemistry, advocated links with industry similar to those he had been used to in England. On Council the long-term chairman of the Buildings and Grounds Committee, John Yencken, a former research chemist and now a member of a management consultancy firm, successfully pressed for changes in the University's patents policy to encourage researchers to think about how their discoveries might be developed. The Earth Scientists sought to work closely with the mining industry, introducing a scheme by which researchers in industry could spend time in the school as visiting fellows.

A venture from the early 1970s illustrates the ANU's bumpy entry into the world of commerce. A.J. Parker, a Professorial Fellow in the Research School of Chemistry, devised a new process for extracting and refining copper, and patented it on behalf of the University. The school agreed to devote substantial resources to developing the process for commercial use, at the same time hinting at some misgivings about the commercial nature of the project by banishing Parker and his team to old huts separate from the Chemistry building. To run this and possible future projects, Council created a private company, ANUMIN Pty Ltd, wholly owned by the ANU, chaired by Yencken and with other senior staff as directors, but sufficiently removed to ensure that the University remained untainted by commerce. Yencken secured modest backing from Australian companies and, when this proved insufficient, attracted substantial support from the United States.

Solar energy dishes at White Cliffs in western New South Wales.

The project was, as Birch described it, a scientific and technical triumph but a commercial disaster. Before it could make any money, the price of copper dropped so low that it was not worth proceeding. In due course Parker moved to a chair at the new Murdoch University in Western Australia. ANUMIN eventually followed him, for the nominal sum of seven dollars. For the ANU's aspiring entrepreneurs it was a chastening experience.

So too was the University's next significant incursion into commerce. This grew out of work in the Research School of Physical Sciences on the development of solar energy for commercial use. The 1976 review committee had doubts about the project's intellectual merit, suggesting that the research team look elsewhere for support. On the eve of an election, the New South Wales government decided that the prospect of developing solar energy was politically attractive, and offered to provide funding through the Electricity Commission for a solar power station at a remote site. Council, tempted by a figure approaching one million dollars, enthusiastically agreed, and to manage the project set up a company called Anutech Pty Ltd.

The solar energy project led to the installation of a series of large reflective dishes at White Cliffs in western New South Wales, and some useful research relating to small steam engines. But the project team encountered major problems in building and commissioning the installation so far from anywhere, and completion was long delayed. While the power station eventually achieved its designed output, this was insufficient for the town's needs without a stand-by diesel generator. The plentiful and ecologically sound supply of electricity that many had hoped for failed to materialise. The station was operated on an experimental basis for some years, and eventually mothballed.

Nevertheless, it was one of the more successful systems of its type, and the University extracted itself from a potentially embarrassing situation with a relatively clean face.

The legacy of the project was Anutech. In the early 1980s an external consultant recommended that the University set up a technology marketing company to exploit its intellectual resources. The concept was not new: in 1959 the University of New South Wales, whose charter specifically required it to aid by research the practical application of science to industry and commerce, had established Unisearch, and this was followed over the next two decades by several other 'search' companies, mostly attached to institutes of technology. So far, no other university had followed the Unisearch lead.

The consultant's suggestion was taken up by John Morphett, who had served as Laboratory Manager in Physical Sciences and then as part-time Company Secretary of Anutech. Morphett, an avuncular-looking former Army officer, went about his business with military determination. He told Ian Ross that, with a University subvention and a bank loan together totalling some $100 000, he could develop a freestanding commercial operation which would give the University a significant return for its investment. Ross, who was now Acting Vice-Chancellor after Low's departure and who shared Morphett's entrepreneurial zeal, grasped the proposal and carried it through Council. Anutech was promptly transformed into the University's marketing arm for academic commercial products and Morphett was appointed Chief Executive (and later Managing Director). The company was to be self-sustaining and was to operate, in such matters as the employment and dismissal of staff, under conditions set by the commercial rather than the academic world. At the same time it was made subject to restrictions not usually imposed on private enterprise, including a prohibition against touting for business. Nor was it to have an exclusive right to develop University research for the marketplace.

John Morphett, Chief Executive Officer of Anutech from its inception in 1979 and Managing Director from 1987. Cartoon by R. Clement, 1991.
Australian Financial Review.

Anutech, its ambit thus redefined, began modestly, not in the areas of science and engineering familiar to the established 'search' companies, but with consultancies to provide archaeological and environmental surveys relating to road and mining developments. To provide a cash flow, Morphett took Anutech into the business of selling computers at discounted rates to ANU staff and students. The enterprise grew to become the largest and most successful commercial company attached to a tertiary institution, and a model for others in Australia and other parts of the world. In 1991 it moved from its original quarters in the wooden huts once occupied by Canberra University College to a new building on the University's perimeter, on a site especially chosen to symbolise the interaction between the ANU, commerce, industry and government. In 1995 it was involved in projects ranging from managing diverse international aid programs in Southeast Asia to manufacturing sophisticated scientific instruments. Its annual turnover had grown to $45 million and it had donated $2.4 million to the University, as well as substantial indirect benefits to departments and the University as a whole.

Marshalling academics for commercial outcomes has been likened to droving cats. Hence the success of Anutech was a significant management achievement. It also reflected the ANU's research and teaching achievement: the company was able to prosper because the University had so much to offer.

Only a small proportion of the academic staff were involved in marketing their discoveries or expertise, and many remained aloof from any form of commercial activity. Yet there was no avoiding the gradual adoption by the University of the forms and culture of the marketplace. When the Annual Report for 1963 had appeared with a colour cover and glossy paper, Council members had complained that it was not in good taste for an academic institution to appear so lavish. Thirty years later such concerns would appear quaint, as the University competed with other employers to attract staff and with other tertiary institutions to attract students, especially from overseas. From 1988 the ANU paid market salary loadings to academic staff in certain disciplines and fields. Staff undertook marketing campaigns to recruit students, who were sometimes referred to as clients, a term made more appropriate by the reintroduction of partial fees in 1989. Even the motto, which carried in the raw translation 'First to learn the nature of things' implications quite different from what Lucretius had intended, was enlisted in the service of marketing, and placed brazenly in English at the foot of ANU advertisements. (The emphasis was later corrected through the insertion of a comma after 'First'.)

As well as influencing the University's image, the marketing imperative helped shape the content and presentation of courses. Here there were dangers: courses could be invented or restructured to accord with fashions that might be short-lived. On the other hand, the need to demonstrate that the ANU offered students more than alternative institutions, or that one department offered better courses than another, led to a renewed emphasis on good teaching, symbolised by the introduction in 1992 of Vice-Chancellor's Awards for Excellence in Teaching. And competition encouraged inventive thinking. Innovative teachers in the research schools as well as The Faculties devised new degrees to meet existing student demands or create new ones. Degrees and diplomas introduced during the early 1990s included several specialist

Bruce Stening, Professor of Management, with students in the Managing Business in Asia program, 1994. Photograph by Gary Schafer.
Canberra Times.

degrees in Asian Studies, a BA in Development Studies, a BSc in Resource and Environmental Management, Masters degrees by coursework in International Relations and International Law, a Graduate Diploma in Scientific Communication, and a Master in Business Administration which focused on Managing Business in Asia (and thereby saved an acronym). Several of these courses quickly proved to be outstanding successes.

A much riskier business was the introduction of certificated courses commissioned and paid for by external funding organisations. Following the Dawkins revolution, several universities looked to such arrangements as a major source of revenue. These placed them in a situation of potentially conflicting responsibilities: while they had traditional obligations to the students to impart knowledge and understanding, and to examine their achievement objectively, they also had to meet the expectations of the commissioning bodies. The ANU entered this new area gingerly with a course introduced in 1991 at the request of the Department of Foreign Affairs and Trade for junior officers in the department, and styled the Graduate Diploma in Foreign Affairs and Trade, which left no doubts about what it was intended to do. The course was to run initially for four years; and as that period neared an end, teachers in the program looked forward to the contract being renewed. Monash University, however, put forward an alternative proposal which seemed to the department to offer a higher level of innovation and flexibility at significantly less cost. The lesson was clear: if the University wished to compete in the marketplace it would have to work hard to win and retain clients.

None of this was entirely new. The aborted Foreign Affairs diploma was reminiscent of the course offered by Canberra University College to diplomatic cadets and funded by the then Department of External Affairs, which had been abandoned 41 years earlier when the department decided it was no longer required. Nor was there anything new about competing for students or negotiating deals to attract staff. What *was* different was the extent to which the ANU, along with universities throughout Australia, had embraced marketing strategies and philosophies. In the 1990s many staff wondered whether the University, in selling its products, was also selling its birthright.

Coombs, as usual, was quick to detect the trend. In his autobiography *Trial Balance*, published in 1981, he remarked that the great threat to the future of universities was 'the tendency of Governments and their servants to apply to universities and their work the values and the standards of the market place'. A decade later Eugene Kamenka, Professor of the History of Ideas in the Research School of Social Sciences, watched the trend with profound dismay. A Russian Jew who had emigrated from Berlin to Sydney at the age of nine in 1935, he had studied philosophy under John Anderson at the University of Sydney and joined the Department of Philosophy in the Research School of Social Sciences in 1955, first as a student and later as a member of staff. In 1969 the History of Ideas Unit was created around him. A man of courtly manners, benign visage and ample girth (a visiting wit once said that he required not so much a chair as a *chaise longue*), and one of the University's most fluent and stimulating speakers on any subject he cared to address, he published extensively on nationalism, Marxism and other revolutionary movements, human rights and legal theory. He was an academic entrepreneur of the traditional sort, whose trade was people and ideas. Under his leadership, the History of Ideas Unit attracted over more than two decades many of the world's most outstanding thinkers and writers, including Q.R.D. Skinner from Cambridge; Shlomo Avineri from the Hebrew University, Jerusalem; J.P. Plamenatz from Oxford; J.G.A. Pocock from Washington University, St Louis; Sir Isaiah Berlin, the President of the British Academy; and D.N. Winch from Sussex.

As a follower of Anderson, Kamenka had inherited a commitment to freedom of thought and to the concept of universities as bastions of critical thinking about the societies around them. Now he found those beliefs challenged. Universities supposed to be dedicated to truth and accuracy were compromised by the values of the marketplace: 'We have adopted the language of the advertising media. If you read any university's description of itself as it attempts to attract students, it's scandalous. If a commercial firm did it we would call it false advertising.' Now money determined everything, and as a result education was suffering. In a valedictory lecture, delivered in 1993 just six months short of his retirement (which was tragically followed three weeks later by his death from cancer), he warned of the threat to traditional values:

Eugene Kamenka, Professor of the History of Ideas, RSSS, and eloquent critic of the university in the marketplace, in 1985.

> The central function of a university is to promote, sustain and impart knowledge and intellectual capacity. On that all its other functions depend. The humanities and the sciences, not the skills of management, communication, making or saving money, offering care and compassion, are the core from which a university derives its values, ideals and irreplaceable social functions.

Was there a middle way? Symbolically, University House suggested that there might be. In the early 1970s, the House was facing financial crisis. Costs were rising and occupancy rates were falling, as increasing numbers of postgraduate students, for whom residence was no longer compulsory, chose to live in houses and flats off campus. At the end of 1971, University House had accumulated a deficit almost three times the size of its annual subvention. It appeared that the gracious living, as conceived by the Academic Advisers and implemented by the first Master, Dale Trendall, would soon be a thing of the past. Long-term residents commented ruefully on the deteriorating quality of meals. A decision in 1972 to separate the room tariff from the meal tariff meant that staff, scholars and visitors no longer necessarily ate together and that much of the collegiate atmosphere of the House was lost. Faced with a choice between maintaining tradition and yielding to financial imperatives, Trendall's successor Sir Rutherford Robertson and his colleagues seemed unsure which way to turn.

Robertson had started to bring the ship around when in 1973 he resigned to become Director of the Research School of Biological Sciences. He was succeeded the next year by Ralph Elliott, formerly Professor of English Language and Literature at Flinders University of South Australia, a German-born Chaucer scholar who as a boy had wanted to be a hotel manager. With an exuberant manner and a flair for public relations, he seemed made for the job. Adding to his credentials, he had just spent a year at University College, the oldest of the Oxford colleges, where he had seen that even in Oxford changes were being introduced to increase revenue.

Building on changes that Robertson had initiated and adding many of his own, Elliott, with the help of astute managers, worked hard to make University House pay. Daily meals in the Hall were abandoned and a Cellar Bar built as a cost-effective alternative; rooms were renovated to cater for more demanding clients; membership was widened to encourage University staff and outsiders to make use of the facilities; the House was vigorously promoted as a conference and reception venue. At the same time, Elliott sought to maintain something of collegiate tradition by organising weekly House dinners and occasional grand feasts, and encouraging cultural activities, such as musical performances and poetry readings. By 1980 University House was breaking even, without the help of a subsidy.

Later masters and managers continued the commercial emphasis, implicitly upholding tradition by marketing heritage. In the mid-1990s the House was returning substantial profits and achieving occupancy rates that were the envy of many Canberra hotels and motels. While it had long ceased to be, as its founders had intended, a college for graduate students, who now occupied about a quarter of the total available rooms, it served the University in other ways: as a national venue for conferences and seminars; as a meeting place where, in the Bistro, Cellar Bar or the shade of the Fellows Garden, colleagues from across the campus could exchange ideas, hatch new projects, and plan for the future; and as a place to entertain and accommodate visitors to the ANU from outside Canberra.

And because so many visitors now arrived from the airport or some other part of town, it no longer mattered that University House was, in accordance with Brian Lewis's original plan, facing the wrong direction.

Ralph Elliott, Master of University House from 1974, at a function in 1986 to mark his coming retirement.

The ornamental pond at University House in the 1990s.

A new generation of students

14

Who were the students?

Despite what Peter Karmel called 'the cult of the big', the ANU remained, in student numbers, a medium sized university. The 1976 figure of 5058 undergraduates increased to 8051 in 1995, while postgraduate numbers rose more sharply from 851 to 2327. Expansion of both groups was concentrated in the 1990s. While Masters' degree and graduate diploma candidates accounted for much of the postgraduate increase, the numbers of PhD scholars nearly doubled. Although the ANU's share of PhD students throughout Australia fell from 12 to 5 per cent as the degree became more common, the high proportion of such candidates remained one of the University's distinguishing features.

Vacation Scholars Jodie Garrett from the University of Queensland and Brett Yeomans from the University of Adelaide conduct an experiment in the Research School of Chemistry in January 1992. Introduced by Bart Bok at Mount Stromlo in the 1950s, the Vacation Scholarship Scheme aimed to encourage recent graduates to proceed to further studies. Photograph by Graham Tidy.
Canberra Times.

From 1976 to 1982 undergraduate numbers in fact fell, as they did in other universities not cushioned by quotas. Then there was a slow and erratic revival until 1990, when new undergraduate enrolments rose suddenly by 18 per cent. These broad trends, as well as variations from one year to the next, were due to various changes: in demography, government policies (especially relating to tuition fees and scholarships), economic conditions and employment prospects, and public attitudes to participation in higher education.

In the late 1970s and early 1980s fewer students went straight from school to university. At the ANU school leavers dropped alarmingly by one-third, while part-timers increased. Hence the undergraduate population aged significantly, from an average age of 21 in 1976 to 26 in 1982. In that year over one-quarter of undergraduates were at least 30 years old. Where many students had once attended university to receive something loosely described as 'a general education' or because it was the thing to do, the new generation of students had a clearer idea of what they were there for. More often now, a degree was seen as a means to an end, the end being employment in an increasingly competitive job market. Worsening employment prospects in the mid-1980s helped make universities more attractive to school leavers, who made up a growing proportion of new enrolments. By 1986 the average age of ANU undergraduates had fallen back to 20. In the early 1990s the undergraduates remained collectively, like their colleagues throughout Australia, both young and earnest.

The gender balance continued to move gradually in favour of women. In 1982, female students for the first time made up a majority of new undergraduate enrolments, and from 1985 there were more undergraduate women on campus than men. The proportion of female postgraduates also grew year by year, from 32 per cent of the total in 1985 to 45 per cent in 1995. For undergraduates and postgraduates combined, females outnumbered males from 1991.

Examinations in the Sports Union Gymnasium, mid-1993. Although continuous assessment helped spread the work through the year, examinations still helped concentrate the mind at the end of year-long or semester courses. Photograph by Graham Tidy.
Canberra Times.

Until 1984, most aspiring undergraduates who met the basic admission requirements were permitted to enrol at the ANU. Teachers and administrators worried that the quality of students was declining, and sought to improve standards by increasing the number of National Undergraduate Scholarships. The exception was the Faculty of Law which, like law faculties in other universities, maintained consistently high admission standards. As pressure for places grew, the University was able to raise entry levels, and by the 1990s there was intense competition for places in other faculties, especially the Faculty of Economics and Commerce. The high quality of students was suggested by the large proportion, over one-third, who proceeded to Honours or postgraduate degrees.

During the late 1970s, the numbers of interstate students—meaning those outside the Canberra–Queanbeyan region—declined, partly because fewer public servants were being transferred (with their children) from other capitals. In 1976 interstate students made up one in three of all undergraduates; six years later this figure was one in four, rising in the late 1980s and early 1990s to reach one in three again by 1995. These figures suggested that, as in previous years, most undergraduates were attracted to the ANU because it was close to home. Yet new undergraduates, asked in 1993 why they chose the ANU, gave almost equal weight to the specific courses offered, with the University's reputation coming not far behind. That reputation was confirmed in the 1990s by several official and unofficial surveys, including the *Good Universities Guide*, first published in 1991, which gave the ANU an 'excellent' rating for staff-student ratios, commended the quality of the library, and remarked that 'opportunities to continue beyond the undergraduate level are without parallel anywhere in the country'. Quality Assurance reviews conducted by the government in 1993 and 1994 placed the ANU in the top band for teaching and research led to additional funding. Many academics regarded such assessments with scepticism. Nevertheless, their impact on potential students, especially those from other countries, was often telling.

Teachers and administrators closely monitored employment figures for ANU graduates from one year to the next. Generally they mirrored national employment trends; and generally ANU students had a better chance of finding full-time employment than the average Australian university graduate, owing in part to the proximity of the Commonwealth public service. Not surprisingly more ANU graduates took jobs in the public than in the private sector. The proportion of ANU graduates entering the public sector was the highest of all Australian universities and the proportion entering the private sector was the lowest.

In 1976 Anthony Low had warned against adjusting degree courses (except in special cases) to the perceived needs of future employers. The ANU, he said, should not focus on target vocations, but should encourage its graduates to be versatile, able to accommodate themselves quickly to the needs of a changing society. Nearly two decades later, the University continued to offer a balance between traditional scholarship and professional training. Nevertheless, few students enrolled at the ANU (or any other Australian university) in the 1990s without some idea of how their degree would lead them towards a specific career.

Anxious faces search for end-of-year results on the notice board outside the Chifley Library in 1987.

Student politics

In 1976 Elizabeth O'Brien finished her degree and completed her term as President of the ANU Students' Association. Except for a year's break in 1970, she had been a full-time or part-time student from 1969, and a prominent figure on campus. During 'the Troubles' she was at the forefront of student politics, contributing especially to the radical feminist movement and the efforts to get courses in Women's Studies up and running. Known in the Chancelry as 'the barefoot contessa', owing to her preference for attending Council meetings shoeless, her departure from the campus marked an end to a turbulent era of student activism. (Two years later she came back to run the campus community radio station 2XX, where in 1996 she was still Station Co-ordinator.)

The new executive of the Students' Association, headed by Jon Nicholson as President, leaned like its predecessors to the left; but its members also believed that the Association's activities should not be influenced by politics. Their main interests were close to home, such as student accommodation, cheaper books, fortnightly flea markets and campus entertainment. They were also keen to improve the popular image of students, much dented in previous years, and to improve relations between students and staff across the campus. Later executives followed this pattern, generally avoiding ideological issues. Ian Warden, resident satirist on the *Canberra Times* (and a PhD student in History in the early 1970s until he realised, as he put it, that his thesis would have a readership of three: its examiners), remarked in 1978 that the mass of ANU students was orthodox and boring, and that the current editor of *Woroni* was as ideologically committed as his neighbour's golden retriever. Jack Waterford, another former ANU student and *Canberra Times* journalist (and later its Editor) who had marched with megaphone in hand at the head of many demonstrations, lamented in the mid-1980s that students had not organised a memorable or well-attended demonstration since 1972.

Waterford conceded a tendency among old revolutionaries to romanticise the past and mourn its loss. Yet there could be no denying that student politics in later years were often unedifying. In the absence of any issue to compare with conscription or apartheid, the campus, like other campuses throughout Australia, became a battleground between left and right which reflected and sometimes parodied political conflicts outside the University.

The big issue of the late 1970s and early 1980s was voluntary student unionism. Under the University statutes, all students were obliged to pay a General Services Fee, part of which was allocated to the Students' Association, which in turn paid a fee on behalf of each of its members to the Australian Union of Students (AUS). Both the local association and the national body were dominated through the 1970s by the left. Both were outspoken not just on educational matters, but also in support of such causes as Palestinian Liberation.

Michael Yabsley, former student politician, in 1980, when he contested a seat in the House of Representatives.
Canberra Times.

In 1976 an Arts student, Peter Berzins, sought exemption from membership of the Students' Association because its policy of supporting abortion law reform conflicted with his religious principles. The case led to questions being asked in parliament, where the Minister for Education in Malcolm Fraser's Liberal-National Party government, Senator John Carrick, initially resisted pressure to intervene, stressing the need to uphold the University's autonomy. Berzins eventually paid his fees; but his resistance contributed to a national campaign by Liberal students who, emboldened by the government's attempts 'to pull the trades unions into line', sought to destroy compulsory student unionism, especially membership of the much despised AUS.

The issue involved matters of principle of a kind that face every democracy. Yet the pursuit of high principles often degenerated into low farce. The campaign for voluntary unionism on the ANU campus was coordinated by an Economics student, Alistair Walton, and an Arts student, Michael Yabsley, leading lights in the ANU Liberal Society who, having failed to win control of the Students' Association, sought to impose their views by other means. These included purloining all the copies of the 1978 *Orientation Handbook* in order to insert a Liberal advertisement, and systematically disrupting Association meetings, a tactic which resulted in some forcible evictions and the occasional brawl. At one meeting in 1978, after several 'serjeants-at-arms' had been unable to throw Walton out, the left-controlled meeting, in desperation, called in the police. The New South Wales Young Liberals, the official youth arm of the Liberal Party, thought their ANU colleagues had gone too far; but Walton responded that the ANU Students' Association was like parliament, where the Opposition had a right to pursue its own ends. Yabsley claimed that he and his colleagues were fighting for 'fairness, justice and the Australian way of life—the rights of the individual'. He later became a New South Wales government minister.

In the meantime, the ANU Liberals urged their friends in parliament to introduce legislation to ban compulsory unionism at the ANU. While Carrick remained opposed, most of his Cabinet colleagues, including the Prime Minister, who had experienced rough treatment at the hands of student demonstrators, supported voluntary unionism. Despite vigorous protests by the ANU Council, a march by students on Parliament House, and some division within government ranks, parliament in 1979 amended the ANU Act to ensure that, while the institutions would continue to collect fees, the money would be passed on to the various societies in proportion to their membership. The constraints were removed after Labor's return to power in 1983.

While the number of serious politicians varied from year to year, there were never more than could comfortably fit into the often chaotic offices of the Students' Association in the Union Building. Usually only a quarter of eligible students bothered to vote at the annual elections for the Association executive. Nevertheless, one successful candidate claimed that the ANU was one of the most politically conscious universities in the country.

During the 1980s the Association continued to be controlled by the left in various guises, sometimes allied with mainstream Labor politics and sometimes not. The exception was in 1982 when, after a Committee on Disputed Returns overturned the result of a previous election, an unusually large number of voters elected the President of the Liberal Society and Arts/Law student, Gary Humphries, as President of the Association. Humphries promised reform; and while some commentators confessed to some uncertainty about what he stood for, one of them remarked that he sounded more reassuring than the 'wild and incoherent ravings' of the left. He later became an ACT government minister, from which vantage point he reflected that the campus was a good training ground for federal and state politics.

At the 1989 election students turned out in larger than usual numbers to elect Back on Track candidates, who stood for 'down to earth competence and an end to obsessive ideology'. While the group emphasised that they were not a political party, their commitment to improved services and value for money suggested that they knew how to win votes. After two years in office, they were defeated by the Green Alliance, which emphasised environmental issues and student welfare. The Greens were inclined to the left; but in keeping with political trends throughout the country, they were also keen to present themselves as good managers.

The Dawkins revolution gave students an issue that most of them could agree on. In order to increase the funds available for higher education, the government introduced in 1989 the Higher Education Contribution Scheme, or HECS, which required all undergraduates and postgraduates, excepting recipients of exemption scholarships, to contribute an annual fee, initially set at $1800 for a full-time student undertaking a standard program of study, and payable in advance or deferred until after the student had entered the workforce. As the Labor government in the 1970s had abolished fees, many students regarded HECS as a betrayal of Labor principles, and the link between the student left and mainstream Labor became increasingly tenuous.

At the same time the government, having signalled that its priority was to provide

Gary Humphries, candidate for the presidency of the Union in 1981.
Canberra Times.

Students express their view of the Dawkins revolution: the minister hangs in effigy from a bridge on campus in 1988. Further downstream a burning coffin marks the death of free education.
Photograph by Warwick Merton.
Canberra Times.

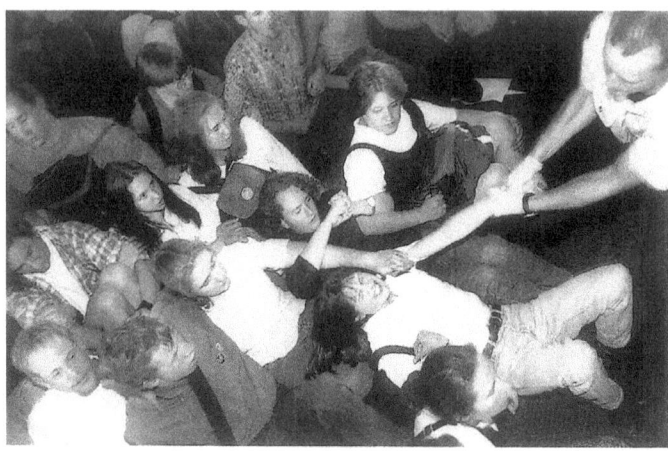

The occupation of the Chancelry recalls similar protests 20 years earlier...

the necessary funding for school leavers to enter university, took the unprecedented step of allowing universities to impose as a substitute for HECS charges their own fees on certain postgraduate courses, specifically those designed for professional upgrading or extension in employment. These arrangements transferred some of the responsibility for funding higher education to the universities, along with some of the opprobrium. The advantage to the universities of introducing fees was that they were allowed to retain them. The ANU, like other universities, therefore proceeded to impose fees comparable with the HECS charges on a variety of Masters and graduate diploma courses. Yet no sooner was the system in place than the government laid down revised guidelines requiring university fees to be at least double the HECS contribution (as discounted for payment in advance). Graduate students everywhere were understandably alarmed, not least because of the implied possibility of future increases. Then in 1993 the government relaxed the guidelines to allow universities to extend their charges to all postgraduate courses, whether or not they were related to obtaining professional qualifications. The ANU, again in common with other universities, took the hint, and set down fees for the following year for most programs comprising coursework or a combination of coursework and research. Programs devoted solely to research were excluded owing to the University's research commitment. And to ensure that the fees were restricted to students who had a capacity to earn sufficient to pay their way, they were applied only to those enrolled on a part-time basis.

The Postgraduate and Research Students' Association protested that graduate tuition fees breached the University's principles of access and equity, and many staff members agreed. Yet so long as the fees were applied only to those students who were likely to be already in the workforce, and who in many cases were sponsored by their employers, resistance was contained. In 1994, however, the University sought to impose an annual fee of $5000 from 1995 onwards on students in the Legal Workshop and gave notice that it intended to make this eight-month course fully self-funding.

Uproar followed. The Legal Workshop, which followed the LLB course and led to the award of a Graduate Diploma in Legal Practice, was full time; and, as the means by which most students completing their law degrees qualified to practise as lawyers, it was in effect compulsory. If students were required to pay the full cost of the workshop, the total expense of qualifying in law, including accrued HECS payments from previous years, could be over $24 000. Although the University suggested that practising lawyers would have little difficulty repaying their debts, students in the Law Faculty rebelled, pointing out that students who were already well into their courses would be obliged to pay fees they had not been told about in advance. Others joined them, seeing the charge as the thin edge of a wedge that could open the way to substantial fees on all full-time graduate courses, and undergraduate courses as well.

The proposal to impose fees for the Legal Workshop came to Council for approval in September 1994. Two days before the scheduled meeting, students occupied the Mills Room in the Chancelry Building, as part of the wider National Day of Action in a campaign against fees called by the National Union of Students, the successor to the AUS. On the day of the meeting, they demonstrated with the help of a double bass, clarinet, drums and a juggler, but the proposal went ahead. An eight-day occupation of the Chancelry by about 150 students helped force the issue back onto Council's agenda. At its next meeting, preceded by another storming of the Chancelry, Council narrowly rejected a rescission motion, but agreed to various compromises, including inquiries into the Legal Workshop and into loan schemes which would allow students to repay the fees once they had graduated.

... although this time the students protest in style. Photographs by Martin Jones.
Canberra Times.

Some students engaged in the Chancelry occupations imagined they were re-enacting the protests of twenty years earlier that had survived in legend. There were certainly resemblances: the sense of injustice, the sit-in tactics, the venue, the frustration of the University administration that eventually led to police being called in to drag the demonstrators away. But there were also differences: the protesters of the 1990s, unlike their predecessors, were described by a reporter as 'peaceful and orderly' (notwithstanding injuries sustained by a pro vice-chancellor and a security guard, and significant damage to property), vacuuming the Mills Room daily, covering the furniture with plastic sheets, and even organising a formal dinner one evening. Above all, while both generations took a stand on matters of principle, the issues of the 1990s related more to the pockets of the protesters than to their hearts and minds.

International students

In the late 1940s and early 1950s the University sent its scholars overseas for postgraduate training. Forty years later all Australian universities were engaged in a determined drive to bring overseas students to Australia.

Foreign students had always made up a large proportion of ANU postgraduates. During the 1970s and 1980s about one postgraduate in three came from overseas. By the mid-1990s, following the introduction of full fees, the ratio had fallen to about one in four. Undergraduates from overseas averaged 4 per cent of all ANU undergraduates in the 1970s, increased to a maximum of 8.4 per cent in 1986, and settled to 5.6 per cent in the mid-1990s. By that time, undergraduate and postgraduate students combined made up some 13 per cent of total student numbers,

International students during Orientation Week in the late 1980s.

expressed as effective full-time student units (EFTSUs), which placed the ANU in the middle range of Australian universities in terms of their overseas student components. What made the ANU unusual was the high percentage of postgraduates, who comprised a little over half the overseas total.

Until the 1980s a large proportion of overseas students came from developing countries and were supported by scholarships offered by the University, or by the Australian government through the Colombo Plan or other development assistance programs. An Overseas Students Charge, estimated at 20 to 30 per cent of the full cost of a student's education, was introduced in 1980. Midway through the decade the government began to look to education as a source of export income. The Overseas Students Charge was gradually raised, and in 1988 the government announced that subsidy arrangements would be phased out and that overseas students would be required in future to pay full fees. Universities were encouraged to become entrepreneurs and to play their part in developing a new industry in the export of education and training services.

The ANU entered the field in 1987 when a team led by Deane Terrell, Dean of the Faculty of Economics and Commerce, visited Hong Kong, Kuala Lumpur and Singapore, bringing back with them preliminary enrolments for 21 students, who became the University's first full fee paying students. Two years later the University set up an International Education Office to market the ANU overseas. As other Australian universities were doing the same thing, the ANU found itself in a highly competitive marketplace, where success was determined as much by the quality of marketing as by the quality of the 'product'. By 1995 full fee paying students, supported by themselves, their family, their friends or their employers, made up 87 per cent of all overseas enrolments.

The University consistently maintained a policy of treating full fee paying students no differently from any others. Nevertheless, the changes in funding arrangements inevitably influenced the way in which overseas students (excepting postgraduate research scholars) were perceived within the University. Where they had once been beneficiaries, now a large majority of them could be defined literally as clients who received a service for a fee. Some courses, such as the MBA 'Managing Business in Asia' program, which reserved one place in three for overseas students, were shaped or adapted to meet overseas student needs.

The changes also influenced where students were coming from. In the mid-1980s the main sources were Malaysia, Papua New Guinea, Hong Kong, Singapore, the United States and Britain. A decade later, the largest numbers came from Hong Kong, Malaysia, Indonesia, China, Singapore and the United States. There was a marked difference between the origins of postgraduates and undergraduates. Postgraduates, who usually received some form of sponsorship, came chiefly from China, Indonesia and the Philippines, while undergraduates, who more often than not paid full fees, came mostly from Malaysia, Hong Kong and Singapore. About seventy countries were represented on campus, with undergraduates from Malaysia and Hong Kong making up the two largest overseas student groups.

While undergraduates enrolled in all faculties and a wide range of courses, the Faculty of Economics, later styled Economics and Commerce, had always attracted the largest numbers of overseas undergraduates. In the mid-1990s, some 30 per cent of overseas students were studying for degrees in Commerce, followed by Arts, Science, Economics and Commerce/Law. Overseas postgraduates were most numerous in the Research School of Pacific and Asian Studies, where there were large numbers researching for PhDs and many others pursuing Masters or graduate diploma courses, especially in some aspect of Development Studies. There were also large groups of PhD scholars in the Faculty of Arts, the Research School of Physical Sciences and Engineering and the Research School of Social Sciences.

Statistical reports made international students into a distinctive group, but in most respects they were far from homogeneous. Students from particular countries, including Malaysia, Singapore and Hong Kong, formed national associations which provided a focal group for social activities. Other friendship groups formed in University House, the colleges and the halls of residence, especially those which provided self-catering facilities. In 1992 some enterprising undergraduates formed the International Students Society, which published a newsletter, offered assistance on educational and welfare matters, and promised to ensure that the University gave full fee paying students their money's worth.

The new emphasis on marketing led to surveys which asked detailed questions about the overseas student population. The results were encouraging. A 1994 survey revealed that most overseas students, whether postgraduate or undergraduate, chose the ANU because of its reputation, either in general, in research or in their specific field of interest. Once settled in Canberra, they were impressed by the helpfulness of teaching and administrative staff, the quality of University facilities and the advantages of living and studying in Canberra. On the other hand, some offered the complaint familiar to residents of Canberra that the city was boring, with too little night life. Nevertheless, over 90 per cent of students said they would recommend the ANU to a friend or relative.

The full fee paying students of the 1990s benefited from the University's efforts to generate income from the education export industry. They also inherited a tradition of pastoral care that reached back to the days of Canberra University College. From the time they were met at the airport to the occasion of their farewell formal dinner, they were shepherded through their courses with the aid of support services widely recognised to be among the best in Australia. While the ANU was more bureaucratised than in earlier years, it was still small enough to maintain some of those traditions of student care which ranked alongside academic reputation as valuable marketing tools.

The language of marketing was pervasive: at a 'Going Home Dinner' in 1993, the Graduate Affairs Officer even suggested jokingly that the University's (projected) alumni association could be seen as a means of providing 'after sales service'. Nevertheless, the ANU's relationship with international students was not solely commercial. Foreign postgraduate scholars had always been an integral part of its research activities. A few schools and departments relied on overseas scholars to maintain their research programs. When in the 1980s it seemed that government policies would impede the supply of students from overseas, there was an outcry, with some departments protesting that they could not manage without them.

The University continued to provide educational services to developing countries, using some of the income received from full fee paying students to offer scholarships. This helped allay any suspicions that its recruitment policies were purely market-driven. Postgraduate and undergraduate overseas students were also valued for their contribution to the 'internationalisation' of the University, and hence to its educational and cultural enrichment. Arrangements with universities in Asia, Europe and North America enabled ANU undergraduates to spend up to a year at overseas institutions, while students from overseas institutions could spend up to a year at the ANU. These and other programs helped maintain the international perspective that had been an integral part of the ANU since its inception.

New graduates in the late 1980s.

From dark matter to the Roman family

15

 A commitment to research

Most weekdays in 1992, Susan Serjeantson, Professor of Human Genetics, rose at 4.00 a.m., wrote and read until breakfast with her family at 7.00, and left for the fifteen-minute drive to the John Curtin School where she arrived about 8.30. Her routines at work differed from day to day, depending on how many meetings or seminars she had to attend; but most of her time was spent conducting research in the laboratory, where she remained until 5.30 p.m. Tall, slim and softly spoken, self-effacing yet single-minded, in many ways she exemplified the dedicated and successful researcher.

Born near Sydney in 1946, Serjeantson had attended the universities of New South Wales and Hawaii, and had spent several years pursuing research in Papua New Guinea before joining the ANU in 1976. For the next seventeen years she worked as part of a small team, first as a research fellow and from 1988 as professor and group leader, on a project to improve the effectiveness of organ transplantation by developing ways of identifying antigens, the foreign substances present in donor organs which often lead to tissue or organ rejection. The project began in the early years of surgical transplantation and was transformed by the emergence of DNA techniques in the early 1980s. These allowed Serjeantson and her colleagues, including dedicated PhD students, to analyse the genes responsible for encoding transplantation antigens and to suggest methods which vastly improved the potential for matching donors with recipients, a process especially critical in bone marrow transplants. The techniques they developed were adopted in laboratories throughout the world.

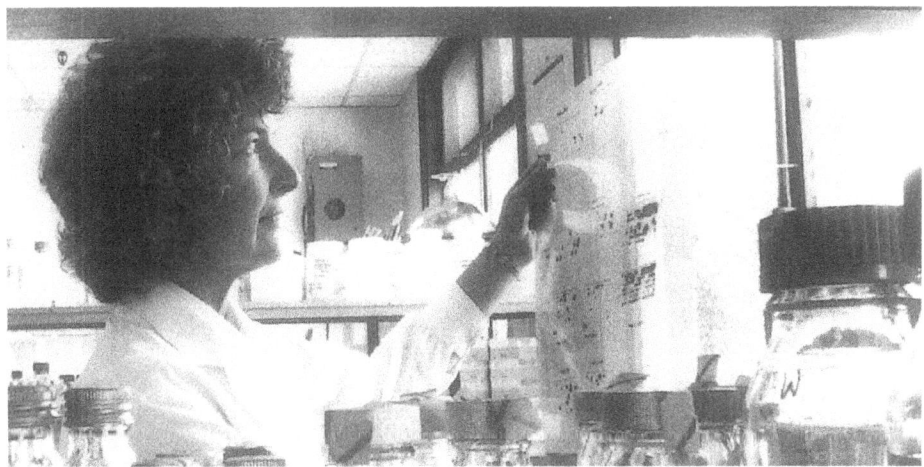

Sue Serjeantson in the laboratory, 1992.
Photograph by Graham Tidy.
Canberra Times.

Their research also led to unexpected contributions to knowledge about the origins of the peoples of the Pacific. Having analysed genetically, in the course of their transplantation work, large numbers of Micronesian and Polynesian volunteers, they were able to contest the traditional view of physical anthropologists that these two groups were closely related, suggesting instead that Polynesians were more likely to have come from South-east Asia across New Guinea to the islands of Polynesia without island-hopping through Micronesia.

In 1992 Serjeantson received a National Clunies Ross Award for Science and Technology, which specifically acknowledged the success of her work in transferring science from a laboratory to a technological environment. It also referred to her persistence in pursuing valuable research over a long period. Much of her time in the laboratory was spent in the slow, meticulous collection of data from DNA testing, gradually extending the bounds of knowledge, like 'little drops of water ... dripping away at stone'. Yet she never found the work monotonous. She told Ann Moyal in 1993:

> one of the most wonderful things I think in science, in the laboratory, is to experience the first extraction of DNA from blood, because you're shaking up all this protein and digesting it with proteinase [an enzyme which acts as a catalyst] and precipitating it with ethanol, and all of a sudden out pops this beautiful pure DNA in long swirling strands that one can actually visualise with the naked eye.

Iain McCalman at his desk, 1995. Photograph by Heather McCalman.

As so often happens to talented researchers, her achievements in the laboratory helped take her out of it: for most of 1993 she was Acting Director of the John Curtin School and later that year she was appointed Director of the Institute of Advanced Studies and the University's first female Deputy Vice-Chancellor.

Iain McCalman, Professor and Associate Director of the Humanities Research Centre from late 1993, rose at 5.00 a.m. and worked for two hours on his laptop computer until interrupted by the appearance of two small boys demanding breakfast. A twenty-minute bicycle ride brought him to the office by 8.45. Born in Nyasaland in 1947, he had come to Australia in 1965, taken an ANU Honours degree in History in 1970, followed by an ANU MA and a PhD from the University of Melbourne. He taught and researched at several universities and colleges of advanced education, passing through the Research School of Social Sciences in the mid-1980s, and returning to a tenured position in the Faculty of Arts in 1987, where his success as a teacher won him an inaugural Vice-Chancellor's Award for Excellence in Teaching.

Energetic and wiry, in 1994 he spent about half his time on the work of the Humanities Research Centre: organising the seven annual conferences relating to the HRC theme, chairing and attending the twice-weekly work-in-progress seminars, selecting the visiting fellows for the 1995 theme on Africa, planning the annual summer school for postgraduate and postdoctoral students, supervising and editing the Centre's quarterly *Bulletin* and numerous published collections of conference papers, communicating with colleagues in the humanities spread around Australia and the world, and trying to win extra resources to enable the Centre to fulfil its local, national and international roles. In the first semester he also taught a well-attended undergraduate course on history and literature in the Faculty of Arts and held regular meetings with the four postgraduates working under his supervision in the Graduate School.

The remaining time was devoted to his own projects on British cultural history, including writing prefaces for the paperback editions of his two books, *Radical Underworld* and *Horrors of Slavery*, both dealing with the rich, strange underworld of ideas that circulated among artisan revolutionaries, ex-slaves, thieves, pornographers, preachers, prisoners, artists and writers in late eighteenth-century Britain and the West Indies. He also prepared and delivered five papers in universities in Britain and the United States, and spent much time editing the *Oxford Companion to British Culture: the Age of Romanticism and Revolution*. In 1993, in recognition of these and other achievements, he was made a Fellow of the Royal Historical Society and a Fellow of the Academy of Social Sciences in Australia.

In addition to being much the same age and early risers, Serjeantson and McCalman had in common a commitment to research. Yet their immediate objectives and methods were so different that the term 'research' scarcely seems sufficient to embrace them both. Where Serjeantson sought to learn more about the human body by interpreting the results of scientific experiments, McCalman pursued understanding of the past through documents. Where Serjeantson spent much of her time at a bench, making use of indispensable scientific equipment, McCalman's research time was mostly spent combing record offices, archives and libraries, reading semi-literate scrawled notes of spies and informers, polemical pamphlets, prosecution reports of government legal officials, fugitive novels, poems and newspapers, as well as keeping up with books and articles by fellow historians and literary critics. Serjeantson worked as part of a team; McCalman (until he became involved in the *Oxford Companion to British Culture*) worked on his own. Serjeantson and her team presented most of their findings in articles in specialist journals, and wrote in a style intended for their scientific colleagues; McCalman wrote books as well as articles, and aimed to reach general readers as well as his peers in history, literature, politics and related disciplines. Serjeantson expected her work to have practical applications for patients undergoing organ transplants; McCalman expected no immediate benefits, beyond the hope of resurrecting lost ideas, visions and social possibilities, and so contributing to larger understandings of humankind.

Yet the link between them was strong. They and their fellow researchers across the campus shared a commitment to the idea of research as a means of advancing the boundaries of knowledge and understanding. They also shared a belief that research, in whatever form it might take, was something that no advanced western nation could afford to be without. This was their association with the founders of the University and the researchers of previous decades, and it was sufficient to give an underlying coherence to the University's research endeavour.

Work in progress

In other respects, that endeavour was most remarkable for its diversity. At any one time, hundreds of research projects were being conducted across the campus. These were often described in work-in-progress seminars, which gave researchers the opportunity to test their theories and findings on colleagues before exposing them to the wider world. Some projects might involve many researchers, including academics from outside the ANU, continue for decades, and lead to major books or discoveries. Others might be the work of a single researcher, last less than a year, and result in a short article in a scholarly journal.

ANU annual reports sought to convey the research achievement by listing the year's publications (until the list became too long for inclusion) and describing a selection of projects in detail. In attempting to represent research over the past two decades, we follow this lead and identify projects, not as a definitive list of outstanding achievements, but rather to illustrate the range and diversity of the ANU's research activity.

Dark matter

ANU scientists at the Mount Stromlo and Siding Spring Observatories (MSSSO) remained at the forefront of international research in astronomy and the related field of astrophysics. Major contributions during the 1970s and 1980s included the discovery that disc galaxies such as the Milky Way have origins far more complex than had previously been understood, and that shells around elliptical galaxies, the other main form of galaxy in the universe, result from mergers between the galaxies. ANU astronomers also provided convincing evidence that about 90 per cent of disc galaxies take the form of 'dark matter', the unseen matter in the galaxies' haloes.

Astronomy and astrophysics illustrate graphically how knowledge advances, as one discovery builds on another. In 1990 staff at MSSSO began a collaborative project with scientists in the United States to test the theory that dark matter comprised objects collectively known as 'massive compact halo objects', or MACHOs. Such objects give out no light themselves but occasionally deflect the light of background stars, thereby offering evidence of their existence. If a star is observed over a period of a year, the chance of such an event being observed is about one in two million.

The MACHO project set out to observe many millions of stars on a continuous basis, making use of the oldest telescope at Mount Stromlo, known as the Great Melbourne Telescope, which had been built in 1868 and transferred to Canberra in

---

GRADUATE PROGRAMS

The list of Graduate Programs in 1996 suggests the diversity of the University's research and teaching activities.

Anthropology
Astronomy and Astrophysics
Biochemistry and Molecular Biology
Business Administration
Chemistry
Computer Science and Technology
Commerce
Demography
Earth Sciences
East Asian Studies
Economics
Epidemiology and Population Health
Engineering
Ecology, Evolution and Systematics
Geographical Sciences
History
Law
Linguistics
Literature and Art
Mathematical Sciences
Medical Sciences
Music
Neuroscience
Philosophy
Physical Sciences
Plant Sciences
Political Science and International Relations
Prehistory and Archaeology
Psychology
Public Policy
Quaternary and Regolith Studies
Resource Management and Environmental Science
Sociology
Southeast Asian Studies
Statistics
Scientific Communication
Science and Engineering of Materials
Visual Arts
Women's Studies

1953. The telescope was modernised and brought under computer control, and the survey began in 1992. By late 1994, the program had made 26 000 exposures of 20 million stars, and had discovered 50 MACHO 'events', accumulating more quantitative data than any other project in the history of astronomy. The ultimate significance of the MACHO project lay in what it revealed about the total quantity of matter in the universe, which would determine its ultimate fate of either expanding to infinity or eventually returning to the primeval Big Bang with which it all began.

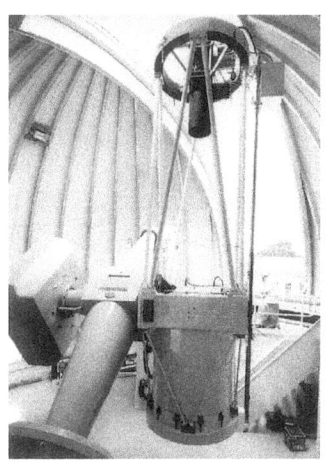

The MACHO project at Mount Stromlo made use of the 50-inch Great Melbourne Telescope, pictured 30 years earlier in chapter 10.

Ion probes and synthetic rocks

Ted Ringwood served as Director of the Research School of Earth Sciences from 1978 to 1983 and as Professor of Geochemistry until his premature death in 1993. In 1991, when accepting the V.M. Goldschmidt Medal of the Geochemical Society (USA), awarded in recognition of major achievement in geochemistry and cosmochemistry, he reflected on the spectacular improvement in our understanding of the earth over the preceding 25 years. It was now possible to investigate in a laboratory the chemical and physical properties of materials which occur in the earth's mantle and core. These advances, he said, 'are now setting the stage for a fundamental enquiry into the dynamical behaviour of the mantle and into the nature of the engine that drives the system and ultimately, I hope, into the origin of the Earth itself'.

William Compston and Ian Willis from the Research School of Earth Sciences with the instrument Compston invented, a Sensitive High Resolution Ion MicroProbe, better known as SHRIMP. Photograph by Guilio Saggin in 1989.
Canberra Times.

The research school was widely acknowledged as a world leader in several areas of geophysics and geochemistry. Research during John Jaeger's time on the theory of continental drift led to a program in palaeomagnetism during the 1970s. Work in geochronology during the 1980s, using an ion-probe instrument developed at the ANU, revealed insights into the evolution of the earth's crust. (The instrument, which fills an entire room, was later manufactured commercially by Anutech.) Much of the school's research had practical applications: for example, by providing a detailed chronology for the old geological terrains in Australia, the ion-probe generated valuable data for mineral exploration. As a by-product of fundamental research, Ringwood developed a synthetic rock which he called SYNROC, which was widely recognised in the mid-1990s as promising the safest method so far invented for disposing of high level nuclear waste.

In the Faculty of Science, Douglas Haynes had been given leave by his employer, the Western Mining Corporation, to enrol for a PhD degree and 'find out all about copper'. His research showed that continental basalts will release copper to circulating hot ground waters and that, under certain geochemical conditions which depend on geological age and setting, the copper is then trapped as copper sulphide in large bodies of copper ore. Having made this discovery in the laboratory, Haynes and his colleagues set out to locate sites which fulfilled the necessary geological conditions. They found one at the Olympic Dam, near the northern tip of Lake Torrens in South Australia. There were no indications on the surface of the existence of an immense deposit. Production began in 1988 and was expected to continue for several hundred years, yielding a total revenue (in 1990s values) exceeding $50 billion. While the ANU had been an expensive undertaking, this one project promised to pay for it many times over.

Shock tunnels, accelerators and mathematical models

In the early 1960s, engineers in the Physics Department in the Faculty of Science set out to reproduce in devices known as shock tunnels the aerodynamic conditions which exist when space vehicles re-enter the earth's atmosphere at orbital speeds. In 1969 the major ANU shock tunnel became the first in the world to reproduce re-entry speeds of up to eight kilometres per second. As well as enabling researchers to diagnose aerodynamic flows, shock tunnels produced heated gases that were used for spectroscopic studies, the analysis of the chemical nature of substances by examination of their spectra. Assisted by contracts from space agencies in the United States and Europe, shock tunnel research continued into the 1990s, with emphasis on developing laser techniques for measuring gas temperatures and densities under the extreme conditions of vehicle entry into planetary atmospheres. This work had direct applications for developing a new generation of aerospace engines.

The year 1975 signalled a turning point in the Department of Nuclear Physics in RSPhysS with the installation of a new generation heavy ion accelerator, known as a 14UD Pelletron. For a time the highest voltage electrostatic machine in the world, it continued to operate efficiently, beyond its original specifications, providing the prerequisite for a productive research program. Nuclear physicists used accelerated heavy ion beams to explore the shapes of atomic nuclei and the mechanisms by which they could form and decay. The 14UD Pelletron was also applied to accelerator mass spectrometry, an ultra-sensitive technique used to measure minute concentrations of naturally occurring radioisotopes. One of these, Chlorine-36, is a unique 'marker' of many hydrological processes, allowing scientists to determine, for example, the age of water basins or to investigate problems of salinity in one of Australia's major agricultural areas, the Murray–Darling basin.

In contrast with team research using large-scale equipment, Rodney Baxter worked alone with little more than pen, paper and personal computer to explore basic questions relating to the nature of matter. When a substance transforms from gas to liquid, or liquid to solid, its individual molecules remain the same, but their collective behaviour changes markedly. Baxter was one of the few scientists in the world to develop mathematical models which accurately explain examples of this behaviour. An ANU PhD and member of the Department of Theoretical Physics in RSPhysS from 1965, he received international physics prizes, including the Boltzmann Medal of the International Union of Pure and Applied Physics in 1980 and the American Physical Society's Heinemann Prize in 1987. In 1992 he was appointed (concurrently with his ANU positions) Royal Society Research Professor at Cambridge University.

Rodney Baxter in 1983.

Surface forces

By the mid-1990s, the Young Turk Barry Ninham had become one of the longest-serving professors in the University, having been appointed to a chair in RSPhysS in 1970, at the age of 35. Although he was styled Professor of Applied Mathematics, he insisted that the title was unimportant. In his view, 'the tyranny of discipline' inhibited the exchange of ideas among scientists. His own area, surface science, encompassed chemistry, physics, mathematics, biology and earth sciences. 'You can't find an apt name for the work we do here', he told the *ANU Reporter* in 1993. 'I think we should sometimes call it natural philosophy and be done with it.' Irrespective of their scientific backgrounds, Ninham and his colleagues sought 'ultimately to understand structure and function and how, in nature, molecules self-assemble into weird and wonderful shapes, exemplified by the diversity of life on earth'.

Some of the major questions in this field relate to the forces that exist between solid surfaces separated by a liquid, when the surfaces are almost touching. Such forces control colloid science, lubrication and adhesion. Their behaviour was explained by theoretical models until Jacob Israelachvili, a member of the Department of Applied Mathematics who had worked at Cambridge on forces between surfaces separated by gases, designed and demonstrated an apparatus capable of measuring the force between two smooth panes of mica immersed in a liquid. As the panes come within a minute distance of one another, the measured force shows up the grainy molecular nature of the liquid.

Such measurements have applications in various industries, including printing, food and mineral processing, and the surface forces apparatus was successfully marketed around the world. When Israelachvili moved to a chair in California, others in the department continued to develop the technology. A versatile new instrument was manufactured and marketed in 1995.

Muscle disease

Michael Denborough in the lab ...

Research in the John Curtin School continued to concentrate, as Florey had intended, on the science behind clinical medicine, that is, the molecular and cellular basis of medicine. From the 1970s to the 1990s there was a gradual shift in emphasis towards clinical outcomes, partly to satisfy public expectations that a school of medical research should have demonstrable relevance to the people's health. That relevance was evident in the many areas of medicine explored in JCSMR: pain and drugs, the molecular structure of viruses, immunity, genetic responses to disease, the initiation and spread of cancer, reproduction, transplantation, neurological disorders such as impaired vision and multiple sclerosis, environmental conditions affecting the incidence of disease, and more.

Nevertheless, the school continued to emphasise the benefits of long-term research, of pursuing specific lines of inquiry wherever they might lead. This was the school's comparative advantage over other universities and medical research institutes. Many projects extended over decades, gradually accumulating knowledge and sometimes yielding spectacular outcomes.

... and on the streets. In the early 1980s he founded the Nuclear Disarmament Party. Here he is being arrested during a protest against an armaments marketing exhibition, held in Canberra in 1991.
Canberra Times.

Michael Denborough joined the Department of Clinical Science in 1974 and devoted himself over the next two decades to exploring the syndrome known as malignant hyperpyrexia (MH). In 1960 he was working in the Casualty Department of Royal Melbourne Hospital when a 21-year-old student was brought to him with an injured leg. The patient was less concerned about his leg than with the prospect of having to receive a general anaesthetic, as ten members of his family had died as a result of anaesthesia with ether. Denborough described the syndrome, and ten years later, having studied reports of similar cases in the world literature, he established a link between MH and an inherited muscle disease. Pursuing the problem at the John Curtin School, he and his colleagues conducted biochemical and physiological experiments on a particular breed of pigs which responded to anaesthesia in a similar way to humans who suffered from MH. Having discovered the nature of the muscle disorder, they developed a test to establish susceptibility to MH in families known to be affected and to identify which anaesthetics could be used in individuals susceptible to MH. As well as saving many human lives, the discoveries were of practical value to the pig industry. In 1982 Denborough was awarded a gold medal at the Fifth International Congress on Neuromuscular Diseases in Marseilles, where the syndrome of malignant hyperpyrexia was named after him.

The immune system

Another of the John Curtin School's continuing interests was the way in which humans combat viruses. In 1973 Peter Doherty and Rolf Zinkernagel in the Department of Microbiology discovered how a gene complex in the cells of vertebrates operates as a 'flag' to attract T-cells (the body's defences) to cells infected with a virus. The T-cells then kill the infected cells. The gene complex, MHC (major histocompatibility complex), is genetically different in each individual, and this difference, known as polymorphism, prevents viruses wiping out whole communities. This discovery, and later work on the biological role of MHC, had a profound international impact on immunology, and won for Doherty and Zinkernagel the Paul Ehrlich Prize and the Albert Lasker Prize, an award of near-Nobel eminence.

Cancer

Drawing on research which began in the 1970s, Chris Parish's laboratory in the Division of Immunology and Cell Biology in JCSMR developed a novel family of sugar-based anti-cancer drugs. One class of drugs inhibits the spread of cancer by preventing cancer cells from migrating through the walls of blood vessels and entering new tissues. Another class starves solid cancers of blood supply by preventing the growth of new blood vessels into the tumours. The sugar-based drugs have considerable clinical potential, as they are subtle in their mode of action and should have minimal side effects.

Chris Parish in 1987. Photograph by Julie Faulkner.

Research in the Department of Biochemistry in The Faculties was directed towards management of the drastic weight loss and progressive weakness caused by tumours. Studies on animals with different types of cancers indicate that a combination of chemical agents which inhibit muscle breakdown can delay the development of wasting. Such mediation should sustain patients receiving stressful treatments such as chemotherapy and radiotherapy.

Vision and optics

Visual sciences began at the ANU when Peter Bishop succeeded Sir John Eccles in 1967 as head of the Department of Physiology. Where Eccles had studied motor neurons in the spinal cord to probe the workings of the brain, Bishop and his colleagues studied sensory cells in the visual system, attempting to unravel how information in the images formed within the eye is analysed by nerve cells of the eye and brain.

Research on vision could be approached from a physical as well as a biological direction. In 1988 the University created a Centre for Visual Sciences to bring

In 1982 Peter Bishop, left, uses a plotting table and mirror to explore the properties of binocular visual neurones, while Shigeru Yamane, visiting fellow, checks the settings on a Zeiss fundus camera, used here to guide the alignment of the two eyes.

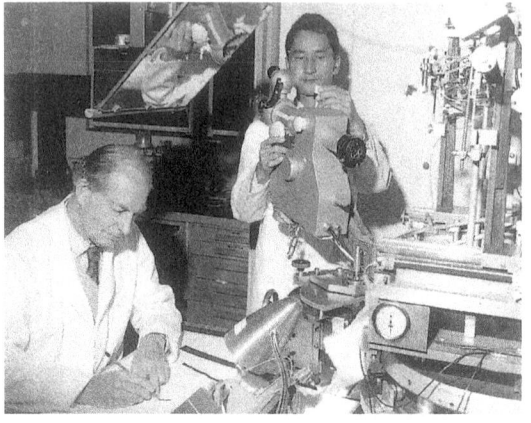

Hans Buchdahl in 1973, after being awarded the Thomas Ranken Lyle Medal of the Australian Academy of Science for research in mathematics and physics conducted in Australia.

Allan Snyder, left, with colleagues Yuri Kivshar and John Mitchell of the Optical Sciences Centre, 1995. Photograph by Darren Boyd.

together many people on campus with interests in natural and machine vision. Researchers associated with the Centre conducted comparative studies on humans and other mammals, birds and insects, drawing links with artificial seeing systems. Research on insects opened the way to the development of novel technologies which promised, among other things, benefits for blind people.

The ANU also had a long history of involvement in the related field of optics, in one direction through the work of Hans Buchdahl, Professor of Theoretical Physics in the Faculty of Science from 1962 to 1985 and later a University Fellow. Buchdahl sought to explain optical aberrations, developing computational schemes that were incorporated into the design of high performance optical systems, such as those used in satellites.

Optics was another area which attracted researchers from various disciplines. An Optical Sciences Centre, created within RSPhysS in 1988 around Allan Snyder, an unconventional American from the Age of Aquarius, quickly became a world centre for research on optical fibres and vision. Again, research benefited from synergies (a term then coming into fashion) between biological and physical approaches. Research on insect vision, for example, stimulated theoretical work leading to significant discoveries about optical fibres, which in turn suggested the possibility of designing a number of unique optical fibre devices with high commercial potential.

Research in optics was strengthened by the amalgamation in 1987 of a number of laser groups to form the Laser Physics Centre, which encouraged cooperation in the use of major laser facilities, with programs in photonics, spectroscopy, materials science and atomic physics. In the 1990s, scientists in the Optical Sciences Centre developed theoretical design concepts for novel, non-linear photonic devices with the potential to revolutionise telecommunications. These concepts, involving the creation and interaction of so-called 'spatial solitons', were realised experimentally by colleagues in the Laser Physics Centre, who demonstrated the attraction and spiralling of optical solitons in non-linear media, the seemingly bizarre pro-cesses proposed by Snyder and his team in 1991, for use in optical switching.

The chemistry of cages

In 1958 Alan Sargeson had joined Frank Dwyer in the John Curtin School to work in the relatively new field of biological inorganic chemistry. With the foundation of the Research School of Chemistry in 1967, the group—now led by Sargeson after Dwyer's death—moved to the new school, where in 1975 he made a discovery which was to retain his interest for the next twenty years and which, in the world of chemistry, became invariably associated with his name.

Sargeson and his colleagues showed that it was possible through a straightforward chemical reaction to create organic molecules that would trap metals. These encapsulating molecules, which became known as 'sarcophagine cages', effectively isolated the metals from the substances in which they occurred.

This process was shown to have many potential uses. The group produced a new class of detergents and a nylon-like compound which removed almost every trace of copper, zinc, cadmium, mercury or lead from water. In the 1990s they were exploring how the cages might be used as imaging agents to provide images of organs such as the brain and heart. The technique also had potential as a means of combating Wilson's Disease, a genetic disorder whose sufferers have no natural mechanism for eliminating the copper which accumulates in their liver and brain cells.

Population health

J.C. Caldwell, who succeeded W.D. Borrie as head of the Department of Demography in 19-70, was a firm believer in the value of social and anthropological approaches to demographic research. An inveterate traveller, he spent much of his time in the field, often in the remote villages and crowded towns of developing countries throughout the world. Empirical research translated into theory: his 1982 book, *Theory of Fertility Decline*, showed how the changing flow of wealth between generations and within families influenced fertility.

In Nigeria in the mid-1970s, he became interested in the influence of maternal education on child survival. Pursuing the subject in South India and Sri Lanka, he moved gradually into the fields of mortality, morbidity and epidemiology. In 1988 he was appointed Advisor to the Rockefeller Foundation on Health Transition and head of a new Health Transition Centre in the Department of Demography, which aimed to explore the cultural, social and behavioural determinants of health change and discover ways of improving health around the world. About this time, he and his colleagues, including his wife Pat Caldwell, began to investigate the causes of the AIDS epidemic in sub-Saharan Africa.

The Health Transition Centre soon moved to a new

Demographers in the field: I.O. Orubuloye (ANU PhD and Professor at Ondo State University), Jack Caldwell and Pat Caldwell interview a Yoruba 'Queen', interim ruler between male chiefs, Nigeria, 1990.
By courtesy of J.C. Caldwell.

part of the University, the National Centre for Epidemiology and Population Health, where Caldwell continued to work after his formal retirement in 1993. Established with Commonwealth government funding, the National Centre undertook research and training in epidemiology, health economics, sociology, statistics and population studies, providing an institutional link between medicine and the social sciences much as Coombs and his colleagues had contemplated in the mid-1940s.

Efficient plants

When RSBS was founded in the late 1960s, one of the areas identified for investigation was the water economy of plants, an appropriate topic for a predominantly arid continent. In the 1970s Ralph Slatyer, Professor of Environmental Biology (and later a Director of the school) initiated a research program on photosynthesis, seeking to discover the relationship between carbon gain, which is the basis of plant growth, and water loss. In due course Barry Osmond (a later Director) elucidated a variety of methods by which different kinds of plants capture carbon. Research by other team members showed how stomata work to optimise the ratio of water vapour and carbon dioxide exchange.

Further investigation demonstrated that the efficiency of a plant's use of water could be assessed by measuring the relative amounts in plant tissue of the two stable isotopes of carbon, because of discrimination between the isotopes during photosynthesis. Such measurements made it possible to identify varieties of agricultural crops that use water with better than average efficiency. For Australia alone, the potential economic gains were impressive. If genetic selection could be used to increase the efficiency of food crops by just 1 per cent, the potential benefits in a dry year would be several million dollars. By the 1990s researchers were reaping rewards from the techniques of genetic engineering. According to an external review in 1995, the school's work on water efficiency was at the cutting edge of plant molecular and physiological research. It was also an outstanding example of teamwork, unexpected outcomes, and the steady accumulation of knowledge and expertise over some 25 years.

Understanding the environment

The Centre for Research and Environmental Studies developed as its makers, Sir John Crawford and Frank Fenner, had intended it should, bringing together various disciplines and offering a unified response to environmental issues in Australia and other parts of the world.

One of its projects in the 1980s was to devise computer-based methods for the analysis of resource and environmental issues and for environmental management. Led by Henry Nix, the Centre's head from 1986, a research team developed a system to incorporate data on the attributes of landscape and biology that regulate key physical and biological processes, such as climate, vegetation, topography, geology and soils. The information is linked to computer models of biophysical processes which help researchers describe and interpret the changing environment.

The system has many uses, relating for example to agriculture, forestry, park management, pest control, tourism and water use. With the help of CRES researchers, national, state and local governments can develop balanced environmental plans that successfully accommodate competing interests.

Saving forests in Nepal

In 1975 the Department of Forestry became closely involved in an Australian government project to save forests in Nepal. The project covered two regions, inhabited by about half a million people who were heavily dependent on fodder from the forests to feed farm animals and on forest wood for cooking and heating. The country was facing a critical shortage of forested land and forest products necessary to sustain its mainly rural, subsistence economy.

ANU foresters, led by the head of the Forestry Department, David Griffin, conducted research into the causes of the deterioration of the forests and provided practical help to the villagers. Where previous aid activities had attempted to impose western styles of management, which turned out to be inappropriate to the circumstances, the Nepal–Australia Forestry Project achieved remarkable success through working closely with local panchayats (councils) and villagers. Over the next decade, more than 6000 hectares of government owned and community land were replanted, many nurseries were established, and scores of villagers were trained as nurserymen. The next stage of the scheme, now managed by Anutech, concentrated on technically feasible and socially acceptable methods of managing and harvesting new and remnant old forests in the context of community forestry.

David Griffin, right, and colleagues in Nepal, 1986.

Economics and policy

ANU economists were never far removed from policy issues. Within the context of Australia's fourfold increase in unemployment since 1975, researchers in RSSS contributed to international literature on the economics of the labour market and to the analysis of unemployment in Australia and other parts of the world. The Centre for Economic Policy Research provided advice to Australian government departments and international agencies including the World Bank. Individual members of the centre, acting as consultants or serving on government committees, made recommendations which sometimes had far-reaching effects on government income and savings on expenditure, such as the introduction of the Higher Education Contribution Scheme, which required all tertiary students to pay something towards the cost of their education, and a tighter assets test for old age pensions, which promised to save the Australian taxpayer up to one billion dollars in the first eight years of its operation.

The Australia–Japan Research Centre, a legacy of Sir John Crawford's close relations with Japan, had a similar practical orientation, with major projects on specific trading commodities, Japanese corporate organisation, the internationalisation of Japanese financial markets, and economic reform in China. Ross Garnaut's report on *Australia and the Northeast Asian Ascendancy*, originally prepared in RSPacS as a report to government, helped shift the country's thinking about its economic future.

Law and society

In view of the pervasive influence of the federal system in Australia, it is not surprising that academic lawyers at the ANU focused much of their attention on federalism. Geoffrey Sawer continued to work in the area until and beyond his retirement from RSSS in 1975. Leslie Zines, a member of the Faculty of Law from 1962 and a professor from 1973, analysed the recent role of the High Court in reshaping both the federal aspects of the Australian constitutional system and the relationship of the citizen to state and Commonwealth governments. His study *The High Court and the Constitution*, first published in 1981, became required reading for judges of the High Court and counsel who appeared before it. In 1988 he explored federal issues in Australia, Canada, New Zealand, Britain and the European Community in a series of lectures at Cambridge, later published as *Constitutional Change in the Commonwealth*.

Although gregarious, Sawer as a researcher was a productive loner, who created no school of research lawyers and left no following. When Sawer left, the Law Department in RSSS wound down, to be wound up again with new appointments in the late 1980s. Researchers in the mid-1990s, including Zines (now retired from the Faculty of Law) and a former Chief Justice and Pro-Chancellor of the ANU, Sir Anthony Mason, carried forward his interests in the law and government; others joined in multidisciplinary projects to open up new areas of social and political theory. The 'Regard' Project, for example, analysed how the good regard of other members of a community functioned as a force for social order.

The Australian people

As the founders had intended, much of the University's research in the social sciences and humanities focused on Australia and Australians. Although Manning Clark had retired in 1975, he continued to present his inimitable view of the nation's past and speak out on the issues of the day. The sixth and final volume of *A History of Australia* was published in 1987, four years before his death.

Ken Inglis worked at the ANU from 1962 to 1994, with a spell as Professor of History and then Vice-Chancellor at the University of Papua New Guinea from 1967 to 1975 and several visiting appointments, including Professor of Australian Studies at Harvard. Soon after joining Clark's Department of History in the School of General Studies in 1963, he set out to explore the meaning of Anzac Day, which had so far attracted little serious historical attention. The Anzac tradition became 'a base from which to explore areas of Australian history not yet well mapped' and inspired *The Australian Colonists* in 1974. As a professorial fellow (briefly) and professor in RSSS from 1975 to 1994, he maintained his interests in Australians at war and the impact of war on Australians, digressing to write a history of the first 50 years of the Australian Broadcasting Commission (later Corporation) and to play a crucial role in creating the eleven-volume series *Australians: A Historical Library* (1987–88), a project which involved many other researchers not only at the ANU but throughout the university system.

Ken Inglis in 1994. Photograph by Loui Seselja, National Library. *By courtesy of K.S. Inglis.*

Inglis also served as chairman of the editorial board of the *Australian Dictionary of Biography* which, after the difficulties surrounding its birth, was one of the ANU's most successful collaborative ventures. With headquarters in RSSS, the series drew on the expertise of working parties and individual writers throughout Australia. By 1990 twelve volumes had been published, covering in more than seven thousand entries the period from 1788 to 1939 and representing, as the Melbourne writer and critic Stephen Murray-Smith said in a review, a 'remarkable gift to the nation'. In 1993, when the first volume for the period 1940 to 1980 appeared, the project looked set to continue in perpetuity.

ANU researchers remained at the forefront of work relating to the composition of the Australian population, including immigration and cultural diversity. W.D. Borrie and his colleagues in the Department of Demography coordinated the National Population Inquiry, publishing in 1975 their first report, which analysed population trends in the preceding century and forecast future movements. By showing the effects of population growth on society and the environment, they provided for the first time a systematic basis for immigration policy-making. Charles Price, a Professorial Fellow in Demography, and Jerzy Zubryzcki, Professor of Sociology in The Faculties, explored the processes of migration and settlement. In RSSS, James Jupp edited *The Australian People*, subtitled *An Encyclopedia of the Nation, its Peoples and their Origins*, which was published to mark the bicentenary of European settlement in 1988 and which spawned a small Centre for Immigration and Multicultural Studies.

At the launch of the bicentennial encyclopedia, *The Australian People*, in 1988, Prime Minister Bob Hawke sets Editor James Jupp straight about his (Hawke's) Cornish inheritance, while Paul Bourke, Director of RSSS, looks on.

Many projects focused, from different disciplinary perspectives, on Aboriginal Australians: anthropological studies of communities and the relations between them, historical surveys, archaeological studies which built on the work that John Mulvaney had begun. In 1983 Noel Butlin exploded traditional assumptions about the size of the Aboriginal population at the time of European settlement, then turned his hand to the economics of Aboriginal societies. In the 1960s, F.L. Jones, Fellow and later Professor of Sociology in RSSS, had conducted the first major demographic study of the Aboriginal population; 30 years later, researchers in the National Centre for Epidemiology and Population Health and the Centre for Aboriginal Policy Research,

Wang Gungwu in 1979.

a small unit in the Faculty of Arts, were analysing social change in Aboriginal populations and generating data which contributed to government policy-making.

Asia

The University's research on Asia ranged across countries, centuries and disciplines. In the Faculty of Asian Studies, Pierre Ryckmans (writing as Simon Leys) won international awards for his publications on China. In RSPacS, C.P. FitzGerald's successor as Professor of Far Eastern History, Wang Gungwu, served the University from 1968 to 1986, including a term as Director of RSPacS. Born in Java in 1930 to Chinese parents, Wang had attended university in Nanjing before the Communist revolution, and had then taken out degrees from the University of Malaya in Singapore and the School of Oriental and African Studies at the University of London. At the time of his appointment to the ANU he was Professor of History at the University of Malaya in Kuala Lumpur. He published widely on Chinese history and politics and on the Chinese diaspora in South-east Asia. An eloquent speaker, he was in frequent demand to comment on contemporary events in Asia.

The ANU continued to be a world centre for the study of South-east Asia. Research on Indonesia included historical, anthropological and archaeological surveys, ethnographic films, and studies of the economy which built on the early work of H.W. Arndt. Notable publications included Anthony Reid's two-volume survey of *Southeast Asia in the Age of Commerce* (1988–93), from the fifteenth to the seventeenth centuries. The University also remained at the forefront of scholarship on Vietnam, chiefly though the work of David G. Marr in RSPacS.

The research agenda responded to changes within Asia and in Australia's relationships with Asian countries. To fill a gap in Australian scholarship, RSPacS set up a Northeast Asia Project in 1989, focusing on Taiwan and Korea. In the mid-1990s, Yang-hi Choe-Wall, a native of Seoul and an expert on the Korean language, whose translations from English into Korean included Manning Clark's *Short History of Australia*, was editing the world's first extensive encyclopedia on Korea in English.

Past and present

Historical research was not restricted to Asia and Australia. The University became an antipodean centre for scholarship on British and Irish history, chiefly through the work of Oliver MacDonagh and F.B. Smith, and visitors and students who came to RSSS to work with them. In several books, Smith brought new understandings to disease, health and medicine in nineteenth- and twentieth-century Britain. MacDonagh's publications during his sixteen years as a professor at the ANU included acute analyses of Irish history and culture, a study of Anglo-Irish conflict over two centuries, a two-volume biography of the nineteenth-century Irish patriot Daniel O'Connell, and an elegant exploration of the 'real and imagined worlds' of Jane Austen (published in 1991, after his retirement).

Much historical work centred on the Pacific islands. Oskar Spate distilled decades of profound scholarship into a three-volume publication *The Pacific since Magellan* (1979–88), which promised to remain one of the world's great works on the Pacific and one of the ANU's great contributions to the world. Pacific researchers continued to play a part in the events and places they were studying, just as Spate and J.W. Davidson had done in earlier years. In 1995 Brij Lal, a historian attached to RSPAS and the Faculty of Arts who had written extensively on Fiji history and politics, was appointed by the Fiji government to a committee of three to review the constitution established after the 1987 military coups.

T.H. Rigby, who first joined Canberra University College in 1955 and retired as Professor of Political Science in RSSS in 1990, built up a corpus of publications on Soviet politics and history, including major studies of *Lenin's Government* (1979) and *Political Elites in the USSR* (1990), and was one of the few scholars to comprehend the fatal weaknesses in Soviet economic statistics. The radical and unforeseen changes in the communist world from 1989 emphasised the value of his expertise and the long-term research that lay behind it.

Harry Rigby in 1985. Photograph by Marlee Maxwell.

Language

ANU researchers were responsible for most linguistic work relating to the Pacific islands and a large proportion of research on the languages of Australia and Southeast Asia. These three areas account for some two thousand languages, or about one-third of the languages of the world. The surveys begun by Stephen Wurm in RSPacS in the 1950s culminated in 1981, with the publication of the first part of the *Language Atlas of the Pacific Area*.

In the 1990s, the RSPacS linguists joined with anthropologists and prehistorians in the school to study the peoples of Austronesia, a linguistic term which refers to a family of languages found in Indonesia and the Philippines, the coastal and island areas of Melanesia, and throughout the Pacific. The project aimed to explore the dispersion of Austronesian speakers which began some six thousand years ago, as they moved southwards from Formosa, eventually reaching Madagascar in the west and Easter Island in the east. The linguists traced the historical development of these languages, publishing a *Comparative Austronesian Dictionary* which contained vocabulary from some eighty languages representative of the family tree; the prehistorians studied archaeological evidence of migration; and the anthropologists examined social parallels that still exist between contemporary Austronesian societies.

Meanwhile, R.M.W. Dixon, Professor of Linguistics in the Faculty of Arts from 1970, worked with his colleagues to record and document Aboriginal languages, including fifty or so that were still in use

The first record of the name 'kangaroo' appears in James Cook's journal of the *Endeavour* in 1770. 'Kangaroo' is one of 10 000 entries in the *Australian National Dictionary*, produced over ten years in the Faculty of Arts and published in 1988.

and another fifty that had died out. As well as compiling academic grammars chiefly of interest to linguists, the team prepared dictionaries and literacy materials to ensure that unique evidence of Aboriginal culture survived.

The Roman family

Ancient Rome, said Beryl Rawson, Professor of Classics in the Faculty of Arts, 'is a complex, urbanised, sophisticated, affluent society which has much to tell us about our own society'. Like her prehistorian colleague John Mulvaney, Rawson was a prominent advocate of the relevance of the humanities, enjoying the rare distinction of having feature articles written about her in airline club and newspaper magazines.

Rawson joined the ANU in 1964, served for a time as Dean of the Faculty of Arts, and became Professor in 1989. Throughout this period her research concentrated on the family in ancient Rome. Looking at old evidence in new ways, she described relationship patterns and showed how they were often similar to those existing in modern families. Contrary to the widely accepted view that the concept of childhood dated from the seventeenth century, she demonstrated that Roman children were 'not just little adults', but real children, 'tugging on adults' togas'.

Rawson's publications won praise at home and abroad. In the 1990s she convened a series of conferences at the Humanities Research Centre, which attracted scholars from throughout the world and confirmed the University's status as an international centre for the study of ancient Rome.

Beryl Rawson, with the model of ancient Rome in the Department of Classics, Faculty of Arts, at the time of her appointment as professor in 1989. Photograph by Stuart Hay.

Measuring achievement

How was the University's overall research achievement to be assessed? In the 1970s the task was relatively easy. The Annual Report for 1975 affirmed the ANU's academic standing by listing the year's publications, outlining selected research programs, and referring (in the Vice-Chancellor's report) to the numbers of ANU academics who were members of the learned academies. Each category suggested impressive achievement, enabling the Vice-Chancellor, Anthony Low, to assert that of all the universities created across the world since the Second World War, none had achieved a greater reputation for scientific and scholarly work.

That may well have been true. But where was the proof? As other Australian institutions strengthened their own research reputations and competed vigorously for diminishing funds, people in government and in other parts of the higher education system looked for precise evidence for such confident assertions. The review process which Low had initiated hastened the trend towards precision. Reviews implied comparisons. Initially these were qualitative and highly subjective; but as reviewers became more searching and the government more demanding, the research schools in particular sought to prove their worth by presenting some hard figures.

Under the leadership of Paul Bourke, Director of RSSS, the University entered the complex field of performance indicators. Bourke was familiar with detailed quantitative research through his work on nineteenth-century voting patterns in the United States. Soon after his arrival at the ANU in 1985, he published for the Commonwealth Tertiary Education Commission a paper entitled *Quality Measures in Universities*, which drew attention to the potential uses of publication and citation data gathered by the Institute of Scientific Information, based in Philadelphia. These records show, among other things, the number of times individual publications are cited in major international scientific journals. Bourke initiated a data survey, modest by later standards, for the review of RSSS in 1988, and a more substantial study of the Institute of Advanced Studies for the 1990 Stephen review.

Increasingly complicated and refined studies followed. Responding to an approach from the University of Sussex, Bourke and his colleague Linda Butler embarked on an ambitious project to replicate for Australia a proposed database designed to render machine readable all British entries in the Institute of Scientific Information indices from 1981 to 1990. The companion studies would permit comparisons between British and Australian research output, and suggest how quantitative indicators might be used to evaluate research in modern multidisciplinary universities. That collaboration provided the basis for the creation in 1992 of the Performance Indicators Project in RSSS, which prepared detailed analyses relating to the past and future of Australian science, including the distribution of fields of research among Australian university science departments and patterns of international collaboration among Australian universities. Within the ANU, the Project embarked on a bibliometric survey for the projected reviews in 1995 of all research schools, centres and the Institute as a whole, intended to provide an impartial assessment of the impact of Institute research relative to that of other Australian universities.

How much significance could be attached to these analyses? Bourke was quick to point out their limitations, especially in relation to the humanities and social sciences, where research often found its way into books rather than the international journals captured by the citation data banks, and scholars in any case were not bound by convention to acknowledge every work that influenced them. For the natural sciences too there were many traps. The irreverent Barry Ninham, Professor of Applied Mathematics, claimed on returning from outside studies leave in 1994 that science citations had become 'quite meaningless': 'virtually no one at the cutting edge of research in my fields reads the literature, and all exchange is by personal interaction'. As Bourke recognised, tacit linkages, as they were called, rather than formal interaction through publications, were becoming increasingly significant, and electronic communications were hastening the trend. In certain areas of scholarship, the pace of research was accelerating so fast that traditional means of publication, and hence the methods designed to assess their impact, were becoming redundant. Would the revolution in electronic communications signal the fate of 'traditional' performance indicators, just as the computer revolution had allowed them to come into being?

Nevertheless, whatever the future of performance indicators, in the 1990s research performance was a major issue for resource allocation in higher education, and a subject of special importance to the ANU. As Geoffrey Brennan, Bourke's successor as Director

---

THE BOYER LECTURES AND THE ANU

The list of annual Boyer Lectures, Australia's most prestigious lecture series, offers disinterested testimony to the way in which the University helped nourish the intellectual life of the nation. Between 1959, when the series began (initially as the ABC Lectures) and 1995, there were 34 annual series of Boyer Lectures, excluding three presented by two or more lecturers. Ten were given by current or former ANU staff (including Geoffrey Bolton, who was also a PhD graduate), two more by former students (Bernard Smith and R.J.L. Hawke) and one by a future Visiting Fellow (the former Vice-Chancellor of Sydney University, Sir Bruce Williams).

1961 W.D. Borrie *The Crowding World*

1963 J.D.B. Miller *Australia and Foreign Policy*

1965 Sir John Eccles *The Brain and the Person*

1968 W.E.H. Stanner *After the Dreaming*

1970 H.C. Coombs *The Fragile Pattern: Institutions and Man*

1973 Sir Keith Hancock *Today, Yesterday and Tomorrow*

1976 Manning Clark *A Discovery of Australia*

1979 R.J.L. Hawke *The Resolution of Conflict*

1980 Bernard Smith *The Spectre of Truganini*

1981 J.A. Passmore *The Limits of Government*

1982 Sir Bruce Williams *Living with Technology*

1985 Helen Hughes *Australia in a Developing World*

1992 Geoffrey Bolton *A View from the Edge: An Australian Stocktaking*

of RSSS, pointed out in 1991, if the University did not provide the government with reliable data for assessing its research performance, it would be vulnerable to 'back-of-the-envelope stabs'. Bibliometric evaluation was 'simply something we must do'.

The 1995 review of the Institute showed that the exercise to date had been well worth the effort. Although the reviewers recognised the limitations of such evaluation, they noted especially the work of the Performance Indicators Project, observing that publications by members of the Institute tended to be cited more often than those by members of institutions selected for detailed comparison. They were also impressed by an analysis of highly cited publications, which showed that the Institute outperformed its 'comparator institutions', sometimes by more than twofold. The reviewers concluded that these quantitative measures confirmed the results of peer group assessment.

Similar conclusions could be drawn for the University as a whole. This chart, based on citation figures for the period 1988 to 1992, shows the six areas of science (excluding the social sciences) where the ANU is most active. As well as demonstrating the University's large share of the publishing output of all Australian science, it shows that the overall impact of those publications was far greater than their numbers might otherwise suggest.

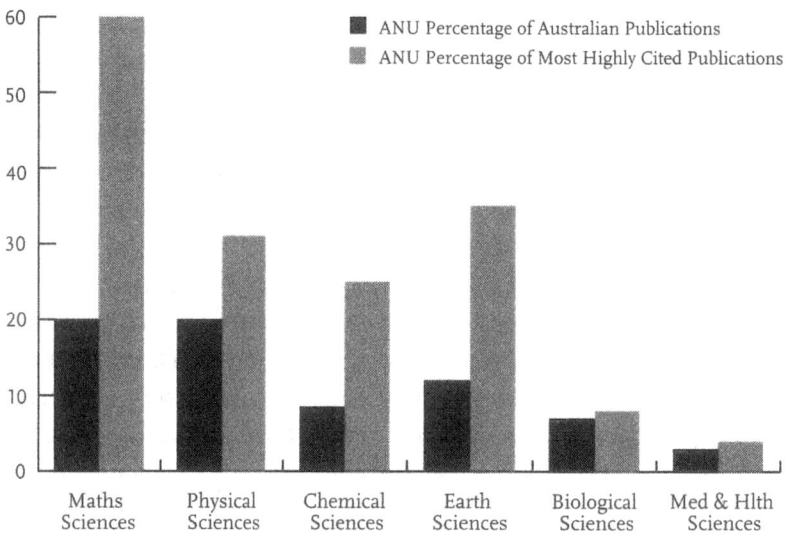

The Science Citation Index, produced by the Institute for Scientific Information in the United States, indexes over 3000 scientific publications. It covers publications from all major Australian research institutions, including all universities, the CSIRO and other government organisations.

The chart shows the proportions of Australian publications, in six relevant fields, that have an ANU author; and ANU proportions of the most highly cited publications in each field. Citations are recorded against a publication when it is referred to in other publications. The more citations a publication receives, the higher visibility is has in the international research community. The Performance Indicators Project database, compiled in RSSS, enables the most highly cited publications (in this case, the top 1 per cent) to be identified, together with their institutional affiliation.

The ANU diaspora

The University's influence could be measured in other ways. Each year's Annual Report listed instances of academic staff giving expert advice and assistance to federal and state government departments and to other institutions, both within Australia and overseas. By the 1990s the list ran to many hundreds of individual entries and included secondments, consultancies, committee memberships, and large and small contributions to specific projects.

More difficult to quantify was the University's impact through its graduates, its staff who moved on to appointments in other institutions, and staff from other institutions who came to the ANU for any period between a few weeks and a year. The visitors' program in the schools and centres was by far the most extensive in Australia. The Research School of Earth Sciences, for example, in the decade to 1994, welcomed over 400 visitors for between one and twelve months, including 285 from outside Australia. As well as ensuring a continuing flow of information and ideas, visitors helped confirm the national and international significance of ANU research.

The influence of ANU graduates varied from one discipline to the next. The University remained at the forefront of teaching and research in prehistory (though in keeping with current fashion, the term 'prehistory' was no longer used in departmental titles). In the 1990s the ANU still accounted for most graduates with chairs in prehistory and directly related areas. Likewise, ANU graduates in linguistics filled over half the Australian teaching positions in the field. In Applied Mathematics, Barry Ninham remarked in 1993 that eighteen of the research fellows who had come out of his department were now full professors at other institutions in Australia and abroad. On a larger scale, the National Centre for Development Studies had produced by 1993 some 900 alumni who were, according to a review submission prepared by RSPAS, 'a powerful resource for regional economies and for the School's networks within the region'.

For evidence of the University's international influence, figures from the Department of Demography in RSSS were hard to beat. The department attracted students from every continent. Of the 200 students who graduated between 1959 and 1988 with a PhD, a Master's degree or a diploma in Demography, 58 per cent came

Distinguished graduates in diverse fields:

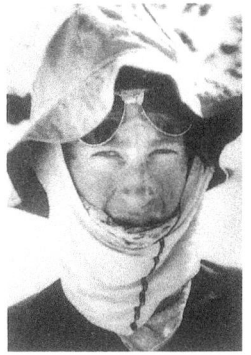

Tim Macartney-Snape, BSc 1980: mountaineer, photographed in 1990 on the summit of Mount Everest.

Cheong Choong Kong, PhD in Mathematics, 1964: Managing Director and Chief Executive of Singapore Airlines.

Louise Vardanega, LLB Hons 1975: Director of the Australian Government Solicitor's Office, ACT Region. Photograph by Branco Ivanovic, 1990.

Peter Corris, PhD in Pacific History, 1970: crime writer. Photograph by Peter Cotton, 1991.

from Asia, 15 per cent from Africa, 12 per cent from Australia and New Zealand, 8 per cent from North America, and the remainder from the Pacific, Europe, Latin America and the Caribbean. While many returned to the countries from which they had come, others remained in Australia, left Australia for overseas, or moved via Australia from one continent to another, so that the department functioned as an international clearing house for studies in demography. Of the 74 students who were awarded PhDs during the period, by the mid-1990s about a quarter occupied chairs or positions of equivalent status in research institutions in various parts of the world.

The Research School of Chemistry measured its influence through the locations and positions of its former graduates, postdoctoral fellows (which it included in its definition of 'alumni') and research fellows. Detailed lists showed how the school had permeated universities, research institutions, government and private industry over a period of 25 years. In 1993, 117 doctoral graduates, former postdoctoral fellows and former research fellows occupied research, teaching or administrative positions in over 30 Australian tertiary institutions, while another 118, including 28 full professors in 13 countries, were members of tertiary institutions abroad. Of those who had moved outside universities, 24 were members of CSIRO, including the head of one division, and many occupied senior positions in government and industry worldwide, including a senior public servant and science adviser to the Australian government, the managing director of a technological enterprise in South Australia and the research director of a multinational company in the Netherlands.

Beth Heyde, PhD in Biochemistry, 1966: Principal Secretary, Government Business and International Scientific Liaison, CSIRO. Photograph by Bob Cooper, 1996.

Penny Chapman, BA Hons 1972: Head of Television, ABC.
By courtesy of ABC Television.

In mathematics and statistics, the impact of the ANU was profound. Between 1959 and 1986, the University graduated 168 PhDs in these fields, over 20 per cent of the national total. In 1989, ten of the sixteen professors of statistics in Australia had been associated with the Department of Statistics in RSSS, either as students or staff, and seven had ANU PhDs. The department that Patrick Moran had created was an international force, especially in the area of applied probability. In the 1990s, however, the relative influence of the department (now a Section in the School of Mathematical Sciences), as measured by direct links through graduates and former staff, was gradually receding, as the discipline gathered strength in other universities. The ANU had been the cradle of advanced statistical research in Australia.

Across the disciplines, the University had generated a vast intellectual diaspora that would have gladdened the hearts of its makers.

The University in 1995

The view from Red Hill across the lake to the campus, with balloons in the early morning.

Students

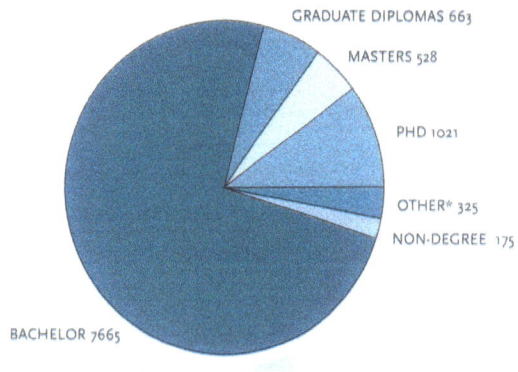

GRADUATE DIPLOMAS 663
MASTERS 528
PHD 1021
OTHER* 325
NON-DEGREE 175
BACHELOR 7665

* Includes cross-institutional courses, undergraduate diplomas and graduate certificates.

Undergraduate Students by Faculty

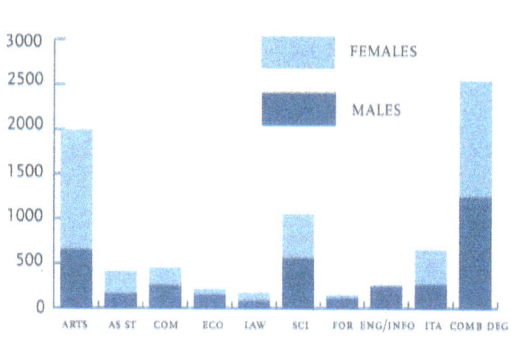

Origins of Undergraduate Students

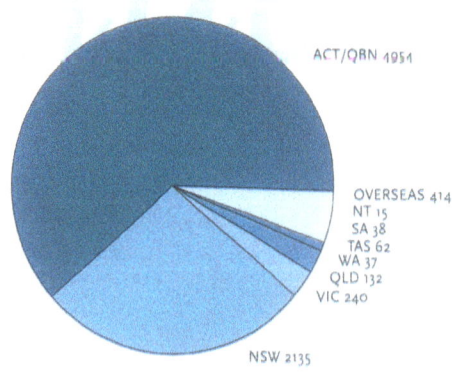

ACT/QBN 4954
OVERSEAS 414
NT 15
SA 38
TAS 62
WA 37
QLD 132
VIC 240
NSW 2135

Origins of Postgraduate Students

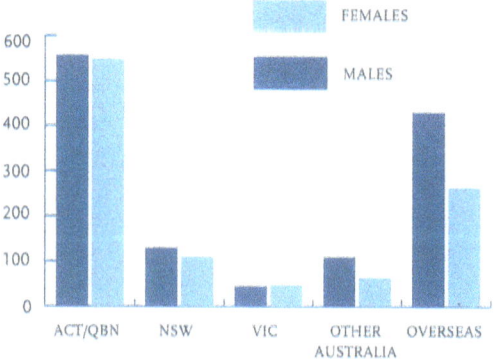

Staff

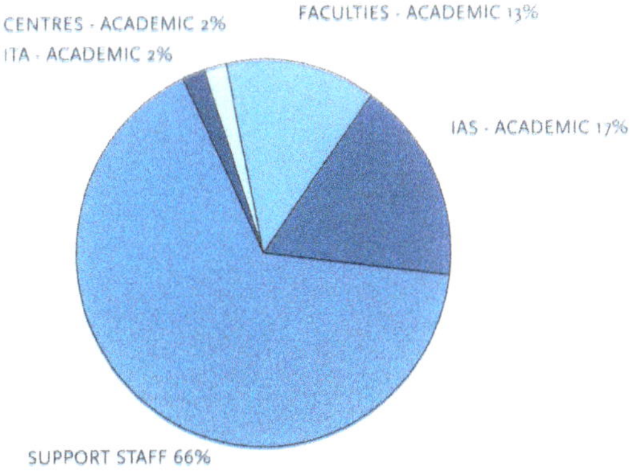

CENTRES - ACADEMIC 2%
FACULTIES - ACADEMIC 13%
ITA - ACADEMIC 2%
IAS - ACADEMIC 17%
SUPPORT STAFF 66%

* Includes administration, library, technical, service areas and independent operations.

IAS Academic Staff

RSPHYSSE 14%
JCSMR 13%
RSSS 12%
RSBS 14%
MSSSO 3%
RSISE 2%
SMS 3%
RSES 7%
RSPAS 19%
RSC 11%

SOURCE: ANU STATISTICAL HANDBOOK 1995

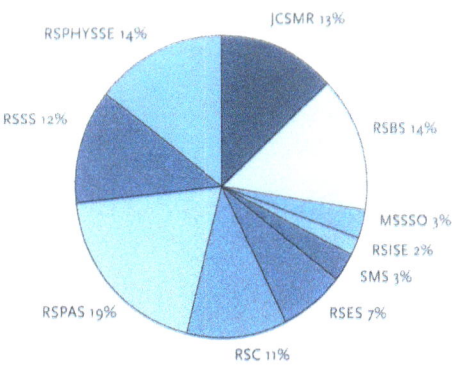

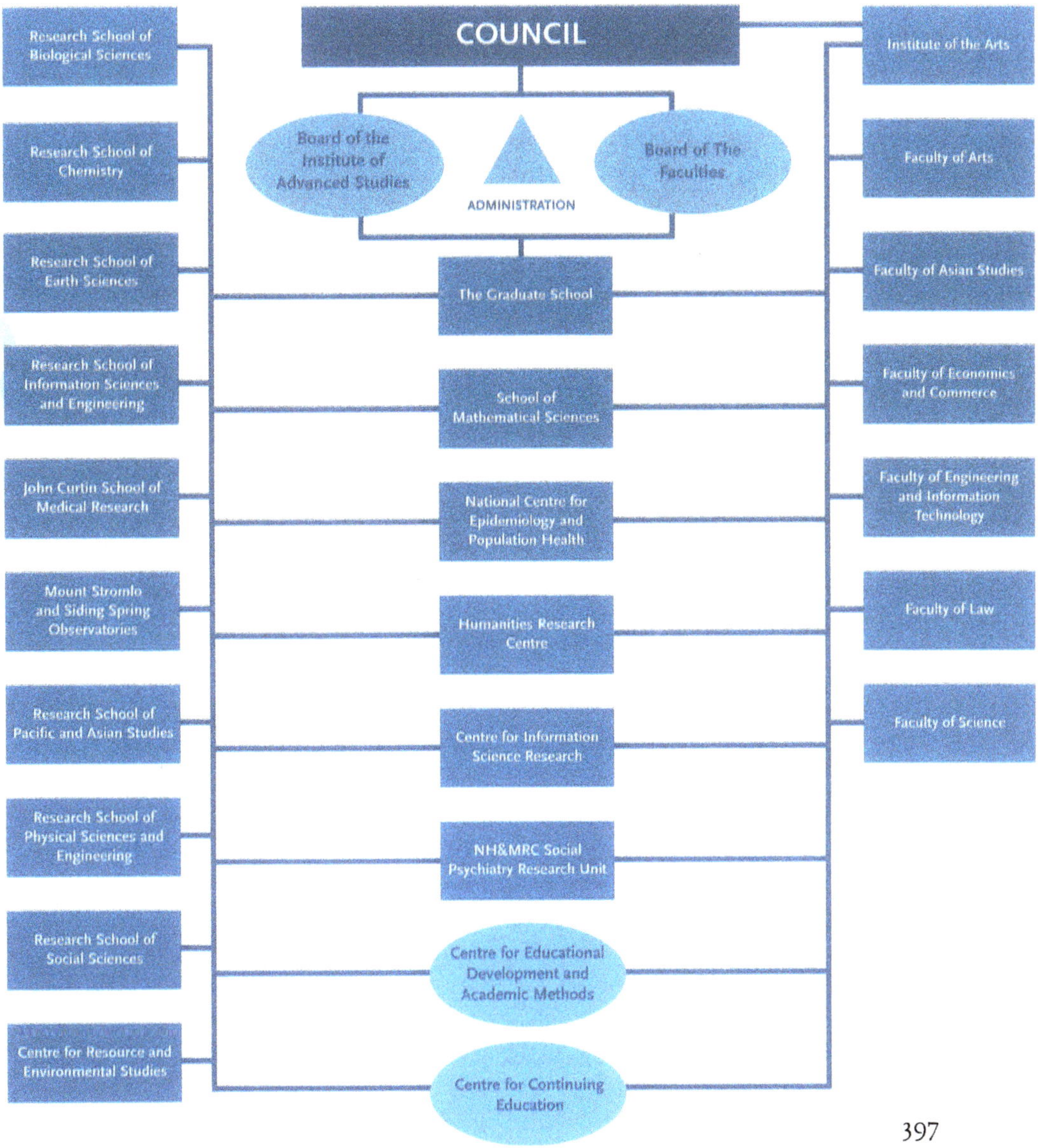

COUNCIL

- Research School of Biological Sciences
- Research School of Chemistry
- Research School of Earth Sciences
- Research School of Information Sciences and Engineering
- John Curtin School of Medical Research
- Mount Stromlo and Siding Spring Observatories
- Research School of Pacific and Asian Studies
- Research School of Physical Sciences and Engineering
- Research School of Social Sciences
- Centre for Resource and Environmental Studies

Board of the Institute of Advanced Studies — ADMINISTRATION — Board of The Faculties

- The Graduate School
- School of Mathematical Sciences
- National Centre for Epidemiology and Population Health
- Humanities Research Centre
- Centre for Information Science Research
- NH&MRC Social Psychiatry Research Unit
- Centre for Educational Development and Academic Methods
- Centre for Continuing Education

- Institute of the Arts
- Faculty of Arts
- Faculty of Asian Studies
- Faculty of Economics and Commerce
- Faculty of Engineering and Information Technology
- Faculty of Law
- Faculty of Science

Sir Keith Hancock in 1965, the year of his retirement as Professor of History, RSSS.
The Australian.

The past and the future 16

 Retirement

Ken Inglis, at a grand occasion preceding a two-day seminar to mark his retirement in 1994 as W.K. Hancock Professor of History, told a story about Hancock in later life:

> One day, when he was into his twentieth or so year of retirement, he came into my room—*his* room, as I suspect he still thought of it—shut the door, and asked if I had heard that there was a danger of so-and-so being appointed our next Director. 'I don't know about you', he said, 'but if that happened I should feel obliged to resign.' He didn't have to.

As Inglis pointed out, Hancock remained a Visiting Fellow longer—in fact much longer—than he had been a professor. He continued to research, write and publish (including the second volume of his Smuts biography and a pathbreaking environmental history of the Monaro region south of Canberra), to participate in University affairs, to give radio broadcasts, and to offer paternal advice to young scholars about their thesis topics and the craft of history. He was still attending seminars until six months before his death in 1988, aged 90.

For many academics, obliged to retire at the age of 65, the transition from employment to retirement meant little beyond less money and more freedom, especially from administrative chores. This applied most obviously to those engaged in full-time research. Noel Butlin, aged 64, ceased formal employment in RSSS one afternoon in 1986 and arrived at the usual time the next morning to get on with the job of writing two more books, one on the economy of Aboriginal Australia, the other on Australia's colonial economy, both of which were published after his death from leukaemia in 1991. John Passmore, retiring in 1979, moved freely between the History of Ideas Unit, where he was a Visiting Fellow, and McMaster University in Canada, where he was Chief Editor of a major project to publish a new edition of the works of Bertrand Russell. His fellow philosopher Jack Smart, retiring in 1985, and the mathematician Bernard Neumann, in 1974, continued in the mid-1990s to write, accrue honours, and bicycle to the campus each day from opposite sides of town. Inglis spent much of his first year as Emeritus Professor visiting his scattered family, finishing one book, starting another, presenting and attending seminars, and taking a meticulous editorial pencil to numerous theses and prospective books, including this one.

The transition meant more for academics in The Faculties. John Mulvaney, freed in 1985 from the burdens of undergraduate teaching, became a Visiting Fellow in RSSS, then honorary Secretary to the Academy of the Humanities, published a book and several articles, and continued to speak out, often angrily, about issues relating to heritage and the humanities. In 1988 he was awarded the ANZAAS Medal for unrolling the historical map of Australia's Aboriginal people. Mulvaney's successor as Professor of Prehistory, Isabel McBryde, retired at the end of 1994, earlier than she need have done, in order to devote herself to research and writing. Like many of her colleagues, she was soon overwhelmed by requests to read theses, present papers and attend committees, and had to remind herself of her purpose in retiring. There were others, of course, who took the meaning of 'retirement' seriously. Hancock's successor, John La Nauze, when asked as he approached retiring age what he planned to do, replied that he was going to make toys for his grandchildren; though he did write a delicate memoir of the academic and essayist Walter Murdoch.

Isabel McBryde in 1989.

Inglis, anticipating retirement, looked forward to retaining a room (smaller than his current one), paper clips and ('if I'm lucky') a modem. Academics engaged in experimental science, if they wanted to keep working, usually needed more. For them retirement was often a wrench. While many retained access to a laboratory, equipment and technical assistance, these were generally less than they had been used to, and there was always the prospect of the facilities diminishing or disappearing entirely. Adrien Albert, who reached the age of 65 in 1973, regarded retirement, according to his friend and colleague Des Brown, as 'a grievous blow'. Although he had organised for himself a visiting fellowship in the Research School of Chemistry, for some time he lamented his fate as 'a discard on the scrapheap' and blamed the University for letting it happen. Gradually he adjusted to his changed circumstances and settled down to work, accepting invitations on several occasions to visit the United States, conducting experiments, preparing new editions of his publications, and writing two books, one of which, on food, drugs and poisons in the human body, won him the Olle book prize from the Royal Australian Chemical Institute. He continued working, exercising daily in the gym and frequenting a Canberra coffee shop (where he eventually learned that women were not the ogres he had once thought them) until shortly before his death in 1989, aged 82.

Frank Fenner in 1981. Photograph by Stephen Berry.

When Frank Fenner retired in 1979, he moved from the Director's office in the Centre for Resource and Environmental Studies back to the John Curtin School. Over the past decade he had played an increasingly important part in the program to eradicate smallpox throughout the world, and in the last three years had been Chairman of the Global Commission for the Certification of Smallpox Eradication. In 1980, when the World Health Organisation officially declared that smallpox had been eradicated, he began the massive task of preparing, as senior author, a history of this remarkable achievement. Published in 1988, the book provided a detailed account of the disease and the campaign to eradicate it, and offered lessons for preventive medicine in the future. Writing history appealed to him: he also edited and wrote large portions of a *History of Microbiology in Australia* (1990). In the mid-1990s he was working on a history of rabbit control and a second edition of a history of the

Australian Academy of Science, which he had first written (with a colleague) during his years at CRES.

The ANU's most controversial retirement was that of Sir John Eccles in 1966, three years after winning the Nobel Prize and two years before the statutory date. Eccles left the University to take up a research position at the Institute for Biomedical Research in Chicago, where he was promised 'virtually unlimited funds' and the opportunity to continue working indefinitely. While he stated that the offer was too good to refuse, and that he would have accepted it irrespective of retirement considerations, he was also critical of mandatory retirement at 65. The Australian tabloids made the issue a front page story, implying that the ANU had forced him out.

In fact, the University had already arranged for Eccles to continue working with his own equipment in new laboratories, though no longer as head of the Department of Physiology. He would also be appointed University Fellow, a status reserved for exceptional retirees and so far accorded only to Hancock. This position would be available for up to three years and included a substantial stipend. But Eccles evidently regarded the matter as one of principle. Eighteen months earlier he had told the Australian Association of Gerontology that Australia did not make best use of its older people and had called for more flexibility in determining the age of retirement,

Above and below: Sydney *Sun*, 16 February 1966. *Centre*: Melbourne *Herald*, 17 February. 1966.

mentioning the 'psychological cruelty' that often occurred when a person left the workforce. Now, rather than expose himself to that cruelty, he embarked on a new life (with a new wife) in a new country, never to return to Australia. While his colleagues in the John Curtin School gave him a lively send-off and the University commissioned the artist Judy Cassab to paint his portrait, senior members of the administration remained sore at the manner of his going.

Eccles was right to anticipate many productive years ahead: after moving from Chicago to the State University of New York at Buffalo, he eventually 'retired' to Switzerland, where he continued to publish and inspire until well into his eighties. For Oliphant, on the other hand, the transition at the age of 65 from a position of authority to one of grace and favour was a difficult one. He was offered a University Fellowship for two years and honorary appointments thereafter. His colleagues urged him to engage in 'biographical writing' (which would cost their school no money), but he found it difficult to devote himself continuously to writing 'without the relaxation of active experimental work'. Everyone was delighted when he was invited to become

Two past and one present head of RSPhysS at 'Founders Day' in 1984. Founders Day, which includes a morning of seminars, is held each year close to Sir Mark Oliphant's birthday. Left to right: Sir Ernest Titterton, John Carver and Oliphant.

Governor of South Australia (where he was soon joined in the office of Lieutenant-Governor by his old colleague, Walter Crocker, who had returned to Adelaide at the end of a distinguished diplomatic career).

There was no perfect solution to the problem of retirement from the University, any more than society at large had solved other problems of growing old. Eccles pointed to the economic benefits of older people working longer; Fenner, 30 years later, saw no reason why academics over 65 should 'plug the system up', especially when so many young people were trying to join it. In the mid-1990s, when 'grey power' forced the abolition of the compulsory retirement age, the University's administrators wondered how many academics would choose to remain beyond 65. Two things were certain: if salary budgets remained unchanged, for every member of staff who stayed longer, another would have to retire younger, or one or two aspiring academics would have to wait; and if the age of 65 ceased to have significance, the traditional concept of academic tenure (if it had not been abolished already) would eventually lose meaning.

The parts and the whole

No one vantage point offers a comprehensive view of the whole University. The RSPhysSE library in the Cockcroft Building affords a fine view of Lake Burley Griffin, but other parts of the campus are hidden. The postgraduate student in physics who conducts all his work in the school library and the nearby laboratories and workshops might easily forget, except at graduation time, that the rest of the University exists. Just over the ridge, the John Curtin School seems remote from those parts of the campus frequented by undergraduates. The laboratory technician, working in one of the wings of Florey's H-shaped building, need venture abroad only to visit the Sports Union or the bank.

The Coombs Building, home of RSSS and RSPAS, is turned in on itself. The research fellow investigating some aspect of Asian culture, when she is not on field trips, spends most of her time in her office or across the road in the Menzies Building of the University Library, sometimes visiting the National Library to make use of its extensive Asian collections. A few hundred metres away, the Director of the Canberra School of Music can watch, through a closed-circuit television located in his office, students and staff rehearsing and performing on the stage of Llewellyn Hall. Although he often attends meetings in the Chancelry, where he represents the interests of the school and contributes to University policy-making, his main concern is what goes on within his own building.

On the opposite side of campus, the terrace at the front of Bruce Hall once

THE PAST AND THE FUTURE

Photograph by
Bob Cooper

commanded views along University Avenue to City Hill, one of inner Canberra's focal points. Now trees interrupt the vista; but the Economics and Commerce undergraduate standing there may imagine *her* University stretched out along either side of the promenade: lecture theatres, faculty offices, the Union quadrangle and, close by, the Chifley Building of the University Library. The research schools (except for RSC) and the Chancelry seem remote.

Perhaps the best outlook, appropriately, is from the R.C. Mills Room on the top floor of the Chancelry. Moving from one side of the room to the other, the spectator can survey much of the campus in all its diversity and perhaps reflect on the University as a whole. But the senior officers who spend much time in the Mills Room at meetings of Council and the academic boards have little time for gazing and reflecting: the immediate needs of running the University keep getting in the way.

These contrasting perspectives suggest a University in parts, a characteristic shared in varying degrees by most universities around the world. Although many people and projects bridge the gaps, the parts remain the object of individual loyalties that are often more powerful than loyalties to the larger institution, especially when the individual research schools and faculties are forced to compete with one another for diminishing resources. The ANU also shares with other universities an inherent tension between its central administration and governing bodies and its faculties and schools. While the strains do not compare with those that have threatened or undermined some multi-campus universities, they are nevertheless more evident than in traditionally organised universities. Their origins lie in the establishment of the four foundation research schools, each with academic autonomy. The purpose of the University structure, as conceived by the Academic Advisory Committee in the 1940s, was chiefly to provide the schools with a protective umbrella. According to Oliphant, Florey, Hancock and Firth, the vice-chancellor and senior officers were to defend and promote the schools, without interfering in their administration. If they defended too meekly or interfered too obviously, members of the schools protested. In the mid-1950s Oliphant, smarting under Melville's administration and a supposed domination by the social scientists, toyed with the idea of abandoning the University structure entirely and rearranging the natural science schools as an institute of scientific research. Thirty years later, the bitter complaints by scientists that the University administration had failed to provide them with adequate research funds were in the same tradition of resistance from the periphery. Although increasing government intervention from the late 1980s made the research schools more vulnerable and therefore more dependent on Chancelry protection, they nevertheless retained substantial academic and budgetary autonomy.

The most significant structural feature of the ANU remains the division between the Institute and The Faculties. The incorporation of Canberra University College in 1960 created what was sometimes referred to as two universities in one; and while no physical gap separated the two parts of the campus, the perceived gulf was profound. Ken Inglis recalled Hancock in the early days of amalgamation saying that he and his colleagues in the History Department, RSSS, should get together more often with the chaps on the other side of the creek, presumably forgetting that the two History departments were in fact on the same side.

Various attempts were made to bring the Institute and The Faculties closer together, especially by Sir John Crawford, who promoted new research centres as bridging structures; and by Peter Karmel, who promoted the Graduate School as a third element in the structure, partly to reduce the distance between the other two. But such initiatives were always premised on the assumption that the Institute must retain its distinctive character, and hence its claim to special funding. In the days of relatively generous government funding, Crawford was able to present the University as a single financial entity, so that the School of General Studies benefited from funds that might have been intended for the Institute. But as money for higher education became harder to get and more precisely linked to student numbers, the Institute was obliged to reassert its separateness. In 1990, the first review of the Institute recommended separate block funding; and although that was a relief to senior members of the University, the decision drove another wedge between the two parts of the University and transferred the Institute's vulnerability to the bridging structures, including the Graduate School. The review also recommended that the Institute have its own Director, at the level of Deputy Vice-Chancellor, who would oversee its affairs, including its place in Australia's system of academic research, and provide leadership on issues beyond the responsibility of individual units.

The process of reviewing one half of the University, while paying little attention to the other, widened the gap. Richard Campbell, Professor of Philosophy in the Faculty of Arts and Chair of the Board of The Faculties, urged the 1995 Institute reviewers to remember that the ANU was 'One University', and that any major changes to the Institute would have an inevitable impact on The Faculties. 'The first, and most important, point which needs to be made is that this review is not just about the future of the Institute of Advanced Studies; *it is about the future of the University as a whole.*' The review committee responded to this and other submissions by recommending more joint appointments,

Photograph by
Bob Cooper

with flexible arrangements for the subdivision of time between teaching and research.

Was there an alternative? A few people had argued for many years in favour of radical change. The chemist Arthur Birch suggested in the 1960s that the ANU should set up an honours school, where 'highly selected' undergraduates enrolled in a three-year course which would be much more demanding than the ordinary degree. This, he said, would make full use of the unique resources of the Institute and enhance the University's national role. Three decades later the applied mathematician Barry Ninham argued along similar lines for a national undergraduate school which would exploit the whole University's teaching and research capacity. But both Birch and Ninham unashamedly used the word 'elite'; and anything that smacked of 'elitism' was unlikely to make much headway in the 1960s, when it was 'un-Australian', or the 1990s, when it was 'politically incorrect' (except for elite athletes). In addition to meeting widespread community resistance, the concept of an elite undergraduate school, with its implications of extra funding, would be fiercely opposed by other universities.

There were other ways of redesigning the University, both to maximise use of its resources and to help it cohere. Yet people who favoured change also saw dangers in tampering with the status quo. Nothing could be done without the approval of government; and in the context of the unified national system, the government was unlikely to look favourably on anomalies. The Institute was already anomaly enough, without the University seeking to create new ones. And if the government was invited to consider major restructuring, including the ways in which the Institute and The Faculties were funded, what might happen to the University as a whole? So Campbell, on behalf of The Faculties, firmly upheld the existing structure, including separate funding for the Institute, merely suggesting that current arrangements could be made to work better.

Was structure the heart of the problem? Don Aitkin, reflecting on academic institutions generally, concluded that structures are not as important as ideas and people: 'Given good ideas and good people almost any structure can be made to work'. Susan

Serjeantson told a conference on 'The Modern Vice-Chancellor' in 1994 that 'If you can recruit and retain talented staff, all else will flow', which recalled Alf Conlon's advice nearly 50 years earlier, 'pick the men and the rest will look after itself'. Following this policy, the makers of the University adjusted its structures to fit the available people, often creating jobs to suit an individual's interests and qualifications. With decreasing budgets, this became harder to do. Also, the ANU, in common with other public institutions, was obliged to follow more rigorous appointment procedures which acknowledged the need for equality of opportunity. Nevertheless, as late as the 1980s people were occasionally appointed to jobs created for them, especially in the Institute, which easily accommodated the minor structural changes that such appointments entailed.

Implicit in the notion that individuals are more important than structures is the assumption that some of those appointed to senior positions will be able to lead. Ever since the Interim Council put its faith in Florey, Oliphant, Hancock and Firth, the University looked to outstanding scholars to provide academic leadership, which meant setting research directions, recruiting more junior staff, and giving the University as well as the individual schools intellectual coherence. Hancock's failure to get his men, Firth's eventual refusal to come and Florey's indecision suggested that this faith was largely misplaced. Yet the makers of the University continued to see outstanding leadership as the surest means of guaranteeing the enterprise's success.

Academic leadership is an elusive concept, partly because it conflicts with the collegial notions that are so much a part of university tradition. Academics are generally keen to be led, but only if the leader follows their directions or adheres to the status quo. At the ANU, the peculiar character of the research schools made leadership issues especially complicated from the outset. The confusion was embodied in the office of director, whose functions were never clearly defined. As it happened, three of the four research schools began without directors, leaving authority in the hands of the individual professors, many of whom demonstrated impressive qualities of leadership and did give their departments a clear sense of direction. Moreover, some members of staff interpreted academic freedom to mean the freedom to do exactly as they wished, without reference to any community of interest at the departmental, school or University level. Although such views existed in all universities, they were more evident in the Institute, where a significant number of academics believed they were conferring a favour on the University by being there. In such circumstances, even the most capable leaders sometimes had difficulty, as Hancock might have put it, turning their rabble into a team. Leadership qualities were insufficient without a corresponding capacity for what one reviewer called 'followership' and a commitment to the collective good.

The Faculties, in the meantime, were administered along more traditional collegial lines, with elected deans who conducted the business of their faculties in accordance with the majority decisions of their constituencies. This difference in patterns of governance contributed to the contrasting cultures of The Faculties and the Institute. By the 1990s, however, the nature of academic leadership was changing throughout the University, in response to demands by the government for greater accountability within the higher education system. Confronted with the prospect of dwindling research funds and increasing government intervention, academics in the Institute were more inclined to accept that directors and deans should play a large role in managing the schools and determining priorities. Similarly, The Faculties moved gradually, and somewhat reluctantly, towards managerial styles of governance, with deans accountable to the vice-chancellor rather than to the faculty that had elected them.

Perhaps surprisingly, the roles of the vice-chancellor had not changed fundamentally since Copland's day, though the duties of the office had become much more complicated and onerous. His (and not, as yet, her) most difficult task was to mediate between the often conflicting interests of his University constituency and the government that paid the bills. Oliphant's requirement—'Give us a person to bully'—was still shared by many senior academics nearly half a century later, though most of them expressed their desire rather more subtly. On the other hand, the government required the vice-chancellor to account for the expenditure of public funds. Just as Prime Minister Menzies and the Commonwealth Treasury had expected Melville to keep a tight rein on free-spending and free-thinking academics, Dawkins demanded that the 'chief executive officers' of tertiary institutions demonstrate responsible financial management and provide their institutions with strategic leadership and a strong sense of direction. The difference was large, but it could also be seen as one of degree.

The other major role of the vice-chancellor was to help bind the University together, a function made more demanding from 1960 by the absence of a single, effective academic board (excepting the Professorial Board, which rarely met). The vice-chancellor symbolised the University and could enhance its sense of unity. The most successful vice-chancellors understood the challenges presented by the University's anomalous structure and, through imaginative leadership, worked hard to surmount them.

 ## The past in the present

In the mid-1990s the ANU was, as it always had been, a unique institution, not just in Australia but in the world. Yet it had moved gradually closer to the more familiar pattern of Australian universities. The trend had begun even before the ANU Act was passed, when Coombs and his colleagues, who had conceived the University as a means of helping rebuild the country after the war, put their faith in expatriate scholars who were deeply imbued with English university traditions and more interested in seeking to recreate Oxbridge in the antipodes than in responding to immediate national needs.

'National needs' was, in any case, a wartime concept which had trouble surviving the peace. Pansy Wright remarked a few weeks after the Japanese surrender that 'the fine frenzy of enthusiasm for knowledge that was apparent in the danger periods of the war is giving way to the burrowing performances of rodents'. Coombs's wartime vision faded, though not entirely, as Australians tried to put the war behind them. But

Oxbridge was not the answer. That vision too, though initially realised in University House, became quickly blurred, partly because only one of the four Academic Advisers promptly accepted an appointment as Director of a school and partly because institutions rarely translate unchanged from one country to another.

Left to their own devices, the newly appointed academics behaved as academics tended to do in other Australian universities, forming departments and getting on with their own research. This is what the philosopher John Passmore meant when he referred in 1972 to 'a natural tendency for universities which were at first conceived of along unorthodox lines to revert to orthodoxy'. So, in the 1950s, the ANU took on many of the characteristics of a traditional Australian university, albeit without the teaching, with subprofessorial staff responsible to their professors and professors responsible chiefly to themselves.

The incorporation of undergraduate students in 1960 deprived the ANU of its most obvious claim to uniqueness. Nevertheless, the University, through its senior officers, continued to assert its singularity, a task made more difficult by the Commonwealth's assumption of responsibility for the system as a whole. The system of higher education which developed in the 1960s opened the universities to the masses, and at the same time made them dependent on Commonwealth financial support, more likely to be regarded as public institutions and hence more subject to external controls, exercised by the AUC and its successors from 1959 to 1987 and later by government departments. One effect of these controls was to draw the ANU more comprehensively into the national system.

In the 1970s the University lost its 'special relationship' with government and was forced to compete with other universities, all determined to ensure that it should be no better (and preferably worse) off than it was already. The new era of financial stringency hastened the trend. As Ian Ross remarked in 1976, for twenty years the ANU had enjoyed patronage and benevolence previously unknown by universities in Australia. Now it faced the prospect of being 'stirred into an homogenized Australian university mixture'. Few members of the University, on either side of the campus, found that prospect to their taste.

By the 1990s the ANU had moved a long way from the institution that Coombs, Conlon and Wright had talked about during their wartime meetings. Yet in some respects the University in the 1990s had more in common with Coombs's original vision than with the rarefied concepts discussed at All Souls in the late 1940s or with the University that evolved in the 1950s. John Dawkins and his successors spoke about national needs and research priorities much as Coombs and his colleagues, especially Sir Frederic Eggleston, had done in the 1940s. What was new under Dawkins was the *requirement* that the system as a whole respond to the government's assessment of national needs. While the new system encouraged universities to be more diverse, it also introduced unprecedented levels of government regulation and imposed strict guidelines for the allocation of government funds. In such circumstances, the ANU's efforts to remain distinctive became even more of a struggle.

So the University changed, as Conlon had predicted it would, to reflect the society of which it was a part. Yet at the same time it reflected much of the vision that had inspired its creation. This capacity to adapt to current circumstances without sacrificing old ideas and structures that were worth keeping was the key to its success, as it was and is with any institution. When members of the University either ignored tradition, as they sometimes did when they embraced the language of the marketplace, or clung to the past too tenaciously, as they did most noticeably in the John Curtin School, they put the institution at risk.

Had the efforts to maintain the difference been worth it? The achievements of the past half-century suggested that they had. By remaining unique, the ANU had contributed uniquely, as its founders hoped it would, to Australian society and the world of research. When we view the University in its parts, the nature of its contribution is easy to identify. Individual academics and departments have done much for Australia and the world, whether in relation to the elimination of smallpox, the exploration of disc galaxies, the elucidation of Australia's national accounts, or any one of many other research accomplishments, without which the nation would be much the poorer. In specific fields, such as demography and the earth sciences, ANU academics created for Australia a culture of research where none existed before. Individual staff members continued to win recognition through prestigious awards and prizes, receiving collectively many more major international awards than their colleagues in any other Australian university. They continued to be the largest university group in the academies of Science, the Social Sciences and the Humanities; and if outsiders sometimes raised an eyebrow at the ANU dominance of the local academies, they could scarcely question the continuing prevalence of ANU academics and former academics among the Australian Fellows of the Royal Society (29 out of 56 in 1995), Corresponding Fellows of the British Academy (3 out of 4), and the Foreign Associates of the National Academy of Sciences of the United States (4 out of 14).

Viewed more broadly, the University's achievement may be seen in the collective contributions of over 30 000 graduates, including nearly 4000 PhDs, who were awarded their degrees before 1996; in the impact of vast numbers of publications and reports; and in the cumulative effects of advice to governments by members of staff. As Bill Hayden, Governor-General and former Labor politician, remarked in 1993, the ANU was 'one of the great reservoirs of information, thought and analysis in Australia'. Through its teaching and research activities, its graduates, staff and visitors, the University helped stimulate an Australian commitment to research.

The ANU also showed, much as Johns Hopkins University had done in the United States in the late nineteenth century, the role research could play in the making of a university. Wang Gungwu, who left the Research School of Pacific Studies in 1986 to become Vice-Chancellor of the University of Hong Kong, reflected in 1994 on what he had learnt from the ANU:

> I would say that the most important thing I took away with me was the sense of how a university could be built upon the quality of research it produces, because the ANU always struck me as an example of how quickly a university, totally new and unknown, could achieve international recognition through research.

The University of Hong Kong, on the other hand, had begun like other universities as an undergraduate institution, and had won an outstanding reputation for the quality of its graduates, without much emphasis on research. Wang encouraged his colleagues to embrace research, seek research funding and engage in postgraduate teaching. By the time he retired in 1995 (and returned to the ANU as a University Fellow), the numbers of research students at the University of Hong Kong had experienced 'a spectacular rise', and the university had achieved what Wang regarded as an appropriate balance between teaching and research. 'Now that', said Wang, 'was inspired by ANU'.

Futures

The makers of the University in the 1940s and 1950s planned buildings to serve its needs for up to 50 years. Beyond that, they were absorbed by immediate challenges, such as recruiting staff, creating a new department or completing a series of experiments. Oliphant looked ahead, never far enough, to finishing his big machine; Florey forecast many years of painstaking medical research and warned the public, overcautiously as it turned out, not to expect remarkable results; Hancock, trusting in his men, preferred to let the future look after itself. When the architect Brian Lewis attempted to describe the completed institution, he got it (through little fault of his own) spectacularly wrong.

The introduction of triennial funding in the 1960s gave the future a horizon. Although the founders of the Research School of Chemistry tried to imagine what their school would look like in 25 years, most people concerned with the future of the University were preoccupied with planning for the ensuing three years. The review process, introduced systematically from the mid-1970s, extended the horizon to ten years; and Karmel's 1987 Strategic Plan presented a framework for the next five. Reviews of the Institute took place in 1990 and 1995. After the second, both the reviewers and the reviewed concluded that this was too often: reviews were taking so much time, money and effort that they were interfering with teaching and research. The 1995 panel proposed that future reviews should occur not fewer than seven years apart; and the Strategic Plan announced in that year was intended to cover the next decade.

Experience suggested that, for planning purposes, seven to ten years was about right. However, Geoffrey Brennan, Director of RSSS, urged his colleagues, gathered at a seminar to discuss the future of the University, not to forget the long view: 'the only real measure of "success", the only proper yardstick for our future, is our capacity to produce great scholars and nurture great work—work that will in a hundred and fifty years time be seen as truly major'. On the other hand, for those (including Brennan) engaged in the day to day running of the University, seven to ten years often seemed a long time. Given the pace of change in higher education, the future seemed increasingly unpredictable and outside the University's control.

As the ANU approached its fiftieth anniversary year in 1996, there were many areas of uncertainty. One related to industrial relations, an issue that affected universities throughout Australia. For several weeks the campus was disrupted by a dispute, the most serious for a decade, during which academic and general staff, now joined in a single union, applied work bans and the general staff imposed pickets which threatened to undermine teaching and research programs and interfere with student recruitment. The conflict arose in part from the government's new system of enterprise bargaining, which was ill suited to academic institutions where productivity could not be measured in dollars and cents. Although harmony was eventually restored, the episode damaged morale and offered a further challenge to collegial government. Would traditional notions of the university community survive a system of industrial relations fashioned for the marketplace? And if they failed to do so, what would be the effects on teaching and research?

While workplace issues caused alarm, there was also cause for optimism. Between 1993 and 1995 the Commonwealth government undertook a series of quality assurance reviews of teaching, research and community service in higher education. On each occasion, the external panel placed the ANU in the top band of Australian universities. Then in 1995 the external reviews of individual research schools and centres offered resounding confirmation of the Institute's achievements. The panel for RSES concluded that the school was 'one of the top five or so earth science research institutions in the world'. RSBS was described as 'a distinguished, major international centre of outstanding research and teaching in biology', which 'fully measures up to the fundamental objective of the Australian National University to be one of the world's great research institutions'. RSC had achieved distinction 'well beyond the fondest hopes of its founders', while RSPhysSE was 'working well beyond the limits of its resources' to produce outstanding research and scholarship. The JCSMR reviewers remarked that the school was 'vital for the health of the nation'; although it had been through 'difficult periods', it was now working with 'renewed vigour' and 'fulfilling its research and development responsibilities with distinction'. The research performance of RSSS was likewise judged to be outstanding and 'on an upward trend', while RSPAS was described as 'a world renowned centre and unrivalled Australian focus for the study of societies, cultures, economics, politics, history and environments of Asia and the Pacific'. MSSSO, the centres and the newer schools all received similar endorsements. Drawing on all these reports, the review of the Institute as a whole concluded that 'the IAS is now a world player in every field in which it has well established scholarly and research activity'.

Yet enthusiastic reviews did not necessarily secure the future; and while the Institute review confirmed the role and mission of the Institute and proposed a modest increase in funding, the government rather than the reviewers would have the final say.

Meanwhile, as the makers of the University in the mid-1990s contemplated many possible futures, teachers, students, researchers, performers and administrators across the campus were getting on with their respective jobs. One of them, Nugget Coombs, approaching ninety, still a Visiting Fellow in CRES and regarded by many as the greatest living Australian, was developing ideas on how Aboriginal communities

Deane Terrell, Vice-Chancellor from 1994, who would lead the University into its second 50 years.

Nugget Coombs, philosopher and visionary, in 1990. Photograph by Heide Smith.
Heide Smith Photography.

fashioned their own institutions to meet the needs of contemporary Australian society. We had hoped, when we began work on this history, to conclude with Coombs producing another publication. But life is not so tidy; and as we complete this chapter, Coombs is in hospital recovering, with characteristic determination, from a stroke, and uncertain whether he will write again.

We can nevertheless end with an appreciation of Nugget Coombs as the person who contributed more than any other to the making of the ANU, who gave it a vision that is still relevant after 50 years, and who recognised that the continuing potency of any vision depends on its capacity to adapt to the times.

List of Chancellors and Vice-Chancellors

Chancellors

R.C. Mills was Chairman of the Interim Council from its inception in 1946 until the election of the first Chancellor in 1951, when he became Deputy Chairman (in effect, permanent chairman) of the Council. When Mills died in 1952, he was succeeded as Deputy Chairman by H.C. Coombs. From 1959 to 1968 Coombs was styled Pro-Chancellor.

1951–1961	Lord Bruce
1961–1965	Sir John Cockcroft
1965–1968	Lord Florey
1968–1976	H.C. Coombs
1976–1984	Sir John Crawford
1984–1987	Sir Richard Blackburn
1987–1990	Sir Gordon Jackson
1990–1994	Sir Geoffrey Yeend
1994–	P.E. Baume

Vice-Chancellors

1948–1953	Sir Douglas Copland
1953–1960	Sir Leslie Melville
1960–1967	Sir Leonard Huxley
1968–1973	Sir John Crawford
1973–1975	R.M. Williams
1975–1982	D.A. Low
1982–1987	P.H. Karmel
1988–1993	L.W. Nichol
1994–	R.D. Terrell

Abbreviations

AUC	Australian Universities Commission
CISR	Centre for Information Science Research
CRC	Cooperative Research Centre
CRES	Centre for Resource and Environmental Studies
CSIR	Council for Scientific and Industrial Research
CSIRO	Commonwealth Scientific and Industrial Research Organisation
HRC	Humanities Research Centre
IAS	Institute of Advanced Studies
JCSMR	John Curtin School of Medical Research
MSSSO	Mount Stromlo and Siding Spring Observatories
NH&MRC	National Health and Medical Research Council
RSBS	Research School of Biological Sciences
RSC	Research School of Chemistry
RSES	Research School of Earth Sciences
RSISE	Research School of Information Sciences and Engineering
RSPacS	Research School of Pacific Studies (to 1993)
RSPAS	Research School of Pacific and Asian Studies (from 1994)
RSPhysS	Research School of Physical Sciences (to 1990)
RSPhysSE	Research School of Physical Sciences and Engineering (from 1991)
RSSS	Research School of Social Sciences
SGS	School of General Studies

Sources

Official records

'Look at the Basic Papers'
> Ross Hohnen to the authors, 1992.

The official records of the University are vast. They include published annual reports of the research schools, faculties and the University as a whole; news publications, the most important of which are the *ANU News* and its successor the *ANU Reporter*; and some 400 000 individual files, which we refer to collectively in the notes as the ANU Archives.

The ANU Archives are subject to the provisions of the Commonwealth Archives Act. Most of them are located in the University and are maintained by the Records Section in the University's Central Administration, pending disposal or transfer to the Australian Archives for permanent retention. They include minutes and papers of Council, the academic boards, the research schools and the faculties; records relating to each research school, faculty and centre; reports and papers relating to internal and external reviews of various parts of the University; subject records; and individual staff and student records. Further information about the content and arrangement of the ANU Archives is available in *A Guide to Central Records*, produced by the University in 1992. We have also consulted selected records in research schools and faculties.

The University of Melbourne Registry holds records relating to the Canberra University College.

Papers relating to the early history of the ANU are located in the Australian Archives, especially in the Commonwealth Office of Education record group. Some collections of private papers also include official and semi-official records, including original and duplicate documents.

The Students' Association keeps minutes of meetings from the 1960s to the present. The two most significant student publications are the annual *Orientation Handbook* and the newspaper *Woroni*.

Private records

'... if the story of any event of importance were derived by historians purely from the official documents there would be no true history'
> Sir Mark Oliphant to David Hodgkin, 25 Feb 1969, ANU Archives.

Many people associated with the University have assembled collections of private papers. Some collections relate to specific research projects. Others, more significant from our perspective, relate generally to the making of the University and how the institution works. Some collections comprise only a few files; others occupy many metres of shelf space.

We have perused, either comprehensively or selectively, the following collections:

Australian Archives
   H.C. Coombs Papers (M448/1; M1505/1; A4311)

ANU Archives
    Correspondence between Hugh Ennor and Sir Howard Florey 1948-56
    A.J. Birch Working Papers
    H.C. Coombs Papers
    J.W. Davidson Papers
    F.J. Fenner Papers
    W.K. Hancock Papers
    D.A. Low Papers
    M.L. Oliphant Papers
    G. Sawer Papers

ANU Library
    H.W. Florey Papers relating to the ANU

Barr Smith Library, University of Adelaide
    W.R. Crocker Papers
    M.L. Oliphant Papers

Basser Library, Australian Academy of Science
    F.J. Fenner Papers
    E.W. Titterton Papers

National Library of Australia
    H.C. Coombs Papers (MS802)
    Sir Douglas Copland Papers (MS3800)
    Sir John Crawford Papers (MS4514)
    L.F. Crisp Papers (MS5243)
    Charles Daley Papers (MS1946)
    John Dedman Papers (MS987)
    Sir Frederic Eggleston Papers (MS423)
    University Association of Canberra Papers (MS470; MS487)
    Jack Waterford Papers (MS7930)
    S.C. Yocklunn Papers (MS2064)

Noel Butlin Archives Centre, ANU
    L.F. Fitzhardinge Papers
    W.K. Hancock Papers (P96)

University of Melbourne Archives
    R.D. Wright Papers

Oral history

> '*Don't believe everything they tell you*'.
> **Many people, often.**

The ANU Oral History Project
Notwithstanding the warnings, we have benefited greatly from the oral reminiscences of people associated with the University. In 1990 the University initiated an oral history project, which later merged into our research for this book. Interviews were conducted by Daniel Connell (DC), S.G. Foster (SGF) and Mary T.N. Varghese (MNV). A series of four interviews conducted by R.A. Gollan in 1982 were transcribed and incorporated in the project.

    The tapes and transcripts are held in the ANU Archives. Some interviews are subject to restricted access.
    Arndt, Heinz Wolfgang 1990 (DC)

SOURCES

Binns, Joan Linnett 1994 (SGF)
Borrie, Wilfred David (Mick) 1982 (RAG)
Bouquet, Mary Grace Cummings (Molly) 1990 (DC)
Burton, Herbert (Joe) 1982 (RAG)
Butlin, Noel George 1990 (SGF)
Catcheside, David Guthrie 1991 (SGF)
Clark, Charles Manning Hope 1991 (SGF)
Coombs, Herbert Cole (Nugget) 1992 (SGF)
Craig, David Parker 1991 (SGF)
Crocker, Sir Walter 1991 (SGF)
Croft, Patricia 1982 (RAG)
Cumpston, Helen 1991 (DC)
Curtis, David Roderick 1992 (SGF)
Fenner, Frank John 1990 (DC)
FitzGerald, Charles Patrick 1991 (SGF)
Fitzhardinge, Laurence Frederic 1982 (RAG) and 1992 (SGF)
Gascoigne, Sidney Charles Bartholomew (Ben) 1990 (DC)
Gibb, Cecil Austin 1991 (SGF)
Gollan, Robin Allenby 1993 (SGF)
Hambly, Arthur Neville 1990 (DC)
Hamilton, William Stenhouse 1994 (SGF)
Karmel, Peter Henry 1995 (SGF)
Kent, Ann Elizabeth and Ward, Robin Lynette 1994 (MNV)
Low, Donald Anthony 1994 (SGF)
Mathews, Russell Lloyd 1991 (SGF)
McCullagh, Peter John 1992 (SGF)
McQueen, Humphrey Denis 1994 (SGF)
Melville, Sir Leslie 1990 (DC)
Nichol, Lawrence Walter 1995 (SGF)
O'Brien, Elizabeth; and Riddell, Diana Betty 1994 (SGF)
Oliphant, Sir Mark 1990 (DC)
Packard, William Percival 1994 (MNV)
Padgham, Stephen; Robinson, Ashton Scott; and Swinbank,
   Christopher John 1994 (SGF)
Passmore, John Arthur 1991 (SGF)
Plowman, Colin George 1994 (SGF)
Robertson, Sir Rutherford (Bob) 1990 (DC)
Rosenberg, Harry 1992 (SGF)
Ross, Ian Gordon 1994 (SGF)
Sawer, Geoffrey 1990 (DC)
Spate, Oskar Hermann Khristian 1990 (DC)
Walsh, Gerald Patrick 1994 (SGF)
Wang Gungwu 1994 (SGF)
White, Patricia Marie 1991 (SGF)
Whitten, Wesley Kingston 1992 (SGF)

In addition, Alan Manning conducted a series of interviews with senior members of the University in 1963: a transcript is held in the ANU Archives. The University also holds television and radio interviews with prominent members of staff.

Interview in the Basser Library, Australian Academy of Science
   Titterton, Ernest William (1980)

Interviews in the National Library of Australia
  Burton, Herbert (Joe) (1982)
  Carver, John Henry (1976)
  Copland, Sir Douglas (1967-68)
  Firth, Sir Raymond (1974)
  Florey, Howard Walter, Lord (1967)
  Huxley, Sir Leonard George Holden (1971)
  Melville, Sir Leslie Galfreid (1973)
  Wheare, Sir Kenneth (1975)
  Wright, Roy Douglas (Pansy) (1976)

Interview in the University of Melbourne Archives
  Wright, Sir (Roy) Douglas (Pansy) (1986)

Bibliographies

Two bibliographies of published sources have been especially valuable:

Naomi Caiden, 'A Bibliography for Australian Universities', in E.L. Wheelwright (ed.), *Higher Education in Australia*, Cheshire, Melbourne, 1965; and

Roy MacLeod, History of Australian Universities: A Working Bibliography, Research School of Social Sciences, ANU, 1990.

Sources of illustrations

Most of the illustrations in this book are taken from what we loosely refer to as the 'ANU Collection'. This is spread around various parts of the University, especially the Public Affairs Division, the Records Section and ANU Photography. The term also includes smaller collections in JCSMR (which, in the early years, provided photographic services to the whole University), MSSSO, the Buildings and Grounds Division, and several other divisions or departments. Where no source is indicated, the original illustration is located within the ANU Collection and may be traced through the Public Affairs Division.

Early chapters make extensive use of photographs taken by the Commonwealth Department of Information (1939-49), which are described as 'Australian Official Photographs', and the Australian News and Information Bureau (1949-72). These were often commissioned by the University and do not form part of the collection of official photographs held by Australian Archives. We therefore describe them as forming part of the ANU Collection.

Where possible we have provided the date or approximate date of each photograph and have acknowledged its photographer. We apologise to photographers whose work appears without acknowledgement.

Notes

These notes are intended to give a broad view of the sources of information, without being comprehensive. They do not include references to sources which are evident from the text. Nor do they include detailed references to the official records described on page 417 as 'ANU Archives'. Where no sources are given, readers may assume that the information is based on evidence in the ANU Archives.

Detailed references, including references to specific files in the ANU Archives, are included in a computer database of the book, which is held by the University. The ANU Archives are not open to general access. However, researchers may seek further details of references by writing to Central Records at the University and referring to *The Making of The Australian National University*.

ADDITIONAL ABBREVIATIONS USED IN NOTES

AA	The Australian Archives	NLA	National Library of Australia
ADB	Australian Dictionary of Biography	OHP	ANU Oral History Project
BGS	Board of Graduate Studies	pt	part
esp	especially	ser	series
inc	including	uni	university
J	Journal	UP	University Press

1   The Planners

3-19   Coombs wrote about the origins of the ANU in his *Trial Balance*, Macmillan, South Melbourne, 1981, pp. 195–200. He and others talked about the early years on various occasions, including a series of interviews for ABC Radio in 1963 with the journalist Alan Manning (transcript in ANU Archives). *ANU News*, Aug 1974, focuses on 'The Coombs contribution'. Milton Lewis worked carefully through some of the archival sources and produced two long papers in 1966 and 1969. His research provided the basis of a published address by Sir John Crawford, *The Australian National University: its Concept and Role*, ANU, 1968. Lewis also produced A national research university: the origins and early years of the Australian National University, MA thesis, ANU 1972; 'The idea of a national university: the origins and establishment of the ANU', *J of the Australian and New Zealand History of Education Society*, 8/1, 1979; and 'Canberra as a cultural centre: the aspirations of the Canberra University Movement', *J of the Royal Australian Historical Society*, 65/1, 1979.

A wartime meeting

3-4   Coombs is quoted by Wright in the interview conducted by Manning, 1963. On Conlon: *Alfred Conlon*, privately published, Sydney, 1963; Peter Ryan's entry in *ADB* vol 13; information from Peter Ryan, 1992. The portrait of Wright is drawn from the Wright Papers, Uni of Melbourne Archives, augmented (especially in relation to the origins and spelling of his nickname) by information from Meriel Wilmot Wright. The Uni of Melbourne Archives also hold interviews conducted with Wright in the 1980s (inc one on the ANU, conducted jointly with Coombs). Also Henry Harris, *The Balance of Improbabilities: A Scientific Life*, Oxford UP, Oxford, 1987, p. 50. The journalist's comment on his charm is from C. Pybus, *Gross Moral Turpitude*, Heinemann Australia, Port Melbourne, 1993, p. 105. The main source for Coombs is his autobiographical *Trial Balance*. Also several OHP interviews, including the interview with Coombs himself.

	1988; R. Gollan in Australian Academy of the Humanities, *Proceedings*, 1987–89; G.C. Bolton, *Australian Historical Association Bulletin*, Aug–Nov 1989; and D.A. Low in *Proceedings of the British Academy*, 82, 1992. There are many assessments of his place in Australian historiography.
24-5	Oliphant's response to the invitation is to Coombs, 2 Oct 1946, Coombs Papers, AA. Hancock talks about his exhaustion and desire to return to Australia in wartime letters to C.R. Badger, Hancock Papers, P96/23, Noel Butlin Centre, ANU. Hancock as vice-chancellor: Mills to Hancock, 2 Jan 1946, Hancock Papers, ANU Archives. 'Slap-up arrangements': Hancock to G.C. Allen, Hancock Papers, ANU Archives. He outlines the problems to J. Medley, 23 Oct 1946, Hancock Papers, ANU Archives.
25	Florey details his concerns in several letters in the Wright Papers.
25-6	Coombs persuades Chifley, 13 Jan 1947, Coombs Papers, AA. Cabinet gives its approval, 31 Jan 1947, Agendum 1291, AA.
26-7	These manoeuvres are in Conlon to Wright, 24 Sep 1946 and 18 Jan 1947, Wright Papers, 8/6/1. Firth is mentioned in Conlon's undated letter (Mar–Apr 1946), Wright Papers, 8/1/8. Firth discusses his association with the ANU in an oral history interview with M. Murphy, 1974, NLA. Firth responds favourably to Mills, 28 Mar 47, Coombs Papers, AA.
27	Rivett to Florey, 21 Feb 1947, Florey Papers. Eggleston to Medley, 18 Feb 1947, Eggleston Papers, ser 12, MS423, NLA.

Oxford and Canberra

27-50	The minutes of the Academic Advisory Committee and the Interim Council are essential sources for the remainder of this chapter. Full sets are held in the ANU Archives.
27-32	The manoeuvres in 1947 are well documented in the Wright Papers, 4/1/3 and 8/2/1; and the Coombs Papers, AA.
27-30	Wright tells Mills of his anxieties, 7 Feb 1947, CRS A1876, OEN1/1 pt 3, AA. Copies of his 'Sketch plan for the establishment of the Australian National University' are in the Wright Papers, 4/1/1; and the Coombs Papers, AA. Oliphant tells Wright he is ready to sign, 21 May 1947, Wright Papers, 4/1/3. Wright explains his strategy to Oliphant, 21 May 1947, Wright Papers, 4/1/3. Crisp's advice: 24 Apr 1947, Wright Papers, 4/1/3; and his 'Comments on Professor Wright's report on his visit to Britain', Mar 1947, Wright Papers, 4/1/1,

	and Interim Council papers. Wright complains to Coombs about the Interim Council, 12 Aug 1947, Coombs Papers, AA.
30-2	Many letters in the Wright Papers and the Coombs Papers, AA, refer to the selection of a vice-chancellor. In addition: Medley to Mills, 24 Sep 1947, CRS A1876, OEN1/1 pt 3, AA; Rivett to Eggleston, 27 Aug 1947, Eggleston Papers, ser 12, MS423, NLA; and Rivett to Mills, CRS A1876, OEN1/1 pt 3, AA. Osborne recorded discussion on the Interim Council in his notebook, 24 Oct 1947, ANU Archives. In 1938 Copland had 'talked himself out of the job' of Vice-Chancellor at the Uni of Melbourne. See G. Serle, *Sir John Medley: a Memoir*, Melbourne UP, 1993, pp. 22–28.

Easter 1948

33	Florey explodes to Oliphant, 21 Feb 1948, Florey Papers. Foster explains the situation to Osborne, 4 Mar 1948, ANU Archives; and to Wright, 3 Feb 1948, Wright Papers, 8/2/2. Wright to Osborne, 22 Mar 1948, Wright Papers, 4/1/5, plans Florey's recreation; Hancock, *Country and Calling*, p. 239, suggests that their efforts were not wasted. Copland tells Osborne about gaining face, 6 Mar 1948, ANU Archives. Complete sets of the conference papers and minutes of proceedings are in the ANU Archives, with selections in various private papers.
34-5	The paper on Basic Policy, 10 May 1948, and Rivett's advice, 2 Jun 1948, are with the minutes of the 20th Interim Council meeting.

Designing the schools

35-42	The proposals of the Academic Advisers are in the Basic Papers, ANU Archives.
35-8	Florey's proposals are drawn chiefly from his papers of 7 Apr 1945, 1 Jun 1946 and 19 Dec 1947; and from the papers of the conference on Medical Research, 3–4 Apr 1948, inc his Suggestions for further procedures in setting up Medical Research Institute, 2 Apr 1948.
38-9	Oliphant's views are set out in the Interim Council minutes, 13 Jan 1947; Comments on the Foundation of a National University in Canberra, with particular reference to the proposed School of Physical Sciences, 8 Feb 1947; and Research School of Physical Sciences — aims, organisation and finance, Apr 1948, with Interim Council minutes, 14 May 1948. 'Passionate belief': Memo on

	Scholarships and Fellowships in the School of Physical Sciences, 8 Dec 1947, Interim Council minutes, 13 Feb 1948.
39-40	Hancock's letter to Mills, 16 July 1947, and his Note on the cost of a School of Social Sciences, 5 Apr 1948, are in the Basic Papers. His comments on planning are in *Country and Calling*, p. 238. On 'growing points': Hancock to Coombs, 31 Mar 1947, Coombs Papers, AA. On 'Ideas without men': Hancock to L. Melville, 22 Dec 1956, Vice-Chancellor's confidential papers relating to the appointment of Hancock.
40	Eggleston's writings on the proposed school of Pacific Studies include Notes on the proposals for a graduate school in Canberra, undated [1946]; and an untitled paper, 26 Sep 1946: Eggleston Papers, ser 12, MS423, NLA. W.G. Osmond, *Frederic Eggleston: An Intellectual in Australian Politics*, Allen & Unwin, Sydney, 1985, pp. 264-77, sets Eggleston's relationship with the ANU in the context of his intellectual development.
40-2	Firth's plan, in Basic Papers, is dated 30 Jan 1948. The differences between Firth and Eggleston emerge in the papers of the Pacific Studies conference, and in correspondence, inc Eggleston to Copland, 13 Apr 1949, CRS A1876, OEN1/1 pt 4, AA. 'Culturally Europeans': Firth to Copland, 17 Jan 1949, with Interim Council minutes, 11 Feb 1949; also Firth interview, NLA. The joint Copland–Eggleston plan, 16 Mar 1949, is in the Basic Papers.

Two gentlemen on a park bench

43-50	This narrative has been pieced together from many sources, inc the minutes of the Interim Council and the Academic Advisory Committee; papers relating to the early history of RSSS, ANU Archives; correspondence at CRS A1876, OEN1/1 pt 4 and OEN4/1 pt 2, AA; Hancock Papers (esp a file labelled 'Signing Off'), ANU Archives; Copland Papers, NLA; Eggleston Papers, NLA; Crocker Papers, Barr Smith Library, Uni of Adelaide; and Crocker OHP.
46	Wheare confirms that he had no intention of coming permanently to Australia in an interview with Catherine Santamaria, 1975, NLA.
48-9	Osmond, *Frederic Eggleston*, includes valuable insights into Eggleston's background and outlook. Crocker OHP offers vivid recollections of his two old friends.

3 Pioneers

Recruiting

51-9	This section draws on various files in ANU Archives. In addition, on Borrie's appointment: conversation with the authors, 13 Apr 1992; Hancock to Copland, 8 Dec 1948, Copland Papers, MS3800, box 137, NLA. Sawer and the bench: Sawer OHP.
51-5	On Nadel: Firth to Hancock, 9 Mar 1949, Hancock Papers, ANU Archives; ANU Archives; and obituary by J.D. Freeman in *Oceania*, 27/1, Sep 1956. On Crocker: Hancock to A.P. Rowe, 1 May 1949, Hancock Papers, ANU Archives; Hancock to Crocker, 18 Feb 1949, Hancock Papers; Copland to R.A. Hohnen, 20 Jun 1949, ANU Archives; and Copland to Mills, 2 May 1949, CRS A1876, OEN4/1 pt 2, AA; correspondence and notes in the Crocker Papers; and Crocker OHP. On Davidson: Hancock to Davidson, 26 May 1949; and Davidson to Hancock, 20 Aug 1949, Hancock Papers. FitzGerald tells the horoscope story in his autobiographical *Why China?*, Melbourne UP, 1985, and in his OHP interview. Copland praises him to Eggleston, 7 Oct 1949, Eggleston Papers, ser 12, MS423, NLA. On Sawer: Copland to L.F. Giblin, 25 Aug 1949, Copland Papers, MS3800, box 138, NLA; and Eggleston to Copland, 1 Sep 1949, ANU Archives. N. Kaldor praises Swan to Coombs, 7 Sep 1948, Coombs Papers, AA. Reservations about Swan: Copland to Medley, 31 Oct 1949, Copland Papers, MS3800, box 138, NLA; and Copland to his secretary, J. Morrish, 13 Jan 1950, Copland Papers, MS3800, box 139. Hancock is cautious about Swan, to Copland, 16 Feb 1949, Hancock Papers, ANU Archives. Swan wrote an obituary of Brown for the *Economic Record*, 47/117, Mar 1971. Eggleston to Copland, 1 Sep 1949, hopes for balance: ANU Archives. Wright's mixed views of Ennor: to Osborne, 1 Jul 1948, ANU Archives; and to R. Gerard, 13 Dec 1948, Wright Papers, 8/2/2, Uni of Melbourne Archives. Wright on Albert: to R. Gerard, 13 Dec 1948, Wright Papers, 8/2/2. Letters regarding appointment of Fenner and Eccles are in the Florey Papers and on official files. Betting on the youngsters: Wright to R. Gerard, 13 Dec 1948, Wright Papers, 8/2/2. On Titterton: J.O. Newton, 'Ernest William Titterton 1916-1990', *Historical Records of Australian Science*, 9/2, Dec 1992. The measured reference is in the ANU Archives. The beginnings of the Department of Astronomy are detailed in

the official records, ANU Archives. Oliphant OHP adds to the story.

58-9 Consideration of women: Firth to Hancock, 9 Mar 1949; and Hancock to Copland, 11 Aug 1948, Hancock Papers.

The lure of Canberra

59-61 Davidson said 'Yes' to Hancock, 19 Mar 1949, Hancock Papers, ANU Archives; and Sawer said 'Yes' to Copland, 12 Sep 1949, ANU Archives. Freeman mentions Nadel's walk in the *Oceania* obituary. Hohnen refers to Council's view of 'the Oliphant mast' in a letter to Mills, 7 Jan 1950, CRS A1876, OEN1/1 pt 4, AA. The attractions of the ANU: Davidson to Hancock, 20 Aug 1949, Hancock Papers; Eccles' statement for the Council of the Uni of Otago, quoted in Eccles to Copland, 24 May 1950, ANU Archives; also Eccles, 'My Scientific Odyssey', *Annual Review of Physiology*, 39, 1977, pp. 5–7; Fenner OHP; and FitzGerald OHP and *Why China?* 'The call of the kookaburra': Hancock to Copland, 9 Aug 1948, ANU Archives. Crocker expresses his enthusiasm to Hancock, 7 Mar and 12 May 1949, Hancock Papers, with additional information from Crocker OHP.

Overseas scholars

61-4 Information about the overseas scholars has been compiled from Interim Council Annual Reports, minutes of the Interim Council and Academic Advisory Committee, and many files in ANU Archives, supplemented by occasional references in the private papers of Florey, Wright, Crocker and Hancock, and OHP interviews, especially Butlin, Gollan and Ross. Henry Harris writes about his experience as a scholar in *The Balance of Improbabilities: A Scientific Life*, Oxford UP, Oxford, 1987. Ross Hohnen helped us with information about the scholars and their later careers.

A shed in a paddock

64-7 David Dexter, a former Registrar (Property and Plans), compiled a detailed history of the site, esp before the creation of the ANU. This was published as *The ANU Campus*, ANU 1991, which includes numerous appendices.
'A shed': *Sydney Morning Herald*, 28 Mar 1950. Osborne tells L.F. Crisp about his hopes, 3 Jun 1947, CRS A1876, OEN1/1 pt 3, AA. Crocker writes to Hancock, 7 Sep 1950, Hancock Papers; also his *Travelling Back: the Memoirs of Sir Walter Crocker*, Macmillan, South Melbourne, 1981; private recollections, written in 1953, in the Crocker Papers, Barr Smith Library, Uni of Adelaide; and OHP interview. Bunker's complaints: 6 Dec 1951 and 21 Apr 1952, Florey Papers. Ennor tells Florey about the sheds, 2 Feb 1953, Florey Papers.

Academics and architecture

67-74 The minutes of the Interim Council and the Academic Advisory Committee include lengthy discussions of architectural matters.

67-70 Coombs suggests an architectural competition to Daley, 2 Nov 1945, Daley Papers, MS1946, 1/6, folder 52. Wright commends Lewis to Oliphant, 25 Nov 1947, Wright Papers, 4/1/3. 'All Souls and a rooming house': Wright to Firth, 1 Dec 1947, Wright Papers, 4/1/3. Lewis on the Advisers: 16 Jan 1948, Wright Papers, 8/2/2. Oliphant on Lewis: Memorandum on the Past and Future of the University, [Dec 1955–Jan 1956], ANU Archives; Foster on Lewis: to Wright, 3 Feb 1948, Wright Papers, 8/2/2.

71-4 The *Sydney Morning Herald* article is dated 28 Jun 1950. Hancock sets out his ideas for University House at the Easter conferences, 1948. He confides to Copland about 'the wife factor', 8 May 1948, ANU Archives. The description of University House borrows from F. West, *University House: Portrait of an Institution*, University House, Canberra, 1980. Hancock praises University House in *Professing History*, Sydney UP, Sydney, 1976, pp. 29–30; as does Oliphant in his Memorandum on the Past and Future of the University, [Dec 1955–Jan 1956], ANU Archives; and Florey (grudgingly), to Hancock, 20 Nov 1954, Florey Papers. Oliphant quotes Menzies in a letter to Florey, 26 Aug 53, Florey Papers; also S. Cockburn and D. Ellyard, *Oliphant: the Life and Times of Sir Mark Oliphant*, Axiom, Adelaide, 1981, p. 173. Menzies made similar comments about University House to Ennor: Ennor to Florey, 23 Sep 53, Ennor–Florey Correspondence, ANU Archives. On Menzies' early connection with Lewis: A.W. Martin, *Robert Menzies: a Life*, vol. 1, Melbourne UP, Melbourne, 1993, pp. 23, 30. Florey takes no nonsense: to Ennor, 21 Mar 1949, Florey Papers.

A genuine university

75-6 Copland refers to 'propaganda missions' in his paper, Basic Problems of Academic Policy, Jul 1949, ANU Archives. Copland

76	confesses to Hancock about his optimism, 13 May 1948 and 22 Apr 1949, Hancock Papers, ANU Archives. Spate remembers Copland in his OHP interview. Copland tells Hancock about Hohnen, 22 Dec 1948, Hancock Papers. Hohnen tells E.H. Clark about the pattern forming, 18 May 1950, ANU Archives. Copies of Sawer's verse are in the Noel Butlin Centre, ANU, and the National Library. Ideas about the Master of University House include Oliphant to Hancock, 13 Mar 1951; and Crocker to Hancock, 25 May 1951, Hancock Papers, P96/23, Noel Butlin Centre, ANU.		

76 Ideas about the Master of University House include Oliphant to Hancock, 13 Mar 1951; and Crocker to Hancock, 25 May 1951, Hancock Papers, P96/23, Noel Butlin Centre, ANU.

76-7 Osborne on the coat of arms: 3 Jun 1947, Office of Education CRS A1876, OEN1/1 pt 3, AA. Oliphant on 'worn-out conventions': Cockburn and Ellyard, *Oliphant*, p. 160. An Aboriginal motif: Geoffrey Sawer's diary, 30 Apr 1951, by courtesy of Geoffrey Sawer; and BGS minutes, 30 Apr 1951. Oliphant saves the day: BGS, 18 Sep 1953; Council minutes, 9 Oct 1953. All other references to the coat of arms are from the official file on the subject in ANU Archives.
Discussion of the motto is from the official file. Also BGS minutes, 6 Nov 1953.

78 The academic dress saga emerges from the official file, supplemented by BGS papers, 24 Jul 1953.

78-9 Florey tells Ennor about the Academic Advisory Committee's deliberations on titles, 27 Oct 1948, Ennor–Florey Correspondence, ANU Archives. Sawer records Copland's stand on 'professor' in his diary, 6 Jul 1951.

79-80 The opening of the RSPhysS laboratories is recorded on audio tape in the ANU Archives, and reported in *ANU News*, Sep 1952. The installation of the first Chancellor is reported in *ANU News*, Mar 1953, and recorded in numerous photographs. A silent film of the occasion is now lodged in the National Film and Sound Archive. Crocker's occasional regrets: J.D.B. Miller to Crocker, 11 Feb 1965, Crocker Papers, 9/1, Barr Smith Library, Uni of Adelaide.

81 Sawer remembers Copland's announcement of his resignation in his OHP interview. Oliphant to Florey, 9 Oct 1952, looks forward to a change: Florey Papers. Florey to Oliphant, 4 Feb 1953, on the 'intolerable mess': Florey Papers. Crocker on Copland: *Travelling Back: the Memoirs of Sir Walter Crocker*, Macmillan, South Melbourne, 1981, p. 172; Crocker to Hancock, 7 Feb 1952 and 12 Jan 1953, Hancock Papers, P96/15/2, Noel Butlin Centre, ANU; also Crocker's private recollections, written in 1953, in the Crocker Papers, Barr Smith Library, Uni of Adelaide; and OHP interview. For other assessments of Copland: Hohnen, 'Leadership in the Academic Community', *Economic Record*, Mar 1960; Butlin, Coombs, Hamilton, Mathews, Oliphant and Sawer OHP interviews; and M. Harper's entry, *Australian Dictionary of Biography*, vol. 13.

81-2 Copland records his meetings with Menzies and Cabinet in confidential paper, The Vice-Chancellor's Notes on the medical School, 29 Jan 1953, ANU Archives. 'A rather high-minded group of people': Copland to Hohnen, 13 Dec 1952, ANU Archives.

4 Research begins

Opportunities

83-4 Copies of Sawer's verse are in the Noel Butlin Centre, ANU, and NLA. FitzGerald's shopping: Report of the Interim Council, 1946–1949, p. 14, ANU Archives; and his OHP interview. McDonald's visiting: Report of the Interim Council, 1946–1949, p. 14. The comments by Butlin, Paton, Hogbin and Capell are from reports which they prepared for the Easter conferences, 1948. Curtis's reflections are from his OHP interview.

The John Curtin School of Medical Research

85-92 F. Fenner published an outline history of the early years of JCSMR in the *Medical Journal of Australia*, 24 Jul 1971.

85-7 On Albert and the Department of Medical Chemistry: correspondence in ANU Archives and in the Florey Papers, ANU Library; D.J. Brown's obituary in *Historical Records of Australian Science*, 8/2, Jun 1990, and other obituaries in Albert's personal file, ANU Archives; information from Ian Rae, Victorian Uni of Technology, who is writing Albert's biography; and Fenner OHP.

86-7 Ennor and Biochemistry: Ennor–Florey Correspondence, ANU Archives; Rosenberg OHP; Whitten OHP; F.C. Courtice's obituary in *Records of the Australian Academy of Science*, 4/1, Nov 1978, which includes the American visitor's comment on 'Prof'.

87-8 Florey discusses his research objectives in his interview with H. De Berg, 1967, tape 220, NLA. Harris's wry comment is in his autobiographical *The Balance of Improbabilities: a Scientific Life*, Oxford UP, Oxford, 1987, p. 62. A 'loathsome desideratum': Mackaness to Florey, 20

89-90	Oct 1955, Florey Papers, ANU Library. Fenner and the Department of Microbiology: Fenner's 'Valediction', 11 May 1973, when he retired as Director of JCSMR, Fenner Papers, ANU Archives; correspondence with Florey in the Florey Papers; *ANU Reporter*, 1 May 1981; Fenner and F.N. Ratcliffe, *Myxomatosis*, Cambridge UP, Cambridge, 1965; Fenner (ed.), *History of Microbiology in Australia*, Brolga Press, Canberra, 1990; and Fenner OHP.
90-1	The research on the hypertensive rats is related in letters from Mackaness to Florey, Florey Papers; supplemented by other letters in the Florey Papers, and Whitten OHP.
91-2	Eccles and the Department of Physiology: Curtis OHP; and Eccles, 'My Scientific Odyssey', *Annual Review of Physiology*, 39, 1977, which includes on p. 11 the concluding quotation.

The Research School of Physical Sciences

92-5	S. Cockburn and D. Ellyard, *Oliphant: the Life and Times of Sir Mark Oliphant*, Axiom, Adelaide, 1981, provides a useful background to Oliphant's career. The discussion of Oliphant also draws on his OHP interview, several of his publications in scientific and popular journals, and numerous reports in the press. Oliphant's optimistic comments are from the Melbourne *Argus*, 5 Jan 1951. The sort of science he wanted to do: 5 Jun 1947, Wright Papers, 4/1/3, Uni of Melbourne Archives. Hancock remarks on Oliphant's optimism, 25 Dec 1957, Florey Papers. The enthusiastic journalist is H.C. McKay in the Sydney *Daily Telegraph*, 16 Mar 1952. Wentworth and Evatt are quoted in Hansard, 10 Nov 1954. Copland on 'the Birmingham thing': 28 Jun 1953, ANU Archives.
95-6	Titterton wrote about 'Nuclear Physics at the Australian National University', *Australian Journal of Science*, Dec 1951. J.O. Newton's obituary of Titterton is in the *Historical Records of Australian Science*, 9/2, Dec 1992.
96-8	Jaeger wrote about 'Geophysics at the Australian National University — a tentative programme', *Australian Journal of Science*, Oct 1951. His obituary, by M.S. Paterson, is in the *Biographical Memoirs of Fellows of the Royal Society*, Nov 1982.
98-9	Astronomers have been diligent chroniclers of their past. Relevant papers include: A.R. Hyland and D.J. Faulkner, 'From the Sun to the Universe — The Woolley and Bok Directorships at Mount Stromlo', *Proceedings of the Astronomical Society of Australia*, 8/2, 1989; S.C.B. Gascoigne, 'Australian Astronomy since the Second World War', in R.W. Home (ed.), *Australian Science in the Making*, Cambridge, Cambridge UP, 1988. Also Gascoigne OHP. On Woolley: S. Davies, 'R.v.d.R. Woolley in Australia', *Historical Records of Australian Science*, 6/1, 1984. Woolley wrote about 'Astrophysics at the Australian National University', *Australian Journal of Science*, Feb 1952.

The Research School of Social Sciences

100	Fitzpatrick's comment is to A. Fabinyi, 29 Aug 1957, Brian Fitzpatrick Papers, 29/2(a), MS4965, NLA. (We thank Marivic Wyndham for this reference.)
103	Moran's paper on The role of Statistics in the Australian National University is in the Florey Papers. Copland tells Crocker about Moran and the scientific left, 13 Jun 1951, ANU Archives.
104-5	The Popper appointment is the subject of a file in the ANU Archives. C. Pybus, *Gross Moral Turpitude*, Heinemann Australia, Port Melbourne, 1993, p. 205, mistakenly attributes the rejection of Popper to Eggleston. A. Boyce Gibson, Uni of Melbourne, denounces Popper to Copland, 22 Jun 1950, ANU Archives. Florey on Jews, 17 May 1950, is in the Florey Papers. Copland tells Wheare 'Florey's doubts have to be taken very seriously', 13 Jun 1950, ANU Archives.
105	Sawer on 'clubbable' appointments: to Hohnen, 19 Jun 1950, ANU Archives. Hancock pronounces on such matters in *Professing History*, Sydney UP, Sydney, 1976, p. 33. Partridge offers his views on Social Philosophy in the ANU *Annual Report*, 1953.

The Research School of Pacific Studies

106	On FitzGerald: OHP interview; and his inaugural lecture, *The Character of Far Eastern History*, ANU, Canberra, 1955.
106-7	H.E. Maude remembers Davidson in the *Journal of Pacific History*, 8, 1973. Melville expresses doubts about Davidson to Sir John Crawford, 21 Jun 1960; Crawford's response, to L.G.H. Huxley, 19 Dec 1960, is more liberal.
107-8	Spate and the geographers: Spate, *The Compass of Geography* (inaugural lecture), ANU, 1953; J.N. Jennings and G.J.R. Linge, *Of Time and Place: Essays in Honour of OHK Spate*, ANU Press, Canberra, 1980, esp the 'personal impression' by T.M. Perry; Spate, *On the Margins of History: from the Punjab to Fiji*, RSPacS, 1991; and Spate OHP. Spate on 'man and land': RSPacS faculty board

	paper, The Research School of Pacific Studies: its future role and organization, Jul 1958.
108-9	The official papers on the Lindsay case are voluminous. They are supplemented by Crocker OHP and correspondence in the Crocker Papers, Barr Smith Library, Uni of Adelaide.
109-10	On Nadel: Nadel, Research projects in Anthropology, Feb 1951, ANU Archives; D. Freeman, 'Siegfried Frederick Nadel, 1903–1956', *Oceania*, 27/1, Sep 1956; M. Fortes, 'Siegfried Frederick Nadel 1903–1956: a memoir', in Nadel, *The Theory of Social Structure*, Melbourne UP, Melbourne, 1957; and notes by A.C. Mayer, by courtesy of R.A. Hohnen. Stanner is quoted on 'men in anthropology' in D.E. Barwick, J. Beckett and M. Reay, 'W.E.H. Stanner: an Australian anthropologist', in Barwick, Beckett and Reay (eds), *Metaphors of Interpretation: Essays in Honour of W.E.H. Stanner*, ANU Press, 1985, p. 26. Stanner's essay 'The Dreaming (1953)' is in his *White Man got no Dreaming: Essays 1938–1973*, ANU Press, Canberra, 1979, p. 23.

The creative imagination

110-12	N. Brown, *Governing Prosperity: Social Change and Social Analysis in Australia in the 1950s*, Cambridge UP, 1995, discusses the broad intellectual background to Australian universities in the 1950s.
111-12	Conlon tells Wright the social science side is 'stuft' in an undated letter, Oct 1950, Wright Papers, 8/6/1. Oliphant expresses his dismay to Eggleston, 8 Nov and 4 Dec 1950; Eggleston responds, Nov 1950: Eggleston Papers, ser 12, MS423, NLA. Eggleston's lament to Hancock is in the Eggleston Papers, ser 1. On Eggleston as an old man: Crocker's personal recollections in the Crocker Papers; Crocker OHP; and W.G. Osmond, *Frederic Eggleston: an Intellectual in Australian Politics*, Allen & Unwin, Sydney, 1985, pp. 276–77. Conlon's 'law' is in *Alfred Conlon*, privately published, Sydney, 1963, p. 29.

5 Academic freedom and leadership

113-43	N. Caiden's bibliography in E.L. Wheelwright (ed.), *Higher Education in Australia*, Cheshire, Melbourne, 1965, includes many articles relevant to this chapter.

The University and the government

113	Copland to Menzies on academic freedom, 31 Jan 1948, Menzies Papers, MS4936, 1/8, NLA: we owe this reference to A.W. Martin. Rowe's list is in his *If the Gown Fits*, Melbourne UP, Melbourne, 1960, p. 51. Copland expands on the meaning of academic freedom in his paper, Basic Problems of Academic Policy, Jul 1949, ANU Archives. Copland's account of the foundation stones speeches, 24 Oct 1949, is in Prime Minister's Department, CRS A461/1, J340/1/7 pt 1, AA.
114	The exchange with Lang is in Hansard, 4 and 15 Mar 1949. Mills had occasion to remind the Secretary of the Prime Minister's Department of the precedent, 14 Mar 50, Office of Education CRS A1876, OEN1/1 pt 4.
115	Menzies on *The Place of a University in the Modern Community* (address at CUC commencement 1939), Melbourne UP, Melbourne, 1939, p. 30. For Casey, Ennor to Copland, 28 Aug 1950; and Copland to Ennor, 28 Sep 1950, Copland Papers, MS3800, box 139, NLA; also W.J. Hudson, *Casey*, Melbourne UP, Melbourne, 1986, p. 222. For Kent Hughes, Copland to Bruce, 5 Jan 1953, Copland Papers, MS3800, box 70, ser 34. Oliphant tells Florey about objections to the John Curtin School, 26 Aug 1953, Florey Papers, ANU Library. The 'honest broker': audio tape recording of opening of RSPhysS laboratories, 1952, ANU Archives: also Oliphant to Florey, 26 Aug 1953, Florey Papers. Copland's satisfaction: Copland to Bruce, 18 Aug 52, Copland Papers, MS3800, box 70, ser 34. Menzies on funding for higher education, Hansard, 6 Nov 1951.
115-16	The Copland superannuation issue is discussed in letters in the Coombs Papers, AA; the Wright Papers, Uni of Melbourne Archives; and in Interim Council minutes. (Copland, as it happened, was sadly impecunious in later life.) Copland protests about Goodes, 17 Mar 1950, and Mills responds, 23 Mar, Office of Education CRS A1876, OEN1/1 pt 4; also Mathews OHP. Rivett urges firmness, 1 Mar 1951, Copland Papers, MS3800, box 141.
116	The Auditor-General story draws on ANU Archives, supplemented by letters in the Florey Papers; *Canberra Times*, 10 Nov 1953; *Argus*, 12 Nov 1953; Melville OHP; and information from R.A. Hohnen and W.S. Hamilton.

'No Melville, no money'

116-18	The circumstances of Melville's appointment have been reconstructed from ANU Archives and the Florey Papers, ANU Library.

Sober administration

119-20 Copland assesses Melville in a letter to Hohnen, 10 Oct 1953, ANU Archives. Coombs expresses his satisfaction to Florey, 23 Jun 1955, Coombs Papers, M448/1, AA. Oliphant complained often to Florey: e.g. 17 Aug 1955, and, on Melville, 10 Nov 1956, Florey Papers. The financial ceiling is explained in Council papers, 14 Dec 1956; also several letters in the Florey Papers, the Coombs Papers, AA, and a note by Wright, Oct 1956, in the Wright Papers, 4/2/1, Uni of Melbourne Archives.
Florey and Oliphant press for Birch's appointment in various letters in the Florey Papers. Coombs explains to Florey the need for restraint, 23 Jun 1955, Coombs Papers, AA.

Freedom with discretion

120-1 The Country Party member is Archie Cameron, in Hansard, 5 Jul 1946. Hohnen on 'witch-hunting': to R.G. Osborne, 25 Oct 1948, ANU Archives. Casey on long-haired communists: Hancock to Florey, 19 Nov 1954, Florey Papers. (Note Hancock on Casey in *Professing History*, Sydney UP, Sydney, 1976, p. 33–34, as an example of Hancock's capacity for self-deception.) Gullett and Keon are in Hansard, 28 Aug 1952; and Gullett's questions, 16 Sep 1952. Copland tells the Secretary of the Department of Immigration about Lindsay, 14 Dec 1950, Copland Papers, MS3800, box 139, NLA.
On ASIO activities: Gollan OHP; and his ASIO file, CRS A6119/79, item 680, AA.

122 Spate's problems are in Casey to Copland, Copland Papers, 11 Sep 1952, MS3800, box 143, which concludes: 'We will now approach Stanner but am having him checked out first by Spry [the head of ASIO]. In future I'll do this about any fellow for any appointment whatsoever.' The Worsley affair is in ANU Archives; also Copland to Bruce, 18 Aug 1952; Bruce to Copland, 29 Aug 1952, Copland Papers, MS3800, box 70, ser 34; and Copland to J.F. Foster, 1 Sep 1952, Copland Papers, MS3800, box 142. Letters relating to Inall are in the Crocker Papers and the Oliphant Papers, both in the Barr Smith Library, Uni of Adelaide.

123 Florey's warning to Oliphant, 1 Feb 1956, is in the Florey Papers. C. Pybus, *Gross Moral Turpitude*, Heinemann Australia, Port Melbourne, 1993, shows that there was more to this case than met the eye. The Diamond case is documented in the official records, ANU Archives, supplemented by letters in the Ennor–Florey Correspondence, and Coombs Papers, both in the ANU Archives.

123-4 For the Mason case: ANU Archives; Ennor–Florey Correspondence; Florey Papers; Hancock Papers, P96/15/2, Noel Butlin Centre, ANU; and correspondence between S.G. Foster and S.F. Mason in 1993–94.

124-6 The debate on Indochina is in the *Canberra Times*, Apr 1954; and on the Bandung conference, *Canberra Times* and other newspapers, April 1955. FitzGerald OHP comments on Menzies and the journalist. Davidson's comment to Fitzpatrick, 4 May 1955, is in the Brian Fitzpatrick Papers, 29/2(a), MS4965, NLA (with our thanks to Marivic Wyndham.) Melville expresses his unease to Florey, 27 May 1955, Florey Papers. Spate remembers the Bandung incident in an article in the *Canberra Times*, 16 Apr 1989. Sawer's verse, entitled '1954', is in the Noel Butlin Centre, ANU, and NLA.

Return of the native

126-7 The main source for correspondence relating to Hancock's return is the Hancock Papers, P96/15/2 and 7, Noel Butlin Centre, ANU. Other correspondence is in ANU Archives and the Florey Papers. A copy of Hancock to La Nauze, 18 Nov 1953, on the Canberra hoodoo is in the Coombs Papers, ANU Archives. Wright on the longest job application is in his 1986 interview, Melbourne Uni Archives.
The newspaper clippings are: *Sydney Morning Herald*, 27 Nov 1954; Brisbane *Courier-Mail*, 15 Jan 1955; and Melbourne *Herald*, 15 Jan and 10 Feb 1955.

129 'The return of the native' is *Sydney Morning Herald*, 22 Mar 1956. Butlin OHP remembers the announcement of Hancock's appointment; and Ennor to Florey, 30 Mar 1956, comments on Melville's triumph.
Crawford explains 'Why I left the public service in 1960' in a note for the NLA, 28 Jul 1983, Crawford Papers, MS4514, box 193, NLA. Comments on his appointment are in *Nation*, 18 Jul 1959; and *Daily Telegraph*, 5 Aug 1959.

Hancock at the crease

130 Hancock on 'the Father figure' and 'the rabble': to Florey, 11 Mar 1957, 1 Nov 1955 and 6 Feb 1956, Florey Papers. He discusses the wool seminar in *Professing History*, p. 36.

130 On the foundation of the *Australian*

	Dictionary of Biography: R.A. Gollan, 'Canberra History Conference', *Historical Studies*, Nov 1957; A. Mozley (Moyal), 'The Australian Dictionary of Biography', *Historical Studies*, Nov 1960; and Fitzhardinge OHP (RAG and SGF).
130-1	Hancock and students: Gollan in 'Hancock: some reminiscences', *Historical Studies*, 13/51, Oct 1968, pp. 303-6; obituary by Gollan in Australian Academy of the Humanities, *Proceedings*, 1987-89, pp. 61-3; Gollan OHP; Butlin OHP; Binns OHP; and conversation with M. Steven. Much has been written about Hancock's contribution, inc obituaries by K.S. Inglis, *Age*, 15 Aug 1988; and D.A. Low, 'William Keith Hancock 1898-1988', *Proceedings of the British Academy*, 1992; also J. Barrett to S.G. Foster and M.M. Varghese, 3 Jul 1994. On Hancock's use of metaphor in his writings: K. Tsokhas, 'Reflections on the life and work of W.K. Hancock', *Round Table*, 1990, pp. 216-18. The exchange with Menzies, which we owe to A.W. Martin, is in the Menzies Papers, MS4936/1/14/117, NLA. Gammage told us the cricket story in 1994.
131-2	Hancock's warning to Albert, 30 Nov 1955, is in the Florey Papers. On chaps and wreckers: Clark OHP; Clark, *A Historian's Apprenticeship*, Melbourne UP, Melbourne, 1992, pp. 8-9; and Hancock, *Professing History*, p. 33.
132	A. Moyal (Mozley) relates the early history of the *ADB*, and quotes from Hancock, in *Breakfast with Beaverbrook: Memoirs of an Independent Woman*, Hale & Iremonger, Sydney, 1995, ch. 9. Also Gollan, Clark and Fitzhardinge (RAG and SGF) OHPs.
132-3	The Lindsay case is documented in great detail the eight parts of his personal file, ANU Archives; pt 5 includes a Chronicle of Events from 1950 to 1960. There is also extensive correspondence in the Crocker Papers and the Oliphant Papers, Barr Smith Library, Uni of Adelaide. Additional material is drawn from the Wright Papers and from Gollan OHP. The reference to 'Sir Fox' is in Hancock, *Professing History*, p. 38. P. Coleman, *Memoirs of a slow learner*, Sydney, Angus & Robertson, 1994, p. 77, presents a different perspective on the case.
133-4	Hancock on the Pacificos, in private: to Florey, 4 Apr 1957, Florey Papers; and in public, *Professing History*, p. 38. Gollan OHP augments the official record about the plans for the Coombs Building; and Coombs comments on the building that bears his name in his OHP interview.

Florey's decision

135-40	This account is based on numerous private letters and documents, chiefly in the Florey Papers, but also in the Ennor–Florey Correspondence, ANU Archives; and in the papers of Coombs, AA and ANU Archives; Wright, Uni of Melbourne Archives; and Oliphant, Barr Smith Library, Uni of Adelaide. The ANU Archives include both the official and the handwritten minutes of relevant Council meetings. T.I. Williams, *Howard Florey: Penicillin and After*, Oxford UP, Oxford, 1984, ch. 8, tells the story from a different perspective. Unhappily, the Emidicta cylinders disappeared from the Florey Papers in the ANU Library many years ago. Coombs OHP and Wright in his Uni of Melbourne interview comment on Florey's indecision. Henry Harris, who worked with Florey at Oxford, mentions Florey's 'totally uncharacteristic indecision' in *The Balance of Improbabilities: A Scientific Life*, Oxford UP, Oxford, 1987, p. 77.
137	According to Williams, p. 284, Ennor understood that Florey's house was to be demolished to make way for an engineering laboratory.
138-9	Ennor's visit to Oxford has been reconstructed from accounts by Florey in the Florey Papers and the Wright Papers; Oliphant in the Wright Papers; Ennor himself in the Florey Papers and the Coombs Papers, ANU Archives; and an especially illuminating letter from Henry Harris to Wright in the Wright Papers.

Two cultures?

140	Hancock repudiates: *Professing History*, p. 31. Oliphant agrees: S. Cockburn and D. Ellyard, *Oliphant: the Life and Times of Sir Mark Oliphant*, Axiom, Adelaide, 1981, p. 266. Snow adumbrated his theme in *The New Statesman and Nation*, 6 Oct 1956, pp. 413-14; and developed it further in the Rede Lectures, delivered at Cambridge in 1959. Quotations here are from the 1956 article and *The Two Cultures and the Scientific Revolution*, Cambridge UP, Cambridge, 1959. The lectures caused a stir at the time and turmoil after F.R. Leavis attacked Snow in 1962.
141	Oliphant's lament to Florey, 17 Aug 1955; and his warning, 20 Dec 1956, Florey Papers. Florey explains the irritation of the Natural Scientist in his report to Council, 2 Jan 1956, ANU Archives. Oliphant's proposal for independent research

143   The 'accursed feud': Hancock to Florey, 1 Nov 1955, Florey Papers. 'Your absence is tantamount to a lack of soul': Oliphant to Hancock, 16 Apr 1952, Hancock Papers, P96/15/2 and 7, Noel Butlin Centre.

       institutes is in his Memorandum on the Past and Future of the University, [Dec 1955–Jan 1956], ANU Archives. He reflected on 'the true humanities', 17 Dec 1951, Hancock Papers, P96/15/2 and 7, Noel Butlin Centre.

6   The college

'A University College for pass men'

144-8   This section draws chiefly on the CUC Annual Reports in the ANU Archives, CUC Calendars in the ANU Library, and papers and correspondence in the Uni of Melbourne Registry, inc minutes of Council and the Professorial Board. T.M. Owen, Secretary to the CUC Council and Registrar from 1939, generously assembled on tape detailed information based on his recollections supplemented by archival records.

144   The Minute Book, 9 Dec 1929, University Association of Canberra, MS740, NLA, records that funds for the College were placed on the estimates on 2 Sep 1929. For the first four years of CUC, see L.D. Lyons, 'A Secretary Looks Back: the Canberra University College 1930–1934', *Canberra Historical Journal*, Mar 1976.

146   Pointed comparisons by the *Canberra Times*, 28 Jun 1945. Also Frederick Watson to Prime Minister Lyons, 19 Jul 1938, Daley Papers, MS1946, 1/3, folder 31, NLA.
The student's comment is in the CUC magazine *Prometheus*, 4, 1937.

145-7   Coombs's view of incorporation is referred to in Hancock to Coombs, 31 Mar 1947, Coombs Papers, AA. Wright's view is in Wright to Florey, 31 Jan 1947, Wright Papers, Uni of Melbourne Archives. Rivett's is in Rivett to Hancock, 31 Jul 1947, Hancock Papers, ANU Archives. The Academic Advisers' views are in the papers from the Easter 1948 conferences, esp the Summary of discussions on 6 Apr. Oliphant tells Copland that undergraduate teaching is unacceptable, 26 Jul 1948, ANU Archives. Hancock dismissed 'a University College for pass men' at the RSSS conference, Easter 1948; also Hancock to Wright, 8 Mar 1947, Wright Papers. Copland avoids the issue, to Rivett, 23 Jul 1948, Copland Papers, MS3800, box 138, NLA.
Garran's Address, 30 Apr 1948, is in the University Association of Canberra Papers, MS487, NLA. Garran takes the initiative in his Report to the Minister on a Reorganisation of the Canberra University College, 23 Oct 1947, ANU Archives. The successful negotiations are reported in the CUC Council minutes and agenda, ANU Archives.

147-8   Wilfred Prest questions Burton's decision, to Copland, 28 Oct 1948, Copland Papers, MS3800, box 138. On Burton: *Herbert 'Joe' Burton 1900–1983*, commemorative pamphlet published by ANU, 1984; Burton OHP; and interview by I. Hamilton, TRC931, NLA.

College types

148-52   Statistical and structural information about the College in the 1950s is in the CUC *Gazette*.

148-9   Clark remembers CUC days in *The Quest for Grace*, Viking, Ringwood, 1990, pp. 182–206; 'Reminiscences', *ANU Reporter*, 23 May 1980; and his OHP interview.

148-9   Sources for this account of College life include Arndt OHP; Ruth Arndt, 'Reminiscences', *ANU Reporter*, 17 Oct 1980; Sawer's diary, by courtesy of Geoffrey Sawer; and information from Patrick Pentony. 'The Canberra Blues' is published in Brissenden's *Gough and Johnny were Lovers*, Penguin, Ringwood, 1984. Murray Todd expresses the College's indignation in 'The Ballad of the Installation', 1952, ANU Archives.

150-1   The Warden of 'Gungahlin', J.O. Clark, reports to the CUC Registrar, T.M. Owen, on the flagpole incident, 21 Aug 1951, ANU Archives. Peter Henderson recalls the occasion in *Privilege and Pleasure*, Methuen-Haynes, North Ryde, 1986, ch. 2. Parkinson reflected on CUC days in a discussion with S.G. Foster in 1992. The CUC Students' Association comments on *Woroni* in its 25th Annual Report, 17 Apr 1956.

Amalgamation

153-9   The moves towards amalgamation are documented in detail in the ANU Archives, most conveniently in a box marked 'Amalgamation papers'. R.A. Hohnen prepared for our use a detailed note on 'ANU's considerations about widening its ambit to include education and training other than for research degrees', 4 Mar 1991; and T.M. Owen assembled information esp relevant to the College's perceptions. Also Milton Lewis's 1969 paper, The Australian National University, 1946–1960, ch. 2.

153   On the Murray Committee: I. McShane, 'Balanced Development': a Study of the Murray Committee on Australian

Universities, MEd thesis, Uni of Canberra, 1995. Oliphant's comment on a spiritual relationship is in Notes of an informal meeting, 1 May 1953, Florey Papers, ANU Library. Oliphant, Partridge and others express their views in minutes of a meeting between BGS and the Committee on Incorporation of CUC, 9 Nov 1955, Coombs Papers, M448/1, AA. Also, for Oliphant, S. Cockburn and D. Ellyard, *Oliphant: the Life and Times of Sir Mark Oliphant*, Axiom, Adelaide, 1981, p. 188.

154-5 Hohnen records Sawer urging caution in 'ANU's considerations', 4 Mar 1991. Coombs's views are in Notes of an informal meeting of the Committee on CUC, nd [Apr 1956]; and in Coombs to Melville, 4 May 1956, Coombs Papers, AA. Representatives of CUC argued their case at the Prime Minister's conference on future of Australian National University and Canberra University College, 23 Jan 1958, verbatim record in ANU Archives. Butlin remembers this meeting in his OHP interview. In addition the official papers, several letters in the Coombs Papers, ANU Archives and AA, illuminate the negotiations during 1959. Menzies had already made up his mind on association before the AUC formally offered its opinion in a report of Oct 1959. The Statement by the Prime Minister: university development in Canberra, 17 Dec 1959, is in the ANU Archives. Crisp on the 'shotgun marriage': *Canberra Times*, 14 Oct 1959. Menzies outlines his requirements to Coombs, 17 Dec 1959, ANU Archives.

156 Oliphant expresses his alarm to Coombs, 13 Jan 1960, Coombs Papers, ANU Archives. Fitzhardinge speaks of the 'newly-weds' in his OHP interview (SGF).

156-8 The detailed negotiations regarding terminology, the library, etc., are recorded in minutes, correspondence, and formal and handwritten notes in the Amalgamation Papers. 'This title [The School of General Studies] was dictated at amalgamation by the I.A.S.': C.A. Gibb to Deputy Vice-Chancellor, 30 Aug 1967, Hohnen Papers on Structure, by courtesy of R.A. Hohnen. Gibb OHP discusses the debate over the library. Clark compliments Melville, 9 Mar 1960, ANU Archives. G.C. Bolton summarises the outcome of negotiations in 'The Canberra Merger', *Vestes*, Jun 1960.

159 Oliphant predicts disaster in his Notes on memoranda and minutes which have been received by me up to Jan. 1, 1959 [unsigned], ANU Archives; and to Wright, 28 Jan 1960, Wright Papers, 4/3/3, Uni of Melbourne Archives. The opinion of the Students' Association is in *Woroni*, 29 Sep 1960. Partridge offers a general assessment of attitudes in *ANU News*, Aug 1960.

7 Setting directions

'There can be no end to the building of a university'

165 Melville's speech is in the *ANU News*, Aug 1960.

168 On Huxley: Bouquet OHP; Hamilton OHP; S.G. Tomlin, 'The new Vice-Chancellor — an appreciation', *ANU News*, Aug 1960; and R.W. Crompton, 'Leonard George Holden Huxley 1902–1988', *Historical Records of Australian Science*, Jun 1991. Mathews OHP discusses Crawford's financial role during Huxley's vice-chancellorship. Huxley reflects on his term of office in *ANU News*, Jun 1968; and in his 1971 oral history interview with Mel Pratt, NLA.

169-72 The question of size is discussed in numerous papers in the ANU Archives. A.R. Hall raises the issue in relation to Australian universities generally in E.L. Wheelwright (ed.), *Higher Education in Australia*, F.W. Cheshire, Melbourne, 1965, pp. 59–61. The main source for Gibb is his OHP interview.

Maintaining the difference

173-6 The 'noble revolution': Stretton to Menzies, 29 Nov 1957, quoted in A.W. Martin, 'R.G. Menzies and the Murray Committee', in F.B. Smith and P. Crighton (eds), *Ideas for Histories of Universities in Australia*, ANU, 1990, p. 94. Stretton's 1964 reflections are in Wheelwright (ed.), *Higher Education in Australia*, pp. 75–6. On the AUC, see A.P. Gallagher, *Coordinating Australian University Development: a Study of the Australian Universities Commission 1959–1970*, Queensland UP, St Lucia, 1982. Partridge on the risks: 'Australian Universities — Some Trends and Problems', *The Australian University*, Jul 1963. Crawford refers to the ANU's 'comparative advantage' and urges fresh thinking in *The Australian National University: its Concept and Role*, ANU, 1968, pp. 22, 20. Oliphant warns Hohnen about undergraduate teaching, 16 Dec 1968, Oliphant Papers, Barr Smith Library, Uni of Adelaide.

'Poor relations'

176-7 Melville's graduation address is published

	in *Vestes*, Sep 1960. Oliphant tells Crawford about being brushed off, 19 May 1969, Oliphant Papers, Barr Smith Library, Uni of Adelaide.
177-8	Papers relating to the history of the library include C. Campbell-Smith, 'The Australian National University Library', *Australian Library J*, Jun 1965; and C.M. James, 'The state of the union: Some effect of the merger of the Australian National University and the Canberra University College 1960 on the Library', 1982, ANU Archives. In 1989 Amirah Inglis prepared a history of the Library as a contribution to the University's submission to the Review of IAS.
178-80	Huxley on 'poor relations': interview in *ANU News*, Jun 1968. Clark on the human heart: *A Discovery of Australia* (Boyer Lectures), ABC, Sydney, 1976. The divine footnote: Gollan OHP. La Nauze on Clark: to Hancock, 3 Nov 1955, Hancock Papers, Noel Butlin Centre, ANU. La Nauze on Clark's *A History of Australia*, vol. 1: P. Ryan, *Quadrant*, Sep 1993. Clark on 'Historical Industries': 'R.C. Mills and M.H. Ellis: a note', *Historical Studies*, Oct 1969, p. 95. Also R.M. Crawford in 'John Andrew La Nauze — tributes on his retirement', *Historical Studies*, Oct 1976; and S. Macintyre, *A History for the Nation: Ernest Scott and the Making of Australian History*, Melbourne UP, Melbourne, 1994, pp. 3-4. Ryan's exchange with Clark is in *Quadrant*, Sep 1993. Crawford sets out his aims in a circular letter to staff, 7 May 1969; and in his address to the Uni of Melbourne, *The Australian National University: its Concept and Role*, ANU, 1968. On maintaining the uniqueness of IAS: Crawford to Oliphant, 21 May 1969, Oliphant Papers, Barr Smith Library.

Governing the University

180-1	Oliphant complains to Hohnen about Council, 15 Feb 1962, Oliphant Papers, Barr Smith Library. L.N. Short discusses lay members of uni councils in Wheelwright (ed.), *Higher Education in Australia*, pp. 122-23. Hamilton OHP mentions the role of Ewens. Huxley discusses the replacement of Bruce in his NLA oral history interview.
181-4	Several OHP interviewees, including Sawer, comment on Coombs's role as chairman. Crawford remarks on his appointment as Chancellor in *ANU News*, Jun 1968. Crawford comments frankly to Coombs on their respective roles, 10 Jul and 21 Jul 1965, Coombs Papers, ANU Archives. Mathews and others discuss Crawford in L.T. Evans and J.D.B. Miller (eds), *Policy*

	and Practice: Essays in Honour of Sir John Crawford, ANU Press, 1987, p. 92. Other estimates of Crawford: Spate in *ANU Reporter*, 9 Nov 1984; *Sir John Crawford 1910–1984*, ANU, 1986; Bouquet, Fenner, Gibb, Gollan, Hamilton, Mathews, Passmore, Sawer, Spate and White OHP interviews; Birch, Working notes on RSC files, p. 120, ANU Archives. Overextended: Hamilton OHP; also Trendall to Crocker, 8 Nov 1964, Crocker Papers, Barr Smith Library, Uni of Adelaide: 'his School sometimes wishes they saw a little more of him'.
184-5	Hohnen on Copland: to Birch, 15 Feb 1991, in Birch's working notes on RSC files, p. 121. Many papers in the ANU Archives relate to Crawford's administrative changes; also Committee on structure and organisation of administration (1967–68), pts 1 and 2, Hohnen Papers, by courtesy of R.A. Hohnen; and Crawford to vice-chancellors and senior staff in other universities, circular, 10 Apr 1968, Hohnen Papers. Crawford tells Coombs of a 'vacuum in the policy field', 8 Jan 1967, Coombs Papers, ANU Archives.
186-7	Oliphant tells Huxley of his wish to resign, 27 Jun 1963, Oliphant Papers, Barr Smith Library. He offers to resign over the approach to Massey in a letter to Copland, 19 Dec 1949, Office of Education CRS A1876, OEN1/1 pt 4, AA. Debate about the composition of the RSPhysS School Committee is in the School Committee minutes, 10 Nov 1966; and Oliphant to Huxley, 5 Apr 1967, and enclosed minutes of a staff meeting, 4 Apr 1967, Oliphant Papers, Barr Smith Library.
187	Ennor as Dean: Council, 8 Sep 1961; Ennor to Fenner, 25 Sep 1961, Fenner Papers, ANU Archives; and Albert, Courtice, Eccles and A.G. Ogston to the Vice-Chancellor, 20 Nov 1961, Fenner Papers. Oliphant tells Florey about Albert's 'palace', 27 Jan 1953, Florey Papers, ANU Library. On Albert's resistance to Dwyer: JCSMR School Committee minutes, 11 Dec 1957, 26 Nov 1958, 22 Feb 1962; and Curtis, Rosenberg and Whitten OHP interviews. Lack of planning: Florey to Wright, 2 Jan 1959, Wright Papers, 4/3/1, Uni of Melbourne Archives; JCSMR School Committee minutes, 29 Mar 1965. Wright's warning to Florey, 22 Apr 1966, Wright Papers, 4/3/1.
188-9	The confrontation with Ennor: JCSMR School Committee minutes, 12 Jul 1966, inc report by Ennor on University administration; JCSMR academic staff meeting, 5 Dec 1966; Gollan OHP; also,

at second hand, McCullagh OHP. On Crawford's appointment as Vice-Chancellor: Mathews in Evans and Miller (eds), *Policy and Practice*, p. 92; handwritten minutes of vice-chancellorship meeting, 25 Jul 1966; official correspondence with Coombs regarding the appointment; and Wright to E. Abraham, 23 Sep 1968, Wright Papers, 4/3/1. Ennor on the architects: to Florey, 15 Mar 1954, Florey Papers, ANU Library. JCSMR staff vote against Ennor, minutes of meeting, 5 Dec 1966. Wright comments on Ennor's departure in his interview in the Uni of Melbourne Archives. Also A.P. Gallagher, *Coordinating Australian University Development*, p. 113. Birch's comment is in his notes on the 'Foundations of the Research School of Chemistry, and its present status', 1992, p. 76, ANU Archives. On attitudes to leadership and democracy in Australian universities at the time, see inter al. L.N. Short in Wheelwright (ed), *Higher Education in Australia*, pp. 122–25.

A new orientation

191-6   The University has published, for internal distribution, two outline histories of the site plan: the first, dated 1973, covers the period 1912–71; the second, dated 1979, covers the period 1971–78; also D. Dexter's *The ANU Campus*, ANU, 1991.

191-3   Lewis's regrets: to Florey, 11 Nov 1952, Florey Papers, ANU Library. On Rudduck: E. Sparke, *Canberra 1954–1980*, AGPS, Canberra, 1988, pp. 72–3. Winston discusses 'Building our Universities' in *Vestes*, Nov 1960. The quotation is from *A History of the Site Plan 1912–1971*, p. 7. Dexter quotes the 'filching' accusation, *The ANU Campus*, p. 94. On other universities, see Bruce Mansfield and Mark Hutchinson, *Liberality of opportunity: Macquarie University 1964–1989*, Hale & Iremonger, 1992, pp. 89–96; D. Hilliard, *Flinders University: the first 25 years 1966–1991*, Flinders Uni, Adelaide, 1991, pp. 17–20. Hamilton OHP augments the minutes of the Advisers on Buildings and Grounds and other files on architectural and planning policies.

193-6   Simpson's proposals are set out in his Site Planning Report, Mar 1969. Additional quotations are from *A History of the Site Plan 1912–1971*. On the Great Hall: Simpson, 'ANU — Great Hall siting. Comments on criticisms of University Ave site', nd [1969], Coombs Papers, M448/1, AA. Trendall's lament, 16 Nov 1968; also 8 Nov 1964, Crocker Papers, Barr Smith Library. On 'vamping the place up': 22 Oct 1968; and on the time to go, 16 Nov 1968, Crocker Papers. Also F. West, *University House: Portrait of an Institution*, University House, 1980, pp. 48–50.

8   Students

Who were the students?

197-200   Statistical information comes from the annual *ANU Statistical Handbook*; unpublished statistics supplied by Phil Telford in the University's Planning Division; and Commonwealth Bureau of Census and Statistics (later the Australian Bureau of Statistics), University Statistics, 1960–76. A. Spaull writes about Dedman in *ADB*, vol. 13; and L.F. Crisp refers to him in *Gravediggers and Undertakers, then and now*, RSSS, ANU, 1974. Gibb describes early visits to schools in his OHP interview. On the early admission scheme, Gibb OHP and his report in the 1970 ANU *Annual Report*, pp. 13–14. Plowman OHP reflects on the backgrounds of students.

'Welcome to the ANU!'

201-3   This section relies chiefly on Orientation Week handbooks and programs. The author of the statement in the 1968 handbook is Craddock Morton. The president of the Students' Representative Council reports on the growth of clubs and societies, May 1963, ANUSA minutes.

Life on campus

203-4   Dinner in University House: F. West, *University House: Portrait of an Institution*, University House, 1980, pp. 37–8. Hawke and the bishops: West, *University House*, pp. 30–1; B. d'Alpuget, *Robert J. Hawke*, Penguin, Ringwood, 1984, p. 66; Sawer OHP; handwritten minutes of an (informal) discipline committee, 25 Feb, 13 Mar 1957, ANU Archives; Oliphant to Melville, 27 Feb 1957, and to Trendall, 28 Feb 1957, Oliphant Papers, ANU Archives. The quotations are from the minutes of the discipline committee.

205-6   The arguments for and against affiliated colleges are set out in a file in the ANU Archives. Huxley quotes one of the wardens in *ANU News*, Jun 1968. A booklet was published to mark Packard's retirement: *Bill Packard: Warden of Bruce Hall. Farewell dinner, 28 June 1986*, ANU, 1986; also Packard OHP. Bush Week 1963: *Age*, 31 Jul 1963; Bush Week 1964: Students' Representative Council, 8 Sep

1964, ANUSA minutes. Burton's comment is in response to letters in *Canberra Times*, 4 Aug 1964. The Union: *Orientation Handbook*, 1970, pp. 24–25; and Plowman OHP.

Teaching and learning

208-12 McQueen, Mathews, Hambly and Ross talk about teaching in their OHP interviews. The Students' Representative Council complains about inadequate teachers, 25 Apr 1965, ANUSA minutes. Selinger's *Chemistry in the Market Place* was first published in 1975 by the ANU Centre for Continuing Education. Lyneham is quoted in the *Canberra Times*, 27 Mar 1993. Clark's reflections are in *The Quest for Grace*, Viking, Ringwood, 1990, pp. 211–12. McQueen discusses his own appointment, Clark's teaching and Clark's view of Gibb in his OHP interview. Clark on McQueen: *Quest for Grace*, pp. 185, 213. Also Gibb OHP. Detailed comments on the semester proposal are in Faculty of Arts and Faculty of Law papers.

'Make love not war'

212-14 J. Spigelman provides an overview of 'Student activism in Australia' in *Vestes*, Jul 1968. The Students' Association Survey, Oct 1966, in ANUSA minutes. Asked whether they supported Australia's commitment to Vietnam (leaving aside the question of conscription), some 66 per cent of those polled said they did while 30 per cent were opposed. Asked whether they approved of the present system of conscription (leaving aside the question of Vietnam), their opinions were about evenly divided. Other comments on campus conservatism: ANU *Annual Report*, 1969, p. 15; Crawford's comments at Directors' and Deans' meeting, 23 Jan 1969, ANU Archives. The President of the Students' Association describes Bruce Hall as 'a mixed blessing', SRC Annual Report, May 1962, ANU Archives. Iremonger on 'Activism at the A.N.U. — the status of involvement': *Vestes*, Jul 1968, p. 141. McFarlane comments in *Orientation Handbook*, 1969. *Canberra Times* report: 19 Sep 1968. *Bulletin* survey: 5 Jul 1969. Chris Cunneen holds newsletters and leaflets from local protest movements. Furness's warning: *Orientation Handbook*, 1972. White reflects on student activities in her OHP interview. Crawford on drugs: 10 Nov 1972. Gould's novella is 'Decency and honour: a documentary', in *The Enduring Disguises: Three Novellas*, Angus & Robertson, North Ryde, 1988.

215-17 The account of Swinbank's activities draws on Padgham, Robinson and Swinbank OHP; a scrapbook and papers held by Swinbank; Gould, 'Decency and honour'; S. Robinson, The Aboriginal embassy, 1972, MA thesis, ANU, 1993; S. Harris, *Political Football — the Springbok Tour of Australia, 1971*, Gold Star Publications, Melbourne, 1972; and recollections of Jack Waterford, *Canberra Times* 22, 29 Apr 1984. On Padgham and the draft resisters: Padgham, Robinson and Swinbank OHP; Plowman OHP; McQueen OHP; a scrapbook and papers held by Padgham; and Jack Waterford Papers, MS7930, NLA. Hohnen's private file on National Service outlines University policy towards the National Service Act, R.A. Hohnen Papers, by courtesy of Ross Hohnen. Hancock writes on *The Battle of Black Mountain: an episode of Canberra's environmental history*, Department of Economic History, RSSS, ANU, 1974; and he refers to the struggle in *Professing History*, Sydney UP, Sydney, 1976, ch. 6. Additional papers are in the Hancock Papers, ANU Archives; and additional information from K.S. Inglis.

The Troubles

217-25 McQueen, Plowman and White OHP interviews have much to say on the student revolt.

217-18 On the changing mood: Report of Local AUS Secretary of the ANUSA (Michael Dunn) at Council of AUS, 1973. For alternative explanations, C.A. Rootes, 'The development of radical student movements and their sequelae', *Australian J of Politics and History*, 34/2, 1988, pp. 182–84. Packard OHP comments on the Kerr demonstration.

218-21 Coombs is quoted from *ANU News*, Oct 1968. Coombs the delinquent: Anon to Coombs, n.d. (Sep 1968), Coombs Papers, MS448/1, AA; and (slightly misquoted) in *Trial Balance*, Macmillan, South Melbourne, 1981, p. 204. Crawford's approach to the students emerges from various papers in the ANU Archives. Also L.T. Evans and J.D.B. Miller (eds), *Policy and Practice: Essays in Honour of Sir John Crawford*, ANU Press, 1987, p. 96, and Plowman OHP.

221-5 Borrie's recommendation of Williams: Hamilton and Plowman OHP interviews. Roe writes in *Woroni*, 1, 24 Feb 1975; and he quotes Gibb in *Woroni*, 26/6, 1974. Council, 13 Sep 1974, includes a paper on 'Student "demands"', which provides an outline of events to that point. Also R. Johnson, 'The Troubles 1974 — the view of the man in the middle', *ANU Reporter*, 27 Sep 1974. Williams' relief: *Canberra*

Times, 12 Sep 1974. Crisp expresses his anger and dismay in *Gravediggers and Undertakers, then and now*, RSSS, ANU, 1974. His speech, reported in *Canberra Times*, 16 Oct 1974, provoked lively debate. Coombs's views are drawn from *Canberra Times*, 21, 27 Sep 1974, 1 Mar 1975; *ANU News*, Aug 1974; *ANU Reporter*, 14 Mar 1975; Council, 13 Dec 1974; and *Trial Balance*, pp. 203–7. Compare with student activities in Queensland: M.I. Thomis, *A Place of Light and Learning*, Queensland UP, St Lucia, 1985, p. 330.

Graduation

225-8 A.W. Martin alerted us to Menzies' letter, 20 May 1966, in the Menzies Papers, MS4936, ser 1, box 15, NLA. The surveys are: S.J. Rawling, *Destinations of Graduates of the Australian National University*, ANU, 1969; and Graduate Careers Council of Australia, *First Destinations of 1975 University Graduates as at 30 April 1976*, Parkville, 1976. Partridge on universities as training institutions: 6 Aug 1968, Coombs Papers, AA. Chapman reflects on her student days in *National Graduate*, Autumn 1994.

9   New initiatives

'Project C'

229-34 The origins of RSC are documented extensively in the ANU Archives. Arthur Birch worked through many of these papers in his retirement and produced extensive working papers. These include personal comments and additional information. His autobiography, *To See the Obvious*, American Chemical Society, Washington DC, 1995, which draws on his working papers, was published after this chapter was written. Craig OHP, and addresses given at an occasion in Oct 1992 to mark the school's 25th anniversary, add to the story.

Biological Sciences

234-7 Rivett's biological sciences proposal is mentioned in the Interim Council minutes, 27 Sep 1946. Fenner outlines early discussions in the Academy in *The Australian Academy of Science: the first twenty-five years*, Australian Academy of Science, Canberra, 1980, pp. 64–6. Also undated comments by Fenner on the proposed school, Fenner Papers, ANU Archives; and correspondence between Fenner and Catcheside, 1961–62, in private possession, Adelaide. Catcheside's ideas are set out in various papers in the ANU Archives, in his OHP interview and in notes made about 1991, in his private papers. He comments on the headship of RSBS in a letter to the Vice-Chancellor, 10 May 1971, in his private papers.

Earth Sciences

238-40 The opposition case within RSPhysS is expressed in papers by Titterton and D.C. Peaslee, Mar 1970, ANU Archives. Oliphant encourages Titterton, 11 May 1970, Oliphant Papers, Barr Smith Library, Uni of Adelaide. Spate's verse, 'Reflections on BIAS, 29.4.70', is in the ANU Archives. The Council debate of 12 Nov 1971 is recorded in the official minutes and, more eloquently, by Spate in an account written on the same day. Ross's version is from the text of an after dinner talk to the IAS Consultative Committee, Sep 1994, by courtesy of Ian Ross. Titterton musters support in letters to several people, 25 Nov 1971, Titterton Papers, ser 1/79, Basser Library. The circumstances of Titterton's removal are set out in several letters in the ANU Archives: Faculty's decision is in Chairman of Faculty to the Vice-Chancellor, 27 Jun 1973. Also J.O. Newton, 'Ernest William Titterton 1916–1990', *Historical Records of Australian Science*, 9/2, Dec 1992.

New teaching departments

241   C.M. Williams, Professor of History, comments on 'gimmickry' to Dean of Arts, 24 Apr 1968, ANU Archives.

241-2 Prehistory: ANU *Annual Report*, 1969; Mulvaney, *The prehistory of Australia*, revised ed, Pelican, Ringwood, 1975; Mulvaney, 'A brief history of the Department of Archaeology and Anthropology', The Department, 1992; *ANU News*, Apr 1969; *Prehistory and Heritage: the writings of John Mulvaney*, RSPacS, 1990.

242-4 The account of the development of Forestry draws on ANU Archives and on *A History of Forestry in Australia*, ANU Press, 1985, by L.T. Carron, a member of the Forestry Department from its inception to 1985 (and subsequently a Visiting Fellow): pp. 263–76. Oliphant comments on 'Technology in the Australian National University', 25 Oct 1961, Oliphant Papers, ser 3, Barr Smith Library. Crisp's remark is to Hohnen, 26 Jun 1961, ANU Archives. Pryor's views are in his paper, 'The Australian Forestry School in relation to the University', 3 Jan 1961, ANU Archives. On the growth of Forestry: *ANU News*, Jun 1968; 'Future of the Department of Forestry', Report of

1965; also paper by Jeanneret on 'The purpose of scholarly publishing' to Canberra Fellowship of Australian Writers, 2 Nov 1965; Council, 12 Nov 1965; and *ANU News*, Mar 1966. The committee, chaired by A. Barnard, reports on ANU Press operations, 3 May 1973: Council, 11 May 1973. Butlin and Croft comment on the history of the ANU Press in their OHP interviews.

268-9 Passmore's observation is a footnote in *Man's Responsibility for Nature: Ecological Problems and Western Traditions*, Duckworth, London, 1974. The visitor was Alexander Carr-Saunders from the Uni of London, who reported to Trendall, 25 Jul 1959, ANU Archives. Coombs comments on Swan in his OHP interview. For other comments on Swan: Butlin OHP, Gollan OHP, and Spate in P. Hasluck, *Diplomatic Witness: Australian Foreign Affairs 1941–1947*, Melbourne UP, Melbourne, 1980.

Papua and New Guinea

269-70 Hasluck comments on the report on economic development in *A Time for Building: Australian Administration in Papua and New Guinea 1951–1963*, Melbourne UP, 1976, p. 141. Also Spate, *On the Margins of History: from the Punjab to Fiji*, ANU, 1991, pp. 89–98. The work of the linguists: *ANU News*, Dec 1966; and Crawford's report to Council, 9 Sep 1966. On Coombs's concern about coordinated studies, see p. 112 above. The origins of the New Guinea Research Unit are drawn from ANU Archives. Also Spate OHP; D.G. Bettison, 'Introduction to the Series', *New Guinea Research Unit Bulletin*, 1, 1963; and *ANU News*, Sep 1966.

271 Spate discusses 'ANU on Bougainville', *ANU News*, Jul 1972. B. McFarlane presents a critical view in 'A strategy for the Pacific rim: the University staff work', *Arena*, 31, 1973, pp. 4–6. Crocombe and Spate consider 'Pacific research: the need for reciprocity', *ANU News*, Nov 1969. Also Crocombe to Plowman, 27 Aug 1968, ANU Archives.

272-3 Establishing the Uni of Papua New Guinea: Spate, *On the Margins of History*, pp. 118–130; and Hasluck, *A Time for Building*, pp. 388–393. Decolonising the New Guinea Research Unit: D.A. Low, paper on the future of NGRU, Council, 13 Jul 1973; Council, 12 Sep 1975; and Low OHP. D. Wade-Marshall and D. Lea outline the history of *The North Australia Research Unit 1973–1993*, ANU, 1993. Somare's address: *ANU Reporter*, 11 May 1979.

The public professor

273 Partridge senses change in 'Australian universities — some trends and problems', *The Australian University*, 1/1, Jul 1963, pp. 16–17. Crawford on 'public service': *The Australian National University: its Concept and Role*, ANU, 1968, p. 19; and 'Public servants and academics in dialogue', *ANU News*, Apr 1970.

274 Titterton's outside activities and the University's concerns are documented in ANU Archives. Note also J.O. Newton, 'Ernest William Titterton 1916–1990', *Historical Records of Australian Science*, 9/2, Dec 1992; and J. McClelland, *Stirring the Possum: A Political Autobiography*, Penguin, Ringwood, 1989, pp. 213–15, 224–5.

275-6 The controversy at the Orientalists conference is reported in *Canberra Times*, 13 Jan 1971. Miller is quoted in G. Langley, *A Decade of Dissent: Vietnam and the conflict on the Australian homefront*, Allen & Unwin, Sydney, 1992, pp. 108–9. G. Clark questions the ANU's motives in a review of J.D.B. Miller (ed.), *India, Japan and Australia*, in *Australian Quarterly*, Sep 1970, pp. 117–20. The origins of the Strategic and Defence Studies Centre: paper for BIAS, 29 Jul 1966; and *ANU News*, Dec 1966. O'Neill summarises arguments about the centre in *ANU News*, Apr 1971.

276-8 The origins of the Centre for Research on Federal Financial Relations: ANU Archives and Mathews OHP.

279 Whitlam on the universities is quoted in *ANU News*, Jul 1973. Richard Campbell, a senior lecturer in Philosophy and Academic Assistant to the Vice-Chancellor, offers some predictions in 'Universities and the Future', *Australian Quarterly*, Apr 1978.

11 A new era

285-306 Low OHP and the Low Papers, ANU Archives, supplement official sources through most of this chapter.

Low at the helm

285-7 Low's graduation address is in the *ANU Reporter*, 26 Sep 1975. Low on the role of vice-chancellor: Report to the University, 11 Nov 1976; on Coombs and Crawford, Low OHP. Plowman's role: Low and Plowman OHP interviews.

287-9 Peter Samuel's *Bulletin* article is 12 Mar 1977. The attack on Clark: Hansard (Senate), 22 Sep 1976. Low's defence: to Carrick, 1 Oct 1976, Low Papers, ANU Archives. The compulsory fees issue is detailed in Council minutes and papers,

289-90 supplemented by White OHP.
Hohnen's departure is recorded in the *ANU Reporter*, 28 Mar 1975. On the administrative restructuring: Low OHP; and Heads of Research Schools minutes, 30 Jun 1975. Ross discusses the 'capacious pouch' in his OHP interview.

'A tighter ship'

290-2 Changes in education funding are outlined by D. Smart, 'The pattern of post-war federal intervention in education', in G. Harman and D. Smart, *Federal Intervention in Australian Education: past, present and future*, Georgian House, Melbourne, 1982, pp. 25–33. Coombs's valedictory address is in the *ANU Reporter*, 30 Apr 1976. On the financial crisis: Ross OHP and his accompanying notes, prepared for this history. Gibson told Council of his fears, 9 Sep 1977. Low presses the alarm button: *ANU Reporter*, 28 Nov 1980; and calls for reduced spending in his Final Report to the University, 11 Mar 1982. Low talks about the threat from Treasury in his OHP interview. Ross OHP discusses the changed relationship with the government.

The University community

293 Hohnen defines 'academic' in a memorandum to Low, n.d. (Jun 1975), Low Papers. Coombs on academics and administrators: to K.E. Enderby, 20 Jan 1973, Coombs Papers, MS802, box 32, NLA.
On cricket: *ANU Reporter*, 23 Nov 1971, 24 Mar 1972 and 15 Aug 1980.

295-7 Molony's comment is in the *Canberra Times*, 9 Dec 1981. The 'realities of modern life', *ANU Reporter*, 2 May 1980. The events of 1982 are recorded in ANU Archives; *ANU Reporter*, 23 Jul 1982; and Ross OHP. Gill, in *ANU Reporter*, 2 May 1980, thinks there is no conflict between collegiality and industrial processes. A decade later, David Penington, Vice-Chancellor of the Uni of Melbourne, thinks otherwise, in 'Collegiality and unions', *J of Tertiary Education Administration*, May 1991.

Mixed reviews

298 This discussion of the reviews of the research schools is based largely on official papers and documents in the ANU Archives, inc the reviews themselves.
The 'distinguished visitor' is Sir Alexander Carr-Saunders, formerly Director of the London School of Economics, who had been invited by A.D. Trendall to comment on 'a research university'.

299 Titterton damns the RSPhysS review in a letter to J. Newton, 19 Aug 1976, Titterton Papers, Basser Library.

302 Low warns about reviews in his Report to the University, 11 Nov 1976.

303-5 A.H. Johns, in *ANU Reporter*, 14 Oct 1988, outlines the beginnings of Oriental Studies. R. de Crespigny, in *ANU Reporter*, 26 Feb 1971, discusses the success of the International Congress of Orientalists. Johns reports to the Faculty of Asian Studies on 'languages in lesser demand', 8 Nov 1976. Ann Kent and Robin Ward comment on teaching in Asian Studies in their joint OHP interview. Johns tells Ross of his concerns, 30 Sep 1976, Low Papers. Opposition to centres includes a Memorandum [to Faculty] from all members of the Japanese Department, 31 Mar 1982, ANU Archives.

305-6 On the changeover from Low to Karmel: Crawford's note, 28 Jul 1983, Crawford Papers, MS4514, NLA; Low OHP; and Karmel OHP.

12 Change without growth

308-37 A publication by the Department of Employment, Education and Training, *National Report of Australia's Higher Education Sector*, Canberra, 1993, provides a useful background to this chapter. Karmel OHP and Ross OHP are relevant for all sections.

Managing

308-10 The Tertiary Education Commission was established as a statutory body in 1977 and added the prefix Commonwealth in 1981. On Karmel: Aitkin, unpublished MS, 1993 (hereafter acknowledged as Aitkin MS), ch. 5; Bouquet OHP; Ross OHP; and White OHP. D. Smart and others discuss 'The Hawke Government and Education 1983–1985', *Politics*, May 1986. Karmel has written and spoken widely on changes in higher education during the 1980s, notably 'Reflections on a revolution: Australian higher education in 1989', *AVCC Papers*, 1, 1989; and 'Higher education — tensions and balances', *J of Tertiary Education Administration*, Oct 1990, which includes at p. 332 the remark on chronic tension.

311-13 The proposal to review current practices: D.N.F. Dunbar to Karmel, 13 Feb 1985, quoted in Aitkin MS, ch. 5. Aitkin also describes the turbulent meeting in JCSMR. Karmel talks about the Strategic

Plan in his OHP interview, and expresses his satisfaction with it in the *ANU Reporter*, 11 Dec 1987. Aitkin pays him tribute in Council, 11 Dec 1987.

Integration

313-14   The quotations from Ross are from his paper, The Institute and the Faculties, 31 Mar 1982. The Report of the Interface Committee is dated 14 Mar 1984. Clark asked a puzzled Stephen Foster about those 'great minds' in the Institute in 1979–80.

315-16   The Review of Graduate Education is dated 20 Nov 1978, and is accompanied on file by the various responses. Spear sets out the history of the Graduate School in 'The ANU Graduate School: origins, current operation and future possibilities', 15 Sep 1992.

Change and resistance in the John Curtin School

317-22   This section draws substantially on ANU Archives, supplemented by Curtis, Fenner, Karmel and McCullagh OHP interviews.

317   Fenner's hopes: 'Reflections on the headship of JCSMR', Aug 1967, Fenner Papers, ANU Archives; and his acceptance of departmental dominance: Director's report to Council, 1 May 1973. Porter talks about his links with Florey in 'Corticomotoneuronal projections: synaptic events related to skilled movement' (The Florey Lecture, 1987), Royal Society *Proceedings*, 1987, pp. 147–48. M. Bouquet committed 'yippee' to a file immediately after telling Porter of the University's offer.

319   On Morris: obituary in JCSMR *Annual Report*, 1988, pp. 71–3; and McCullagh OHP.

Equal opportunity?

323   The table is from M. Sawer, *Towards Equal Opportunity: Women and Employment at the Australian National University*, ANU, 1984, p. 77.

324-6   These paragraphs draw on the Report on conditions of service of female staff, 1 Dec 1964, and associated papers. Moyal's comment is in *Breakfast with Beaverbrook: Memoirs of an Independent Woman*, Hale & Iremonger, Sydney, 1985, p. 132.

326-7   Bok addresses the Australian Federation of University Women on 'Looking ahead for the woman graduate', 13 Jan 1964, copy in ANU Archives. Coombs puts his proposal to the Academic Registrar, 31 Jan 1975: Council papers, 14 Mar 1975.

327-8   Hunter offers a personal view of 'Married women in academia' in *Vestes*, Jun 1975. The Bramley-Ward Report is titled *The Role of Women in the Australian National University*, ANU, 1976. On the impact of the Bramley-Ward Report: Sawer, *Towards Equal Opportunity*, p. 28; and Low OHP. On defining sexual discrimination: Bouquet OHP; and various comments accompanying the Bramley-Ward papers, ANU Archives.

329-32   The complementary report is *Employment of Women at the Australian National University: Report of the Working Party of the Association of Women Employees at the Australian National University to the Vice-Chancellor*, 1984; also *ANU Reporter*, 28 Oct 1983. White OHP discusses Karmel's role in steering the proposals through Council. Hughes is quoted in *The Australian Magazine*, 12–13 Nov 1994. An RSPhysSE report to BIAS on 'Women academics in the IAS', 9 Sep 1992, noted that the numbers of female applicants were 'infinitesimal' and that fractional appointments were 'not practicable in most research areas'. Serjeantson is interviewed by A. Moyal in *Portraits in Science*, NLA, Canberra, 1994, p. 169.

Innovation

332-7   This section draws on annual reports of the University and individual faculties and research schools.

332-3   Mack outlines the history of the Peace Research Centre in *Australia and Peace Research*, Peace Research Centre, 1989. On the origins of the centre: Report of Ad Hoc Committee on the proposal for a Peace Studies Research Centre (with Addendum by T.B. Millar), 20 Oct 1983. The centre was reviewed in Feb 1995.

333-4   Sources for the history of the 2.3 metre telescope include a booklet produced for Opening, 16 May 1984; B. Newell, 'Astronomy is looking up at MSSSO', *Australian Foreign Affairs Record*, Jul 1984; A.W. Rodgers, Paper on MSSSO for BIAS, 1989; and Ross OHP.

334-7   On early computing activities: *ANU News*, Nov 1971; Mathews OHP; and Butlin OHP. Butlin OHP discusses the introduction of personal computers.

13   A new generation of planners

The Dawkins revolution

339-42   The changes of the late 1980s are detailed in government policy documents and outlined in Department of Employment, Education and Training, *National Report of Australia's Higher Education Sector*, Canberra, 1993; also S. Marginson, *Education and Public Policy in Australia*, Cambridge UP, Cambridge, 1993, ch. 6; and W.F. Connell and others, *Australia's*

First: A History of the University of Sydney Volume 2 1940–1990, Uni of Sydney and Hale & Iremonger, Sydney, 1995, pp. 432–34.

339-41 Aitkin reflects on Dawkins in Aitkin MS; and he offered further thoughts as he commented on a draft of this chapter. Karmel critically assesses the reforms in 'Reflections on a revolution: Australian higher education in 1989', *AVCC Papers*, 1, 1989. The Academy of Social Sciences/RSSS seminar is published as *Papers from the Symposium on the Green Paper on Higher Education 20 and 21 February 1988*; the comments on the diagnosis and the remedy are in a paper by G. Withers, 'Higher education and national needs: "The two lights of the world"'. Later discussions include N. Marshall and C. Walsh (eds), *The Governance and Funding of Australian Higher Education*, ANU, 1992. The White Paper is published as Dawkins, *Higher Education: a policy statement*, AGPS, Canberra, 1988; the quotations are at pp. 27 and 103.

342 The letter from Kamenka, Mulvaney and others is in the *ANU Reporter*, 12 Aug 1988. For Rolfe, *Australian Higher Education Supplement*, 5 Jun 1991; and Ninham, *Canberra Times*, 3 Jun 1991. Spate sketched 'Dawkins' Dream' for a seminar in RSSS, 1 Dec 1988.

Amalgamation revisited

343-7 This section is based on documents in the ANU Archives; government policy papers and news releases; articles and commentary in newspapers, inc the *ANU Reporter*; and Karmel, Nichol and Ross OHP interviews.
Ross's article is in the *Canberra Times*, 11 and 12 Apr 1989. The *ANU Reporter*, 14 Apr 1989, quotes Molony at the staff meeting. Dixon's response to Ross is in the *Canberra Times*, 12 Apr 1989. Stiffening resistance: *ANU Reporter*, 26 Aug 1988. Defending the title of professor: *ANU Reporter*, 14 Jul 1989. The ANU soon joined the trend: people who carried the anomalous title of professorial fellow were automatically elevated to the rank of professor. The denouement is reported in the *ANU Reporter*, 11 Aug and 22 Sep 1989. Nichol's views are quoted from his OHP interview and the *ANU Reporter*, 14 Apr 1989.

Music and art

317-51 For music see W.L. Hoffmann, *The Canberra School of Music: the first 25 years 1965–1990*, Canberra School of Music, 1990. Christine James kindly showed us her work-in-progress on the School of Art. This description of the merger draws on Karmel OHP, supplemented by documents from the ANU Archives. The celebration of amalgamation is described in the *ANU Reporter*, 26 Feb 1992. Aitkin discussed 'Music and the verbal arts as university subjects' at the Association of Commonwealth Universities Conference, Swansea, 1993. (Our thanks to Don Aitkin for providing a copy of his paper, a condensed version of which appeared in the *Canberra Times*.)

John Curtin under siege

351 Karmel expressed his suspicions to H. Hudson, 7 Oct 1986, ANU Archives.

352 The figure of 13 per cent is from tables prepared by Karmel.

353 Aitkin's disappointment, and that of his fellow ARC member, are mentioned in Aitkin MS.

353-6 Curtis OHP discusses reactions within JCSMR to the committee's recommendations. The University's responses to government have been traced through Council, BIAS and Heads of Research Schools Committee minutes and papers, and articles in the *ANU Reporter*. The authors attended the rally on 11 Dec 1991 (just as we were starting work on this book). An account of the meeting is in the *ANU Reporter*, 19 Dec 1991. Summaries of speeches and resolutions are in JCSMR submission to Senate Standing Committee on Employment, Education and Training, Jan 1992. The committee's report is titled: The John Curtin School of Medical Research: Report by the Senate Standing Committee on Employment, Education and Training, 1992.

356 D. Penington reflects on university autonomy in 'The institutional perspective: autonomy and the interface with government', in Marshall and Walsh (eds), *The Governance and Funding of Australian Higher Education*. Nichol's departure was discussed widely around the campus and in the press, inc *Canberra Times*, 22 Jun 1992. His perspective on the key issues is in his OHP interview.

The University in the marketplace

356-7 R.D. Wright raised questions about links with industry: to Chifley, 7 Sep 1945; to H.K. Ward 8 Sep 1945; to Coombs 8 Sep 1945: Wright Papers, 8/1/7, Uni of Melbourne Archives. A.A. Burnett and A.J.R. Yencken discuss 'Commercialising University inventions', *ANU News*, Nov 1971. When Crawford, as Director of RSPacS, was offered a seat on the board of a major company, Council decreed (12 Aug 1960) that staff should not have any relationship with an outside organisation that might prevent them making their knowledge and expertise freely available to all. Birch discusses industry links in his working papers, ANU Archives. On RSC generally: reports to Council, 12 Jul 1968, 12 Nov 1976, 12 May 1978, 14 Sep 1979. Yencken on patents: Burnett and Yencken, 'Commercialising University inventions', *ANU News*, Nov 1971. On RSES: reports to Council, 12 Jul 1974, 8 Jul 1977. Also Crawford in support of marketing: 'Notes for an informal address ... to the Victoria Institute of Colleges Staff Association Council', 27 Nov 1970, Crawford Papers, MS 4514, NLA.

357   The copper project: Council, 10 Nov 1972, 13 May 1977; Craig OHP; Ross OHP; and Birch Papers, ANU Archives. The solar energy project: RSPhysS Review, Jul 1976; Ross OHP.

358   This account of the origins of Anutech draws on Council minutes; P. Wing, *This gown for hire: a history of the Australian Tertiary Institutions Commercial Companies Association*, Anutech, Canberra, 1993, pp. 33, 38; Ross OHP; and Notes by I.G. Ross, 27 Oct 1994. Compare with Macquarie's entry into the marketplace: B. Mansfield and M. Hutchinson, *Liberality of Opportunity: a History of Macquarie University 1964–1989*, Hale & Iremonger, Sydney, 1992, pp. 293–95.

359-61   Bad taste: Council, 11 Sep 1964. Market loadings: Paper by W. Williams on 'Market-related and merit loadings for academic staff', 11 Apr 95, ANU Archives. The Faculty of Law report to Council, 12 Oct 1990, remarks on ANU's 'restrictive attitudes' to loadings. Coombs identifies the threat in *Trial Balance*, Macmillan, South Melbourne, 1981, p. 213. Kamenka is quoted from *ANU Reporter*, 12 May 1993; and '"Australia made me" — but which Australia is mine?', John Curtin Memorial Lecture, 16 Jul 1993. He discusses similar themes in *ANU Reporter*, 28 Jul 1989. An obituary of Kamenka by his long-term colleague Robert Brown is in *Canberra Times*, 21 Jan 1994, and Australian Academy of the Humanities, *Proceedings*, 1994, pp. 60–63.

361-2   Problems in University House: A. Albert to B. Thorpe, 1 Oct 1987 (by courtesy of Brian Thorpe) laments deteriorating meals in earlier years; Report of the Committee on the policy and functions of University House, 12 Nov 1971; letters relating to purposes of University House in *ANU Reporter*, 8 Jun, 27 Jul 1973. On changes: F. West, *University House:* *Portrait of an Institution*, University House, 1980; and R.W.V. Elliott, *ANU Reporter*, 9 Dec 1983.

14   A new generation of students

Who were the students?

363-5   Statistical information comes from the annual *ANU Statistical Handbook*; unpublished statistics supplied by Phil Telford in the University's Planning Division; and Department of Employment, Education and Training, *Selected Higher Education Statistics*. On fears of declining standards and proposals to increase National Undergraduate Scholarships: ANU *Annual Reports*, 1982, 1983. On reasons for choosing ANU: ANU Submission to the Committee for Quality Assurance in Higher Education, Sep 1993, p. 39. Scepticism about assessments: e.g. *Campus Review*, 17–23 Mar 1994; *Australian*, 15, 22 Mar 1995; and P. Karmel in *ANU Reporter*, 13 Sep 1993. *Australian*, 5 Apr 1995, reports on the misreading in Singapore of a Quality Assurance assessment, in favour of ANU, and on consternation in other universities.

365   Low's warning is in his Report to the University, 11 Nov 1976.

Student politics

365-7   ANUSA policies in 1977: *ANU Reporter*, 25 Feb 1977. Warden's observation appears in advertisements for and in the *Canberra Times*, May 1994; his 1978 comment is in that year's *Orientation Handbook*. Waterford's lament is in the *Canberra Times*, 22 Apr 1984. Greg Giles has written about voluntary student unionism in *Burning Down the House: a view of the campaign for voluntary student unionism*, Council of South Australian College Student Organisation Inc, 1992. The Berzins case is at pp. 76–80. The book includes a contribution by P. Cardwell (President of ANUSA in 1978), 'Voluntary student unionism: the ANU experience'. The campaign is documented in ANUSA minutes of meetings, Mar-Sep 1978; Yabsley is quoted from the minutes of 7 Jun 1978; also White OHP. A. Major claimed the ANU was a politically conscious uni in *ANU Reporter*, 28 Oct 1988.

367   For most of his term, Humphries was styled Administrator, while the Supreme Court considered whether the results of the previous elections had been properly overturned. His later reflections are in the *Orientation Handbook*, 1990. The Green Alliance: *ANU Reporter*, 26 Feb, 23 Sep

367-9   Our main sources for the fees issue are Council minutes and the *ANU Reporter*, Aug-Oct 1994; also *Canberra Times*, 12, 14 Oct 1994, and selected papers from the ANU Archives.

International students

369-72   S. Marginson, *Education and Public Policy in Australia*, Cambridge UP, Cambridge, 1993, pp. 184–88, discusses the development of the education export industry. A Report and Report Summary of the Survey of International Students at the ANU, 1993, is distributed by the University's International Education Office. The 'after sales service' comment is reported, wryly, in the newsletter, *International Student*, Sep-Oct 1993. Anxieties about the supply of students drying up include G.A. Horridge to Chairman of BIAS, 22 Nov 1986, ANU Archives. On the non-economic benefits of international students: R. Spear, The ANU Graduate School: origins, current operation and future possibilities, 1992, Introduction and Pt 1, p. 12; and D. Terrell in *ANU Reporter*, 7 Jul 1993.

15   From dark matter to the Roman family

A commitment to research

373-6   Moyal's interview with Serjeantson is in *Portraits in Science*, NLA, Canberra, 1994; the quotations are from pp. 166 and 168. Also on Serjeantson and her research: JCSMR Annual Report, 1988; and *ANU Reporter*, 26 May 1993. Iain McCalman provided details to supplement information in official reports.

Work in progress

373-90   These accounts have been garnered from many sources, including annual reports of schools, centres, faculties and the University as a whole; submissions to review committees, esp the University's presentations to the 1990 and 1995 reviews of IAS; reports of review committees; articles on individuals and projects in the *ANU Reporter*; and information assembled for various purposes, including compilations prepared by the Public Affairs Division. In addition, a number of researchers have kindly provided short descriptions of their projects: we have acknowledged their help in the Preamble.

376-7   P. Quinn describes 'Searching for the dark side: the story of the MACHO project', pts 1 and 2, *Southern Sky*, Sep/Oct and Nov/Dec 1993.

377   Ringwood is quoted in Moyal, *Portraits in Science*, p. 134.

379   Ninham attacks 'the tyranny of discipline' in the *ANU Reporter*, 13 Oct 1993.

390   Rawson is quoted in the *Sydney Morning Herald* magazine, *Good Weekend*, 19 Aug 1995.

Measuring achievement

390-2   The origins and parameters of the Performance Indicators Project are set out in P. Bourke and L. Butler, *Mapping Scientific Research in Universities: Departments and Fields*, RSSS, 1993. This is the first in a series of occasional papers published by the project. Ninham's comment is in his Outside Studies Report, n.d. (about Nov 1994), Council papers, 9 Dec 1994. Brennan tells M. Neutze about the necessity of bibliometric evaluation, 15 Oct 1991, ANU Archives. Bourke and Butler prepared the diagram for this history.

The ANU diaspora

393-5   Visitors to RSES: RSES submission to the Review Committee, Feb 1995, pp. 132–33 and tables. Ninham on Applied Mathematics: *ANU Reporter*, 13 Sep 1993. NCDS alumni: RSPAS submission to Review Committee, Dec 1994, p. 14. Demography's influence: *Studies in Demography at the Australian National University*, 9, Jun 1988; 10, Nov 1991. RSC's influence: RSC submission to Review Committee, vol 3, Apr 1995.

16   The past and the future

Retirement

399-402   Albert is quoted in his obituary by D.J. Brown, *Historical Records of Australian Science*, 8/2, Jun 1990, pp. 67–68. Birch makes similar comments about 'forced retirement' in his working notes, Birch Papers, ANU Archives. Fenner in retirement: OHP interview; and *Canberra Times*, 26 Nov 1994. Eccles' resignation led to articles in the *Australian*, *Canberra Times* and *Sydney Sun*, all 16 Feb 1966. Huxley presented the University's view to J.G. Gorton, 21 Feb 1966, ANU Archives. Eccles refers to his retirement in 'My Scientific Odyssey', *Annual Review of Physiology*, 39, 1977, pp. 14–15. Also Curtis OHP; and Wright interview, Uni of Melbourne Archives. Oliphant's departure is the subject of several letters in the Oliphant Papers, Barr Smith Library; the Titterton Papers, Basser Library; and the Wright Papers, Uni of Melbourne

Archives. W. Williams prepared a Background paper on Compulsory Age Retirement, 23 Nov 1995, ANU Archives.

The parts and the whole

404 Oliphant's toys with dismemberment: 'Proposals for the reform of the Australian National University', 23 Jun 1955, Florey Papers, ANU Library; and again, Oliphant to Wright, 28 Jan 1960, Wright Papers, 4/3/3, Uni of Melbourne Archives.
Campbell is quoted from the submission by The Faculties to the 1995 Review of IAS. Ninham's comment is from the *ANU Reporter*, 13 Oct 1993, and Birch's from an undated newspaper clipping, late 1980s–early 1990s, in his working notes.

406 Aitkin refers to good ideas and people in Aitkin MS; Foster noted Serjeantson's comment during the conference.

407 Dawkins refers to 'Chief Executive Officers' in his White Paper, *Higher Education: a policy statement*, AGPS, Canberra, 1988, p. 103.

The past in the present

407 Wright on the rodents: to the Editor, Melbourne *Herald*, 7 Sep 1945, Wright Papers, 8/1/7, Uni of Melbourne Archives.

408-10 The quotations from Passmore and Wright are from papers in the ANU Archives. Hayden is quoted in the *ANU Reporter*, 13 Sep 1993. Wang's comment is from his OHP interview.

Index

Page numbers in **bold** refer to illustrations and captions.

Aarons, Laurie, 201
Aboriginal Australians, research on, 109-10, 241, 387-8, 389-90
Abschol, 215
Academic Advisory Committee
    on the CUC, 146-7
    at the Easter conferences, 1948, 33-42, 43
    establishment of, 23-7
    on the 'ideal' vice-chancellor, 30-2
    and the Interim Council, 28-30, 33, 44-5
    meetings, 28-32
    opposition to Lewis's site plan, 69-70
    role of, 29-30
    on University House, 71, 73
academic autonomy. *see* academic freedom; autonomy of the university
academic boards
    Board of Graduate Studies, 77, 154
    Board of the Institute of Advanced Studies, 158
    Board of the School of General Studies, 158, 220, 221-2
    Professorial Board, 156, 407
    structure of, 156
    student representation, 218-24
academic courses, 332
    computing, 336-8
    CUC, 144-5, 151
    diplomatic studies, 146, 149-51, 360
    engineering, 337-8
    impact of 'commercial' marketing on, 359-60
    inclusion of professional courses, 243-4
    protests against course content, 218, 222-4
    SGS/The Faculties, 202-3, 222-4, 242
    Women's Studies, 222, 246-8, 326
academic dress, 78
academic freedom, 113-26
    and accountability, 174, 407
    government attacks on academics, 288
    impact of outside funding on, 333
    and individual rights, 406
    and service to the public, 273-9
    and Stephen Committee recommendations, 354
    threats from within, 224
academic government
    board structure, 156
    collegial, 295-7, 322, 411
    differences between IAS and The Faculties, 406
    in the IAS, 133
    impact of AUC on, 174-5
    impact of Stephen Committee recommendations, 354
    and managerialism, 340-1, 407

role of Council, 156
styles of management, 310
see also administration
academic honours. *see* awards and honours
academic leadership, 126-43, 301, 406
Academic Salaries Tribunal, 294
academic staff
    as advisers to foreign governments, 107, 108, 389, 393
    as advisers to government, 96, 278-9, 385-6, 393
    calibre of early appointees, 55
    ceilings, 170
    early staff members, 51-9
    gender balance, 58-9, 323, 325, 330
    involved in demonstrations and protests, 217
    market salary loadings, 359
    numbers, 156, **161, 281, 397**
    outside activities, 273-9, 393
    recruitment of, 20-3, 29, 37, 48
    relationship with general staff, 293
    retirement activities, 399-402
    underperformers/non-producers, 268-9, 295
    see also conditions of service
academic staff association. *see* ANU Staff Association
academic structure, **161**, 180-9, **281**, 310, **397**, 403-6
    bridge-building between IAS and SGS, 249-50, 313-16
    centres and units, 248-50
    as defined in 1948, 34-5
    as defined in the 1946 Act, 18
    directors v. deans, 232, 236-7
    duplication of resources caused by, 314-15
    'group' structure, 232, 236
    IAS, 169, 186-9
    overseas models, 27-8, 36, 180
    post-amalgamation ANU, 158
    relationship of individuals to, 405-6
    review recommendations on, 299, 301-2, 305-6
    SGS/The Faculties, 185-6, 240-1
academic titles, 78-9, 176
Academy of Science. *see* Australian Academy of Science
Academy of the Social Sciences in Australia, 266
accelerators, 93-6
    14UD Pelletron, 378-9
    see also homopolar generator
Accounting and Public Finance, Department of (SGS), 245
Acton Guest House, 65
Acton ridge, 194, 195

447

ADB. see Australian Dictionary of Biography
administration
    financial, 81, 116, 289
    industrial relations issues, 294-6, 411
    introduction of strategic planning, 312-13
    management reforms under Karmel, 308-13
    reduction of powers under Low, 289
    restructuring under Crawford, 184
    see also academic government
Administrative and Allied Officers Association, 296
administrative and general staff, 82, 184-5, 289-90
    numbers of, 160, 281, 397
    staff associations, 185, 187, 294-6, 329
    see also academic staff
admissions schemes. see recruitment of students
Aitkin, Don, 307, **311**, 339, 341-2, 405
    management style, 341
    on the Stephen Committee review, 353
Albert, Adrien, **85**, **86**
    appointed to JCSMR, 56
    attitudes towards women, 325
    establishes Medical Chemistry
        department, 60-1
    research, 85-6, 88
    retirement, 400
Alexander, Frederick, 47
All Souls College, Oxford, 30
Allen, F.J., 241
Allen, Leslie H., 77
    at CUC, 144, **145**, 146
amalgamations, institutional
    ANU/CCAE proposal, 343-7
    with CUC, 153-9, 176-80
    with the Institute of the Arts, 343, 347-50
    University of Canberra proposal, 354
American universities, 5, 7
ancient Rome, research on, 390
Anderson, Brian, 334
Anderson, John, 105, 133, 273, 360, 361
Anglo-Australian Telescope, 262-6, **265**
animal experiments, 320
    cats, **91**, 92
    pigs, 380
Anthropology and Sociology, Department of
    (RSPacS), 109-10
anti-apartheid demonstrations, **215**
ANU Club for Women, 293, **294**
ANU Cricket Club, 293-4
ANU General Staff Association, 295-6
ANU Labor Club, 215
ANU Liberal Society, 366
ANU Press, **266**, 266-8
ANU Staff Association, 185, 187, 294
ANU Students' Association, 122, 217
    see also clubs and societies
ANUMIN Pty Ltd, 357
Anutech Pty Ltd, 357-8, 378, 385
Applied Mathematics, Department of (RSPhysS),
    299, 393
applied research. see fundamental v. applied
    research; 'national needs' research
Aquarius Festival, **214**
architects
    Coombs Building, 134, 192

Lewis's plan, 67-74
selection of, 192-3
Winston and Rudduck plans, 190, 191-2
see also site and buildings
Arndt, Bettina, **226**, 226-7
Arndt, Heinz Wolfgang, 209, **226**
    appointed to CUC, 148
    personal attributes, 150
    research, 388
Arndt, Ruth, **226**
art collections, 73, 349
Art History, Department of (Arts), 332
Arts, Faculty of, 185
    academic courses, 203
    optimum size, 172
    review of, 313
    teaching in, 211
Ashby, Eric, 22, 28
Asian Studies, Faculty of, 241, 303-4
    research achievements, 388
    review of, 304-5
assessment methods, 210, 225, 364
    student protests, 218, 222-4
Association of Women Employees, 329
Astronomy, Department of (RSPhysS)
    postgraduate training, 261
    research directions, 98-9
    see also Mount Stromlo and Siding Spring
        Observatories
Atiyah, Patrick, 278
Attridge, Martin, **220**
attrition rates. see failure and attrition rates
AUC. see Australian Universities Commission
Australia-Japan Research Centre, 386
Australian Academy of Science, 234, **252**, 252-3
Australian Academy of the Humanities, 266
Australian Atomic Energy Commission, 254
Australian Dictionary of Biography (ADB), 130,
    131, 132, 387
Australian National Dictionary, 389
Australian National University Press, **266**, 266-8
The Australian People (Jupp), 387
Australian Research Council, 341-2
Australian School of Forestry, 242-3
Australian School of Pacific Administration, 26
Australian Science and Technology Council, 351
Australian Security Intelligence Organisation
    (ASIO), 121
The Australian Ugliness (Boyd), 193
Australian Union of Students (AUS), 366, 369
    fee dispute, 288-9
Australian universities. see state universities; and
    under names of specific institutions
Australian Universities Commission (AUC),
    250, 340
    on ANU's growth rate, 290
    approves establishment of RSC, 230
    relationship with ANU, 174-6
    role of, 173-4
    views on amalgamation with CUC, 155
autonomy of the university
    academics' concerns about government
        interference, 113
    Coombs on, 15, 354

Copland on, 113-14, 115
Dedman on, 114
Eggleston on, 113
increasing intervention under Labor, 340-1, 355-6, 407
and JCSMR funding, 355-6
Menzies on, 114-15
Rivett on, 115-16
and student union fees, 366-7
see also academic freedom; government
Avineri, Shlomo, 361
awards and honours, 251-2, 266

Bachelard, Eric, **345**
Back on Track party, 367
Bailey, Sir Kenneth, 117, 154
Bain, Andrew, 227
Baker, Don, 148, 211
Baldwin, Peter, 340
Bambrick, Susan, 330
Bandler, Faith, 201
Bandung Conference (1955), 124-5
Barisic, Marica, **349**
Barnard, Alan, 130, **199**
Barton, Allan, 245, 308, 310
Basham, Arthur Llewellyn, **303**, 303-4
Bastable, Charles, 175, 226
Baxter, Rodney, **379**
Beadle, Paul, 77
Beazley, Kim, 61, 158
Beck, A.E., 63
Beddie, Brian D., 148
Behavioural Biology, Department of (RSBS), 236, 237
Bellingham, Lois, **82**
Beloff, Max, 43
Belshaw, Cyril, 269-70
Benjafield, D.G., 63
Bennett, J.H., 63
Bensusan-Butt, David, 189, 324
Berlin, Sir Isaiah, 361
Berzins, Peter, 366
Biami people, 270
bibliometric surveys. *see* Performance Indicators Project
Bielenstein, Hans, 151, 303
binary system, abolition of, 340
Biochemistry, Department of (JCSMR), 86-7, 89
Biochemistry, Department of (The Faculties), 381
Birch, Arthur John, 120, 287, 405
    as advocate of industry partnerships, 356
    appointed Adviser and then Dean for RSC, 229-31, 232
    awards and honours, 253, 266
    at opening of RSC, **234**
    on the two part university, 250
Bishop, Peter, 381-2, **382**
Black Mountain Tower, 217
Blackett, Patrick, 95
Blamey, Field Marshal Sir Thomas, 3, 12, 13
Board of Graduate Studies (BGS), 77, 154
Board of the Institute of Advanced Studies (BIAS), 158

Board of the School of General Studies (BSGS), 158, 220, 221-2
Bok, Bart J., 99, **260**, **261**
    and the Anglo-Australian Telescope, 262
    as director of Mount Stromlo Observatory, 260-2
    on equality in conditions of service, 325, 326
Bok, Priscilla Fairfield, 260, 326
Bolton, Geoffrey, 391
Borg, Rigmore Helene, 214
Borrie, Wilfred David (Mick), 58, 221, 294, 383
    appointed head of Demography, 102
    appointed to RSSS, 51
    outside activities, 274, 278
    research, 101-2, 387
Bougainville Copper Pty Ltd, 271
Bouquet, Mary Grace ('Molly'), 289
Bourchier, Murray, 150
Bourke, Paul, **387**, 390-1
Bowler, Jim, 241
Boyd, Robin, 193
Boyer Lectures, 391
Boyle, A.J.F., 63
Bragg, Lawrence, 251
Bragg, William, 251
'brain drain', 4
Bramley, Gwenda, 326-8
Brennan, Geoffrey, 220, 391-2, 410
Brent, Richard, 336-7
Brewster, Don, 201
Brissenden, R.F., 149
British National Institute of Medical Research, 36, 74
Brophy, James, 116
Brown, Sir Allen, **34**, 82, 117, 119, 154
Brown, D.J., 58, 86
Brown, H.P. (Horrie), 54, 55
Brown, Maurice, 78, **82**
Bruce, Stanley Melbourne, 1st Viscount of Melbourne
    awarded honorary degree, 80
    as Chancellor, 79-80, 117-18, 181
    at opening of University House, **80**
Bruce Hall, **205**, 206-7
    as centre for political activism, 215
    conflict over naming of, 178
Bryant, Chris, 345
Buchdahl, Hans, **382**
budget. *see* finances
buildings. *see* site and buildings
Buildings and Grounds Committee, 70, 192-3
Bull, Hedley, 273
Bunker, A.F. (Fred), 66-7, 136-7, 140
Bureau of Mineral Resources, 97, 238
Burgen, Sir Arnold, 300
Burgmann College, 205-6
Burnet, Sir (Frank) Macfarlane, 36
    attitudes towards JCSMR, 37, 57
    awarded Nobel Prize, 252
Burns, Arthur, 275-6, **276**, 295, 302
Burridge, Ken, 63
Burton, Herbert ('Joe'), **41**, **147**, **148**
Burton, John, 16, 124-5
Burton Hall, 205, 207

449

Bush Week, 207-8, **208**
business administration. *see* administration; finances
Butler, Linda, 391
Butler, Stuart, 63
Butlin, Noel George, 64, **102**, **103**, 293, 294
  awarded overseas scholarship, 62-3
  research and publications, 100-1, 267, 387
  retirement, 399
Butlin, Sydney James, 17, 84
Butt Report, 189, 318
Butters, Sir John, 6

Cairns, Jim, 201
Caldwell, Geoffrey, **295**
Caldwell, J.C. (Jack), 278, **383**, 383-4
Caldwell, Pat, 383, **383**
Calwell, Arthur, 14
Cameron, Burgess, 64, 148
Cameron, Donald, 123
Cameron, Sue, **295**
Campbell, David, 148
Campbell, Richard, 404, 405
Canberra
  city design competition, 5, **6**
  ideas for a university for the capital, 6-9
  1950s, described, 59-60, 65-6, 148-9
  planning bodies, 192, 206
  university relationship with, 193-5, 358
Canberra College of Advanced Education (CCAE), 343-7
Canberra Community Hospital, 64, **65**, **66**
Canberra House, 65
Canberra Institute of the Arts. *see* Institute of the Arts
Canberra School of Art, 343, **347**, 347-8
Canberra School of Music, 343, 348
Canberra Technical College, 347
Canberra University College (CUC), 144-59
  academic courses, 144-5, 151
  amalgamation with ANU, 153-9, 176-80, 347
  ANU's initial opposition to, 146-7
  association with the University of Melbourne, 8, 145-6, 149
  attitudes towards ANU, 149
  budget, 144, 147
  buildings, 144, 148
  collaborative efforts with ANU, 130
  incorporation in the ANU Act, 18
  Murray Committee's recommendations on, 151, 152
  origins, 8
  residential halls, 149-50, **150**
  site, 144, 148, 151-2
  staff members, 148, 151
  student numbers, 144, 149, 152, 156
cancer research, 381
Carmody, Alan, 292
Carr, Dennis J., 236
Carrick, John, 288, 366-7
Carslaw, Horatio Scot, 96
Carver, John Henry, 64, 254, **402**
  as Director of RSPhysS, 258, 300, 337

Casey, Richard Gardiner, 115, 120
  involvement in academic appointments, 122, 125, 128
Cassab, Judy, 401
Catcheside, David Guthrie, 235, **235**, 236
Catt, A.J., **103**
Centre for Aboriginal Policy Research, 387-8
Centre for Economic Policy Research, 385
Centre for Immigraton and Multicultural Studies, 387
Centre for Information Science Research (CISR), 336
Centre for Mathematical Analysis, 332
Centre for Recombinant DNA Research, 332
Centre for Research on Federal Financial Relations, 276-8
Centre for Resource and Environmental Studies (CRES), 248-9
  research achievements, 284-5
Centre for Strategic and Defence Studies, 218
Centre for Visual Sciences, 381-2
centres and units, 248-50
see also under names of individual centres/units
chancellor, 181-3
  installation of Bruce, 79-80
  role and function, 181, 286
Chancelry sit-ins
  1974, 222-3, **223**, 224
  1994, **369**
Chapman, Penny, 228, **394**
Cheong Choong Kong, **393**
Chifley, J.B. (Ben), 4, **20**
  biography of, 151
  interest in nuclear physics, 25-6, 38
  meeting with Oliphant in London 1946, 20-1
  as Minister for Post-War Reconstruction, 11
  and the naming of ANU, 14
Chifley Library, 177, **177**
child care facilities, 327
Childers Street Building, **148**
Choy, Alison Low, **350**
Chubb, Ian, 354
Clark, Charles Manning Hope, 130, **148**, 178, 209
  appointed to CUC, 148
  attacks Fraser government, 288
  attitudes towards IAS, 179
  on Canberra in the 1950s, 148
  government criticisms of, 124
  as head of History Department, SGS, 208, 211-12
  outside activities, 273
  personal attributes, 150-1
  and recruitment of women, 325
  relationship with La Nauze, 178-9
  research, 178, 268
  and the student protests, 223
  as teacher, 209-10, **210**
  on Women's Studies, 246
Clark, Ernest H., **34**, **41**, 78
Clark, Gregory, 275
Classics, Department of (Arts Faculty), 172
Clemenger, Joan, 33
Clifford, J.T., 63
Clinical Science, Department of (JCSMR), 380

clubs and societies, 151, 202
    ANU Club for Women, 293, **294**
    ANU Cricket Club, 293-4
    ANU Labor Club, 215
    ANU Liberal Society, 366
coat of arms, 76-7, **77**
Coates, John, 199
Cockcroft, Sir John, 79, 93, 116-17, **181**, 256
Cockcroft Building, **74**
collaborative teaching and research
    Anglo-Australian Telescope, 262-6
    Australian Dictionary of Biography (ADB), 130, **131**, 132, 387
    centres as 'bridges' between IAS and SGS, 249-50
    in chemistry, 232-3
    in computing, 336
    CRC for Robust and Adaptive Systems, 334
    history consortium, 130, 153
    between IAS and SGS, 232-3, 313-16
    with industry partners, 336, 356-9
    with other institutions, 130, 132, 262-6, 332, 336, 387
    solar energy project, **357**, 357-8
    university-wide schools, 332, 382
    see also interdisciplinary research; multidisciplinary research; outside funding
colleges of advanced education, 340, 343-7
collegiate government
    and industrial relations, 295-7, 411
    and managerialism, 322
collegiate life
    impact of managerialism on, 310, 407
    impact of size on, 172
    Nichol's support for, 341
    role of University House in fostering, 110, 203-4, 362
Colman, Ron, 201
Commerce degree, introduction of, 302-3, 332
commercial operations, 357-8, 378, 385
Committee of Enquiry into the Future of Tertiary Education in Australia (Martin Committee), 171
Committee on Australian Universities (Murray Committee), 151-3, 173-4, 212
Committee on National Morale, 11
Commonwealth Observatory. *see* Mount Stromlo Observatory
Commonwealth Office of Education, 12, 22
Commonwealth Scientific and Industrial Research Organisation (CSIRO), 89, 315
    collaboration with ANU, 130
    see also Council for Scientific and Industrial Research
Commonwealth Special Research Centres, 332
Commonwealth Tertiary Education Commission, 311, 312, 340
communism, 120-4
Compston, William, **377**
Computer Centre, 248
Computer Sciences, Department of (Faculties), 336-7
Computer Sciences Laboratory (RSPhysS), 337
Computer Services Centre, 334, 336

computers, 334, 336-7
'Concerned Asian Scholars of Australia and New Zealand' (CASAN), 275
conditions of service
    academic salary levels, 1950s, 59-60
    activities of staff associations, 294-7
    Bramley-Ward Report recommendations, 327-8
    female staff, 324
    industrial disputes, 294-6, 411
    market salary loadings, 359
    sabbatical leave, 83
    salary differential between SGS and IAS, 176, 179
    Sawer report recommendations, 328-30
    working hours for general staff, 308
Conlon, Alfred, **3**, 408
    as Chairman of Committee on National Morale, 11
    medical research institute concept, 12-13, 20
    personal attributes, 3
    and the planning of ANU, 3, 22, 26
    on the social science schools, 111
constitutional law, 100
Contemporary China Centre, 248
Coombs, Herbert Cole ('Nugget'), **2**, **34**, 181, **199**, 411-12, **413**
    and the Academic Advisers, 20, 20-1, 25-8
    on the amalgamation of ANU and CUC, 154, **155**
    on the appointment of Melville, 117-18, 119
    on the appointment of the first vice-chancellor, 31-2
    as Chancellor, 181-3
    at Chancelry sit-in, 1974, **223**, 224
    as Director-General of Post-War Reconstruction, 11-12
    personal attributes, 4
    and the planning of ANU, 3, 4, 13-14, 15-19, 112, 408
    as Pro-Chancellor, 181
    retires from chancellorship, 286
    on the role of women at ANU, 326
    at 'save the JCSMR' rally, 354, **355**
    on students, 218-19, 220, 224
Coombs, Jack, 91
Coombs Building, 134-5, 192
Cooperative Research Centres, 334
Copland, Sir Douglas Berry, **53**, **61**, **82**, 152, 184
    on academic freedom, 113-114
    appointed as first vice-chancellor, 30-2
    at the Easter conferences, 1948, 33, **34**, **67**
    farewell party for, 82
    outside activities, 273
    personal attributes, 81, 119
    plans for RSPacS, 41-2
    and public relations, 75, 81-2
    recruits staff for the social science schools, 51-5
    relationship with Hancock, 45-7
    resigns from ANU, 80-1
    and the University Association, 9
    visit to London, 1949, 45-7
Corden, Max, 324
Cornforth, John, 229-30
Cornick, Mick, 58

451

Corris, Peter, **394**
Cotton, Robert, 277
Council
    membership, 18, 342
    role and functions, 156, 180-1
    see also Interim Council
Council for Scientific and Industrial Research (CSIR), 7, 10, 17-18
    see also Commonwealth Scientific and Industrial Research Organisation
Country and Calling (Hancock), 43, 45-6, 47, 127-8
courses, university. *see* academic courses
Courtice, (Frederick) Colin, 317
Craig, David, 229-31, **234**
Craig, Russell, **295**
Crawford, Raymond Maxwell, 17, **41**
Crawford, Sir John Grenfell, **182**
    administrative restructuring under, 184
    appointed Director, RSPacS, 129
    appointed Vice-Chancellor, 170, 188
    on the AUC, 175
    as Chancellor, 286
    on combining the two parts of ANU, 180, 250
    as Fiscal Adviser, 168, 183
    on the growth rate of ANU, 290
    outside activities, 183-4
    retires from vice-chancellorship, 221
    on the social science schools, 42
    and the student 'Troubles', **219**, 219-11
    as Vice-Chancellor, 183-4, 238
Creative Arts Fellowship Scheme, 349
CRES. *see* Centre for Resource and Environmental Studies
cricket matches, 293-4, **294**
Crisp, L.F. (Fin), **179**, 197-8, 209
    appointed to CUC, 148
    attitudes towards amalgamation, 155
    and the formation of the Student Union, 208
    research, 151
    as Secretary to the Interim Council, 29
    and the student 'Troubles', 220, 224
Crocker, Sir Walter Russell, 44, **61**, 83, 273, **402**
    appointed to RSPacS, 51-2, 61
    career, described, 51-2
    on Copland, 81
    early impressions of ANU and Canberra, 65-6
    resigns from ANU, 80
Crocombe, Ron, 271
Crowley, Frank, 63
CUC. *see* Canberra University College
Cumpston, Helen, 223
Currie, Sir George, 272
Curthoys, Ann, **247**
Curtin, John, 3
    death of, 13, 14
    educational initiatives, 10-11
    interest in medical research, 12, 14
Curtis, David Roderick, 84, **199**, 353, **355**
cyclo-synchrotron, 93-4, 95, 254

Dadswell, Lyndon, 73
Daley, Charles Studdy, **12**, 22, **34**
    and the concept of a national university, 11-12, 18
'dark matter' research, 376-7
Darling, Peter, **293**
Davidson, Alastair, 209
Davidson, James Wightman (Jim), 44, 45, **107**
    on academic freedom, 124, 125
    on academic titles, 79
    appointed to RSPacS, 52, 59, 60
    as Dean, RSPacS, 126
    at Gungahlin, 150
    outside activities, 273-4
    research, 106-7
Davies, A.F., 63
Dawkins, John, **339**, 339-42, 354, **367**, 408
'Day of Rage', 216
de Jong, J.W., 303, **304**
de L'Isle, Lord, **88**
De Vaucouleurs, Gerard, 99
deans. *see* directors and deans
Dedman, John Johnstone, 11, 12, **19**, **114**, 225
    on autonomy of the university, 114
    as Minister for Post-War Reconstruction, 12
    and the planning of ANU, 11, 12, 14, 18-19, 21-2
    as student in SGS, 197-8
Demography, Department of (RSSS), 393-4
    research achievements, 101-2, 383-4, 387
    staff members, 1950s, 102
demonstrations and protests, 212-25
    against apartheid, **215**
    against assessment and course content, 218, 222-4
    Chancelry occupations, 222-3, **223**, 224, 369
    against governing structure, 218-22, 224-5
    'save the JCSMR rally', 354, **355**
    against the Vietnam war, 212, 215-17, **216**
Denborough, Michael, **380**, 380-1
departments
    autonomy of IAS departments, 186, 187
    optimum size, 169-72
    responsibilities of heads of, 185-6
    review recommendations on abolition of, 301-2, 305
    see also academic structure; *and under names of specific departments*
Developmental Biology, Department of (RSBS), 236, 237
Diamond, Sigmund, 123
Dicker, George, **289**
diplomatic studies course, 146, 149-51, 360
directors and deans, 232
    functions as defined in Butt Report, 189
    Karmel on role of, 310-11
    limits on authority of, 317
    role of, 34, 85, 186, 321
disciplinary problems, 204
Dixon, R.M.W. (Bob), 344, 389-90
Dodson, Leigh, 90-1
Doe, William, **318**
Doherty, Peter, 311, **318**, 320, 321, 381
Donagan, Alan, 148
Donaldson, Ian, **249**
Downing, Richard, **41**
drug usage on campus, 214
Dubs, Rosalind, 330, **331**

Dunbar, (David) Noel, **185**, 223
Dunn, Michael, 222, 223
Dunstan, Don, 214
Dwyer, Frank, 187, 229, 383
Dyson, Freeman, 259

early admissions scheme, 199
Easter conferences, 1948, 33-42, 113
Eccles, John (Jnr), **80**
Eccles, Sir John Carew, **85**, **92**
    appointed to JCSMR, 57
    awarded Nobel Prize, 251-2, **253**
    personal attributes, 187
    research, 91-2, 110, 381
    retirement, **401**
    salary loading, 60
Economics, Department of (RSSS), 100-1
Economics, Faculty of, 185, 203, 302-3
Economics and Commerce, Faculty of, 364, 371
Edwards, Jimmy, 58, **254**
Edwards, Vincent, 348
Eggen, Olin Jeuck, 99, **263**, 263-5
Eggleston, Sir Frederic, **34**, **41**, **50**, 408
    attitudes towards Copland, 31
    criticises social science schools, 111
    on government interference, 113
    on the Interim Council, 22, 27
    and the planning of ANU, 16
    plans for RSPacS, 40-2, 44-5
    on staff recruitment, 47-8
Electron and Ion Diffusion Unit, 248
electron synchrotron, 96, 274
Electronic Materials Engineering, Department of (RSPhysS), 337
Elliott, Ralph, 361-2, **362**
Ellis, Malcolm, **132**
Employment, Education and Training, Department of (Commonwealth), 339
Encel, Sol, 268
Engineering and Information Technology, Faculty of, 338
engineering degree, 337-8
Engineering Physics, Department of (RSPhysS), 258, 299
Ennor, Sir Hugh, **85**, **87**
    appointed to JCSMR, 56
    as Dean of JCSMR, 85, 87, 135, 138-9, 141, 187-9
    and establishment of RSC, 229-31
    farewell dinner for, **188**
    personal attributes, 188
    relationship with Florey, 135, 138-40
    research, 86
    resigns from ANU, 188
enterprise bargaining, 411
Environmental Biology, Department of (RSBS), 236, 237
environmental research, 384-5
equal employment opportunity (EEO), 328-32
European historical research, 388
Evatt, Herbert Vere, 16, 95, 100
Ewens, John Q., 181
exchange arrangements, student, 372
Experimental Pathology, Department of (JCSMR), 88-9, 90-1
External Affairs, Department of (Commonwealth), 149

The Faculties, 185
    academic structure, 310-11
    naming of, 180, 250
    relationship with IAS, 314
    see also School of General Studies
Fadden, Sir Arthur, 123
failure and attrition rates, 212, 245
Fallding, Harold, **199**
Far Eastern History, Department of (RSPacS), 106
Fazekas de St Groth, Steven, 110
Federalism Centre. *see* Centre for Research on Federal Financial Relations
fellowships of academic societies, 252-3, 266, 409
Fenner, Frank John, **85**, **90**, 194
    appointed director of JCSMR, 189
    appointed to CRES, 248-9
    appointed to JCSMR, 57, 60
    and the establishment of RSBS, 234-5
    outside activities, 273, 278
    research, 89-90, 400
    retirement, **400**, 400-1
finances, 168, 289, 290
    accounting procedures, 308, 310
    appointment of Fiscal Adviser, 168
    Auditor-General's criticisms of, 81, 116
    'centres of excellence' program, 332
    Commonwealth funding, 1970s, 286-7
    development budget, 16, 81
    freeze during the mid-1950s, 120
    government interference in, 115-16, 292
    impact on education caused by inadequacy of, 361
    Karmel's views on affluence of ANU, 308
    'new initiatives' tax, 291, 308
    outside funding, 97, 270, 271, 277, 333, 360
    recommendations of Stephen committee, 352-5
    and segregation of IAS and SGS, 313-14
    stringency during the late 1970s, 290-2
    triennial funding, 169, 290, 410
    uniqueness of ANU's arrangements, 173
financial benefits from research, 378, 380, 384
Fingleton, Jack, 131
Firth, Raymond
    as Academic Adviser, 26-9, 42
    at the Easter conferences, 1948, 27, 33-5, **34**, **41**
    plans for RSPacS, 40-2
    recruits staff for RSPacS, 51-5
    resigns as Adviser, 41, 44, 126
Fiscal Adviser position, 168, 183
FitzGerald, Charles Patrick
    appointed to RSPacS, 52, 54, 55, 60
    awarded degree, **106**
    establishes Chinese library, 83
    government criticisms of, 124-5
    outside activities, 273-4
    research, 106
FitzGerald, Stephen, **278**
Fitzhardinge, Laurence Frederic, 29, 54, 55, 144
    on the concept of a national university, 8-9

research, 101, 130
Fitzpatrick, Brian, 101, 125
Fleming, John, 151, 156
Flinders University, 246
Florey, Sir Howard, **23, 44, 59**
    as Adviser to JCSMR, 135-7
    appointed as Academic Adviser, 25, 28-9
    attitudes towards Copland, 32, 47, 81
    awarded Nobel Prize, 251
    as Chancellor, **139**, 140, 181
    and the concept of an Australian medical research institute, 13, 16
    declines Directorship offer, 137-9
    on the design and structure of JCSMR, 35-8, 74
    at the Easter conferences, 1948, 33-8, **34, 35**
    personal attributes, 23, 104
    recruits staff for JCSMR, 55-7
    research, 87
    on the role of the director, 37
    visits to ANU, 12-13, 85
Foreign Affairs, Department of (Commonwealth), 333
Foreign Affairs and Trade, Department of (Commonwealth), 360
Forestry, Department of (SGS), 242-4, 385
Forge, Anthony, 242
Foster, John F., 28, 29, 33, 45, 70
'Founders Day' (RSPhysS), 402
14UD Pelletron, 378-9
Franklyn, Charles, 78
Fraser, Malcolm, 201, 264
Freeman, J.D. (Derek), 110
Freeman, Ken, **261**
Fry, Eric, 211
full fee paying students, 370-2
functions of ANU. *see* objectives of ANU
fundamental v. applied research
    funding requirements for fundamental research, 352
    Geophysics approach, 97
    in JCSMR, 87-8, 89
    see also 'national needs' research
funding. *see* finances
Furness, Bryan, 214

Gage, Peter, 321
Gammage, Bill, 131, 201
Gardiner, Laurie, 148
Garnaut, Ross, 213, 386
Garran, Sir Robert, 7, **12**, **152**
    awarded honorary degree, 79
    and the concept of a national university, 11-12, 18
    and the CUC, 8, 144, 147
    on Interim Council, 22
    and the study of Pacific affairs, 16
Garran Committee (1927), 7
Garran Hall, 205, 207
Garrett, Jodie, **363**
Gascoigne, S.C.B. (Ben), 98-9, **261**
Geissler, Marie, **202**
General Services Fee dispute, 288-9
Genetics, Department of (RSBS), 236, 237

Geography, Department of (RSPacS), 107-8
Geophysics, Department of (RSPhysS), 96-8, 237-8
Geophysics and Geochemistry, Department of (RSPhysS), 170
Gibb, Cecil Austin, **172**, 199, 220
    on the size of the university, 172
    as teacher, 210
Gibbney, Jim, **150**
Giblin, L.F., 144
Gibson, Frank, 64, 291, 317
gifts to the university, 96, 274
    Lyttleton-Taylor, **303**
Gill, David, 296
Gollan, Daphne, 247
Gollan, R.A. (Bob), 64, 131, 133, 267, 294
    awarded overseas scholarship, 62
    communist allegations against, 121-2
Golson, Jack, 241
Good Universities Guide, 364
Gooden, Isabel, **102**
Goodes, H.J. (Bert), 12, 22, **34**, 115-16, 119, 180-1
Gore, Michael, **338**
Gorton, John, 205
Gould, Alan, 214, 215
government
    and academic appointments, 117-18, 120-4, 125, 128
    academics' concerns about interference by, 113
    ANU staff as advisers to, 96, 278-9, 385-6, 393
    ANU's relationship with, 15, 113-26, 141, 168, 288, 305-6
    attacks on academic freedom of, 124-5, 288
    attempts to curb students' political activities, 288-9
    Dawkins' education policies, 339-42, 367-8
    education initiatives, pre-1945, 10-11
    and financial management, 115-16
    forces ANU/CUC amalgamation, 153-5, 158
    government initiated research, 276-7
    see also autonomy of the university
Graduate Degrees Committee, 250
Graduate House, 204
Graduate School, 315-16, 352, 404
graduates
    destination of, 225-6, 364-5, 393-5
    numbers of, 84, 173, 287, 363
Graneek, J.J., 177-8
Grant, Olwyn, **202**
Green, Peter, **295**
Green Alliance, 367
Greenwood, Gordon, **41**
Griffin, David, **385**, 385
Griffin, Walter Burley, 5, 6, 64, 196
Grimshaw, Peter, 296
Grounds, Roy, 134
Gruen, Fred, 278
Gullett, Henry ('Jo'), 121, 122
Gum, Colin, 99
'Gungahlin', 149-50, **150**
Gunther, John, 272

Hales, Anton, 240
Hall, R.L., 20

Hambly, Arthur, 209, 233
Hamilton, Bill, 82, 184, **184**, 289
Hancock, Sir (William) Keith, 20, 22, 40-1, **130**
  on the ANU site, 1948, **44**
  appointed as Academic Adviser, 24-5, 28-9
  appointed Director, RSSS, 127-9
  attitudes towards Copland, 32, 46, 47
  early recruiting efforts, 43-4, 47-8
  at the Easter conferences, 1948, 33-5, **34**, **35**, **41**
  on the naming of ANU, 14
  outside activities, 273
  personal attributes, 23, 24
  plans for RSSS, 39-40, 49-50
  plans to join RSSS and RSPacS, 44-5, 133
  resigns as Adviser, 45-6, 47
  retirement, **398**, 399
  on 'two cultures', 143
  and University House, 71
Hancock, Theaden, 24, 46, 47, 128
Hannan, E.J. (Ted), 103, **103**
Hansen, Ragnar, 348
Hardy, Frank, 214
Harris, Henry, 63, 87, 138, 139
Hart, Amanda, **295**
Hasluck, Sir Paul, **41**, 42, 113, 122, 269-70, 275
Hawke, Robert James Lee (Bob), 204, 308, **387**
Hayden, William George (Bill), 332, 409
Haydon, J.F.M., 144, **145**
Haydon-Allen Building, 144
Hayes, Douglas, 378
Health, Housing and Community Services,
  Department of (Commonwealth), 354
Health and Research Employees Association, 296
Health Transition Centre, 383-4
Henderson, Peter, 150
Herbert, William, 348
Hercus, Luise, **304**
Herrera, Juan Jacinto, **350**
Heyde, Beth, **394**
Hieser, Ronald, **199**
Higgins, Chris, 201
Higher Education Contribution Scheme (HECS), 367-8, 385
Higher Education Council, 354
History, Department of (SGS), 209-12, 222
'The History Consortium', 130, 153
History of Ideas Unit, 248, 360-1
Hodgkin, A.L., 252
Hodgkin, David, **184**, 289
Hogan, Warren, **103**
Hogbin, Ian, 84
Hogg, Arthur, **261**
Hohnen, Phyllis, 293
Hohnen, Ross, 75, **82**, 116, 222, 348
  attitudes towards Copland, 81
  and the establishment of RSC, 230-1
  and his 'capacious pouch', 290
  personal attributes, 75
  as Registrar, 67, 184-5
  retirement, **288**, 289-90
homopolar generator (HPG), 93-4, **95**, 254, 254-9, **259**
Hope, Alec Derwent, 148, **150**, 151, 209, 350
housing scheme, 184

Hoyle, Fred, 264
HPG. *see* homopolar generator
HRC. *see* Humanities Research Centre
Hughes, Helen, 329-30, **330**, 331
Hughes, Wilfred Kent, 115
Hughes, William Morris, 101, 130
Humanities Research Centre (HRC), 248, 249-50, 375
Humphries, Gary, **367**
Hunter, Thelma, **246**, 246-7, 327
Huxley, A.F., 252
Huxley, Molly, 293
Huxley, Sir Leonard, **165**, **174**, 207
  and the Anglo-Australian Telescope, 262
  appointed Vice-Chancellor, 165
  personal attributes, 168, 184-5
  research, 248
  and the RSBS proposal, 235

immigration research, 387
immune system research, 381
Immunology and Cell Biology Division
  (JCSMR), 381
Inall, Ken, 122-3, 255
industrial disputes, 294-6, 411
information technology, 334, 336-7
Inglis, Ken, 64, 272, 386-7, **387**
  retirement, 399, 400
Institute of Advanced Studies (IAS), 158
  academic structure, 186-9
  AUC's support for, 175-6
  financial problems, 291
  inquiry into management of research resources, 311-12
  management problems, 311
  1995 review, 404-5, 411
  1990 review, 351-3
  optimum size, 169-72
  origins of name, 157
  relationship with SGS/The Faculties, 176-80, 314
Institute of Anatomy, 33
Institute of the Arts
  amalgamation with, 343, 347-51
interdisciplinary courses, 247-8
interdisciplinary research, 110
  Austronesian research, 389
  facilitating role of NGRU, 270
  see also collaborative teaching and research;
    multidisciplinary research
Interface Committee, 313-14
Interim Council
  conflicts between natural and social scientists, 27
  Easter Conference meetings, 33-4, 43
  first meeting, 22-3
  meeting rooms, 65
  membership, 22
  relationship with Academic Advisors, 28-30, 33, 44-5
  see also Council
International Congress of Orientalists, 28th, 275, 303

International Education Office, 370
International Relations, Department of (RSPacS), 108-9, 132-3, 275
international students, 369-72, 370
International Students Society, 371
internationalisation, 372, 393-5
ion-probe instrument, **377**, 378
Iremonger, John, 213
Israelachvili, Jacob, 311, 379-80

Jaeger, John Conrad, **97**
    as Dean of RSPhysS, 186
    plans for earth sciences, 229, 238
    research, 96-8, 110, 378
John, Bernard, 302
John Curtin School of Medical Research (JCSMR)
    academic government, 187-9
    building, 74, **138**
    clinical orientation, 317-19, 380-2
    criticisms of, 115
    under Curtis, 353
    departmental structure, 140
    divisional structure, 319
    early staff, 55-7
    faculty, 189
    under Fenner, 189, 317
    Florey's design for, 35-8
    funding arrangements, 1990s, 353-5
    management problems, 317-22
    origins, 16
    planning of, 17, 25, 28-9, 37-8
    research achievements, 82, 85-92, 373-4, 380-2, 383
    reviews, 300-2, 317, 322, 411
    School Committee, 137
    Senate committee inquiry into, 355-6
    Stephen committee's recommendations on, 353-5
John XXIII College, 205, 207
Johns, A.H., 304
Johns Hopkins University, 5, 7
Johnson, Lyndon B., 212
Johnson, Richard, 77, 171, 224, 249
Joplin, Germaine, 97, 250
Jordens, J.T.F. (Jos), **304**
Jupp, James, **387**, 387
Jupp, Kathleen, **102**

Kamenka, Eugene, 248, 342, 360-1, **361**
Karmel, Peter, **309**
    appointed Vice-Chancellor, 306, 307-8
    as Chairman of the AUC, 290
    commissions status of women report, 328
    on Dawkins's reforms, 339, 340, 341
    as Executive Chairman of CITA, 343, 348-9
    personal attributes, 307
Kellock, Gené, 77
Kennedy, Laurie, 348
Kenniff Cave, 242
Kent, Bruce, 131
Keogh, Bill, 56-7
Keon, S.M., 121

Kerr, Sir John, 3, 26, 217
Keynes, J.M., 4
Kivshar, Yuri, **382**
Knight, Alan, 199
Knowles, George, 8, 12
Kohlhagen, Dawn, **202**
Korean encyclopedia, 388
Korner, Paul, 322
Kron, Gerald, 99

La Nauze, John Andrew, 127, 128, **178**, 268
    relationship with Manning Clark, 178-9
    research, 178
    retirement, 400
laboratory accidents, 255
Laby, T.H., 6-7
Lagos, George, 255
Lal, Brij, 389
Lang, Jack, 114
Langenbert, Joanne, **220**
Langer, Albert, 220
Langer, Kerry, 220
Laser Physics Centre, 382
Laski, Harold, 62
Law, Department of (RSSS), 100, 386
Law, Faculty of, 185, 240
    academic courses, 203
    admission standards, 198, 364
    Legal Workshop, 203, 368-9
    size limits, 171
Lawley House, 66
leadership. *see* academic leadership
Legge, J.D., 63
legislation, 15-16, 18-19, 180-1, 342
Lennox House, 150, 205, 214
Lewis, Brian, **67**, 191
    ANU's first architect, 67-74
    resigns as architect for JCSMR, 74
    site plan, **68**, **190**
Lewis, C.S., 124
Leys, Simon, 388
library, 177-8, 314-15
    establishment of, 83-4
    post-amalgamation facilities, 157, 158
Lindsay, Lord (Michael), 108-9, 121, 132-3
linguistic research, 389-90
Liu Ts'un-yan, **303**, 303
Llewellyn, Ernest, **348**, 348
Llewellyn Hall, 348
loan schemes for students, 369
Low, Donald Anthony, 272, 365
    introduces system of reviews, 300
    personal attributes, 285-6, 305-6
    research, 130
    as Vice-Chancellor, **284**, 285-306
lunar research, 238
Lyneham, Paul, 209
Lyons, Joseph, 9
Lysenko, Trofim, 103

Macartney-Snape, Tim, **393**
MacCallum, Sir Mungo, 6, 7

MacDonagh, Oliver, 388
MACHO project, 261, 376-7
Mack, Andrew, 333
Mackaness, George, 88-91, 136
MacNamara, Jean, 89
Magarey, Susan, 247, 247-8
Magellanic Clouds, 98-9, 261
Male, Beverley, 202
Malmqvist, N.G.D., 303
managerialism, 308-13, 407
  as government policy, 340-1, 342
Managing Business in Asia program, 359, 360, 371
Mander, Lew, 234
Mannall, Geoff, 150
Mansergh, Nicholas, 43
Maralinga atomic tests, 97
marketing campaigns, 359-61, 370-1
Marr, David G., 388
Marshall, Ian, 91
Martin, Sir Leslie, 17, 173-6, 174
Martin, Ross, 103
Martin committee, 171
Mason, Sir Anthony, 386
Mason, Stephen, 123-4
Massey, H.S.W., 20, 186
Masson, Sir David, 7-8
Masson committee, 7-8
mathematical modelling, 379
Mathews, Russell, 78, 82, 208, 245
  and federalism research centre, 276-8
Mathewson, Don, 333-4
Maude, Harry, 106
Mayer, Adrian, 63
Mayer, Henry, 210
McArthur, Norma, 102, 267, 268
McAuley, James, 3
McBryde, Isabel, 400
McCallum, Frank, 17
McCalman, Iain, 209, 374, 374-5
McCarthy, (Senator) Joseph, 120
McCombe, Tim, 355
McDonald, A.L.G., 29, 34, 83, 83-4, 177
McDonald, John, 102
McDonald, Rod, 199
McDonald, Warren, 192-3
McFarlane, Bruce, 213
McLaren, J.G., 7
McMahon, William, 277
McQueen, Humphrey, 210-12, 211, 222
McRobbie, Michael, 336
Medawar, Brian, 252
Medical Chemistry, Department of (JCSMR), 60-1, 187, 301-2
  research, 85-6, 87-8
medical research institute, early proposals on, 3, 4, 12-13, 35-6
Medley, Sir John, 22, 27, 145
Melbourne Building, 148
Melville, Sir Leslie, 32, 199
  appointment of, 117-18
  and the appointment of Hancock, 128-9
  personal attributes, 119-20, 184
  retires from vice-chancellorship, 165
Meninga, Mal, 295

Menzies, Sir Robert Gordon, 10, 252-3
  and the amalgamation of ANU and CUC, 153-5, 158
  on autonomy of the university, 114-15
  awarded honorary degree, 225, 225
  criticises University House design, 73
  involvement in appointment of Melville, 117-18
  at opening of RSPhysS laboratories, 79
  relationship with Bok, 260, 261
  support for ANU, 18
Menzies Library, 177
Messel, Harry, 254-5, 264
Microbiology, Department of (JCSMR), 89-90, 381
Milky Way, 98-9, 260, 261
Millar, T.B., 268, 275-6, 333
Miller, J.D.B. (Bruce), 133, 274, 275
Mills, Richard Charles, 11, 12, 13, 34, 41
  as chair of the Interim Council, 22, 31
Mills committee, 12, 13-14, 16-18, 20
Mitchell, John, 382
Mockridge, Stahle and Mitchell, 134
Mojé, Klaus, 348
Molecular Biology Unit (RSBS), 236, 237
Molony, John, 295, 345
Monash University, 173, 213, 360
Monte Bello Island, 274
Mooney, Maryanne, 247
Moran, Patrick, 124
  and the Mason case, 124
  research, 102-3, 110
Morison, W.L., 63
Morphett, John, 358, 358
Morris, Bede, 188, 320
  relationship with Porter, 319-21
Morris, Charles, 31, 32
Morris, Edward, 5
Morrish, Joan, 82
Morrison, Allistair, 77
Morrison, Bill, 151, 188
motto, 76, 77, 87, 181, 359
Mount Stromlo and Siding Spring Observatories (MSSSO), 333-4, 411
  establishment of, 337
  research, 376-7
  see also Astronomy, Department of
Mount Stromlo Observatory, 16, 99
  under Bart Bok, 260-2
  collaborative project with the British government, 262-6
  early association with ANU, 58, 98-9
  research achievements, 261
  summer vacation scholarships, 261, 363
  under Woolley, 58, 98-9
  see also Astronomy, Department of
Moyal (Mozley), Ann, 130, 132, 325
multidisciplinary research, 130, 143
  see also collaborative teaching and research; interdisciplinary research
Mulvaney, D.J. (John), 64, 241-2, 242, 342, 390
  research, 387
Munitions Supply Laboratories, Maribyrnong, 61
Murphy, Lynne, 202
Murray, Sir Keith, 151, 152, 155
Murray committee, 151-3, 173-4, 212

Murray-Darling basin salinity, 379
Murray-Smith, Stephen, 387
muscle disease research, 380-1
Myer, K.B., 175
myxomatosis research, 82, 89-90

Nadel, George, 63
Nadel, Siegried Frederick (Fred), **110**, 126
    appointed to RSPacS, 51, 55, 59
    research, 109-10
naming of the university, 14-15
Narellan House, 150
NARU. *see* North Australia Research Unit
Nasioi people, 271
National Aeronautics and Space Agency (NASA), 238
National Board of Employment, Education and Training, 340
National Capital Development Commission (NCDC), 192, 206
National Centre for Development Studies, 393
National Centre for Epidemiology and Population Health, 384, 387
national compensation inquiry, 278
National Day of Action, 369
National Health and Medical Research Council (NH&MRC), 17, 319, 320-1
    Florey's views on role of, 36, 37
    and JCSMR research funding, 353-4
'national needs' research, 407, 408
    in Chemistry, 234
    emphasis in Dawkins' policies, 340
    see also fundamental v. applied research
National Population Inquiry, 278, 387
National Radiation Advisory Committee, 274
National Science and Technology Centre, 338
National Tertiary Education Union, 297
National Undergraduate Scholarships, 199, 207, 364
National Union of Students, 369
natural resources centre. *see* Centre for Resource and Environmental Studies
natural science schools, 186
    see also under names of specific schools
natural v. social sciences, 27, 140-3, 266
Nepal-Australia Forestry Project, 385
Neumann, Bernard, 399
Neumann, Hanna, 32, **325**
Neurobiology, Department of (RSBS), 236, 237
neurophysiology, 91-2
New Guinea Research Unit (NGRU), 270-3
Newstead, Gordon, 257-8, 259
Nichol, Laurie, **294**, **341**, **345**
    appointed Vice Chancellor, 341
    and the proposed amalgamation of ANU and CCAE, 343-7
    resigns from vice-chancellorship, 356
    as Vice-Chancellor, 341-56
Nicholson, Jon, 365
Ninham, Barry, 300, 342, 379, 391, 405
Nix, Henry, 384
Nobel Prize, 251-2
North Australia Research Unit (NARU), 273, 292

Nossal, Sir Gustav, 317
Nuclear Disarmament Party, 380
Nuclear Physics, Department of (RSPhysS), 95-6, 378
Nyholm, Ronald, 229-31

objectives of ANU
    as defined by Coombs, 15-16
    as defined in the 1946 Act, 18
    as defined in the 1987 Strategic Plan, 312-13
O'Brien, Elizabeth, **246**, 246-7, 365
observatories. *see* Anglo Australian Telescope; Mount Stromlo and Siding Spring Observatories
Ochiltree, Margaret, **202**
O'Connor, Mark, 214
Office of Research on Academic Methods (ORAM), 210, 248
Ogan, Eugene, 271
old hospital buildings, **64**, **66**, **138**
Oliphant, Sir Mark, 20, 23, 66, **142**, 262
    on the ANU site, 1948, **44**
    on ANU's 'two cultures', 141, 143
    appointed as Academic Adviser, 24, 28-9
    attitudes towards Copland, 32, 47, 81
    attitudes towards CUC amalgamation, 156
    at Birmingham, **21**
    building requirements, 67, 73-4
    concerns about ANU's 'uniqueness', 176
    criticises social science schools, 111
    on the design and structure of RSPhysS, 38-9
    as Director, RSPhysS, 186
    at the Easter conferences, 1948, 33-5, **34**, **35**
    housing, 60
    HPG project, **254**, 254-9
    meeting with Chifley in London 1946, 20-1
    outside activities, 274
    reactions to the Bramley-Ward report, 327
    recruits staff for RSPhysS, 57-8
    relationship with Melville, 119-20
    research, 93-5
    resigns from directorship of RSPhysS, 255-6
    retirement, 401-2, **402**
    at 'save the JCSMR rally', 354, **355**
    on teaching, 259
    on Titterton's outside activities, 274
    on university symbols, 76
    visit to Australia, 1947, 26
Olympic Dam, 378
O'Malley, King, 5
O'Neill, Robert, 276, **276**
Optical Sciences Centre, 382
ORAM. *see* Office of Research on Academic Methods
Oriental Studies, Faculty of, 241, 303
Orientation Week, 201-2
Orr case, 133
Orubuloye, I.O., **383**
Osborne, Paul, **295**
Osborne, R.G., 29, **34**, 41, 65, **67**
Osmond, Barry, 384
outside funding, 97
    Bougainville Copper Pty Ltd, 271

Centre for Research on Federal Financial
    Relations, 277
commissioned academic courses, 360
Commonwealth Bank, 270
Peace Research Centre, 333
overseas models, 7, 27, 157
    academic structure, 27-8, 36, 180
    buildings, 69, 70-1, 73, 74
overseas scholarship scheme, 29, 61-4
overseas students, 369-72, **370**
Overseas Students Charge, 370
Ovington, J.D. (Derrick), **243**, 244
Oxbridge influences on ANU, 27-8, 36, 110, 407-8
Oxford University Press, 268

Pacific History, Department of (RSPacS), 107
Pacific islands research, 269-73, 389
Packard, W.P. (Bill), 207, **207**
Packer, David, **102**, **103**
Packer, Sir Frank, 256
Padgham, Stephen, 216-17, 228
Page, Sir Earle, **80**
Papua and New Guinea research, 269-73
Papua New Guinea Institute of Applied Science
    and Economic Research, 273
Parish, Chris, **381**
Parker, A.J., 357
Parker, R.S., 14
Parkinson, Sir Nicholas, 150-1
Parsons, R.W., 63
Particle Physics, Department of (RSPhysS),
    255, 258
Partridge, P.H. (Perc), 278
    appointed Director, RSSS, 135
    on the AUC, 174
    on changes in university education, 226
    on political involvement of academics, 273
    on postgraduate training, 179
    research, 105
    on the size of the IAS, 169
Passmore, John, **105**, 105, 350, 408
    research and publications, 105, 268
    retirement, 399
patents policy, 356-7
Paterson, Mervyn, 97
Paton, G.W., 84
Peace Research Centre, 332-3
Penrith, Harry, 201
Performance Indicators Project, 390-2
Pergamon Press, 268
Peters, Phil, **151**
Petrov, Vladimir, 124
Physiology, Department of (JCSMR), 91-2, 381
Pike, Douglas, 130, **131**
Plamenatz, J.P., 361
plant research, 384
Plowman, Colin, 217, 328
    appointed Assistant Vice-Chancellor, 287
    resigns as Academic Registrar, **220**, 221
    and students, 208, 219, 221
Pocock, J.G.A., 361
political activism, students', 212-17, 288-9, 365-8
Political Science, Department of (RSSS), 132

Popper, Karl, 92, 104-5
Population Biology, Department of (RSBS),
    236, 237
Porter, Robert, **317**, 317-22
Post-War Reconstruction, Department of,
    4, 10-11, 12
Postgraduate and Research Students' Association,
    368
postgraduate students
    ANU's declining proportion of Australian
        graduates, 287, 363
    coordination of IAS and SGS training, 250
    development of overall ANU policy on, 179
    dispute over control of, 157-8
    distinctions between IAS and SGS
        students, 200
    diversity of current graduate programs, 376
    early scholars, 61-4
    establishment of the Graduate School, 315-16
    impact of Stephen committee
        recommendations, 352
    introduction of course fees, 368
    numbers of, **160**, 173, 200, **280**, **396**
    opportunities for ANU graduates, 225-6
    origins of, **160**, 200, **280**, **396**
    residential requirements, 203, 204
    scarcity of PhD graduates, 1950, 84
    see also students
Powell, Tony, **151**
Prehistory and Anthropology, Department of
    (SGS), 241-2
Price, Charles, **102**, 268, 387
Princeton Institute of Advanced Study, 7, 27, 157
Professorial Board, 156, 407
professors, role of, 34, 185-6
protests. see demonstrations and protests
proton synchrotron, 254
Pryor, Lindsay, 193, 244
Przybylski, Antoni, 99
Psychology, Department of (SGS), 210, 222
public criticisms of ANU, 287-8
public relations
    Coombs's views on, 89
    efforts of Copland, 75, 81-2
    under Low, 285-6
    role of Bok in promoting astronomy, 260, 261
publications, 266-9

Quality Assurance reviews, 364, 411
Questacon, **338**

Radiochemistry, Department of (RSPhysS), 98
Raggatt, H.G., 97
Ramson, W.S., 269
Rawson, Beryl, 329, **390**
Rawson, Don, **103**
Reay, Marie, 328
Reconstruction Research Grants, 10
recruitment
    and academic freedom, 122-4, 125
    the 'clubbable' criterion, 105
    policy issues, 34, 47-8, 54-5

Stephen committee's recommendation on
    tenure, 352
  of women, 324-5, 330-2, 374
recruitment of students, 198, 199, 364
Refshauge, Richard, 220
'Regard' Project, 386
Reid, Anthony, 388
Reid, Gordon, 277
Renfree, Beverley, 91
research, 83-112, 409
  CRES, 384-5
  Faculties, 374-5, 385-8, 389-90
  JCSMR, 82, 380-2, 383
  measuring, 390-2
  motivations for, 110-12, 251-3, 266-9, 373-6
  MSSSO, 376-7
  RSBS, 235-6, 237, 384
  RSC, 233-4
  RSES, 377-8
  RSPacS, 106-10, 241-2, 389-90
  RSPhysS, 93-9, 378-80
  RSSS, 100-5, 383-7
  until the 1940s, 84
Research Data Network CRC, 336
Research Fellowship Scheme (social sciences), 30
Research School of Biological Sciences (RSBS),
    170, 234-7
  academic structure, 236-7
  early staff, 236
  origins, 234-5
  research, 235-6, 237, 384
  reviews, 301, 302, 411
Research School of Chemistry (RSC), 170, 229-34
  academic structure, 232
  building design, 232, 233
  collaborative relationship with SGS, 232-3
  destination of graduates from, 394
  origins, 120, 229-31
  research, 233-4
  reviews, 301, 411
Research School of Earth Sciences (RSES),
    170, 237-40
  academic structure, 240
  buildings, 66
  collaborative research projects, 238
  links with the mining industry, 357
  origins, 98, 186, 229, 238-9
  research, 377-8
  reviews, 301, 411
Research School of Information Sciences and
    Engineering (RSISE), 337
Research School of Pacific and Asian Studies
    (RSPAS), 371, 411
Research School of Pacific Studies (RSPacS)
  appointment of Academic Adviser to,
    26-7, 28-9
  changes name, 332
  criticisms of, 111-12
  early staff, 51-4
  Easter Conference meeting on, 40-2, 113
  female appointments to, 331
  meaning of 'Pacific', 17, 40-2
  origins, 16
  planning of, 17, 40-2

  relationship with RSSS, 40, 42
  research, 106-10, 241, 242, 389-90
  reviews, 301, 411
Research School of Physical Sciences and
    Engineering (RSPhysSE), 337, 411
Research School of Physical Sciences
    (RSPhysS), 79
  academic structure, 186-7
  adopts faculty structure, 189
  budget, 21, 25, 39, 186
  buildings, 67, 73-4, 74, 138
  under Carver, 258, 300, 337
  changes name, 337
  early staff, 57-8
  'Founders Day', 402
  innovations in the 1980s, 337
  under Jaeger, 186
  under Oliphant, 186, 254-9
  Oliphant's blueprint for, 38-9
  opposes establishment of RSES, 238-9
  origins, 16
  planning of, 17-18, 24, 28-9
  research, 93-9, 378-80
  reviews, 298-300, 357, 411
  school committee, 187
  site, 1950, 94
  under Street, 298-300
  theoretical v. experimental focus, 20-1
  under Titterton, 186-7
  workshops, 95
Research School of Social Sciences (RSSS), 46
  criticisms of, 111-12
  departmental structure, 103
  early staff, 43-4, 54-5, 103
  Easter Conference meeting, 41
  Eggleston's views on objectives of, 48-50
  female appointments in, 331
  under Hancock, 130-5
  intra-school innovative activities, 332
  origins, 16
  planning of, 17, 24-5, 28-9, 39-40
  relationship with RSPacS, 40, 42
  research, 100-5, 383-4, 385-7
  reviews, 298, 301, 302, 411
residential halls and colleges, 169, 205-7
  denominational colleges, 205
  'Gungahlin', 149-50, 150
  mixed-gender accommodation, 207
  'moral tutors', 206
Resources Review Committee, 311-12, 316
reviews, 298-305, 322, 410, 411
  Faculties, 298, 302-3, 304-5
  IAS, 298-302, 351-3, 404-5, 411
  Quality Assurance, 364, 411
Richardson, J.E., 171
Richardson, Sir Frank, 123
Riddell, Diana, 217, 220, 225
Rigby, T.H. (Harry), 389
Ringwood, Ted, 238, 239, 316
  as Director of RSES, 239, 377
  research, 378
Rivett, Sir David, 7, 11, 16, 35, 234
  on autonomy of the university, 115-16
  on Interim Council, 22, 31

on the naming of ANU, 14
personal attributes, 7
Robertson, Sir Rutherford, 196, 236, 361
Robinson, Derek, **345**
Robinson, John, **150**
Rochester Medical School, 27
Rodgers, Alex, **261**
Roe, Julius, 222, 223
Rolfe, Barry, 342
Rosenberg, Harry, 86, **88**
Ross, Ian Gordon, 64, 198, **209**, 239, 291
  efforts to integrate the university's parts, 313-16
  on the proposed amalgamation with CCAE, 344
  support for Anutech, 358
  as teacher, 209
Rowe, A.P., 113
Royal Military College, Duntroon, 208
Rubbo, Sydney, 56
Rudduck, Grenfell, 190, 191-2
Russell, Bertrand, 104
Rutherford, Lord, 93
Ryan, Peter, 179
Ryan, Susan, 227, 308, 328
Ryckmans, Pierre, 388

sabbatical leave, 83
salaries. *see* conditions of service
Samuel, Peter, 201, 287
'sarcophagine cages', 383
Sargeson, Alan, 234, **383**
satellite technology, 260
Sawer, Geoffrey, **101**, 149
  appointed to RSSS, 51, 54, 59
  coat of arms design, **77**
  as Dean of RSSS, 127
  outside activities, 274
  research, 100, 386
  on teaching at ANU, 76
Sawer, Marian, **328**, 328-30
Scarf, Frank, 98
Schmeisser, Jörg, 348
scholarships
  National Undergraduate Scholarships, 199, 207, 364
  overseas scholarships scheme, 30, 61-4
Schonland, Basil, 117
School of Art. *see* Canberra School of Art
School of Forestry. *see* Australian School of Forestry
School of General Studies (SGS), 158
  academic courses, 202-3, 222-4, 242
  academic structure, 185-6
  admission standards, 198, 364
  early admissions scheme, 199
  faculty and departmental structure, 240-1
  lack of 'uniqueness' in, 176
  optimum size, 170-2
  origins of name, 157
  postgraduate students, 179
  relationship with IAS, 176-80
  renaming of, 180, 250
  student profile, 197-200
  see also The Faculties; *and under names of specific departments*
School of Mathematical Sciences, 332
School of Music. *see* Canberra School of Music
School of Oriental Studies, 185, 303
  see also Asian Studies, Faculty of; Oriental Studies, Faculty of
Science, Faculty of, 153, 185
  research, 378, 382
  teaching in, 211
Scott, Roger, 343
Secretary, role and functions of, 185
Selinger, Ben, 209
Sellbach, Udo, 347-8
semester system, 210
semiconductor science, 337
Senate committee on JCSMR, 355-6
'Sepoy seminar', 130
Serjeantson, Susan, 331, **373**, 373-4, 405-6
Serle, Percival, 130
sex discrimination and sexual harassment, 328-9
Shakespeare, Arthur, 348
Sherrington, Sir Charles, 91
shock tunnels, 378
SHRIMP, **377**, 378
Siding Spring Mountain, 262, **262**, **265**
  see also Mount Stromlo and Siding Spring Observatories
Simpson, Lois, **350**
Simpson, Roy, 193-6, **196**
Sir William Dunn School of Pathology, Oxford, 12, 13, 36
site and buildings, **44**, 64-7, **160**, 166-7, **168**, **169**, **280**, **396**
  Boyd's criticism of, 193
  ceremonial group, 193-4
  conflicts with Canberra planners, 192
  Coombs Building, 134-5
  CUC, 144, 148, 151-2
  early buildings, **64**, **65**, **66**
  JCSMR, **138**
  landscape design, 71, 193
  laying of foundation stones, 1949, 114
  Lewis's plan, 67-74, **68**, 190
  naming policy, 134
  old hospital buildings, **138**
  opening of RSPhysS laboratories, 79
  overseas models, 69, 70-1, 73, 74
  precedence of functional needs, 192
  relationship with Griffin's plan, 196
  relocation of the 'gateway' to ANU, 193-6
  RSC, 232, 233
  RSPhysS, **138**
  selection of architects, 192-3
  Simpson's plan, 193-4
  Winston and Rudduck's designs, 190, 191-2
Sitsky, Larry, 348
size of the university, 169-72
Skinner, Q.R.D., 361
Slatyer, Ralph, **236**, 278, 384
Smart, Jack, 399
Smith, Bernard, **199**, 200, 391
Smith, F.B., 388
Smithies, Arthur, 43
Snow, C.P., 140, 141

Snowy Mountains Hydro-Electric Authority, 97
Snyder, Allan, **382**
social life, 293-4
    campus events, 1950s, 110
    Canberra, 1950s, 149
    students, 207-8
    University House functions, 110, 203-4
social medicine, 13, 16
Social Philosophy, Department of (RSSS), 103-5
    social philosophy, defined, 49
social science schools
    academic government in, 186
    communism witch-hunting in, 120-4
    criticisms of, 111-12, 115, 141
    joint faculty meetings, 133
    publishing in, 268-9
    'women only' positions, 331-2
    see also under names of specific schools
Soejono, R.P., 241
solar energy project, **357**, 357-8
Somare, Michael, **273**, 273
Spate, Oskar Hermann Khristian, **107**
    awarded honorary degree from UPNG, 272
    and communism, 122
    on Dawkins' reforms, 342
    impressions of Copland, 75
    outside activities, 274
    on plans for RSES, 238, 239
    research, 107-8, 269, 271-2, 389
Spear, Ray, 316
Spiegler, Marlene, 199
Spock, Benjamin, 214
sporting activities, 293-4
staff. *see* academic staff; administrative and general staff
Stanner, W.E.H. (Bill), 3, **109**, 204
    appointed to RSPacS, 52
    on equality in conditions of service, 324-5
    research, 109-10
Stanton, Robin, 338
state universities, 4-5
    ANU's contributions to, 63, 75
    Commonwealth assumes full financial responsibility for, 286-7
    impact of Murray committee report on, 173-4
    postgraduate training, 173
    student numbers, 1960, 171
    see also under names of specific universities
Statistics, Department of (RSSS), 102-3, 395
Steele, Colin, **337**
Stening, Bruce, **359**
Stephen, Sir Ninian, 351, 355
Stephen committee review, 351-3
Stone, Julius, 3
Storry, Richard, 63
Stoyles, Megan, 212
Strategic and Defence Studies Centre, 275-6, 332
strategic planning, 312-13, 316, 410
    reactions from JCSMR to, 319-20
Street, Robert, **298**, 298-300
Stretton, Hugh, 173, 175
strikes and pickets, 296-7, 411
Stuart, Ricky, **295**
student life, 214

clubs and societies, 151, 202
demonstrations and protests, 212-17
drug usage, 214
1950s, 151
political apathy of students, 365-6
student numbers, **160**, 168, 197, 363-4, **380**, **396**
    all universities, 1960s, 173
    CUC, 144, 149, 152, 156
    international students, 369-70
    and 'national' role of ANU, 171, 364, 405
student politics
    government interference in, 288-9
    1960s/1970s, 212-17
    opposition to Dawkins' policies, 367-8
    voluntary student unionism campaign, 366-7
Student Union, 208
students, 197-228, 363-72, **364**, **365**
    career opportunities, 225-6, 364-5, 393-5
    demographic profile, 197-200
    disciplinary problems, 204
    fees, 367-8
    gender balance, **160**, **280**, **396**
    international students, 369-72, **370**, 393-4
    origins of, **280**, **396**
    participation in decision-making, 218-24
    recruitment of, 359
    socio-economic background of, 199-200
    see also undergraduate students; postgraduate students
Students' Representative Council (SRC), 213
    see also ANU Students' Association; Australian Union of Students
study leave, 83
subsidised research, issues involved in, 271, 276-8, 332-3
Summerhayes, Judith, 202
superannuation, 295, 324-5
Supercomputer Facility, 336
surface forces, 379-80
Sutherland, Alexander, 5
Sutherland, Helen, 202
Swan, Trevor, 43, **54**, 133, 268-9, 294
    on academic titles, 79
    appointed to RSSS, 54, 55
    outside activities, 274
    research, 269-70
    on subsidised research, 277
Swinbank, Chris, 215, 216-17, 228
Sydney Metropolitan Water Board, 97
synchro-cyclotron, 93
synchrotron, Birmingham, **21**, 259
SYNROC, 378
Systems Engineering, Department of (RSPhysS), 334, 337

Taxonomy Unit (RSBS), 236
Taylor, Ross, 240
teaching, 208-12
    and assessment, 210
    'excellence' awards, 359, 374
    and research links, 88-9, 147, 153
    standards, 209
    tutorial system, 209

INDEX

telescopes, 98, 262
    Anglo-Australian Telescope, 262-6, **265**
    Farnham Telescope, **99**
    Great Melbourne Telescope, 261, 376-7, **377**
    Solar Telescope, **99**
    2.3 metre, 333-4
Terrell, Deane, 293, **345**, 370, **411**
Tertiary Education Commission, 287
Thatcher, Margaret, 264
Titmuss, R.M., 43
Titterton, Sir Ernest, **96**, **239**, 264, **402**
    appointed to RSPhysS, 58
    criticises RSPhysS review, 299-300
    as Dean of RSPhysS, 186-7
    internal opposition to, 240
    opposes establishment of RSES, 238-9
    outside activities, 274
    research, 95-6
    'Titterton's tower', 192
Toad Hall, 206
Todd, Murray, 148
town-gown orientation of site, 193-5
Town v. Gown cricket matches, 294
Trendall, Dale, 110, **111**, **204**, 361
    on the loss of ANU's uniqueness, 196
triennial funding, 169, 410
Trudeau, Pierre, 214, **214**
Turner Hostel, 150
'Two Cultures' concept, 140-3
two-part university, 404-5
    Crawford's efforts at integration, 180, 250
    Stephen committee's emphasis on retaining, 352
    tensions between ANU and CUC, 176-80

undergraduate students, 363-4
    numbers of, **160**, **280**, **396**
    origins of, 198, **280**, **396**
    proposed honours school, 405
    residential accommodation for, 205-7
    see also students
UNESCO's 'Man and Biosphere' program, 278
unified national system, 340, 343
unions, 294-7
uniqueness of ANU, 173, 405, 407-9
    in academic course offerings, 203
    AUC's support for, 175-6
    loss of the vision of the founders, 195, 196
    national student body, 171
    role of academic structure in maintaining, 250
Unisearch, 358
United States of America, 5
units, 248-50
    see also under names of individual units
Universities Commission, 11
University Association of Canberra, 8-9, 11-12
University Health Service, 214
University House, **72**
    changing role and functions, 196, 361-2
    commercial emphasis, 361-2
    Dining Room, **72**
    high table, 203-4, **204**
    Lewis's design of, **68**, 71-3, **72**
    ornamental pond, **362**
    role of the Master, 76
    social activities, 203-4
    social role, 110
University of Adelaide, 4-5
University of Melbourne, 4, 8, 145-6, 149
University of New South Wales, 173
University of Papua and New Guinea, 272
University of Sydney, 4
university traditions, 75-80
Urban Research Unit, 248
Ursula College, 205, **206**, 207, 217

Vacation Scholarship Scheme, **261**, 363
Vardanega, Louise, **393**
vice-chancellor, role of, 183, 286, 407
vice-chancellors, appointment of, 30-2, 116-18, 165, 188, 221, 285, 306-8
Vice-Chancellor's Advisory Group, 289
Vice-Chancellor's Awards for Excellence in Teaching, 359, 374
Vietnam War protests, 212, 215-17, **216**
vision research, 381-2
visiting staff, 29, 52, 249, **393**
voluntary student unionism, 366-7
Voorhoeve, Clemens, 270

Waddell-Wood, Sue, **247**
Walker, Ronald, 11-12, 32
Walker committee, 11-12
Walsh, Richard, 212, 213
Walter and Eliza Hall Institute, 36
Walton, Alistair, 366
Walton, Ernest, 93
Wang Gungwu, 315, **388**, 409-10
War Organisation of Industry, Department of, 11, 12
Ward, E.J. (Eddie), 22
Ward, Frederick, 73, 184
Ward, Hugh, 89
Ward, J.M., 41
Ward, Marion, 326-8
Ward, R.G., 272
Ward, Russel, **199**, 200
Warden, Ian, 365-6
wastage rates. see failure and attrition rates
Waterford, Jack, **215**, 366
Webb, Leicester, 54, 267
Weeks, Philippa, 209
Weise, Bernt, **349**
Wentworth, W.C., 95
Western, Bernadette, **202**
Western Samoa, 107
Wheare, K.C., 20, 46, 49
White, Harold, 8, 9
White, Patricia Marie, 223, **289**
White Cliffs project, **357**, 357-8
Whitlam, E.G. (Gough), 158, 264, **265**, 277
    on contemporary role for universities, 278-9
Whitlam, H.F.E., 144
Whitlam, Tony, 201
Whitten, Wes, 83

463

Wight, Martin, 108-9, 132-3
Wilkes, G.A., 63
Williams, C.M., 62, 64
Williams, Jim, 337
Williams, R.M. (Robert), **221**, 221, 223, 240
Williams, Warwick, 328
Williamson, Darrell, 338
Willis, Ian, **377**
Wilson, J.T., 96
Wilson, Lillian, **102**
Wilson, Sir Roland, 43, 117-18, 119
Wilson's Disease, 383
Winch, D.N., 361
Winston, Denis, 190, 191-2
Woden Valley Hospital, 318
women, 58-9, 323-32
    academic staff numbers, 323, 325-6
    EEO policies, 330-2
    inquiries into the role of, 326-9
    policies on employment of, 324-5, 330
    senior appointments, 374
    social club, 293, **294**
    student numbers, 364
    'women only' advertised positions, 331-2
Women's Studies course, 222, 246-8, 326
Wood, George Arnold, 273
'The Wool Seminar', 130, 143
Woolcott, Richard, 150, **151**
Woolley, Richard van der Reit, 16, **99**, 262
    appointed Professor of Astronomy, 58
    and the planning of RSPhysS, 17
    research, 98-9
workshops, 91, **95**
Woroni, 151
Worsley, Peter, 63, 122
Wright, Sir (Roy) Douglas (Pansy), 3, **34**
    on the appointment of staff, 22, 29, 38, 55
    attitudes towards Copland, 31-2
    on Interim Council/Council, 22-3, 26, 181
    personal attributes, 3-4, 32
    and the planning of ANU, 3, 408
    plans for a medical research institute,
        4, 12-13, 20
    proposes overseas scholarships scheme, 61
    relationship with Florey, 12-13
    visit to UK and USA, 1947, 27-8
Wurm, Stephen, 268, **270**, 389

Yabsley, Michael, **366**
Yamane, Shigeru, **382**
Yang-hi Choe-Wall, 388
Yencken, John, 356, 357
Yeomans, Brett, **363**
Yocklunn, Sir John, 201
Yuncken Freeman Architects, 193

Zhou Enlai, 278
Zines, Leslie, 386
Zinkernagel, Rolf, 381
Zubryzcki, Jerzy (George), 387